1,000,000 Books

are available to read at

www.ForgottenBooks.com

Read online
Download PDF
Purchase in print

ISBN 978-1-330-41244-2
PIBN 10056482

This book is a reproduction of an important historical work. Forgotten Books uses state-of-the-art technology to digitally reconstruct the work, preserving the original format whilst repairing imperfections present in the aged copy. In rare cases, an imperfection in the original, such as a blemish or missing page, may be replicated in our edition. We do, however, repair the vast majority of imperfections successfully; any imperfections that remain are intentionally left to preserve the state of such historical works.

Forgotten Books is a registered trademark of FB &c Ltd.
Copyright © 2018 FB &c Ltd.
FB &c Ltd, Dalton House, 60 Windsor Avenue, London, SW19 2RR.
Company number 08720141. Registered in England and Wales.

For support please visit www.forgottenbooks.com

1 MONTH OF FREE READING

at

www.ForgottenBooks.com

By purchasing this book you are eligible for one month membership to ForgottenBooks.com, giving you unlimited access to our entire collection of over 1,000,000 titles via our web site and mobile apps.

To claim your free month visit:

www.forgottenbooks.com/free56482

* Offer is valid for 45 days from date of purchase. Terms and conditions apply.

English
Français
Deutsche
Italiano
Español
Português

www.forgottenbooks.com

Mythology Photography **Fiction** Fishing Christianity **Art** Cooking Essays Buddhism Freemasonry Medicine **Biology** Music **Ancient Egypt** Evolution Carpentry Physics Dance Geology **Mathematics** Fitness Shakespeare **Folklore** Yoga Marketing **Confidence** Immortality Biographies Poetry **Psychology** Witchcraft Electronics Chemistry History **Law** Accounting **Philosophy** Anthropology Alchemy Drama Quantum Mechanics Atheism Sexual Health **Ancient History Entrepreneurship** Languages Sport Paleontology Needlework Islam **Metaphysics** Investment Archaeology Parenting Statistics Criminology **Motivational**

DICTIONARY
OF
WORDS, FACTS, AND PHRASES

DICTIONARIES.

THE READER'S HANDBOOK OF ALLUSIONS, REFERENCES, PLOTS, AND STORIES. By the Rev. E. C. BREWER, LL.D. With an Appendix containing an ENGLISH BIBLIOGRAPHY. Crown 8vo. cloth extra, 7s. 6d.

AUTHORS AND THEIR WORKS, with the Dates. Being the Appendices to 'The Reader's Handbook,' separately printed. By the Rev. E. C. BREWER, LL.D. Crown 8vo. cloth limp, 2s.

A DICTIONARY OF MIRACLES: Imitative, Realistic, and Dogmatic. By the Rev. E. C. BREWER, LL.D. Crown 8vo. cloth extra, 7s. 6d.

FAMILIAR SHORT SAYINGS OF GREAT MEN. With Historical and Explanatory Notes. By SAMUEL A. BENT, A.M. Crown 8vo. cloth extra, 7s. 6d.

THE SLANG DICTIONARY: Etymological, Historical, and Anecdotal. Crown 8vo. cloth extra, 6s. 6d.

WORDS, FACTS, AND PHRASES: a Dictionary of Curious, Quaint, and Out-of-the-Way Matters. By ELIEZER EDWARDS. Crown 8vo. cloth extra, 3s. 6d.

London: CHATTO & WINDUS, 111 St. Martin's Lane, W.C.

WORDS, FACTS, & PHRASES

A DICTIONARY OF

CURIOUS, QUAINT, & OUT-OF-THE-WAY MATTERS

BY

ELIEZER EDWARDS

'A quaint and curious volume of forgotten lore'—POE'S *Raven*

A NEW EDITION

LONDON
CHATTO & WINDUS
1897

PRINTED BY
SPOTTISWOODE AND CO., NEW-STREET SQUARE
LONDON

PREFACE.

My aim in this work has been to comprise within the compass of a single volume a mass of curious, out-of-the-way information acquired during years of labour and research from sources not easily accessible to general readers. I have further attempted to render the book interesting, as well as useful, by making it familiar in style rather than formal, and by keeping it free, as far as possible, from technicalities, dry details, and scientific terms.

When I first commenced the work, it did not occur to me that it would be either desirable or necessary in all cases to cite authorities. Some of the articles in the book are, consequently, unsupported by other testimony than my own. I think it may be well for me, therefore, to state that in all such cases the evidence, or the authority upon which I relied, was such as to convince me that it was trustworthy.

I can scarcely hope that the nearly four thousand articles which the book contains will each be found strictly accurate. Authorities, even of the highest repute, differ greatly; sometimes two, three, or even more, give different explanations of one word or subject. One case which I will mention is a good illustration of the difficulty of arriving at exact results, even in simple matters of fact. When I proposed to give the height of St. Paul's Cathedral, I found no fewer than seven different statements in as many separate publications. Haydn, in the 'Dictionary of Dates,' gives it as 404 feet, and the others varied from 356 to 410 feet. To ascertain with absolute certainty, I applied to the surveyor of the Cathedral, whose assistant, Mr. George McDowel, informed me in reply that, having personally measured the building, he was able to state positively that the height from the level of the street on the south side is 365 feet. This statement *differs from every one of the authorities I had consulted*.

In some instances, where I found that opinions and statements as to one subject varied very considerably, I have cited the different authorities; in others I have given the explanation which appeared to be the best supported. Other instances are those in which the evidence did not appear to be strong enough to warrant a positive expression of opinion. In these cases I have used the expressions 'perhaps,' 'probably,' 'there seems reason to believe,' and others, to denote that the explanations given are not to be taken as conclusive.

The accurate character of the contents of the book has, of course, been my chief object. I have, however, endeavoured as much to make the manner attractive as to render the matter trustworthy. But, after all, although I hope and believe that the book is free from serious error, I am quite aware that faults both of manner and matter will be discovered. I can only say in respect of these, that I shall feel obliged if those who detect error, or can suggest improvement, will kindly communicate with me, so that, in future editions, defects may be remedied.

E. EDWARDS.

HARBORNE, BIRMINGHAM:
October 1881

A LIST

OF SOME OF THE AUTHORITIES CONSULTED FOR THE PURPOSES OF THIS BOOK.

Amos, Sheldon	*The Science of Law.*
Angus, Dr.	*Handbook of the English Tongue.*
Bailey, N.	*Dictionary,* 1735.
Bartlett, J. R.	*Dictionary of Americanisms.*
Beckmann, John	*History of Inventions.*
Brand, John	*Popular Antiquities.*
Brewer, Dr.	*Reader's Handbook; Dict. Phrase and Fable &c.*
Chambers, W. and R.	*Encyclopædia &c.*
Charnock, R. S.	*Local Etymology.*
Chatto	*History of Playing Cards*
Clarke, Dr. Adam	*Commentary on the Bible.*
Cotgrave, R.	*French and English Dictionary.*
Cunningham, Peter	*Handbook of London.*
De Quincey, T.	*Opium Eater &c.*
De Vere, A. T.	*Studies in English.*
D'Israeli, I.	*Curiosities of Literature.*
Earle, John	*Philology of the English Tongue.*
English Cyclopædia—Various articles.	
Fairholt, F. W.	*Dictionary of Terms in Art.*
Gentleman's Magazine—Various volumes.	
Gould, E. S.	*Good English.*
Grose, F.	*Glossaries &c.*
Hallam, H.	*Constitutional History.*
Hoare, Archdeacon	*English Roots.*
Hook, Dr.	*Church Dictionary.*
Hotten, J. C.	*History of Signboards.*
Jamieson, J.	*Scottish Dictionary.*
Jevons, Professor	*Money.*
Johnson, Samuel	*Dictionary.*
Knight, Charles	*Penny Cyclopædia.*
Lake, W.	*Inventions and Discoveries.*

LIST OF AUTHORITIES CONSULTED.

Locke, John	Human Understanding &c.
Lubbock, Sir J.	Origin of Civilisation &c.
Marsh, G. P.	Lectures.
Müller, Max	Various works.
Nares, Archdeacon	Glossary.
Nichols, J.	Literary Anecdotes.
Notes and Queries—Sixty volumes.	
Philological Society	Proceedings.
Phillips, Sir R.	Million of Facts.
Power, John	Handy Book about Books.
Pulleyn, W.	Etymological Compendium.
Richardson, C.	Dictionary.
Sala, G. A.	Various.
Stillingfleet, Bishop	Origines Britannicæ.
Stow, John	Chronicles.
Strutt, Jos.	Sports and Pastimes.
Talbot, Fox	English Etymologies.
Taylor, I.	Names and Places.
Tooke, Horne	Diversions of Purley.
Trench, Archbishop	Study of Words &c.
Verstegan, R.	Restitution of Decayed Intelligence, 1635
Wedgwood, H.	Dictionary of English Etymology.
Wharton	Law Lexicon.
Wood, E. J.	Curiosities of Clocks and Watches.
Worcester, Dr.	Dictionary.
Wright, T.	Domestic Manners of the Middle Ages.
Wright and Halliwell	Reliquiæ Antiquæ.

WORDS, FACTS, AND PHRASES.

A

A. Up to a recent period it was considered correct to use the article 'an' before every word beginning with *u*, whether the sound were long or short. Dr. Johnson always so used it, saying 'an useful article,' &c. The rule is now relaxed. It is held that the sound of the *u*, as in the word just quoted, should be the guide rather than the orthography; and as the sound in the word 'useful' is identical with that in 'youth,' the article 'a' is proper in both cases. All words, therefore, beginning with a long *u* should be treated as though commencing with *y*; the 'a' being invariably used.

A 1. This is the symbol of a first-class vessel at Lloyd's. The letter A refers to the character of the hull of the ship, and is assigned to a new ship for a number of years varying from four to fifteen, according to the material used and the workmanship. After the original term has expired, the 'A' may be 'continued' for a further specific term, on condition of certain specified repairs, &c. The figure 1 refers to the state of anchors, cables, and other fittings. Vessels of inferior character are classified under the letters Æ E & I. The term A 1 has latterly come into common use, to denote anything of undoubtedly good quality.

Abaft. See AFT.

Abandon. From the Latin *ab*, from, and *bandum*, a flag; meaning 'to desert one's colours.'

Abbeys. The first abbey founded in Britain was at Bangor, in the year 560. One hundred and ninety abbeys were suppressed by Henry VIII., in 1539. They contained nearly 50,000 persons, and their united annual incomes amounted to 2,853,000*l*.

Abbot. From a Syriac word, *abba*, signifying 'father.' The word 'abba' is used in this sense in the verse Romans viii. **15.**

Abdication differs from resignation, inasmuch as 'abdication' is done purely and simply, whereas 'resignation' is in favour of some other person.—*Wharton's Law Lexicon.*

Aberdeen. The ancient and correct orthography of this local name was 'Aberdon,' from *Aber*, the mouth of a river, and *Don*, the name of the river upon whose banks the city is built.

Abernethy Biscuits. In 'Notes and Queries,' June 21, 1873, a correspondent says that the late eminent surgeon replied to a patient who told him that he took his biscuits every morning at breakfast: '*My* biscuits! I've nothing to do with them! They were called after the baker who introduced them, whose name was *Abernethy*.' The correspondent adds that in his 'student days' he 'lodged with the party to whom the above was said.'

Aberystwith is so called from its situation near the mouth (*Aber*) of the *Ystwith*, a river which enters the sea at a short distance.

Abigail. Applied as a general term for a female domestic servant. The origin of this use of the name may be found in 1 Sam. xxv. 41, where Abigail says to David: 'Behold, let thine handmaid be a *servant* to wash the feet of the servants of my lord.'

Aborigines. 'This word is explained in every dictionary, English, Latin, or French, as a general name for the indigenous inhabitants of a country. In reality it is the proper name of a peculiar people of Italy, who were not indigenous, but were supposed to be a colony of Arcadians. The error has been founded chiefly on the supposed derivation of the word from *ab origine*. Never was a more eccentric etymology—a preposition with its governed case made plural by the modern final *s*!'—*H. J. Pye, Poet Laureate*, 1790–1813, quoted by Hone in the 'Table Book,' p. 638, edit. 1878.

Above, Over, Upon. These three words are almost synonymous, but there is a clear distinction between them, when applied literally. *Above* means a greater altitude, but it does not imply verticality. The moon and stars are *above* us, at considerable intervals of space; but they are not always *over* us, as a cloud is over the sea; nor are they *upon* us, as a man's hat is upon his head. The hat and the cloud are *above*, but the moon is not *over*, nor are the clouds *upon* us.

Above mentioned is a term used in composition to denote

something previously written. The expression is figurative, and is taken from the ancient method of writing on scrolls, so that everything previously mentioned in the same roll must be *above*.

Above Par, Below Par. These are common Americanisms. *Par* is a commercial term signifying that certain stocks or shares can be bought on the Stock Exchange at their nominal value; as when 100*l*. worth of London and North-Western Railway stock can be bought for 100*l*., there being neither premium nor discount. *Par*, therefore, may be taken to mean level or average. It is used in America to denote the state of health or spirits of a person. 'Below par' means low in health or spirits; 'above par' signifies in better health or spirits than usual.

Abscond. This word originally meant to conceal or to hide. Horace Walpole in one of his letters says: 'Virette *absconds*; and has sent M. de Pecquigny word that he shall *abscond* till he can find a proper opportunity of fighting him.'

Absinthe. The name is from the Syriac *Ab-sintha*, cause or author of sleep.

Absolom. It is a very general belief that Absolom was caught by the hair of his head in the tree, and that when his mule passed away he was left so hanging. There is nothing of the kind stated in the Scriptural account; we are distinctly told that his 'head' caught hold of the oak. He was probably caught in the fork of a branch by the neck. The expression 'he was yet alive' when Joab saw him, seems to imply that he was nearly dead. The weight of Absolom's hair (2 Sam. xiv. 26) when 'polled' or cut annually was equal to about 4 lbs. 2 ozs. of our weight.

Absurd. From the Latin words *ab*, from, and *surdus*, deaf. The allusion is to a reply such as is given by a deaf man to a question he has not heard distinctly.

Ac. This prefix to the names of places is derived from the Anglo-Saxon *ac*, an oak: *e.g.* Acton, which means the dwelling or town among the oaks.

Academy. From Academus, the name of the owner of the grove near Athens where Plato taught philosophy.

Accolade. From the Latin *ad*, to, and *collum*, the neck. This word was used to denote the ancient ceremony of conferring knighthood, which was by the sovereign laying his arms round the young knight's neck and embracing him. The accolade is now represented by the monarch touching the shoulder of the kneeling recipient with a sword, and addressing him by his christian name, bidding him rise, as 'Arise, Sir John.'

Accord. From the Latin *ad*, to, and *chorda*, the string of a musical instrument. Thus things that are in accord are in unison or harmony.

According to Gunter. In America this phrase is used in the same sense as the English 'according to Cocker.' Gunter was an English mathematician of great eminence, who died in 1626. His name is known in connection with 'Gunter's scale,' and the surveying chain, which is always spoken of as 'Gunter's chain.'

Accouchement. From the French *à*, to, and *couche*, a bed.

Account Current. The symbol *a/c* means 'account current.' It is often improperly used as an abbreviation of the word 'account,' in the sense of description or narrative.

Accumulate. From the Latin *ad*, to, and *cumulus*, a heap.

Ace at Cards. From the Latin *as*, a unit.

Acerbity. From the Latin *acerbus*, unripe; inferentially 'sour, rough.'

Aches. Isaac D'Israeli, in the 'Curiosities of Literature,' says: 'Swift's own edition of "The City Shower" has "old a-ches throb." A-ches is two syllables, but modern printers who had lost the right pronunciation have aches as one syllable, and then to complete the metre have foisted in "aches *will* throb." Thus what the poet and the linguist wish to preserve is altered and finally lost.'

Butler uses it as a dissyllable:—

> Can by their pains and a-ches find
> All turns and changes of the wind.
> *Hudibras*, iii. 2, 407.

and Shakespeare in the 'Tempest' makes Prospero threaten Caliban:—

> If thou neglect'st or dost unwillingly
> What I command, I'll rack thee with old cramps,
> Fill all thy bones with a-ches; make thee roar
> That beasts shall tremble at the din.

John Kemble always pronounced the word as a dissyllable, but endured much ridicule for doing so. The word seems now to be finally settled as a monosyllable.

Acorn. From the Anglo-Saxon *ac*, the oak, and *corn*, grain, or fruit.

Acre. The word 'acre,' which comes from the Latin *ager*, a field, originally meant an open space—a campaign, without reference to its size. It is still retained in that sense in the names of places: as Castle-acre, West-acre, &c. 'God's-acre' was the space around a church. The word now signifies a definite area. The English acre contains 43,560 square feet; the Scotch, 6,150 square yards. The Irish acre is equal to 1 English acre, 2 rods, and 19 perches. The Welsh contains about 2 acres English. The French acre is 54,450 square feet.

Acrobat. From a Greek word signifying 'to run on tiptoe.'

Acropolis. The citadel of Athens. At first Acropolis was the only name of the city, which was so called from Acrops, the founder. Afterwards when the city extended over the adjoining plains, the name Acropolis was confined to the citadel and the hilly ground adjoining.

Act of Uniformity. This Act, which was passed in 1661, for regulating public worship, &c., obliged all the clergy to subscribe the Thirty-Nine Articles. Upwards of 2,000 conscientious ministers left the Church of England and became dissenters, rather than submit.

Actresses. In the time of Shakespeare the female characters were always acted by boys. In the Epilogue to 'As You Like It,' Rosalind says, '*If I were a woman*, I would kiss as many of you,' &c., which proves that the player was not a female.

The earliest known mention of female performers upon the stage occurs in Coryat's 'Crudities,' published in 1611, but probably written some years before. When Coryat was at Venice, he went to a theatre, and he says, 'Here I observed certain things that I never saw before. For I saw women acte, a thing that I never saw before, though I have heard that it hath sometimes been used in London. . . . . they performed with as good a grace, action, gesture . . . . as ever I saw any masculine actor.'—Edition 1776, vol. ii.

Women were not allowed to act in stage-plays, in England, until after the Restoration. Charles II., in 1662, granted a licence for a theatre in Dorset Gardens, London. One of the clauses of the licence was as follows:—'Whereas the women's parts in plays have hitherto been acted by men in the habits of women, at which some have taken offence, we do permit and give leave for the time to come, that all women's parts be acted by women.'

Mrs. Coleman, who played Ianthe in Davenant's 'Siege of Rhodes,' in 1656, was probably the first English actress.

Adam Smith. The title of Smith's great work, 'The Wealth of Nations,' was perhaps suggested by Dryden's lines:—

> The winds were hush'd, the waves in ranks were cast
> As awfully as when God's people passed,
> Those, yet uncertain on whose sails to blow,
> These, where the *wealth of nations* ought to flow.

Ad captandum. This Latin phrase means 'in such a plausible manner as to attract notice.' The full phrase in Latin is *ad captandum vulgus,* to catch the attention of common or ignorant people.

Address Cards. The enamel of address cards is produced by the brushing over the card a mixture of 'Kremnitz white,' which is a fine variety of white lead. When dry, the surface is wiped with flannel dipped in powdered talc, and polished by vigorous rubbing with a hard brush.

Addle. There were two distinct Anglo-Saxon words which have been modernised into this form. The first, *Aδel*, signified a disease; from this we get *addle*, rotten. The other, *Æδlian*, to earn, thrive, or gain, is still in use as *addle* in Lancashire and the adjoining counties, where it is common to hear a man say he 'car *addle* thirty shillings a week.'

> I *addle* my ninepence every day.
> Richard of Dulton Dale.

In the sense of thriving, Halliwell quotes from Tusser:—

> Where ivy embraceth a tree very sore,
> Kill ivy, or tree will *addle* no more.

Adieu. This is purely French. In its original form it was *à Dieu*: literally 'To God,' but in its full sense expressing 'To God I commend you.'

Adjective. From the Latin *ad*, to, and *jactus*, from the verb *jacio*, to throw: meaning 'to throw or change the noun into a descriptive word,' or adjective. All adjectives are derived from nouns.

Adjourn. From the French *à*, to, and *jour*, a day: meaning 'to put off or postpone *to* (another) day.'

Adjutant. From the Latin *adjutans*, assisting. Hence the Adjutant of a regiment is one who assists the Major.

Ad libitum. This Latin phrase, or its contraction *ad lib.*, is often met with in English books or papers. Its literal meaning is 'at pleasure'; and it generally means 'as much as you please,' 'as far as you please,' &c.

Admiral is from Amir, an Arabic word for 'leader.' The syllable *al* is supposed to be a misplacement of the Arabic article *al*, 'the' or 'an.'

Admire. The Americans retain the old English use of this word in the sense of *wonder at*. Shakespeare speaks of 'most admired disorder,' which sounds like nonsense to modern English ears, but which an American would understand to mean 'in a wonderful, or extraordinary state of disorder.' They also use the word in the sense of *to desire very much*. Thus, in New England, it is not uncommon to hear such phrases as 'I should *admire* to go to Paris,' &c. It is still used in some parts of England in the sense of 'to wonder at.' Not long ago an old woman in Oxfordshire told a clergyman that 'if he saw her husband he would quite *admire* him, he looked so ill.'

Ad valorem. This is a Latin phrase signifying 'according to the value.' Thus, an *ad valorem* duty of 20 per cent. means a duty of 20 per cent. upon the value of the goods.

Advent. From the Latin *ad*, to, and *venio, ventus*, to come; applied to the coming of Christ.

Adverbs. Adverbs are, speaking generally, only convenient forms of abbreviation, enabling us to use a *word* where otherwise a *phrase* would be necessary. Thus we say *here* instead of 'in this place'; *then*, for 'at that time'; *thus*, for 'in that manner.' A large number of adverbs are formed from adjectives by adding the termination *ly*, which means *like*, but the principle of abbreviation still holds good; as in the case of *foolishly*, for 'in a foolish manner'; *hastily*, for 'in a hasty manner'; and *wisely*, 'like a wise man.'

Advertise. The accent was formerly placed on the middle syllable of this word. Ben Jonson ('Fox,' iv. 1) has :—

I therefore
Advértise to the state, how fit it were, &c.

and Shakespeare ('3 Henry VI.,' act iv. sc. 5) says :—

I have advértised him by secret means.

The original meaning of the word, according to Halliwell, was 'admonish.' Ben Jonson used it in this sense, in the words 'Let me advertise you,' meaning '*let me admonish you.*'

Advertisement. The earliest known advertisement is contained in a newspaper entitled '*Perfect Occurrencies of euery daie*;

iournall in Parliament, and other Moderate Intelligence, No. 13, From Fryday March the 26th to Fryday April the 2, 1647.' It is the advertisement of a book called '*The Divine Right of Church Government*, Collected by sundry eminent Ministers in the Citie of London, and is printed and published for Joseph Hunscot and George Calvert.'

Adult Schools. The first school exclusively for adults was established at Bala, in Merionethshire, in 1811, by the Rev. T. Charles.

Aërated. This word is often spelled by printers 'æra:ed,' than which nothing can be more erroneous. It is a word of four syllables, and should be pronounced as though written a-e-ra-ted. The same rule applies to aëronaut, aërial, &c.

Æsthetics. Probably the first use of this word in English literature was by Carlyle in his 'Essay on Richter' ('Edinburgh Review,' 1827), where he accompanies it with the following note: 'From αισθάνομαι, to feel. A word invented by Baumgarten (some eighty years ago) to express generally *the Science of the Fine Arts*, and now in universal use among the Germans. Perhaps we also might as well adopt it; at least if any such *science* should arise among us.'

Ætheling, a general title given to the king's eldest son by the Anglo-Saxons; corresponding to the modern 'Prince of Wales.'

Affidavit is based upon the Latin word *fides*, faith. In the middle ages the schoolmen formed the word *affidare*, to pledge one's faith; hence 'affidavit,' a certificate that some one has pledged his faith.

Affinity of the English and Dutch Languages. The close resemblance of the Friesic dialect to modern English was perhaps never better shown than in a song translated from the former by Mr. Bosworth, and published in the 'Book of Beauty', 1834, as follows :—

Modern Friesic.	English.
Hwat bist dhou Libben ?	What art (be'st) thou, Life ?
Ien wirch stribjen	A weary strife
Fen pine noed in soargh.	Of pain, need and sorrow ;
Lang oeren fen smerte	Long hours of grief (smart)
In nochten-ho koart !	And joys—how short (curt)
Det foed wine de móars.	That vanish (fade) on the morrow.
Deadh hwat bist dhou ?	Death, what art thou ?
Ta hwaem allen buisge	To whom all bow,
Fen de scepterde kening ta da slave ;	From sceptred king to slave ;
De lætst bæst freon	The last best friend,
Om uns soargen to eingjen	Our cares (sorrows) to end,
Dhyn gebiet is in t'græf.	Thy empire is in the grave.

Affix, Prefix. An 'affix' in grammar is a syllable placed at the end of a word, by which its exact meaning is modified or made clearer. A 'prefix' is a syllable placed at the beginning of a word for the same purpose. Thus, the word *clean* means an entire absence of dirt; the affix *ly* alters the word to 'cleanly,' which means a person free from dirty habits. The prefix *un* completely reverses the meaning, as the word 'unclean' signifies something dirty, or the opposite of clean.

Affluence. From the Latin *affluo, affluens,* to flow to. Wealth may be said to flow to the rich, without effort on their part.

Affront. From the Latin *frons,* the forehead. The word means 'to meet front to front; to encounter.'

Afraid. This word originally did not necessarily convey the idea of terror. 'To affray' meant 'to startle with sudden or unexpected noise or disturbance.' Chaucer uses the word 'afraid' to denote being awakened by the singing of birds:—

> Me met thus in my bed all naked
> And looked for the, for I was wakëd
> With small foules a grete hepe
> That had *afraide* me out of my slepe
> Through noise and sweteness of her song.

Africans. The children of the blackest Africans are born white. In a month they become pale yellow; in a year brown; at four years, dirty black, and at thirty, glossy black. The blood of blacks and whites is of the same colour. The colouring matter of blacks is supposed to be due to bilious secretions in the mucous membranes underneath the cuticle.—*Sir R. Phillips.*

Aft, Abaft. Both these are nautical terms derived from the word 'after,' in the sense of 'behind.' Thus a seaman will say the captain is '*abaft* the mainmast,' when he is between the mainmast and the stern; or 'he is gone *aft,*' signifying that he is gone towards the stern.

After us the Deluge. This was a saying of Madame de Pompadour. It is generally attributed to Metternich.

Against, Again. 'To ride again,' or 'against,' formerly meant 'to ride to meet.' Chaucer says:—

> And praide hem for the riden *again* the queene
> The honour of his regne to sustene.

Agate. The petrifaction so called was named from the river Achates in Sicily, where it was first found.

Age of Women. The delicacy as to mentioning the age of

women is no piece of modern sensitiveness. In the Old Testament, although great numbers of women are mentioned, there is but one —Sarah, Abraham's wife—whose age is recorded.

Agenda. This word in its original signification relates to the order of the offices or services of the Church. In ordinary life, it is the memorandum of the various items of business which are to be brought before a council, or committee, for discussion or settlement.

Aggravate. From the Latin *ad*, to, and *gravis*, heavy; hence to aggravate a trouble is to make it heavier to bear. Its use in the sense of 'provoke' or 'irritate' is improper.

Aghast. *Gast* was the Anglo-Saxon name for 'ghost' or 'spirit.' To 'stand aghast' is therefore to stand as though frightened by the apparition of a ghost.

Agony. Comes from a Greek word signifying to contend for a prize, or to struggle for the mastery in a prize-fight.

Agriculture. This term is from the Latin *ager*, a field, and *cultura*, cultivation.

Ague, from the French *aigu*, sharp. The French say *fièvre-aigue*—acute fever. In English the word *aigu* has been altered to 'ague,' and its meaning confined to intermittent fevers.

Air-bladder. The air-bladder of fishes is the provision within their bodies which enables them to rise or fall in the water. Near the bottom, the weight of the superincumbent waters compresses the air-bladder, and consequently the *body* of the fish shrinks until its bulk is of equal weight with the water it displaces. In the middle and upper regions the bladder expands in proportion, so that the body of the fish is always equiponderant with the water in which it floats. Thus according to the dilatation or contraction of the air-bladder, the fish can regulate its depth in the water at pleasure.

Airs. Conceited people are said to 'give themselves airs.' This proverbial saying is closely allied to the phrase, 'puffed up with pride.'

Aisle. From the Latin *ala*, a wing. The word 'aisle' means something added 'by the side of,' as the *aisles* of a church, which run by the side of the nave. The word as used to denote the passages by which the seats in places of worship are approached is a corruption of *alley*, a passage. The north aisle of the choir of Lincoln Cathedral was formerly called the *Chanter's alley*. 'Mr.

Olden did say that when he came to be churchwarden he would make the Puritans come up the middle *alley* on their knees to the rails.'—1638. *Waltington, Hist. Notices*, i. 70.

A-kimbo. The derivation of this word is obscure. It is probably related to the Keltic *kam*, or *cam*, crooked. Cotgrave, in 1611, has 'carrie his armes a-kemboll,' which he illustrates by comparing the attitude to the two handles or 'eares' of a pot or cup. Mr. Wedgwood connects it with the Italian *a-schimbo*, awry, crookedly. Dryden has :—

> The *kimbo* handles seem with bearsfoot carved,
> And never yet to table have been served.

Halliwell has 'arms on kemboll, *i.e.* a-kimbo.'

Al is an Arabian particle corresponding to the English word 'the.' It is a prefix of many English words, in which it is equivalent to definiteness, as *Alkoran*, The Koran.

Alabama. The name of this American State is composed of three Indian words, signifying 'Here we rest.'

Alabaster is so called from Alabastron, a place in Egypt where it is found in great abundance.

Alarum, Alarum-bell, &c. Probably from the old Norman-French word *larum*, a thief. One can easily believe that in the Norman times it was necessary to have on each estate a *larum* bell, that is a thief-bell, to give notice of the presence of robbers. Instead of the modern 'Stop thief!' the ancient cry would be '*a larum! a larum!*' Our modern word 'alarm' evidently arose in this way. The modern French form of the word is *larron*.

Alas! This English interjection is a compound of the Latin words, *ai*, denoting grief, and *lassus*, weary.

'**Alas, Master, for it was borrowed**!' This, from 2 Kings vi. 5, is a mistranslation. The Hebrew words *vehu shaul* signify 'and it hath been sought.' The true meaning of the text is 'Alas! the axe-head is fallen into the water, and we have sought for it in vain.'—*Adam Clarke.*

Albert is a contraction of the Old English name Ethelbert. It was first abbreviated to Ealbert, and afterwards to Albert. According to Verstegan, it means 'noble conceited, or advised, or of noble conceit or adviscment.' It is perhaps needless to say that the word 'conceit' is here used in its original sense of 'power of apprehension, understanding, acumen, judgment.'

Albert Chains. When Prince Albert visited Birmingham in

1849, the jewellers of the town presented him with a watch chain such as are now in use. They have ever since been called 'Alberts.'

Albino. An Albino is a white negro (*albus*, white), so first called by the Portuguese. Albinoes are also found among white people. The characteristics are extreme whiteness of the skin, white or very pale flaxen hair, and pink eyes. The wool of the negro Albino is generally perfectly white. It is now known that these characteristics are the result of a peculiar disease, to which some animals, as the domestic rabbit, are also liable.

Album is derived from the Latin *albus*, white; hence its application to unprinted books as receptacles for manuscripts or drawings.

Alcohol is the English form of an Arabic word *alkohl*, the spirit or essence. In the original the word exactly corresponds in meaning with our word 'ethereal.' There is but one source of alcohol—sugar. From whatever vegetable product alcohol has its origin, whether grain, fruit, roots, or sap, the sugar contained in it is the only source of the spirit. In some plants the sugar exists in the saccharine condition; in others, as in grain, it is present in the form of starch, which is converted by artificial means into sugar. The fermentation of saccharine fluids produces alcohol in a diluted form. It is afterwards separated from the watery portion of the fluid by distillation.

Alcove. An Arabic word which comes to us through the Spanish *alcoba*, a place in a room railed off to hold a bed of state.

Alderman. Most of the English Dictionaries derive this term from the Anglo-Saxon word *ælder*, older, and *man*. There is, however, strong reason to believe, with Verstegan, that it means 'of *all the men* chief.' *Alder* was a noun of multitude, signifying 'all of us,' or all that are concerned, and *alderest* meant 'first or chief of all' in a company, and is so used by Chaucer, in many words, one of which completely upsets the 'elder' theory. This is the word *alder-eldest*. Chaucer would not be likely to use a tautological form like this, if *alder* had meant 'elder.' Then he makes the Host of the Tabard propose that the best narrator of a tale shall have a supper 'at our alder-cost,' meaning at the cost *of all*, and it is settled that the Host, on their setting out on their pilgrimage in the morning, shall lead the way as 'alder-cock,' that is the cock, or leader, of all. Halliwell makes the case stronger by quoting the word 'alder-youngest,' a term which upon the 'elder' theory would be absolutely ridiculous.

Alderney Cows. There are certainly not a hundred cows approaching the pure Alderney breed in the entire island of Alderney; yet one dealer advertises in the 'Times' that he annually imports 'from the island' upwards of 1,000 cows! He does not tell us by what process they are produced.

Ale. This name for malt liquor was probably introduced into England by the Danes, as the name *öl* is still the name for malt liquor among the Scandinavian nations. The Anglo-Saxons used the word *beor* until the irruption of the Danes, but the word *beer* was gradually disused, and the name *ale* was general until the introduction of hops from Germany in the reign of Henry VIII. With the hops came again into use the German or Saxon word, *bier*, or beer, which was at first applied only to the hopped liquor to distinguish it from ale—that which was unhopped. Although unhopped ale is no longer in use, both names are retained, but are used roughly to designate strength. In some counties ale signifies 'weak,' and beer is 'strong,' but generally the name *beer* is applied to the weaker products of the brewery, and *ale* to the stronger, the varying degrees being designated by X, XX, XXX, and so on.

Ale-conner was an officer appointed by Courts Leet or Corporations to test the quality of the ale supplied within their separate jurisdictions. The name is a corruption of Kenner, one who *kens* or knows.—See FLESH-CONNER.

Alert. *Erte* in old French was a watch-tower. *Estre à l'erte* was 'to be on the watch;' hence *à l'erte*, alert, watchful, vigilant. See INERT.

Alexandria. In reading or speaking in *Latin*, this name is pronounced *Alexan-dri'a*, but in English it is properly *Alex-a'ndria*, the accent being placed on the third syllable.

Aliens. By the English law an alien is one born out of the allegiance of the sovereign, unless his father be a British subject. Formerly aliens were subject to many disabilities, but under the Act 7 and 8 Vic. c. 66, these were much mitigated. An alien can now acquire nearly all the rights of natural-born subjects, by memorialising the Home Secretary and taking a prescribed oath. He cannot, however, become a member of a municipal corporation, of Parliament, or of the Privy Council.

Aliquant, Aliquot (in arithmetic). An *aliquant* part of a number is one that *cannot* be multiplied so as to produce that number. Thus 3 is an *aliquant* part of 10, because thrice 3 are 9, and 4 times 3 are 12. An *aliquot* number, on the contrary, is one which *can* be multiplied so as to produce the number; thus, 5 is an *aliquot* of 15 and 20, because 3 times 5 are 15, and 4 times 5 are 20.

Alkali. From the Arabic *al*, the, and *kali*, the plant from the ashes of which soda was first obtained.

Alkanet root is a root containing a stain of a deep red colour, which it will only impart to oils, fats, and spirits. It is used for colouring hair-oils, and for deepening the colour of mahogany. It will only impart a dirty-brown tinge to water.

Alley. Bailey defines this as 'a walk in a garden. Some say that an "alley" is different from a "path" in that an alley should be only broad enough for two persons to walk abreast, but that the breadth of a path is not determined.'

Alligator. The name arose from the expression of a Spanish sailor on board an English ship, who seeing an alligator in one of the tropical rivers of America, said ' that's a *lagarto*,' *lagarto* being the Spanish word for lizard.

All serene. This slang expression is derived from the Spanish word *serena*, which is used in Cuba as a countersign by sentinels. It is equivalent to the English phrase, 'All's well.'

Allow. This word formerly had the meaning of 'approve.' The baptismal service says 'nothing doubting but that He favourably *alloweth* this charitable work.' Latimer in one of his sermons (Parker Society's ed. p. 176) says, 'Ezekias did not follow the steps of his father Ahaz, and was well *allowed* in it.'

Alloy. We derive this word from the French term *à la loi*, 'according to law.' The meaning is gold or silver reduced in value by admixture with inferior metals in accordance with regulations established by law.

Gold and silver before being made into coins are *alloyed* with baser metals to increase their hardness or capacity for wear. Thus 'standard gold' in English law means twenty-two parts of pure gold to two of alloy, and one pound of 'sterling silver' consists of eleven ounces, two pennyweights of 'fine' silver, and eighteen pennyweights of alloy.

Allude. This word is gradually losing its proper signification, which is 'to hint at, to intimate slightly, to suggest.' Yet in newspapers we daily see it used in the sense of 'to mention,' or 'to state.' Dean Alford once wrote 'I did not *allude to it*, I distinctly mentioned it.'

Alma Mater, a Latin phrase generally applied by scholars to the University at which they graduated. The literal meaning is 'a benign mother.'

Almack's. This well-known place of assembly in King Street, St. James's, was built by one Mac Call, a tavern-keeper, in 1759. He was originally a poor Highlander, who, having made his way to London, inverted the syllables of his name to disguise his Northern origin. As *Almack* he opened the tavern and the celebrated rooms which were known as Almack's for the greater part of a century. They were afterwards called 'Willis's Rooms.'

Almanac. The derivation of this word is uncertain. Some derive it from the Arabic *al*, the, and *mana* or *manah*, a reckoning or diary. Verstegan derives it from the Anglo-Saxon *al-moan-heed*, 'to wit, the regard or observations of all the moons; hence is derived the name of almanac.' Another derivation is from the Anglo-Saxon *All monath*, all the months. The earliest known English almanac is 'John Somer's Calendar,' written at Oxford in 1380. The earliest English *printed* almanac was published by Richard Pynson in 1497. 'Poor Robin's Almanac' was commenced in 1652. 'Moore's Almanac,' for many years the most popular in England, circulating by hundreds of thousands, was established about the beginning of the 18th century. (Haydn says, '1698 or 1713.') On October 20, 1603, James I. granted a patent to the Stationers' Company 'for the sole printing of *Primers, Psalms, and Almanacs*,' which continued in force until 1775, when it was upset by the Court of Common Pleas in favour of a bookseller named Carnan. Almanacs were for a long time subject to a duty of 1*s*. 3*d*. per copy, but this was abolished in 1834. In all legal proceedings, 'the *almanac* to go by is that annexed to the Book of Common Prayer.'—*Wharton*.

Alms. This word is a curious example of the English fashion of shortening words in common use. It came to us from the Latin *eleemosyna*, which in the form *eleemosynary* we still retain as an adjective. The noun has in course of time assumed the following forms—almosine, almosie, almous, almose, almesse, almoyn, almes, and finally, as at present, alms. Johnson says, 'this word has no singular'; while Todd, on the contrary, says it is 'without a plural.'

Aloof. This is a nautical term slightly altered. To *luff* a ship is to keep her closer to the wind, or so to steer as to meet the wind. In the case of a hostile vessel of war being discovered to leeward, a merchantman would 'luff' in order to keep a*loof*.

Alpha and Omega. *Alpha* is the first letter in the Greek alphabet, and *Omega* the last. 'I am Alpha and Omega, the first and the last' (Rev. i. 11).

Alphabet. This word is composed of the names of the first two letters of the Greek alphabet—Alpha and Beta. It corresponds exactly to the English 'A B C,' as in the phrase, 'He does not know his A B C,' meaning *alphabet*. The alphabets of different nations vary in the number of letters, as the following table will show :—

English .	. 26	German .	. 26	Arabic .	. 28
French .	. 25	Russian .	. 35	Persian .	. 32
Italian .	. 20	Latin .	. 25	Hebrew .	. 22
Spanish .	. 27	Greek .	. 24	Sanscrit .	. 44

Bentley, in whose day I and J, and U and V were considered identical, says :—' It is a mathematical demonstration that these twenty-four letters [that is, of the English alphabet] admit of so many changes in their order, and make such a long roll of differently arranged alphabets, not two of which are alike, that they could not be exhausted, though a million of million of writers should each write a thousand alphabets a day for a million million of years.'

The following verse contains all the letters of the alphabet, reckoning I and J as one :—' And I, even I, Artaxerxes the king, do make a decree to all the treasurers which are beyond the river, that whatsoever Ezra the priest, the scribe of the law of the God of Heaven, shall require of you it shall be done speedily' (Ezra vii. 21).

Alps. The word *Alp*, or *Alb*, is Keltic, and signifies 'white.' Its application to the white tops of the mountains of the Alps is a natural one, and it is singular that the names of nearly all the great mountains of the earth have some reference to their snow-covered summits. *Snow*don; Mont *Blanc*; *Sna*fell, in the Isle of Man; *Sneeuw* Bergen, at the Cape of Good Hope; *Snee*hatten (*Snow*-hat), in Norway; *Snee*koppe (Snowhead), in Bohemia; *Weiss*horn (*White*horn) and Tête *Blanche* (*White*head), in Switzerland, as well as the names of many other mountains in languages not so familiar, all show that they are of a descriptive character.

Alto-rilievo, Italian, *high relief*. The word *rilievo*, being Italian, is pronounced as though written *ree-le-aý-vo*, with the accent on the third syllable.

A.M. or **M.A.** The rule followed by the editors of both the Oxford and Cambridge Chronicles as to the position of these initials, is that where the context is in Latin, the form is A.M., and where English, M.A. For instance, in the table 'Distributiones Foedorum' we find 'A.M.,' and in the 'Lists of Members of Colleges' 'M.A.'

Amalgamate. Metals are amalgamated when they are combined or united with mercury. Tin, for instance, is *amalgamated* with mercury for the purpose of 'silvering' looking-glasses. George Hudson, the Railway magnate of the period 1843-50, used this word to denote the union of two railway companies. At a meeting at York he announced that the 'North Midland,' of which he was chairman, had 'amalgamated' with the 'Midland,' which then ran from Derby and Nottingham to Rugby only. From that time the word has come into general use in a similar sense.

Amateur, originally French, from the Latin *amator*, a lover. Hence an 'amateur' is a *lover* of any particular art, but does not practise it professionally.

Amber is so called from the German word *ambern*, from *anbrennen*, to burn. The German name for the fossil is *bernstein* or burnstone. Dr. Girtanner is of opinion that amber is an animal substance produced by ants, as wax is by bees. He states that the old pine forests are inhabited by large ants, which form hills of five or six feet in diameter; and that it is in these ancient forests, or in places where they have been, that fossil amber is usually found. Freshly-formed amber is of the consistence of honey, or half-melted wax; it is of a yellow colour; gives the same results on analysis, and hardens in a solution of common salt. The fact that ants are found more frequently than other insects in fossil amber supports Dr. Girtanner's theory.

Ambidexter, from the Latin *ambo*, both, and *dexter*, skilful, is a term applied to persons who can use the right and left hands with equal facility.

Ambition, from the Latin word *ambio*, I go round. The allusion is to the practice among the ancient Romans of *going round* to canvas for votes by a person desirous or ambitious to obtain a certain office.

Ambush, from the French *en*, in, and *bois*, a wood or bushes.

Amen. The meaning of this word at the end of a prayer is *so be it*. At the end of a Creed it signifies *so it is*. The word is Hebrew, and is equivalent to 'yea,' or 'truly,' used intensively.

In the Prayer Book the word Amen is sometimes printed in ordinary type, and sometimes in italics. Dr. Pinnock, in his 'Laws and Usages of the Church,' gives the following explanation :— 'When the *Amen* is in the same type as the text to which it is appended, it is to be said by the same person or persons who utter the text. When it is in a different type from the text, it becomes a *response* by itself, and is to be said by the congregation.'

Amen Corner. Before the Reformation the clergy walked annually in procession to St. Paul's Cathedral on Corpus Christi Day. They mustered at the upper end of Cheapside, and there commenced to chant the *Paternoster*, which they continued through the whole length of the street, thence called Paternoster Row, pronouncing the *Amen* at the spot now called Amen Corner. Then commencing the *Ave Maria*, they turned down Ave Maria Lane. After crossing Ludgate they chanted the *Credo* in Creed Lane. Old Stow mentions Creed Lane, and adds that Amen Lane 'is lately added thereto,' from which it may be inferred that the processional chanting ended at that spot. Amen Lane no longer exists.

Amende honorable. This phrase now signifies a manly acknowledgment of a fault, with an honorable retractation, apology, and, if necessary, reparation. Formerly it was a disgraceful punishment for offences against public decency or morality. Bailey describes it as a 'disgraceful sort of punishment, where an offender is delivered up to the common hangman, who having stripped him to his shirt, and put a rope about his neck and a wax taper in his hand, leads him to the court, where he is to beg pardon of God, the king, and the court.'

America, the name applied to the New World, is derived from Amerigo Vespucci, a native of Florence. He visited the eastern coasts of the western hemisphere a few years after their discovery by Columbus, and having impudently given the name 'Tierra de Amerigo' to the newly-discovered country in some maps that he published, the name was adopted, and is still in use. The earliest printed book in reference to America was printed at Rome by Silber in 1493. It is a translation of a letter of Columbus, by De Cosco, into Latin, and bears the title 'Epistola Christofori Colom: de Insulis Indiae supra Gangem nuper inuentis.' It was published a few months after the discovery of America. There is a copy in the British Museum. Printing was introduced into Mexico and other Spanish settlements at a very early period. The first book printed in any of the English settlements was a crown octavo edition of the Psalms. The title ran thus:—'The Psalms in

Metre, faithfully translated for the use, edification, and comfort of the saints in publick and private, especially in New England, 1640.' The book was printed by Stephen Day at Cambridge, Massachusetts. In the 'running title' the word 'psalm' stands on each left-hand page, but on the opposite or right-hand pages it is spelt 'psalme.' *Thomas's History of Printing in America.*

Americanisms. A large number of words and phrases not generally to be found in English dictionaries are used colloquially in America, many of which would be looked upon by purists as vulgarisms, and indeed are so classed by Americans. If the origin of these peculiarities be traced, it will be found that a large proportion of them are still current, or, at any rate, within living memory have been current in rural localities in England. The appellation *Americanism* is, notwithstanding, quite correct. The original words or phrases have, for the most part, become obsolete in the mother country. Their survivorship, therefore, in America partakes of the nature of a revival or of a new life. But there is another class in which entirely new words and phrases have been adopted in America to suit the varying and novel exigencies of a new country. Such words or phrases are, therefore, true *Americanisms*. Many of these have been inserted in this book, but their American origin has been distinctly pointed out in every case. Few persons are aware that the peculiar intonation of American speech is simply a survival of the *patois* of the East Anglian districts, from which the earliest settlers emigrated. Not only the nasal sounds, but many American phrases are quite common in Suffolk among the farmers and the peasantry, and a stranger passing an afternoon in Woodbridge market might fancy himself in Massachusetts.

American Flag. It is a curious fact that the stars and stripes are both to be found on George Washington's shield. The engraving on this page is from a brass in the church of Brington in Northamptonshire, where several generations of the Washington family were buried. The stars are five-pointed, and the stripes are alternately red and white as in the flag. This coincidence has led many to suppose that the devices were adopted in compliment to Washington, but the flag seems to have been a gradual out-

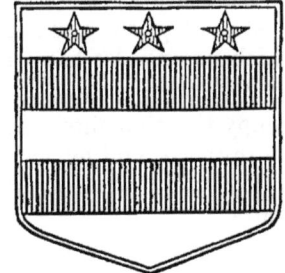

growth, and in its original form was merely a modification of the English, the Union Jack being retained and the red field split up into thirteen stripes of alternate red and white to represent the thirteen colonies. A flag almost identical with this was used by the East India Company as far back as 1704, the thirteen stripes being the same, and the only difference being that it was cantoned with St. George's cross instead of with the Union Jack.

American Postage Stamps. The portraits on the various denominations of the U.S. postage stamps are as follows:—

Cent.		Cent.		Cent.	
1	Franklin	6	Lincoln	15	Webster
2	Jackson	7	Stanton	24	Scott
3	Washington	10	Jefferson	30	Hamilton
5	Taylor	12	Clay	90	Perry

American States. The States of Alabama, Mississippi, Kentucky, Illinois, Ohio, Missouri, Arkansas and Wisconsin, were all so called from the Indian names of their chief rivers.

Amethyst. From a Greek word signifying a remedy against drunkenness, it being supposed that wine drunk from a cup made of amethyst would not intoxicate.

Ammonia. This name is derived from the temple of Jupiter Ammon in Egypt, near which muriate of ammonia was first made by burning the dung of the numerous camels belonging to pilgrims and other worshippers.

Among the Gods. This expression arose from the fact that the ceiling of Drury Lane Theatre was formerly painted in imitation of a blue sky and fleeting clouds, among which great numbers of Cupids were disporting themselves. As the ceiling extended over the gallery, its occupants were said to be 'among the gods.'

Amour propre. A French phrase, literally 'proper love.' Applied in English to that proper amount of self-respect or self-esteem which no one else has a right to disregard or intrude upon.

Amusement formerly meant something to *muse* on, or to occupy the thoughts. Richardson has, 'Here I put my pen into the inkhorn, and fell into a strong and deep *amusement*, revolving in my mind with great perplexity the amazing change of our affairs.'

Ancestor 'differs from predecessor, in that it applies to a natural person and his progenitors, whilst the latter is applied to a corporation, and those who have held offices before those who now fill them.'—*Wharton.*

Ancestry. The ascending scale of lineal ancestry in legal phraseology formerly ran thus :—1 Pater, 2 Avus, 3 Proavus, 4 Abavus, 5 Atavus, 6 Tritavus, 7 Tritavipater, 8 Proaviatavus.—*Wharton.*

Ancient City Customs. The origin of the City officers counting horsenails, &c., every year at Westminster Hall is thus described in Blount's 'Ancient Tenures,' 1815 :—

'Walter le Brun, farrier, in the Strand, in Middlesex, was to have a piece of ground in the parish of St. Clement, to place a forge there, he rendering six horseshoes for it. This rent was antiently wont to be paid to the Exchequer every year; for instance in the reign of King Edward I., when Walter Marescullus paid at the *crucem lapideam* six horseshoes with nails, for a certain building which he held of the King *in capite* opposite the stone cross; in the second year of King Edward I.; in the fifteenth year of King Edward II.; and afterwards. It is still rendered at the Exchequer by the mayor and citizens of London, to whom in process of time the said piece of ground was granted.'

The chopping with the *Whittle* is thus described :—

'Walter de Aldeham holds land of the King, in the More in the county of Salop by the service of paying to the King yearly at his Exchequer two knives [whittles] whereof one ought to be of that value or goodness that at the first stroke it would cut asunder in the middle a hasle rod of a years growth and of the length of a cubit, which same service ought to be done in the middle of the Exchequer in the presence of the treasurer and barons every year on the morrow of St. Michael; and the said knives to be delivered to the chamberlain to keep for the Kings use.'

Ancient Dancing Custom. By a note in Reed's 'Shakespeare,' we learn that in dancing 'A Kiss was antiently the establish'd fee of a lady's partner.' So in Lovel's 'Dialogue betweene Custom and Veritie,' 1581—

> But some reply what foole would daunce,
> If that when daunce is doone
> He may not have at ladye's lips,
> That which in daunce he woon?
> *Brand's Popular Antiquities,* vol. ii., p. 87.

Ancient Dwelling Houses. Wright, in his 'England in the Middle Ages,' says that in the time of William I., and for some time afterwards, the mansions of the nobility were built mainly of wood. He adds, 'I am not aware that there are any known remains of a stone mansion in this country older than the reign of Henry II.'

Ancient Games. In 'Erondells French Garden,' published in 1605, is a curious list of games then in use:—'They played at *cardes*, at *cent*, at *primcoe*, at *trumpe*, at *dice*, at *tables*, at *lurch*, at *draughts*, at *perforce*, at *pleasant*, at *blowing* [qy. blow-point?], at *queenes-game*, at *chesses*,' and 'the maydens did play at [cross] *purposes*, at *sales*, to *think*, at *wonders*, at *states*, at *vertues*, at *answers*.'

Ancient Law as to Innkeepers. By the laws of Edward the Confessor, if a man lay three nights at an inn, the host was answerable if he afterwards committed any offence. The first night—*uncuth*, or unknown night—he was reckoned a stranger. The second night—'twa night'—he was a guest. The third night he was looked upon as an *agenhinde* or domestic.

Ancient Lights (*law term*). The undisturbed enjoyment of daylight and air for ventilation for twenty years and upwards gives a right which cannot afterwards be disturbed.

Ancient Meal-Times. Wright, in his 'Domestic Manners of the Middle Ages,' &c., p. 155, says—' Until comparatively a very recent date, the hour of dinner, even among the highest classes of society, was ten o'clock in the forenoon. There was an old proverb which defined the divisions of the domestic day as follows:—

> Lever à six, dîner à dix,
> Souper à six, coucher à dix;

which is preserved in a still older and more complete form as follows:—

> Lever à cinq; dîner à neuf;
> Souper à cinq; coucher à neuf;
> Fait vivre d'ans nonante et neuf.'

Which may be translated—

> Get up at five, and dine at nine;
> Take supper at five; go to bed at nine,
> And you'll live till your years are ninety and nine.

In Chaucer's day the hour of *prime* was the usual dinner time. *Prime* was one of the canonical hours in the Romish Church, and was probably about nine o'clock. In the 'Schippeman's Tale' the monk calls for dinner at prime, as follows:—

> Goth now your way, quod he, al stile and softe
> And let us *dyne* as sone as ye may,
> For by my chilendre, it is *prime* of day.

Ancient method of sealing Deeds. Verstegan in the Glossary attached to 'Restitution' has '*Gewang*, the cheeke or wang; hereof the side teeth are called wang teeth. Before the use of Seales was in England, divers writings had the wax of them bitten with the *wang tooth* of him that passed them; which was also mentioned in Rime, as thus—

> In witness of the sothe
> Ich han bitten this wax with my wang tothe.'
> *Restitution, &c.*, e lit. 1655, p. 174.

Ancient Money. Silver and gold coins were anciently struck of such weights that one of them represented the value of some animal. Thus the word *kesitah* (Genesis xxxiii. 19), translated 'pieces of money,' is literally *a lamb*; and the Latin *pecunia*, from which we get *pecuniary*, is derived from *pecus*, a general name for sheep and smaller animals. In early times coins were stamped with the figures of a horse, a bull, or a hog, and bore the names of those animals. Afterwards, as values changed, the figures stamped on the coins no longer represented their value in cattle, and then arose the angel, the rose, the eagle, &c.

Anenst. Chaucer uses this word in the sense of 'against,' and Ben Jonson ('Alchemist,' act ii.) has

> And right *anenst* him a dog snarling-er.

The word is still in use in Warwickshire in the sense of 'opposite.'

Aneroïd Barometer. This barometer measures and indicates the pressure of the atmosphere by means of a metallic spring of extreme delicacy, no mercury, alcohol, or other liquid being used. The word is properly pronounced an-e-ró-id.

Angel. This was the name of an ancient English coin, originally of the value of 6*s.* 8*d.*; but for a long period, its value was 10*s.* The coin was so called from its obverse bearing the figure of the Archangel Michael overcoming the Dragon. An old verse in which its name appears is a very convenient 'ready reckoner'; it runs thus:—

> Compute but the pence
> Of one day's expense,
> So many pounds, *angels*, groats, and pence,
> Are spent in one whole year's circumference.

So that if a penny a day be spent, the amount at the end of the year will be equal to one pound, one angel, one groat, and one penny, or 1*l.* 10*s.* 5*d.* Twopence a day is equal to two pounds, two angels, two groats, and two pennies, or 3*l.* 0*s.* 10*d.*, and so on.

Anglesey. The Angles were a German tribe who came over with the Saxons after the departure of the Roman, to help the Ancient Britons to resist the Picts. The Angles afterwards took possession of the northern, and the Saxons of the southern parts of England. The Angles also founded a colony in the island of *Mona*, which thenceforward became known as Anglesey, or Anglesea, which means the *ey*, *ea*, or island of the Angles.

Anglo-Saxon. The compound term *Anglo-Saxon* first occurs in the life of Alfred the Great. His contemporary Asser calls that prince *Angul-Saxonum Rex*, King of the Anglo-Saxons. The employment of the term as a designation of the language and literature is much more recent.—*G. P. Marsh.*

Anglo-Saxon Language. 'There is no proof that *Anglo-Saxon* was ever spoken anywhere but on the soil of Great Britain; for the *Heliand* and other remains of *Old* Saxon are not *Anglo-Saxon*, and I think it must be regarded, not as a language which the colonists or any of them brought with them from the Continent, but as a new speech resulting from the fusion of many separate elements. It is therefore indigenous, if not aboriginal.'— *Marsh's Lectures on the English Language.* Although a large number of alien words have been added to the English language during the present century, while the number of Anglo-Saxon words remains the same, it will be seen by the following table (which is condensed from Marsh) that the proportion of Anglo-Saxon used by the best modern writers is on the increase:—

		Per cent.
Swift—*Political Lying*	employs of Anglo-Saxon words	68
Johnson—*Preface to Dictionary*	,, ,,	72
Junius—*Letters*		76
Hume—*History of England*	,,	73
Gibbon—*Decline and Fall*	,,	70
Mrs. Browning—*Cry of the Children*	,,	92
Robert Browning—*Blougram's Apology*	,, ,,	84
Tennyson—*In Memoriam*	,,	89
Ruskin—*Elements of Drawing*	,, ,,	84
Longfellow—*Miles Standish*	,, ,,	87

In the New Testament Matthew averages 93; Luke, 92; John, 96; and the Romans, 92 per cent. Chaucer's *Canterbury Tales* has 90. Spenser's *Faery Queene*, 86.

Anglo-Saxon Numerals. 'Our Saxon fathers formed words for the numerals up to nine, but there their power of invention seems to have abandoned them, for *ten* is not an original word. It comes from the Saxon verb *tynan*, to close, to shut in or up, expressive of the simple fact that when the calculation had gone on to the extent of the ten fingers, one after another having been turned in, both hands were found " closed " or " shut in." Eleven is simply the *an lif*, " one left," of our Saxon fathers, as was the case after both hands were closed, and twelve is the contracted form of *twa-lif*, " two left." After twelve the numerals are simply compounds of *ten* and the lower numbers, until we arrive at twenty, which consists of the dual *twain*, and the old word *tig*, meaning ten.'—*De Vere, Studies in English*, pp. 261-262.

Anglo-Saxon Wills were transcribed three times on the same sheet of parchment. They were then read over in the presence of witnesses, and cut off from each other with a waved or indented line. The copies were then given to three several persons for safe custody.

Animals Drinking. All carnivorous animals lap up water with the tongue. Herbivorous animals, as the horse and the ox, suck it up.

Animal Names as Verbs. Many English verbs are metaphors derived from the names or habits of animals. Thus, we ' crow over ' a person like a cock ; we ' quail,' as that bird does in presence of danger ; we ' caper,' as a goat (*caper*) ; we ' duck ' our heads ; we ' ferret ' a thing out ; we ' dog ' a person's footsteps ; we ' sneak ' like a snake ; we ' strut ' like an ostrich (*strouthos*) ; and so on.

Annie Laurie. The heroine of the popular song was the daughter of Sir Robert Laurie of Maxwelltown. In his family register he thus recorded her birth :—' At the pleasure of the Almighty God, my daughter Anna Laurie was born upon the 16th day of December, 1682 years, and was baptised by Mr. Geo. Hunter of Glencairn.' Annie Laurie was married in 1709, to James Ferguson, of Craigdanoch, and was mother of Alexander Ferguson, the hero of Burns's song ' The Whistle.' The composer of the song ' Annie Laurie ' was William Douglas of Fingland, in the Stewartry of Kirkcudbright.

Annul, Disannul. Contrary to all analogy, the prefix *dis* in the second of these words has no negative quality, the two words having precisely the same meaning, that of making void or nullifying. Chaucer uses the word *adnul* in the same sense. Dr. Johnson says of *disannul*, ' It ought to be rejected as ungrammatical and barbarous.' There is a similar want of analogy in the case of the word *unloose*, which has precisely the same meaning as the verb to *loose*.

Answer. This word, now so common, is derived from an Anglo-Saxon legal term, *answarian—an*, against, *swaran*, to swear —meaning ' a reply upon oath.'

Antediluvian Population. Whiston calculated that in the year A.M. 1482 the population of the earth was nearly 550,000,000,000! Burnet, by adopting the principle of quadruple multiplication for each hundred years, showed that at the end of the first century there were 10 persons; at the end of the second, 40; at the end of the third, 160; and by carrying this on he supposed that 10,737,418,240 persons were alive at the end of the sixteenth century! The present population is supposed to be about 1,450 millions.

Anthem. The meaning of the word is 'verses sung alternately by opposite sides of a choir.' Dr. Johnson thinks it is derived from *anti*, opposite, and *hymnos*, a hymn; but other authorities say it is from the Greek compound *anti-phon*. The latter theory is certainly better supported than Dr. Johnson's.

Antipodes. This is derived from two Greek words, *anti*, opposed to, and *pous, podos*, a foot. It means those who stand exactly opposite each other on the earth's surface—*i.e. feet to feet*. This word has no recognised singular. It is pronounced an-tip'-o-dees.

Antiquity of Smoking. Long before tobacco was introduced into England smoking was commonly practised. The favourite 'smoke' was the dried leaves of coltsfoot. In the 'Historie of Plantes,' by Dodoens, translated by Henrie Lyte, and published 1578, is the following passage :—' The parfume of the dryed leaves [of coltesfoote] layde upon quicke coles, taken into the mouth of a funnell or tunnell helpeth such as are troubled with the shortness of winde and fetch theyre breath thicke and often.'

In 'The Travels of Evliya Effendi,' translated by Von Hammer (vol. i. part 2, p. 12), it is stated that an old Greek building in Constantinople was converted into a mausoleum in the early part of the sixteenth century. At the time of the alteration it was computed that the building was a thousand years old. In cutting through the walls to form windows, a tobacco-pipe, which even then smelt of smoke, was found among the stones.

The learned Dr. Petrie, the acknowledged chief of Irish antiquarians, says :—' Smoking-pipes of bronze are frequently found in our Irish *tumuli* or sepulchral mounds of the most remote antiquity. On the monument of Donogh O'Brien, King of Thomond, who was killed in 1267, and interred in the Abbey of Corcumrae, in the county of Clare, he is represented in the usual recumbent posture, with the short pipe or *dhudeen* in his mouth.'

Antithesis is defined by Dr. Worcester to be a figure in rhetoric by which contraries are opposed to contraries. A fine example of *antithesis* is contained in the verse, Isaiah v. 7 : ' He looked for judgment, but behold oppression ; for rightcousness, but behold a cry.' This remarkable verse is, however, still more noteworthy in the original, from the fact that the words placed antithetically are almost identical. .' He looked for judgment (*mishpat*), but behold oppression (*mishpach*) ; for righteousness (*zĕdākah*), but behold a cry (*zĕghākah*).'—*Earle*, p. 550.

Anywhen, Somewhen. Both very good and useful words, which ought to find their way into ordinary English. Fifty years ago they were in common use in Surrey.

Apocryphal, from the Greek *apo*, from *krupto*, to hide. It is becoming usual to employ this word as synonymous with *false*. It has no such meaning. An apocryphal book is one the authorship of which is *not known*. The letters of Junius are, strictly speaking, *apocryphal*, because it is not known who wrote them.

Apoplexy. The ancient Greek name for this disease was *apoplexia*, stupor (*Apo*, from, *plesso*, to strike). The word has, by some, been thought to come from a Greek term signifying *Apollo-struck*, in allusion to the rays of the sun, which were called 'the arrows of Apollo.' This, however, probably referred to the sudden seizure which is now known as sun-stroke.

Apostle James. There were two apostles named James— 'James the son of Zebedee' (Matthew x. 2, 3), and James who is called in Galatians i. 19, 'the Lord's brother.' The latter was the writer of the 'General Epistle of James.'

Apostle Spoons. The earliest known mention of an 'apostle spoon' is the following entry in the books of the Stationers' Company, A.D. 1500 :—' A spoyne of the gyfte of Master Reginald Wolfe, all gylte with the pycture of Saint John.'

Apothecary. The earliest mention of an apothecary in England is by Anderson in his 'History of Commerce,' vol. i. p. 319. He tells us that King Edward III., in the year 1345, gave a pension of 6*d*. a day to Coursus de Gangeland, an apothecary of London, for attending and taking care of his Majesty during an illness in Scotland.

Apotheosis. The best authorities now pronounce this word with the accent on the *e*, to which they give the long sound as in *theme*. Garth says :—

  Allots the prince of his celestial line
  An apothéosis and rites divine.

Appal. Most dictionaries erroneously derive this word from the

Latin *pallere*, to look pale. It is from the old English word *pall*, to deaden, to deprive of vitality by age, sudden terror, or the like. Chaucer speaks of a man who had lost his vigour through age, as 'an old *appalled* wight'; and Stow, speaking of Severus, says that he was '*appalled* with age, so that he was constrained to keep his chamber.'

Apparatus. This is a Latin noun, from the verb *apparo*, I prepare. The word in English is both singular and plural. The 'Penny Cyclopædia' has the word *apparatuses*, but the example has not been followed.

Apparition in its original meaning conveyed no notion of the supernatural. It simply signified *appearance* in the sense of the thing appearing.

Appetite. 'An Esquimaux boy, says Parry, "ate in one day $10\frac{1}{4}$ pounds of solid food, and drank $1\frac{1}{2}$ gallon of fluid." A man of the same nation ate 10 pounds of solids, including two candles, and drank $1\frac{1}{2}$ gallon. A soldier of seventeen, named Tarare, ate 24 pounds of leg of beef in 24 hours, and on another occasion consumed all the dinner prepared for fifteen persons.'—*Sir R. Phillips.*

Applaud. From a Latin word signifying 'to clap the hands approvingly.' 'Acclamation,' is approval expressed by the voice; 'applause' is, partly at any rate, by the hands.

Apples were first cultivated in America in 1629, having been imported from England by the Governor of Massachusetts. Governor's Island in Boston Harbour was given to Governor Winthrop in 1632, on condition that he should plant an orchard upon it.—*New York Sun*, 1854.

Apple-pie order. A few years ago the origin of this phrase was the subject of discussion in the pages of 'Notes and Queries.' The most probable derivation is that which attributes it to a corruption of *alpha-beta order*, that is alphabetical order; but even this is doubtful.

Appliqué is a French term used in ornamental art to designate enrichments made separately, of different materials, and *applied*, or fastened to, articles of furniture. Such are Chinese plaques let into, or attached to, sideboards, cabinets, &c.

Appraise. From two Latin words meaning 'to set a price to.' It was formerly, and much more correctly, written *apprize*.

Appreciate. This word is frequently used improperly in the sense of *highly* valued or esteemed. Its true meaning is to *set a just value on*; in fact, it is almost identical with 'appraise.'

Apprentices not eating Salmon. There is a tradition current through the whole length of the valley of the Severn, that formerly a clause was usually inserted in the indentures, by which the masters bound themselves not to feed their apprentices on salmon more than three days a week. Some years ago the editor of 'Notes and Queries' offered a reward of 5l. for the discovery of an indenture having this clause, but the reward has never been claimed. A similar belief exists on the banks of the Tyne and in Scotland.

Approaches, in military engineering, are sunken trenches or protected roadways, by which soldiers, while approaching some point of attack, are protected from the fire of an enemy. The most extensive system of approaches known in military history were those formed during the siege of Sebastopol in 1854-5. No less than 70 miles of sunken trench were excavated, and these were supplemented by the use of 60,000 fascines, which are long faggots; 80,000 gabions, or cylindrical baskets open at each end and filled with earth; and upwards of a million bags, which being filled with sand were piled up to protect the men in the trenches or at the batteries.

Approbate. This obsolete English verb, signifying 'to approve,' has been revived in America, where it is used in the sense of 'license.' In New England a tavern-keeper is '*approbated*' to sell spirituous liquors; and preachers are '*approbated*' or licensed. Dr. Worcester in his 'Dictionary' gives the following as a quotation from the old English chronicler Hall:—'The cause of this battle every one did allow and *approbate*'; and Todd in his edition of Johnson quotes from Sir T. Elyot's 'Governor,' fol. 226, 'All things contained in Scripture is *approbate* by the whole consent of all the clergie of Christendom.'

Appurtenances. This word is now almost confined in its use to the lawyers, who speak of the *appurtenances* of a house or farm. The word originally meant the viscera of animals, or what is now called, colloquially, the 'pluck.' The '*purtenance* of a lamb' is mentioned in Exodus xii. 9.

Apricot. More properly, as formerly, *apricock*. The word is from the Latin *præcoqua*, a name given to the fruit from its ripening earlier than ordinary peaches. It is a native of Armenia, and was brought into Europe in the time of Alexander the Great. It is now common in all the western countries. It was first cultivated in England about the middle of the sixteenth century. It grows as a standard in the south of England, but in the north requires the protection of a wall facing the south.

April Fools. There is a tradition among the Jews, that the custom of making fools on the first of April arose from the fact that Noah sent out the dove on the first of the month corresponding to our April, before the water had abated. To perpetuate the memory of the great deliverance of Noah and his family, it was customary on this anniversary to punish persons who had forgotten the remarkable circumstance connected with the date, by sending them on some bootless errand, similar to that on which the patriarch sent the luckless bird from the windows of the ark.

Apron. This word is found in all the dialects of the Gaelic: in Irish it is *aprun*; in Cornish, *appran*; and in the Highlands of Scotland it is *aparan*. Brockett gives *nappern* as the pronunciation in the North of England. The word seems to be allied to the French *naperon*, a linen cloth or napkin.

Aquafortis is the ordinary name for sulphuric acid. The words are Latin, and their literal meaning is *strong water*.

Arabic Numerals. The 'figures' in general use as numerals are not Arabic. They are really (with two exceptions) the first ten *letters* of the Egyptian alphabet, and they are found upon the mummy bandages almost identical in form, with the exception of the 5 and the 8, with the figures now in common use. The following engravings, in which their exact forms are shown, are taken from Brüttner's 'Comparative Tables of Alphabets,' copied in Eichhorn's first volume of the Old Testament:—

1 2 3 4 ꝑ 6 7 ⅄ 9 ο

Egyptian Letters.

The true Arabic numerals are totally unlike. They are given below:—

True Arabic Numerals.

'The numeral figures 1, 2, 3, 4, 5, 6, 7, 8, 9, which we now employ, were made use of in Europe for the first time in 1240, in the Alphonsean Tables, made by the order of Alphonso, son of Ferdinand, King of Castile, who employed for that purpose Isaac

Hazan, a Jew singer of the Synagogue of Toledo, and Aben Ragel, an Arabian.'—*Isaac D'Israeli, Curiosities of Lit.* vol. i. p. 160.

Arable. Bailey has '*To Are* (a contraction of *arare*, Latin), to plow.' Arable land, according to this definition, is *ploughable* land. We have lost the word Are, but retain *ear*, to plough. (See Gen. xiv. 6; Deut. xxi. 4; 1 Sam. viii. 12; Is. xxx. 24.)

Arch. There is reason to believe that the Ancient Egyptians and the Assyrians were acquainted with the principles upon which the arch is constructed, but it was certainly unknown to the Greeks. The Romans introduced it, and in their hands the rigid horizontal style of Greek architecture soon gave way to more rounded forms. From the Romanesque it gradually passed to the Gothic, or pointed style, and now arches of all imaginable lines of curvature are common all over the world. The largest stone arch in England is at Chester, its span being 200 feet. The centre arch of Southwark Bridge, which is of iron, is 240 feet span.

Archbishop. An archbishop is '*enthroned*' when he is invested with the archbishopric. A bishop is '*installed.*'

Archery. It is quite clear that the use of bows and arrows was common in England before the Conquest, and was not, as some have supposed, introduced by the Normans. As Wright ('England in the Middle Ages') points out, 'the names bow (*boga*) and arrow (*arewe*), by which they have always been known, are taken directly from the Saxon; whereas, if the practice of archery had been introduced by the Normans, it is possible that we should have called them *arcs* and *fletches*.' The enormous distance to which the ancient bowmen could shoot their arrows is often alluded to by the older poets and dramatists. The word 'score' in the language of archers meant twenty yards, and 'a mark of twelve score' meant a mark or target placed 240 yards away. Shakespeare ('2 Henry VIII.' iii.) makes Falstaff praise Old Double as a good shot in the following words:—'He would have clapped i' the clout at *twelve score* and carried you a forehand shaft at fourteen, and a fourteen and a half, that it would have done a man's head good to see.' These seem incredible distances, but Drayton ('Polyolbion,' S. xxvi. p. 1175), speaking of Robin Hood and his men, says that:—

    At marks full *forty score*, they used to prick and rove.

But surely *that* must be an *un*licensed stretch of the poet!

Archipelago. From the name *Archos Pelagos*, first or chief sea, given by the Greeks to the Ægean Sea, and as this sea abounds in small islands, the name has become a word to designate a cluster of islands wherever situate.

Arctic. The word 'arctic' is derived from the Greek name for the constellation of the Bear, *Arctos*, and arctic means 'near Arctos'—that is, in the extreme north.

Ard. This is a Saxon termination of personal names denoting natural tendency; as Goddard, good-tempered; Giffard, liberal; Drunkard, sottish; Sluggard, lazy; and many othe

Area of London. The district under the charge of the City and the Metropolitan Police—'Greater London,' as it has been called—covers 687 square miles. The 'City' contains only 632 acres, which is eight acres less than one square mile.

Arena, literally 'a sandy place.' It was the name given by the Romans to that part of an amphitheatre where the gladiators fought, which was strewed with red sand to conceal from the view of the spectators any blood which might be spilt.

Around. This word is used in America in the sense of near. An 'American Police Gazette' quotes a witness as saying, 'I was standing *around* when the fight took place,' and Bartlett in his 'Dictionary of Americanisms' says, 'A friend assures me that he has heard a clergyman in his sermon say of one of the disciples, that "he stood *around* the Cross."'

Arras were hangings for rooms, first made at Arras, in France, in the fourteenth century. They were woven stuffs having simple patterns, something like modern wall-papers.

Arresting a Dead Body. 'It is a popular error that a creditor can arrest or detain the body of a deceased debtor; and the doing such an act is indictable as a misdemeanour.'—*Wharton.*

Arrive is from the Latin *ad*, to, and *ripa*, a bank or shore. The allusion is to landing from a boat or ship.

Arrowroot is so named because the South American Indians apply the root of the plant from which it is made to wounds caused by poisoned arrows.

Art is the power of doing something not taught by nature: as to walk is natural, to dance is an *art*.

Artemus Ward. This name, adopted as the pseudonym of Charles F. Browne, the American humourist, was borne as a real name, though with the 'u' changed to an 'a,' by a distinguished

American general of the Revolutionary War, and also by a jurist of some note in Massachusetts.

Artery. This word is from two Greek words signifying to preserve or protect air. The Greeks used the word *arterion* as the name for the windpipe.

Artesian Wells. These wells were so named from one at *Artois* in France, which was the first sunk with a full knowledge of the principles involved. The Chinese have from time immemorial used wells of this description, and they have also been in use for centuries past in the neighbourhood of Vienna. Artesian wells are only possible in certain localities. Where there are pervious strata lying between impervious beds the water percolating through will be imprisoned; lying upon the lowest, and rising to some point in the highest, where a pervious stratum brings it to the surface, and it escapes in the form of springs. If, however, a shaft can be sunk to the lowest point, the water of the whole basin will press upwards for escape and will rise to a level, corresponding to the greatest height to which the imprisoning strata reach. The Artesian Well at Grenoble, near Paris, throws the water to the height of 32 feet above the surface at the rate of more than 500 gallons every minute.

Artichokes. 'The artichowe (the globe artichoke) was introduced in time of King Henry the Eight.'—*Hakluyt*, 1599.

Artificer, Artisan. An 'artificer' is one who requires intellectual refinement or artistic skill in the exercise of his profession or art. An 'artisan' is one whose work requires no further knowledge than the general rules and practices of his trade.

Artificial Teeth. The earliest known allusion to artificial teeth is by Martialis, in the first century (Epigr. xii. 23). The lines following are a free translation :—

> You use, without a blush, *false teeth* and hair :
> But Lælia, your squint is past repair.

Ben Jonson mentions false teeth in the 'Silent Woman' (1609).

Artillery. This word originally comprised various instruments of warfare, as bows, arrows, crossbows, &c. The most ancient military body in Europe—the Honourable Artillery Company of London—was instituted by Henry VIII. in the year 1537 for the encouragement of *archery*. The verse 1 Sam. xx. 40 says, ' And Jonathan gave his *artillery* unto his lad.' Fairfax has :—

> His heart unworthy is, Shootress divine,
> Of thine *artillery* to feel the might.

Asbestos is an incombustible fibrous mineral, so soft and pliable that it may be woven into cloth. The ancients wrapped dead bodies in cloth of this kind, before cremation, in order that the whole of the ashes might be preserved.

Ash Wednesday. The first day of Lent is so called from the ancient custom of sprinkling ashes upon the heads of those who were condemned to do penance on this day.

Ask, or **Axe.** The latter, although now accounted vulgar, is the correct form of the word. The Anglo-Saxon form was *axian*. Chaucer uses the word *axe*; and in Wycliffe's Bible it is—'Or if he *axe* a fish.' The word was sometimes spelt 'aks,' from which the transition to 'ask' is very easy.

Asparagus. This name is said to be from the Latin *à*, intensive, and *sparasso*, to tear, in reference to the strong prickles or spikelets of some species of the plant. This word is frequently pronounced 'Sparrow-grass.' Some years ago a charade was circulated which was attributed to a certain alderman:—

> My first is a little thing vot hops (sparrow);
> My second brings us good hay crops (grass);
> My whole I eats vith mutton chops (sparrow-grass).

Mr. Fox Talbot says:—'There is some reason to think that Sparrow-grass may be a genuine Northern term. "Sparrow," indeed, is wrong; but the real word may have been *Spear-grass*. For the plant comes up like a multitude of little spears; and our ancestors used to take notice of such similitudes.' As old gardeners called the plant 'sperage,' Fox Talbot is perhaps right, and *asparagus* a piece of modern affectation.

Assassin. This word is derived from a military and religious Order formed in Persia by Hassan ben Sabah, about the middle of the eleventh century, and called 'Assassins,' from their immoderate use of Hashish, or Indian hemp, used as a stimulant in Eastern countries. They are said to have nerved themselves for their horrible work by the excitement produced by Hashish; so that an assassin, strictly, is not a secret murderer, but a drunken maniac.—*Brand*.

Assay. This word is now confined to the testing of gold and silver, but it formerly had a far wider significance in the sense of essaying, or trying. There was an officer of the king's household called the 'Assayer,' whose duty it was to *assay* or test the food supplied at the royal table. Chaucer says contemptuously:—

> Thyne Assayer schalle be an hounde
> To assaye thy mete before the.

Assets. From the French *assez*, sufficient. The word originally meant property of a deceased person sufficient (*assez*) to pay his debts and legacies. The application of the word to the property of insolvent debtors is comparatively modern.

Assigns. This word is now only used in the plural. The singular form, *assign*, has been supplanted by the word 'assignee.'

Assize. In Scotland this word means a jury. A Scottish assize consists of fifteen men. The verdict need not be unanimous, as in England, but is given by the majority. The verdict may be 'guilty,' 'not proven,' or 'not guilty.' The verdict of 'not proven' is *legally* equivalent to one of not guilty, as the accused person is discharged from custody, and cannot be tried again for the same offence. See JURY.

Astonish. From the Anglo-Saxon *stunian*, to stun. It has, however, some affinity with the Latin *attonitus*, thunderstruck, and with the English *astound*.

Astronomy. The oldest map of the heavens is in the National Library at Paris. It was made by the Chinese, about the year 600 B.C., and contains 1,460 stars.

Atom. From two Greek words, signifying so small that it *cannot be cut*.

Attorney. This word at one time had a far wider significance than it has now. In a 'Short Catechism' published in 1553, quoted by Archbishop Trench in his 'Select Glossary,' Jesus is spoken of as 'Our only attorney . . . between God and Man.'

Attorney, Solicitor. The designation *attorney* was abolished by the late Act of Parliament altering the constitution of the Courts of Law. Formerly, all proceedings at Common Law were carried on by *Attorneys*. *Solicitors* conducted proceedings in the Courts of Equity. The term *Solicitor* applies now to both branches of the profession, and is the only one in use to designate legal practitioners below the rank of barristers.

It is often disputed whether or not attorneys or solicitors are entitled to wear gowns. In 'Notes and Queries,' April 1858, Mr. John Fenwick, of Newcastle-on-Tyne, says—' When I was admitted in Easter Term, 1813, an attorney in the Court of Common Pleas, I had to stand on the table of the Court, arrayed in *the gown of an attorney*, i.e. a gown in shape and form in every respect as that of a Serjeant-at-law, with this difference that the serjeant's gown is of silk, and the attorney's of stuff. I well remember paying a shilling for the use of the gown.'

Au courant. A French phrase, which means 'well-acquainted with.' In English composition it is used in such sentences as—'He kept himself *au courant* of all that was passing around him.'

Auction. The Americans say 'Sales *at* Auction.' The first auction in England took place about 1715. An old magazine has the following:—'Elihu Yale, an American, brought such a quantity of goods from the East Indies that he had not room enough in his house in London for them, so he had a public sale, and this was the first sale by auction in England.' Elihu Yale was buried at Wrexham, Denbighshire, and on his tombstone are the words:—

> Born in America, in Europe bred,
> In Afric travelled, and in Asia wed,
> Where long he lived and thrived; in London dead.

Haydn ('Dictionary of Dates') says:—'The first auction in Britain was about 1700, by Elisha Yale, a Governor of Fort George in the East Indies, who thus sold the goods he had brought home.' Haydn is wrong; 'Elihu Yale' is the name inscribed on the tomb. This Yale was the founder of the celebrated college in New Haven (Conn.) which bears his name.

Audacious. This word is now seldom used but in a bad sense. Originally it meant fearless, intrepid, or commendable boldness. Milton says:—

> Thence many a league
> As in a cloudy chair ascending, rides
> Audacious.

And Shakespeare has 'Audacious without impudency'; which now-a-days seems almost a contradiction.

Audi alteram partem. A Latin phrase, signifying 'hear the other side.'

Au fait. A French phrase, in frequent use in England. It means 'fully acquainted with the matter.' The familiar saying 'up to' is a very good equivalent.

August. Augustus Cæsar gave his name to this month, which had been previously known in Rome as *sextilis*. In Gallia, however, and in other remote parts of the empire, the ancient name for this month was *Eaust*, or *Aust*, i.e. harvest; and this similarity, as in the case of July (which see), no doubt suggested the change. It is curious that the French have never adopted the Roman *August*, either in spelling or pronunciation. They continued to use the ancient name, altering the spelling first to *Aoust*, and then to its present form, *Août*. The Dutch word for harvest is *Oegst*, or *Oogst*.

Australia. The first indication of Australia on any map is in a small map of the world which forms the vignette to a Dutch work, *Journael vande Nassauche Vloot*, under Admiral l'Hermitte, in 1623–4–5–6. The place indicated is to the West of Cape Carpentaria of the present map, and is marked, 'Land eendracht.'—*Trübner's American and Oriental Literary Record*, 1879.

Australian Aborigines. The last aboriginal native of Tasmania, a woman, named Trucanini, died on May 8, 1876, aged 73 years.

Authorship of the Church Catechism. 'The late Mr. Brand informed me that in a copy of "Bishop Beveridge on the Church Catechism," 1705, is the following note by Dr. Ellison, Vicar of Newcastle-upon-Tyne, dated 1708:—"Dr. Alexander Nowell, Dean of St. Paul's, composed the *Church Catechism*, as far as the article on the Sacraments, which article was drawn up by Bishop Overall, Dr. Nowell's successor in the deanery."'—*Churton's Life of Nowell*, p. 184.

Avast. This is the nautical term for 'stop'; it is a corruption of the Italian *basta*, enough.

Ave Maria. A Roman Catholic form of prayer to the Virgin Mary. The name is derived from the first two words in Latin, which signify 'Hail, Mary!' The word *Ave* is of two syllables, and is pronounced '*A-ve*.'

Average formerly meant work done for the lord by the *avers*, or draught-cattle of the tenant.—*Wedgwood*.

Avocation. This word, within the last few years, has been much used in a wrong sense, as a synonym for *vocation*, to which its meaning is exactly opposite. A man's *vocation* is his calling —the occupation or business to which he is called. An *avocation* is something which *calls him away from his vocation*.

Avoirdupois. 'This term comes from the Old French *Avoirs-de-poids*—goods that are sold by weight, and not by measurement.' —*Wedgwood*.

Avoirdupois and Troy Weights. Although one pound avoirdupois or 'imperial' weight contains 16 ounces, and one pound Troy weight only 12 ounces, the actual proportion is as 17 to 14.

Awful. This slang word, which is made to do duty for every adjective in the language by turns, seems to have originated in America. Bartlett, in his 'Glossary of American Words and Phrases,' 1859, says: 'Everything that excites surprise is *awful* with them' [the New Englanders]: and he quotes 'awful hill,' 'awful nose,' 'awful custom,' 'awful eaters,' 'awful cold day,' 'awful handsome,' 'awfully given to smoking,' &c. He does not, however, quote anything so absurd as 'awfully jolly,' which is so common among young ladies in the old country.

Awkward. The word *awk* signifies 'the left as opposed to the right.' A left-handed man is therefore an awkward man. Anything clumsily done is said to be awkwardly done—that is, done as though with the left hand. *Dexter* means 'right as opposed to left.' Hence, a right-handed man does things dexterously, or with dexterity.

B

Baal. 'This word is to this day a name of the sun in Irish: as in *Bel-ain*, a year (*i.e.* a "sun circle"); and *La-Bal-tinne*, midsummer day—*i.e.* "the day of the fire of Baal," from the huge fires that are to this day lighted on that anniversary.'—*Fras. Crossley.*

Babbler. This word, from its occurrence in almost all languages, is supposed to have some traditionary connection with the confusion at *Babel*. At Babel there was confusion of tongues, and now when a man talks in a confused and inarticulate manner, he is said to 'babble.'—*Dean Hoare, English Roots.*

Babies' Corals. The use of corals by infants while teething is at least two hundred years old. Addison, who was born in 1672, says in No. 1 of the 'Spectator,' that he has been told that at two months old he 'would not use his coral until they took the bells from it.'

Bachelors. By Act of Parliament, 7 William III. 1695, a tax was laid upon all bachelors of twenty-five years of age and upwards. The amount varied from one shilling a year for a common person to 12*l.* for a duke. Bachelors were charged in 1785 with extra duties upon servants.

Bachelors' Buttons. 'Now the similitude that these floures have to the jagged cloath buttons ancientlie worne in this kingdom gave occasion to our gentlewomen and other lovers of floures in these times to call them bachelors buttons.'—Quoted by *Nares*, edit. 1822, p. 23.

Bacon. Most dictionaries give as the origin of this word the Anglo-Saxon *bacan*, to bake, but as bacon is never baked, it does not seem to be the correct etymon. The word is more likely to have come to us from *bece*, the Anglo-Saxon name for the beech tree, the triangular-shaped nuts, or *mast*, of which were given as food to hogs intended to be converted into bacon, for the purpose of hardening their flesh. The phrase 'Save your bacon' arose at the time of the Civil Wars in England, when housewives in the country had to take extraordinary precautions to save their principal provision, bacon, from the greedy appetites of soldiers on the march.

Back and forth. In New England this phrase is used instead of its English equivalent, 'backwards and forwards.'

Backgammon. From the Danish *bakke*, a tray, and *gammen*, a game. The word *blot*, used in the game to signify leaving a piece exposed, is Danish for *naked*. Backgammon was probably introduced by the Danes when they first invaded England. The Anglo-Saxons called it 'Tables.' The game is of great antiquity, and is supposed to have been known to the Greeks. Homer alludes to this or a similar game in the following two lines of the first book of the 'Odyssey':—

> Before the door they were amusing themselves at *tables*,
> Sitting on the skins of oxen which they themselves had killed.

Badger. This word applied to a trader is common in old plays and books. In the 'State Papers, Domestic Series,' vol. 1547-1580, is the following:—'Dec. 17, 1565. Note of certain persons upon Humber side, who buy up great quantities of corn, two of whom are authorised *badgers*.' By 5 Eliz. c. 12, *badgers* are to be licensed annually under penalty of 5*l*. The word means corn-dealer.

Baffle. The original meaning of this word was 'to unknight.' The ceremony on these occasions seems to have been of the most contemptuous nature, one part of it being to hang the recreant up by the heels. Spenser, in the 'Faerie Queene,' describes it thus:—

> And after all for greater infamie,
> He *by the heels him hung* upon a tree
> And *bafful'd* so, that all who passed by
> The picture of his punishment might see.
> B. VI. vii. 7.

Shakespeare also makes Falstaff say:—

> An I do not, call me villain and *baffle* me.
> 1 *Hen. IV.* Act i. sc. 2.

And in Act ii. sc. 4 :—
>If thou do it half so gravely . . . . *hang me up by the heels,* &c.

The French have *bafouer,* to deride, scoff at, mock, revile, abuse.

Bagatelle. A writer in 'Notes and Queries,' April 28, 1866, says that an Act of Parliament having passed, prohibiting the game of nine-pins in public houses, the Act was evaded by substituting nine holes for the nine pins. This, he thinks, was the origin of bagatelle. A similar prohibition of the game of nine-pins in the United States was evaded by adopting the game of ten-pins, which is still popular in America. See TEN-PINS.

Bagnio. This word, which is simply the Italian for *bath,* contains a history within itself. In the profligate times of the Stuarts, the public baths became places of assignation, where the worst forms of licentiousness could be indulged in. At length the word became a synonym for a brothel, and in that sense only is it understood at present. See HUMMUMS.

Bagpipes. Mr. M. A. Lower, in his 'Wayside Notes in Scandinavia,' 1874, says it is 'a curious fact that bagpipes were invented in Norway, and thence imported into Scotland during the period when a portion of the country fell into Scandinavian hands.'

Baize, from the Dutch *baaij.* The Flemish refugees brought the name and the method of making the material to England in the sixteenth century.

Baked Meats, in the language of our ancestors, did not mean baked joints, as with us, but was applied to *meat pies.* Cotgrave, in his 'French and English Dictionary,' translates *baked meats* by the word *pastisserie,* or pastry ; and on the other hand, *pastisserie* is rendered 'baked meats.' But the meaning is clearer in a passage quoted by Nares from an old play, 'The White Devil,' where one of the characters is made to say—

>You speak as if a man
>Should know what fowl is coffined in a *baked meat*
>Afore it is cut up.

See COFFIN.

Baker's Dozen. This phrase arose from the custom of the trade to allow thirteen penny rolls to each dozen sold. The same custom still holds good in the wholesale book-trade ; a publisher's 'dozen' is thirteen copies.

Balance. *Lanx* is the Latin word for a dish, or the scale of a balance. *Bilanx* was a Low Latin term for two dishes hanging from a beam supported in the middle, forming a pair of scales; hence our word 'balance.'

Balance. This word is generally used throughout America in the sense of 'remainder'; thus they say, 'the *balance* of a speech,' 'the *balance* of the people,' the '*balance* of the day,' &c.

Balcony. The first balcony, or belconey, as it was originally called in England, was put up in Covent Garden by Lord Arundel in the seventeenth century. Up to about the year 1815 the accent was on the second syllable of this word. Rogers, in his 'Table Talk,' says, 'Con'template is bad enough, but bal'cony makes me sick.' See BARBICAN.

Bald. This is the past participle of the verb *to ball*, and the meaning of it is the head reduced to the smoothness of a ball by the loss of hair. It was anciently written 'balled.' Thus Chaucer says—

His head was balled, and shone as any glass.

Balderdash. Originally the froth or lather made by barbers in dashing balls of soap backwards and forwards in hot water.

Bubbly spume, or barber's balderdash.—*Nash*, 1599.

Bal, Bally. This prefix to the names of many localities in Ireland is the Irish word *baile*, a town, a village. The termination is generally descriptive: thus, Bally*more* is 'the great town'; Bally*shannon*, the 'town on the river Shannon.'

Ball, Bullet. These words, both in French and English, are derived from the same source. In England, however, a bullet is the missile discharged from a rifle or gun, and a ball is sent from a cannon. In France, it is *balle de fusil*, and *boulet de canon*.

Ballad. Verstegan, in his 'Glossary,' says, '*Lay*, a song. It is sometimes written *Ley*, and sometimes *Leid*; of this cometh our name of *Ballad*, which is as much in signification as a song of an act or deed done.'—*Restitution*, &c., edit. 1655, p. 178.

Ballad Singers. Anciently ballad-singers, rope-dancers, and others of similar occupations were compelled to take out licences. In the 'London Gazette' of April 13, 1682, there is the following notice:—'Whereas Mr. John Clarke of London, bookseller, did rent of Charles Killigrew Esq. the licensing of all ballad-singers for five years; which time is expired at Ladyday next. These are therefore to give notice to all ballad-singers that they take out licenses at the Office of the Revels at Whitehall for singing and selling of small books, according to an ancient custom. And all persons concerned are hereby desired to take notice of; and to suppress all mountebanks, rope-dancers, prize-players, ballad-singers, and such as make show of motions and strange sights, that have not a license in red and black letters, under the hand and seal of the said Charles Killigrew Esq. Master of the Revels to His Majesty that they may be proceeded against according to law.'

Ballast. From Provincial Danish, *bag-læs*, the back load. When a ship has to return home without a cargo, it is necessary to carry a quantity of stones, or other worthless material, to preserve the equilibrium of the vessel. This is the *bag-læs* of the Danish, and hence 'ballast,' which has the same signification. For many years vessels from Newcastle, after discharging a cargo of coals in London, took in at Erith on the Thames a quantity of *ballast*—that is, gravel or other earth—which they discharged on arriving at the Tyne. In the course of time the accumulation on the banks of the river formed huge hills on both sides. When railways were constructed in the neighbourhood the material was used to form embankments, and to cover other portions of the lines. From this circumstance the word 'ballast' has come into general use, both in England and America, for the final layer of earth upon the surface of new railways.

Balloon is from the French *ballon*, a large ball. The first ascent of a balloon was in June 1783, when a fire-balloon, thirty-five feet in diameter, made by Montgolfier, rose to a height of 1,500 feet. In September of the same year a larger one went up, carrying a sheep, a cock, and a duck, all of which descended in safety. On the following November 21st, Professor Charles and the Marquis d'Arlandes ascended in a Montgolfier, and remained in the air twenty-five minutes, sailing for some distance in the neighbourhood of Paris. A few days afterwards, December 1, Charles, with a companion named Robert, ascended in a balloon filled with hydrogen, and made much in the same manner as at present. Navigation of the air is, upon the whole, less dangerous than navigation of the sea. It is computed that out of 1,500 aëronauts making 10,000 ascents, only fifteen lives have been lost.—Condensed from *Chambers's Encyclopædia*.

Balloon Post. During the siege of Paris fifty-four balloons were despatched, carrying two and a half millions of letters, weighing altogether ten tons. The first balloon was sent up on September 23, 1870; the last on January 20, 1871. One which left on November 30, 1870, has never been heard of, and is supposed to have been lost at sea.

Ball's Pond, near London, is 'so named from one John Ball, who kept a house of entertainment here about the middle of the seventeenth century, having for its sign, "The Salutation." A large pond, which remained till the commencement of the present century, was probably in his day frequented by duck-hunters, and by them coupled with the name of their host. A token issued by him bears the inscription, "John Ball at the boarded house neere Newington Greene." '—*Lewis's Islington.*

Balm is a contraction of 'balsam.'

Baltic Sea. Cluverius says that the Baltic Sea is so named from *balteus*, a belt, because the strait or entrance to the sea has always been called the 'Belt.'

Banbury Cakes are of great antiquity. In 'A Treatise of Melancholy, by T. Bright, Doctor of Physic, 1586,' is the following paragraph :—' Sodden wheate is a grosse and melancholicke nourishmente, and bread, especiallie of the fine flower unleavened : of this sorte are bagge-puddings, or panne puddings made with flower, frittars, pancakes, such as we calle *Banberrie Cakes*, and those greate ones confected with butere, egges, etc., used at weddings; and howsoever it be prepared rye and bread made thereof carrieth with itte plentie of melancholie.'

Bandanna, the name for silk pocket-handkerchiefs, is of Spanish origin; *bandano*, in that language, meaning a 'neckerchief.'

Bank. It is generally believed that this word is derived from the Italian word *banco*, a shop counter, but this is thought to be an error. The word is a literal translation of the Italian *monte*, meaning a common fund, or joint stock. Public loans for the service of the State were known by the name *monti*. The Banks of Venice and Genoa were formed by uniting several Government loans; and as they lent money to poor and deserving persons, they were called *monti di pietà*, which means literally 'banks of charity,' or charity banks. The first regular banker in London was Francis Child, who established 'Child's Bank,' in the reign of Charles II. The old banking-house was pulled down, and new premises erected on the site near Temple Bar, in 1879. On these premises the business is still carried on under the style of Child and Co. The Bank of England was established in the reign of William and Mary, A.D. 1695. It commenced business in Grocers' Hall, in the Poultry. An early mention of the word bank, as a place of deposit for money, is in the Authorised Version of the Scriptures, Luke xix. 23 : 'Wherefore then gavest not thou my money into the bank?'

Bank Notes are always called 'Bank Bills' in America.

Banks of Rivers. In looking down a river, the bank on our left side is the left bank; that on our right side is the right bank.

Bankrupt. From the Italian *banco,* a bench or counter, and *rotto,* broken; in allusion to the practice of breaking the benches or tables of those money-changers who became insolvent.

Banns of Marriage. The earliest existing canonical enactment on this subject is in the eleventh Canon of the Synod of Westminster, A.D. 1200; which enacts that no marriage shall be contracted without banns thrice published in the church, unless by the special authority of the bishop.—*Wilkins, Concilia Magnæ Brittaniæ,* i. 507. During the Commonwealth banns might either be published in churches, or by the bellman, or crier, on marketdays, at the nearest market town to the residence of the parties. Marriages might be celebrated before magistrates, whose certificate was valid proof of legal marriage. A copy of a certificate of a marriage performed before a magistrate at Chester in 1654 is to be found in 'Notes and Queries,' October 9, 1858. This certificate recites that the intention of marriage had been 'published at the Market Cross in Chester, three market-days in three several weeks; viz. the 7th, 14th, and 21st days of June, 1654.'

Banquet. What is now called 'dessert' was formerly the *banquet,* and was usually served in a separate apartment. Massinger ('Unnat. Comb.') says, 'We'll dine in the great room, but let the musick and banquet be prepared here.' And Taylor, in the 'Penniless Pilgrim,' has—'Every meale foure long tables furnished with all varieties, our first and second course being threescore dishes at one boord, and after that alwayes a banquet.'

Bantam. A small species of domestic fowl, brought originally from Bantam, a town in Java.

Banter. The verb 'to banter' is derived from the name of 'a set of scholars called "banterers," who make it their employment to talk at a venture, lye, and prate what nonsense they please.'—*Life of Anthony à Wood,* 1649.

Baptismal Name. Lord Campbell held that a letter may be a good baptismal name. In the case 'The Queen *v.* Dale' (17 'Queen's Bench Reports,' p. 66) he said : 'I do not see that there is any reason for supposing that the magistrate's actual name is not

J. H. Harper. There is no doubt that a vowel may be a good Christian name; why not a consonant? I have been informed by a gentleman of the bar, sitting here, on whose accuracy we can rely, that he knows a lady who was baptised by the name of " D." Why may not a gentleman as well be baptised by a consonant?'

Barb. The barb on an arrow, or a fish-hook, is the beard-like (*barba*, the beard) projection, directed backwards to prevent it from losing its hold.

Barbarian. Gibbon says that *barbar* was the imitative sound applied by the Greeks to the *language* of tribes whose speech was harsh and unintelligible. It was adopted by the Romans in the same sense. Ovid says of himself when banished to Pontus, '*Barbarus hic ego sum quia non intelligor ulli.*' 'Here I am a barbarian, *because I am understood by no one.*'

Barbecue. This word, according to the dictionaries, means to roast an animal whole, as an ox, or a hog. Ingoldsby, in the 'Lay of St. Cuthbert,' says :—

And the barbecu'd sucking-pig's done to a turn.

The word barbecue is probably formed from *barbe*, beard, and *queue*, tail; meaning 'from head to tail,' the whole body.

Barber, from the Latin *barba*, the beard. The business of hair-cutting is generally united with the legitimate office of the barber. Barbers existed from very early ages. Ezekiel, in the first verse of the fifth chapter, says : 'And thou, son of man, take thee a barber's razor, and cause it to pass upon thy head and upon thy beard.'

The verb *to barb*, meaning to shave, is not often met with. In ' Pepys's Diary,' under date November 27, 1665, it occurs :—' To Sir G. Smith's, it being now night, and there up to his chamber and sat talking, and I *barbing* against to-morrow.'

Randle Holme, in his curious book on 'Heraldry,' gives us some curious details as to barbers. 'A barber,' he says, 'is always known by his checque parti-coloured apron; neither can he be termed a barber, or poler, or shaver till his apron be about him.' His instrument case contains his looking-glass; a set of horn combs with teeth on one side and wide for the combing and readying of long, thick and strong heads of hair,' 'a rasp to file the end of a tooth, &c.' Several curious names of beards are mentioned: the *pick-à-devant* beard is a sharp-pointed one ; a *cathedral* beard is one trimmed so as to be very broad at the bottom, spreading like the tail of a fish; the *forked* beard is a broad beard ending in two points; 'the *mouse-eaten* beard, where the beard groweth scatteringly, not together, but here and there a tuft.' The *British* beard 'hath long *mochedoes* [moustachios] on the higher lip hanging down either side the chin, all the rest of the face being bare,' &c. 'Scizzors' in this article is written '*cisers*.'

Barber's Pole. Anciently barbers performed minor operations in surgery, and in particular, when bleeding was customary, it was to the barber that the patients applied to be bled. 'To assist this operation, it being necessary for the patient to grasp a staff, a stick or pole was always kept by the barber-surgeon, together with the fillet or bandaging he used for tying the patient's arm. When the pole was not in use the tape was tied to it, so that they might be both together when wanted, and in this state pole and tape were hung at the door as a sign. At length, instead of hanging out the identical pole used in the operation, a pole was painted with stripes round it in imitation of the real pole and bandage, and thus came the sign.' Lord Thurlow, in a speech in the House of Lords, July 17, 1797, said that 'by a statute, still in force, barbers and surgeons were each to use a pole [as a sign]. The barbers were to have theirs blue and white, striped, with no other appendage; but the surgeons', which was the same in other respects, was likewise to have a galley-pot, and a red rag, to denote the particular nature of their vocation.' The last barber-surgeon in London was a man named Middleditch, of Great Suffolk Street, in the Borough. He died there in 1821. Mr. Timbs, in his 'Autobiography,' says, 'I have a vivid recollection of his dentistry.'

Barbican. This word is not, as is currently supposed, from the Anglo-Saxon *burgh kenning* or 'town-watching' tower. It comes from the Persian *bala klaneh*, a projecting turret over a gateway, and the word exactly describes a mediæval barbican. The term 'balcony' comes from the same root.

Barclay and Perkins's Brewery was founded, in a small way, early in the eighteenth century, by Edmund Halsey, who having made a fortune, married his daughter—an only child—to Lord Cobham. At Halsey's death it was not considered fit that a peer should continue the business. It was accordingly transferred for 30,000*l.* to a Mr. Thrale, a clerk in the house, security being taken upon the property. Thrâle paid off the debt in eleven years, and afterwards became M.P. for Southwark and High Sheriff of Surrey, dying in 1758. His son was the Thrale with whom and with whose pretty wife Dr. Johnson was on such friendly terms. He got into difficulties, but his wife 'begged and borrowed' enough to retain the brewery. At his death, in 1781, Dr. Johnson, the executor, sold the entire concern for 135,000*l.* to David Barclay, the head of the banking firm of Barclay and Co., who placed in it his nephew and Mr. Perkins, who had been manager in Thrale's time; and so arose the great firm of Barclay and Perkins. The brewery now covers about 14 acres of ground.

Praise-God Barebone. This enthusiast's real name was Barbon. His baptismal name was undoubtedly 'Praise-God.' He was a leather-seller in Fleet Street, and was M.P. for London in the Parliament called, after him, the *Barebones Parliament.* He was imprisoned in the Tower in 1662, but whether he died there or was released is not known. His son was a great builder and projector, and became 'Dr. Barbon,' but was generally known as 'Damned Dr. Barebone.' He built the houses in Red Lion Square, and in Essex Street, Strand.

Barge-board, a term used in architecture, is a corruption of the term 'verge-board.'

Baring Brothers. The founder of this celebrated mercantile house was John Baring, a German, who established himself in business at Exeter in the first half of the eighteenth century. Two of his sons removed the business to London in 1770, where it has grown to be one of the largest trading concerns in the world. The various members of the firm have been as much distinguished intellectually as for their commercial eminence.

Barley grows wild in the mountains of Himalaya, where it is, apparently, indigenous.

Barley Sugar. Barley does not enter into the composition of this sweet, nor has the word any right to be in the name. It is a corruption of the French term *brûlé,* burnt. Barley sugar is, therefore, burnt sugar, or, in French, *sucre brûlé.*

Barnacles. This word is often used by old people to signify 'spectacles.' It may have been formerly the common name for them. The word 'barnacles' is used by farriers as the name of an instrument by which they hold a horse by the nose. As spectacles are supported by the nose, there is some analogy.

Baronet. Anciently there were two degrees of barons—viz. those by feudal tenure, and those who were summoned to Parliament by writ of summons. These latter were called *baronets.* Both were styled *Honourable,* and both were entitled to wear coronets. The distinction in time ceased to be recognised, and the title 'baronet' fell into abeyance. It was revived by James I.,

May, 22, 1611, when eighteen were created, each of them paying 1,000*l.* for the honour. This money was ostensibly for improvements in the province of Ulster. In connection with this application of the fund, all baronets were allowed to place in their shield of arms the noted *Lamh derg Eirin*, or red hand of Ulster, forfeited by the O'Neil family. Some have thought that modern baronets are entitled to be called. Honourable, and to a distinctive coronet, but they forget that in everything but the name the two kinds of baronets are distinct. A modern writer has said, 'there is as much difference between the two as between a Roman Consul in ancient Britain, and a British Consul in modern Rome.'

Baron of Beef. The baron of beef is a double sirloin, a joint which is usually served at great public entertainments, and at the English Court on Christmas Day. The name 'baron' was probably applied in jocular allusion to the sirloin, a Baron being higher in rank than a Sir, or knight.

Barrack. From the Gaelic *barrack*, brushwood; hence *barracha*, a hut, or booth. The original barracks were huts made of the branches of trees. 'Before the gates of Bari he lodged in a miserable hut or barrack composed of dry branches, and thatched with straw.'—*Gibbon.*

Barrel. A cylindrical wooden vessel made of *bars*, or staves hooped together.

Barristers' Bags. These are either red or dark blue. Strictly speaking, red bags are reserved for Queen's counsel and serjeants, but a stuff gownsman may carry one if presented therewith by a 'silk.' Only red bags may be taken into court, blue ones must be left in the robing-room. There are no restrictions as to the colour or use of solicitors' bags.

Barristers' Fees in bygone days. A barrister's fee was anciently an angel, or ten shillings. The following couplet, quoted in Nares' 'Glossary,' puts this pretty plainly :—

UPON ANNE'S MARRIAGE WITH A LAWYER.
Anne is an angel; what if so she be ?
What is an angel but a lawyer's fee ?

Bassoon. The bassoon is a musical instrument which was originally called a bass-horn.

Batch. A batch of bread is as much as is *baked* at one time. A baker was formerly called a 'batchter' or 'baxter.'

Bath. In 'The Office of the Justices of the Peace,' by William Lampard, 1588, p. 334, is the following :—' Such two justices may

.... licence diseased persons (living of Almes) to travel to Bathe or to Buckstone for remedie of their griefe.' This is probably the origin of the saying, 'Go to Bath.' The words 'remedie of their griefe' seem to point to mental disorder, if so, 'Go to Bath and get your head shaved' implies that the waters of that city were in good repute for the cure of mental derangements.

Batlet, Bat. Touchstone, in 'As You Like It,' says, 'I remember the kissing of her *batlet*.' The batlet, or battledore, as it is now called, was the prototype of the modern mangle. It consisted of a flat piece of wood about two feet long and six inches wide, with a thin short handle at each end. The linen to be 'mangled' was coiled round a roller and placed upon a flat table; the batlet was then used with all the pressure the operator could put upon it to roll the linen backwards and forwards until it was smooth. The cricket-bat is evidently named after this instrument. The batlet is still used in Yorkshire.

Batta. This name is applied to allowances made to military officers on service in India, in addition to their regular pay. The word is Hindustanee, and signifies *allowance*.

Battersea was anciently 'St. Peter's ea' (*ea*, island).

Battle Bridge, now King's Cross, is the traditional site of the great battle between Boadicea, the queen of the Iceni, and Suetonius Paulinus, the Roman general. The bridge was over the river Fleet.

Battledore and Shuttlecock. Battledore in this phrase is the Spanish *batidor*, a beater or striker. Shuttlecock (evidently a corruption of 'shuttle *cork*'), the feathered *cork* which is driven to and fro by the players, as a *shuttle* moves in a loom.

Battle of Waterloo. Mr. A. J. Dunkin, of Dartford, shows in 'Notes and Queries,' July, 1873, that the first intelligence of this battle was brought to England by Mr. Charles Fowler, an architect, who afterwards built Hungerford Market, and obtained the first prize for a design for new London Bridge.

Battle Royal. Battle-royal is a term used in cock-fighting, signifying a kind of free fight between three, five, or seven game cocks, which are made to fight until all are defeated but one, who is then declared to be the victor.

Bauble. A bauble was originally an implement having lumps of lead hanging by short leather thongs from the end of a short stick, for beating dogs, &c. Afterwards a similar instrument, ornamented burlesquely, was used by a fool at court, as symbolic of his office.

Baxter's Maxim. Dean Stanley, in speaking at Kidderminster, said that the maxim attributed to Baxter, 'In necessary things unity, in doubtful things liberty, in all things charity,' was 'dug out of an obscure German treatise.' W. L. Bowles, the poet, who had it inscribed over a doorway of his house in the Close at Salisbury, always attributed it to Melancthon. It seems clear that Baxter was not its author.

Bayonet. This word is said to have been derived from Bayonne, in France, where, it is stated, bayonets were first made in 1640, or, as others say, were first used at the siege in 1665. As they are mentioned by Cotgrave, in 1611, as 'a great knife to hang at the girdle,' this cannot be correct. They were perhaps so named from having been made at Bayona, in Toledo, so famous for the excellent temper of the swords manufactured there. The first mention of this weapon in the English service is in a proclamation of Charles II., April 2, 1672, where it is directed that 'the rest of the soldiers of the several troopes are to have and to carry each of them one matchlocke musket, with a collar of bandileers, and also to have and carry a bayonet or great knife.'

Bayswater. From a *Quo Warranto*, of the time of Edward I., we learn that this locality was then held by one *Bainiardus*, as tenant, from the Abbot of Westminster. In other parts of the same document his name is written *Baynardus*. In 1653, the 'common field at Paddington' is described as being near to a place called '*Baynards watering*.' In 1720 the same lands are mentioned as being in the occupation of Alexander Bond of 'Bears Watering.' The 'common field' is the piece of land lying between Craven Hill and the Uxbridge Road, upon which there were formerly a number of excellent springs of water. Bayswater, therefore, is a corruption of *Baynards waters*, or springs.

Bay-window, Bow-window. A bay-window is one so formed that it forms a projection outside, and a recess or bay inside. A bow-window is a similar window, but its front is a segment of a circle, or *bow-shaped*. Every bow-window is a bay-window; but no window is a bow-window unless its front be rounded. See, ORIEL.

Beadel, Bedel, or Beadle, for the word is spelled in three different ways, is the name of an officer of a court, whose office it is to summon or *bid* persons to attend the sittings. A parish beadle's duties were formerly to *bid* persons to attend divine service. See BID.

Beak or Magistrate. Mr. W. H. Black, in a note to his 'Ballad of Squire Tempest,' says this term was derived from a Mr. Beke, who was formerly a resident magistrate for the Tower Hamlets. See HOOKEY WALKER.

Beam. Verstegan, in a Glossary of Anglo-Saxon words, says, '*Beom*, a tree; we use the name now for the tree when it is squared out, calling it a *beam of timber*, whereby is meant a tree for building, for *timbering* in our old English is building.'—*Restitution*, &c., edit. 1655, p. 163.

Bear. A *bear* in Stock Exchange phraseology is one who looks forward to a fall in stocks, and sells in the hope of being able to buy at a lower price before the time comes for delivery. The name is supposed to be derived from the story of the man who sold a bear's skin before he had caught or killed the bear. See BULLS AND BEARS.

Beard. The earliest known mention of shaving is in the Bible (Genesis xli. v. 14), 'And he [Joseph] shaved himself and came in unto Pharaoh.' There are several directions as to shaving in Leviticus, chaps. xiii. xiv. and xxi., and there are allusions to the practice in many other parts of Scripture. Shaving the beard was introduced by the Romans about 300 B.C. Scipio Africanus was the first Roman who shaved daily. Under Hadrian, the beard was allowed to grow, and the practice remained in fashion till the time of Constantine. The custom of shaving arose in France in the time of Louis XIII., who came to the throne when he was young and beardless. In England the fashion has frequently changed. The Anglo-Saxons wore their beards until the Conquest, when they were compelled to follow the example of the Normans, who shaved. This custom was, however, soon discontinued, for Edward III. is represented on his tomb at Westminster wearing a very long beard. Beards were universally worn from that time until the reign of Charles I. In the time of Charles II. the moustache and whiskers only were worn, and soon afterwards the practice of shaving became general throughout Europe. The revival of the custom of wearing the beard dates from the time of the Crimean War, 1854-5. Jews are forbidden to shave, cut their nails, or bathe, for thirty days after the death of a father, mother, brother, sister, wife, son, or daughter The growth of beards was regulated by statute at Lincoln's Inn in the time of Queen Elizabeth. Primo Eliz.: 'It was ordered that no fellow of that house should wear a beard above a fortnight's growth.'—*Regist. Hosp. Linc.* iv. f. 345. But fashion prevailed, and in the following year all previous orders touching beards were repealed.—*Nichols, Progresses of Eliz.* an. 1562, p. 26. In an old drama, by Lyly, quoted by Nares, one of the characters, a barber, thus addresses a quondam apprentice:—' I instructed thee in the phrases of our elegant occupation, as, "How, sir, will you be trimmed? Will you have your beard like a spade, or a bodkin? A penthouse on your upper lip, or an alley on your chin? A low curle on your head like a bull, or dangling lockes like a spaniel? Your mustachoes sharpe at the ends like shoemakers aules, or hanging down to your mouth like goats flakes? Your love-lockes wreathed with a silken twiste, or shaggie to fall on your shoulders?"'

Bearing Reins. The use of these reins is very ancient. In Osburn's 'Ancient Egypt,' Sethos (1610 B.C.) is represented as using them; so that when Joseph rode in Pharaoh's chariot it is probable that bearing reins were used.

Bear's Grease. The reputation of bear's grease as an ungent for the hair is of long standing. In 1562, W. Bulleyn published a 'Booke of Simples,' in which he says (fol. 76), 'The beare is a beaste whose flesh is good for mankynd; his fat is good, with Laudanum to make an oyntment to heale balde-headed men to receive the hayre agayne.'

Bear sucking his paws. There is a common belief that, when deprived of his natural food, the bear sustains life by sucking his paws. It is curious that the same belief is common in Surrey as to the badger, which, by-the-bye, is the only English bear. The badger never leaves his hole when snow is on the ground, lest his foot-tracks should betray him; 'but,' said a gamekeeper, not long ago, 'he lies and sucks his paws, and that's all the food he gets; but when the snow goes away, he comes out quite fat.'

Beauty only skin deep. The first known, if not the original, use of this phrase occurs in Ralph Venning's 'Orthodoxe Paradoxes,' 3rd ed., London 1650, p. 41. 'All the beauty of the world tis but skin-deep, a sunne-blast defaceth it.'

Beaver. Workmen in many parts of England call their afternoon meal beaver or bever. It is an old name for an afternoon meal which was in use before the introduction of tea, the name of which has superseded the older term. The following will show its application:—' Betimes in the morning they break their fast; at noon they dine; when the day is far spent they take their beaver; late at night they sup.'—*Gate of Languages*, 1568. 'He is none of those same ordinary eaters that will devour three breakfasts, and as many dinners, without prejudice to their bevers, drinkings, or suppers.'— *Beaumont and Fletcher, Woman Hater*, i. 3.

Beaver Hats. The earliest known detailed mention of beaver hats is the following, from Stubbes' 'Anatomy of Abuses,' 1580:— 'And as the fashions be rare and strange, so is the stuff whereof their hats be made, divers also; for some are of silk, some of velvet, some of taffety, some of sarcinit, some of wool, and, which is more curious, some of a certain kind of fine haire; these they call *bever hattes*, of xx, xxx, and xl shillings price, fetched from beyond the seas, from whence a great sort of other varieties doe come besides.' It is, however, known that Henry III. possessed '*unum capellum de Bever cum apparatu auri et lapidibus preciosis.*'

Bedford Row is not so named from any connection with the Russell family, but from the circumstance that Sir William Harper, who was Lord Mayor of London in 1562, left the land on which it stands for the foundation of a school and other charities in the town of Bedford.

Bedlam. A corruption of the word Bethlehem, which was the name of a religious house in London, converted into an asylum for lunatics in 1546. It is believed to be the oldest asylum for lunatics in Europe, though there is one in Spain which claims priority. Some authorities give the date of the foundation of Bethlehem Hospital a year later, 1547.

Bedridden. From the Anglo-Saxon *bed-rida*, one who *rides* or is permanently borne on a bed.

Bedstead. *Stead*, or *sted*, was an Anglo-Saxon word, signifying 'a place.' Spenser has—

> They nigh approached to the stead
> Where as those maremaids dwelt.—*Faerie Queen.*

It is obsolete in this exact sense, but we still say, 'We must send some one else in his *stead*,' and we use it in the compound 'bedstead,' which did not originally mean a movable stand on which beds are laid, but a recess in a room where the bed was placed. We still say 'instead of' for 'in the place of,' and a 'farm-stead' is the chief place on a farm.

Beefeater. There is reason for thinking that the derivation of this word from *buffetier* is erroneous, and that the modern name of the royal servants is also the original one. At any rate, the following extract from 'Histrio-mastix,' iii. 1, 93–101 [*circa* 1585–1600], quoted in Simpson's 'School of Shakespeare,' vol. ii. p. 47, shows that it has been in use nearly three hundred years:—

 Steward. These impudent audatious serving-men scarcely beleeve your honour's late discharge.
 1st Servant. Beleeve it? by this sword and buckler no; stript of our liveries, and discharged thus?
  Mavortius. Walke, sirs, nay, walke; awake, yee drowsie drones
    That long have suckt the honney from my hives;
    Begone yee greedy beefeeaters. . . . . .
    The Callis Cormorants from Dover roade
    Are not so chargeable as you to feed.

Bee-line. The term 'bee-line' is used in America exactly in the sense in which we say 'as the crow flies,' that is, perfectly straight. The following is a curious example of its use: 'Sinners, you are making a bee-line from time to eternity.'—*Dow's Sermons*, vol. i. p. 215.

Beer, in the names of places in the Holy Land, means a well; thus Beer-Sheba is the well or fountain of an oath (*shabah*, an oath).

Beer is spoken of by Xenophon in his history of the retreat of the Ten Thousand. It was well known to the Romans as the beverage of Northern Europe.

Beldame. Literally, *fair lady*. 'The name given to a woman who lives to see the sixth generation descended from her.'—*Lansdown MS.*

Belfry. This word, in English, is improperly confined in signification to the chamber in a church tower in which the bells are hung. It means 'a tower,' and is common in mid-Latin, German, and French; in which languages it appears in the forms *beffroi*, *berfroi*, *bervrit*, *bergan*, *bertefredum* and *belfredum*. Its true significance is a tower for defence, or a watch-tower. A tower may be properly called a belfry, although there may not be a bell within it.

Believe. The country people in Durham and Northumberland use this word in a sense having nothing in common with 'belief.' With them it means 'in the evening,' 'towards night,' &c. It is probably a corruption of 'by-the-eve.' Chaucer uses *beleved* in the sense of 'left.'

Belittle. This is a pure American verb. It means 'to make smaller; or lower in character.' ' In an editorial in the *New York Times*, January 10, 1859, the following sentence occurs in reference to a debate in the House of Representatives:—' Upon a motion being made for a committee of investigation, the usual attempts were made to *belittle* the press, and treat its censures with contempt.'

Bell. To ' bear the bell ' is a proverbial expression to denote one who has achieved some distinction. By some it is thought to allude to the practice of attaching a bell to the neck of the most courageous sheep in a flock; but a more probable origin is in the custom which formerly prevailed of giving silver bells as prizes in horse-racing, the winner of a race being said to ' bear away the bell.'

Belladonna. Italian for ' fair lady.' It is the name of a poisonous plant—*Atropa bella donna*—formerly used by ladies as a cosmetic, and for dilating the pupils of the eyes.

' **Bell, book, and candle.**' In the Middle Ages this was a form of excommunication in use among Roman Catholics. The bell was tolled to summon the people; the sentence was read from a book, and a candle was extinguished by being thrown upon the ground; which last was supposed to represent the fate of the criminal.

Bell-hanging. The use of bells in dwelling-houses, for the purpose of summoning domestics, was not known in England until after the time of Queen Anne.

Bellows. ' Bellows were certainly in common use in Anglo-Saxon times, for the name is Anglo-Saxon, *bœlig* or *bylig*; but as this meant only a bag, it is probable that the Anglo-Saxon bellows was of very rude character. It was sometimes distinguished by the compound name *blast-bœlg*, a blast-bag, or bellows.'—*Wright*. A MS. of the fourteenth century, now in the British Museum (MS. Reg. 10 Edward IV.), shows a man blowing a fire with bellows almost identical in shape with those now in use. It is copied in Wright's ' Domestic Manners in the Middle Ages,' p. 144.

Bells. The earliest mention of bells as applied to the purposes of Christian worship is by Polydore Vergil, who states that Paulinus, Bishop of Nola, a city of Campania in Italy, first adapted them to his church in the year 400. They were used in Scotland in the sixth century, but not in England until near the end of the seventh. The Jewish high priests were directed (Exodus xxviii. 33) to wear ' bells of gold,' alternating with pomegranates, upon the hem of their robes. This is the earliest Biblical allusion to bells.

Bells. 'Formerly alarms of fire were given by ringing the church bells backwards.'—*Nares*, p. 39.

Bendigo. The original name of this celebrated Australian goldfield was Bandicoot Creek, from the Bandicoot, a small animal of the opossum species, which formerly frequented the spot in large numbers.

Beneath. This is compounded of the Anglo-Saxon prefix *be*, and an obsolete Old English word, *neath*, from the Anglo-Saxon *neothra*, under. Although we have discarded 'neath,' we still preserve 'nether' and 'nethermost.'

Benefit of Clergy. An ancient custom of law, under which the clergy, urging the Divine command, 'Touch not mine anointed, and do my prophets no harm,' claimed immunity from punishment at the hands of civil officers. Even after conviction of criminal offences, they could plead 'Benefit of Clergy' in arrest of judgment. 'He was then put to read in a *Latin* book, of a Gothic black letter, and if the ordinary of Newgate said *Legit ut Clericus*, i.e. he reads like a Clerk, he was only burnt in the hand, and set free; otherwise, he suffered Death for his crime.'—*Verstegan*. Benefit of Clergy was abolished by Act of Parliament, 7 & 8 George IV. c. 28. See NECK-VERSE.

Bequeath. Verstegan gives the origin of this word in his Anglo-Saxon Glossary, as follows: '*Cwith*, a will, or testament. Hereof remaineth yet our word *bequeath*.'—*Restitution*, &c. p. 167.

Bereft is bereaved.

Berkshire. This name is derived from *barruc*, a polled or pollard oak, and *scyre*, a shire; from the Shiremotes of that county being anciently held in the shade of a large polled oak-tree.

Berwick. This is a contraction of Aber-wick, the meaning of which is a town (*wick*) at the mouth (*aber*) of a river.

Beseech, originally 'beseek'—which gives the exact meaning—which is 'to seek something from another.'

Beside, Besides. Great care is necessary in deciding which of these two words should be used in writing a sentence. *Beside* is a preposition, and should be used whenever it means 'by the side of,' or 'outside of'; as, 'He was sitting *beside* me when it happened'; or 'He is quite *beside* himself.' *Besides* is also sometimes a preposition, as when it is used to signify 'in addition to,' as, '*Besides* all this, between you and us there is a great gulf fixed.' But *besides* should always be used where the sense is adverbial, as signifying 'beyond,' or 'moreover,' as in the two lines from Dryden—

Besides, you know not while you here attend
Th' unworthy fate of your unhappy friend.

Beth, in the names of places mentioned in Scripture, is the Hebrew *beth*, a house. Thus, *Beth-lehem* is 'the house of bread'; *Beth-el*, 'the house of God'; *Beth-saida*, 'house of mercy.' In Birmingham there is a thoroughfare called 'Betholom Row,' in which is an old Jewish burial-ground. *Beth-Olom*, 'the house of Eternal Rest.'

Better, Best. The Persian word for good is *beh*; the comparative *behter*, which means 'better,' and the superlative *behtereen*, which means 'best.' Both the English and Persian languages belong to the Indo-Germanic group, and we doubtless had formerly some corresponding word to the Persian *beh*, good, which has disappeared from the language. The Anglo-Saxons had *behefe*, gain, benefit, which we retain as 'behoof.' Does this point to the same root?

Between hay and grass is a proverbial expression in America, equivalent to the English word 'hobble-de-hoy'—that is, a youth between boyhood and manhood.

Beverage. This word has had many changes in orthography; it is found spelled 'biberedge,' 'beverege,' and 'beveridge.' It comes from the Italian *bevere*, to drink. Hearne ('Glossary to Robert of Gloucester's Chronicle') defines it as 'reward, consequence. 'Tis a word now in use for a Refreshment between Dinner and Supper.' It is now limited in its signification to liquid refreshment.

Bible. From the Greek, *ta biblia*, 'The Books.' The name Bible was given to the Sacred Writings by St. Chrysostom, in the fourth century. The present (1880) version of the Bible originated in a suggestion made by Dr. Rainolds, an eminent Puritan, at the Conference at Hampton Court, January, 1604. In the following July the king (James) suggested the appointment of fifty-four scholars for the preparation of this version, and instructed his bishops that, whenever a living of 20*l.* a year fell vacant, they should inform him, in order that he might recommend one of the translators to the patron. This was all James did on behalf of the translation with which his name is associated. The expenses (about 3,500*l.*) were paid by Barker, the printer and patentee. Forty-seven of the fifty-four accepted office, and they were divided into six companies, of which two met at Westminster, two at

Cambridge, and two at Oxford. The Westminster companies translated the Old Testament, to the end of the Second Book of Kings, and the Apostolic Epistles. The Cambridge bodies translated from the First of Chronicles to the end of Canticles, and the Apocrypha. The Oxford companies completed the Old Testament, and translated the Gospels, the Acts, and the Apocalypse. The final revision was conducted in London, by two delegates from each of the six companies. These twelve met daily for nine months, in the Hall of the Stationers' Company. The work of translation and revision lasted from 1607 to 1610. About 1810, a painstaking person made the following calculations and statements :—

'The Authorised Version of the Bible contains—

	Old Testament	New Testament	Total
Books	39	27	66
Chapters	929	260	1,189
Verses	23,214	7,959	31,173
Words	592,439	181,258	773,697
Letters	2,728,100	838,380	3,556,480

The middle chapter, and the shortest, is Psalm cxvii. The twenty-first verse of the seventh chapter of Ezra contains all the letters of the alphabet, reckoning I and J as the same letter. The nineteenth chapter of the Second Book of Kings and the thirty-seventh chapter of Isaiah are alike. The shortest verse is John xi. 35.' The divisions of chapters into verses were made by Stephens in 1551.

Bid. The old word *bid*, to invite, as used in the verse (Matthew xxii. 9), 'As many as ye shall find, *bid* to the marriage,' is from the Anglo-Saxon *Beodan*, to invite, or entreat. It now seems almost obsolete. We however retain it in the compound *forbid*. We 'invite' a person to our house; we *forbid*, or prohibit, him from entering it. 'Have I not *forbidden* her my house?'— *Merry Wives of Windsor*. The word *bid*, as used of an offer of money for a commodity, is from a different root. In this sense, *bid* comes from the Anglo-Saxon *biddan*. See BEADLE.

Bigamy. The offence known by this name should properly be called polygamy, *i.e.* having a plurality of wives or husbands living at the same time. *Bigamy*, in its original and canonical sense, 'consists in a man marrying two virgins, one after the death of the other; or in marrying a widow once.'—*Wharton*. A second marriage, after the death of the first wife, is sometimes called Digamy.

Bigot. According to Camden, this word arose from the French pronunciation of the English phrase, 'By God!' uttered as an oath by Rollo, Duke of Normandy, when he refused to kiss the foot of Charles the Foolish, his father-in-law. Cotgrave's Dictionary, published in 1611, has the following:—'*Bigot*, an old Norman word signifying as much as *de par Dieu*, or our "for God's sake!" made good French, and signifying an hypocrite, or one that seemeth much more holy than he is, also a scrupulous or superstitious fellow.'

Bilboes are the fetters in which the ankles of refractory or mutinous sailors are confined, when they are sentenced to be put in irons. The word is derived from Bilboa, in Spain, where they were first made. Some bilboes found in the Spanish Armada are preserved in the Tower.

Billiards. The invention of billiards is by some attributed to a Frenchman named Devigne, who lived in the time of Charles IX. of France. Bouillet says it originated in England. Strutt thinks it is only the game of 'paille-maille' (the original of croquet) transferred from the ground to a table. Who discovered it is not known, but the time of its introduction seems to have been about the middle of the sixteenth century. Spenser alludes to it in 'Mother Hubbard's Tale'; and Shakespeare, in 'Antony and Cleopatra.'

Billion. The word is a contraction of *bi-million*, literally *millions twice*. In England and the Colonies the meaning is a million of millions. In France, on the Continent, and in the United States, it is a thousand millions.

Bill of Exchange. In 'Notes and Queries,' July 28, 1877, is a copy of an Italian bill of exchange drawn at Milan March 9, 1325. It was payable on the 9th of October following. The amount is mentioned as 'Lib. XIV.'

Binnacle. This word is a corruption of *bittacle*. It means the enclosed box in which a ship's compass is placed and permanently fixed. The name is from the French *habitacle*.

Birch. Bailey, with dry humour, in his 'Dictionary' says: 'BIRCH [*Birce* Sax. *Birckenhaum* Teut.] This is well known to schoolmasters.'

Birch's, Cornhill. This celebrated house for good things was established by one Horton, in the reign of George I. The proprietor, Alderman Birch, was Lord Mayor in 1815. He was not only a confectioner; he was poet, dramatic writer, and Colonel of the City Militia. He wrote the inscription for the statue by Chantrey of George III. now in the Council Chamber, Guildhall. The shop front in Cornhill remains as it existed 150 years ago.

The Alderman died in 1840, but had previously (1836) disposed of his business to Messrs. Ring and Brymer.

Birchin Lane. Stow says that this is properly Birchover Lane, 'so called of Birchover, the first builder and owner thereof, now corruptly called Birchin Lane.'

Bird, in the original Anglo-Saxon, *brid*, is literally the young of birds, as *earnes brid*, an eagle's young; hence the German *brut*, a hatch of young, and the English *brood* and *breed*. In this sense Shakespeare uses the word 'bird' in ' Hen. IV.' act v. sc. 1.:

> Being fed by us you used us so
> As that ungentle gull the cuckoo's *bird*
> Useth the sparrow.

Properly the word *fowl* is the general term applicable to the feathered race as a whole, but this word is now only used for *domestic* fowl, and the name of the young animal has become the general term to signify the feathered tribes.

Birdlime. The second syllable of this word is the German *leim*, glue. The Dutch word for glue is *lym*; the Scandinavian nations spell it *lim*.

Birmingham trade discounts. The prices of nearly all the goods manufactured at Birmingham are regulated by discounts or allowances from nominal list prices. These discounts range from a mere fractional percentage to a maximum of 80 or 90 per cent. To the general public this seems unaccountable and open to endless fraud, but practically it is found to work well, to prevent fraud, and to be absolutely the only plan by which the business of the town could be carried on. As an illustration, we may take the case of a brassfounder—that is, a maker of hooks and bolts, and the innumerable articles of brass that are in constant use in every house. All his goods are represented to customers by means of drawings in his pattern-book, and some of these books contain thousands of different objects. Each of these has a *nominal* price printed in the book. The *real* price is arrived at by a deduction or discount from the nominal. The nominal price of a particular item has been calculated and fixed, we will say, when copper—which is the chief raw material in making brass—is at 100*l*. the ton, and the current rate of brassfounders' discount is 30 per cent. Now, if copper should suddenly rise in price to 150*l*. the ton, the manufacturer does not *raise his prices*, but he *reduces his discount*. Instead of 30, he only allows 20 per cent. So in the opposite case of a fall in copper to 70*l*. the ton. He then *raises his discount* say to 40 per cent., and in this way *reduces the value* of all his five or six thousand different articles by a single stroke of the pen. Thus, by the simple process of altering the deduction to be made from a fictitious basis, the *cost* of finished goods follows that of the raw material, although their nominal price remains unaltered.

Birthplace of Napoleon III. It has been stated over and over again that the Emperor Napoleon III. was born at the Tuileries. Mr. Bertrand Payne, the author of the 'Index of Biography,' says this is erroneous. 'A friend of mine,' he writes, 'submitted a proof to the illustrious original, who then and there made three slight corrections in it with his own hand, one of which was to expunge the word "Tuileries," and to substitute "Rue Ceruti (now Lafitte)."'

Biscuit. This word is a compound of the French words *bis*, twice, and *cuit*, baked. Originally the bread for use on shipboard, made in thin flat cakes as now, was baked twice, in order to secure the requisite hardness and dryness.

Bis dat qui cito dat. This Latin proverb is from the works of Publius Syrus, a Roman poet of the time of Julius Cæsar. It means 'He gives twice who gives quickly.'

Bishop. Dr. Chance, in 'Notes and Queries,' points out that the English word bishop, and its French equivalent, *évêque*, are both derived from the Latin *episcopus*, and yet neither word has a single letter belonging to the other. He gives the gradations as follows: Episcopus, episcop, piscop, biscop, bishop; and in French episcopus, episc, epesc, evesc, évesque, évêque.

Bishop's Apron. This apron represents the short cassock which was formerly worn alike by bishop, priest, and deacon. The 74th Canon enforces its use upon all the clergy, but it is now confined to the bishops. The short cassock differed from the long one in having no collar or sleeves, and in its extending only about two inches below the knees.

Bishops in Parliament. Before the time of Henry VIII. certain abbots held manors from the Crown for which they owed military service, and in right of which they were *lords* and were summoned to Parliament. From this arose the custom of bishops sitting as peers. Although, however, they are called 'lords spiritual,' they sit as *temporal peers* in right of baronies.

Bishopric, Kingdom. The terminating syllables of both these words are from the Anglo-Saxon. They called a kingdom *Cyning-*

dome, or *Ciningric*, indiscriminately. Verstegan says '*dom* and *ric* signify both one thing, to wit the jurisdiction or dominion belonging to some publick person. And whereas we say a King*dom*, they say in Germany a Kining*ric*; but whereas we say a Bishop*ric*, they say a Bishop*dom*.'—*Restitution*, &c., edit. 1655, p. 168.

Bissextile. This is a word derived from the Latin *bis*, twice, and *sextus*, sixth. The extra day in February every fourth year is called an *intercalary* day. Under the Julian, or Roman system, this intercalary day was inserted in the Calendar between the 24th and 25th of February. According to the peculiar method of reckoning among the Romans, the 24th of February was called the 'sixth before the Calends of March.' Every fourth, or leap year, this sixth (*sextus*) was reckoned twice (*bis*), and was called *bissextus*. From this we get the word *bissextile*, meaning leap year.

Bit for a horse. From the Anglo-Saxon, but whether from *bitol*, a bridle, or *bitan*, to bite, is uncertain.

Bitter end. This phrase, which originated at the time of the American civil war, is probably founded upon the verse Proverbs v. 4, 'But her end is bitter as wormwood.'

Bivouac is a military term corrupted by the French from the German *bei-wache*, an additional watch. There is an old English term in Bailey, biovac or bihovac, meaning a night guard of the whole army in apprehension of danger, but the latter word is now obsolete, and the French word is completely Anglicised.

Bi-weekly, Tri-weekly. These are words used to express something that happens, or is published twice or three times within a week. It is wrong. They mean something occurring once in two or three weeks.

Black. It is singular that this word originally signified 'pale.' In the Anglo-Saxon an old writer speaks of *Se mona mid his blacan leohte*—'the moon with her pale light.' Another praises the beauty of *blac hleor ides*—'the pale-cheeked maiden.' 'Then,' as Mr. Wedgwood says ('Etymology, vol. i.), 'as a pale complexion takes a blueish tint, the designation has passed on to make the darker colours of the spectrum, and finally in English black, a total absence of all colour. The words bleak and bleach are from the same root as the word black. In the north of England *blake*, as applied to butter or cheese, means 'yellow'; *blakeling* is a local name for a yellow ammer, and Ray has "as blake as a paigle," i.e. cowslip.'

Black Doll at marine-store shops. Formerly cast-off clothes were bought in large quantities for the purpose of being shipped to uncivilised countries; and a black doll gaily dressed was exhibited in front of the houses of dealers in cast-off garments as a sign that the owner dealt in such goods for exportation to Africa.

Black-edged Paper. In 'Social Life in Former Days,' by E. D. Dunbar, of Lea Park, Forres, there is a copy of a letter from Lord Donne to an ancestor of the Author, inviting him to the funeral of the Countess of Murray. The letter was dated January 5, 1683, and was written upon paper edged with black. Black-edged paper is mentioned in Addison's comedy of 'The Drummer,' which appeared in 1715. In act iv. sc. 1 there is an allusion to 'my lady's mourning paper—that is, blacked at the edges.' It does not seem to have come into general use, for in 'Mann and Manners at the Court of Florence,' 1740–86 (Bentley, London, 1876) is a copy of a letter from Mann to Walpole, dated January 28, 1745. The letter was written on paper with narrow mourning border, referring to which, the writer says, 'I believe you never saw anything like it before; here everybody uses it but myself. I begged a sheet for this occasion only, and another to keep as a curiosity. Madame Royale was very unpolite to dye just at the beginning of Carnival to deprive us of all our diversions.' The lady who had just died was the mother of the Grand Duke of Tuscany.

Blackguard. The earliest mention of this term that the compiler of this book has met with is in the 'Churchwardens' Account of St. Mary-at-Hill, London, 17 & 19 Edward IV.' (quoted by Brand, vol. ii. p. 231), where, under date 1532, is 'Item, received for iiij. Torches of the Black Guard, iiij*d*.' What this 'black guard' consisted of is not mentioned, but the following seems to show that the name was formerly applied to link-boys—that is, boys who ran with lighted torches, links, to light passengers in the streets in dark weather :—

> Love is all gentleman, all joy,
> Smooth are his looks, and soft his face,
> Her [Belinda's] Cupid is a blackguard boy
> That rubs his link full in your face.
> *Sackville, Earl of Dorset.*

The name, however, seems also to have been applied to a low class of servants in the kitchen of the king. In the 'Calendar of State Papers' there is the following entry :—'Aug. 17, 1535. Sir William Fitzwilliam to Mr. Secretary Cromwell: Refusal of the workmen to work for less than 6*d*. a day. Two of the ringleaders had been for some time of the *Blackguard* of the King's kitchen.' From various circumstances it seems to have been the duty of these blackguards to watch over and remove from one palace to another, when the Court changed its residence, all the cooking utensils and even coals. These, being the lowest, meanest, and dirtiest of the retainers, were called the *black guard*.

Black Letter. This is the modern name for the Old Gothic or Old English letter, introduced into England about the middle of the fourteenth century. When, about a century later, printing was introduced, the types were cast in this character in imitation of manuscript. All the early printed Bibles, and all the books printed before 1500, are in this character, and are called Black Letter books.

Blade. The Anglo-Saxon word for a shoot or leaf of grass or corn was *blæd*. The name is applied to the cutting part of a knife or sword from the similarity in shape. We still say a 'blade' of grass. See SHOULDER-BLADE.

Blank. From the French *blanc*, white. Hence a blank page means a white page.

Blanket. It is doubtful whether the etymology of blanket from the name of a Bristol Mayor is correct. Spenser uses the word *bloncket* for liveries or coats; and in 'Cole's Dictionary' *blanquet* is used to designate a delicate white pear, '*Pyrum subalbidum*, a *blanquet* pear.' This seems to point to the French *blanc*, white, as the root. Kersey also has the word *blankers* for white garments. The transition from *blanquet*, a white livery, to an undyed woollen material similar to that of which liveries are made, seems easy and natural. The woollendrapers still sell a cloth which they call 'livery cloth.'

Blaze. In England a white mark in the forehead of a horse is called a *blaze*. In America the word is used to denote pieces of bark cut from the trees in a forest, at short distances from each other, so that travellers may, by observing the white marks left, retrace their steps. The term is also used by the American Government when they plot out new roads or mark 'lots' for sale. The rule is, 'three *blazes* in a perpendicular line on the same tree indicate a legislative road; the single *blaze*, a settlement, or neighbourhood road.'—*Carlton*. The word is also used metaphorically; as, 'Champollion died in 1832, having done little but *blaze* out the road to be travelled by others.'—*Nott's Chronology, Ancient and Scriptural*, p. 36.

Blind-man's-buff. Taylor, the Water-Poet, in his 'Great Eater of Kent,' 1630, says, ' Gregorie Dawson, an Englishman, devised the unmatchable mystery of Blindman buffe.'

Blithe, Blithesome. The original meaning of *blithe* or *blithesome* was 'yielding milk.'—*Bailey*. This seems doubtful. Milton has—
> And the milkmaid singeth *blithe*.

Bloater. To blote, or blōt, fish is, in Scandinavia, to soak them preparatory to curing them by smoke. When cured fish, under the name ' blōt fish,' were first brought to England from Sweden, it was naturally thought that ' blōt ' had reference to the smoking process, and hence to blote, or bloat, in English has come to signify curing fish by smoking. The term is an old one. Nares quotes from Beaumont and Fletcher, ' I have more smoke in my mouth than would *blote* a hundred herrings '; and, from Ben Jonson, 'You stink like so many *bloat*-herrings newly taken out of the chimney.' The original word *bloat* means 'to swell'; as we speak of 'a bloated toad.' Strange that the same word should signify dried, and therefore shrunken; and its exact opposite, swollen and distended.

Blockhead. This comes from a play upon the word 'block,' the name of the wooden mould upon which hats are shaped, and it was used to designate the shape or fashion of the hat itself. Our forefathers often exercised their wits upon the subject. Beaumont and Fletcher have, ' Though now your blockhead be covered with a Spanish block '—that is, a hat of Spanish fashion. In ' Wits' Recreations ' (Epigram 456) is the couplet:—
> A pretty *block* Sextinus names his hat,
> So much the fitter for his *head* by that.

Blood is thicker than water. Many think that this saying originated with Commodore Tatnall, of the United States Navy, who assisted the English in the Chinese waters, and, in his despatch to his Government, justified his interference by quoting the words. It is, however, an old English proverb, and is to be found in Ray's ' Collection of English Proverbs,' published in 1672. Walter Scott, too, makes Dandie Dinmont say, ' Weel! *blude's thicker than water*; she's welcome to the cheeses and the hams just the same.'

Blood-heat. The average temperature of the human body is from 98 to 100 degrees. This heat is maintained within one or two degrees whether in arctic or tropical climates. It does not vary whatever the sensations of heat or cold may be. Any deviation from the average, whether the temperature falls or is raised, is injurious, and if it be great is soon fatal. The *mammalia* generally have about the same temperature as man. Fishes, reptiles, and insects do not differ greatly from the warmth of the air or water in which they live, but the temperature of birds is from eight to ten degrees higher than that of man.

Bloom on the Grape, Plums, &c. The bloom upon fruit is a provision of nature to prevent water from settling, to the detriment of the fruit. Where it is rubbed off damp accumulates, and decay commences.

Blowpoint. Nares describes this as a 'childish game, consisting perhaps of blowing small pins or points against each other. Probably something like push-pin.'

> We pages play at *blowpoint,* for a piece of a parsonage.
> *Return from Parnassus,* iii. 1.

Blue. Bailey gives an extraordinary etymon to this word. He has it in his 'Dictionary' as follows :—' Blue [*Blaw*, Teut. probably of *l'eau,* the water, *because of its representing the colour of the sky*], sky colour.'

Blue-Book. This term in America has a different signification from that which it has in England. The American Blue-Book is similar to the English Red-Book. It contains lists of all persons in authority in the government, the law offices, and in the various civil, military and naval departments.

Blue Nose. This is a slang name in America for a native of Nova Scotia. Haliburton, in 'Sam Slick,' gives the following account of its origin :—' "Pray, sir," said one of my fellow-passengers, "can you tell me the reason why the Nova Scotians are called *Blue Noses* ?" " It is the name of a potato," said I, "which they produce in the greatest perfection, and boast to be the best in the world. The Americans have, in consequence, given them the nickname of *Blue Noses.*"'

Blue Ribbon of the Turf. Lord Beaconsfield originated this phrase, so frequently quoted in reference to the great race, the Derby. He gives, in his 'Biography of Lord George Bentinck,' an account of its origin. Lord George had given up racing to become the leader of the Conservative party, and was defeated in Parliament a few days before the horse *Surplice,* which he had sold, won the coveted prize. The two events troubled him greatly. 'It was in vain to offer solace,' says Disraeli. 'He gave a sort of stifled groan. "All my life I have been trying for this, and for what have I sacrificed it ? You do not know what the Derby is,' he moaned out. "Yes I do; it is the Blue Ribbon of the Turf." "It *is* the Blue Ribbon of the Turf," he slowly repeated, and sitting down at a table, he buried himself in a folio of statistics.'

Blue-stocking. In the time of Dr. Johnson, Mrs. Thrale and other ladies held weekly assemblies for meeting literary men. A Mr. Stillingfleet was an eminent member, who excelled in conversation. His dress was peculiar, and he wore blue stockings. When he was absent he was greatly missed, and it was common to say, ' We can do nothing without the *blue stockings*.' By degrees the name became applied to the ladies who attended, and the assemblies received the name of Blue-Stocking Clubs. Hence literary ladies are called ' *blue stockings* ' in England, France and Germany.

Blunderbuss. An old English name for an empty-pated fool. Woolston, ' Sixth Discourse on Miracles,' p. 50, says, ' No wise man ever reprehends a *blunderbuss* for his bull any other way than by laughing at him,' and Pope speaks of ' a *Blunderbus* of Law.' The name appears to have been applied to the gun so called, from its similarity in sound to the Dutch name for the firearm, *Donderbuss*, literally, thundertube.

Board of Green Cloth. The duties of this ' Board' were formerly of a much more minute nature than at present. In Mr. Cunningham's 'Handbook of London' is a copy of an order, as follows :—' Board of Green Cloth, 12th June, 1681. Order was this day given that the Maides of Honour should have cherry tarts instead of gooseberry tarts, it being observed that cherry's are at threepence per pound.'

Board of Trade. ' Cromwell seems to have given the first notion of a Board of Trade. In 1655 he appointed his son Richard, with many Lords of his Council, judges and gentlemen, and about twenty merchants of London, York, Newcastle, Yarmouth, Dover, &c., to meet and consider by what means the trade and navigation of the republic might be best promoted.'—*Thomas's Notes of the Rolls.*

Boar's Head in Eastcheap. This inn, celebrated for all time as the scene of Falstaff's roysterings, was burnt down in the Great Fire of London. It stood upon the exact site of King William's statue at the end of King William Street.

Bob 'was not originally a diminutive of Robert, but merely the Teutonic *bub* or *bube*, signifying boy.'—*Fox Talbot.*

Bobadil. The name of the swaggering captain in Ben Jonson's comedy was probably adapted from that of the governor of Cuba who sent Columbus home in chains, which was Babadilla.

Bobby. This term was first applied to policemen in reference to Sir Robert Peel, who organised the police force. 'Peeler,' from the same source, is used in Ireland in reference to the rural police.

Bodkin. This word originally meant a dagger. It is so used by Chaucer, and by Beaumont and Fletcher. This definition makes Hamlet's 'bare bodkin,' which was to make his quietus, more intelligible.

Bodkin. 'To ride bodkin.' Dr. Payne, formerly Archdeacon of St. David's, gave the following explanation of this saying:—'Bodkin is *bodykin* (little body), as *manikin* (little man), and was a little person to whose company no objection could be made on account of room occupied, by the two persons accommodated in the corners of the carriage.'

Body-snatching. This offence, common enough a few years ago, is now rendered unnecessary by judicious legislation. The earliest known case of body-snatching occurred in 1777, from a burial-ground near Gray's Inn Lane. The gravediggers themselves raised the corpse of a Mrs. Jane Samsbury, and were tried at Guildford for the offence. It was ingeniously contended that, as they took nothing but the body, there could be no crime, as the body could not be held to be the property of anyone. The men were, however, convicted, and imprisoned for six months.

Boer. The word 'Boer,' applied to the Dutch inhabitants of the country districts of the Cape of Good Hope, is the German name for farmers and agriculturists. The English word 'boor' originally had the same significance.

Bogie. The goblin with which silly nurses frighten children. There are many ways of spelling the word, as *boggart, boggard, boggè, boggle, boggybo, bugan, boguesh, bogy,* and *bogle.* They all seem to have been derived from the Celtic *bwgan,* a spectre.

Bogus. The 'Boston Daily Courier' of June 12, 1857, has the following upon the origin of this word:—'The word "bogus," we believe, is a corruption of the name of one *Borghese,* a very corrupt individual, who, twenty years ago, or more, did a tremendous business in the way of supplying the great West, and portions of the South-West, with a vast amount of counterfeit bills, and bills on fictitious banks, which never had an existence out of the "forgetive brain" of him, the said "Borghese." The Western people, who are rather rapid in their talk, when excited, soon fell into the habit of shortening the Norman name of Borghese to the more handy one of *Bogus*, and his bills, and all other bills of like character, were universally styled "bogus currency."'

Boiling point of water. At the level of the sea, water boils at a temperature of 212 degrees, but as we ascend, the boiling point becomes gradually lower. At the Hospice of Mount St. Bernard on the Alps, which is at an elevation of 8,600 feet above sea level, water boils at something less than 200 degrees. This compels the monks to live almost entirely upon baked, roasted, or fried food, as its nutritious qualities cannot be extracted at a lower temperature than 212 degrees. The monks are consequently debarred from many comforts through not being able to make their boiling water so hot as that of their neighbours in the valleys below. At the city of Mexico, the boiling point is 200 degrees; at Quito it is 194; and on the Donkia mountain, in the Himalaya range, Dr. Hooker found it 180 degrees.

Bolt. This word is used in many senses, but they are all referable to the original meaning of an *arrow*. The word was originally spelt *boult*. Chaucer has 'a featherless *boult*,' and we read of a man taking a *boult* from his quiver. Besides this primitive meaning, we have 'thunder*bolt*' as applied to lightning, which everybody knows darts like an arrow, and a door is *bolt*ed by a piece of straight iron *shot out* of a socket. '*Bolt* upright' means 'straight as an arrow'; a horse *bolts* when he starts off suddenly, as an arrow from a bow; and a hog *bolts* his food when he shoots it into his stomach without mastication.

Bombast. A mixture of cotton and silk yarn, so called, was used in the time of James I. to stuff or pad the enormous breeches used at that time. Hence bombast, or bombastical, is applied to anything spoken or written in an inflated style.

Bombay is a corruption of *Bom Bahia*, 'good bay,' the name given to the locality by the Portuguese when they took possession.

Bombazine, a fabric much in use forty years ago for ladies' dresses, derived its name by corruption from the Greek *bombyx*, a silkworm. The name was at first applied to silk itself, and finally to a fabric made for mourning dresses, in which silk was the chief material.

Bombs. Hone says that the first bombs were thrown, on the 24th March, 1580, upon the town of Wachtendonck, in Guelderland. He adds that 'the invention is commonly attributed to Galen, Bishop of Münster.'

Bonâ fide. This phrase is frequently pronounced by imperfectly educated people as though the latter word were one syllable only. Its proper division into syllables is bo-nâ fi-de; the accent is on 'fi.' The literal meaning is 'in good faith.' *Bonafides* is 'good faith.'

Bone to pick. It is the custom in Sicily for the father of a bride to hand the bridegroom a bone, saying, ' Pick this bone; you have undertaken a more difficult task.'

Bonfire. From the Scandinavian *baun-fire*, a beacon-fire.

Boniface. This name is probably applied to publicans from the legend mentioned in the 'Ebrietatis Encomium,' which relates that Pope *Boniface* instituted indulgences for those who should drink a cup after grace, to his own memory, or to the pope for the time being, which cup is proverbially called St. Boniface's Cup.

Bonne-bouche. French; literally, *a good mouth*. Used in England as equivalent to *tit-bit*, or in reference to some rare old wine, as ' Now I'll give you a *bonne-bouche*. This is a bottle of the celebrated Comet Port of 1811.'

Bonnet is from the Gaelic *bonaid*, a head dress.

Book (see **Volume** before reading this article). The Gothic tribes used slips of wood for writing tablets, and the wood of the beech being found most suitable for the purpose, its Anglo-Saxon name *boc* became the origin of the English *book*, and the German *buch*. As slips of wood could not be rolled, like the Latin *volumen*, they would naturally be gathered together like leaves of modern paper. One of the oldest manuscripts in existence, 'The Upsala Copy of the Mæso-Gothic Translation of the Scriptures,' is written on sheets of vellum arranged as a *book*. The superior convenience of that form led to its adoption in Rome early in the Christian era; though the *Rolls* were continued to be used in the Northern nations down to a comparatively recent period.

Books. A folio volume is composed of sheets of paper folded so as to make two leaves; a quarto (4to), four; an octavo (8vo), eight; a duodecimo (12mo), twelve, &c.

Bookbinding in cloth. 'The originator of Binding in Cloth was Mr. R. E. Lawson, of Stanhope Street, Blackfriars, and the first book bound in cloth was a manuscript volume of music, which was subsequently purchased by Mr. Alfred Herbert, the marine artist. On this volume being shown to the late Mr. Pickering, who was at that time (1823) printing a diamond edition of the Classics, he thought this material would be admirably adapted for the covers of the work. The cloth was purchased at the corner of Wilderness Row, St. John Street, and 500 copies were covered by Mr. Lawson, with glue. Shakespeare's plays were also issued in this form, and these books were the first books bound in cloth.'—ED. *Notes and Queries*, Feb. 18, 1865.

Boot. The original meaning of boot was a leathern bag. In Spanish, at the present day, the same word, *bota*, means a leathern bag or skin for carrying wine, and a leathern covering for the foot and leg.

Boot-jack, Roasting-jack. Foot-boys, who had frequently the common name of Jack given them, were kept to turn the spit, or pull off their masters' boots; but when instruments were invented for both these services, they were both called *jacks*.

Boot of a carriage. The word probably comes from the French *boîte*, a box. The 'boots' of ancient carriages were projections from the sides, in which the attendants were carried sideways. In Hoefnagel's picture of Nonsuch Palace, 1582, the attendants upon Queen Elizabeth are represented as sitting in a 'boot' of this kind. 'Monday, April 26, 1669, was the first time the Oxford Flying Coach went to London in one day. It had then a "boot" on each side.'—*Oxoniana*, iv. 220.

Booty comes from the Gothic *botyan*, to profit. Hence booty is something that the soldier derives profit from. We have 'a bootless errand,' 'what boots it?' and 'so much to boot'; all of which are from the same root. In Canada, 'booty' means a man's personal luggage on a journey.

Bosh. This word, which was first applied at the Universities to anything nonsensical or trashy, is a pure Turkish word, signifying empty: *bosh làkirdi*, in the same language, means 'nonsense.'

Bosky, a word used frequently by Shakespeare, and other old dramatists, in the sense of wooded, umbrageous, &c., is the French word *bosquet*, a grove or thicket. Milton uses the word in 'Comus,' e.g.:—

> I know each lane and every alley green,
> Dingle or bushy dell of this wild wood,
> And every *bosky* bourn from side to side.

Boss, for master. This American word is the modern form of the Dutch *Baas*, of the same meaning. It has descended from the original Dutch settlers of New York. At the Cape of Good Hope the word is used in its native form, *Baas*, to signify the head of a household.

Botanical nomenclature. In botany the name of each plant consists of at least two words. The first is the name of the *genus*, and the second that of the *species*. Thus the generic name for the oak is *Quercus*, of which the white oak is one of the species. Accordingly, the Latin word *alba*, which signifies *white*, is added, and we get *Quercus alba*, as the botanic name of the white oak. When three names are given, the third signifies that the plant is a variety. Thus the name *Quercus ilex crispa* is that of a variety of the evergreen (*ilex*) oak having curled leaves (*crispa*).

Bothered, in the sense of confused. Grose derives this from *both-eared*; that is, from two persons speaking to a third at the same moment, one to each ear, so that he is confused or *bothered*; understanding neither.

Bottle of hay. To 'seek a needle in a bottle of hay' is a common expression. Shakespeare makes Bottom ('Mid. Night's Dream,' act iv. sc. 2) say, 'I have a great desire to a *bottle of hay*.' The phrase originally signified a quantity of hay tied in a bundle, to be carried out for foddering cattle. The word comes from the French *boteau*, a bundle.

Bottles. The bottles mentioned in Luke v. 37 were the skins of goats, which in those days were used for storing wine. Old 'bottles' of this kind would be liable to burst, from the pressure of the fermentation of new wine; hence new wine had to be put into new bottles. (See Psalm cxix. 83.)

Bought and sold. This was formerly a proverbial expression, to signify completely disposed of, done for, ruined by being outwitted; e.g.:—

> It would make a man mad as a buck to be so *bought and sold*
> *Comedy of Errors*, iii. 1.

> Jockey of Norfolk, be not too bold,
> For Diccon thy master is *bought and sold*.—*Rich. III.* v. 3.

> Then were the Roman Empire *bought and sold*,
> The holy Church were spoyl'd and quite undone.
> *Har. Ariost.* xvi. 33.

Boulevard. This French term, which is the exact equivalent of the English word bulwark, is the name given in France to the ramparts or fortifications by which towns were formerly surrounded.

They have, for the most part, been dismantled, and the spaces they occupied have been laid out as broad streets, the sides of which are planted with trees. These, which in Paris are the finest thoroughfares, are still known as Boulevards.

Bowie-knife. This formidable weapon took its name from 'Colonel Jim Bowie,' a desperate and daring character, born in Logan Co., Kentucky, who is said to have invented it.

Bows. '*Bowes*, at the very first invention of them, were made of *boughs* of trees; and so, accordingly, in our ancient language, took that name.'—Verstegan, *Restitution of Decayed Intelligence*, edit. 1655, p. 161.

Bowyer. A bowyer was one who made bows for archers; hence the surname.

Box Harry. To 'box Harry,' among commercial travellers, is to avoid the usual *table d'hôte*, and to take something substantial at tea-time, in order to save expense.

Bo ʒ. This seems to have been formerly used as a contraction for bushel; the symbol ʒ being the same mark of contraction as used in 'Vi ʒ' (which see). In a bill of charges for a dinner given by Lord 'Leiyster,' as Chancellor of Oxford, September 5, 1570, is the following item :—'For ij bo ʒ, a pecke and a haulfe pecke of flower, to Mr. Furnes, at ijs viid the bo ʒ, vis iiijd.'—*Collectanea Curiosa*, vol. ii. p. 4.

Brace, from the Anglo-Saxon *bracear*, to bind, to tie up. A *brace* of pheasants has come to mean two, because they are usually tied together in pairs; but the word *brace* refers only to the fastening, and might with propriety be applied to three or four birds as well as to two. Two partridges or grouse are not a *brace* until they are tied or braced together. See COUPLE.

Bradshaw's Guide was started in 1839 by George Bradshaw, a printer in Manchester. The time tables were at first printed on a broad sheet. The first *Monthly Guide* was issued Dec. 1841. It consisted of 32 pages, and gave 'tables' relating to 43 lines of railway. Its information was confined to English railways. It contained neither map nor advertisements.

Braham the vocalist, whose real name was Abraham, made his début at the Old Royalty Theatre in 1787, he being then in his thirteenth year. He was described in the bills as '*Master Abrahams.*' He was a pupil of Leoni.

Brahma-pootra, the name given in England to a peculiar breed of domestic fowls, is a slightly altered form of the Sanscrit *Brahma-putra*, 'Brahma's son.'

Brain. The average weight of a man's brain is 46 ounces. The weight, however, varies greatly in different individuals, but it is usually about one-35th of the weight of the body. Lord Campbell's brain was 53¼ ozs., and was perfectly healthy. Cuvier's was the heaviest on record—59 ozs.—but it was not quite healthy. In quadrupeds the relative weight is remarkably less. In dogs it is one-120th; in horses, one-450th; in the sheep, one-750th; and in the ox, one-800th. This shows that there is a direct relation between weight of brain and intelligence, the animals named being ranged in the order of their mental capacity and docility.

Bramble. There are no fewer than sixty-three varieties of the common bramble classified and named by botanists as being found in England. Fifty-eight of these have been found in the county of Warwick.

Bran. This is a corruption of the word *brown*. Bran is the *brown* husk or covering of wheat.

Bran-new is brand-new; that is, so new that the mark or brand of the maker is not worn away or rubbed off. *Spic and span new* is said to be cloth just taken off the spikes or spanners used in stretching it. Another derivation of the latter will, however, be found under SPIC AND SPAN NEW, which see.

Brandy. Mr. Fox Talbot thinks that the German *branntwein*, from which our word brandy is derived, is corrupted from *brand-wein*, and that the meaning is not burnt wine, but burning wine, that is, wine which burns the mouth and throat. In Bretagne brandy is called *gwin-artan*, wine of fire.

Brandy-and-water. The earliest known mention of brandy-and-water as a beverage occurs in 'A Treatise on Diet,' by Dr. Velangin, London, 1768. Speaking of a hard-working lawyer, the doctor says, 'He had lately, through custom more than choice, given in to the too fashionable use of drinking *brandy and water*.'

Brat. This word, which is now applied to an ugly, ill-favoured, ill-behaved, dirty child, originally simply meant *offspring*. Archbishop Trench mentions this, and gives the following quotation from Gascoigne's 'De Profundis':—

> O Israel, O household of the Lord,
> O Abraham's *brats*, O brood of blessed seed,
> O chosen sheep that loved the Lord indeed.

Bravo! Well done! This is an Italian word naturalised in England in the masculine form, which with us is used indiscriminately. The Italians say *bravo* to a male performer, *brava* to a lady, and *bravi* to two or more performers or singers.

Brawl. This word seems to have sadly deteriorated in meaning. In the 'New World of Words,' a dictionary published in 1696, it is defined to be 'the dance with which all balls are begun, wherein the persons dance in a ring or not forward, continually pulling and shaking one another.'

Brawn. Tooke says the name of this once favourite dish is from bawr-en, boar's flesh, but this etymology is doubtful. The word is, with greater probability, derived from the name of Brawn, a celebrated cook who kept the 'Rummer' in Queen Street, London. King's 'Analogy between Physicians, Cooks, and Playwrights' opens thus:—'Though I seldom gat out of my own lodgings I was prevailed on the other day to dine with some friends at the Rummer in Queen Street. . . . Mr. Brawn had an art,' &c. A grandson of this Brawn kept the public-house at the old Mews Gate at Charing Cross.

Brazen-nose College. The term brazen-nose or brasenose is a corruption of the word *brasen-house*, or brewing-house.

Bread, Loaf. Verstegan has 'Laf or Hlaf, for so was it most written, was with our Ancestors their most usual name for bread, though they had also the word *breod*.'— *Restitution*, &c. edit. 1655, p. 178. It has been estimated that the average daily consumption of bread by Englishmen is one pound. The average for Frenchmen is estimated at $2\frac{1}{4}$ pounds. The proportions of beef and mutton would be in an inverse ratio. The price of the quartern loaf was $4\frac{3}{4}d$. in 1745, which is the lowest within the last 150 years. It was $22\frac{1}{2}d$. in 1800, and $21\frac{1}{2}d$. in 1812, which are the highest prices recorded within the same period. See LADY.

Bread and butter. 'I know on which side my bread is buttered.' This proverb occurs in Heywood's 'Dialogue,' &c., 2nd part, 7th chap., printed in 1546.

Bread-stuffs. The Americans do not use the word 'corn' as a general name for all kinds of grain, but confine it exclusively to Indian corn or maize. Hence they have adopted the term 'bread-stuffs' for wheat, meal, flour, &c. The word arose soon after the acknowledgment of American independence. The earliest known instance of its being used officially is in a 'Report of the Secretary of State on Commercial Restrictions' (Washington, Dec. 16, 1793).

The words are these : ' The articles of exports . . . . are *bread-stuffs*, that is to say Bread-grains, meals, and bread.'

Breaking of bread. This phrase, so frequently used in the New Testament to signify a meal, is explained in Beckman's ' History of Inventions.' He tells us that 'among the ancient Romans all articles of food were cut into small morsels before being served at table. . . . For cutting meat, persons of rank kept a carver, who was designated the *scissor*, or *carptor*, and who had the only knife placed on the table. The bread was not cut at table. It more nearly resembled flat cakes than large loaves like our own, and could easily be broken; hence mention is so often made of the *breaking of bread*.'

Breeches. Among the ancient Greeks wearing breeches was a mark of slavery. To ' wear the breeches ' now-a-days has a very different signification. The phrase ' to wear the breeches ' is common to most of the northern nations of Europe. The French have it, and the Dutch say ' De vrouw draagd'er de brock.' The Germans say ' Sie hat die Hösen '—' she has the breeches.'

Breeches Bible, sometimes called the ' Geneva Bible.' This translation of the English Bible was undertaken by Protestants who fled to Geneva during the reign of Queen Mary. It is called the ' Breeches Bible ' from the curious translation of Genesis iii. 7, 'and they sewed fig-tree leaves together and made themselves *breeches*.' The first edition was printed at Geneva in 1562. It contained two very curious printer's errors—Matt. v. 9, ' Blessed are the *place*-makers '; Luke xxi., ' Christ *condemneth* the poor widow.' About 130 editions of this Bible were printed between 1562 and 1611. Copies are erroneously supposed to be of great value. From 20s. to 30s. is about the value of good copies of the later editions.

Breeze, Breezes. These terms are applied to the smaller kind of cinders left by the combustion of coal. In the neighbourhood of London *breeze* (singular) is principally used by the brickmakers. In the neighbourhood of Birmingham, *breezes* (plural), after being washed carefully, are used by the smiths for their forges. The term is probably a corruption of *débris*.

Brequêt Watch Keys. These ingenious keys, which turn round if it should be attempted to wind the watch in the wrong direction, were so named after the inventor *Brequêt*, a celebrated watchmaker of Paris in the eighteenth century.

Brethren, Children. These two words have a double plural. *Brether* and *childer* were the original plurals of brother and child. The old plural form *en* having been suffixed, the words have become doubly plural.

Brevet is a commission conferring on an officer (not below the rank of captain) a degree of rank immediately above that which he holds in his particular regiment. It does not, however, confer the corresponding increase of pay. There is no 'brevet' rank in the Royal Navy.

Brewers and Bakers in the Anglo-Saxon times, when found guilty of breaking the laws regulating their trades, were placed in what 'Domesday Book' calls 'cathedra stercolaris,' and ducked in *stercore*, that is, stinking water. The *cathedra*, or chair, was akin to the *ducking stool*, used for the punishment of scolding women. One of these chairs or stools is still preserved in the Town Hall of Leominster. See DUCKING STOOL.

Brewers' Marks. The mark X on brewers' casks is a handy method of intimating the original Latin names for the varying degrees of strength:—

    1st. Simplex—which is single X,   or X.
    2nd. Duplex—which is double X,   or XX.
    3rd. Triplex—which is triple X,   or XXX.

Brewster is an ancient name for a brewer. Brewster Sessions are the sittings of magistrates to grant publicans' licences.

Bribe. This word is, perhaps erroneously, supposed to be derived from the French *bribe*, a morsel of bread given to a beggar. Bribery, in old English, did not mean secret corruption, but theft, rapine, open violence, or official extortion. Dame Julyana Berners, in the 'Boke of St. Alban's,' classes thieves and *brybours* together. Lord Berners, in his translation of Froissart, describes the captain of a band of irregular soldiery, called *Companions*, as 'the greatest *brybour* and robber in all Fraunce.' Formerly he who extorted was the briber; now he who corrupts by payment of money, or by other valuable consideration, is the briber, exactly the opposite of the old meaning, though both are equally dishonest.

Brick Building. The oldest brick building, except those built by the Romans, in existence in England is said to be Hurstmonceaux Castle, in Sussex, which was erected by De Fiennes, treasurer to Henry VI. It was dismantled about a century ago by one of the Dacres, but the ruins still present a very picturesque appearance.

Bridal, applied to a marriage-feast, is from the Anglo-Saxon *bryd-eale*, signifying bride-ale; large quantities of ale being consumed by our forefathers on these occasions.

Bridal Custom. The custom of throwing a shoe after a bride comes from the Jewish custom of handing a shoe to a purchaser of land on the completion of a contract (see Ruth iv. 7). Parents also gave a shoe to the husband on a daughter's marriage in token of yielding up their authority. See SHOE AT WEDDINGS.

Bride Cake. 'Our bride cake, which invariably accompanies a wedding, and which should always be cut by the bride, may be traced back to the old Roman form of marriage by a *confarreatio*, or eating together.'—*Lubbock, Origin of Civilisation*, p. 85.

Bridegroom. Verstegan, in his Anglo-Saxon Glossary, spells this *bridgrome*, and defines it thus:—'The Groom of the Bride, because on the marriage day he serveth and waiteth on the table of the bride.'

Bridle. The insertion of the letter *r* in this word has somewhat obscured the derivation. It means that by which the bit is held. In the Icelandic the old form is preserved, *bitell*, and in Danish it is little altered, being *bidsell*.

Brief. Formerly the pleadings in a suit at law were so voluminous that half the time of a court might have been taken up in the mere reading of formal matter. It was therefore ordered that a *brief* summary should be prepared for use in court. This was the origin of the modern brief. An old epigram shows the origin clearly:—

> Here lies old Gripe, a wealthy lawyer he,
> Who six and eightpence had for each decree,
> Death with a *ca. sa.* took the knave in tow,
> To *brief his pleadings* in the world below.

Brig comes to us from the word brigand or brigant, a robber. A brigante was a pirate, and a pirate's ship was a brigantine. These vessels were built on a peculiar model, which was copied in our navy. The name brig is a contraction of brigantine.

Brimstone is a corruption of *brynstone*, the Anglo-Saxon for 'burning stone,' from *bryne*, burning.

Britain. The Celtic name according to Camden, was Prydhain.

The Romans latinised this into Britannia, from which word the present name is derived.

Britannia Metal, sometimes called Tutania, is generally made by melting together 100 parts of tin and 10 parts of metallic antimony. Some makers add small quantities of bismuth and copper.

British Museum. This institution originated in a bequest of Sir Hans Sloane, who had collected a large number of works of art, specimens of natural history, curiosities, books, and manuscripts at a cost of upwards of 50,000*l*. The collection was offered, in terms of his will, in 1753, to the British Government upon condition of 20,000*l*. being paid to his family. The offer was accepted; the funds being raised by a lottery. Montague House, Bloomsbury, having been bought for 10,250*l*., the collection was removed thither, and the Harleian and Cottonian Libraries having been added, the new institution, under the name of the British Museum, was opened in 1759. The old house has entirely disappeared, and the present magnificent building stands upon the site formerly occupied by the mansion and its gardens. When first opened, the number of visitors was limited to forty-five per day. It is now not uncommon for 50,000 persons to pass through the building on a holiday.

British production of Iron. According to published statistics, the weight of the iron produced in Great Britain, in a recent year, by 629 blast furnaces, was $6\frac{1}{2}$ millions of tons. The human mind can hardly grasp these enormous figures, but some conception of the prodigious bulk of the mass of iron they represent can be realised, when it is known that the iron produced in that single year would form a solid wall from London to Birmingham (112 miles), 5 feet in thickness, and $11\frac{1}{2}$ feet in height.

Broad Arrow. 'Used as a Government mark, is thought to have had a Celtic origin; and the so-called arrow may be the ⇐ or *â*, the broad *a* of the Druids. This letter was typical of superiority either in rank or authority, dignity or holiness, and is believed also to have stood for king or prince.'—*Wharton*. As a Government mark for stores it is supposed by others to have been adopted during the time (1693-1702) when Lord Sydney, afterwards Earl of Romney, was Master-General of the Ordnance. Lord Sydney's crest was a barbed dart's head, very similar in form to that now in use as the Government mark.

Brocade. From the French word *broche*, a sort of awl, needle, or bodkin used in embroidery.

Brochure. A small book, *stitched*, not bound; so named from the French *brocher*, to stitch; a pamphlet.

Broker. The word broker comes to us from the shores of the Baltic, where a braker, or bracker, is a public inspector, whose duty it is to examine goods, report upon their quality, and reject any that may be damaged or unsound. In St. Petersburg, tallow is quoted with or without 'brack,' i.e. brokerage. Bailey gives a curious explanation of the origin of the term broker. It is reproduced here, although its correctness is extremely doubtful:— 'Broker, of the word break, because in former times none but bankrupts were permitted to follow that employment.'

Bronchitis. This term came into general use about 1850 or 1851. John Leech published a sketch in 'The Month' for December, 1851, which was entitled ' Scene from the last *new* fashionable complaint—Bronchitis.'

Bronze Coinage. In the year 1860, the old copper coinage was called in, and the present bronze substitutes were issued. From that date to 1873, 2,652 tons of metal were coined, producing upwards of 53 millions of farthings, 164 millions of halfpence, and 170 millions of pennies. The nominal value was about 1,100,000*l*.—*Jevons*.

Broom. A broom is so called because originally made from the fine twigs of the *broom* plant, *Cytisus Scoparius*. Brooms made of other twigs are birch-brooms, heath-brooms, bass-brooms, &c.

Brother Jonathan was Jonathan Turnbull, Governor of Connecticut, under Washington, who had such confidence in him, that, when in doubt or difficulty, he was in the habit of saying, 'I must consult brother Jonathan.' The name is now accepted as the national American designation. This is the generally received origin, but the term, it seems, was in use long before. In a pamphlet published in 1643, entitled 'the Reformado precisely characterised by a transformed Churchwarden at a Vestry, London,' the following passage occurs :—' Queene Elizabeth's monument was put up at my charge when the regal government had fairer credit among us than now, and her *epitaph* was one of my *Brother Jonathan's* best poems before he abjured the university, or had a thought of *New England*.'

Brown Bess—the musket. Bess is a corruption of *buss*, the ancient name for the barrel of a fire-arm. We retain the original word in Arquebuss and Blunderbuss. Arquebuss was a crossbow with a barrel; it was formed from *arc*, or bow, and *buss*, a barrel, and was originally *arc-et-buss*, that is, bow and barrel.

Brown study. This has been thought to mean *brow* study. It is more probably one of the group of similar phrases, in which colours are employed to designate characteristics or temper; as 'black melancholy,' 'blue devils,' 'green-eyed monster,' 'yellow stockings,' 'blue stockings,' 'white feather,' &c. &c.

Bruit. This is the only purely French word in the English Authorised Version of the Bible. It occurs in Jeremiah x. 22, and again in Nahum iii. 19. Adam Clarke says, 'Why this silly French word is huddled in, I am at a loss to divine. Certainly there are at least half-a-dozen English words which would express the same meaning,' which is noise, uproar, clamour, angry dispute, &c.

Brunt. To bear the brunt of anything is to receive the heaviest of the shock. To be in the brunt of a battle is to be in the front, or taking the lead. The word is derived from the custom of hanging a bell on the leading beast of a herd, which the others readily follow. The Servian name for bells of this kind is *bronza*. The Grisons call the first mule in a train the *brunza*—the bell mule—the bell itself being called *brunzinna*, and *portar la brunzinna* meaning being the first in anything. This exactly corresponds to the English *bearing the brunt*, and is the origin of the phrase.—*Wedgwood*.

Brush. This word is found in nearly every language in Europe to signify a whisk made of brushwood or twigs, to clear away dust or rubbish. The following are a few of its forms: *brossa, brosser, brusg, brusco, brusca, bruske, brosse, broza, brozar, bruis, brist, bruscia, brustia, brastie, broustia, börste, burste, brous, brousso, brosse, brossette, bruskr, borste.*

Brusque is a French word, which has been introduced into English to soften the harshness of the native words of similar signification. The English terms, blunt, rough, and abrupt, when applied to manners, all imply censure; but *brusque* simply conveys the idea that the person to whose manners it is applied wants polish.

Bucellas. The wine so called is made at the village of *Bucellas*, near Lisbon.

Buckwheat. This is a corruption of *beech*-wheat; the corn is so called from the similarity of the shape of its grains to the mast or nuts of the beech-tree.

Bucket was originally *water-budget*, or water-bag (French, *bougette*, a small bag). A water-budget in heraldry is a very honourable blazon, having been conferred as a reward for some courageous act in supplying an army with water. Guillim, in his 'Display of Heraldry,' thinks 'the three mighty men in David's army who broke through the host of the Philistines, and drew water from the well of Bethlehem, deserved to be remunerated with such armorial marks on their coat armours for their valour.'

Budge Row, in London, was so called from the numbers of sellers of 'budge' who formerly lived there. Budge is the dressed skins of lambs, with the wool remaining.

Buff—the colour. The bull of the wild cattle common at one time in England was called 'buffe,' or 'buffle' (hence, buffalo), and the skin when dressed, so as to remain soft, was much esteemed. It was called 'buff-leather,' and was coloured of a peculiar shade of yellow; similar to that which is now known universally as *buff colour*.

Buffalo Robe. The skin of the buffalo is always in America called a *robe*. A 'buffalo robe' is the skin of the buffalo dressed without removing the hair, and used as we use travelling-rugs. 'The large and roomy sleigh, decked with *buffalo-robes*, red-bound, and furnished with sham eyes and ears.'—*The Upper Ten Thousand*, p. 4.

Bug. This word originally meant a goblin. The Welsh word *bwg* means a ghost. The Hebrew word, which in Psalm xci. 5 is represented by 'terror,' was in the early translations rendered *bug*, the verse being 'Thou shalt not need to be afraid of any *bugs* by night.'—*Mathew's Trans.* 1537.

Bug-a-boo. Bogill, or bogle, are Scotch names for a phantom. *Bogill* also means a figure dressed up to scare birds away, and *bogill-bo* a hobgoblin. Hence *bug-a-boo*, empty terror, or groundless alarm. See BUG and BOGIE.

Bugbear. The first syllable signifies an empty terror (see BUGABOO). The second—bear—is probably a corruption of 'bird.' A bugbird was probably a stuffed falcon, or hawk, set up to frighten small birds from a farmer's crops.—*Fox Talbot*.

Bugle, Bugle-horn. The derivation of the word 'bugle' is from an old name for a bull. In Latin, the word *buculus* is an ox, or bull. In English, bugle and bull are synonymous; but the former is obsolete, except in the extreme southern counties. At Newport (Isle of Wight), Fareham (Hants), and other towns in that district, the 'Bugle' is a favourite sign for a tavern, denoted by a painting of a bull. 'Bugle,' the musical instrument, was originally the *horn* of a bugle or bull, with its tip cut off, used for making what the French call *buglement*, a bellowing sound. As in Anglo-Saxon times hunters made their signals by means of a horn of this kind, the term bugle-horn, or bugle, came naturally to denote an instrument of metal producing a sound of similar character. Horns of oxen are still used by boys for frightening birds from cornfields in the South of England. Shakespeare ('As You Like It,' iii. 5) mentions '*bugle* eye-balls,' and in 'Winter's Tale,' iv. 3, '*Bugle* bracelet.'

Buhl-work is furniture made of wood, tortoiseshell, or other costly materials pierced and inlaid with metal, pearl, or other contrasting substances. The art took its name from that of the inventor, André Charles Buhl, who was extensively employed by Louis XIV. in the embellishment of the Palace of Versailles.

Bull—a blunder. So called from Obadiah Bull, a lawyer of the time of Henry VII., noted for his repeated blunders.

Bull and Bear. These Stock-Exchange terms have been explained by saying that a *bull* is one who does what he can to *toss up* the prices of Stocks, and a *bear* is one who wishes to *bear them down*. See BEAR.

Bull-baiting. Although bull-baiting was a cruel pastime, it was also a fulfilling of the law; for, formerly, no butcher was allowed to offer for sale the flesh of any bull that had not been baited. The goading of the animal into fury was supposed to have some influence upon the flesh. In a similar belief, the flesh of a hunted hare was thought superior in flavour to that of one which had been shot; and a present of 'a hunted hare' was considered to be a special compliment. In the Records of the Corporation of Leicester, the following 'order' appears as having been made:—'At a Common Hall, held on Thursday before St. Simon and St. Jude, 1467,' 'No butcher to kill a bull till baited.' At Winchester, it was ordered (30th Henry VIII.): 'That from hensforth ther shal be no bulstake set before any mayor's dore to bayte any bull, but onlie at the bull-ringe within the saide cytie.'

Bullfinch. The training of bullfinches to whistle particular airs is carried on principally in Germany. Not less than nine months of careful training are requisite. It begins when the bird is a mere nestling, and is continued until after the first moulting; for all that has been previously acquired is apt to be lost at that period, or is very imperfectly remembered. They are seldom taught more than a single air.

Bully-boy. This curious phrase often appears in American newspapers, and is thought to be indigenous to that country. It is, however, an old English saying, as the following quotation from 'Deuteromelia,' &c., published in London, 1609, will show :—

> We be three poore mariners,
> Newly come from the seas,
> We spend oure liues in ieapordy
> Whiles others liue at ease ;
> Shall we goe daunce the round, the round,
> And shall we goe daunce the round,
> And he that is a *bully-boy*,
> Come pledge me on the ground.

Bumpers. In America the buffers of a railway carriage are called *bumpers*.

Bumper, a full wine-glass. In Catholic times, the first toast at a dinner was the health of the Pope, which was given in French, *au bon Père,* 'to the good Father,' and always in a full glass. The French pronunciation of the *n* in *bon* partakes somewhat of the sound of *m*, so that the transition to 'bumper' was easy and natural.

Bumbailiff is a corruption of 'bound bailiff,' a sheriff's officer who is bound under heavy penalties to perform his duties with regularity, good conduct, and integrity.

Bun. The original signification of bun is anything round, thick, lumpy. The French *bondon,* a bung, is the same word slightly altered. The Italians have *bugno,* meaning any round knob, a boil, &c. In English we have bun, a round cake; bunion, a round swelling on the foot; bung, bunch and bundle. The first known mention of buns is in a comedy by Knaresby, called 'Cupid's Mask,' which was first acted in 1676. The cross upon what are called hot-cross buns is a symbol of Christ, and the practice of so marking the buns is probably derived from the bread of the Eucharist used in the Greek Church, which is impressed with the Greek cross. It is worthy of note that it is the form of the Greek cross which is impressed on the English buns; the Latin cross is never used.

Bungalow is the name given in India to the houses of Europeans. They are generally entirely on the ground floor, have a verandah completely surrounding them, and the roofs are heavily thatched to keep out the heat arising from the sun's rays.

Bunker's Hill, in America, where the celebrated battle was fought, was, in the seventeenth century, the property of George Bunker, who gave it his own name. He was a Charlestown man, and died in 1664. There is a Bunker's Hill in the parish of Laughton, near Gainsboro', Lincolnshire; another near Newtownbury, in the county of Wexford; and another on Lord John Scott's estate, in Warwickshire. There are also several places so marked on the Ordnance Maps of Norfolk and Suffolk.

Bunny, or Bun, applied to rabbits. Bun is a Scotch word signifying 'tail.' Scotch people say of a hare that she 'cocks her bun.' The word bunnie or bunny is a diminutive, meaning *little or short tail*, and in this sense it is particularly applicable to the rabbit.

Bunkum. A tedious speaker in Congress being interrupted and told it was no use to go on, for all the members were leaving the House, replied, 'Never mind, I'm talking to Buncombe.' Buncombe county, in North Carolina, was the district he represented.—*Bartlett's Dictionary of Americanisms.*

Bunting, the cloth used for flags. In Somersetshire, to 'bunt' meal is to sift it. The material formerly used for making the sieves for the various degrees of fineness was woven of finely-twisted woollen yarn, and was called 'bunting.' From its toughness, and capacity for hard wear, it was seen to be a suitable material for making flags. It is now made for no other purpose, wire netting having superseded it for making sieves.

Burden of a song. 'Bourdon' is the drone of a bagpipe, hence a running accompaniment or repetition of musical sounds or words is called the 'burden.'

Burglar is from the Gaelic *buar glacair*, a cattle-lifter.

Burrow—of a rabbit or other animal. This is the same word as burgh, burg, and borough. Its primary sense is a 'place of shelter,' a 'fortress.' It comes from the Anglo-Saxon *beorgan*, to protect or fortify. A castle or fortress in Wales is called *caer*, and a rabbit-burrow is *cwning-gaer*—the fortress of the coney or rabbit.

Burton Ale. Burton has been celebrated for the excellence of its ale for 270 years at the least. In 1610 one Benjamin Wilson commenced brewing in Burton with such success that he soon had several competitors. In Shaw's 'Staffordshire' the name is spelt Pailson, but an inspection of the parish books shows this to be a misprint. In 1712 its reputation had extended to London. In the 'Spectator' (No. 383), published in that year, we are told that Sir Roger de Coverley went to Vauxhall Gardens and there regaled himself on 'a glass of Burton ale and a slice of hung beef.'

Bury. The Anglo-Saxon word *birige* meant to bury or inter, and also to hide. *Birgen* meant a grave, and it also meant hidden. Many English words are derived from this root; for instance, potatoes are stored for winter in a deep trench called a 'potato *bury*.' Rabbits *burrow* for themselves holes in banks. One who retires into solitary life is said to be '*buried* in seclusion,' and the *barrows*, or artificial mounds erected over the dead, were anciently called berghs or burrows. From these berghs the Germans applied the name berg to hills generally, and metaphorically to high places, as notable cities. From this again we got *bury* for places noted for *high* sanctity, as Canterbury, Salisbury, St. Edmondsbury, &c. &c.—*Verstegan*, pp. 164–65.

Burying without coffins. The custom of burying without coffins was formerly very prevalent. In a table of fees payable to the Vicar of St. John's, Isle of Thanet, A.D. 1577, are these items:—

	s.	d.
For marriage and banns	3	6
For *burial in a sheet only*	0	6
For churchyng a woman	1	0
Poorer sort to pay only	0	9

In the year 1638 the table of fees for Birchington in the same island contains the items:—

	d.
A coffined grave	8
Noe-coffined grave	6

Soon after this it was made compulsory to bury all corpses wrapped in woollen cerements. The following is a copy of an original affidavit in the possession of R. Rising, Esq., of Horsey, in the county of Norfolk:—

Borough of Harwich, in the County of Essex, to Wit.

Sarah, the wife of Robert Lyon, of the parish of Dovercourt, in the Borough aforesaid, husbandman, and Deborah, the wife of Stephen Driver, of the same parish, husbandman (being two credible persons), do make oath that Deborah, the daughter of the said Stephen and Deborah, aged 18 weeks, who was on the 7th day of April instant interred in the parish churchyard of Dovercourt in the borough aforesaid, was not put in, wrapped, or wound up, or buried in any shirt, shift, sheet, or shroud, made or mingled with Flax, Hemp, Silk, Hair, Gold, or Silver, or other than what is made of sheep's wool only, or in any coffin lined or faced with any cloth stuff or any other thing whatsoever, made or mingled with Flax, Hemp, Silk, Hair, Gold, or Silver, or any other material but sheep's wool only.

{ The mark × of Sarah Lyon.
 The mark D of Deborah Driver.
   Witness, B. Didier.

Taken and sworn the fifteenth day of April, 1769, one of His Majesty's Justices of the Peace.   G. DAVIES.

Burying on the south side of churches. The feeling in favour of burying on the south side of churches is probably a traditionary one, dating back to the time of sun-worship. Early burial-places in Switzerland and other continental countries are always found on the southern slopes of hills.

Burying suicides at cross-roads. 'It was usual to erect crosses at the junction of four cross-roads, on a place *self-consecrated*, according to the piety of the age; and it was not with a notion of indignity, but in a spirit of charity, that those excluded from holy rites were buried at the crossing roads, as places next in sanctity to consecrated ground.'—*British Magazine*.

Bustle. This word seems to be derived in some way from the bubbling of a boiling liquid, an action which makes a great stir. In Iceland at the present day *bustla* means to bustle, and also to make a splash in the water. The word in English was originally spelt *buskle*. Halliwell quotes from a writer, A.D. 1555, 'It is like the smouldering fire of Mount Chimæra, which boiling long time with great *buskling* in the bowels of the earth, doth at length burst forth with violent rage.'

Butcher, from the French *boucher*; Provençal, *bochier*, from *boc*, a goat. Literally, 'a slaughterer of goats.' So also, in Italian, from *becco*, a goat, comes *beccajo*, a butcher.

Butcher's meat in olden time. In Stow's 'Chronicles,' under the year 1592, he tells us that 'It was this year enacted that butchers should sell their beef and mutton by weight, beef for a halfpenny the pound, and mutton for three-farthings; which being devised for the great commodity of the Realm (as it was thought) hath proved far otherwise, for at that time oxen were sold at six and twenty shillings and eight pence the piece, fat wethers for three shillings and four pence the piece, fat calves of the like price, a fat lamb for twelve pence. The butchers of London sold penny pieces of beef for the relief of the poor, every piece two pounds and a half, sometimes three pounds for a penny; and thirteene, sometimes fourteen, of these pieces for twelve pence. Mutton eight pence the quarter, and an hundredweight of beef for four shillings and eight pence. What price it hath grown to since needeth not to be set down. At this time also, and not before, there were foreign butchers permitted to sell their flesh in Leadenhall Market, at London.'

Butler. Two origins of this word seem equally probable. The one is from *butt.* The person who has charge of the butts, or barrels containing drinkables. The other is from the French *bouteillier,* from *bouteille,* a bottle, in the same connection.

Butter. This name seems to signify shaking. 'In Bavaria *buttern* or *butteln* is to shake backwards and forwards; a *butter-glass* is a ribbed bottle for shaking up salad dressing. *Buttel-trüb* means thick from shaking. *Butter-schmalz* means grease produced by shaking, that is, *butter,* as distinguished from *gelassene-smalz*— dripping, that is, grease that sets by merely standing.'—*Schmeller,* quoted by *Wedgwood.*

Butterfly. In Germany there is a large moth which infests dairies, and lives upon butter and milk. In Low German and Holland it is called the butterfliege (*fliege,* fly). Other names for the dairy moth are *buttervogel,* butter bird; *molkendieb,* whey thief; and *milchdieb,* milk thief. This, there is little doubt, has become the general name for the whole race; though some think the name is a corruption of the English phrase 'flutter fly.'

Buttons. Tailors generally put two buttons on the back of a coat, although there are no button-holes and the buttons serve no purpose. The origin of the custom is that a hundred years ago, when every gentleman carried a sword, the sword-belt was suspended by two buttons in this position. The buttons have been retained, although the sword has been discarded.

Butty. This is a slang word, much in use in the Midlands as a name for a companion, or partner in a piece of contract work. A '*butty* collier' is one who contracts with the mine owner to raise the coal at so much per ton, employing other men to do the actual work. The word is from the Gipsy dialect. A *booty pal* is a fellow-workman—literally, a *work brother.* In the mouths of navvies, or rough workmen, *pal* would soon be dropped, and *butty* would represent the original phrase.

Buxom. From the Anglo-Saxon *boga*, a bough, and *sum*, some. In the Old English it was *boughsome*, i.e., easily bent to one's will. The original meaning of the word buxom is 'obedient' or 'pliant.' It was not uncommon for letter-writers to use the phrase 'Your buxom servant' before the signature. Verstegan says it is 'Pliableness or *bow*someness, to wit, humbly stooping or bowing down in sign of obedience.' Chaucer writes it 'buxsomness.'

The following are good examples of the original meaning of the word:—

Great Neptune stonde amazëd at their sight,
Whiles on his broad rownd backe they softly slid,
And eke himselfe mourn'd at their mournful plight,
Yet wist not what their wailing meant; yet did
For great compassion of their sorrow, bid
His mighty waters to them *buxome* bee.—*Faerie Queene*, iii. 4, 32.

For holy church hoteth all manere puple
Under obedience to be, and *buxum* to the lawe.—*Piers Plowman*.

Dean Trench quotes the following from an ancient form of submission:—'I submit myself unto this holy Church of Christ, to be ever *buxom* and obedient to the ordinances of it.'

Buying a pig in a poke. This saying is said to have originated in a trick of a countryman who put a cat into a poke, or sack, and sold it in a market as a sucking-pig, the buyer not having taken the precaution to inspect it before paying his money. The discovery of the trick is said to have originated another saying:— 'Letting the cat out of the bag.'

Buzz the bottle. This is a common expression at wine parties, when the bottle does not contain sufficient to fill all the glasses. It means, 'equally divide what is left.' The word *buzz* meant anciently *to empty*. Perhaps the word *booze* comes from the same root.

Bye-law. *By* is an old Danish word signifying town, burg, or borough. It is still retained in many names of places, as Grimsby, Derby, Whitby, all of which towns were re-named by the Danes. The term *bye-law* is therefore 'the law of the *by* or town.'

By Jingo. *Jenco*, in the Basque language, is the name of the devil.

By'r Lakin. *Lakin* is a contraction of *Ladykin*, which is a diminutive of endearment for lady. Thus, *our Lakin* meant 'our dear lady,' and was usually applied to the Virgin Mary. The contracted form *By'r Lakin* was frequently used by the old dramatists as a kind of oath, as in the 'Tempest,' iii. 3, '*By'r Lakin!* I can go no further, sir'; and in the 'Midsummer Night's Dream,' iii. 1, '*By'r Lakin!* a parlous fear!'

Byron or Birron. Sir William Knighton ('Memoir,' vol. i. p. 423; Bentley, 1838) says that Lord Byron was asked by Sir R. Milbanke how he pronounced his name, Byron or Birron, to which he replied, ' B-y, sir, spells *by*, all the world over.'

Byron and Shelley. 'It is a singular fact that both Byron and Shelley were lineally descended from William Sidney, the great-great-grandfather of Sir Philip Sidney.'—*Notes and Queries*, December 1870.

Byron and Waller. Byron ('English Bards') says:—

> So the stretched *eagle* quivering on the plain,
> No more through rolling clouds to *soar* again,
> Viewed his own *feather* on the fatal dart
> And winged the *shaft* that quivered in his heart.

Waller has :—

> The *eagle's* fate and mine are one,
> Which on the *shaft* that made him die,
> Espied a *feather* of his own,
> Wherewith he wont to *soar* on high.

C

C or K. The Keltic alphabets had no *k*, but the letter *c*, at the commencement of their words, was almost invariably hard. Many attempts have been made to restore the hard sound of *c*, in words of Keltic origin, where it is followed by the letter *e*, but as they have been for the most part unsuccessful, it is now becoming usual to use the letter *k*, as in the word Keltic. The letter *k* is also now used in similar words derived from the Greek, as Keramic, instead of Ceramic.

Cab. Up to the year 1823 the word cab was slang for a house of bad repute. In that year, we are told ('Gentleman's Magazine,' part i. p. 463), under the date April 23, that '*Cabriolets* were, in honour of his Majesty's birthday, introduced to the public this morning. They are built to hold two persons besides the driver (who is partitioned off from his company), and are furnished with a book of fares for the use of the public, to prevent the possibility of imposition. These books will be found in a pocket hung inside of the head of the cabriolet. The fares are one-third less than hackney coaches.' These cabriolets had covers or hoods something like the present 'hansoms,' but the driver sat on a perch, over the right wheel. A comic song of the period has :—

> In days of yore when folks got tired,
> A hackney coach or a chariot was hired;
> But now along the streets they roll ye,
> In a shay, with a kiver, called *cabriólay*.

'Cabriolet' soon became shortened to *cab*. In Macaulay's 'Life and Letters,' he tells his sister that after the division in the House on the first Reform Bill he 'called a *cabriolet*.' Two months afterwards, he tells her that he 'called a *cab*.' Cabs are often spoken of as the 'Gondolas of London.' The allusion first occurred in 'Mayfair,' a satire, published anonymously by Harrison, of Old Bond Street, in 1827. The couplet in which the words were used is :—

> There beauty half her glory veils
> In cabs, those *gondolas on wheels*.

Cabbages. Cabbages were introduced into England in the sixteenth century. Evelyn, writing about 1680, says, ''Tis scarce a hundred years since we first had cabbages out of Holland. Sir Anthony Ashley of Wiburg St. Giles, in Dorsetshire, being, as I am told, the first who planted them in England.'—*Acetaria*, sec. ii.

Cabinet Councils. This phrase seems to have been originated by Lord Bacon, who, in his 'Essays,' says : 'The practice of France, in some kings' times, hath introduced Cabinet Councils.' At a 'Privy' Council the Sovereign presides, but at Cabinet Councils the Royal presence is unnecessary. Cabinet Councils had their origin in the time of George I., who, being ignorant of the English language, could take no part in the deliberations of his Council. The ministers, therefore, consulted in his absence, and informed him of the result. The custom thus established by accident, brought about a complete change in the machinery of government.

Cad. Probably derived from *cadet*, a younger son. The younger sons of the nobility were no doubt looked upon with something like scorn by their elder and richer brothers. Hence the depreciatory remark, 'Oh, he's only a *cad*,' i.e. he's only a *cadet*, having no property, and therefore not worth notice. When omnibuses were first introduced, the conductor was always known as the 'cad.' In Dickens's earlier works, the word frequently appears in this sense.

Cadger. In falconry, the hawks were taken to the field on a wooden frame, carried on a man's shoulders. This was called a *cadge*, and the man who carried it was the *cadger*.

Caer, in the names of Welsh localities, means a fortified wall or castle. Thus, 'Caermarthen' is the castle of Merlin or Merdkin; the latter portion of the name being modernised to its present form.

Cake comes from the verb 'to cook.' The German name for a cake is *kuchen*, and pancakes are called *pfann kuchen*.

Calamity. 'Another ill accident is drought, and the spindling of the corn; insomuch as the word *calamity* was first derived from *calamus* (stalk), when the corn could not get out of the stalk.'—*Lord Bacon*.

Calcutta. The name of this city is derived from a *cutta*, or temple, dedicated to the Hindû goddess, *Caly*.

Calendar. From the Latin *Calendæ*, the first day of each month.

Calf's-head. The practice is almost universal amongst inn-keepers and *restaurateurs* of writing upon bills of fare the name of this dish in the plural possessive case, thus: 'Calves' Head.' Sometimes the announcement is even more absurd, being 'Half a Calves' Head.'

Calico. The name of this fabric is derived from the town of Calicut, in the East Indies, where a similar cloth was manufactured. It was first brought to England by the East India Company in 1631. In America, the word 'calico' is exclusively used for printed cotton goods. The white cloths which we call 'calicoes' are 'shirtings' in the States.

Căller. This old English word meant fresh and cool; as, 'the caller air,' 'caller gooseberries,' &c. The only relic of the word now seems to be the cry of the Scottish fishwives—'Caller herrins!' The word is in none of the modern dictionaries, but Grose has it in his Glossary.

Calomel. This name, which means 'beautiful black,' was originally given to the Æthiop's mineral, or black sulphuret of mercury. It was afterwards applied in joke by Sir Theodore Mayerne to the chloride of mercury, in honour of a favourite negro servant whom he employed to prepare it. As calomel is a white powder, the name is merely a jocular misnomer.—*Hooper's Medical Dictionary*.

Callous, from the Latin *callus*, skin hardened by labour.

Caltrops, abbreviated from *cheval-traps*, are instruments consisting of four spikes of iron radiating from a common centre in such a manner that, however thrown, one spike will stand upright.

They were formerly in use to prevent the passage of cavalry. At the time of the Chartists' agitation, in 1839, thousands of these deadly weapons were said to have been made in the neighbourhood of Birmingham, in readiness to be used against the troops.

Calvary. The phrase '*Mount* Calvary' is not warranted by any expression in Scripture. It is true that the old masters usually depicted the Crucifixion as having taken place on the summit of a hill; but, as we are told that the locality was 'the place of a skull,' or cemetery, there are reasons for believing that the solemn event occurred in one of the *valleys* 'round about Jerusalem.'

Cambric. So named from being first manufactured at Cambray, in France. It was first worn in England in 1580, at which time, according to Stow, it was accounted a great luxury.

Camel. The ordinary load of a camel is from nine to ten hundredweight. The speed of the animal carrying this burden is about two and a half miles an hour. The average day's journey is from thirty to thirty-five miles.

Camel, the Ship of the Desert. The origin of this saying is in George Sandys's 'Paraphrase of the Book of Job,' 1610. It occurs in the couplet:—

Three thousand camels his rank pastures fed,
Arabia's wandering ships, for traffic bred.

Camellia. This beautiful flowering evergreen was brought originally from Japan by a Spanish Jesuit named *Kamel*; hence the name.

Cameos are gems formed from precious stones, having two distinct layers or strata of different colours. The darker stratum is left to form a background, the object to be represented being left in relief by cutting away the surrounding parts. The onyx is generally used for this purpose. Cameo-cutting was known to the Babylonians, the Egyptians, and the Greeks, the latter of whom brought the art to great perfection. It was also practised very extensively in ancient Rome. Shell cameos are of Sicilian origin. The art was carried to Rome about 1805. It is still carried on there and in Paris.

Camomile. From a Greek word signifying *earth apple*, so called because the flowers of the camomile smell like apples.

Camp-followers are non-combatants who follow an army in the capacity of servants, water-carriers, hostlers, *cantiniers*, laundresses, &c. In Indian warfare the number of such persons is enormous. In 1839, when a Bengal army of 15,000 men left

Shikarpoor for Afghanistan, 85,000 camp-followers were in attendance, and the commander took six weeks' provisions for the entire 100,000 people.

Canada. Charleroix says that this name is from an Iroquois word *Kannata*, a collection of huts. There is, however, a Spanish tradition that some Spanish explorers visiting the country and finding no mines, or other appearance of riches, said, *Aca Nada*, 'here is nothing,' which being repeated by the natives to subsequent visitors from Europe, was supposed to be the name of the country.

Canadian Lakes. The Canadian Lakes have been computed to contain 1,700 cubic miles of water, or half the fresh water in the world. They extend from east to west, over $15\frac{1}{2}$ degrees of longitude, with a difference of latitude of $8\frac{1}{2}$ degrees. They receive the drainage of nearly half a million of square miles of country.

Canal. This is derived from the Anglo Saxon word *canel*, a channel.

Canary. These favourite song-birds are natives of Madeira, the Canary Isles, and the Cape Verde Islands. In its wild state the canary is green, or greenish-yellow tinged with brown, and is not unlike the English bird called the greenfinch. Canaries were first brought to Europe in the early part of the sixteenth century. Most of the domesticated birds are now bred in confinement, and many distinct varieties are known to bird-fanciers. The wild birds have louder and clearer notes than the tame varieties, and when caught and brought to England fetch extraordinary prices.

Cancel. This word comes from the Latin *cancellus*, lattice-work. Deeds and other writings were formerly cancelled by being marked with lines which crossed the writing in both directions like lattice-work. Among the smaller class of tradesmen, to this day, an entry in an account book is cancelled by being 'crossed out,' and the saying, 'cross it out of your books' is very common. The designation 'chancellor,' or cancellor, is from the same root. 'A chancellor is he whose office it is to look into the writings of the Emperor, to cancel what is written amiss, and to sign that which is well.'—*Jus Sigilli*, 1678. The chancel of a church was so called, because anciently it was divided by *lattice-work* from the body of the church.

Candidate, from the Latin *candidus*, white, so called from the custom among the Romans for persons seeking to be elected to offices of state, arraying themselves in white togas; they were thence named *candidati*—i.e. candidates.

Cannel Coal. Various suggestions have been made as to the derivation of cannel. Some think it is 'candle' coal, others canal (pronounced cannel) coal, from its having been first brought to Liverpool by the Duke of Bridgwater's canal. ' Blome's Britannia,' published 1673, has, ' Wigan is famous for fuel . . . . especially for the coal called *cannel.*' Woodward ('Fossils of England,' 1729) speaks of *canal coal.* The word seem to be of Celtic origin, and comes from the same root as the word kindle. In Welsh, *cynnew* is kindle, *cynnud* is fuel, and *cynnenawl,* the pronunciation of which is something like *kenyol,* is ignitible. Cannel is evidently a modern form of this latter word.

Cannibal. This word is probably a corruption of the term 'caribales,' a form under which Columbus designates the Caribs ('*propter rabiem caninam anthropophagorum gentis*'), as in French *appétit de chien.—Trench.*

Cannon. Shakespeare, in 'King John,' act ii. sc. 1, mentions cannons, that ' have their bowels full of wrath, to spit forth indignation,' &c., and a few lines further on he speaks of ' bullets wrapped in fire.' Shakespeare here was at fault in his chronology. John died in 1216, but cannon were not then invented. Haydn says, ' the first piece was a small one contrived by Swartz, a German cordelier, soon after the invention of gunpowder in 1330.' They were first used at the battle of Cressy, 26th August, 1346. Edward III. had four pieces there, which gained him the battle. They were then called bombards.

Cannon Street, London. This should properly be ' Canon' Street. It was named after the canons of St. Paul's. The implements of war, so called, were not in use when the street was named.

Canny. There is no error more frequent than the application of this term to Scotchmen in the sense of low cunning, excessive prudence, or roguish sagacity. This word canny has no connection with these qualities, and its meaning is exactly opposite, being equivalent to gentle, innocent, propitious, pretty. Jamieson says, ' It is applied to persons or things having pleasing or useful qualities.' ' Canny man,' in addressing a stranger, means ' worthy man,' and the term is used exactly as in England we say ' My good man.'

Canopy. The usual derivation from the Greek word for gnat or mosquito, with the ingenious guess that canopy originally meant a couch, with curtains to keep out these insects, is unsatisfactory. The more probable theory is that a canopy was originally a tent. The Italian name for the material of which tents are made is *canapa*, in Latin it is *cannabis*, in French *canevas*, and in English *canvas*. Our word canopy and the French *canapé* are evidently derived from the Italian *canapa*. It will be observed that in each language quoted the syllable *can* is retained.

Cant. In 'English Villanies,' 1683, the writer says:—'This word, "canting," seems to be derived from the Latine verbe *canto*, which signifies in English to sing, or to make a sound with wordes, that is to say, to speake. And very aptly may canting take his derivation from singing, because canting is a kind of musicke, and he that can cant best is the best musician.' This is in allusion to what are now called Chanters, *i.e.*, men who go about and in whining tones solicit alms. In a 'Dictionary of the Terms of the Canting Crew,' &c., published early in the last century 'Canting Crew' is thus defined:—'Beggars, gypsies; also Dissenters in Conventicles, who affect a disguised speech, and distinguish themselves by a peculiar snuffle and tone as the shibboleth of their party.' Mr. Wedgwood ('English Etymology') thinks that 'the real origin is the Gaelic *cainnt*, speech, language, applied in the first instance to the special language of rogues and beggars, and subsequently to the peculiar terms used by any other profession or community.'

> The Doctor here,
> When he discourseth of dissection,
> Of *vena cava*, and of *vena porta*,
> The *meseræum* and the *mesentericum*,
> What does he else but *cant?* or if he run
> To his judicial astrology
> And trowl the trine, the quartile and the sextile,
> Does he not *cant?* Who here can understand him?—*B. Jonson.*

Cant and Slang. These words are frequently used as if they were identical in meaning, which is not the case. 'Cant' is a sort of secret dialect by which thieves, gipsies, and other low persons make themselves mutually understood. Slang is composed of transient forms of expression much affected by swells and others who desire to appear familiar with the ways of the town. Thus a thief, using cant expressions, may say that he has 'prigged a wipe,' or 'cracked a crib,' meaning that he has stolen a handkerchief, or broken into a house. When, however, a languid swell tells you that he 'was at a *tea-fight* last night, and met *any quantity* of *awfully jolly* girls,' he indulges in slang of the worst kind. It is but fair to say that many words which were pure slang at first have become incorporated with the language, taking their places among words of far more reputable origin.

Canteen is from the Italian *cantina*, a wine vault.

Canter is an abbreviation of 'Canterbury gallop,' and is an allusion to the easy ambling pace adopted by pilgrims to à-Beckett's shrine.

Canterbury is a corruption of the Anglo-Saxon *Cantwara-byrig*—the forts or strongholds of the Cantwere, or men of Cant [Kent]. *Cantwara* was the ancient genitive plural.

Canvas for artists is kept by the artists' colourmen ready for use. The sizes used for portraits are known as 'kit-cat,' which is 36 × 29 inches; 'three-quarters,' 30 × 25 inches; 'half-length,' 50 × 40; 'Bishop's half-length,' 56 × 45; 'Bishop's whole-length,' 94 × 58.

Caoutchouc, from the Indian word *cuckucu*, India-rubber, is pronounced *caoo-chook*.

Cap-à-pié. A military term, applied in the middle ages to a knight fully armed with weapons for defence and attack. The words are French, meaning 'head to foot.'

Cape Horn was so named by Shonten, a Dutch sailor, who first 'doubled' it, from the name of his birth-place, Hoorne, a village on the Zuyder Zee.

Capel, in Welsh local names, signifies 'chapel.'

Caper, to skip about in a frolicsome manner, is derived from the Latin *caper*, a goat, in allusion to the habit of that animal of suddenly jumping about without any apparent reason or object.

Capers. The capers used in cookery are not berries, as is commonly thought. They are the unopened flower-buds of the caper-bush (*Capparis spinosa*). They are principally imported from Sicily, Italy, and the South of France. Capers seem to have been used as a sauce for boiled mutton in Shakespeare's time. In 'Twelfth Night,' i. 2, Sir Andrew Aguecheek says, 'Faith! I can cut a *caper!*' to which Sir Toby Belch replies, 'and I can cut the mutton to 't.'

Caprice, from the Latin *caper*, a goat. The allusion is to the sudden and apparently whimsical antics of the goat, which leaps and skips about in a freakish, fantastical manner, with no apparent motive, but merely from *caprice*.

Capuchin, from Latin *caput*, the head. A Capuchin monk or nun is one who wears a hood or cowl as part of the monastic habit.

Carat. The weight used by jewellers and goldsmiths. The word is derived from the name of the seed of the Abyssinian coral tree (*Erythrina Abyssinica*), which, being very small, and very equal in size, were originally used in weighing gold and precious stones. When artificial weights were made, the name was retained.

Cards. Playing-cards are known to be of Eastern origin, but when, or by whom, first introduced cannot now be ascertained. It is, however, tolerably certain that they originated in Arabia, and were brought into Europe during the Crusades. In an ancient 'History of the Garter' there is an extract from a wardrobe account of Edward I., dated 1377, in which a game called the 'Four Kings' is mentioned. As Edward, before his accession to the throne, resided for some years in Syria, he may have learned to play cards while in that country. They were certainly introduced into Europe in the fourteenth century, and they are said to have been brought to Viterbo by the Saracens in 1379. From the fact that an entry occurs in the Treasury books of France of 'fifty sols of France paid to Jacquemin Gringonneur for three packs of cards for the amusement of the King'. (Charles VI.) in the year 1393—one year after that king lost his reason—it has been erroneously stated that they were invented for his amusement; but they were certainly known in France before Charles ascended the throne, for in the romance 'Renard le Contrefait' it is mentioned that they were in use in 1340.

From a passage in Ascham's 'Toxophilus,' 1545, quoted by Singer, the price of cards at that time appears to have been about twopence a pack. 'He sayd a payre of cards cost not past ii.*d*.' The word 'payre' at that time meant a set or pack. Lord Bacon speaks of 'a pair of cards' in this sense. The term 'deck,' which is in common use in America, is a survival of another old English form. Thus in '3 Henry VI.' act v. sc. 1:

> But whiles he thought to steal the single *ten*,
> The king was slily fingered from the *deck*.

And in the 'Two Maids of Moreclacke,' temp. 1609:

> I'll deal the cards, and cut you from the *deck*.

And also in 'Solimus, Emperor of the Turks,' 1638:

> Well, if I chance but once to get the *deck*
> To deal about and shuffle as I would.

In an Act of Parliament of 1463 the importation of playing cards, amongst other things, was forbidden, as being injurious to native manufacturers and tradesmen. This seems to show that cards were commonly made in England at, or even earlier than, that date. In Elizabeth's reign Edward Darcy obtained a patent for making cards. The Card-makers' Company was incorporated by Charles I. in 1629. Up to 1767 all playing-cards were white at the back. In that year John Berkenhout took out a patent for 'marking them on the back by dicing, colouring, flowering, so as to render them different in appearance from the cards now in use, and thereby prevent the inconvenience arising from mixing two packs, which are not thus distinguished from each other.' In Queen Anne's time, 1711, an Act of Parliament was passed imposing a tax upon cards. In a 'Book of Presidents' [precedents], compiled by Thomas Phaer, the translator of the first seven books of the 'Æneid,' and printed in 1565, there is a form of indenture of apprenticeship, in which the prohibition to play at cards or dice appears.

Carding Wool is to comb it with a *carduus*, or thistle. The *teasel*, a plant grown expressly for this purpose, is a *thistle*, the name being slightly altered.

Career is the French *carrière*, a road, a highway.

Caret, Latin *caret*, from *careo*, to want, is the mark ($\wedge$) in writing to signify that something has been omitted or is wanting.

Caricatures. Caricatures, which are now almost confined to the comic periodicals, were formerly issued singly on stout paper for framing. The most celebrated caricaturist of modern times was John Doyle, better perhaps known as H.B. from the monogram ID which his publications bore. It is formed by doubling his initials, and placing one set over the other; thus: $\frac{ID}{ID}$. One authority says Doyle adopted the monogram because all his drawings were executed with H.B. pencils, H.B. in this case meaning 'hard black.'

Carmine, from *kermes*, the dried bodies of European insects, somewhat similar to the Mexican cochineal insect. They produce a scarlet dye almost equal to true cochineal.

Carnival. This is derived from the Italian words *carne*, flesh, and *vale*, farewell. It was originally applied to a festival or feasting-time just before the commencement of Lent. During this festival people ate to their full of flesh meat, which was forbidden during the time of Lent.

Carol means 'a dance.' The French have *carole* and *querole*, the Bretons *korole*, and the Welsh *koroli*, all of which signify dancing. A *chanson de carole* was originally a song to accompany a dance. Afterwards the word *carol* was applied to the song itself.

Carotid Artery. The word 'carotid' is derived from a Greek word signifying to produce sleep. The carotid arteries convey blood to the head, and are so named from the opinion of the ancients that an increased flow through them produced sleep or stupefaction.—*Brand.*

Carouse. Johnson derives this from the German *Garausz*, which is most improbable. Worcester and Armstrong both give the Gaelic *craos*, a large mouth, which is equally unlikely. Gifford, from Rich's 'English Hue and Cry,' explains *rouse* to be 'a bumper,' and a *carouse* to be a pledging of each other in bumpers.' The word *rouse* was certainly in use by Shakespeare and his contemporaries in the sense of drinking heavily: 'The king doth wake to-night and takes his *rouse.*'—*Hamlet*, act i. sc. 4. Beaumont and Fletcher, in 'The Loyal Subject,' act iv. sc. 5, having just mentioned a full glass, say:

> Take the *rouse* freely, sir;
> 'Twill warm your blood and make you fit for jollity

And in the 'Knight of Malta,' iii. 4 :

> I've took, since supper,
> A *rouse* or two, too much.

The word seems, from the following passage from Dekker's 'Gul's Hornbook,' to be of Danish origin : ' Tell me, thou soveraigne skinker, how to take the German's *upsy-freize*, the Danish *rowsa*, the Switzer's *Stoop of Rhenish.*'

Carp. This fish is a native of the south of Europe, and is mentioned by several of the classic authors of Rome under the name of *cyprinas*. The exact date of its introduction into England is unknown. Its name does not occur in the Anglo-Saxon Dictionary of Ælfric, who died in 1051. The earliest known reference to the carp in English occurs in Dame Juliana Berners' 'Boke of St. Albans,' published in 1486, where, speaking of the carp, she says that 'it is a deyntous fysshe, but there ben but few in Englonde, and therefore I write the less of hym. He is an euylle fysshe to take. For he is so stronge enarmed in the mouthe that there may be no weke harnays hold him.'

Carpenter. *Carpentum* is the Latin word for a car. *Carpentarius* signified a maker of cars or wagons, a wheelwright. This is the original signification of 'carpenter' in English. The Germans call a carpenter a *Zimmermann*, that is, a timber-man. An old English name for a carpenter, according to Verstegan, was 'woodsmith.'

Carpet Knights are 'such as have studied Law, Physic, or other arts or sciences, whereby they have become famous, and seeing that they are not knighted as Soldiers, they are not therefore to use the Horseman's Title or Spurs; they are only termed simply *miles*, and *milites*, Knight, or "Knights of the Carpetry," or "Knights of the Green Cloth," to distinguish them from those Knights that are dubbed as Soldiers in the Field.'—*Randle Holmes, Academy of Armour*, iii. 57.

Carriages. The verse Acts xxi. 15, in the Authorized Version, runs as follows: 'And after those days we took up our carriages and went up to Jerusalem.' Many people are surprised to be told that this means that the Apostles walked, and carried their luggage with them; but so it is. The word translated 'carriages' means *that which had to be carried*. In Cranmer's Bible, 1539, the passage is rendered: 'We toke vp oure burthens'; and in the Geneva version, 1557, 'We trussed vp our fardeles.' Dean Alford translates it, 'We made ready our baggage.'

Cars. Americans never 'travel by rail,' or 'go by train'; they always 'take the cars,' or 'go by the cars.'

Carte blanche is a French phrase which means, literally, a blank sheet of paper. Giving a man *carte blanche* means that he has no written directions, but is at liberty to act as he pleases in the matter entrusted to him.

Cartes de Visite. The photographic portraits so called were originated by the Duke of Parma, who, in 1857, had his portrait photographed by M. Ferrier, at Nice, and copies affixed to his visiting cards. The fashion thus initiated soon extended to Paris and London, and the name, although no longer applicable, is now used all over the world for portraits of the size of a lady's visiting card.

Carving at table. Anciently there were separate words for carving the different kinds of game and poultry, and persons using the wrong term were looked upon with some pity and contempt.

Dr. Salmon, in his 'Receipts,' published in 1696, enumerates the following: 'Leach that brawn. Lift that swan. Rear that goose. Spoil that hen. Fract that chicken. Sauce that capon. Unbrace that mallard. Unlace that coney. Dismember that heron. Disfigure that peacock. Display that crane. Untach that curlew. Unjoin that bittern. Allay that pheasant. Wing that quail. Mince that plover. Wing that partridge. Thigh that pigeon. Border that pasty. Thigh that woodcock. Break that hare.'

Caryatides, literally 'maidens of Caryæ,' are figures of women used instead of columns in architecture. So named from the handmaidens in the temple of Diana in Caryæ.

Cash. 'Originally, "cash" meant that which was *encaissé*, i.e. put into the chest or till. Strictly speaking, it should consist of actual specie, and the word is used in some English banks to include only coin of the realm. But I find that bank cashiers use it with every shade of meaning. Some take Bank of England notes to be *cash*. Others go so far as to include cheques upon other banks of the same town, and even country notes.'—*Professor Jevons, Money, &c.* p. 250.

Castanets. The word is derived from the Spanish *castana*, a chestnut; the allusion is to the cracking sound of a chestnut which bursts when roasting, which the instruments called castanets are supposed to imitate.

Caste, which is the Hindu word for 'rank,' was borrowed by the Indians from the Portuguese *casta*.

Casus belli, a Latin phrase often met with in the newspapers, means some act, or circumstance, which renders war inevitable or unavoidable.

Catch a Crab. This phrase originated with the Italians, who have several proverbial sayings of similar import. *Chiappar un granchio* is used exactly in the same sense as our 'catch a crab.' *Pigliare un granchio* means to commit a blunder; and *Pigliare un granchio a secco*, 'to catch a crab on dry land,' is used when a person pinches his finger.

Catching a Tartar. Arvine's 'Cyclopædia' states that in a battle between the Russians and the Tartars a Russian soldier called to his captain, saying, he had caught a Tartar. 'Bring him along, then,' was the captain's reply. 'Ay, but he won't let me,' replied the soldier. It then came out that the Tartar had caught him. 'So,' says Arvine, 'when a man thinks to take another in, and gets himself bit, they say, "he's caught a Tartar."'

Catch-penny. This well-known term for anything brought out for sale with a view to entrap unwary purchasers, originated in the year 1824, just after the execution of Thurtell for the murder of Weare. This murder had created a great sensation, and Catnach, the celebrated printer of Seven Dials, in London, made a very large sum by the sale of Thurtell's 'last dying speech.' When the sale of this speech began to fall off, Catnach brought out a second edition, with the heading ' WE ARE alive again!' the words ' we are' being printed with a very narrow space between them. These two words the people took for the name of the murdered man, reading it ' WEARE alive again'; and a large edition was rapidly cleared off. Some one called it a 'catchpenny,' and the word rapidly spread, until Catnach's productions were usually so styled, and the word became adopted into the language.

Catchup. This name, which is variously spelt catsup, catchup, ketchup, and kitchup, is a corruption of the Chinese word *kitjap*, the name given to an inferior kind of soy made in China, and often sold in England in substitution for real soy.

Catchword. A catchword is the first word of a page of printed matter, printed at the right-hand corner at the bottom of the page preceding, to assist the reader. The earliest book printed with catchwords was an edition of ' Tacitus,' printed at Venice, about 1469, by Johannes de Spira.

Catechism. The ' English Church Catechism ' is intended as an explanation of the vows of baptism. Up to the time of James I., the Catechism consisted only of the repetition of the baptismal vows, the Apostles' Creed, and the Lord's Prayer. The additional portions, relating to the Sacraments, were added after the Conference at Hampton Court, in 1604.

Caterpillar. The etymologists are all at variance as to the origin of this word. Can it be, as suggested, compounded of the English word *cater*, to provide provisions, and the French *piller*, to steal? This derivation, at any rate, has the merit of being descriptive; a caterpillar does *cater*, by *stealing* from our gardens.

Cat-gut. Corrupted from gut-cord. It is usually made from the intestines of the sheep. The fine gut used for fishing-tackle is made by taking silkworms by the head and tail, just as they are about to spin, and stretching them until they break. When treated in this way, the material of which the silk would have been spun forms transparent cords. These, when dry, are 'silkworm-gut. Silkworm-gut is generally in lengths of twelve to fifteen inches.

Cathedral. A *cathedra* was a chair in which the Greek and Roman philosophers sat to deliver their learned orations. The name was also given to the seats in which the early Christian bishops sat. Churches furnished with bishops' seats or thrones were thence called 'cathedrals'; and hence, a cathedral-city is called the 'seat' of a bishopric.

Cat-in-pan. In the old song, 'The Vicar of Bray,' the following verse occurs:—

> When George in pudding time came o'er,
> And moderate men looked big, sir,
> I turned a *cat-a-pan* once more,
> And so became a Whig, sir.

Dr. Pegge says: 'The word *cat* is no doubt *cate*, which is an old word for a cake, or other omelette, which being fried, and consequently having to be *turned in the pan*, does very aptly express the changing of sides in politics or religion.' 'To turn a "cat in the pan" is to turn head over heels. A common saying amongst children in Staffordshire.'—*Dr. Fraser.* Mr. Thrupp, in 'Notes and Queries,' suggests that this may be a mispronunciation of the old French phrase, *tourner côte en peine,* which certainly comes very near to the meaning in the song of 'The Vicar of Bray.'

Cats are believed to have been brought first into England from Cyprus by merchants who came to Cornwall for tin. It is generally supposed that the name is Teutonic. If so, it is a curious coincidence that the modern Persian name for cat is *catto.*

Cat's-paw. To make a *cat's-paw* of a person is to employ him to do something dangerous, shameful, or degrading, which you will not do yourself. The reference is to the fable of the monkey, who, having roasted some chestnuts, and finding them too hot to touch, caught a cat, and holding her fast, used one of her paws to rake the nuts out of the fire.

Caucus. Gordon ('Hist. of the American Revolution') speaks of this word as having been in use in 1724. Dr. Trumbull, of Hartford, Conn., says, 'its origin is the Indian *cau-cau-as'u,*' which he defines or translates as 'one who advises, urges, encourages, &c.' *Am. Philog. Assoc. Trans.* 1872. In 'Webster's Dictionary' is a quotation from 'The Political Passing-bell,' a Parody on 'Gray's Elegy,' Boston, 1789:—

> That mob of mobs, *a caucus,* to command,
> Hurl wild dissension round a maddening land.

Cauliflower. Most etymologists derive this name from the Latin *caulis,* a cabbage; but Gerard, in his 'Herbal,' makes it a purely English word. Cole, or colewort, was the generic name for all plants of the cabbage tribe, and Gerard writes, ' *Coleflore,* or after some *colie-flore.*' The modern word *kale* is allied to *cole.*

Caveat emptor. This is a Latin phrase signifying ' let the purchaser beware, or take care of himself.' It was formerly held that a buyer must be bound by a bargain under all circumstances. Chief Justice Tindal, in giving judgment in the case ' Brown v. Edgington' (2 Scott N.R. 504), modified this ancient rule. He said, ' If a man purchases goods of a tradesman without in any way relying upon the skill and judgment of the vendor, the latter is not responsible for their turning out contrary to his expectation; but if the tradesman be informed, at the time the order is given, of the purpose for which the article is wanted, the buyer relying upon the seller's judgment, the latter impliedly warrants that the things furnished shall be reasonably fit and proper for the purposes for which it is required.'

Cayenne Pepper is the powder of the dried pods and seeds of the Capsicum plant.

Ceiling. This word is not derived from *cœlum,* the canopy of heaven, as its orthography would intimate. It is from *seal,* to close up, and was formerly used to signify wainscoting generally. That which we now call the ceiling was formerly the *upper seeling,* to distinguish it from that which ' seeled' the sides of walls.

Celery. Celery is the cultivated variety of the English weed *smallage.* It was introduced into kitchen gardens in this country about the time of the Reformation, by some Italians, who gave it the Italian name *celleri.* Evelyn (1669) says, ' Smallage and sellery are to be sown in March.'

Celt. The proper pronunciation of this word is as though spelt with the initial K. Some of the best modern writers spell it ' Kelt.'

Cemetery. The earliest English cemetery, as distinct from churchyards and burial-grounds connected with places of worship, is that at Kensal Green, which was consecrated November 2nd, 1832. ' Great truths are sometimes embodied in single words, and this so with the word " cemetery." That word means *sleeping-place*; it is a truly Christian name to give to a burying-place; it implies that such as slumber there, sleep for a great awakening.' —*Boyd.*

Cenotaph. From the Greek *kenos,* empty, and *taphos,* a tomb. A cenotaph is a monument erected to the memory of a person whose body is buried elsewhere. Most of the monuments in St. Paul's Cathedral are cenotaphs.

Censer. Abbreviated from *incenser*.

Censure at one time meant giving an opinion which might be either good or bad. Its use is now confined to the latter sense.

Census, a Latin noun, now fully Anglicised. Its original meaning was the amount of property a Roman possessed, but in English it is confined to the decennial counting of the population. The first regular *census* was taken in 1801, from which time it has been taken at regular intervals of ten years. Since 1836, when the new system of registration came into use in England, the method of taking the census has been greatly improved, and its scope much widened, so as to include a larger number of subjects and details.

Cent. The American coin called a *cent* is the hundredth part of a dollar. Its value is about the same as that of an English half-penny. The French centime is the hundredth part of a franc, and is about the value of one-tenth part of an English penny.

Centurion. A centurion in the Roman army was an officer commanding a hundred men, or the sixteenth part of a legion. His position corresponded to that of a captain in the British service.

Ceramic. (Greek, *keramos*.) Contrary to the ordinary rule in English, under which *c* before the vowel *e* is soft, the *c* in this word is hard, and the word is pronounced *keramic*. It is becoming usual to spell the word with the inital K.

Cereals. Corn, such as wheat, barley, &c.; so called from *Ceres*, the Goddess of Agriculture.

Chacun à son goût. A French proverb, frequently used in England. It means, 'Every one to his own taste,' and is generally used satirically, as, 'Well! I didn't think he'd associate with people of that kind; but' (with a shrug), '*chacun à son goût.*'

Chaffing. In some counties, when a man has been guilty of inflicting personal chastisement upon his wife, it is customary for the neighbours to empty a sack or two of chaff in front of the offender's door, to signify that *thrashing* had been done there. This is called 'chaffing.' The general term may perhaps have had its origin in this curious custom.

Chain Cables were first employed on shipboard in 1811. The first vessel to use them was a West India ship, the *Penelope*, Captain Brown. They were invented and patented in 1808 by a navy surgeon named Slater.

Chaise. Two hundred and fifty years ago the ordinary vehicle used by the upper classes for conveyance to each other's houses, and to court, was the 'sedan chair.' In 1624, hackney coaches, drawn by horses, were introduced under the name of hackney *chairs*. The modern word *chaise* is a corruption of the latter word. The substitution of *s* for *r* in the word is supposed to have first taken place in France.

Chaldaic and Hebrew. That these two languages were contemporaneous is proved from Genesis xxxi. v. 47, where Laban calls a heap of stones *Jegar sahadutha*, which is pure Chaldaic, whilst Jacob calls it *Galeed*, or *Ga-lêd*, which is pure Hebrew.

Chalk Farm. This name has nothing whatever to do with chalk. It is derived from the name of two villages which formerly existed in this locality, and whose names are found on old maps—Upper and Lower *Chalcot*.

Chalk for cheese. In Nicholas Grimald's 'Translation of Cicero,' published 1568, there is an address to the reader, in which the following words occur:—' And wanting the right rule they take chalke for cheese, as the sainge is.'

Chalking the Door. In Scotland a landlord gives his tenant notice to quit by 'chalking the door.' The 'chalking' is done by a ' burgh officer,' upon the verbal authority of the landlord. It is usual, though not necessary, for the officer to give notice to the tenant of the object of his visit.

'Chambers's Journal' was commenced on February 4, 1832, about six weeks before the advent of the ' Penny Magazine.'

Champagne. In the seventeenth century a monk named Perignon had charge of the vineyard belonging to the abbey of St. Peter Hautvilliers, Champagne, and he also superintended the making of the abbey wines. In the course of his experiments he discovered 'Sparkling Champagne.' The inmates of the abbey kept the secret and the enjoyment of the delicious liquor entirely to themselves for a long time. A present was at length sent to Louis XIV., soon after which champagne became known to the outer world. A hundred years ago Moët and Chandon thought six thousand *bottles* in one year an enormous production. Their successors—one only of many firms—now bottle annually about 200,000 *dozens*. The peculiar cork used was also invented by Perignon, who died in the year 1715 at a very advanced age. Champagne is freed from sediment by a very ingenious process.

When first filled, the bottles are placed with the necks downwards, which are afterwards gently agitated at intervals, so that the whole of the sediment falls into the necks. The bottles are then taken singly, and while they are bottom upwards the corks are withdrawn and the sediment allowed to escape. They are then filled up with some flavouring and strengthening liqueur, recorked and wired, and so made ready for sale.

Champion. The ancient *champions* were those who in the wars between the English and Scotch decided by single combat the matters at issue. These duels were called *acrefights*, or campfights, and the combatants were called *champions* from the *champ* or field on which they fought.

Chance. Strauss, in 'The Old Faith and the New,' says, 'Chance is the result of hitherto undiscovered causes.'

Change from the Old Style to the New. In the month of September 1752 there were but nineteen days, and there was no new moon. The following is from Parker's 'Ephemerist' for that year:—

SEPTEMBER HATH 19 DAYS.

First quarter . . . . 15 day at 1 after.
Full moon . . . . 23 day at 1 after.
Last quarter . . . . 30 day at 2 after.

M D	HOLYDAYS and others	Moon south	Moon sets
1	*Giles Abbott*	3 A 37	8 A 7
2	*London burnt*	4 . 26	8 . 24

'According to Act of Parliament passed on the fourteenth day of His Majesty's reign, and in the year of our Lord 1751, the Old Style ceases here, and the New takes place; and consequently the next day which in the Old account would have been the third is now to be called the fourteenth, so that all the intermediate nominal days from the second to the fourteenth are omitted, or rather annihilated this year, and the month contains no more than nineteen days, as the table at the head expresses.'

THE NEW STYLE BEGINS.

14	Holy Cross	5.15	9 A 28
15	———	6.3	10.18

Change of Surname. Seton, in his 'Law and Practice of Scottish Heraldry,' says, 'It appears to be the established law of both England and Scotland that surnames may be assumed or changed at pleasure, independently of any royal, parliamentary, or judicial authority.' In the case of 'Leigh v. Leigh' (1808) Lord Eldon is reported to have said, 'The King's license is nothing more than permission to take the name; it does not give it.' In the Scottish Court of Session, in 1835, the Lord President Hope said, 'There is no need of the authority of this Court to enable a man in Scotland to change his name.' The practice of enrolling a deed-poll in Chancery is simply to secure a record of the change of name. It does not confer the name.

Changes in the meaning of Words. The following abridgment of a table prepared by Dr. Angus shows the gradual manner in which many English words have become utterly changed in meaning from their original signification:—

Boor	Cultivator	Cultivator, rough in manner	Boorish, uncivilised
Villain	A farm labourer	A labourer, low in morals	An immoral bad man
Pagan	A villager	A villager ignorant of the Gospel	One ignorant of the Gospel
Clumsy	Benumbed with cold	Benumbed, awkward	Awkward from any cause
Lewd	Of the laity; vulgar, ignorant	Ignorant, vicious	Vicious
Miscreant	Misbeliever	Misbeliever, grossly vicious	One grossly vicious
Preposterous	Putting behind what should be before	Putting, &c., and so absurd	Absurd

Change-ringing. The number of changes that can be rung increases enormously with the number of bells. Three bells allow six changes; four bells will produce twenty-four changes; whilst the number that can be rung upon twelve bells amounts to upwards of four hundred and seventy-nine millions.

Channel Islands. These islands—Guernsey, Jersey, Sark, &c.—have never been made part of the United Kingdom. They were united to the English *crown* by Henry I. as a portion of the Duchy of Normandy, and so still remain, being governed by their own laws.

Chap is an abbreviation of the word *chapman*—one who sells in a cheaping or market. Todd says, 'If the phrase be a *good chap*, it implies a dealer to whom credit may be given; if simply a *chap*, it designates a person of whom a contemptuous opinion is entertained.' The general application of the word to a boy or youth of inferior position is of modern usage.

Chapel, from *capa*, a chest. The word was originally applied to the chest in which the relics of a saint were deposited; afterwards to the apartment in churches or cathedrals in which the chest was kept. These chapels were separately dedicated, and were known by the name of the saint whose relics they contained, upon whose anniversary special services were performed therein.

Chaperon. This word is frequently incorrectly spelt *chaperone*, with the final *e*. The word is not feminine, although it is generally applied to a lady. It means a hood, and when used metaphorically signifies that the married lady shields her youthful *protégée* as the hood shields the face. The orthography should therefore be 'chaperon.' The word 'chaperoness' is used in the 'Devil's Law Cure,' a play written about the year 1620.

Chapter and Verse. 'The proverbial expression of "chapter and verse" seems peculiar to ourselves, and I suspect originated in the Puritanic period, probably just before the civil wars under Charles I., from the frequent use of appealing to the Bible on the most frivolous occasions practised by those whom South calls "those mighty men at chapter and verse." '—*D'Israeli's Curiosities of Literature.*

Charcoal. Wood, when cut of proper lengths and stacked for firewood, was formerly called *coal*. Bailey defines 'coal-fire' to be 'a heap of *fire-wood* for sale, so much as will make a load of coal when burnt.' This fire-wood, when properly charred or burnt, is *charcoal*, or, as Bailey calls it, 'coal.'

Charge of the Light Brigade. Tennyson, when he wrote this celebrated poem, had evidently in his mind some recollection of Michael Drayton's 'Battle of Agincourt,' one stanza of which is as follows :—

> They now to fight are gone,
> Armour on armour shone,
> Drum now to drum did groan,
>   To hear was wonder.
> That with the cries they make,
> The very earth did shake,
> Trumpet to trumpet spake,
>   Thunder to thunder.

Charles's Wain. This common pseudonym for the constellation *Ursa Major* is probably a corruption of *Ceorles wain*, 'countryman's wagon.'

Charlies. The old watchmen who were superseded by the present police force were called Charlies, or Charleys. According to Wheeler ('Noted Names of Fiction,' p. 71), the name of

Charlies was given to the old bellmen and watchmen from King Charles I., who in 1640 extended and improved the watch system of the metropolis.

Charlotte. This name as used in cookery as 'Charlotte russe,' 'Apple charlotte,' &c., is found in Harl. MS. 4016, which contains bills of fare, recipes, &c., from A.D. 1380 to 1425 or thereabouts. The orthography there is 'Charlette.'

Charm. In the sense of a charm or incantation this word is derived from the Latin *carmen*, a song. In the sense of grace, loveliness, beauty, in fact all that we express by the word 'charming,' it is from the Greek *charma*, which is from the root *charis*, signifying favour, gracefulness, beauty, &c.

Charterhouse. The name of the Charterhouse in London is a corruption of the word *Chartreuse*, that is 'Carthusian.' The Charterhouse was originally a Carthusian monastery founded in 1371, but was seized by Henry VIII. The present charity was founded by Thomas Sutton, Nov. 1, 1611. Sutton died Dec. 12 of the same year.

Charwoman. The verb 'to char' is a very old term almost gone out of use in England. It seems to be derived from the Anglo-Saxon *cyre*, or *cyran*, to turn, and Richardson says that a charwoman is one who goes out to take a *turn* at work. 'Char' was formerly used to signify any odd job, whether done for hire or otherwise. In Ray's 'Collection of Proverbs' is 'That char is char'd, as the good wife said when she had hanged her husband.' The word, spelt *chore*, is in very common use in the United States.

Chatterpie, a term frequently applied to a great talker, is an old name for the magpie. 'The pie still chattereth.'—*Sir P. Sydney.*

Chaucer's Inn, the 'Tabard.' The old tavern immortalised by Chaucer as the 'Tabard' was burnt down in the great fire of 1676. Upon its restoration the name was changed to the 'Talbot' or Dog, under which name it remained until about 1873, when it was demolished, and a glaring ginshop, called as though in mockery 'The Old Tabard,' was erected in its place.

Cheap. This word is from the Anglo-Saxon *ceapian*, to buy. An article, if well bought, was said to be *good-cheap*. If too much had been paid for it, it was said to be *bad-cheap*. It is now only used for 'good-cheap,' and the prefix 'good' is dropped as being superfluous.

Cheap Newspaper in Ireland. The 'Belfast Evening Telegraph,' the first halfpenny evening newspaper issued in Ireland, was started Sept. 1, 1870.

Cheapside. In the third year of Edward II. it was ordered that 'no man or woman should be so bold as henceforward to hold common market for merchandise in Chepe, or any other highway within the city except Cornhill after the hour of nones' [midday prayers], and it was also forbidden under pain of imprisonment to 'scour pots in the roadway of Chepe to the hindrance of folk who were passing.'

'**Cheers but not inebriates.**' Cowper used this phrase in reference to tea, but it had been previously applied by Bishop Berkeley to Tar-water. In the 217th paragraph of his work 'Siris' the good bishop says that tar-water 'is of a nature so mild and benign, and proportioned to the human constitution, as to warm without heating, *to cheer but not inebriate*, and to produce a calm and steady joy, like the effect of good news.'

Cheese. This word has evidently some affinity with, if it is not formed from, the verb to squeeze. The curds are squeezed into a mass to form cheese. The Anglo-Saxon word for 'squeeze' is *cwysam*, and in Low German it is *quesen*; the Spanish name for cheese is *queso*.

Chemistry comes from the Arabic *kimia*, something hidden.

Chenille. This favourite trimming for ladies' dress has a very appropriate name. *Chenille* is the French name for a caterpillar.

Chep, Cheeping, Chipping. These words in the name of a place, as Chepstow, Chipping Norton, Chepping Hill, and Chippenham, always signify market. Cheapside and Eastcheap were ancient market-places in London. There is a Cheapside in many old towns—Leicester for instance—and a Corn-Cheaping at Worcester and Coventry.

Cherries were first brought into Europe from Kerasunt in the Black Sea by Lucullus, about the year 70 B.C.

Cherry Fairs were meetings in 'cherry orchards' for the young and gay on Sunday evenings—not to buy and sell cherries, but to enjoy themselves. Cherry orchards did not necessarily grow cherries, but were similar to what we now call tea-gardens, where, by the way, little tea is ever sold.

> They prechen us in audience
> That no man schalle hys soule empeyre,
> For all is but a *chery fayre*.—*Gower*.

Thys lyfe is but a *chery faire.*—*Bodl. MS.* 221.
Therfore be the werldes wele.
It fary's as a *chery feyre.*—*Ashmole MS.* 61, folio 6.

Cherubim. In several parts of the Bible this word is printed with a final *s*—'*cherubims.*' This is wrong. The singular of the word is *cherub,* the plural is *cherubim,* without the *s.*

Chess. It 'may now be considered certain that, under the Sanscrit name of *chaturanga,* a game essentially the same as modern chess was played in Hindustan nearly 5,000 years ago.'—*Chambers's Encyclopædia.*

Chested. Anciently when a dead person was placed in a coffin he was said to be 'chested.' Chaucer has 'He is now ded, and nailed in his cheste.' In the heading of the 50th Chapter of Genesis the word is used in reference to Joseph, of whom it is said, ' v. 26, *he dieth and is chested.*'

Chester, Caster, Cester. 'Places whose names terminate with either of these words were sites of castles *built by the Romans.*'—*Wharton.*

Cheval-glass. *Cheval* is the French word for 'horse'; a cheval-glass is a large looking-glass mounted on a wooden frame or *horse,* which can be moved about on wheels or rollers. The word *horse* is frequently used in combinations, as towel-horse, clothes-horse, &c.

Chewing the Cud. The cud is called *quid* in Surrey; hence perhaps a *quid* of tobacco.

Chiaro-oscuro. An Italian phrase, literally 'light and shade,' but according to Fairholt it 'means not only the mutable effects produced by light and shade, but also the permanent differences in brightness and darkness.'

Chickens. This is a double plural. *Chick* is the singular; *chicken* the old plural; 'chickens' with the final *s* is a modern corruption.

Chignon. The chignon, so fashionable a few years ago, was not a novel introduction. It was in use a hundred years ago, and is mentioned in the following terms in the 'Lady's Magazine' for 1777, p. 374: 'The fourth [curl] descends towards the *chinion,* and measures six inches in length, and two and a-half or three in diameter. . . . The *chinion* is pretty full and descends rather lower than it used to do.' In 'L'Art de la Coiffure des Dames Françoises' by Legros (Paris 1768), are engravings and descriptions of the head-dresses of that day, in which chignons are figured, and the word is spelled as now, '*chignon.*'

Child-king. The earliest mention of the regal dignity descending to a child is in 2 Kings xi., where we are told that Jehoash was anointed king when seven years of age.

Child's Coral. The well-known toy with bells, &c., and a piece of coral at the end, which is generally suspended from the necks of infants, is with the greatest probability supposed to have had its origin in an ancient superstition, which considered coral as an amulet, or defensative, against fascination; for this we have the authority of Pliny.

Chiltern Hundreds. The Chiltern Hills are a range of chalk eminences, separating the counties of Bedford and Hertford, and passing through the middle of Bucks, to Henley in Oxfordshire. They comprise the Hundreds of Burnham, Desborough, and Stoke. They were formerly much infested by robbers. To protect the inhabitants from these marauders, an officer of the Crown was appointed, under the name of the 'Steward of the Chiltern Hundreds.' The duties have long ceased, but the office—a sinecure with a nominal pay—is still retained. A member of the House of Commons cannot resign, but acceptance of office under the Crown vacates his seat. Whenever, therefore, an M.P. wishes to retire, he applies for this office, which being granted as a matter of course, his seat in Parliament becomes vacant; and he holds the office until some other member wishes to retire.

Chimney. It seems to be generally thought that the chimney, in its present sense of a funnel from the fireplace or hearth to the roof of a building, was unknown to the ancients. The writer has, however, in his possession, a photograph of the 'Maison de Boulanger' at Pompeii, in which a chimney from the mouth of the oven to the height of the external walls is distinctly visible. The earliest form of chimney in England is seen in the ruins of Rochester Castle, where there are fireplaces to each apartment, from which chimneys are carried up in the thickness of the wall, a few feet above the fireplace, where they terminate in horizontal openings through the outer wall.

Chine is an old English word signifying a cleft, or a piece cut out. It enters into the name of several places in the Isle of Wight, as in Blackgang Chine.

Chinese name for a Book. The Chinese call a book *Shoo*. They write it with two characters, one of which means 'pencil,' the other 'speak.'

Chirk. This word is in common use in the New England

States of America, in the sense of lively, cheerful, or in good spirits. It is an old English word which in the mother-country has been modernised into *chirp*. In England, a bird 'chirps' when he is lively; in America, a sick person when recovering is said to be 'chirk.' Chaucer has 'chirkith,' in the sense of 'chirpeth.'

Chocolate. From two American-Indian words, *choco*, sound, and *alta*, water, from the sound in triturating the cacao-nut with water.

Chopping and Changing. The word chopping, in this familiar phrase, was probably originally 'chapping,' an old term for dealing. The term 'chapman' is not yet quite extinct as a legal phrase; and the words cheap, chepe, chipping, cheaping, all refer to marketing, or buying and selling.

Christian. 'The disciples were called *Christians* first at Antioch.'—*Acts* xi. 26.

Christmas Custom. The custom of stealthily hiding money and other presents in the stockings of children after they have retired to bed on Christmas-eve—which presents are said to be sent by Santa Claus—is derived from a Continental practice. On St. Nicholas-eve presents are secretly hidden in children's shoes and slippers, and the little ones are told that these presents were brought through the windows—though they were shut—by St. Nicholas. The custom is founded upon a tradition that St. Nicholas, in his lifetime, was in the habit of throwing purses of money in at the windows of poor maidens, to be used by them as marriage-portions.—*Brand*.

Christmas Tree. 'The Christmas tree has become a prevailing fashion in England, and is by most persons supposed to have originated in Germany. Such, however, is not the fact. The Christmas tree is from Egypt, and its origin dates from a period long anterior to the Christian era. The palm-tree is known to put forth a branch every month, and a spray of this tree, with twelve shoots on it, was used in Egypt at the time of the winter solstice, as a symbol of the year completed.'

Christopher, as a Christian name, is usually given to one born on Good Friday; the word means 'Christ bearer.'

Chronology of local Printing. Mr. Power, in his 'Handy Book about Books' (Wilson, 1870), gives the dates of the introduction of printing in a large number of places in Great Britain. The following are some of the earliest:—

	A.D.		A.D.
London	1474	Abingdon	1512
Oxford	1481	Cambridge	1521
Edinburgh	1507	Winchester	1545
York	1509	Bristol	1546
Beverley	1510	Worcester	1548

Chum. From the Armenian word *chom*, 'to live together.'

Church. Verstegan gives the origin of this word from the Anglo-Saxon *ciric*, as follows:—'*Ciric*, by abbreviation *Kirk*, and by thrusting in *c, h*, it was first alienated to *Chirche*, and since, further off, by making it *Churche*.'—*Restitution*, &c. p. 168.

Church Bells. 'Though churchwardens have a general power to manage everything connected with the fabric of their church, this power does not extend to the bells, so far as to enable them to decide, independently of the minister, when they shall be rung for purposes not directly connected with the summoning parishioners to worship. It is perfectly clear law that the churchwardens have no power to order that the bells shall be rung, on this or that occasion, without the permission of the minister.'—*Whittaker's Almanack.*

Churches not standing due east. Aubrey (MS. Ashmolean Museum) says, 'In days of yore, when a church was to be built, they watched and prayed on the vigil of the dedication, and took that point of the horizon where the sun arose on the morrow, for the east, which makes that variation so that few stand true, except those built between [qy. about the time of?] the two equinoxes.'

Churchyards. Strutt ('Manners and Customs,' vol. i. p. 69) tells us that, 'before the time of Christianity, it was held unlawful to bury the dead within the Cities, but they used to carry them out into the fields, hard by, and there deposit them. Towards the end of the sixth century, Augustine obtained of King Ethelbert a Temple of Idols (where the king used to worship before his conversion), and made a Burying-Place of it; but St. Cuthbert afterwards obtained leave to have Yards made to the Churches, proper for the reception of the dead.'

Churl. This was originally spelt 'ceorl' and was a general term for a tenant at will. There were two kinds of churls; one paid a rent in money, the other—called also 'sockmen'—yielded work and not rent, tilling the demesnes of his thane or lord, and having a portion of land as his recompense.

Churn. In the old Northern languages, *kern*, as at present used in Germany, meant the pith, marrow, or choicest part of anything. Hence our word *kernel*. In Dutch, the word *kernjen* means to separate the *kern* of the milk by agitation or churning.; and from the same root we get our words 'churn' and 'churning.' Our word 'curds' is evidently another form derived from the same origin.

Cicerone. This Italian word is now naturalised in England, and is found in all our dictionaries, the definition being ' a guide who shows, and loquaciously describes or explains curiosities.' 'The term probably arose from the ironical exclamation, *E un Cicerone* (He is a Cicero), referring to the excessive garrulity of the Italian guides.'—*Brand*.

Cigars. In the 'Distresses and Adventures of John Cockburn' (London, 1740, p. 139), the earliest known mention of cigars occurs. Cockburn was put on a desert island in the Bay of Honduras, swam to the mainland, and travelled thence on foot to Porto Bello, a distance of 2,600 miles. He appears to have met with some friars, who gave him some 'seegars' (*sic*) to smoke, which they supposed would be very acceptable. 'These,' he says, ' are leaves of tobacco rolled up in such a manner that they serve both for a pipe and tobacco itself.'

Cinderella and the Glass Slipper. This pretty tale of a 'little cinder girl' comes to us from the French; but the translator made a curious mistake, which has been so long current in English that it seems like sacrilege to disturb it. In the original the slipper is described as *pantoufle en vair*, that is, a slipper made of fur (*vair*). The translator, being more familiar with the sound than the sense, read this as if it were *verre*, that is, glass; and the *glass* slipper, we suppose, will remain for ever a part of the story.

Circulating Libraries. The earliest of which there is any record was established at Dunfermline in 1711. Allan Ramsay started one in Edinburgh in 1725. The first in London was opened in 1740, at No. 132 Strand, by a person named Wright. This library was afterwards carried on by Batho, who was succeeded by Bell.

Circumstance comes from the Latin *circum*, around, and *sto*, to stand. Hence circumstances are adjuncts, incidents, or events *surrounding* or attending a fact.

Citizen of the World. In 'England's Path to Wealth and Honour,' by Puckle, published in 1700, one of the characters introduced is made to say, 'An honest man is a *citizen of the* *world.* Gain equalizeth all places to me.' This is believed to be the earliest use of the phrase in English. The Greeks used *cosmopolites* in the same sense.

City. The word city was not used in England until after the Conquest; before which time the metropolis was called Londonburgh.

City Officers. The officers of the Corporation of London formerly competed at auction for the purchase of their appointments; the highest bidder, whether suitable or otherwise, obtaining the office. The following advertisement is cut from an old newspaper, October 31, 1770:—

'The Committee for letting the lands and tenements of the City of London, in the account of the Chamberlain thereof, do hereby give notice that they will sit in the Council Chamber of the Guildhall of the said City THIS DAY, the 31st of October instant, at four of the clock in the afternoon, to lett, by Public Auction, a Lease for twenty-one years, from the 27th day of December next, the Office or Place of one of the sixteen Sea Coal Meters of this City, in lease to Mr. Heneage Robinson; of which further information and printed particulars may be had at the Comptroller's Office at Guildhall aforesaid.

'At the same time the Committee will sell, by Public Auction, the office or place of the Clerk of the Papers of the Poultry Compter, vacant by the death of Mr. George Wade.

'N.B.—That by an order of the Court of Common Council of the 14th of March, 1755, it is ordered that all persons who shall agree for the purchase of any place or office belonging to the City or Bridge-house, shall, at the time of their contracting for the same, deposit ten pounds per cent. of the purchase-money; which deposit shall be forfeited in case of non-performance of their contract.

'D. SEAMAN, Comptroller.'

Clap-trap. This phrase seems to have been derived from the *clap-net*, used for trapping larks and other birds. Bailey says that '*clap-trap* is a name given to the rant that dramatic authors, to please actors, let them go off with; as much as to say, to catch a clap of applause from the spectators at a play.'

Clarence. The royal title of Duke of Clarence is taken from the small town of Clare in Suffolk. The first Duke of Clarence was Lionel, the third son of Edward III., who became possessed of the manor of Clare by his marriage with the heiress in 1362. Subsequent dukes have been Thomas, second son of Henry IV.;

George, brother of Edward IV.; and William, son of George III., who afterwards became King William IV.

Classic. This term is of Latin origin, and is derived from the social economy of Rome. One man was said to be of the second class, another was in the third, but he who was in the highest was said emphatically to be of *the* class—*Classicus*, as we say, 'men of rank,' meaning those of the *highest* rank. By an obvious analogy the best writers were termed *Classic*, that is, of the highest class.

Claymore. The word *claymore* is often used by Sir Walter Scott and other Scottish writers to denote a sword. The dictionaries give the Gaelic word *Claidheamb* as the origin. As it is sometimes found written *glaymore*, it is more likely to be the inverted form of *Morglay*, the sword of Sir Bevis of Southampton, a weapon so famous that its name became a general one for a sword. The name morglay was derived from the Norman *glaive de la mort*, the 'sword of death.' Beaumont and Fletcher often use the word *morglay*, e.g.:—

> Talk with the girdler or the milliner,
> He can inform you of a kind of men
> That first undid the profit of these trades,
> By bringing up the form of carrying
> Their *morglays* in their hands.—*Honest Man*

> Had I been accompanied with my toledo or *morglay*.
> *Every Woman in her Humour.*

Cleanliness is next to Godliness. The author of this phrase, quoted by John Wesley, is not known. Something similar to it is found in the 'Talmud,' and Plutarch tells us that amongst the ancient Egyptians 'health was no less respected than devotion.' A Jewish lecturer, on December 3, 1878, reported in 'The Jewish World,' said, 'This well-known English phrase had been taught by the Rabbins of the "Talmud" many centuries ago, both as a religious principle and a sanitary law.'

Clearing House. The Bankers' 'Clearing House' is an establishment instituted in Lombard Street, London, in 1775, for the purpose of facilitating the adjustment of daily accounts between the various banking establishments, by merely paying the *balance* found to be due upon a comparison of the debits and credits. This is done by each bank having an account with the Clearing House, which is balanced daily. 'Chambers's Encyclopædia' gives a copy of a daily statement, showing that transactions to the amount of nearly a million and three-quarters sterling may be settled by a cheque for 5,000*l*. A copy of the account is annexed :—

		GLYN.		
Debtors	Balance	—	Balance	Creditors
£	£		£	£
280,000	20,000	Barclay	—	260,000
50,000	10,000	Bosanquet	—	40,000
110,000	—	Commercial	10,000	120,000
115,000	5,000	Currie	—	110,000
50,000	5,000	Fuller	—	45,000
100,000	10,000	Hanbury	—	90,000
110,000	—	Hankey	5,000	115,000
280,000	—	Jones	20,000	300,000
150,000	—	Lubbock	10,000	160,000
200,000	—	Masterman	15,000	215,000
50,000	—	Olding	5,000	55,000
65,000	5,000	Spooner	—	60,000
165,000	5,000	Union	—	160,000
	60,000		65,000	
		Dr.	60,000	
			5,000	

Messrs. Glyn have therefore to give a cheque on the Bank of England for 5,000*l.*, which balances the entire day's transactions.

Cleave. This word has two directly opposite significations. In one sense it means to adhere, to stick to, to be attached to; as in Job xxxviii. 38, 'The clods *cleave* fast together'; and in Matt. xix. 5, 'For this cause shall a man leave father and mother and shall *cleave* to his wife.' The original Anglo-Saxon word having this meaning was *clifian*. In the other sense it means to divide, to part asunder, to separate, as in Psalm cxli. 7, 'as when one cutteth and *cleaveth* wood'; and in Deut. xiv. 6, 'Every beast that parteth the hoof and *cleaveth* the cleft into two claws.' The original Anglo-Saxon in this sense was *cleafan*.

Cleeves. An obsolete plural of the word 'cliff':—

<blockquote>
She sang and wept, O yee sea-binding <i>cleeves</i>,
Yield tributary drops, for vertue grieves.
Browne's Pastorals, 1, 4, p. 110.
</blockquote>

Cleveland in Yorkshire is the 'land of *cleeves*,' or cliffs.

Clef, in music. *Clef* is the French word for *key*. It gives the key, or interpretation, of the music which is to follow.

Cleopátra. The accepted English pronunciation of this word places the accent on the letter *a*, which is sounded as in the word father.

Clerical Error. A clerical error is an error in writing, made inadvertently, not from ignorance. The word is from *clericus*, or clerk.

Clever. The Americans apply to this word the meaning of good-natured, well-disposed, honest, &c. 'A clever fellow' with them is a good-hearted, well-disposed, genial, or, as we should say, a 'good sort of fellow.' 'The landlord of the house was a very *clever* man, and made me feel quite at home.'—*Crocket, Tour Down East*, p. 22.

Cliff. 'In our ancient language the cut off, or broken mountaines on the sea sides, are more rightly and properly called cliffs than by the name of Rocks or Hills, that appellation being more fitting unto the inland mountains, but the name of clifft, coming from our verbe to cleave, is unto these more aptly given, for that they seeme unto our view as cleft or cloven from the part that sometime belonged to them.'—*Verstegan, Restitution,* &c., p. 80, edit. 1655.

Climatic influence upon Animals. In transporting animals from one climate to another, it is seldom that they become fully acclimatised. Their progeny, however, even in the first generation, are found to be better adapted than their parents to the new state of things. The following remarkable instance of this modification in the case of some greyhounds is mentioned by Sir Charles Lyell. Some Englishmen engaged in mining operations in Mexico, at the height of 9,000 feet above the level of the sea, finding the locality abound with hares, imported some greyhounds from England to hunt them, but as the barometer at that great height seldom stood at more than 19 inches, 'it was found that the greyhounds could not support the fatigues of a long chase in this attenuated atmosphere, and before they could come up with their prey, they lay down gasping for breath; but these same animals have produced whelps which have grown up and are not in the least degree incommoded by the want of density in the air, but run down the hares with as much ease as the fleetest of their race in this country.'—*Principles of Geology,* 11th edit. vol. ii. p. 297.

Climb. In England this word is always used in the sense to mount, to rise, to ascend. In America, it seems, people climb *down*. Mr. H. W. Beecher, who may be considered a competent judge of correct English, in describing his visit to Oxford, says, 'To *climb down* the wall was easy enough.' And in the 'Star Papers,' p. 41, we find, 'I partly *climbed down*, and wholly clambered back again.'

Climbing Plants. Some plants, in entwining themselves round sticks or other supports, turn to the left, as the hop; others, as the convolvulus, turn to the right.

Clincher. Something that settles a point or argument. This application of the word is said to have arisen from two notorious liars being matched against each other. 'I drove a nail through the moon once,' said the first. 'Yes,' said the other, 'I remember the circumstance, and I went round to the back and *clinched* it.'

Clipper. The origin of this name for a fast-sailing vessel has been much debated. The following, from 'Alice Lorraine,' vol. iii. p. 2, seems plausible :—' The British corvette, *Cleopatra-cum-Antonio*, was the nimblest little craft ever captured from the French and her name had been reefed into " Clipater " first, and then into " Clipper," which still holds sway.'

Clocks. The earliest clocks were called 'horologes.' Horologes were first contrived to move by the dropping of water, and these were known to the Romans a century and a half before the Christian era, under the Greek name of *clepsydræ*. Julius Cæsar is said to have found a native water-clock in Britain, 55 B.C. Afterwards sand-glasses (*clepsammia*) were invented, and such a time-measurer was used by St. Jerome. Alfred the Great, however, did not use either of these contrivances, but measured his time by the burning of wax candles of different length and size, each weighing 12 pennyweights, being 12 inches long, and burning four hours, so that six of them burnt exactly 24 hours. To prevent the wind from causing them to 'gutter' or to burn too quickly, he enclosed each in a framework, the sides of which were made of horn, scraped so thin as to be transparent. Pacificus, Archdeacon of Verona, is said to have been the inventor of wheel clocks, in the early part of the ninth century. The first wheel clock in England seems to have been set up in St. Paul's Cathedral in London in the 13th century; a record of the allowance to be made to the clock-keeper, dated 1286, being still in existence. Chaucer, who was born in 1328 and died in 1400, mentions the word clock, but it is doubtful whether he did not mean merely the *bell* which rung out at the hour of prime, first three strokes, then four, then five, and then one; the thirteen strokes representing Our Lord and the Twelve disciples. Chaucer is speaking of a cock, and his words are :—

>Ful sikerer was his crowing in his loge
>Than his a *clock* or any abbey orologe.

which may be modernised :—

>Full surer was his crowing on his roost
>Than is a *bell* [at prime] or any abbey clock.

The earliest known mention by that name, of a clock with a dial and striking apparatus, available both for seeing and hearing, is contained in a work of Reginald Pecock, Bishop of Chichester, written about 1449. The book is called, 'The Repressor of overmuch Blaming of the Clergy,' and in it the Bishop says, 'In all Holi Scripture it is not expressid bi bidding, counseiling, or witnessing, or bi eni ensaumbling of persoon, that men schulde make and vse *clockis* forto knowe the houris of the dai and nygt; for thou [though] in eeldist daies, and thou in Scripture menshioun is maad of orologis, schewing the houris of the dai bi schadew maad bi the sunne in a cercle, certis neuere saue in late daies was eni *clok* telling the houris of the dai and nygt bi peise and bi stroke, and open it is that nouwhere in Holi Scripture is expresse mensioun of eni suche.' From this he proceeds to argue that many things are lawful in the church that are neither mentioned nor implied in Scripture. There is a clock of the date 1543 still in going order in the place where it was originally set up at Hampton Court Palace. The initials of the maker's name are N. O. The oldest clock in England is now at the Museum of Patents at South Kensington. The compiler has been favoured with the following description of this interesting clock, by Mr. George Wallis, of the South Kensington Museum:—' It was made at Glastonbury Abbey by Peter Lightfoot, one of the resident monks, in 1325. In Elizabeth's reign it was removed from Glastonbury to Wells Cathedral, and worked there until about forty years ago, when it was laid aside in the crypt of the cathedral to make room for a new clock. The Dean and Chapter of Wells having *lent* it to the Patent Museum for exhibition, a few new brass wheels were made to take the place of some of the iron ones which had been lost, and the clock was made to tell time once more. It is interesting from its very early date, and connection with Glastonbury Abbey, as also from being the work of one man. It indicates time of day and night, and the age of the moon. The framing of the whole is of wrought iron, and it is fastened together by mortice, tenon and cotters. Two bells are placed, on which it strikes the quarters, and a larger bell, on which it strikes the hour. My resident colleague next door, tells me that he frequently, when all is still, and the wind favourable, hears this 555 year-old machinery striking the hour on the larger bell. I am, unfortunately, too deaf to be able to verify this.'

The terms clock and watch seem to have been formerly used interchangeably; Shakespeare, 'Love's Labour Lost,' iii. i. speaks of

> A woman that is like a German *clock*,
> Still a-repairing; ever out of frame;
> And never going aright; *being a watch*,
> But being watched that it may still go right.

A 'clock' shows and strikes the hours; a 'quarter-clock' strikes the quarters as well; a 'time-piece' shows the hours without striking them; a 'watch' is a portable time-piece for the pocket; a 'repeater' is a watch which has a contrivance by which it can be made—at pleasure—to repeat or strike the hours, and sometimes the quarters; a 'chronometer' (*chronos*, time, *metron*, a measure), is a watch of the best kind, made especially for astronomical purposes.

Closet. The diminutive of *close*, an enclosure, meaning any small place which can be closed.

Clothing, Costume. The distinction, not usually fully recognised, between clothing and costume, is that *clothing* is composed of the garments which are used for the purposes of shelter, or protection from the inclemencies of cold or heat, whilst *costume* consists of such garments as are worn either to suit the varying caprices of fashion, or from a proper sense of that which is in consonance with good taste, or with a correct notion of that which is becoming.

Clove. The clove is the unexpanded flower-bud of *Caryophyllus aromaticus*. The plant is a native of the islands in the Chinese seas.

Clown. From the Latin *colonus*, a husbandman. It was formerly spelt 'colone.' The original meaning was 'one who tills the ground.' The adjective 'clownish' still retains the original signification.

Clubs. The modern clubs in London and other large towns originated in London after the close of the Napoleonic wars, or about 1815. A number of military and naval officers being then placed upon half-pay, found themselves compelled to economise, and they originated the United Service Club, where they could dine together at far less expense than dining separately. The success of the experiment speedily led to the establishment of others, and the system is now in operation in almost every large town in the kingdom. Carlyle, in 'Frederick the Great,' vol. i. p. 111, says that 1190 'was the era of chivalry orders and *Gelübde*; time for Bodies of men uniting themselves by a Sacred Vow " Gelübde," which word and thing have passed over to us in a singularly dwindled condition. "Club" we now call it; and the vow, if sacred, does not rank very high.'

Clue, or Clew. A *clew* is a ball of thread or twine, which being unwound and left on the ground in passing into a labyrinth, or intricate subterranean passage, is a guide to find the way back. Hence, metaphorically, it is used to designate the discovery of some evidence which an officer of justice, in pursuit of a criminal, hopes may guide him in his search.

Clumsy is from hands stiffened or frozen, and contracted so as to be incapable of grasping anything. The word is general in Northern Europe, as in Iceland *klumsa*, Old English *clomsid*, Low German *klomen*, Swedish *klumsig*, and Dutch *kluntet*. Piers Plowman has 'thou *klompsist* for cold,' and Wicliff, ' Our hondis ben aclumpsid.'

Coach. The earliest coaches in England were called ' whirlicotes.' The mother of Richard II., who in 1360 accompanied him in his flight, rode in one of these vehicles. Coaches, properly so called, were brought from the Continent in 1580. In 1601, the year before the death of Elizabeth, an Act was passed to prevent men from riding in coaches, as being effeminate. The first coach seen in Scotland was that of the queen of James VI., afterwards James I. of England. The ' Diary ' of Robert Birch records that, after the king's departure for England, the queen, on May 30, 1603, ' came to Sanct Geill's Kirk, weill convoyit with coches, herself and the prince in hey awin coche guhilk came with hir out of Denmarke in 1599, and the English gentelwemen in the rest of the coches.'

Coal as fuel. Seacoal Lane, near Snow Hill, in London, is mentioned under the name of ' Secollane ' A.D. 1253. The name is no doubt derived from sea-coal, which was brought up the river Fleet in barges. In the year 1316 the Parliament petitioned Edward II. to prohibit the use of coal on the ground of its being injurious to health, and a proclamation was issued forbidding its use. On account of the high price of wood, the proclamation was little heeded, and after a short time the use of sea-coal—as it was then called to distinguish it from charcoal—became general.

Coast is from the Latin *costa*, a rib, or side ; hence the side or frontier of a country. The term '*sea*-coast' shows that it was not originally confined to the *sea margin* of a country, and in the New Testament it is used of the country *within the borders*. Thus, Matthew ii. 16—' All the children that were in Bethlehem and in all the *coasts* thereof ' ; and Mark v. 17 :—' They began to pray him to depart out of their *coasts*.'

Coat of Arms. Knights originally had their armorial bearings embroidered on their coats or outer garments.

Coat of many colours. The expression 'coat of many colours,' used in Genesis xxxvii., is literally a coat made of strips of different coloured cloth. Coats made in this way were worn by persons of distinction in Persia, India, and some parts of China down to the present day.—*Adam Clarke.*

Coax. *Cokes*, in old English, was a simpleton or gull, probably from the old French *cocasse* or *cocosse*, imbecile. To cokes or coax one is to make a cokes or fool of him, by wheedling or gulling him into doing something.

Cobalt. From the German *Kobold*, a devil. Ores of this metal were so named by the workers in the silver mines, before its value discovered, because they were so hard as to be almost unworkable, the hardness being attributed to the malice of the Kobold, or devil.

Cobbler. This is an American word for a drink, as sherry-*cobbler*, &c. The word cobbler is perhaps derived from the English adjective 'cobby,' brisk, hearty, lively. As the drink gives rise to feelings of this kind, it may be supposed that a *cobbler* is something which makes a man *cobby*.

Coblentz is a corruption of *Confluentes*, the name given to the place by the Romans from its situation at the confluence of the Rhine and Moselle rivers.

Cobweb. In the Anglo-Saxon *attercop* was the poison-spider (*atter*, poison, *cop*, spider), so that cobweb should be *cop*web.

Cochineal. The Spanish word for a woodlouse is *cochinilla*, the diminutive of *cochina*, a sow, from some fancied resemblance in shape. When the Spaniards went to America they transferred the name to the insect producing the scarlet dye, which is somewhat similar in appearance. It is curious that in some parts of England a wood-louse is called a wood-sow.

Cockade. The black cockade is the badge of the House of Hanover, and is worn only by servants of the Royal Family, and by those of naval, military, and court officers. The servants of officers in the navy use a small oval cockade which does not rise above the crown of the hat. The fan-like rays on the military cockade are supposed to represent the bursting of a shell. Sir Bernard Burke, Ulster King-at-Arms, in a letter to a correspondent, March 6, 1860, said that '*commissioned* officers of volunteer corps are entitled to the privilege of having cockades in their servants' hats.'

Cock-a-hoop. A crested cock (old French *hupé*, crested, proud). The term is applied to vainglorious, conceited persons, who carry their heads thrown backwards, as a peacock does.

Cock and bull story. The pope's bulls were named from the *bulla*, or seal, which was attached. The seal bore the impression of a figure of St. Peter, accompanied by the cock. Hence after the Reformation any tale or discourse that was unheeded was on a par with a pope's bull, which was a 'cock and bull affair.'

Cockchafer. Probably *clock*-chafer. Clock was an old name for a beetle. In the Anglo-Saxon *ceafor* or *ceafyr* also meant a beetle. In German *kafer* has the same signification. In the Swabian dialect it is *chäfer*.

Cocker. 'According to Cocker.' Edward Cocker, a writing-master, engraver, and arithmetician, was born in 1632 and died about 1673. He is said to have published fourteen engraved copybooks. He published some time before 1664 the 'Tutor to Writing and Arithmetic.' His work was for a long time the standard authority on arithmetic; hence the phrase. In an edition of Cocker's 'Pen's Triumphs,' published in 1657, is his portrait, with the following lines:—

> Behold rare Cocker's life-resembling shade,
> Whom envy's clouds have more illustrious made;
> Whose pen and graver have displayed his name,
> With virtuosos' in the book of fame.

In Wing's 'Ephemeris,' 1669, is an advertisement as follows: 'Cocker's Compleat Arithmetician, which hath been nine years his study and practice. The piece so long and so much expected.' Cocker also published a dictionary, of which a posthumous edition (the third) appeared in 1724.

Cock-fighting is supposed to have been introduced into England by the Romans, with whom it was a favourite amusement. It was forbidden by Statute 39 Edward III., again in 1569, and 1654, but has only been vigorously put down within the last forty or fifty years.

Cockney. This word, now exclusively applied to a resident of London, originally signified a milksop, or one who had been over-petted or spoiled. The following passage from Nash's 'Pierce Peniles,' 1592, shows the meaning of the term at that date: 'A young heyre or cockney—that is his mother's darling,' &c. &c.— *Collier's Reprint*, p. 21. Mr. Wedgwood, in his 'Dictionary of Etymology,' says that 'the original meaning of cockney is a child too delicately nurtured—one kept in the house and not hardened by out-door life; hence applied to citizens as opposed to the hardier inhabitants of the country, and in modern times confined to the citizens of London.'

Cocksure. This appears to be a corruption of the French phrase '*À coup sûr*,' which means 'certainly,' 'indubitably,' 'to be sure.'

Cocoa-nut fibre. In preparing the fibre for the manufacture of matting, &c., the husks of cocoa-nuts are steeped in water for six, or even twelve months. They are then beaten with sticks to cause the fibres to separate. Cocoa-nut matting wears longer in wet or damp situations than when used in a dry place.

Coddle. This expressive word is derived from 'codlomb' or 'cadelamb,' a tender delicate lamb, brought up by hand, nursed, and *coddled*. A pet lamb is still called in many parts of England a 'cade lamb.' Mr. Cockayne, in 'Spoon and Sparrow,' p. 26, says 'coddle is the frequentative of *cade*, to pet.'

Codlin. One meaning of the old English word 'coddle' is to boil slightly. A 'codlin' apple is therefore an apple fit for coddling —*i.e.* good for making puddings.

Coffee. The coffee-plant is supposed to be a native of Abyssinia, but its early history is obscure. It was carried from Arabia to Batavia by Wiesser, a Dutchman, and was successfully cultivated there. Some of the plants were sent over to the botanical garden at Amsterdam, from whence the Paris garden obtained one. A cutting was sent from France to Martinique, in 1720, and from that plant the whole of the trees in the West India Islands have been propagated. '1637. There came in my tyme to the College, Oxford, one Nathaniel Conopios, out of Greece. He was the first I ever saw drink coffee, which custom came not into England till thirty years after.'—*Evelyn's Diary*, 1637.

Coffee-houses. The first coffee-house in England was opened in Oxford, by a Jew named Jacobs, in 1650; the first in London was established by a Greek named Pasquet, in George Yard, Lombard Street, in 1652. Coffee-houses were suppressed by proclamation in 1675, but the order was revoked in the following year.

Coffin, from the Greek *cophinus*, a basket. It formerly meant in English the raised crust of a pie. See BAKED MEATS.

> Therefore if you spend
> The red-deer pies i' your house, or sell them forth
> Cast so, that I may have their *coffins*.
> Ben Jonson, *Staple of N.*, ii. 3.

Coffins. Formerly, corpses were buried, being merely wrapped in winding-sheets. Coffins came into use in the sixteenth century. In the Vestry Minutes of St. Helen's, Bishopsgate, under date March 5, 1564, is the following minute :—' *Item.* That none shall be bury'd within the church unless the dead corpse be coffined in wood.'

Cohen. The name, among Israelites, spelled Cohen, Cahn, Cahen, Kahn, or Kohn, signifies that the person bearing it is a descendant of Aaron. Persons of this name, being priests by descent, do not enter Hebrew cemeteries, as their doing so would involve legal pollution. (See Levit. xxi. 1, 11.)

Cohort. A cohort in the Roman army was the tenth of a legion, or from five to six hundred men.

Coke. Coke is to coal what charcoal is to wood. In both cases the gaseous and aqueous fluids, and the bituminous elements, are driven off by heat in close chambers, until nothing but the carbonaceous base remains. Coal produces coke to the extent of fifty-five to seventy-five per cent. of its weight.

Coldstream Guards are so named from the town of that name in Berwickshire, where, in 1660, General Monk raised the regiment known at first as Monk's regiment. When Parliament agreed to give Charles II. a brigade of guards, this corps, under the name of *Coldstream Guards*, was included in it. With the exception of the 1st Regiment of Foot, the Coldstream is the oldest corps in the British service.

Cold Tea. In the early part of the last century this was a cant term for brandy. In the 'Spectator,' 'Tatler,' and 'Guardian,' mention is often made of a 'keg of cold tea,' as an appropriate present for a lady.

Coliseum at Rome. The Coliseum was so named from its being ornamented with a *colossal* statue of Nero. It is stated that the enormous structure was completed in one year by the compulsory labour of 12,000 Jews and Christians.

Colonel. This title is derived from the Spanish. The original name is *Coronel*, which may account for the English pronunciation. Spenser ('State of Ireland') says, ' Afterwards their *Coronell*, named Don Sebastian, came forth to intreat that they might part with their armes like souldiers.'

Colour. There are but three true, or primary colours—red, blue, and green. All other shades are compounds of two of these

K

which are called secondary, or of all three. From these compounds, which can be varied indefinitely, all possible varieties of colour or shade are composed. The three secondary colours are violet, from blue and red; orange, from yellow and red; and green, from blue and yellow.

Coloured Glass. The colours are given to glass by metallic oxides. Ruby-coloured glass is produced by oxide of gold; the finest amber-colour by oxide of silver; blue, by oxide of cobalt; purple, by oxide of manganese; green, by oxide of copper or iron; and the beautiful canary-colour, by oxide of uranium. The colouring power of the oxide of cobalt is so great that a quarter of an ounce will give a blue colour to half a ton of molten glass. Opacity in glass is produced by a mixture of phosphate of lime (burnt bones) and common arsenic.

Coloured Rain is due to the presence of enormous quantities of vegetable pollen, carried occasionally to great distances by the wind.

Collar of S.S. 'The most likely conjecture is that the "S" stands for "Soverayne," the favourite motto of Henry IV. There is ample evidence that the collar of S.S. was originally a badge of the House of Lancaster.'—*Gentleman's Magazine*, 1842–3.

Collects were originally short prayers offered by the minister at the close of each service, in which the previous devotions were *collected* in an epitomised form for more easy recollection.

Collide. This verb, which is generally thought to be an Americanism, is in 'Bailey's Dictionary.' He defines it thus:—'To beat, knock, or beat together; to dash one against another.' The word was also used by Burton (1621), in the 'Anatomy of Melancholy,' part i. sec. 1 :—'The outward being struck or *collided* by a solid body, still strikes the next ayre.' Sir Thomas Browne also (1646) uses it in 'Vulgar Errors':—'The inflammable effluences discharged from the bodies *collided*.' The Latin *collido* means 'to dash together.'

Coltsfoot is the name of a common herb, which is reputed to be beneficial in cases of cold. The name is a corruption of *cold's food*. Botanists have given it the name *Tussilago*, from the Latin *tussis*, a cough, and *laganum*, a lozenge.

Columbine The name of this flower comes from the Latin *columba*, a pigeon, because when the outer petals are pulled off the remainder resembles a pigeon.

'**Come into the Garden, Maud.**' The metre of this exquisite lyric of Tennyson's was looked upon as *absolutely* new when it appeared in 1855. Something very closely resembling it had been, however, used by Dryden, in whose fragmentary poem, 'Of a Scholar and his Mistress,' are the following lines:—

> Shall I marry the man I love?
> And shall I conclude my pains?
> Now bless'd be the Powers above,
> I feel the blood bound in my veins;
> With a lively leap it began to bound,
> And the vapours leave my brains.

Come it strong. Draw it mild. These terms were originally used by the leader of a metropolitan orchestra to violinists when he wished them to play loud or softly.

Comes to grief. Browning has made this classical. In his poem, 'Hervé Riel,' he has the line:—

> Not a spar that comes to grief.

Coming of age. 'It was long ago settled in the courts of law that the full age of twenty-one years is completed on the day preceding the anniversary of a person's birth; that if born just before midnight on January 1, he may do any legal act just after midnight on December 31, though not having *lived* twenty-one years by nearly forty-eight hours.'—*Notes and Queries*, Nov. 1862. Thus, on 'a devise, the question was whether the testator was of full age or not, and the evidence was that he was born on January 1, *in the afternoon*, and died *in the morning* of December 31, twenty-one years after. And it was held that he was of full age, for that there shall be no fraction of a day.'—*Law Dictionary*.

Coming to the scratch. This was originally a phrase used by boxers. In the prize-ring it was usual to make a distinct mark or *scratch* in the turf, dividing the ring into two equal parts. 'To come to the scratch' meant to walk to the boundary to meet the antagonist.

'**Comin' through the Rye.**' The original version of this song was entered at Stationers' Hall, June 29, 1796. It was sung by Mrs. Henley, at the Royal Circus, in a pantomime called 'Harlequin Mariner.' The opening lines are:—

> If a body meet a body going to the fair,
> If a body kiss a body, need a body care?

Commandments. The Commandments were set up in churches in 1564, by the order of Queen Elizabeth; 'but there is no authority whatever for placing the Apostles' Creed and the Lord's Prayer in churches.'—*Notes and Queries*, January 25, 1868.

Commercial Terms. Mr. Burgon says that the Lombards introduced most of the commercial terms now in use; and he instances debtor, creditor, cash, usance, bank, bankrupt, journal, diary, ditto, and £ s. d., which originally stood for *libri*, *soldi* and *denari*.

Comme il faut. No French phrase is more commonly heard in England than this. It means 'as it should be.' Thus we say, 'She behaved with the greatest propriety; quite *comme il faut*.'

Commodity. This word originally meant convenience, advantage, benefit, or profit. Thus Ben Jonson speaks of the 'commodity of a footpath'; and Hooker says, 'Men seek their own commodity.'

Commodity of brown paper. This phrase is very common among the old dramatists. It always has the meaning of a custom among young rakes of the period, when in want of money, of buying merchandise upon credit, which they sold for ready money, at a loss. Thus in Green's 'Quip for an Upstart Count,' we find, 'So that if he borrow an hundred pounds, he shall have forty in silver, and threescore in wares, as lutestrings, hobby horses, or brown paper.' So, in 'Measure for Measure,' iv. 3, we have, 'First here's young Master Rash, he's in for a commodity of brown paper and old ginger, nine score and seventeen pounds'; that is, he is charged 197*l*. for a lot of stuff not worth more, probably, than half the money. Nares, from whom this article is quoted, well says, 'Such schemes have been heard of in later times.'

Comparisons are odorous. This phrase is generally, but wrongly, attributed to Mrs. Malaprop. It was written by Shakespeare, and occurs in 'Much Ado about Nothing,' act iii. sc. 5. What Mrs. Malaprop really *did* say ('The Rivals,' act iv. sc. 2) was—'No caparisons, miss, if you please; caparisons don't become a young woman.'

Compete. Familiar as this word now seems, it is of very modern introduction. It does not appear in the dictionaries earlier than 1820. It is of Scottish origin.

Competitor means one who strives to attain the same object. It is now always used to signify a rival, but it formerly meant just the opposite, being used for one who assisted in carrying out some joint intention. It is so used by Shakespeare in 'Antony and Cleopatra,' v. 1:—

That thou my brother, my *competitor*
In top of all design, my *mate* in empire,
Friend and *companion* in the front of war.

Complected. A common Americanism. 'Pale *complected*,' 'dark *complected*,' mean, respectively, of a pale, or of a dark complexion.

Compos mentis, Latin, meaning 'of sound mind.' *Non compos mentis* is 'not of sound mind.'

Comrades. From the Spanish military term *camarades*; that is, men who sleep in the same *camera*, or chamber.

Conceited formerly meant inclined to jest, or to be playful, and is so constantly used by the old dramatists.

Concerning Snakes in Ireland. This phrase is constantly cropping up as a genuine quotation. It, however, does not refer to Ireland in any way, but to Iceland. In a translation of Horrebow's work, 'The Natural History of Iceland,' London, 1758, chapter xlii. is headed 'Concerning Owls,' and is as follows:—'There are no owls of any kind in the whole island.' Chapter lxxii. is entitled 'Concerning Snakes,' and the entire chapter is as follows:—'No snakes of any kind are to be met with throughout the whole of the island.' The application of the phrase to Ireland probably at first arose from a printer's error.

Conclave, from the Latin *con*, and *clavis*, a key, meaning a room that can be locked up. The original signification is the locked-up apartment in which the cardinals meet to elect the pope.

Concrete. The first concreted foundation of any magnitude was that of the Post Office on the east side of St. Martin's-le-Grand. 'When the ground was cleared, the site was a maze of cesspools and wells of various depths, interspersed with brick foundations of various ages from the time of the Romans to that of the great fire.' Sir Sidney Smirke, despairing of a foundation upon the ordinary plan, caused 'an open flooring, many feet above the level,' to be made, and 'from that height was cast down the concrete mixture, that by heat, expansion and adhesion, formed one solid rock and main foundation, the entire length and breadth of this vast and ponderous edifice.'—*Elmes, C. E.*

Conger Eel. The conger eel is the king eel. The name is from the Icelandish *kongr*, a king.

Congregation. The largest congregation ever assembled to listen to a preacher was on October 7, 1857, the day appointed as a fast at the time of the Indian Mutiny, when the Rev. C. H. Spurgeon preached at the Crystal Palace to 23,000 persons.

Congress. English writers on American affairs speak of *The* Congress, using the definite article. This form has long been disused by Americans, who always speak of 'Congress' as we do of 'Parliament,' as though it were a proper name.

Connecticut, the American State, is so called from the Indian name of its principal river.

Connoisseur, Dilettante. 'The "connoisseur" is "one who knows," as opposed to the dilettante, who only "thinks that he knows." The connoisseur is one *cognisant* of the true principles of art, and can fully appreciate them. He is of a higher grade than the *amateur*, and more nearly approaches the artist, whose rules of action he is familiar with, but does not practise.'—*Fairholt.*

Conquest. This word is applied in Scotland to all real property acquired by purchase, donation, or even exchange. See PURCHASE.

Consequence. This is an ill-used word. Its primary meaning is something that follows or results from some cause or principle. The following quotation from South is a good example of the proper use of the word :—' That which brought sin into the world must, by necessary *consequence*, bring in sorrow too.' Yet the word is in common use in the sense of *importance*, with which it has no affinity whatever. We hear people spoken of as 'persons of consequence'; and the phrase 'it's of no consequence' is on every one's lips, but both phrases are wrong. Dr. Johnson, perhaps, seems to justify the usage, by giving as a definition, 'Importance, moment,' but he is singularly unfortunate in the quotation he cites in support, and which, by curtailing, he has considerably modified. The full sentence is:—

<blockquote>
But 'tis strange,
And oftentimes to win us to our harm,
The instruments of darkness tell us truths ;
Win us with honest trifles, to betray us
To deepest consequence.
</blockquote>

Johnson, however, only quotes the words that are here printed in *italics*. In relying upon this, there seems every reason to think, with Mr. E. S. Gould ('Good English,' New York, Widdleton, 1871), that Johnson is wrong. By *consequence*, Shakespeare undoubtedly meant *result*, and the word 'deepest' shows it. What the poet meant was that the 'instruments of darkness' lead us, unconsciously, to actions which have the 'deepest,' that is the *most important,* 'consequences' or *results.* Thus it seems that Shakespeare used the word in its very strictest sense, and that Dr. Johnson misunderstood him. The *result,* or *consequence,* is that the language has been vitiated by a word being generally used in an inconsequential and improper sense.

Conservative. Canning seems to have been the first to use this word in a political sense. In a speech at Liverpool in March, 1820, speaking of the middle class, he said, 'Of that important and *conservative* portion of society, I know not where I could look for a better specimen than I now see before me.' 'The Quarterly Review,' January, 1830, has, 'The Tory, which might with more propriety be called the *Conservative* Party.'

Consols. This familiar word is an abbreviation of the term *consolidated annuities,* a class of stock of which a large portion of the British National Debt is composed. The interest is three per cent., and the market price of *consols* is an index to the value of all other securities. The accent is on the final syllable.

Conspiracy has been defined as an agreement for an unlawful purpose, or to effect an unlawful purpose by lawful means.

Constable. A Constable was originally an officer of dignity attached to the king's person. He was the *Comes-stabuli,* the Count of the Stable, corresponding to the modern Master of the Horse. Afterwards the Constable became master of outlying fortresses, in which sense we still use the word to designate the *Constable of the Tower,* the *Constable of Chester Castle,* &c. In this way the Constable became the officer of the king's peace in any district to which he might be appointed. Petty, or deputy constables, were afterwards appointed for each parish or hamlet, and these officers are now almost the only representatives of an office which was formerly of vice-regal dignity.

Constant. Probably this is the word 'consistent' with the middle syllable omitted. Constancy and consistency are certainly closely allied in meaning.

Contagion means disease communicable by *contact,* either with the diseased person himself, or his clothing, or something that he has been in contact with. Infection is disease, propagated by contamination of the atmosphere by malaria; by the effluvium from the bodies of diseased persons, or from decaying or putrid animal or vegetable matter.

Contango. This is a Stock Exchange slang corruption of *continuation*. It is used to denote the premium paid by a buyer of stock to the seller, when, upon settling day, he wishes the bargain to remain open.

Contemporary, or Cotemporary. The modern use of 'cotemporary' is condemned by most good authorities. The rule seems to be that before a consonant the prefix *con* is proper, as in contemporary and consequent, but before a vowel the *n* is omitted, as in coeval, co-operate, coincident, coexistent, &c.

Continent. This word was formerly used in the sense of continuous, or connected. Thus Brerewood says, 'The north-east part of Asia, if not *continent* with the west side of America, is the least disjoined by sea.' And Verstegan, 'Restitution,' &c. edit. 1655, p. 78, 'That our isle of Albion hath been *continent* with Gallia hath been the opinion of divers, as of Antonius Volscus, Dominicus Marius Niger,' &c.

Control. This word has greatly changed in meaning. Originally it meant to *check* a man by keeping a *counter-roll*, or duplicate of accounts of transactions with him. The word in use for the same purpose at the present day is *counterfoil*, which is the old name for the portion of a wooden tally kept in the Exchequer; the original or *stock* being held by the person advancing money. See TALLY.

Conundrum. This word appears to have formerly had a wider signification than at present. Bailey defines it as a 'quaint expression, word, or sentence.'

Cony, or Coney, is the old English name for the rabbit. It is used in the Bible as the translation of a Hebrew word which certainly does not mean the rabbit. The cony of the Old Testament is thought to have been the daman, or ashkoko, an animal similar in form and size to the guinea pig, but having very distinct characteristics allying it to the elephant and rhinoceros. Cuvier said, that although damans are thickly covered with fur, they are, excepting the horns, little else than rhinoceroses in miniature. They are common in Syria and Palestine, sheltering themselves in the holes of rocks, but not burrowing, for which its feet are not adapted. See RABBIT.

Cook, Kitchen. 'Our words cook and kitchen are the Anglo-Saxon *côc* and *cycene*, and have nothing to do with the French *cuisine*.'—*Wright, Domestic Manners of the Middle Ages.*

Cookery Book. The earliest known cookery book was printed at Venice in 1475. It is in Latin, and its full title is 'Platinæ de Obsoniis et Honestâ Voluptate et Valetudine Libra.'

Coolies are a distinct tribe of aborigines inhabiting the hill country in India. From many of them being employed as labourers in Bombay, the name is now used by Europeans in Hindustan to denote labourers in general, whether natives or emigrants from China or other tropical or semi-tropical countries.

Cooper. A cooper is one who makes coops. Coop is a general term, meaning a something to confine, or to *contain*. Formerly the word coop was used for a cask or barrel to contain liquids. The Germans still use *küpe* for a tub or vat, and *küpfer* for one who makes tubs. We still say 'cooper' for a tub-maker, and the word coop, a tub, still remains in our dictionaries, but it is not used.

Cooper is a word of modern introduction to denote a liquor of intermediate strength between porter and stout. The name is said to have arisen from the practice at large breweries of allowing the coopers a certain daily quantity of stout and porter, which the men mixed to obtain a drink of equal strength.

Coping Stone is *capping* stone.

Copper derives its name from *Cyprus*, where it was first discovered by the ancient Greeks.

Copperas, sometimes called 'green vitriol.' This is a sulphate of iron, and contains no copper whatever. When exposed to the air, it effloresces, and, absorbing oxygen, changes from green to a reddish colour, whence it is called in French *couperose*, of which the English name is a corruption.

Copper Coinage. 'The earliest Hebrew coins were composed chiefly of copper, and the metallic currency of Rome consisted of the impure copper called *aes* until B.C. 269, when silver was first coined.'—*Jevons*. The present British bronze coinage was issued on December 1, 1860, superseding the wretched coppers which had been current up to that date.

Copper-plate Printing. The date of the invention of copper-plate printing can only be inferred. Evelyn, in the 'Abridgments of Specifications of Patents,' Printing, p. 26, says, 'The art of engraving and working from plates of copper, which we call prints, was not yet appeared, or born with us until about the year 1490.'

Copper Sheathing. The first ship to which a sheathing of copper was applied was His Majesty's ship *Alarm*, in 1761. In a newspaper of October 14, 1765, is the following :—'It is now believed that the sheathing of ships of war with copper will become a general rule; for though the expense be great at first, yet upon the whole, it is said to be cheaper, as the worms can never injure them.'

Copy, from the Latin *copia*, abundance. It was frequently used in the phrase, *copiam scripturæ facere*, to impart the knowledge of a writing; and eventually *copia* came to signify a transcript of a writing, or, as we say in English, a copy.

Copyhold. So called because the holder has no deeds except a *copy* of the rolls made by the steward of a manor.

Copyright. The entering a book or other work at Stationers' Hall does not *confer* a copyright; it is merely evidence that the copyright—which is inherent in the work itself—is the property of the author, or his assign, whose name is registered in the books of the company. No action, however, can be brought for infringement of copyright unless the book is 'entered.' The fee payable on 'entering' a work is 5s. A 'certificate of entry' costs another 5s. Copyright endures for the life of the author, and for seven years after his death; but if that time should terminate within forty-two years from the date of first publication, then the right is to endure until forty-two years have elapsed. In the case of works published after the author's death, the copyright is the property of the owner of the manuscript for forty-two years from the date of the first publication.

Copyright of private Letters. 'The receiver of a private letter is the owner of the paper upon which it is written, but the copyright belongs to the writer, and it cannot be published without his consent.'—*Wharton*.

Coquette. Mr. Wedgwood thinks this word comes from the French *coqueter*, to call, as a cock to his hens; to strut and swagger as a cock does among hens. A 'coquette' is one who lays herself out for the admiration of the male sex, as a cock does among his females.

Coral. The origin of this word is very poetical. It is from two Greek words signifying the 'daughter of the sea.'

Corbleu. A profane French interjection. It is a softening of *Corps de Dieu*.

Core. The 'core' of an apple or other fruit is the *cœur*—the heart.

Cork is the outer bark of the evergreen oak, *Quercus suber*. It is not the true bark or skin of the tree through which the sap circulates, but a spongy layer of cellular tissue formed outside it. After a few years, this outer covering falls off. In Spain and Portugal, the great cork-growing countries, this process is anticipated, for the bark is removed every six or eight years, the trees continuing to yield good crops for 100 to 150 years. There is a fine specimen of the cork tree in the deer park at Hampton Court. Corks as stoppers were in use in Cato's time (201 B.C.). 'Lighter than cork' is an Horatian comparison. The peculiar cork stoppers for champagne bottles were invented by a Benedictine monk named Perignon at the Abbey of Hautvilliers, about A.D. 1670. The name cork is derived from *cortex*, the bark of a tree.

Corn. In England this word is applied alike to wheat, barley, rye, and oats. In Scotland its use is almost confined to oats. In the United States it is exclusively used to designate maize, or Indian corn; other cereals being spoken of collectively as 'grain,' and wheat being known as 'bread-stuff.'

Cornelian, the stone, so called from *cornu*, a horn, from its transparency resembling that of a horn or a finger-nail.

Cornet, the musical instrument, is from *cornu*, the Latin word for horn. Literally, cornet is a small horn.

Cornish Names:—

> By Tre, Pol, and Pen,
> You shall know the Cornish men.

Fuller, after quoting this old proverb, says :—' These three words are the dictionary of such surnames as are originally Cornish, and though nouns in sense, I may fitly term them prepositions. *Tre* signifieth a town; hence Trefry, Trelawny, Trevannion, &c. *Pol* signifieth a head; hence Polwheel. *Pen* signifieth a top; hence Pentire, Penrose, Penkevil, &c.'

Cornwall. The ancient British name of this county was *Cernyw*, a name they must have received from the Latin *cornu*, a horn. The Romans, who traded here for tin, called it *Cornubia*, which name it bore until the Saxons imposed the name of *Weales* upon the British, who retreated into the fastnesses west of the Severn and the Dee. The latter portion of the name Cornubia was then dropped, and the word Wales substituted, forming the name 'Corn-Wales,' of which the present, Cornwall, is a corruption.

Coroners. The name of 'coroner' is from the Latin *corona*, a crown, and it implies that a coroner represents the Sovereign, in the performance of the duties of his office. There were coroners in 925, but it is not known what their duties were. The office of coroner as now existing was created by Act of Parliament, in 1276, in the reign of Edward I. A coroner is the only officer known to English law who can investigate a crime, and examine witnesses upon oath in reference thereto, anterior to any accusation being made against any person of having committed it. All other magistrates must have an accused person actually arrested and brought before them, to enable them to adjudicate.

Cosher is a term used by the Jews to designate such food as, according to their law, it is right or proper for them to eat. *Tryfa*, on the contrary, signifies that which is forbidden. The word *tryfa* literally signifies that which has been torn by wild beasts.

Costermonger. Originally, a seller of *costards*, a fine description of apples brought from Holland, the Dutch name of which is from *kost*, food, and *œord*, nature; that is, 'natural food.' Costermongers are now itinerant dealers in fruit, fish, and vegetables. It is said that there are 30,000 costermongers in London alone. The term is a very old one. Ben Jonson, in the 'Alchymist' (iv. 1), has—

> Her father was an Irish *costar monger*.

Cosy. This comfortable word is of recent introduction. It is not found in any of the older dictionaries, and even Latham can find no example of its use earlier than in 'The Recreations of a Country Parson.' The word seems to have been derived from the Scotch. 'Cosiely' is found in Allan Ramsay, and Burns has a line in the 'Holy Fair':—

> While some are *cozie* i' the neuk.

Coterie. Coterie is derived from the Latin *quot*? 'how many?' or 'how much?' A coterie, originally, was a company of merchants who united for some special venture or speculation, each contributing his *quota* of money or goods, and receiving his *quota* of profit. In the present day a 'coterie' is an exclusive or select number of persons, combined for some special purpose; but the word seems to convey the notion that the members of a coterie have some intrigue on hand, or some sinister purpose in view.

Cotswold Hills. So named from the Anglo-Saxon *cote* and *wold*, as meaning a place where there are no growing woods.

Cottage. 'A cottage is a house without land belonging to it.'—4 Edward I. Stat. 1. By the Stat. 31 Eliz. c. 7, 'No man may build a *house* unless he lay four acres of land to it'; so that a cottage originally meant a house that had not that quantity of land belonging to it.

Cotton. This word is adopted from the Arabic *kotun*, meaning the same article. In Egypt it is called *gotun*. The Spanish *algodon* is evidently the same word, with the article *al* prefixed. No fibre can be spun into yarn of such extreme fineness as that of cotton. Messrs. Houldsworth, of Manchester, have produced yarn so fine that a single pound of it would measure 4,000 miles in length.—*Chambers's Encyclopædia*. In 1721 an Act of Parliament was passed imposing a penalty of 20*l*. for selling calico or cotton-cloth. Before 1774, the use of chintz or printed calico for dresses was illegal; and persons were frequently fined for wearing them. Eighty persons were convicted in 1768, before the Lord Mayor of London, for 'wearing chintz gowns, and were fined 5*l*. each.'

Cotton to. 'To "*cotton to* one" is a cant phrase in the United States, signifying to take a liking to one, to fancy him; literally, to stick to him, as cotton-wool does to clothes.'—*Ogilvie*.

Countergate. In the 'Merry Wives of Windsor,' iii. 3, Shakespeare uses this word:—

> Thou might'st as well say, I love to walk by the *countergate*, which is as hateful to me as the smell of a lime kiln.

Counter here evidently means 'prison.' Debtors' prisons in London were formerly called *counters*, or *compters*. There were several of them: as the 'Poultry Compter,' the 'Giltspur Street Compter,' the 'Wood Street Compter,' &c. The atmosphere of prisons in pre-Howard days was very offensive; hence Falstaff's objection to pass the gate, the *reek* from which he thinks as objectionable as that of a lime-kiln.

Counterpane is a mispronunciation of the French *contrepoint*, the name applied to producing patterns by the process of needlework called 'quilting.'

Counties of Towns. There are twelve cities and five towns in England which are 'Counties Corporate,' or counties of themselves, and which have consequently their own sheriffs. These cities are London, Chester, Bristol, Coventry, Canterbury, Exeter, Gloucester, Lichfield, Lincoln, Norwich, Worcester, York. The towns are Kingston-upon-Hull, Nottingham, Newcastle-upon-Tyne, Poole, and Southampton.

Country-dance has nothing to do with the country or with country people. It is from the French *contre-danse*; a dance in which the partners stand *contre*, or opposite to each other.

Coup d'état (pronounced *koo-day-tah*). This French term means a sudden stroke of policy whereby the existing state of government is upset or subverted. Such was the celebrated act of Napoleon III., when, on December 2, 1852, under the pretext of saving society, he, with the aid of his army, virtually destroyed the Republic which he, as President, had sworn to conserve. The English language, happily, has no name for such acts.

Coup d'œil. A French term used in art. It means as much as may be comprehended by the eye at one view; the general effect of a picture as seen at a glance.

Couple. There are few words in the English language so frequently misapplied as the unfortunate word *couple*. The root of the word is a Hebrew noun, meaning 'a fetter,' but we get it from the Latin *copula*, a joining, and it should never be used except in the sense of *two joined together*. A man and his wife are properly 'a couple'; so are two hounds, when strapped together; but two eggs are not a couple; two sovereigns are not a couple; nor are two days a 'couple of days.' Two rabbits, or two ducks, when alive and running about, are not couples; but when killed, and tied in pairs for sale, they become couples. The word 'pair,' or the numeral 'two,' should be used in all cases when speaking or writing of two things alike, but not united. See Brace.

Coupon. Coupons are certificates of interest attached to transferable bonds, each certificate having thereon the date it becomes due. There are usually as many certificates as there are payments of interest to be made before the principal becomes due. The name *coupon* is from the French *couper*, 'to cut,' and they are so called because as they become due they are *cut off* and presented for payment.

Court-cards. This is a corruption of 'coat-cards,' *i.e.* cards having *coated*, or dressed, figures; as, King, Queen, Knave. Ben Jonson uses the phrase 'coat-card.'

Court Circular. The few paragraphs of news respecting the movements of Royalty are supplied to the daily papers by an officer at Court specially appointed for the purpose. The custom was instituted in 1803, by George III., who was annoyed at the incorrect statements in reference to Royal movements which the papers inserted. The name 'Court Circular' was, however, not given until 1813. The first Court Newsman was a Mr. Doane, whose son succeeded him and held the office until 1863, when he retired. The present holder of the office is Mr. Beard. He has to supply the papers with daily records of the proceedings of the Queen, the Prince of Wales, and the Court generally; and also to report levees, drawing-rooms, State-balls and concerts, the meetings of the Cabinet, deputations to Ministers, and any other information which the Government wish to be made public. The 'Court Circular' *newspaper* has nothing whatever of an official character.

Court of Pie-poudre. All the dictionaries say that this Court, which was anciently held in fairs and markets, was 'so called from the dusty feet of the suitors.' This is not *strictly* accurate; the name is derived direct from the old French *pied puldreaux*, 'a pedlar.' The Court was, therefore, the Court of such small itinerant dealers as frequented these marts. The derivation of *pie-poudre* from 'dusty foot' is therefore only *secondary*; not *from the dusty feet of the suitors*, but because most of the suitors were persons *the name of whose calling* was derived from French words signifying *dusty feet*.

Cousin German, applied to first cousins, signifies that they are from the same *germ*, or origin. Mr. Fox Talbot thinks that the word 'cousin' was formerly *consang*, from the Latin *con*, union, and *sanguis*, blood.

Cove. Slang for 'a man.' This word has so bad a reputation that it is not admitted into modern dictionaries. It appears always to have been *slang*; for Bailey defines it thus:—'A little harbour for boats; also a man (*cant*).' He also has it in the compound 'Abram-cove, a naked or poor man (*cant*).'

Covent Garden. The market in London so called was so named from its having been originally the garden of the Convent of St. Peter. The square was erected in 1633, but it has since been rebuilt.

Coventry. The name of this city is not derived from 'convent,' as some suppose, but from *Cune*, or *Coven*, the name of the stream on which it is built. Drayton, who lived in the neighbourhood, says, in his 'Polyolbion,' xiii. p. 922:—

<blockquote>With *Cune*, a great while missed
Through *Coventry* from whence her name at first did raise.</blockquote>

And, in a note, 'otherwise *Cune-tre*, that is, the town upon *Cune*.' Skinner also says, '*Vel à Coven fluvio, nam in diplomate prioratus dicitur Cuentford.*'

Coverlet is the French *couvre-lit* (*lit*, a bed).

Covey (of birds). This is a corruption of the French noun *couvée*, a brood; the French noun is derived from the verb *couver*, to hatch. The word is pronounced *kuv'-ve*.

Coward. This word is probably derived from the Norman-French *coue*, the tail, in allusion to the fact that most animals when frightened put the tail between their legs. Some have thought it a corruption of 'cow-herd,' and say that it was a term of reproach used by the Normans to the Anglo-Saxons; but this is improbable, because the term 'cow-herd' is pure Saxon, and would not be likely to be familiar to the Norman invaders. Coward in heraldry is applied to 'a lion or other beast having his tail hanging between his hind legs.'

Cow-catcher. Cow-catchers are instruments fixed in front of locomotives in America; so that if cattle stray upon the railroad, they are caught on a sort of shelf, and so prevented from getting under the wheels, and endangering the train.

Cowl. The name 'cowl' is applied to the revolving top of a chimney, or to the ventilators of the drying-chambers of hop-kilns or malthouses, from its supposed likeness to the cowl worn by monks.

Cowper. Mr. Fisher, of Waterford, writing to 'Notes and Queries' (April 4, 1874), says:—'My wife saw some years ago a letter from the poet Cowper to the late Mrs. Charlotte Smith, the poetess, in which he stated that the pronunciation of his name was *Cooper*.'

Coxcomb. 'This word tells us nothing by its spelling, but it did when spelt, as it used to be, *cock's-comb*; when the [imitation] comb of a cock was a token which fools or jesters wore.'—*Trench*.

Coxswain. The word *kog*, in all the Scandinavian languages, and in the Dutch, means a ship, or boat; the Welsh word *cwch* has the same meaning. The idea conveyed by the word is something round and hollow, and we have this idea in the English word *keg*, and the Scottish word *cog*. The word *coxswain*, therefore, is, etymologically, a young man (swain) who has charge of a *kog*, or boat. We have the tautological term *cock-boat*, in which each syllable has the same meaning. See 'King Lear':—

> The fishermen that walk upon the beach
> Appear like mice, and yon tall anchoring bark
> Diminished to her *cock*. Her *cock* a buoy
> Almost too small for sight.

Craft. This word, now signifying cunning, evil, subtlety, fraud, or trickery, formerly meant skill, talent, or ability. Thus, smith-craft was the trade of a blacksmith; metre-craft was the art of poetry; and leech-craft the science of medicine. We still retain the word craft as a generic name for a sailing vessel employed in a trade or craft; in the compounds witchcraft and handicraft; and in apprentices' indentures, where a boy is bound for a term of years that he may learn the art, trade, or *craft* of his master. Deceit was anciently called *overcraft*, in the same way in which we still speak of a man as being over-cunning or over-reaching.

Cram, Ram. There seems some affinity in these two words. Shakespeare uses them in precisely the same sense:—

> You *cram* these words into mine ears;

and

> *Ram* thou thy faithful tidings in mine ears.

Cravat. This word is derived from a regiment of *Croats*, in the service of Austria, part of whose uniform consisted of linen bands round their necks. The French raised a regiment in the seventeenth century and adopted the Croat uniform. The regiment bore the name of 'The Royal *Cravat*.'

Cray is the English form of the French *craye*, or *craie*, chalk. We have the same root in the word *crayon*. The river *Cray* rises in the chalk hills of Surrey, and gives its name to Croydon (anciently Craydiden), Foot's Cray, St. Mary's Cray, Paul's Cray, and Crayford.

Crayfish. There is no doubt that this is the French *écrevisse*. ' Trace, however, the word through three successive spellings; *krevys* (Lydgate), *crefish* (Gascoigne), and *craifish* (Holland), and the chasm between écrevisse and crayfish is bridged over.'—*Trench*.

Creole. A Creole is a person born in the West Indies or South America *of European parents*. The name is often erroneously applied to persons of mixed white and black parentage. There are distinct names for each degree of admixture. The offspring of a pure white and a pure black is a Mulatto. See MULATTO.

Crescent, from the Latin *crescens*, to grow. This word had originally no reference to shape. It was applied to the moon when in a state of apparent increase in size, in distinction to the word *wane*, which denoted its apparent decrease. Not long ago a newspaper writer spoke of the 'crescent moon' as being visible at six o'clock in the morning which is an impossibility, as it is only the

L

waning moon which can be seen at that time. The 'crescent' has nothing to do with the Turks or their religion. It was the ancient symbol of the city of Byzantium. Warburton, in 'The Crescent and the Cross,' 1845, vol. ii. p. 356, says it arose from the fact that 'Philip, the father of Alexander the Great, meeting with great difficulties in carrying on the siege of this city, set the workmen one dark night to undermine the walls. Luckily for the besieged, a young moon suddenly appearing, revealed the design, which accordingly miscarried; in acknowledgment whereof, the Byzantines erected a statue to Diana, and the crescent became the symbol of their city.'

Cribbage. This is an old game at cards. Hall, 'Horæ Vicaræ,' 1646, p. 150, says, 'For cardes, the philologie of them is not for an essay. A man's fancy would be sum'd up in cribbage.'

Cricket. The earliest known mention of this game occurs in an affidavit made anno 40 Elizabeth, by John Derrick of Guildford, in reference to a 'A Garden withelde from the Towne,' in which the deponent says :—'When he was a scholler in the free schole of Guildeford, he and severall of his fellowes did runne and play there at crickett and other plaies.' Nares gives as one of the definitions of this word 'a stool with four legs.' In an old play, the 'Maids of More-Clacke' (1609), is the following dialogue, which shows that a stool of this kind was the original 'wicket' :—

Tutch. What do you call it, when the ball, sir, hits the *stool?*
Filbon. Why, '*out.*'
Tutch. Even so am I; out; out of all hope ever to come in to crown my poor age at his table.

The word cricket is mentioned in the old song, 'Of noble race was Shenkin.' The date is uncertain, but it is probably of the seventeenth century at latest. The stanza in which it occurs runs thus :—

> He was the prettiest fellow,
> At football or at *cricket*;
> At hunting chase, or nimble race,
> How featly he could prick it.

Some authorities have contended that the word 'cricket' is a diminutive of the Saxon *cricc*, a staff. The ball was originally struck by a *criccette*, or short staff or stick.

Crimson. The Italian name for 'kermes' is *cremisi*, hence crimson. See CARMINE.

Crinoline, from Latin *crinis*, hair, so called from expansive skirts having been originally made from horsehair.

Cripple, from the Anglo-Saxon *creopere*, a creeper.

Crochet. A French term applied to a certain kind of knitting. The word is the diminutive of *croc*, a hook, and means literally the *little hook* with which the work is performed. It is pronounced *cro-shay*. The English word 'crotchet' is from the same root. It signifies some *crooked* fancy or whim.

Crocketts on the angles of Gothic spires were not mere ornaments, but were intended to do duty as ladders. In Sir Christopher Wren's report to the Bishop of Rochester on the state of Westminster Abbey, he describes the spire he intended to place on the central tower, and says:—' The angles of pyramids [*i.e.* spires] in Gothic architecture were usually enriched with the flower the botanists call *calceolus*, which is a proper form to help workmen to ascend on the outside to amend any defects without raising large scaffolds upon every slight occasion.'

Crone. This word, usually applied contemptuously to a disagreeable, ill-tempered old woman, is derived from an old Anglo-Saxon term for a ewe that has lost her teeth.

Crony is from the Teutonic *knonen*, to whisper, to tell secrets.

Crooked Money. The common belief that crooked money is lucky is of ancient date, as may be seen from the following extracts from 'Fox's Book of Martyrs':—' He sent to him his servant secretly .... with a *bowed* [*i.e.* bent] *groat*, in token of his good heart towards him,' &c., A.D. 1562. ' Also when she had *bowed* a piece of silver, to a saint, for the health of her child,' &c., A.D. 1584.

Croquet. This is the old French word for a bandy or hockey-stick. The circumflex over the *e* in the final syllable is improper, and is not used in the original French word.

Crosier. 'A crosier is the pastoral staff of an archbishop, and is to be distinguished from the pastoral staff of a bishop; the latter terminating in an ornamented *crook*, while the *crosier* always terminates in a cross.'—*Hook's Church Dictionary.* The crosier is always carried before an archbishop. *He* carries a *crook* like other bishops.

Cross. The Roman Catholic, and all the Protestant churches, adopt what is called the *Latin cross*, as an emblem. The lower limb of this cross is considerably longer than the other three. The Greek cross has all the limbs of equal length. St. Andrew's cross consists of two shafts of equal length, crossed diagonally in the form of the letter X. The Greek cross is sometimes called the cross of St. George, and is blended with that of St. Andrew and St. Patrick to form the flag called the Union Jack.

Crosspatch. Patch was at one time a term of contempt. It did not, as Nares suggests, necessarily mean a fool, but signified what we now mean by a *contemptible* fellow. Shakespeare has ('Midsummer Night's Dream') :—

<blockquote>A crew of patches, base mechanicals.</blockquote>

Crosspatch is the only remnant of the word. It is very expressive of a cross, ill-tempered, disagreeable person.

Cross Posts. In the year 1720 the delivery of letters was greatly facilitated by the institution of 'cross posts,' a system introduced by Mr. Ralph Allen, whose services in this respect are immortalised by Pope, in the lines :—

<blockquote>Let humble Allen, with an awkward shame,
Do good by stealth, and blush to find it fame.</blockquote>

Crotchet. In the 'Ladies' Dictionary,' 1694, this word is defined as 'the hook whereto ladies chain their watches, seals, and other matters.' From this we get the word 'crotchet,' as the name of the note in music, in allusion to its hook-like form.

Crouch. This word is corrupted from the old English word *couch*, 'to conceal.' 'Fierce tigers *couched* around.'—*Dryden.* 'And thu schalt mak him *cowche*, as doth a quaile.'—*Reliq. Antiq.* p. 69.

Crowbar. Probably from the old British word *cro*, a curve. If so, the original form of the word would be *croed-bar*, that is, a 'curved bar,' which is exactly applicable; the modern 'crow-bar' being curved to make it more effective as a lever.

Crowd. This was an old English name for a fiddle or violin:

<blockquote>Hark how the minstrels 'gin to shrill aloud,
Their merry music that resounds from far;
The pipe, the tabor, and the trembling <i>crowd</i>,
That well agree withouten breach or jar.—<i>Spenser.</i></blockquote>

This word in America is used as a synonym for company, or assembly. In a discussion in the House of Representatives at Washington, Mr. Elliot, of Kentucky, proposed the Rev. John Morris for Chaplain to the House, and said :—' He is just the man to pray for such a *crowd* as this.'—*Bartlett, Dictionary of Americanisms*, Boston, 1859.

Crown. The Imperial State Crown, worn by Queen Victoria at her coronation, weighs 39 oz. 5 dwts. It was made by Rundell and Bridge, in 1838. It contains the famous ruby given to the

Black Prince by the King of Castile, in 1367, and a very large sapphire, bought by George IV. Besides these, there are 16 other sapphires, 11 emeralds, 4 rubies, 1,363 brilliant diamonds, 1,273 rose diamonds, 147 table diamonds, 4 drop-shaped pearls, and 273 other pearls.

Crucible, from the Latin *crux*, genitive *crucis*, a cross. Melting-pots were originally marked with a cross, from a superstition that evil spirits would thereby be prevented from marring the chemical operation. Hence the name.

Crumpet is said to be derived from 'crumb-bread'; that is, bread baked without crust. There was an Anglo-Saxon word, *crompeht*, wrinkled, which survives in our word 'crumpled,' which some have thought to be the origin of crumpet; and Mr. Fosbroke, in his 'British Monachism,' says that pancakes, or 'crumcakes,' as they were called, were eaten at Barking Nunnery before the Dissolution, and suggests that this may be the derivation of 'crumpet'; but 'crumb-bread' seems the most probable.

Crusted Wines. The *crust* deposited on the sides of bottles containing wine is composed of *argol*, which is a crude cream of tartar, sparingly soluble in alcoholic fluids. As the wine matures —that is, as the sugar in it is converted into alcohol—the wine becomes less capable of holding the *argol* in solution, and it is consequently deposited in the form of *crust*.

Crystal or Flint Glass. The pure colourless glass which is now called 'flint glass' was formerly made only at Venice, and when the manufacture was first brought to England, the name of 'Venice Glass' was for a long time retained. Stowe tells us that 'Venice Glass' was first made in England in the time of Queen Elizabeth.

Crystal Palace. The name 'Crystal Palace' was applied by Douglas Jerrold, in 'Punch,' to the building in Hyde Park in which the Great Exhibition of 1851 was held. After its close, the materials of which it was composed were sold to a Company, for 70,000*l.*, and removed to the present site at Sydenham. The first column was erected on August 5, 1852, and the 'Palace' was opened by the Queen, June 10, 1854.

Cubit, from a Latin word signifying the elbow. A measure of length; originally the distance from the elbow to the extremity of the middle finger. The Hebrew cubit was about twenty-two inches, the Roman seventeen and a half inches.

Cuckoo-spit, or Frog-spit, are names given to a frothy exudation seen in summer, on the stems of plants, particularly on willow-trees. It is caused by an insect (*cicada spumaria*) known commonly as the 'froth-fly,' or 'frog-fly,' which pierces the bark of the plants, and lays its eggs in the aperture. As the eggs are hatched, some irritation is set up which causes the juices of the plant to exude in groups of frothy matter, within which the young insects are concealed.

Cucumbers. Cucumbers were known to the ancients, being mentioned by Virgil, and other writers. They were first cultivated in England, 1538 A.D., having been introduced from Holland.

Cul-de-sac, French, literally 'the bottom of a bag.' Usually in England applied to a court or street open only at one end. In the Midland Counties, places of this kind are called 'pudding-bag streets.'

Culprit. This word is now improperly used to denote a person actually proved to be guilty of a criminal offence. The term is only properly and strictly used to denote a prisoner *who is on his trial.* Blackstone says it is an abbreviation of *culpa,* 'guilty,' and *prit,* 'ready'; which words were used by the clerk of arraigns to signify that he was ready or prepared to prove the prisoner's guilt. Etymologists, however, do not agree as to the origin, but they all say that 'culprit' was the proper designation of a person accused before a judge of some crime, but not convicted.

Cum grano salis, a Latin phrase, meaning literally, 'With a grain of salt.' In English, it is used in such sentences as, 'I don't quite believe what they say; I shall accept it *cum grano salis*'—that is, with some doubt.

Cum multis aliis, Latin, meaning 'there are many other similar things'; but in English its use implies that it would be a waste of time to mention them all. *Aliis* is a word of three syllables—*a-li-is.*

Cunning. This word had formerly the meaning of *understanding.* In Foxe's 'Book of Martyrs' he gives at full length the confession of one Thorpe, a martyr, in which is the following sentence:—'I believe that all these three persons [in the Godhead] are even in power, and in *cunning,* and in might; full of grace and of all goodness.'

Cupboard. The second syllable of this word is a modern corruption. It was originally *bur,* 'an enclosure'; *bur,* in various shapes, is common to most Northern European languages. In

Norman-English, *boor* was a 'parlour.' In Iceland, *uti-bur* is an outhouse.' In Anglo-Saxon, *swefn-bur*, a 'sleeping-chamber'; *cumena-bur*, a 'guest-chamber.' In Swedish, *hönse-bur*, a 'hen-coop.'

Cups and Saucers were anciently known in Cheshire as 'counterfeits and trinkets.'—*Bailey.*

Cur, applied to a dog, is a contraction of the term *curtailed dog.* Under the old forest laws, all dogs belonging to unqualified sportsmen, or inferior persons, had their tails cut short, and were called 'curtails.' This afterwards became *curtall* (which is still applied to a horse whose tail is docked), and finally *cur*, which is always used in a bad or reproachful sense.

Curaçoa. Oranges which fall from the trees in an unripe condition have the acrid and bitter properties of the skin of ripe oranges, but in a more concentrated form. They are used in flavouring the liqueur which is called *Curaçoa*.

Curate. The word *curate* means one who has the 'cure of souls.' It was originally applied to any clergyman in charge of a parish, whether rector, vicar, or what we now call *curate*. It is now exclusively limited in its application to the assistant minister of one who has the 'cure of souls,' and so is misapplied; as indeed are nearly all the titles given to the English clergy.

Curfew Bell. It is commonly believed that the *curfew bell* was instituted by William the Conqueror. There is, however, reason for thinking that William merely ordained that a custom which was already in use in some places should be universally applicable. Peshall, in his 'History of Oxford' (p. 177), says:— 'The custom of ringing the [curfew] bell at Carfax, every night, at eight o'clock, was by order of King Alfred, the restorer of our University, who ordained that all persons at the ringing of that Bell should cover up their fires, and go to bed; which Custom is observed to this day; and the Bell as constantly rings at eight, as Great **Tom** tolls at nine.'

Curmudgeon. Mr. Graham thinks the word is derived from *corn mudgin*, an old English name for a corn merchant. 'Corn mudgins' were dealers in corn who were unpopular, as it was thought that they hoarded and kept up the price of corn to serve their own interests. Hence the word came to signify an avaricious monopolist. When Dr. Johnson was compiling his great dictionary he could find no derivation of this word. He inserted a query on the subject in the 'Gentleman's Magazine,' in reply to which some one anonymously informed him that it was probably a corrupt pronunciation of the French words, *cœur*, which means 'heart,' and *méchant*, 'bad'; 'a bad heart.' Johnson inserted this explanation, adding, as his authority, 'From an unknown correspondent.' Dr. Ash, who evidently did not understand French, and who published a dictionary in 1775, gave the following absurd definition of the word:—'Curmudgeon (*s*. from the French, *cœur*, unknown, and *méchant*, correspondent), a miser, a churl, a griper.'

Currants. The 'currants' of the grocers' shops are really grapes. They are the fruit of a seedless variety of the common vine which is cultivated in Greece and the islands of the Archipelago. The grapes are simply dried in the sun upon the ground; and then packed in barrels for export. The Zante 'currants' are considered the best. The name is derived from *Corinth*, near which place they were first extensively cultivated.

Curry favour. To curry a horse was to rub him down, comb him, and dress him. *Favel* was a general name for a chestnut horse, derived from the French *faveau*, the colour of fallow land or chestnut. The phrase was originally 'to curry Favel,' but it has been corrupted. The saying no doubt originated in the case of a favourite horse *Favel*, to curry whom well was a sure passport to the favour of his master.

Curse is from the Anglo-Saxon *Corsian*, to execrate by the sign of the cross. Blackstone speaks of the *corsned* as 'a morsel of execration, being a piece of bread or cheese which was consecrated with a form of exorcism, desiring of the Almighty that it might cause convulsions, and paleness, and find no passage if the man was really guilty, but might turn to health and nourishment if he were innocent.'

Curse of Scotland. Amongst old whist-players, the nine of diamonds is often spoken of as the 'curse of Scotland.' It is probably a corruption of the phrase 'Cross of Scotland,' and as the nine 'pips' on the cards were formerly printed somewhat in the shape of a St. Andrew's cross, there seems great reason for believing that this is the true origin.

Curtain Lecture. These words occur as a marginal reference in Sir R. Stapleton's 'Translation of Juvenal's Sixth Satire,' A.D. 1647, lines 267-8, which he renders as follows:—

| THE CURTAIN LECTURE. | Debates, alternate brawlings, ever were I' th' marriage bed; there is no sleeping there. |

Dryden (1693) introduces the words into the text :—

>Besides what endless brawls by wives are bred,
>The *Curtain Lecture* makes a mournful bed.

Curtain Road, Shoreditch, marks the site of one of the earliest theatres in London. *The Curtain* is mentioned by Stubbs in his 'Anatomie of Abuses,' in 1583, as the name of a theatre in this locality. It is supposed to have been so named from its being the first theatre to adopt a green curtain.

Custom and Law. Before 1824, the weights and measures used in England varied considerably in different parts of the country. Thus there was one *bushel* customary at Winchester, and another at York. One *stone* for meat in London, and another, 6 lbs. heavier, in the north. In 1824 the first attempt was made to secure uniformity by statute. This was further extended by 5 & 6 Will. IV. c. 63, and by subsequent legislation. By the Act just quoted, any other *stone* than that of 14 lbs. was declared to be illegal; and it was enacted that any bargain or sale made by any other stone should be void, the seller having *no power to recover by law any money for goods so sold.* That law was made more than half a century ago, yet in London, to the present time (1880) all meat is sold, and publicly quoted in the newspapers as having been sold at so much 'per stone of 8 lbs.' In the Midland counties, the customary butcher's wholesale weight is the 'score of 20 lbs.'; and the carcases of pigs are accordingly sold and quoted in the papers at so much 'per score.' The stone of 8 lbs. is mentioned in a bill of fare of Philip and Mary, quoted in 'Collectanea Curiosa.' The item runs thus :—'Item Whyt Sewet, vj. stone viij. pownde to the stone.'

Cut of his jib. The foremost sail of a ship is called the jib, and its shape indicates, to some extent, the class of vessel bearing it. At sea, particularly in war time, every vessel coming in sight is carefully scanned, and if the strange craft looks suspicious, the man on the look out expresses his opinion by saying 'He don't like the cut of her jib.' The expression is easily transferred by Jack to the personal appearance of any person to whom he may feel a dislike.

Cut your stick. A writer in 'Notes and Queries,' who dates from Glasgow, says this phrase originated as follows :—'About the year 1820 a song was sung in the Salt Market, Glasgow, beginning—

>Oh I creished my brogues and I cut my stick.

The song related the adventures of an Irishman, and, of course, the 'cutting of the stick' referred to the common practice in Ireland of procuring a sapling before going off. It afterwards became the practice, when anyone ran off or absconded, to say, 'That chap has cut his stick too,' and thus the phrase originated and spread over the country. Americans claim the origin of this phrase. They say it arose from the fact that runaway slaves usually cut a great stick before starting, to help them on their way. Advertisements of runaway slaves were headed with woodcuts of a negro with a stick and bundle over his shoulder. Some have thought that the phrase may have originated in a printing office, where a compositor, who wanted a holiday, said, 'I shall cut the stick [composing stick] for to-day, and have a walk instead.'

Cutting off with a shilling. Blackstone says that 'The Romans were wont to set aside testaments as being *inofficiosa*, deficient in natural duty, if they disinherited or totally passed by any of the children of the testator. But if the child had any legacy, however small, it was a proof that the testator had not lost his reason or his memory, which otherwise the law presumed. Hence, probably, has arisen that groundless error of the necessity of leaving the heir a shilling, or some express legacy, in order to disinherit him effectually. Whereas the law of England makes no such constrained suppositions of forgetfulness or insanity, and therefore, though the heir, or next of kin, be totally omitted, it admits no *querela inofficiosa* to set aside such a testament.'

Cutty Pipes. Probably from the city of *Kutaieh*, in Asia Minor, where a soft white stone is found, which is used by the Germans in the manufacture of pipes. It may, however, be from the Scottish word *cutty*, signifying short : 'Weel done, *cutty sark*.'—*Burns*.

Cwm, in Welsh local names, means a hollow, a deep sheltered valley, a place between hills.

Cwt., a hundred weight. In this symbol *C* is the Roman numeral letter for one hundred, and *wt* are the first and final letters of the word weight.

Cyder. This liquor was formerly called *sizer*. The word is used by Chaucer in the 'Monke's Tale,' line 65, which runs :—
'This Sampson neyther siser dronk ne wyn.'

Cynical, from a Greek word signifying *dog-like*. Hence applied to persons of snarling, snappish, ill-natured disposition.

Cynosure, from two Greek words signifying a *dog's tail*. It is a name for the constellation Ursa Minor, which contains the Polar Star. As mariners are guided by this star, so they are constantly fixing their gaze upon it. Hence Milton's metaphor—

The *cynosure* of neighbouring eyes.

D

Daffodil. This flower is the *asphodel* of the Greeks. The Italians called it *affodillo*, the French *fleur d'affodille*, and we adopted their name, but incorporated the article *d'* with the name, making it 'daffodil.'

Dagger. This name is derived from the Spanish *daga*, a sword. It is commonly believed that the dagger in the City arms was added by Richard II. to commemorate the slaying of Wat Tyler by Sir Richard Walworth in 1381. This, however, is an error; the City arms had the dagger long before the time of Walworth. It represents the sword of St. Paul, the patron saint of the Corporation.

Dagger Scene in the House of Commons. It is well known that during the French Revolution, Burke created a great sensation by suddenly throwing a dagger upon the floor of the House of Commons, vociferating, 'There is French fraternity for you! Such is the poignard which French Jacobins would plunge in the heart of our Sovereign.' It is said that Sheridan threw great ridicule upon this theatrical exhibition by saying, 'The gentleman has brought his knife with him; but *where's the fork?*' At any rate, the matter created great amusement at Burke's expense. In the 'Life of Lord Eldon,' by Twiss, the author says that, 'The dagger had been sent to a manufacturer at Birmingham as a pattern, with an order to make a large quantity like it. At that time the order seemed so suspicious, that, instead of executing it, he came to London and called on my father at the Secretary of State's office to inform him of it, and ask his advice, and he left the pattern with him. Just after, Mr. Burke called, on his way to the House of Commons, and upon my father mentioning the subject to him, he borrowed the dagger to show in the House. They walked down to the House together, and when Mr. Burke had made his speech, my father took the dagger again and kept it as a curiosity.'

Dahlia. This flower is a native of Mexico. It was brought thence within the present century, and was first cultivated in Europe by Dahl, a Swedish botanist. It was brought to England about the year 1804, and was first cultivated in the French garden at Holland House. Kensington. There is now an infinite variety in the shape, colour and size of the flowers. The name is derived from Dahl, who introduced it.

Daily News. The first number of this paper appeared January 21, 1846. At that time Charles Dickens was editor; his father, John Dickens, was the manager; Douglas Jerrold was assistant editor, and Bradbury and Evans were the printers; Albany Fonblanque and John Forster were leader writers; Father Prout (Mahoney) was Roman correspondent, and George Hogarth, Dickens's father-in-law, was musical critic. Sir William Jackson, Sir Joseph Watkins, and Mr., afterwards Sir Joseph Paxton, were amongst the principal proprietors.

Daily Newspaper. The first daily paper published in England was 'The Daily Courant,' the first number of which appeared on March 11, 1702. It was 'printed by E. Mallet, against the Ditch at Fleet Bridge.'

Dainty originally meant a venison pasty; the word is derived from the French *daine*, a deer.

Dairy is from the old English word *dey*, a farm servant, usually a female, whose duty it was to make cheese and butter, attend to the calves, poultry, and other odds and ends of a farm. The 'deyry' was the department under her care. Halliwell defines *caseale* as a 'deyhouse where cheese is made.' In Gloucestershire, a dairy is still called a 'deyhouse.'

Dam. The phrase 'don't care a dam' is usually thought to be a piece of profanity. It is not so, however. The *dam* is a small coin current in India, and the phrase is equivalent to 'don't care twopence.'

Damask. This word has two distinct meanings. The one derived from the name Damascus, applied to linen or other fabrics woven so as to show, by various intersections of the threads, diaper patterns, or other ornamental devices. The other meaning, that of a red colour, though formerly used generally, is now almost confined to the *damask* rose. The well-known quotation from Shakespeare—

> She never told her love,
> But let concealment, like a worm i' the bud,
> Feed on her *damask* cheek—

is an early example of its use in a sense which is now practically obsolete. Another occurs in Cowper's translation of Milton's Italian Sonnet to Charles Deodati :—

> Yet think me not thus dazzled by the flow
> Of golden locks, or *damask* cheek.

And Lord Lytton used it in ' What will he do with it ? ' in which he speaks of ' a sensation which gave that softness to the eye, and that *damask* to the blush.'

Damask Rose. 'The Damaske rose [was brought to England] by Doctour Linaker, King Henrie the Eight's physician.'—*Hackluyt*, 1599.

Damning with faint praise. This phrase is from Pope's epistle to Dr. Arbuthnot :—

> Damn with faint praise, assent with civil leer,
> And without sneering, teach the rest to sneer.

Damsel. This word originally meant a young person *of either sex*. Historians mention ' *damsel* Louis-le-gros,' ' *damsel* Richard, Prince of Wales.' It was afterwards used as the diminutive of ' dame,' the wife of a knight; a knight's daughter being entitled a ' damsel.'

Damson is derived from Damascus, from whence the damson tree was first brought to Europe.

Dances. Nearly all the European nations have their distinctive dances. In England, what is called the ' country dance ' and the ' hornpipe ' seem indigenous. In Ireland, the ' jig '; in Scotland, the ' reel '; in France, the ' quadrille ' and the ' cotillon '; in Germany, the ' waltz ' and the ' gallopade '; in Spain, the ' fandango '; in Naples, the ' tarentella '; in Poland, the ' mazurka ' and the ' krakoviech '; and in Russia the ' cossac ' are all characteristic dances, suitable in their quick or slow movements to the national idiosyncrasies.

Dandelion. The name is a corruption of the French *dent de lion*, lion's tooth, from some fancied resemblance of the leaves to the teeth of the lion. The Greek name *Leontodon* has the same meaning.

Daniel Lambert was probably the fattest man that ever lived. He was born at Leicester in 1770, and died at Stamford, 1809. His weight was 739 lbs. He was 9 feet 4 inches round the waist, and the calf of his leg was 37 inches in circumference. The compiler of this book was one of a group of eleven young men, who in the year 1841 stood within a buttoned waistcoat which had once belonged to Lambert.

Dardanelles. The strait so-called was named from two castles guarding its entrance, which were known as the Dardanelles, the name being taken from the neighbouring town *Dardanus*, so named from *Dardanus*, the mythical founder of Troy.

Darling is the Anglo-Saxon *deorling*, the diminutive of *deor*, dear. Darling is, therefore, 'little dear,' and should not be applied by children or young persons to people older or bigger than themselves.

Dartford Brent. On the Dover road, just outside Dartford, is a very steep hill overlooking the town, called the 'Brent.' This is probably a corruption of the old English adjective Brant, meaning steep; obsolete now, except in Northumberland. The Northumbrians still speak of a 'brant' hill. Bailey has 'brant' in his Dictionary. East Brent in Somersetshire, and Brent Tor in Devon, are other examples of local names derived from this root-word.

Dashes under words in writing. One dash ——— under a word is understood by a printer to signify that the word is to be printed in *italics*; two dashes ═══ intimate the wish of the writer that the word so marked shall be printed in SMALL CAPITALS. Three dashes ≡≡≡ signify LARGE CAPITALS.

Data, a Latin plural noun, literally signifying *things given* or *granted*. In English it means facts or premisses admitted, or granted, from which conclusions may be drawn. Thus we say 'His case was founded upon certain data,' or 'He had no data to go upon.'

Dauphin. This was the title formerly borne by the eldest son of the kings of France. In 1349 Humbert, the last of the princes of Dauphiné, having no issue, left his dominions to the king of France on condition that the king's eldest son should be styled the Dauphin. After the Revolution of 1830 the title was abolished.

Davy Jones's Locker. It is a common thing among sailors to say of a person who is dead that he is 'gone to Davy Jones's locker.' Smollett, in 'Peregrine Pickle,' says, 'Davy Jones, according to the mythology of sailors, is the fiend that presides over all the evil spirits of the deep.' A 'locker' in sailor's phraseology is something that locks up, or keeps anything safe. Hence to go to Davy Jones's locker is to be placed in the Devil's lock-up.

Dawn. Anciently the day was said to *daw*. Drayton says, 'Morning daws,' and in 'Reliq. Antiq.' are two examples: 'Day daweth,' p. 7; and 'The daye, wenne hit dawe,' p. 244. The transition was probably at first to 'dawing,' the *dawing* of the morning, then by contraction to *dawn*, the present form.

Day. A day in law includes the whole twenty-four hours, without reference to the season of the year or the amount of light or darkness. An obligation to pay on a certain day is discharged if the money be paid before twelve o'clock at night. If A binds himself to pay money ten days after the death of B, and B dies on the 1st of a given month, the money will not be due until twelve o'clock of the night of the 11th. Where a tenancy expires on a given day, the key may be tendered to the landlord at any time before midnight of that day.—*Wharton*. See COMING OF AGE.

Days in each month. In the Calendar of Julius Cæsar the distribution of days in each month was more convenient than at present. The Calendar commenced with March, and all the *odd* months, as 1, 3, 5, 7, 9, 11, had thirty-one days each, while the even numbers 2, 4, 6, 8, 10, 12, had thirty each, except in leap year, when February, which was the last month in the year, had but twenty-nine. This excellent arrangement was altered to gratify the frivolous vanity of the Emperor Augustus, who thought it derogatory that the month which bore his name should have fewer days than the one named after Julius. He therefore took one day from February and added it to August.

Daysman. An old English word for an arbitrator or umpire. It is used in Job ix. 33, 'Neither is there any *daysman* betwixt us.' Also it is used in an old play quoted by Nares:—

> If neighbours were at variance they ran not streight to law,
> *Daiesmen* took up the matter and cost them not a straw.
> *Newe Custome.*

Spenser has 'dayes man' in the 'Faery Queene,' viii. 28. It is also used by some of the old Puritan writers in reference to Christ, who is called the *Daysman* between God and man. The origin is not accurately known; Nares says 'from his fixing a day for decision,' but this is hardly satisfactory.

Days of the week. The English names of the seven days of the week are derived from those of pagan deities, or natural objects of worship to which each day was dedicated; thus:— *Sunday*, Sun's day. *Monday*, Moon's day. *Tuesday*, from Tuisto or Tuesco, a Saxon god. *Wednesday*, Woden's day, from Odin or Woden, also a Saxon idol. *Thursday*, Thor's day. Thor was worshipped by all the northern European nations. *Friday*, Friga's day, from Friga, the Scandinavian Venus. *Saturday*, Saterne's day.

Dead. This word is employed as part of many phrases in English seafaring life, in a sense opposed to *real* or active, as 'dead-lights,' which are wooden shutters to protect cabin windows in stormy weather; '*dead* wind,' a wind blowing directly against a ship's course, or, as seamen say, '*dead* against us.' There are many other phrases in which it occurs, as 'dead eyes,' 'dead flat,' 'dead rising,' 'dead ropes'; 'dead wood,' which consists of timber fastened internally to the keel, to give rigidity to the vessel; and 'dead reckoning,' which is a calculation of a ship's place at sea, made independently of celestial observations.

Dead as a herring. It is a rare thing, even for fishermen, to see a really live herring. The fish dies the instant it is taken out of the water.

Dead Sea. Lieutenant Symond, in 1841, made a trigonometrical survey of the country between Jaffa and the Dead Sea, by which he ascertained the surface of the latter to be 1,311 feet below that of the Mediterranean, or nearly a quarter of a mile. The water of the Dead Sea contains upwards of 26 per cent. of saline matter, that of the ocean varying from 3 to 4. No living object has ever been found in the waters of the Dead Sea.

Dear, Daughter. 'I have somewhere read that *deore*, now spelt "dear," meaning beloved, also signified a "daughter." If this be correct, and certainly *dear* is Erse for daughter, it conveys a very pleasing idea, as suggesting that any object of tender affection was called dear, as being like a daughter to one.'—*Dean Hoare*, p. 32.

Dearest. This word originally had the meaning which we now express by the word *direst*. Shakespeare makes Hamlet say, 'Would I had met my *dearest* foe in heaven.' The word dear, meaning 'beloved' or 'precious,' is from the Anglo-Saxon *deor*; but dear, in the sense of 'hateful,' is from *derian*, to hurt. The Scotch have *dere*, to annoy.

Death by burning. Anciently women convicted of capital offences were burnt to death. A writer in 'Notes and Queries,' Sept. 21, 1850, states that he was present at the execution by burning of a woman in March 1789. The 'Gentleman's Magazine' of the period gives the following details:—'Nine malefactors were executed March 18, 1789, before the debtors' door at Newgate. Three men and one woman—Jane Grace, for coining; four men for burglary, and one for highway robbery. They were brought upon the scaffold about half-an-hour after seven, and turned off about a quarter past eight. The woman for coining was brought out after the rest were turned off, and fixed to a stake and burnt, being first strangled by the stool being taken from under her.' This was the last execution of the kind. In the following year an Act was passed (30 Geo. III. c. 48) 'For discontinuing the judgment which has been required by law to be given against women convicted of certain crimes, and substituting another judgment in lieu thereof.'

Death of Nelson. The first stanza of this well-known ode is adapted from one written on the death of the Duke of Cumberland—the butcher of Culloden. The original ran thus:—

> O'er William's tomb, with silent grief opprest,
> Britannia mourns her Hero, now at rest;
> Not tears alone, but praises too she gives,
> Due to the guardian of our laws and lives;
> Nor shall that laurel ever fade with years,
> Whose leaves are watered with a nation's tears.

Death Warrant. It is a mistake to believe that the sovereign signs the death warrant of a criminal left for execution.—*Wharton.*

Death Warrant of Charles I. The original warrant for the execution of Charles I. is in the library of the House of Lords. 'It was produced by Colonel Harker after the Restoration, and was the evidence upon which those who had signed it were excepted from the Indemnity Act.'—*J. H. Pulman, Librarian to the House of Lords.*

Debate. This word formerly signified to fight. Nares thinks this was the primitive sense. Spenser ('Faerie Queene,' II. i. 6) has 'Well could he tourney, and in lists *debate*'; and in '2 Henry IV.' iv. 4, Shakespeare speaks of the '*debate* that bleedeth at our doors.'

Debt of Nature. The origin of this phrase is probably the following from 'Quarles's Emblems,' 12, 13:—

> The slender *debt to nature's* quickly paid,
> Discharged perchance with greater ease than made.

Decanter. The French phrase *de cant* is used of anything set on edge, as a beam half raised, yet not turned over. We have the word 'cant' in the sense of an angle or corner; and to *cant* anything is to raise it on the edge or corner. Hence to 'decant' is to pour off from a bottle by tilting it, or placing it on an angle; and a 'decanter' is that into which the liquor is so poured.

Decedent. In Pennsylvanian law, a deceased person is called a *decedent*, or the *decedent.—Bartlett.*

Decking Churches at Christmas. This custom seems to be an attempt to realise the verse which occurs in the first lesson in the service for Christmas-eve :—'The glory of Lebanon shall come unto thee; the fir-tree, the pine-tree, and the box together, to beautify the place of my sanctuary.'—*Isaiah* lx. 13.

Decoction. A decoction is a solution of any organic matter made by boiling it. See INFUSION.

Decoy, properly 'duck-coy'; from *coy,* an old English word, meaning to allure. Shakespeare has, ' I'll *coy* their hearts from them.'

Defeat was formerly used in the sense of disfiguring the *features.* Thus, in 'Othello,' i. 3, we have, 'Defeat thy favour with an usurped beard'; and, in the ' Comedy of Errors,' 'And careful hours with Time's deformed [*qy.* deforming ?] hand have written strange *defeatures* in my face.'

Defence comes from the verb 'to fence,' to fortify by enclosure. A *fenced* city, often mentioned in the Scriptures, is a city defended by a *fence* or protected by walls. 'Defend' was often used by the old writers in the sense of *forbid;* as in the line,

Great Jove *defende* the mischiefs now at hand.
Ferrex and Porrex, Old Plays, i. 129.

Defender of the Faith. It is commonly believed that this title was first borne by Henry VIII. In his case, however, it was but a revival. In a marginal note to the dedication to Charles II. of Basire's 'Sacrilege Arraigned' (London : 1668), is the following :—' 'Tis a gross error to think that the King of England's title of Defender of the Faith is no older than King Henry VIII. For 300 years ago, in the old writs of K. Rich. II., to the Sheriffs, the old style runs :—" *Ecclesia, cujus nos Defensor sumus et esse volumnus."* ' A note by Christopher Wren, Dean of Windsor, appended to Peck's 'Memoirs of Cromwell' (4to. 1740), runs as follows :—' That King Henry VII. had the title formerly of Defender of the Faith appears by the Register of the Order of the Garter in the Black Book now in my hands by office '—p. 86.

The title was not, however, at that time hereditary, and it died with Henry VII. The hereditary title '*Defensor Fidei*,' or Defender of the Faith, was, we are told, 'conferred' by Pope Leo X. upon Henry VIII., in 1521, as a reward for writing against Luther. It seems, however, that he was merely reviving a title that had been borne by Henry's father.

De Foe. The real name of the celebrated author of 'Robinson Crusoe' was Daniel Foe. His father, a butcher of Cripplegate, who originally came from Elton in Northamptonshire, was James Foe. Both father and son were busy men amongst Dissenters about the year 1700, and the son, to distinguish him from the father, was always called Mr. 'D.' Foe. His letters to Lord Halifax, written in 1705, are signed in three different forms—'D. Foe,' 'De Foe,' and 'Daniel De Foe.' He afterwards adopted De Foe or Defoe as his usual surname, and he has been known ever since as Daniel Defoe.

Dei Gratia. This phrase, meaning 'by the grace or favour of God,' has been a part of the royal style of the sovereigns of England from the time of Offa, King of Mercia, A.D. 780. Some of the kings varied the phraseology to *Dei dono, Divina providentia,* and *Christo donante. Dei gratia* was also part of the style of the Archbishops of Canterbury, from the time of Theodore, A.D. 676, to that of Thomas à-Beckett, A.D. 1170. *Dei gratia* is now exclusively royal. The Archbishop of Canterbury is so '*by Divine providence.*'

Deism and Theism. Both these words signify a belief in the existence of God. The first is, however, applied in a bad, and the second in a good sense. A Jew, and, indeed, every believer in one God, is a *theist*. A *deist* is one who hesitates to accept the theory of a *Divine Revelation*, and is hence looked upon as an enemy to all religion.

Déjeûner à la fourchette, French; literally, 'a breakfast with a fork.' Applied in England to morning or mid-day meals of light character.

Delaware took its name from Lord De la Warr, who colonised it in 1610, and died in what is now Delaware Bay.

Delegate. A 'Delegate,' in the Congress of the United States, is the representative of a 'Territory,' which is a district not yet made into a 'State.' He has the right of debating, but cannot vote.

Delighted. This word formerly meant 'deprived of light.' D'Avenant uses the word in this sense in a poem 'On Remembrance of Mr. William Shakespeare,' where, addressing his brother-poets as having lost their chief light by Shakespeare's death, he calls them '*delighted* poets.'

Delirious. From two Latin words *de*, from, and *lira*, a furrow, meaning to wander out of the furrow, or track; to go out of the straight line.

Deliver. This word formerly meant 'active,' 'nimble.' There are numberless instances of its use in this sense, of which two or three examples must suffice:—

> Having chosen his soldiers of nimble, leane, and *deliver* men.
> *Holinshed*, vol. i. N. 6, col. 1.
> All of them being nimble, quick, and *deliver* persons.
> *Ibid.* vol. ii. C. col. 5.
> Like bulls set head to head with mere *deliver* strength.
> *Drayton's Polyolbion*, Song 1, p. 662.

Delph. This name for earthenware is derived from *Delft*, a town in Holland, where extensive potteries existed from A.D. 1300.

Demean. There is a modern custom of using this word as though one who 'demeaned' himself disgraced himself. Nothing can be more opposed to the true signification of the word. The proper meaning of the word is expressed in the word 'demeanour,' which simply means behaviour, either good or bad. If the word 'mean' is to be used in a compound, having a bad sense, it should be '*be*mean,' not *de*mean.

Demerit. This word has come to mean the exact opposite of its signification three or four centuries ago. Polydore Vergil ('Hist. of Engl.' 295 Camd. Soc. 1846) says:—'He [Edward the Confessor] was buried in the churche at Westminster, and successivelie, for his "demerits" escribed emonge the Saincts.' Shakespeare, in 'Othello,' has:—

> And my *demerits*
> May speak, unbonneting, to as proud a fortune,
> As this which I have reached.

Demi-john, French *dame-jeanne*, a large glass bottle of spherical shape, covered with wicker-work. The name is corrupted from *Damaghan*, a town in Persia, once famous for its glassworks. The word in English is being gradually superseded by 'carboy.'

Demise does not mean 'decease.' At the death of a monarch there is a demise of the crown, that is a descent (*demissio*) of the office to another, not a 'demise' of the person of the sovereign.

Demon. This word in the original meant a divinity below the rank of the gods. Cooke, in his 'Hesiod,' says:—

> Holy *demons* by great Jove designed
> To be on earth the guardians of mankind.

Demoralise. Dr. Webster seems to have coined this word. When Professor Lyell was in the United States, he called upon Webster, who, in reply to questions, said he had 'only coined one word, the verb to "demoralise," and that, not for the dictionary, but for a pamphlet published in the last century.'—*Travels in the U. States*, p. 53.

Dent. There are many words derived from *dens*, a tooth, as dentist, dentifrice, dental, &c., but the word *dent* does not appear in its place as a noun meaning a tooth. It is, however, to be found in 'Bailey's Dictionary' under the word 'battlements,' which he says are 'The turrets of houses built flat, and a piece of masonry on the top of a building or wall like a dent.'

Deodand. Up to the year 1846, a coroner's jury had the power to order the forfeiture of any animal or chattel which had caused the death of a human being. In the latter years of the custom it was usual to commute the forfeiture into a money payment. Thus it was common for a verdict to be somewhat in this form :—'Accidental death, with a "deodand" of £5 on the horse.' The name is derived from two Latin words signifying 'given to God,' and it was supposed to propitiate the wrath of God. Deodands were abolished by Act of Parliament, 9 & 10 Vict. c. 52.

Deo Volente, usually contracted to *D.V.*, is a Latin phrase meaning 'God being willing.' The phrase is divided into syllables thus—De-o vo-len-te.

Depart originally had the meaning of dividing, parting, or separating. In the old marriage service, the words denoting the life-long nature of the union were 'till death us depart.' This is modernised into 'till death us do part.'

Depôt. This word is used almost universally in the United States to signify a railway station.

Deptford was formerly called and written 'Depeford,' from a deep ford over the river Ravensbourne just before it widens into what is now called Deptford Creek.

Derange, Deranged. It is curious that these words do not appear in any but the most modern dictionaries. Paley uses the word 'deranged' in 'Evidences,' prop. 2.

Derby. The great race called 'the Derby' was instituted in the year 1780 by the Earl of Derby, whose name was applied to it.

Derive, from the Latin *de*, from, and *rivus*, a stream. The word originally meant to draw off (*de-rivus*) water from a river or stream.

Derrick. A crane is called a derrick from the name of Derrick, the Tyburn hangman in the 17th century, who made gibbets. In an old work, 'Bellman of London,' 1616, his name is mentioned:—'He rides circuit with the devil, and Derrick must be his host.'

Descant. We now confine the use of this word to its secondary meaning of speechifying, as 'the honourable member then *descanted* at considerable length on the,' &c. It was originally a musical term for a song in parts for different voices, as opposed to 'plain song.' 'The cuckoo was said to sing plain-song, and the nightingale to *descant*.'—*Nares*.

Desk, Pulpit. In the New England States the word 'desk' is always used instead of pulpit; it is also used figuratively for the clerical profession, as 'I intend one son for the bar, the other for the desk.'

Dessert is from *desservir*, to remove the cloth, or clear away. The word is therefore improperly applied to fruits, &c. placed 'on' the cloth, or with the substantial part of a dinner, as in dinners à la Russe. The word in America is used to denote the course in which puddings, pies, jellies, &c. appear *at dinner*. It is never, as with us, applied to the fruits, &c. which follow a dinner. See BANQUET.

Desultory, from the Latin *de*, from, and *salio*, to leap. A rider in a circus who leaps from the back of one horse to another is a 'desultor'; hence 'desultory' means going in a sudden or abrupt manner from one occupation or study to another.

Detriment, from the Latin *de*, from, and *tritus*, the past participle of the verb *tero*, to rub. Hence to injure, to hurt, to damage.

Deuce. Bede, according to Sharon Turner, in his 'Commentary on Luke,' mentions demons appearing to men as females, and to women as men, which demons, he says, the Gauls call *Dusii*. This is the presumed origin of our word 'deuce.'

Deuteronomy, from two Greek words meaning *second* and *law*. The fifth book of Moses is so named from its being mainly a repetition or second edition of laws previously enunciated.

Devel. It is a curious fact that in the gipsy dialect the word *Devel* means God. It is supposed to be connected with the Sanscrit word *deva.—Kuhn.*

Devil. It is the opinion of many philologers that the name of God is derived from *Good spirit*, shortened by long use to good or god. In the Anglo-Saxon the word 'god' is used in the sense of 'good' as well as to designate the Almighty, and it is only known by the context which is intended. By a similar process Satan may have been known as *the Evil Spirit*, which shortened by usage would become *the Evil or th'evil*, easily corrupted into *Devil*. In the Anglo-Saxon the word *yfel* signifies both evil and devil. The common synonyms of this word, *Old Nick, Old Scratch*, and *Old Harry*, are all derived from Northern sources. 'Old Nick' is from the Finnish *Nœki* or North-German *Nickel*, both meaning a demon. 'Old Scratch' is from *Scrat* or *Schrat*, a Scandinavian wood demon; and 'Old Harry' is from *Hari*, or *Herra*, Scandinavian terms identical with *Baal* or *Beel* in *Beelzebub*. The common pictorial representations of the devil are entirely copied or derived from Greek and Roman mythology. The pitchfork is the two-pronged sceptre of Pluto, the King of Hell. The blackness is also from Pluto, who was named *Jupiter Niger*, the black Jupiter. The horn, tail, and cloven feet are from the Greek *satyri* or satyrs.

Devil among the Tailors. This phrase arose in connection with a riot at the Haymarket on an occasion when Dowton announced the performance for his benefit of a burlesque entitled 'The Tailors, a Tragedy for Warm Weather.' At night many thousands of journeymen tailors congregated in and around the theatre and by riotous proceedings interrupted the performances. Thirty-three of the rioters were brought up at Bow Street the next day. A full account of the proceedings will be found in 'Biographica Dramatica' under the heading 'TAILORS.'

Devil and Bag o' Nails. One of the witnesses on the trial of Catlin, Patterson, and others, for conspiracy ('Remarkable Trials,' 1765, vol. ii. p. 14), said, 'He went into a public-house the sign of "The Devil and Bag o' Nails," for so the gentry called it among themselves, though its real sign was, "The Blackmoor's Head and Woolpack," by Buckingham Gate.'

Dexterity, from the Latin *dexter*, right, as opposed to left— hence a man who works skilfully with his right hand is said to be *dexterous*.

Dextrine, sometimes called British gum, is made by subjecting ordinary starch to a great heat, when it changes to a substance not unlike gum arabic. It is the adhesive preparation used for postage stamps, for which it is better adapted than gum, as it is more elastic and consequently is less brittle or liable to chip off.

Diæresis is the name given to the mark ¨ when placed over a vowel, as in the word 'aërate.' Its object is to show that the vowel so marked is to be sounded independently, the word just quoted being pronounced *a-e-rate*. The word 'diälysis' has the same meaning.

Diamond is a corruption of the Greek word *adamant*, meaning untameable or refractory. The Greeks called the diamond *adamant* because of its excessive hardness.

Diamond of the first water. There is some appropriateness in this phrase because of the resemblance to the sparkling of water, as in a dewdrop. Mr. Fox Talbot thinks, however, that the expression originated in a mistake. He supposes that the Anglo-Saxons spoke of 'the finest or purest hue' or colour (Anglo-Saxon *hiw*, colour). The Normans supposed this word to be their own *ewe*, water, and applied it in that sense.

Diaper, corrupted from the French *d'Ypres*, the manufacture having been introduced at the town of Ypres in Flanders.

Dick's Hatband. Many proverbial sayings have 'Dick's hatband' for their subject, as 'As queer as Dick's hatband,' &c. They all allude to Richard Cromwell, who found the crown unsuitable to his head.

Dick, or Rich? In 'Timon of Athens,' act i. sc. 2, is the line:

> Much good *dick* thy good heart, Apemantus.

The context seems to show that this is an error, and even suggests the correct reading. The last line of Apemantus's grace is—

> *Rich* men sin, and I eat root;

upon which, drinking as a sort of toast to himself, he continues—

> Much good rich [*i.e.* enrich] thy good heart, Apemantus.

Dieu et mon Droit. This motto, which means 'God and my right,' was the parole given to his army, at the battle of Gisors, by Richard I., Sept. 20, 1198. It was first adopted as the royal motto of England by Henry VI. in the fifteenth century.

Diffidence, which now means mistrust of one's own powers, originally meant want of confidence in others. Milton speaks of 'diffidence of God,' and in another place says 'Be not diffident of wisdom.' Bentley mentions 'Reasons for suspicion and diffidence.'

Dig. The Anglo-Saxon word from which 'dig' is derived was *dician*, to make a ditch, and the word digger was originally confined to the meaning of one who made a ditch or dyke.

Dilapidate. From the Latin *dis*, apart, and *lapis*, a stone, signifying the disintegration or decay of stone, as in a ruinous building. It is now commonly improperly used in the general sense of decay or ruin in anything, so that it is common to hear men speak of 'a dilapidated hat!'

Diminutives are words in which the primitive or original meaning is lessened or diminished, as in bullock, hillock, duckling, and lambkin. They are also used as terms of endearment, as Johnny, for John; Tommy, for Tom; wifie, for wife; darling, for dear, &c.

Dine with Duke Humphrey. A correspondent of 'The Gentleman's Magazine,' March 1794, p. 210, says, 'This proverb originated from the accidental circumstance of a wit in the seventeenth century being shut up in the Abbey of St. Albans, where the remains of Humphrey, the good Duke regent, are yet to be seen, while a party of his friends who came down to that borough on an excursion were enjoying a convivial dinner at the White Hart Inn.' The proverb, however, seems to have been known at an earlier period than this story refers to, and it meant to have no dinner to eat. The phrase perhaps arose from the custom of making a part of Old St. Paul's Cathedral, which was called Duke Humphrey's Walk, a common place of meeting. People short of a dinner used to promenade this spot in the hope of meeting some one who would invite them.

Dinner Custom. The custom of ladies and gentlemen walking in pairs to the dining-room is of comparatively recent origin. Even now, in some old-fashioned country homes, the lady of the house leads the way, followed by the other ladies in single file, the gentlemen bringing up the rear. A writer in 'Notes and Queries' says that in 1790 his mother was greatly shocked on board a man-of-war in Leith Roads by an officer asking her to 'take his arm,' and that he remembered her speaking with indignation of 'the fellow's impudence.' Another writer in the same paper (April 1862) says that 'a lady who died in 1840, and whose daughter was born in 1798,' told him that 'when she first saw a lady *hook* herself to the arm of a gentleman in a ball-room, she felt so indignant that she remarked to a friend, "If my daughter were introduced and did that, I should take her home immediately."'

Dinner-time. In the 'Haven of Health,' by Thomas Cogan, physician, published in 1584, we are told that, 'When four houres bee past after breakefaste, a manne may safely take his dinner, and the most convenient time for dinner is about eleven of the clocke before noone. The usuall time for dinner in the Universities is at eleaven, or else where about noone.'

Dint. The expression 'by dint of' is very common. The word is the Anglo-Saxon *dynt*, force, as of a blow. A dint is a blow strong enough to make a *dent*. Milton speaks of 'that mortal *dint*' and Addison has 'by *dint* of arms.'

Diploma is a Greek term meaning anything folded double. It was originally a messenger's or traveller's passport written on two leaves for convenience of carriage. In modern times it signifies the written certificate of membership granted by learned or artistic bodies.

Diplomatics (from 'diploma') is the science of deciphering ancient writings, assigning their date, &c. It is said to have originated with a Jesuit of Antwerp, named Pakebrock, about the year 1675; but Mabillon, in 1681, published a work on the subject in six folio volumes, in which the matter is gone into fully, and the bases laid for all future investigations. This term has nothing in common with the word *diplomatic*, as used in relation to international politics.

Directory. In the British Museum there is a copy of a Directory entitled 'The names of all such Gentlemen of Accompts as were residing within ye City of London, Liberties and Suburbs thereof, 28 Novembris, 1595, anno 38 Elizabethe Reginæ.' This is the first known work of the kind. The next was published in 1677. It is entitled 'A Collection of the Names of Merchants living in and about the City of London.' It was 'Printed for Samuel Lee, and are (*sic*) to be sold at his Shop in Lombard Street.' The names are 1,790 in number, and follow in alphabetical order. There is a separate list of forty-four Bankers, under the heading 'Goldsmiths who keep running Cashes.' Twenty-seven of these had their places of business in Lombard Street. The book contains the name of the father of Pope, the poet, thus: 'Alexander Pope, Broad Street.' The late Mr. J. C. Hotten reprinted the book in 1863. The first 'Directory,' so called, was compiled by James Brown in 1732, and was printed by Henry Kent, in Finch Lane.

Its title was 'The Directory, or List of Principal Traders in London.' Kent afterwards published an annual edition, and realised a fortune. The first 'Post Office Directory,' according to Haydn, was published in 1800; it contained 300 pages. From that time it has been published annually.

Dirge, a contraction of the word *dirige*. It is the name by which an ancient solemn anthem of the Roman Catholic Church was known.

Disaster (*aster*, a star) is a word formed at a time when the stars were believed to influence human actions. It conveys the notion that calamity is caused by an unfavourable planet or star. The idea is embodied in Judges v. 20: 'The stars in their courses fought against Sisera.'

Discard. The original meaning of this word was to throw out of the hand such cards as were useless. We now at *Cribbage* throw out cards for the crib. In the old-fashioned game *Quadrille*, the eights, nines, and tens were *discarded*, the pack being thus reduced to forty cards.

Disease. This word, divided into dis-ease, gives its exact meaning, 'absence of ease.' It was formerly used both for bodily and mental distress. In Wycliff's translation of the Bible we read: 'In the world ye shall have disease.'—*John* xvi. 33. In an old play, quoted by Nares, 'The Woman Killed with Kindness,' it is employed as a verb —:

> Fie, fie, that for my private discontent,
> I should disease a friend, and be a trouble
> To the whole house.

Disguised as a gentleman. This phrase originated in a play of the poet Cowley, in 1661. In the comedy of 'The Cutter of Coleman Street,' act i. sc. 5, Colonel Jolly and Captain Worms are chaffing Cutter, who boasts that he, 'like the King himself, and all the great ones, got away in a disguise'; to which Jolly replies, 'Take one more disguise, and put thyself into the habit of a gentleman.'

Dished, in the sense of ruined or frustrated, is a contraction of the old English word *disherit*, for disinherit. A person is said to be *dished* when property he expected to inherit is left to some one else. Byron, in 'Don Juan,' asks :—

> Where's Brummel? Dished!

Dislocate. Johnson derives this from the Latin *dis*, and *locus*, a place. Mr. Fox Talbot thinks it more likely that its root is the old English *loc*, or *lock*, a joint (see Fetlock). This is much nearer the sense of the word 'dislocate' than Johnson's theory.

Disparage. From the Latin *par*, equal, the French derive the word *parage*, equality of birth, blood or lineage. Hence to match a person with one of inferior condition is to 'disparage' him. Anything done to 'lower' a man in his own estimation, or in that of others, 'disparages' him.

Dissenting Chapel. The first dissenting chapel or 'meeting-house' in England was at Wandsworth, Surrey. It was opened as a place of worship, November 20, 1572.

Dissever, Disannul. The negative prefix in these two words has no effect whatever on the signification. Sever and dissever both mean to separate or cut off; annul and disannul are alike in signification.

Dissimilation. 'We have long had "assimilation" in our dictionaries, but "dissimilation" has yet scarcely found its way into them, but it speedily will.'—*Trench* (1851).

Distillation is the process of separating alcohol from fermented liquors in which it is present. It is effected by taking advantage of the fact that alcohol, or spirit, boils, and is consequently converted into steam at 170 degrees of heat, while water does not boil under 212 degrees. If, therefore, a mixture of alcohol and water be heated to 180 degrees, the spirit will pass off in steam or vapour, the water still remaining in its liquid condition. The alcoholic vapours are carried through pipes surrounded with cold water, and are there re-condensed, falling out at the lowest point in a liquid form.

Distressed. The Americans apply this word (which they pronounce dis-tress'-ed) to anything which they think unfit, improper, or not good enough for the purpose—*e.g.* 'Why,' said the pedlar to the Widow Bedott, who had selected an article for her wedding dress, 'a body 'd think 'twas some everlastin' old maid, instead of a handsome young widder that had chosen such a *distressëd* thing for a weddin' dress.'—*Widow Bedott Papers*.

Ditto. This is the English form of the Italian word *detto*. In the original it means 'as aforesaid.'

Ditty, Inditing. According to Verstegan, both these words come from the Anglo-Saxon word *Diht*, or *Dight*, which he defines as follows:—'Meeter or rime; hereof cometh our name of *dities*, for things that be *deighted*, or made in meeter. *Dighting* or *indighting* is also prose set forth in exact order.'—*Restitution*, &c. p. 168.

Diversion is that which diverts, or 'turns us aside,' from the cares and troubles of everyday life.

Dives. The name Dives is generally supposed to have been that of the rich man at whose door Lazarus lay. There is, however, no mention of the name in Scripture. Our version has, 'There was a certain rich man.' This in the Vulgate is '*Homo quidam erat dives.*' So also the expression, 'The rich man also died,' stands in the Vulgate as '*Mortuus est autem et dives.*' No doubt 'dives' became 'Dives' under the belief that it was a proper name. The misapprehension may have been strengthened by the mediæval practice of inscribing pictures founded on the Scriptural narrative with the words *Dives et Lazarus*—'The rich man and Lazarus'—which might lead to the belief that 'dives,' like Lazarus, was a proper name.

Divest, from the Latin *de vestio*, to undress; hence to deprive of. 'Divest' is the opposite of 'invest.'

Divorced persons re-marrying. 'The man will present himself [at the altar] as a bachelor; the woman will come, not as a married person, nor as a widow, but as a spinster. In a word the sentence of divorce will effectually restore the parties to their original state.'—*Macquelin's Practical Treatise on Marriage*, &c.

Dr. Syntax. The work, so popular half a century ago, called 'Adventures in Search of the Picturesque,' was written by an able but eccentric man named William Combe. He wrote the book, and Rowlandson illustrated it. It was published by Ackerman in the Strand, and had, for that time, an almost unexampled 'run.' Combe was extravagant, and ran through, not only an inherited fortune, but also enormous sums earned by his facile pen. He died in the King's Bench prison.

Document. The word document was formerly used as a verb in the sense of to teach, to direct, to instruct. Dryden has, 'I am finely "documented" by my own daughter.'

'**Documents** properly include all material substances on which the thoughts of men are represented by any species of conventional mark or symbol. Thus the wooden score on which a baker and his customers indicate by notches the number of loaves supplied, the old Exchequer tallies, and such like, are "documents" as much as the most elaborate deed.'—*Best, C. J.*

Dodge. 'That homely, but expressive phrase,' as the present Lord Cairns called it in the House of Commons, 2nd March, 1859, is from the Anglo-Saxon *deogian*, to disguise, to colour, to conceal.

Dog. 'Take a hair of the dog that bit you' is advice given figuratively for 'Take a cool glass of ale in the morning after excess in ale over night.' Our forefathers, however, gave and accepted the advice literally and practically. In an old Receipt Book, dated 1670, is the following: 'Take a hair from the dog that bit you, dry it, put it into the wound, and it will heal it, be it never so sore.'

Doggett's Coat and Badge. The first sculling match for this prize is thus recorded in 'The Weekly Journal' newspaper of Saturday, Aug. 15, 1715:—'Monday last six watermen, who were scullers, rowed from London Bridge to Chelsea, for a silver badge and livery, which was won by one John Hope; and this tryal of skill, which is to be performed yearly on the 1st of August, caused a great concourse of people to be then on the River of Thames.' It was founded to commemorate the accession, on August 1st, of George I., and is still annually competed for.

Dog-whipper. Formerly an officer, called a 'dog-whipper,' was appointed to every church. His duty was to drive the dogs out of the church during service. Even so late as 1856, the 'Exeter Gazette' announced that 'Mr. John Pickard, in the employ of the Rev. Chancellor Martin, has been appointed *dog-whipper* of Exeter Cathedral, in the room of Mr. Charles Reynolds, deceased.'

Dole. A portion given in charity; the portion *dealt* to the recipient.

Doll, the name of the little girl's favourite toy, Johnson thinks, is the diminutive of Dorothy. It is, however, with more probability derived from *idol*. The Welsh word for an image is *delw*. Anciently the English word *idol* meant 'something in the place of the real.'

Dollar Mark. Mr. J. E. Norcross, of Brooklyn, N.Y., in writing to 'Notes and Queries,' tells us that, before the establishment of the United States, each province had its own paper currency in pounds, shillings, and pence. The metallic currency was in Spanish dollars. These dollars, from their being of the value of eight reals, were called 'pieces of eight,' by which name Defoe speaks of them in the following extract from 'Robinson Crusoe' (sec. 4.):—'As to my boat, it was a very good one, and that he saw, and told me he would buy it of me for the ship's use; and asked me what I would have for it? I told him that I could not offer to make any price of the boat, but left it entirely to him; upon which he told me he would give me a note of hand to pay me eighty *pieces of eight* for it in Brazil.' Accounts, in the Southern parts of North America, were kept in dollars and reals, and as a distinguishing mark in the books, a cancelled figure of 8 was used, or sometimes the 8 was put between two slanting lines, thus : /8/. A period, or full stop, separated the digits representing the reals or eighths, from those representing the dollar. When the United States adopted the dollar as the money unit, it was found convenient to continue the old mark in the South and to adopt it in the North. The present symbol, $, therefore is this conventionalised form of the old cancelled figure 8, representing the coin of 8 reals. Two other origins have, however, been contended for; the first traces the mark to the Mexican 'Pillar Dollar,' on the reverse of which is the representation of two pillars or columns connected by a scroll. There is a rude resemblance in this device to the present dollar mark. The other theory is that the mark is the union of the two capital letters U and S, meaning United States. There is little doubt, however, that the mark originated in the manner Mr. Norcross points out.

Dome, Cupola. In architecture, a *cupola* is a roof or vault of rounded form. In England the word *dome* is generally applied to such structures, the name having been adopted into the language through a mistake. In Italy, the name *il duomo*, the temple, is given to the principal church or cathedral in a place; and as most of the Italian churches have cupolas, it has been supposed that the word *duomo* referred only to the rounded shape. An Italian, speaking of St. Peter's at Rome, applies the term *duomo*, or temple, to the entire building; an Englishman, speaking of the *dome* of St. Paul's, erroneously limits the meaning of the word to the magnificent cupola by which it is surmounted.

Domesday Book. A book made by order of William the Conqueror, in which the extent and value of lands in England, with the owners' names, were entered. 'It was composed after the two examples of the times of Ethelbert and Alfred. It was laid up in the church of Winchester, and for that reason, as graver authors say, was called "*Liber domus Dei*" [the Book of the Lord God], and by corruption of the last two words, *Domes-day Book*.'— *Verstegan*.

Domine dirige nos, the Latin motto of the City of London,

means 'O Lord, direct us.' It is divided into syllables thus:—
Dom-i-ne di-ri-ge nos.

Donkey. This now common name for an ass was unknown until towards the end of the eighteenth century, and it seems to have originated in London. The earliest known use of the word is in 'A Poetical Answer to Mr. Peter Pindar's Benevolent Epistle to John Nichols,' 1790, where the following lines occur:—

> But, Peter, thou art mounted on a Neddy,
> Or in the London phrase, thou Dev'nshire monkey,
> Thy Pegasus is nothing but a *Donkey.*

It was not until about 1850 that the word 'donkey' found its way into the dictionaries. It is a nickname for the ass, and nothing more.

Don't care a fig is properly 'don't care a *fico*.' *Fico* means a contemptuous snapping of the fingers. Shakespeare has 'a *fico* for the phrase.'

Dormer Window. A dormer window is a vertical window in the sloping roof of a house; so called from its lighting a 'dormitory,' or sleeping-place, from *dormio*, to sleep.

Dote, Fond. Both these words originally meant 'foolish.' We still call an imbecile man a 'dotard,' and say that he is in his 'dotage.' 'Fond' implied weakness, silliness, or simplicity. Shakespeare describes Lear as 'a foolish, *fond* old man'; and, in 'Coriolanus,' tells us that ''Tis *fond* to wail inevitable strokes'; while Ascham mentions the case of a boy who was 'beaten out of all love of learning by a *fond* [that is, foolish] schoolmaster.' It is curious to note that if we say we are 'dotingly fond' of some one, both the words imply that we are making fools of ourselves.

Dotting the i. D'Israeli ('Curiosities of Literature'), in exposing a literary forgery, says, 'Besides that, there were dots on the letter *i*, a custom not practised till the eleventh century.'

Double Christian Names. The earliest known mention of a double Christian name is in a deed poll, 36 Edward III. (anno 1363), executed by 'Stephen, son of John Fylip Curpel of Fineham.' Verstegan says, 'It is often seen in Germany, that either [? each] godfather at a christning, giveth his name to his god son; and therefore it cometh that many have two proper names besides their sirnames.'

Double-headed Eagle. The Eagles of the Eastern and the Western Empires had their heads turned in opposite directions.

When the empires were united under Charlemagne in 802, the two shields were divided perpendicularly, and the halves of each were brought together to form a united shield. The compound shield, therefore, shows only one body, but the two heads are retained.

Doubtful Orthography. The orthography of the English language is far from settled. Dr. Worcester, in his great Dictionary, gives a list of about 1,800 words differently spelt by English writers. Many changes have taken place since Johnson's time: as, for instance, the omission of *k* in the words musick, logick, publick, &c.; and of the *u* in error, emperor, &c. There is still, however, doubt whether 'travelling' should be spelt with *ll*, 'worshippers' with *pp*, 'civilize' with *z* or *s*, 'alchemy' with a *y*, as 'alchymy,' or 'bason' with an *o* or with an *i*, as 'basin.' There is plenty of work for an English 'Academy' on the model of the French one in clearing up these and other doubtful matters in the English language.

Douceur. This is a French word signifying 'sweetness.' In England it is used to designate a gift, or bribe.

Dout is *do out*, as 'dout the candle.' Many other phrases are similarly contracted, as *don*, for 'do on'; *doff*, for 'do off.' To 'doff your hat' is to take, or *do it*, off. See Dup.

Douters. Amongst old-fashioned people, in the midland counties, it is not usual to use *extinguishers* for putting out candles. An instrument is employed similar to ordinary snuffers, but having a pair of flat discs at the end with which to pinch the wick and so extinguish the flame. These are called 'douters,' from the old verb *dout* (which see). The following witty impromptu was sent by a lady, a few years ago, to a friend who had made her a present of a pair of these old-fashioned extinguishers :—

> An age of sceptics this, no doubt,
> Colenso, and such out-and-outers;
> But you, my friend, are doubly bold,
> In sending me a pair of *douters*.
> I doubt the doubtful gift to take—
> But no! I will accept in blindness;
> I'll *dout* the candles for your sake,
> But oh! I'll never doubt your kindness.

Dowager. Strictly speaking, a dowager is an endowed widow; that is, one who has a 'dower' from her late husband, or who has property brought by her to her husband on marriage ('dowry') and settled on herself after his decease. In practice the name 'dowager' is applied to any widowed lady of title, to distinguish her from the wife of the present holder of the title.

Dowdy, from the Scandinavian *Dawdie*, a dirty, slovenly, dawdling, indolent woman.

Dower, Dowry. *Dower* is the estate for life which a widow acquires in a portion of her husband's real estate after his death. *Dowry* is the portion brought by the wife to her husband upon their marriage.

Dowgate, London. A corruption of *Dourgate*, i.e. Watergate.

Dowlas is a kind of linen cloth first made at Dourlaus, a town of Picardy.

Downing Street was named after Sir George Downing, who, according to Wood, was 'a sider with all times and changes, skilled in the common cant, and a preacher occasionally.' He was sent by Cromwell to Holland as resident there. After the Restoration he espoused the King's cause, and was knighted and elected M.P. for Morpeth in 1661. He was afterwards created a baronet. He died in 1684.

Doyleys were so named from a tradesman of that name who first introduced them. The family of the Doyleys were linen and woollen drapers, who lived in a house at the corner of Upper Wellington Street in the Strand, from the time of Queen Anne until about 1850. Dryden speaks of 'Doiley' petticoats, and Steele, in the 'Guardian' (No. 102), of his 'Doiley' suit. Mr. Wedgwood thinks this derivation wrong, and suggests the Dutch *dwaele*, a towel. The Swiss word for a napkin comes even nearer; it is *dwaheli*.

Dozen, from the Teutonic *deux*, two, and *zen*, ten.

Dragoons are cavalry trained to act either on horseback or on foot, as emergencies require. They are so called from carrying a short-barrelled firearm anciently called a *dragoon*.

Dramatic Critics. The writer of the article 'London' in the 'Parliamentary Gazetteer' (Fullarton and Co.), in a note on the early London theatres, says, 'The critics sat on the stage, and were supplied with pipes and tobacco' (vol. iii.)

Drat 'em and **Od rot 'em.** These colloquial terms, used so frequently by old playwriters, and by modern scolds, are probably contractions of 'May the gods out-root them.'—*Notes and Queries.*

Dray, or **Drey,** is the old name for a squirrel's nest. The word is in frequent use among the older poets, e.g.—

> Whilst he from tree to tree, from spray to spray,
> Gets to the woods and hides him in his *dray.*
> *Browne, Pastorals,* i. 5.

> Climbed like a squirrel to his *dray,*
> And bore the worthless prize away.—*A Fable (Cowper).*

Dreshell, or **Threshell,** a flail. This word is frequently confounded with the word 'threshold.' Aubrey says, the inmates of a house he is speaking of 'think not the noise of the "threshell" ill musique.' The word, in the form dreshell, or draishell, was until lately common in the West of England. It is probably a corruption of 'thrashall.' The West of England rustics call the two parts of the draishall by separate names, the *handstaff,* and the *vlail,* or *flegel,* which is 'flying-staff,' from the Anglo-Saxon *fleogan,* to fly. Over the greater part of England the latter term only has been retained, and the compound implement is known only as the 'flail.'

Dresser. The 'kitchen dresser' of our days had an exalted origin. Mr. Wright tells us that in the fifteenth and sixteenth centuries, 'one of the great objects of ostentation in a rich man's house was his plate, which at dinner-time he brought forth, and caused to be spread on a table in sight of his guests. Afterwards, to exhibit the plate to more advantage, the table was made with shelves or steps, on which the different articles could be arranged in rows, one above another. It was called in French, or Anglo-Norman, a *buffet,* or a *dressoir* (dresser), the latter name being given to it because, on it, the different articles were *dressés,* or arranged.'—*Domestic Manners of the Middle Ages,* p. 379.

Drinking Fountains in the seventh century. In 'Hardyng's Chronicle' (ed. by Ellis, p. 162) it is stated that King Ethelfryde

> Mayde he welles in diuerse countrees spred,
> By the hye wayes, in cuppes of copper clene
> For trauelling folke, faste chayned as it was sene.

Drinking Healths. The custom of drinking healths is of great antiquity. A story is current that at an entertainment given by Hengist, in the fifth century, to the British king, Vortigern, the young and beautiful daughter of the host, Rowena, knelt and presented the wine cup to the king, saying as she did so, '*Liever kyning, wass hœl*'—'Dear king, your health'—and this is generally quoted as the origin of the custom. See TOAST.

Dropsy. An abbreviation of 'Hydropisy'; from *hydor*, water.

Drum. This word, so much used a generation or two ago to signify an evening party, and latterly in the phrase 'kettle-drum,' a tea-party, is probably a corruption of the Dutch *drom*, a crowd.

Drum. The 'beats' of the drum, used as signals in the British infantry, were composed by Drum-Major Potter, of the Coldstream Guards.

Drummer. In America, a commercial traveller is called a *drummer*, and travelling in search of business is called *drumming*. 'The expenses of *drumming* amount to no small sum. Besides employing extra clerks, and paying the extra price for their board at the hotels, the merchant has to be very liberal with his money in paying for wine, oyster suppers, theatre tickets, and such other means of conciliating the favour of the country merchant as are usually resorted to by *drummers*.'—*Perils of Pearl Street*, ix.

Drunk as Blazes. This vulgar expression is a corruption of 'drunk as Blaizers.' Bishop Blaize is the patron saint of wool-combers, who, at Leicester and elsewhere, celebrate his festival with marchings and great convivialities. In Sir Thomas Wyse's 'Impressions of Greece,' he mentions this custom, and says:— 'Those who took part in the procession were called *Blaizers*, and the phrase "as drunk as Blaizers" originated in the convivialities common on these occasions.'

Drunk as Chloë. This saying probably refers to the lady of that name, notorious for her drinking habits, so often mentioned by Matthew Prior in his poems.

Drury Lane Theatre was originally a cockpit, which was converted into a theatre in the time of James I. It was pulled down and rebuilt in 1662, burnt in 1672, and a new one built by Wren in 1674. The interior was rebuilt in 1775. In 1791 it was pulled down and rebuilt, being opened in 1794. It was burnt down February 1809, and replaced by the present building, which was opened October 10, 1812. See PIT.

Dryasdust. Scott probably got his first idea of this name from the assumed name of the author of 'Wit Revived, or a New and Excellent Way of Divertissement, Digested into most Ingenious Questions and Answers,' by *Asdryasdust* Tossofacean (London, 1674, 12mo.). Lowndes says a copy was sold at Heber's sale, for 1*l*. 11*s*. 0*d*.—*Bohn*, p. 2958.

Dublin. In the Irish language this is *Dubh-linn,* the meaning of which is 'black-pool.' The name has reference to the fact that the greater part of the site of the city was formerly a black, slimy expanse of mud, through which the River Liffey flowed sluggishly to the sea.

Ducats were first coined in Sicily. They take their name from the word *Ducatus,* which was part of the inscription the earliest bore. *Ducatus* means 'Duchy.'

Ducking-stool. The 'ducking-stool' was an instrument formerly used for punishing scolding wives. It was a chair, fixed at the extremity of a beam, working on a pivot, between two uprights fixed upon a rude cart with low wheels. The offender was fastened in the chair, which was then wheeled to the nearest river, or pond, where the short end of the beam being raised, she was dipped over head in the water. The last 'ducking' was at Leominster, in 1809, when one Jenny Piper was so punished. The stool is still in existence, and has recently (October 1879) 'been repaired by Mr. Arkwright, of Hampton Court, and is now in safe keeping in the Town Hall, where it may be seen upon application.'

Ducks and Drakes. To 'make ducks and drakes' with one's money is an allusion to a game played by boys, who take oyster-shells, or flat stones, and throw them horizontally along the surface of a piece of water, in such a manner that the missiles skim along the surface, touching it many times and again emerging. The first time the stone emerges it is a *duck,* the second a *drake;* and so on, according to the old doggerel—

>A duck and a drake,
>And a halfpenny cake,
>And a penny to pay the baker, &c.

The meaning, in the case of money, is, that the spendthrift metaphorically uses coins, as boys use stones, to make 'ducks and drakes.'

Dudgeon. In 'Macbeth,' act ii. scene 1, Shakespeare has—

>I see thee yet,
>And on thy b'ade and *dudgeon* gouts of blood
>Which was not so before.

The term *dudgeon* was for a long time misunderstood, a 'dudgeon-dagger' being defined as a small dagger. It was correctly explained by Bishop Wilkins, who, in his 'Real Character,' explains 'dudgeon' to be the root of the box-tree; and *dudgeon dagger* 'a small sword whose handle is of the root of box.' Gerrard, under the article

'Box-tree,' writes :—'The root is likewise yellow, and harder than the timber, and of greater beauty, and more fit for dagger-hafts ... Turners and others doe call this wood dudgeon, wherewith they make *dudgeon-hafted* daggers.' The word dudgeon seems afterwards, for brevity's sake, to have been used for 'dagger.' Butler says of his hero's dagger :—

> It was a serviceable dudgeon,
> Either for fighting or for drudging.—*Hudibras*, l. i. v. 379.

'*Gouts* of blood,' in the first quotation, is *drops* : *goutte*, French, a drop.

Duel. *Duellum*, in Latin, signifies a battle between any number of combatants. In the Middle Ages, the use of the Latin word *duo*, two, and of the familiar term 'the dual number,' induced the erroneous belief that the combats between two persons, then so common, must be the *duellum* of the Romans; who, however, had no notion of a practice such as the modern 'duel.' Neither was duelling known to the Anglo-Saxons; but it was probably introduced by the Normans. Up to the time of Elizabeth, trial by duel was a regular judicial proceeding. Duelling declined during the Commonwealth, but revived, and became very prevalent, during the reign of Charles II. Queen Anne, in a Speech to Parliament, in 1712, recommended an Act for its abolition, but it was not passed, and the custom prevailed until 1844, when some new Articles of War were issued, under which any officer 'who shall send or accept a challenge, or who, being privy to an intention to fight a duel, shall not take active measures to prevent it, or who shall upbraid another for refusing, or for not giving, a challenge,' is made liable to be cashiered. Under this rule, the practice may be said to have become obsolete in this country. Duels are still, however, occasionally fought in France, and other Continental countries.

Duffer. A 'duffer' was one who offered inferior goods to the unwary, under the pretence that they were smuggled. In the 'Oxford Journal,' May 25, 1765, is an account of the apprehension of 'an East India *Duffer*, or fellow who pretends to sell ignorant people great bargains of smuggled goods.'

Dulwich College was founded in 1619, by Edward Alleyne, a tragic actor. The pictures in the Gallery were bequeathed, in 1811, by Sir F. Bourgeois.

Dumb-bell. The original dumb-bell was an apparatus contrived like that for ringing church-bells; that is, a heavy flywheel with a weight attached, which was set in motion like a church bell, until it acquired sufficient impetus to carry the gymnast up and down, and so bring the muscles into active play. There is one at New College, Oxford, to the present day. The modern weights, so called, produce similar results, in a less cumbrous and more agreeable manner.

Dun. It is said that this word originated in the name of John Dun, a bailiff of Lincoln, in the time of Henry VII., who was so active in collecting debts, that it became proverbial to say of anyone who was slow to pay, that the creditor must ' *dun* him '; that is, send Dun after him.

Dunce. This word is believed to be from the name of Duns Scotus, a mediæval divine. A more probable theory is that of Dr. Mackay, who derives it from 'the Gaelic *donas*, bad luck; or in contempt a poor ignorant creature. The Lowland Scotch, borrowing from the Gaelic, has *donsie*, unfortunate, obstinate, stupid; whence *dunce*, a poor unfortunate creature, incapable of instruction.'

Dun Cow of Warwick. Guy, Earl of Warwick, is said to have killed a monster cow of a dun colour, which had ravaged the neighbourhood. Some huge bones are shown to visitors at Warwick Castle as those of the veritable dun cow. Professor Owen pronounced the bones to be those of a Mastodon, and Mr. Isaac Taylor says that the tradition is founded upon the conquest of the *Dena gau*, or Danish settlement in the neighbourhood.

Dup the door. This is a common phrase in country places, meaning 'fasten the door.' It is a contraction of the words ' Do up the door.' See DOUT.

Dupe. The word 'dupe' has nothing to do with duplicity. Dupe' originally meant a dove or pigeon, the most guileless and simple of creatures. Even now the word 'pigeon' is used as a synonym for a silly fellow who may be easily plucked.

Durability of Perfumes. 'Among the curiosities shown at Alnwick Castle is a vase taken from an Egyptian catacomb. It is full of a mixture of gums, resins, &c., which evolve a pleasant odour to the present day, although probably 3,000 years old.'— *Piesse's Art of Perfumery.*

Dust to dust. The custom of thrice throwing earth into the grave of a corpse was anciently performed by the priest, as directed by the rubric of 1542. That of 1552 first directed that it should be done by 'some one standing by.' Bishop Cosin says that in his day it was customary in most places for the priest to do it.—*Blunt, Annotated Book of Common Prayer.*

Dutch Auction. A sale in which the auctioneer fixes a high price upon that which he has for sale, gradually reducing it until some one closes with the offer.

Dwarf. This word did not originally convey the sense of smallness, but of crookedness and deformity. In the Scandinavian mythology 'dwarfs' were evil and deformed spirits.

Dwt, a pennyweight. In this symbol *d* is the initial of *denarius*, a penny, and *wt* are the first and final letters of the word weight. See CWT.

E

Eager. Shakespeare, in the first scene of 'Hamlet,' has 'It is a nipping and an *eager* air,' and in the fifth scene, 'And curd, like *eager* droppings into milk, the thin and wholesome blood.' The word 'eager' here is the French *aigre*, which has several meanings,' those bearing upon these quotations being, for the first, *rough, severe, harsh*; and for the second, *acid, sour*. Our word 'vinegar' is compounded of the French *vin*, wine, and *aigre*, sour.

E and O E. These letters are almost invariably found at the foot of merchants' statements of account. They mean 'Errors and omissions excepted.'

Ear of Corn. It is singular that both in the Latin and the Anglo-Saxon the name given to arrows should be derived from that of ears of corn. In the Latin an ear of corn was *spica*, and an arrow was *spiculum*. In the Anglo-Saxon the word 'ear' was used as at present, and an arrow was *earh*.

Earl. 'Before we borrowed the word *honour* we used instead thereof our own ancient word *ear*. For noble or gentle we used *Ethel*. "Ethel" was sometimes in composition abridged to *el*, so as of *Ear-ethel*, it came to be *Ear-el*, and by abbreviation "Earl"; it is as much as to say *honour-noble*, or noble of honour.'—*Verstegan, Vestiges,* &c., p. 247. Earl is the only title of nobility derived from the Anglo-Saxons. William the Conqueror first made hereditary earls, but they were to be called *counts*. The ancient title has, however, held its position to the present day, but the wives of earls are called *countesses*.

Earliest Printed Book. The earliest known complete printed book is a Latin Bible printed by Gutenberg and Fust at Mentz in 1455. A copy of this book is in the British Museum. It is called the 'Mazarine Bible,' from a copy found in the library of Cardinal Mazarin.

Early American Newspaper. Superscription upon one at the State Paper Office, London: 'Boston, Printed by R. Pierce for Benjamin Harris at the London Coffee House, 1690.'

Early English Bibles. 'The first edition of the folio Bible, called "The Great Cromwell Bible," which was the first English Bible issued by authority (1538-1539), and was printed in the reign of Henry VIII., consisted of 2,500 copies, one of which was set up in every church in England, and secured to a desk by a chain. Within three years there were seven editions of this work.'—*Dibdin, Bibliographical Decameron.*

Early English Newspaper. The 'English Mercurie,' 1588, which for nearly a century past was believed to be the first English newspaper, a paper for which mankind was said to be indebted to 'the wisdom of Queen Elizabeth, and the prudence of Burleigh,' was proved, in 1839, by Mr. Thomas Watts, of the British Museum, to be an impudent forgery. One fact which he mentions is conclusive. The paper upon which it is printed bears the arms of the House of Hanover, and the initials 'G. R.' The 'Gentleman's Magazine' for May 1850 says, 'It may be concluded with some certainty that for "the earliest newspaper" we are indebted to the press of James Bettenham of St. John's Lane.'

Early Illustrated Book. The first book containing engravings is a copy of 'Dante's Poems' printed at Florence in 1481.

Early Local Newspaper. In Reid's 'Handbook to Newcastle-upon-Tyne' it is stated that 'The earliest instance of the printing of a newspaper in any prominent town in Great Britain occurred in Newcastle during the sojourn of Charles I. in the North in 1639. He was attended by Robert Barker, the Royal Printer, who issued a news-sheet from time to time.'

Early London Banks. Child's Bank was established in 1663; Hoare's in 1675; Snow's in 1680; and the Bank of England in 1694.

Early mention of Playbills. In the 'Books of the Stationers' Company' there is an entry (October 1567) of a licence granted to

John Charlewood ' by the whole consent of the assistants,' for the 'Onlye ymprinting of all maner of bills for players. Provided that if any trouble arise herebye, then Charlewood to bear the charges.'

Early mention of Railroads. In North's 'Life of the Lord Keeper North' (1676) is the following :—'At that period near Newcastle-on-the-Tyne coals were conveyed from the mines to the banks of the river by laying rails of timber exactly straight and parallel; and bulky carts were made with four rollers fitting these rails, whereby the carriage was made so easy that one horse would draw four or five chaldrons.'

Early Newspaper Advertisements. The earliest known advertisement occurs in the ' Mercurius Elencticus,' No. 45, Oct. 4, 1648, and is as follows :—' The reader is desired to peruse A Sermon Entituled *A Looking Glasse for Levellers*, Preached at St. Peters, Paules Wharf, on Sunday, Sep. 24, 1648, by Paul Knell, M[r]. of Arts. Another Tract called *A Reflex upon our Reformers*, with a Prayer for the Parliament.' This is four years earlier than the one mentioned as the earliest by Mr. James Grant in his work ' The Newspaper Press.'

Early notice of Gas. In the ' Times ' newspaper, May 17, 1800, is an advertisement of a display of ' Philosophical Fireworks,' at the Lyceum Theatre, which states that ' The Theatre will be illuminated by a most curious aëroferic Branch, which is lighted and extinguished in a moment.'

Early Theatres. The earliest theatrical performances in England took place in inn yards. The spectators watched the performances from the open galleries which led to the bedchambers of the inn. The Globe Theatre, which was built on the grounds of the ' Globe Tavern,' was modelled much in the style of an innyard, being without a roof.[1] The galleries, or ' scaffolds ' as they were called, ran tier above tier round three sides of the building over the ' rooms ' which corresponded to our modern boxes. What we call the pit was then the ' ground,' where the common people stood to witness the performances. Shakespeare speaks of this portion of a theatrical audience as ' the groundlings,' and Ben Jonson mentions ' the *understanding* gentlemen of the *ground*.' In Shakespeare's time the price of admission to the ' rooms ' was a shilling, and to the ' scaffolds ' sixpence. The charge for admission to the ' ground ' varied, being in some cases as low as a penny.

[1] It was afterwards thatched, except in the centre, which was left open to give light.

Early use of Hydropathy. Horace Walpole writes to Cole in 1775, 'At Malvern they certainly put patients into sheets just dipped in the spring.'—*Letters*, vol. v., p. 419.

Early Watches. The early watches were driven by catgut pullies instead of chain. In Beckmann's 'History of Inventions,' edit. 1846, vol. i., p. 362, is a note stating that Sir Richard Burton of Sacket's Hill, Isle of Thanet, has a silver watch, presumably of the time of Elizabeth, in which catgut is used in place of chain.

Earn. Comes from an old Teutonic word for harvest, implying to reap the fruit of one's labour. In Dutch the word for harvest is *erne*, and *ernan* is to reap. In German *ernte* means harvest; in Bavarian *arn* is harvest, and *arnen* signifies both to reap and to earn wages (g'arnen).

Earth. 'The earth is the Lord's and the fullness thereof.' It is generally, but erroneously, thought that Prince Albert suggested these words as appropriate for an inscription on the pediment of the Royal Exchange. The correct story is given by the architect (Mr. Tite) in a letter to the 'Times,' March 13th, 1862, from which the following is condensed :—'The figure of Commerce stands in the centre of the group upon an elevated pedestal, which, when completed of proper size, looked very bare, though the defect was not apparent in the model. Sculptor and architect tried various plans to hide the defect—wreaths, festoons, &c.—but all were unsatisfactory. Prince Albert on a visit to Westmacott's studio advised some religious inscription, which he particularly wished should be in English. Mr. Westmacott consulted Dr. Milman, the Dean of St. Paul's, who suggested the words of the Psalmist, which were adopted.'

Earwig. The popular notion is that this insect is named from its supposed propensity to creep into the human ear. This is an error. In old English the word *ear* meant an undeveloped flower-bud, particularly of corn, and *wic* meant a hiding-place or dwelling. The favourite hiding place of the insect under notice is in closely shielded bud-ears of plants, hence the name *earwic*, which was originally so written, but has since been corrupted into earwig.

Easel. The name of the painter's easel is from the German *esel*, an ass.

Easter Dues, or **Easter Offerings.** Under the old laws, the rector of a parish was entitled to tithes of the labour of his parishioners. The Easter offerings now are voluntary contributions as compensation to the clergy in respect of these personal tithes.

Eating-houses in Newfoundland. At the beginning of this century, earthenware plates and dishes were almost unknown luxuries in Newfoundland. At the public eating-houses, iron hoops, some ten inches diameter, were fastened to the tables, and from the receptacles thus formed the customers ate their food.

Ecce Homo, Latin, literally 'Behold the Man,' the words used by Pilate (John xix. 5). It is generally applied to the Saviour. It is divided and pronounced *Ek se ho-mo*.

Ecclesiastes. This canonical book is generally attributed to Solomon, but the authorship is disputed, and it is now thought by the most competent critics to have been written about the year 340 B.C. The verse (chap. i. 12) where the writer says, 'I the preacher *was* king over Israel,' could not have been written by Solomon, as he was king until his death. The allusions to the state of the laws, injustice amongst judges, &c., do not correspond to circumstances in Solomon's time; and the language, according to Dr. Davidson, distinctly points to its origin at a time subsequent to the Babylonian captivity.

Eclipse. An eclipse of the sun is caused by the moon coming in a direct line between the earth and the face of the sun. An eclipse of the moon is caused by the earth coming between the sun and the moon, so that the shadow of the earth is thrown upon the moon.

Eddy. Mr. Wedgwood derives this word from the old Norse *yda*, a whirlpool.

Edict of Nantes. This famous edict was issued April 13th, 1598, by Henry IV. of France to secure to the Protestants the free exercise of their religion. It was confirmed by Louis XIII. in 1610, and by Louis XIV. in 1652. Afterwards, in a fit of caprice, Louis revoked it, October 22, 1685. This step led to a renewal of the persecutions and bloody scenes which had been enacted against the Protestants before the promulgation of the edict. Hundreds, if not thousands, perished by the sword. About half a million of the most intelligent and industrious of the people emigrated, carrying with them immense sums of money, together with many industrial arts. The greater part of these emigrants settled in England, where they established silk manufactures, glass making, and many other trades which up to that time were unknown in England.

Edify, from the Latin *edes*, a building, means to build up.

There was a holy chapel *edified*.

From the same root we get the word edifice.

Educate. This word is from the Latin *educo*, to lead forth. It is often improperly used instead of the word 'instruct.' To educate means to 'bring out' the latent or innate faculties of the mind. To instruct means to 'impart' knowledge, to 'inform' the mind, to teach, to direct.

Effigy. This word originally meant the *features*. In a MS. declaration by Lord Colerain in 1675, bound up in 'Dugdale's History of St. Paul's Cathedral,' in the library of the Earl of Oxford, there is an account of the disinterment of the body of Bishop Braybrooke, who had been buried 250 years. In this account the following words occur:—'On the right side of ye cheek there was flesh and hair visible, enough to give some notice of his *effigy*.'

Eggs as food. The most ancient Scriptural allusion to eggs as food is in Job vi. 6 : 'Is there any taste in the white of an egg ?'

Eglantine. Milton was mistaken in giving the name 'eglantine' to the honeysuckle. The true eglantine is the prickly sweetbriar of our gardens (*Rosa rubiginosa*).

Egyptian Hall. The Egyptian Hall in the Mansion House of the City of London was so called because of its exact correspondence with the Egyptian Hall described by Vitruvius.

Ei, or Ie. This combination is very puzzling, even to persons well acquainted with orthography. A simple rule is that 'ei' should always follow the consonants *c* and *s*, as receive, seize, &c., and 'ie' should follow all other consonants, as belief, thief, &c. There are, however, two exceptions to this rule, the words sieve and siege.

Either, in the sense of 'each.' All the best modern writers condemn the use of the word 'either' in this sense. Lowth says '*Each* signifies both of them, taken distinctly or separately; *either* properly signifies only the one or the other taken disjunctively. For which reason the expression in the following passages seems improper:—"They crucified two others with him, on *either* side one, and Jesus in the midst."—*John* xix. 18. "On *either* side of the river was there the tree of life."—*Rev.* xxii. 2.' In both cases it should be 'on each side.'

Either, Neither. *Either* means one of two. *Neither* means exactly the opposite, that is, not one of two. In the case of each word its meaning is limited to two objects. Yet both words are constantly applied to a greater number of objects; not only in ordinary speech, but in the writings of persons who ought to know better. Such phrases as 'It was either Monday, Tuesday, or Wednesday, but I don't know which,' may be excusable in ordinary speakers; but when a newspaper of position prints in its leading columns a sentence in which we find 'Neither of the three allied powers' we can but wonder. Even Archbishop Trench, as Mr. Gould in his 'Good English' points out, is not free from this error. In 'English Past and Present' Dr. Trench has the following passage:—'*Either* the words were not idiomatic, *or* were not intelligible, *or* were not needed, *or* looked ill, *or* sounded ill, *or* some other valid reason existed against them.' In this sentence there are five definite and one indefinite subject to which the word 'either' is applied or implied by a writer who is one of the highest authorities on the subject of pure English.

Elbow. The ancient *ell*, a measure, was the length of the arm of Henry I. *Elbow* is the bow, or bend, of the ell, or arm.

Electric Telegraph. Arthur Young ('Travels in France,' 1792) says that on October 15th, 1787, he saw at a mechanician's at Paris, an electrical machine and pith-ball electrometer. A wire connected this with a similar one in a distant apartment. Words given to an operator in the first room were read by his wife in the other from the pith-ball motions there. 'Thus,' says Young, 'they have invented an alphabet of motions suitable for besieged cities communicating outside,' &c.

Eleme Figs are brought from Eleme, a small village near Smyrna.

Elephant. The hind legs of the elephant have the knee-joint in front, as in man, so that when the knee is bent the angle is towards the head, and not backwards, as in the horse and most other animals. In lying down, the elephant stretches his legs backwards as a man does in kneeling; but other animals bring the hind legs forwards. The usual load of a full-grown elephant is about 5,000 lbs. The word 'trunk' is a foolish corruption of the old English name *trump*, which was correctly derived from the Latin. Pliny says, 'the elephant can make a noise like a *trumpet*'; hence the name *trump*, which the French still retain (*la trompe*), but which we have discarded for the silly and inapplicable word 'trunk.'

Eleven and **Twelve.** The names of these two numbers are curiously formed in all the languages of the Teutonic stock. Thus 'eleven' means *one left*, i.e. after counting ten; German, *ainlif*. So 'twelve' means *two left;* in Gothic, *twa-lif*. In most other languages the names are formed by adding one, or two, to ten, as in *undecim* and *duodecim*; on the same principle as our higher numbers—thirteen, fourteen, &c.

Eliminate means to 'throw out,' to 'reject,' but it is often erroneously used to signify to select for the purpose of retaining.

Elizabethan. This word has but five syllables, but is commonly pronounced as if there were six. It is properly E-liz-a-be-than— not E-liz-a-be-*thi*-an.

Embden Groats were so named because they were first made at Emden, or Embden, a town on the river Ems, in Hanover.

Embezzle. At one time this word conveyed no meaning of dishonesty. In the will of Matthew Prior, the poet, is the following bequest :—' I leave to Mr. Adrian Drift, the sum of one thousand pounds, to be employed and disposed of at his discretion, hoping that his industry and management will be such that he will not *embezzle* or decrease the same.'

Embowel, Disembowel. Both these words, notwithstanding the negative prefix of the last, have the same signification.

Embrocation. Medical terms have greatly changed in signification within the last 150 years. The word 'embrocation,' for instance, is defined by Bailey to be 'a kind of fomentation wherein the fomenting liquor is let distil from aloft, drop by drop, very slowly, upon the part or body to be fomented.'—*Dictionary*, edit. 1757.

Emerald. It is very singular that there are two words in the Welsh language which together fairly describe the emerald, and closely resemble the name. *Em* is a gem, and *eiriawl* is splendid. The name Emerald came originally from the Greek.

Emerald Isle. The author of this epithet was Dr. William Drennan, of Belfast, who died 1820. It occurs in a poem entitled 'Erin,' of which the fourth stanza runs thus :—

> Arm of Erin! prove strong, but be gentle as brave,
> And, uplifted to strike, still be ready to save,
> Nor one feeling of vengeance presume to defile
> The cause, or the men of the EMERALD ISLE.

In a note Dr. Drennan 'claims the original use of an epithet—the Emerald Isle, in a party song written in the year 1795'; and adds, 'From the frequent use of the term since that time, he fondly hopes that it will gradually become associated with the name of his country, as descriptive of its prime natural beauty, and its inestimable value.'

Emery is so called from Cape Emeri, in the island of Naxos, where the best variety is obtained.—*Brand.*

Emigrate, Immigrate. A person *emigrates from* one country, and *immigrates into* another. Hence, an *e*migrant is a person leaving his native land, and an *im*migrant is one who has arrived at the country of his adoption.

Emmet and **Ant** 'are different spellings of the same word. The different spellings by which they are bridged over are emmet, emet, emt, ant.'—*Trench.*

Empress. The title Empress was applied to Queen Elizabeth by no less an authority than Edmund Spenser, who dedicated 'The Faerie Queene' 'To the Most High, Mightie, and Magnificent *Emperesse,* Renovned for Pietie, Vertve, and all Graciovs Government, Elizabeth, By the Grace of God, Queene of England, France, and Ireland, and of Virginia, Defender of the Faith, &c., Her Most Humble Seruaunt, Edmund Spenser, doth, in all humilitie,' &c. (ed. 1612).

End, as an affix to the number of places, is very common, but its meaning is not always obvious, as some places having that additional name are situated in the middle of a plain, on the top of a hill, and in other localities where the word 'end' seems altogether inappropriate. In the parish of Great Hampden, Bucks, there is a place called Honor-end, as to which the following entries from the parochial register afford some information which may be applicable to other places:—'1678. Mary Harper, the wife of William Harper, who dyed in a barne at Honor-end, *or Inn,* was buried 21 daye of October, 1678.' '1682. Anne Williams, widow, a Traveller, who dyed at Honor *Inne* barne, was buried the 26 of June, 1682.' '1775. Dec. 28th. Mr. John Stone of Honor's *Inn.*' There is no inn now at the place.

Endemic diseases are those which, although attacking a number of people simultaneously, are confined to certain districts or countries, and seem to arise from local causes. They are supposed to be caused by some peculiar poison or malaria generated in the soil; diffused in the atmosphere, and weakened in its effects in proportion to its distance from the place of its origin. Ague is *endemic* in most fenny or marshy districts, and diseases of this type are very prevalent in the dense forests of the tropics. They differ from epidemic diseases in being altogether free from contagion. Endemics are checked by drainage and cultivation, and in some places, formerly almost uninhabitable, they have completely disappeared under these good influences.

Endorse or **Indorse**, from the Latin *in*, in, and *dorsum*, the back. The word originally meant something carried on the back, as elephants were said to be 'endorsed with towers of archers,' but its meaning is now limited to the signatures on the back of bills of exchange, or other commercial or legal documents.

Endowment was formerly limited in meaning to money or other property settled upon a wife by way of *dower*. It has since been extended to money settled to the use of churches, schools, and other charities.

Endue, Endow, and **Indue.** Although Dr. Johnson thinks these are three different verbs, they are probably but variations of the spelling of the same word. Milton has

> More lovely than Pandora whom the Gods
> *Endowed* with all their gifts.

The Common Prayer Book has

> *Endue* them with thy Holy Spirit.

And Hooker has 'God *indued* the waters of Bethesda with supernatural virtue.' All these uses are exactly synonymous. But there is a stronger example in the Bible:—'And Leah said, God hath *endued* me with a good *dowry*.'—*Gen.* xxx. 20.

England. When Egbert, King of the West-Saxons, in 829, had subjugated the other six Saxon kingdoms, he summoned a general council at Winchester, at which it was declared that henceforth Britain should be called England, its people Englishmen, and himself King of England. The name was derived from the Angles, one of the tribes of Anglo-Saxons. Verstegan says, in reference to this change, 'To the affectation of which name of Englishmen it should seem he was chiefly moved in respect of Pope Gregory, his alluding to the name of *Engelisce* unto Angel-like. The name of Engel is yet at this present in all the Teutonic tongues, to wit, the High and Low Dutch, &c., as much as to say an Angel. And if a Dutchman be asked how he would in his own language call an *Angel-like-man*, he would say "ein Englishman," and being asked how in his own language he would or doth call an Englishman, he can give us no other name for him than that he gave before, *ein Englishman*; *Engel* being in their tongue an angel, and English, which they wrote *Engelsche*, angel-like. And such reason and consideration may have moved our former kings upon their best coyn of pure and fine gold to set the image of an Angel.'—*Restitution of Decayed Intelligence*, edit. 1655, p. 117.

English Cathedrals. The longest cathedral in England is that of Winchester, which is 545 feet; the shortest Oxford, which is 154 feet; Lincoln is the widest at the transept, 227 feet; Lichfield the narrowest, 88 feet. The following table gives the length and breadth in feet of some of the largest:—

	Internal length.	Width of transept.
Winchester	545	186
Ely	517	178
Canterbury	514	154
York	498	222
Lincoln	498	227
Peterborough	480	202
Salisbury	452	210
Durham	420	176
Gloucester	420	144
Norwich	411	191
Lichfield	411	88
Worcester	410	130

English Dukes. The first English Duke was Edward the Black Prince, who was created Duke of Cornwall, a title which has ever since belonged to the eldest son of the sovereign, during the life of his parent. He is called *dux natus*, or a born duke, in contradistinction to *duces creati*, or dukes by creation. There were several dukes in the time of the Tudors, but the title in Elizabeth's reign became utterly extinct. James revived it in favour of George Villiers, who was created Duke of Buckingham, and Charles II. conferred the title on several of his illegitimate sons.

English Gold Coinage. The gold coinage of England commenced in the reign of Edward III., the quality of the gold being upwards of twenty-three carats fine, or nearly pure. A pound weight (Troy) of this gold was made into coins of the current value of 13*l*. 3*s*. 4*d*. The price of gold gradually rose, until at the accession of Henry VIII. the product of one pound of gold was 22*l*. 10*s*. Henry, as in the case of silver, debased the gold, and raised the amount of coinage per pound. He reduced the standard to twenty carats, which he made to produce 30*l*. in money, making enormous profits by the change. His successors gradually fell back upon the ancient standard, but in 1604 James I. again reduced it to twenty-two carats, at which it still remains. In 1604 the pound Troy produced 37*l*. 4*s*.; the present coinage value of a pound of standard gold (22) is 46*l*. 14*s*. 6*d*.

English Language. The name *Semi-Saxon* was applied to the English language, as spoken from the middle of the twelfth to the middle of the thirteenth century. From that period to the death of Edward III., in 1377, the term *old English* is applied. From thence to the death of Queen Elizabeth, in 1603, it is called *middle English*; and from that date to the present it has been called *modern English*.

It is a singular fact that among the many thousands of Norman words which were introduced into the English language at the time of the Conquest, not a single pronoun is to be found. Lake, in his 'Inventions and Discoveries,' in comparing the English and the Latin languages, says, "It may be proved that where a Latin verb will admit of but two variations, ours, answering thereto, may be very conveniently extended to eleven in the present tense, six in the past, and twenty-four in the future, with the simple assistance of auxiliaries and emphasis only; and every tense of our verb, it is calculated, will produce ninety-six variations.'

English Printing. It is commonly believed that the earliest book printed in England was 'The Game and Playe of the Chesse,' and that this book was printed in Westminster Abbey in 1474. This, it seems, is a mistake. 'It was,' says Blades, 'translated into English in that year, but was printed at Bruges.' Caxton did not set up his printing press until 1475-6, and it was *near*, not inside, but outside, Westminster Abbey. The second edition of this book, under the title of 'A book of the Chesse Moralysed,' was printed by Caxton *neare* Westminster Abbey in 1480. It is the earliest English book having woodcut illustrations. A copy is in the British Museum.

The earliest book printed in England on 'English made paper' was an edition of Trevisa's translation of Glanville's 'De Proprietatibus Rerum,' which was printed by Wynkyn de Worde, at Westminster, in 1495, on paper made by John Tate at Hertford. A copy of this work is in the British Museum.—*Power, Handybook about Books*, p. 32.

English Salt in France. English table salt is called in France *sel de cuisine*. *Sel anglais* means Epsom salts.

English Silver Coinage. At the time of the Conquest, the pound (Troy) of the silver used for coinage contained 11 oz. 2 dwts.

of the pure metal, and was coined into money of the value of 1*l.* sterling. The quality of the metal used remained the same until the accession of Henry VIII., but the size of the coins had gradually decreased, so that, at that time, a pound weight of silver produced coins of the value of 1*l.* 17*s.* 6*d.* Henry, for the first few years of his reign, retained the ancient standard of quality, but the price of silver continuing to rise, the pound weight of silver was made to produce 2*l.* 5*s.* in money. In 1543 Henry commenced a system of infamous tampering with the coinage. He first reduced the fineness of the silver by 1 oz. 2 dwts. in each pound, leaving only 10 oz. of pure silver; and three years afterwards, he still further reduced it, leaving only 4 oz. of silver in each pound weight. Notwithstanding this wholesale deterioration of the quality, the amount of coins from each pound was increased to 2*l.* 8*s.*, by which Henry secured a profit of 4*l.* 4*s.* upon each pound of pure silver employed. In the early years of the reign of Edward VI. this infamous system was continued; but, in 1551, four years after his accession, the standard of silver was raised to 11 oz. Mary raised it to 11 oz. 1 dwt.; and Elizabeth restored the ancient standard of 11 oz. 2 dwts., which has been continued to the present day. The pound weight is now coined into sixty-six shillings.

Enlist, or **Inlist,** as a soldier, is to enroll one's name *in the list* of soldiers in the service of the State.

Enough and **Enow.** Formerly these two words were used properly, but the word *enow*, which is the plural of enough, is now disused, except by a few old country people. 'Enough' refers to *quantity*, and 'enow' to *numbers*; as *enough* wheat or barley; *enow* turnips, horses, cows, or pigs.

Entangle. *Tangle* was the Anglo-Saxon name for a small bough or twig. Our ancestors used to smear twigs with birdlime to catch birds, which, when so caught, were said to be *entangled*. Hence the modern word, applied to one who is involved in intricate matters from which he cannot disengage himself. 'The Pharisees took counsel how they might *entangle* him in his speech.'—*Matt.* xxii. 15.

Enthusiast originally meant one who believed he had a private revelation from God; a zealot, a fanatic, a visionary.

Envelopes. Before the Penny Postage was introduced by Rowland Hill, envelopes were scarcely known; as the placing of a note, however small, in an envelope, however thin, would have converted the missive into a *double* letter, liable to twice the amount of the ordinary postage. Now, more than two millions of letters in envelopes pass through the Post Office every day. The first envelope-making machine was invented by Mr. Edwin Hill, the brother of Sir Rowland. Envelopes were, however, in use nearly two centuries ago. A writer in 'Notes and Queries,' October 3, 1857, says that he has an envelope which was used as the cover of a letter sent by Frederick the Great of Prussia to an English general. 'The envelope is like those at present in use, except that it opens at the end like those used by lawyers for deeds.' Mr. C. Hopper, in the same periodical (August 29, 1857), says:—' In examining some papers recently, at the State Paper Office, I met with one cut nearly the same as our modern envelopes, and attached to a letter of May 16, 1696, addressed by Sir James Ogilvie to the Right Hon. Sir William Trumbull, Secretary of State; the size was $4\frac{1}{4}$ by 3 inches.'

Epilogue (from the Greek *epi*, upon, and *logos*, a discourse) is properly what is termed a *peroration*; but its use is now confined to short and witty speeches made to audiences at the conclusion of dramatical performances.

Epithet. Worcester says that 'an *epithet* is an adjective denoting any quality, good or bad.' Epithets are, however, not all adjectives, although all adjectives are epithets. Many titles of honour are *epithets*. When we speak of Cardinal Newman we use an *epithet*, although the word 'Cardinal' is not an adjective as thus applied. The term *epithet* is often improperly used to denote nouns of an offensive character, such as 'fool,' 'coward,' and 'villain. These are not epithets; but their adjectives, 'foolish,' 'cowardly,' and 'vile,' are. Another common error is, that an epithet means something insulting or offensive, but it is not so; the words 'handsome,' 'truthful,' 'honest,' 'just,' 'worthy,' are all epithets.

Epsom Races. Races were first established at Epsom in 1711. They have been held annually since 1730.

Equestrian Statue. The oldest equestrian statue in the world is that of the Emperor Marcus Aurelius, in the piazza of the Capitol at Rome. Michael Angelo is said to have been so impressed with the air of motion given to it by the artist, as to have exclaimed to it *Cammina!* 'Move on then!' The statue formerly stood in front of the church of St. John Lateran. Marcus Aurelius was one of the greatest and most magnanimous of rulers the world has ever seen. He died Dec. 23, A.D. 176. De Quincey says, 'Till very lately the etiquette of Europe was that none but royal persons could have equestrian statues. Lord Hopetoun, the reader will observe, is allowed to have a horse in St. Andrew's Square, Edinburgh. True; but he is not allowed to mount him. The first person, so far as I can remember, that, not being royal, has in our island seated himself comfortably in the saddle, is the Duke of Wellington.'

Equinox. The term 'equinox' means literally *equal night*. There are two equinoxes in each year, the vernal and the autumnal. On these occasions the sun passes north, or south, over the equator, and the length of night and day is equal over the entire world. The equinoxes occur about the 21st days of March and September.

Equivocal, from the Latin *æquus*, equal, and *vox*, genitive *vocis*, a word, meaning a word so uncertain that it may be interpreted in either of two ways with equal facility.

Era, or Æra. Derived from A. ER. A., initial abbreviations of *Annus erat Augusti*, which initials were employed by the Spaniards to signify the time when their country came under the domination of Augustus, and they adopted the Roman Calendar. 'Era' differs from 'epoch.' 'Era' means a series of years proceeding from a fixed *point* of time; 'epoch' is the *point* itself. The Christian era began at the epoch of the birth of the Saviour.

Eradicate, from the Latin *e*, from, and *radix*, a root, meaning originally 'to pull up by the root.'

Erase, from the Latin *e*, from, and *rado*, to scrape.

Ermine. So called from its having been originally brought from Armenia.

Errant is an abbreviation of itinerant. Hence, a knight-errant is an itinerant, or travelling knight. Applied first to Don Quixote.

Error, from the Latin *erro*, to wander. Ben Jonson speaks of a voyage as an *error* by sea.

Erse. This is a corruption of the word 'Irish,' and is the name always applied to the original Irish language. The Lowlanders of Scotland call the language spoken by the Western Highlanders *Erse*, wrongly thinking it to be of Irish origin. The Highland language is *Gaelic*.

Eschscholtzia. The beautiful yellow flower so called derives its name from Dr. Eschscholtz, a botanist, who first brought it to Europe from California.

Espalier. Perhaps from the Spanish *espalda*, shoulder. In that language *espaldar* means 'something to lean against,' or 'a support,' and *espaldera*, 'wall-trained fruit-trees.' From this it seems to have been adopted by the French, who use *espalier* for fruit-trees trained against a wall, either by nailing to the wall itself, or on a frame or latticing. Our word is identical with the French.

Esquire. This word, in the primary meaning, is 'shield-bearer.' In the early Middle Ages this was called *scutifer*, from the Latin *scutum*, a shield, and *fero*, I bear. This, in the old French, became *escuyer*, from which the transition to its English form was easy and natural.

'Esquires may be divided into five classes; he who does not belong to one of them may or may not be a gentleman, but is no esquire.

1. Younger sons of peers, and their eldest sons.
2. Eldest sons of knights, and their eldest sons.
3. Chiefs of ancient families (by prescription).
4. Esquires by creation or office, as heralds and serjeants-at-arms; judges; justices of the peace; the higher naval and military officers; doctors in the several faculties; and barristers.
5. Each Knight of the Bath appoints *two* esquires to attend upon him at his installation and at coronations.

No estate, however large, confers this rank upon its owner.'—Wharton.

Established Religion. The earliest established or State-supported religion of which we have any record was that of Egypt. In Genesis xlvii. 22 we are told that when 'Joseph bought all the land of Egypt for Pharaoh,' he made an exception in the case of the priests, for 'the priests had a portion assigned them of Pharaoh . . . . . wherefore they sold not their lands.'

Estates of the Realm. It is generally believed that the three estates of the realm are Queen, Lords, and Commons. Whatever may be meant by the phrase now, it was clear that this was not the original meaning. The Collect for the Fifth of November in the old Prayer Books speaks of 'the King; *and* the three estates of the realm of England assembled in Parliament.' The meaning evidantly was: 1. The Lords Spiritual; 2. The Lords Temporal; 3. The Commons. As the word 'realm' means a 'kingdom, a state, a region,' it is clear that the King or Queen cannot be a part of it.

Estreat means *extract*. When a man is bound under his own recognizances, he engages to do certain things, or pay a certain penalty. The bond in which he makes the undertaking is then enrolled in the archives of the Court in which he is bound. If he fail to carry out his engagement, his 'recognizances are *estreated*'; that is, they are *extracted* from the rolls of the Court, and sent to the sheriff that he may proceed to recover the amount of the penalty as a debt due to the Crown.

Et cetera is a neuter plural, and should, consequently, never be applied to *persons*. It is, however, a common error of newspaper reporters, in closing a list of persons present at a meeting or ceremonial, to add the symbol '&c.' *&* is the modern form of *&*, the *E* and *T* joined together to form 'et.'

Etiquette. This word, which means simply a label or ticket, received its present figurative signification from the fact that an old Scotch gardener, who laid out the grounds at Versailles for Louis XIV., being much annoyed at the courtiers walking over his newly-made grounds, at length had labels placed to indicate where they might pass. At first these labels were not attended to; but a hint from high quarters that in future the walks of the courtiers must be within the 'etiquettes' was promptly attended to, and to *keep within the etiquettes* became the correct thing. The meaning of the phrase was afterwards widened, and is now universally understood.

Euphemism is a term employed to denote the art by which offensive terms are avoided, even when offensive matters have to be described. Thus we say, 'he was taken away'; 'he breathed his last'; or, 'he departed this life'; to avoid the unpleasant images called up by the direct statement that 'he died.' The ancients used many euphemisms to avoid expressions which they feared might be obnoxious to the unseen malignant powers. Thus they spoke of the Furies as *Eumenides*, or benign goddesses, and the stormy Black Sea was called the *Euxine*, or the hospitable.

Eurasian. This word, which is often met with in Indian newspapers, is applied to persons born of European fathers and native mothers. The word is a contracted combination of the two words 'European' and 'Asian.'

Evening Schools. The first evening school for instructing boys and girls who had to work all day was established, in 1806, at Bristol, by the 'Benevolent Evening Schools Society.'

Ever. A common fault in modern speech and writing is the introduction of the word 'ever' where it is entirely useless. For instance, in the phrase 'as soon as *ever* I saw him,' the italicised word is mere surplusage, and adds nothing to the strength, meaning, or elegance of the passage.

Everybody's business is nobody's business. In Izaak Walton's glorious 'Compleat Angler' (part i., c. 2), he says, 'I remember that a wise friend of mine did usually say, "That which is everybody's business is nobody's business."'

Every shepherd tells his tale
   Under the hawthorn in the dale.

'The word "*tale*" here means *tally*, or the account of the flock, which each shepherd numbers or *tells* in the morning; and not a love-tale.'—*Edgeworth's Readings on Poetry.*

Ewer. From the Norman *ewe;* French, *eau,* water.

Ex. A Latin prefix, signifying *out of,* or *beyond,* often used in English composition in the sense of *out of office,* as 'ex-emperor,' 'ex-mayor,' &c.

Exaggerate, from the Latin *agger,* a heap. The original meaning was to heap, or pile up.

Ex cathedra. A Latin phrase, signifying '*from the chair*'; usually applied to opinions or decisions of exalted personages, given in a solemn or judicial manner. See CATHEDRAL.

Exception proves the rule. This proverbial saying is very generally misunderstood. The word *prove* anciently meant 'test,' and is so used in this saying. An old use of the word *prove* occurs in the advice of St. Paul:—'Prove all things,' &c.; which means that we should *test* all things, so as to know which good ones to 'hold fast' to. An exception cannot prove a rule in the modern sense, it tends rather to render it invalid; but an exception may *test* a rule, and in some cases prove it to be wrong, whilst in others the test may show that the so-called exception may be explained. Another theory on the subject is that the very word 'exception' implies that there is a rule; so that the word 'prove' means 'proves the existence of.'

Exchange. Professor Jevons says that exchange is 'the barter of the comparatively superfluous for the comparatively necessary.'

Exchequer. This name is derived from the fact that a

chequered cloth covered the table at which the business of the Court was formerly transacted. In Foss's 'Lives of the Judges' it is stated that this Court 'was sometimes called *Curia Regis ad Scaccarium,* and its name was derived from the table at which it sat, which was a four-cornered board, about ten feet long and five broad, fitted in manner of a table to sit about, on every side whereof is a standing ledge or border four fingers broad. Upon this board is laid a cloth, bought in Easter Term, which is of black colour rowed with strekes, distant about a foot or span, like a chess-board. On the spaces of this *scaccarium,* or chequered cloth, counters were ranged, with denoting marks for *checking* the computations.'

Execution. The last man executed for attempted murder was Martin Doyle, who was hanged at Chester, Aug. 27, 1861. An Act of Parliament had been passed before that date, abolishing the punishment of death for such crimes, but it did not come into operation until the following November—too late to save Doyle's life. The first private execution was that of Thomas Wells, who was hanged in Maidstone Gaol, Aug. 13, 1868, for the murder of Mr. Walsh, station-master at Dover.

Exhibition, in the sense of an allowance of money, as now used in the Universities, where he who 'gains an *exhibition*' has an annual allowance, was formerly in common use. Thus, in the 'Two Gentlemen of Verona,' Shakespeare has :—

> What maintenance he from his friends receives,
> Like *exhibition* thou shalt have from me.

Then Lear complains of being 'confined to *exhibition*': and Othello requires for his wife

> Due reference of place and *exhibition.*

Ex officio. A Latin phrase, signifying 'by virtue of his office.' Thus, we say, 'the mayor of a town is *ex officio* a magistrate.'

Exorbitant, from the Latin *ex,* from, and *orbita,* an orbit or track. Hence to be ex*orbit*ant is to be 'beyond all bounds.'

Extant. This is probably the word *existent* abbreviated by the omission of the middle syllable. That which is not *extant* is that which does not exist, or is not *existent.*

Eye of a Needle. Lord Nugent, when at Hebron, was directed to go out by '*the Needle's eye,*' that is, by the small gate of the city. This explains an obscure passage of Scripture on *riches,* for the gate in question would hardly be high enough to allow a camel to pass, and the animal would have to go down on its knees and crawl to be able to pass.

F

ff in surnames. A few families use the *ff* as though it were the capital letter F, but it is often seen erroneously printed *Ff*. It is now pretty generally thought that the *ff* was originally the manuscript capital, and that the modern F is the same form with merely the shortening of the second downstroke. The process of shortening was probably gradual, as seen by the following figures:—

This theory is confirmed by the fact that in the earliest instances the second *f* has no cross stroke.

Fac-simile. This is now looked upon as an English phrase. It is derived from the Latin *facio*, to make or do, and *similis*, like. It means an exact copy. It is divided into syllables thus—*fac-sim-i-le*.

Factotum, from the Latin *facio*, to do, and *totus*, all. The phrase is an old one. Ben Jonson in one of his plays makes Tip ask

Art thou the Dominus?

to which the host replies,

Factotum here, sir.

And Foulis, in his 'History of the Plots of our Pretended Saints,' 1674, says, 'He was so farre the *dominus fac-totum* in this *juncto* that his words were laws.'

Fagged, in the sense of tired, is merely a contraction of the word *fatigued*.

Faint heart never won fair lady. This is a very old proverb. In 'A Proper New Balad in Praise of my Lady Marques,' printed in 1569, are these lines:—

Then have amongst ye once again,
Faint harts faire ladies neuer win.

Reprint, Philobiblion So. 1867, p. 22.

'The Rocke of Regard,' 1576, concludes as follows :—

> The silente man still suffers wrong, the proverbe olde doth say,
> And where adventure wants, the wishing man ne'er thrives;
> Faint heart, hath been a common phrase, faire ladie never wives.
>
> *J. P. Collier's Reprint*, p. 122.

And in 'Britain's Ida,' by Spenser, canto v. stanza 1, the second line is

> Ah, fool! faint heart fair lady ne'er could win.

Fairy. According to some, from the Persian *peri*. The word came to us through the Arabian, in whose alphabet there is no *p*. In Arabic it, therefore, became *feri*, which word being introduced by the Crusaders, received the broader English sound, *fairy*. Other etymologists derive it from the Low Latin verb *fato, fatare*, from Latin *fatum*, fate, to enchant. In the French this became *faer*, and from the verb the French made the noun *faërie*, an illusion. From this, it is said, the meaning gradually widened to its present signification.

Fairy Rings. Fairy rings are the green circles or portions of circles sometimes seen in pastures. They are produced by mushrooms or other fungi, by the spreading in all directions of their spawn. As the first year's growth of fungus decays, the spawn spreads further, but the decaying fungi have left behind a rich crop of manure, which causes the grass where they have grown to assume a deeper shade of green. As year by year the spawn pushes outward the ring enlarges, while the impetus given to the soil by the first crops of fungi having spent itself, the grass assumes its normal colour, so that the dark green of the grass of the more recent growths still preserves the annular or ring-like form, until sometimes the rings are several yards across.

Shakespeare alludes to the belief that these rings are caused by fairies in the lines :—

> Ye demi puppets that
> By moonlight do the green sour ringlets make,
> Of which the ewe not bites.—*Tempest*, v. 1.

Falconet was the name given in the fifteenth century to a small cannon. As the name of the musket (q.v.) was derived from the sparrow-hawk, so the name falconet was derived from the falcon.

Fall. This word, which is used in America to signify autumn, was formerly current in England in the same sense. Dryden has :—

> What crowds of patients the town doctor kills,
> Or how, *last fall*, he raised the weekly bills.—*Juvenal*.

Izaak Walton, also, in the 'Compleat Angler,' uses it in *The Milkmaid's Mother's answer*, as follows :—

> The flowers do fade, and wanton fields,
> To wayward Winter, reckoning yields.
> A honey tongue, a heart of gall,
> Is fancy's Spring, but sorrow's *Fall*.

Fallow-deer are said to have been introduced into Britain by James VI. of Scotland, who brought them from Denmark, of which kingdom his wife was a princess. When he became King of England, he stocked Enfield Chase and Epping Forest with fallow-deer, and from his herds all the deer in England have descended.

Family, from the Latin *famulus*, a slave. The collective Latin word *familia*, from which our word comes, meant the whole of the slaves in a household.

Fardel. Shakespeare makes Hamlet say :—

> Who would *fardels* bear,
> To groan and sweat under a weary life?

A fardel was a bundle or small pack. An Act of the Common Council of London, August 1, 1554, recites that 'the inhabitants of London and others were accustomed to make their common carriage of fardels of stuffe, and other grosse wares and things thorow [through] the Cathedrall Church of Saint Paul's,' and prohibits the abuse. Randle Holmes says that the difference between a porter and a pedlar is that 'the porter's pack reacheth over his head, and so answerable below, but the pedlar's is a small truss, bundle, or fardel, not exceeding [in height] the middle of his head.'

Fare, Farewell. In the Anglo-Saxon *fare* meant a passage. Verstegan thus explains it :—' FARE, Passage; *Farewel*, Passwel, a well wishing to one's proceedings; mistaken for diet when we say meat-*fare*.' We retain the original meaning in omnibus fare, railway fare, thoroughfare. Bailey gives the Anglo-Saxon *faran* as the root of the word in this sense; and the Low-Saxon *vaeren* as the origin of 'fare' in the sense of diet, cheer, condition.

Farm. This word is derived from the Anglo-Saxon word *feorm*, meaning supper, food, or hospitality. Originally tenants held lands in consideration of supplying their lords with certain specified quantities of food or other necessaries for the use of the manorial household, and this was called the *ferme*. Afterwards this was commuted into a money payment, which was called *ferme* *blanche*, from being paid in silver or white money. Still later the rent was called *ferme* simply, and eventually the land from which the rent was derived was called the *ferme*, or farm.

Farrago. This word is now seldom used in its literal signification, which is a mixture of several sorts of grain or corn. The sweepings of a corn market, where several kinds of corn have been spilled, and are swept into a mixed heap, are properly a *farrago*.

Farrier. From the Latin *ferrum*, iron; hence in English a farrier is a blacksmith who shoes horses with iron.

Farringdon Street. Stow gives the origin of the name Farringdon in his usual quaint manner. He tells us that 'The whole great Ward of Farindon, both intra and extra, took name of W. Farindon, goldsmith of that ward, and one of the sheriffs of London in the year 1281, the 9th of Edward I. He purchased the aldermanry of this ward.'

Farther and **Further.** Which of these two words to use is often a puzzle even to well-informed people. *Farther* means 'more far,' and always signifies a greater distance, as 'I can't walk a step *farther*.' *Further* implies 'addition,' as 'It requires *further* consideration.' 'And *further*, by these, my son, be thou admonished.'—*Eccles*. xii. 12.

Farthing. The word farthing was not always confined in meaning to the fourth of a penny. The Anglo-Saxon *feorthlyng* meant the fourth of any coin. In the 'Grey Friars Chronicle,' printed by the Camden Society, we read:—This yere the kynge made a newe quyne, as the nobylle, half-nobylle and *ferdyng-nobylle*.'

The coin mentioned Matthew x. 20 and Luke xii. 6 as a 'farthing' was the Roman *assarium*, which was the tenth part of the *denarius* or penny, and was equal in value to three of our farthings. Another coin, also called 'farthing' in our translation, Matthew v. 26 and Mark xii. 42, was the *quadrans*, the fourth part of the *assarium*. This 'farthing' was only equal in value to three-fourths of an English farthing. The mite was a still smaller coin, being half the value of the *quadrans*, or about three-eighths the value of one of our farthings.—*Booker, Obsolete Scripture Words*.

Fashions in Dress. 'Parti-coloured coats were first worn in England in the time of Henry I.; Chaplets or wreaths of artificial flowers in the time of Edward III.; hoods and short coats without sleeves, called tabarts, in the time of Henry IV.; hats in the time of Henry VII.; ruffs in the reign of Edward VI.; and wrought caps or bonnets in the time of Elizabeth. Bands were introduced by Judge Finch in the time of James I., and breeches, instead of trunk hose, in 1654. Perukes were introduced after the restoration.'—*Manners and Customs*, London, 1810.

Fashions. This was the old name for a certain disease of the horse. It is alluded to in the 'Taming of the Shrew,' where Petruchio's steed is said to be 'infected with the fashions.' The complaint is a common one now, but not among horses.

Fast and loose was the name in Shakespeare's time of the trick now known as 'pricking the garter,' so often practised upon credulous persons at races and fairs. The ancient name has been transferred from the game itself to the acts of persons who live by their wits, and are said to 'play fast and loose' with other people's property. 'Pricking the garter' is practised as follows. A narrow belt of leather is doubled and then rolled into a circle so as to show an opening, apparently in the centre, into which a novice is invited to place a skewer. By a little adroitness on the part of the man who holds the ends of the strap, the peg can be made to come within or without the loop at his pleasure.

Fatherland. Isaac D'Israeli, in 'Curiosities of Literature,' claims the introduction of this as an English word. He says:— 'Let me claim the honour of one pure neologism. I ventured to introduce the term of "Fatherland" to describe our *natale solum*. I have lived to see it adopted by Lord Byron, and by Mr. Southey. . . . . Fatherland is congenial with the language in which we find that other fine expression "mother-tongue."'

Fathom. A fathom was originally the space between the tips of the middle fingers of a man's two hands when the arms were extended horizontally. It is now legally fixed at six feet. A Jewish fathom was rather more than seven feet.

Feast. They have a singular use of this word in New York. 'I'm feast of it,' which is a common phrase, means 'I'm sick of it,' 'I'm disgusted with it,' 'I loathe it.' The word 'feast' so used is a corruption of the Dutch word *vies*, nice, fastidious.

Feast of reason, &c. The line

The feast of reason and the flow of soul

occurs in Pope's 'Imitations of Horace,' book ii. sect. 1.

Feather in his cap. 'In the 'Lansdowne MS.' 775, fol. 149, in the British Museum, is a description of Hungary, anno 1599, in which it is stated that 'It hath been an ancient custom among them that none should wear a feather but he who had killed a Turk.'

February, from *februum*, a purgative. The name is applied to this month because the Romans celebrated the festival of purification on the 15th of February.

Fee, capital, cattle. 'Our common expression for the payment of a sum of money is *fee*, which is nothing but the Anglo-Saxon *feoh*, meaning alike money and cattle. *Pecunia*, the Latin word for money, is derived from *pecus*, cattle. The same connection of ideas is manifested in the Greek word for property, which means alike possessions, flocks, or cattle.'—*Jevons*. In Sir H. C. Maine's 'Early History of Institutions,' he says, 'Being counted by the head, the kine [cows] were called *capitale*, whence the economical term capital, the law term chattel, and our common name cattle.'

Fellow. In a translation of the Bible, 1549, quoted in Richardson's 'Dictionary Supplement,' we have:—'And the Lord was with Joseph, and he was a luckie *felowe*, and continued in the house of the Egyptian, his master' (Genesis xxxix.) 'Of Moises, the *felow* that brought us out of the land of Egypt, we know not what is become' (Exod. xxxii.)

Fellow was formerly a common name for companion, either male or female. Jephtha's daughter desires that she may go upon the mountains with her *fellows* (Judges xi. 37); and in Psalms xiv. 15 we read, 'The virgins that be her *fellows* shall bear her company.' Girls still speak of their school*fellows*.

Felo de se. These words mean 'a felon of himself'—that is, of the criminal; not of a crime. Hence it is wrong to say that a man has 'committed' felo de se. He 'is' a felo de se. He has 'committed' *suicide*.

Felon. This word had a Gaelic origin. The verb *feall* meant to deceive, betray, treachery, treason; *feallan* is a felon or a traitor; *feall duine* is a worthless man; *feall tair* a traitor, a villain.

Felt Hats. The 'Penny Magazine,' in 1841, stated that 'felt' was invented accidentally by St. Clement, fourth Bishop of Rome. Being persecuted, and obliged to flee, his feet became blistered from long-continued travel. To ease the pain, he placed a layer of wool between his feet and his sandals. The heat, moisture, motion, and pressure worked the wool into a compact and uniform mass, which the bishop, observing, caused to be introduced as an article of manufacture. St. Clement is still considered the patron saint of hatters.

Female. This word is an adjective, and should never be employed as a noun. Such phrases as 'A man with a *female* were seen in a boat just after the ship struck'; or, 'The *females* shrieked,' are in bad taste, and bad grammar. 'A man and a *woman*,' &c., 'The *women* shrieked,' are at once felt to be more appropriate. The improper use of the word 'female' is more common in America than in England. 'In March 1839, a Bill for the protection of the reputation of unmarried females was brought into the House of Delegates, Maryland. The title was afterwards amended by substituting *women* for "females," on the ground that the latter was an Americanism.'—*Bartlett.*

Fence Month, or Defence Month, 'A time during which deer in forests do fawn, and their hunting is unlawful. It begins fifteen days before Old Midsummer and ends fifteen days after it.'—*Manwood's Forest Laws*, part ii., c. 13. By recent legislation 'fence' times have been established in the case of birds and fishes, during which their capture or injury is unlawful.

Fender, an abbreviation of the word *de-fender*, applied to the article of furniture so called, because it defends the floor of a room from ignited fuel from the fireplace.

Fern. Probably from the Scandinavian word *fer*, a feather. The Greeks called fern *pterin*, which also means a feather.

Ferret, from the Latin *fur*, a thief. In French it is *furet*; in Welsh *fured*. The name seems to have originated in the furtive, or stealthy, habits of the animal, so like those of a *fur*, or thief. 'Ferrets are not the subjects of larceny.'—*Wharton.*

Ferry-boat. The earliest known mention of a ferry-boat is in 2 Sam. xix. 18.

Fertility of the Orange-tree. A single tree at St. Michael has been known to produce in one year 20,000 oranges fit for packing, exclusive of the damaged fruit and the waste, estimated at one-fifth more.

Fetlock. Most dictionaries derive this word from the lock of hair near the horse's foot. It is, however, with greater probability, from the Old English word *lock*, a joint, and means the foot-joint. The Anglo-Saxons had *ban-loc*, or bone-joint. In a line of

Beowulf, quoted by Wright in his 'Literature of the Anglo-Saxons,' p. 10, are the words *burston ban-locan*, the juncture or joints of the bones burst.

Fetter Lane. This is a very old name. It is found, with the spelling '*Faytour Lane*,' in a deed dated 1363 (37 Edward III.) Stow says it is derived from *fewter*, an idle fellow; but it more probably arose from *feuter*, an Old English name for dog-keeper. Fetter Lane has been for many generations a favourite abode of bird and dog-fanciers, fishing-tackle makers, *et hoc genus omne*.

Fiacre. This is the French name for a hackney carriage. These carriages were introduced by Sauvage, who lived in the Hôtel S. Fiacre, Paris.

Fiasco. This is an Italian word for bottle or flask. In making the beautiful old Venetian glass, it was the custom of the glass-blowers, if they made any flaw in their delicate work, to turn the article into a common flask—*fiasco*. Hence any failure is called 'a fiasco.' The word is used in the Italian theatres to express dissatisfaction with an actor or a singer. It is not uncommon to hear an audience shout '*Olà, olà, fiasco!*' even when a singer has made only one false note. The origin of its use in this sense is unknown. The word is becoming naturalised in England, and is used to signify an utter failure.

Fiddle. In Mr. Wright's 'Domestic Manners in the Middle Ages' is a woodcut copied from the Harleian MS., No. 603, in which is a representation of an Anglo-Saxon *fithelere* playing on the *fithele*. The ancient fiddle, however, seems more like a cittern or guitar than a modern violin, and the performer does not use a bow. In another woodcut in the same work, taken from a Saxon MS. in the British Museum (MS. Cotton. Tiberius, c. vi.), there is, however, the representation of a performer who uses an instrument almost identical in shape with the violins now in use.

Field. Tooke's derivation of this word from 'fell'd,' a place cleared of timber, is ingenious, but hardly satisfactory. The Germans say *feld*, the Dutch *veld*, and the Danes *felt*. The Anglo-Saxons also said *feld*. All these forms, as well as the word 'field,' are probably corruptions of the Anglo-Saxon word *fold*, which is still in use amongst us almost in its original sense.

Fieldfare. The first syllable of the name of this bird has nothing to do with our word 'field.' The name is a corruption of the Anglo-Saxon *feala-for*, or *fela-far*, meaning something restless, and ever on the move.

Fiend. An Anglo-Saxon word, literally meaning 'enemy.' Verstegan, in reference to this word, sneers at the introduction of the French word 'enemy'; and, with quaint humour, says, 'yet we sometimes call the Devil the *Fiend of Hell*, which is as much as to say, the *Enemy of Hell!*'

Figaro is a character in the play 'Le Barbier de Séville.' Figaro, who is first a barber, and afterwards a valet, manages to outwit everybody by cunning, intrigue, and dexterity. The name has become typical of these qualities.

Fighting like devils, &c. In Lady Morgan's 'Memoirs,' vol. ii. p. 232, the writer, in an extract from her diary, October 30, 1826, in which she describes a compliment paid to her by a Dublin street ballad-singer, gives the following as a stanza from his carol :—

> Och, Dublin City, there's no doubtin',
>   Bates every city upon the say ;
> 'Tis there you'll see O'Connell spoutin',
>   An' Lady Morgan makin' tay ;
> For 'tis the capital of the finest nation,
>   Wid charmin' pisantry on a fruitful sod,
> Fightin' like divils for conciliation,
>   An' hatin' each other for the love of God.

Figures, in arithmetic. The word 'figure' as used in arithmetic is probably a corruption of the word 'finger.' 'Counting on the fingers was the first arithmetic,' and the symbols we employ were called *digits*, that is, fingers. The Latin word *figura* was never employed in relation to numerals, but only in reference to form or shape ; and there seems no reason why the ten characters employed in arithmetic should be called figures, any more than the twenty-six which are employed in writing. The change from 'finger' to 'figure,' when written arithmetic became common, was very easy.—*Fox Talbot.*

Filbert, or Filberd. Probably *fillbeard*, from the nut just filling up the cup or cavity formed by the beards of the calyx. In the ordinary nuts the nut projects far beyond the beard.—*Wedgwood.*

Filibuster. This word, the signification of which is a pirate, has a curious origin. It is derived from the Spanish word *filibote*; but the Spanish word itself is a corruption of the English word *flyboat.*—*Max Müller.*

Filly. A young female horse. This word is generally derived from the Latin *filia*, a daughter, but it is more probably the feminine of 'foal,' the vowel being altered, as in *fox*, feminine *vixen*.

Filter. From the word *felt*, of which strainers for liquids were originally made.

Finch Lane is so called from the church of St. Benet Finke, which was pulled down to enlarge the Royal Exchange. The statue of George Peabody is placed within the ancient churchyard of St. Benet Finke.

Findon Haddocks. Findon haddocks, or 'Finnon haddies,' derive their name from the village of Findon or Finnon, a village of about 200 inhabitants, on the coast, about six miles south of Aberdeen, where the fish are cured in great perfection, and from whence they are sent to all parts of the country, and to the Royal palaces. The fish are dried in the smoke caused by burning green branches of the fir-tree, which is said to impart a bright yellow colour and an agreeable flavour to the fish.

Fine Roman Hand. This phrase is often used in reference to the style of any particular author. The origin appears to be 'Twelfth Night,' act iii. sc. 4, where Malvolio says, 'It did come to his hands, and commaunds shall bee executed; I thinke we doe knowe the sweet *Roman hande*.' The allusion appears to be to the Italian style of caligraphy, which, at the time Shakespeare wrote, was superseding the old English style of handwriting. Aubrey says of Sir Kenelm Digby, that he 'was not only master of a good and gracefully judicious stile, but also wrote a delicate hand both fast and Roman.'

Finger comes from *fang*, that with which anything is seized, or held.

Finger Talking, or Dactylology. The first manual alphabet was that of Dalgarno, published in 1680. At the trial of Mary Sayer for the murder of her husband, in 1713 ('State Trials,' vol. xv. col. 791), it came out in evidence that Sayer was jealous of his wife because of 'conversations incomprehensible to him, as his wife talked [with Noble, her fellow-prisoner] upon her fingers.'

Fire and water. 'I would go through fire and water to serve you.' This saying is a relic of the old trials by ordeal. In the old times when trial by ordeal of fire or water was recognised by English law, both ordeals could be performed by deputy. This was sometimes done for hire, and sometimes out of friendship. The ordeal of fire was passing blindfolded and barefooted through a place where nine red-hot ploughshares were arranged at irregular intervals. In the trial by water the person to be tried was bound hand and foot and thrown into a pond or river. If he swam, he saved his life and redeemed his character. If drowned, he was considered to have met with a just retribution for the crime of which his drowning was held to be proof that he was guilty. The saying 'I would go through fire and water,' &c., was, therefore, equivalent to saying that the person using it was ready to sacrifice life or limb to serve his friend.

Fire Engines with hose-pipes were first used at the great fire in Southwark, in May 1676, which destroyed about 600 houses.

Firkin is from the Anglo-Saxon *feower*, four, and *kin*, a diminutive. It signifies a *small* cask, holding the *fourth* part of a barrel.

First Cannon cast in England. In the fifth 'Report of the Royal Commission on Historical MSS.' is the following note on the MSS. belonging to Sir John Wilson :—' A deed of 30 Elizabeth is a conveyance from Thomas Hog of Buxstedd, Co. Sussex, to James Burgess of a house in Buxstedd which bears this indorsement: " In this house lived Ralp Hog, who at his then furnace at Buxsted, cast the first cannon that was cast in England." '

First-chop. This phrase is used all through the United States as a synonym for 'first-rate.' The word *chop* is Chinese for quality. He looks like a *first-chop* article.'—*Sam Slick in England*, ch. 2.

First Newspaper Report by Electric Telegraph. In 1847 a line of telegraph wires was being laid down between Manchester and Leeds. Mr. George Wilson, well known as Chairman of the Anti-Corn Law League, was a director of the Telegraph Company, and he had several miles of wire placed temporarily, so that the report of the proceedings at the nomination and election of Mr. Cobden could be transmitted to Manchester. The report appeared on the same day in a second edition of a Manchester paper, and is the first newspaper report by electric telegraph on record.

First Railway Time Table. In October 1825, the first railway time table, of which the following is a copy, was issued :—

'STOCKTON AND DARLINGTON RAILWAY.

'THE Company's coach, called the Experiment, which commenced travelling on Monday, the 10th of October, 1825, will continue to run from Darlington to Stockton, and from Stockton to

Darlington, every day (Sundays excepted), setting off from the Depôt at each place at the times specified as under (viz.) :—

'On Monday from Stockton at half-past seven in the morning, and will reach Darlington about half-past nine. The coach will set off from the latter place on its return, and reach Stockton about five. Tuesday from Stockton at three in the afternoon, and will reach Darlington about five.

'On the following days, viz., Wednesday, Thursday and Friday, from Darlington at half-past seven in the morning, and will reach Stockton about half-past nine. The coach will set off from the latter place on its return at three in the afternoon, and reach Darlington about five. Saturday from Darlington at one in the afternoon, and will reach Stockton about three.

'Passengers to pay 1s. each, and will be allowed a package of not exceeding 14 lbs. All above that weight to pay 2d. per stone extra. Carriage of small parcels 3d. each. The Company will not be accountable for parcels of above 5l. value unless paid for as such.

'Mr. Richard Pickersgill, at his office in Commercial Street, Darlington, and Mr. Tully at Stockton, will, for the present, receive parcels and book passengers.'

First recorded Sale of Land. The first sale of land of which we have any record is that mentioned in the 23rd chapter of Genesis. The transaction appears to have been very simple. Abraham wished to buy a field for a burial-place for his family. Ephron, the owner, valued it at 400 shekels of silver (about 50l. of our money), which Abraham agreed to pay. He accordingly went to the gate of the city, and weighed the money, which he paid in the presence of 'all that went in at the gate of the city.' This simple ceremony, without the intervention of lawyers or other officials, made 'the field and the cave that was therein, and all the trees that were in the field, and in all the borders round about,' sure unto Abraham for a possession.

Fish. 'A pretty kettle of fish.' In the eleventh annual 'Report of the Inspectors of Salmon Fisheries,' Mr. Inspector Walpole, in reporting on the fisheries on the coast of Sussex, says (p. 44) :—' The kettle nets, it may be interesting to note, probably derive their name from the old fishing weir, the *kidellus*, or kiddle, which is mentioned in Magna Charta, and many early fishery statutes. In their turn the kettle nets are, I conceive, responsible for the old proverb, " a pretty kettle of fish."' See KETTLE.

Fish, at cards. The word fish' used for counters at cards is from the old word *fisc*, a treasury, a heap of money. From this root we derive the word 'fiscal.'

Fitting to a T. This phrase refers to the T or Tee Square, an instrument used in drawing and mechanics; so called from its resemblance to a capital T.—*Notes and Queries.*

Flag. Before the introduction of playbills, the old theatres exhibited flags on their roofs as a kind of telegraphic advertisement when performances were going on. In Lent, of course, as there were no plays, there were no flags. This is alluded to in the 'Mad World,' printed in 'Dodsley's Old Plays,' vol. v. p. 314 :—
'Nay faith, for blushing, I think there's grace little enough amongst you all; 'tis *Lent* in your cheeks, *the flag's down*'; and 'The hair about the hat is as good as the *flag* upon the pole at a common playhouse, to waft company' (ibid. p. 364.)

Flag-lieutenant. A flag-lieutenant in the navy is an officer who stands in relation to an admiral as an aide-de-camp in the army to a general. It is his duty to see that the admiral's orders are communicated, either personally or by signal, to the various ships of which the squadron is composed. The ship which carries the admiral is called the flag-ship, and her captain is the flag-captain.

Flannel was originally written and pronounced 'flannen.' It is essentially of Welsh origin. The name is derived from the Welsh *gwlanen*, wool.

Flash Money. The word 'flash,' as applied to spurious money, is derived from the name of a village between Buxton and Leek, where a gang of coiners once carried on their dishonest trade.

Flatter. At first sight there would appear to be little connection between flattery and the wagging of a dog's tail, yet in nearly all the Northern languages the same word signifies both, and flattery is certainly derived from the word signifying to wag the tail. In the old Norman, *fladra* signifies to flatter, and also to wag the tail. In Danish, *logre* is to wag the tail, and *loger for een* is to fawn on one. In Dutch, *vleyden* is to flatter, and *vleyd-steerten* is to wag the tail. In the old German, *wedeln* is to wag the tail, and in English, *wheedle* is to gain one's end by flattery.

Fled. Fled is the past participle of the almost obsolete verb to flee. 'Flew' holds the same position in reference to the word 'fly.' In the Midland Counties it is common to hear 'fled' improperly used in such expressions as 'the bird fled away.'

Flesh Conner. An ancient manorial officer. See ALE CONNER.

Fletcher. A fletcher was a maker of arrows. Hence the surname.

Fleur-de-lis. Louis VII. adopted the Iris as his badge when he formed the crusade, which led to its being called *Fleur-de-Louis*. This in the course of time has been corrupted to fleur-de-lis, the name it still retains in France, and in the southern parts of England.

Flight. A flight was a kind of arrow, made specially for long shots. Leland ('Itinerary,' vol. iv. p. 44) tells us that a 'flite shot' was 'as much as the Tamise is above the [London] bridge.'

Flippant. This word originally meant *fluent*, and was used as in the following passage from Barrow :—'It becometh good men in such cases to be *flippant* and free in their speech.'

Flirtation. 'I assisted at the birth of that most significant word "flirtation." Flirtation is short of coquetry, and indicates only the first hints of approximation.'—*Lord Chesterfield*. It was first used by the beautiful Lady Frances Shirley, and arose from the practice of flirting the fan. In 'An Ode to Lord Barrington' (ed. 1784) is an allusion to a stuffed ourang-outang at Paris, of which it is said—

> He once like you could *flirt* a fan,
> And was in truth a pretty man,
> But died by drinking whiskey.

Flock Paper-hangings were invented and patented in France by Jerome Lanyer in 1634.

Floored. This slang term for being disappointed is in allusion to an artist's picture being hung on the lowest row at the Exhibition. A picture so hung is said to be floored.

Florida was so named because it was discovered by the Spaniards on Easter Sunday, which in Spain is called *Pascua Florida*, from its being customary to deck the churches with flowers on that day.

Florin. This coin was so named from its having been first coined at Florence. The first English florin was issued by Edward III. Its value was 6s. There are florins current in Germany, Spain, Sicily and Holland. The modern English florin, or two-shilling piece, was issued in 1849. The first coinage was of smaller size than those now current. They were withdrawn because the letters F.D. (Defender of the Faith) were omitted from the

Queen's title. Richard Lalor Shiel, a Catholic, was Master of the Mint at the time, and it was said that the letters were omitted by his private directions. Whether this was so will probably never be publicly known.

Flour, Flower. Originally flour was spelt *flower*. The French still say *fleur de farine*, i.e. flowers or blossom of meal. In chemistry the word flower is used to signify the fine impalpable powder thrown off in sublimation. We still speak of flower of zinc, flower of sulphur, &c.

Fly, a hack carriage. The name 'fly' originated at Brighton. A Mr. Butcher made an invalid carriage, in shape like a sedan chair, but mounted on wheels. It was drawn by one man, and another, if the *fare* were heavy, pushed behind. It became so much in request that more were constructed and were soon fully occupied. They were much used by George IV. when Prince of Wales, in midnight frolics, and it is believed that he gave them the name 'fly-by-night'; this soon became contracted to 'fly,' and the name is still retained.

F.O.B. These letters, which are often met with in quotations of prices of merchandise, mean 'free on board'; that is, the price includes carriage and all charges upon the goods until they are actually in the ship which is to carry them to their destination.

Focus is the Latin word for 'hearth,' a place where a fire is made. The focus of a convex lens is the point at which the rays of the sun, in passing through, converge so as to set on fire any combustible substance.

Folk. Johnson says this 'is properly a collective noun and has no plural except by modern corruption,' yet he wrote 'Folks want me to go to Italy.' Walker says that '"folks" is the proper orthography.'

Folk-lore. This expressive phrase is said by Trench, in his 'English Past and Present,' to be 'borrowed recently from the German.' This appears to be wrong. Mr. W. J. Thoms, in 'Notes and Queries,' October 6, 1872, distinctly claims to have coined it. The word was first used in the 'Athenæum' August 22, 1846, in an article written by Mr. Thoms, and signed 'Ambrose Merton.' In stating this circumstance Mr. Thoms quotes 'Coriolanus':—'Alone I did it.'

Fond, from *fon*, an idiot—so used by Spenser—originally meant weak, silly, foolish, simple, besotted. See DOTE.

Font. Formerly the baptistery was a portion of a church

partitioned off, and contained a large *font* or *fountain*, in which, when required, adults might be baptized by immersion.

Fool or physician at forty. Plutarch, in his 'Treatise on the Preservation of Health,' tells us that Tiberius said a man was his own physician or a fool.

Foolscap Paper. 'This term has not, as is generally believed, any reference to the water-mark of a cap and bells. The word is a corruption of *folio shape.*'—*De Vere, Studies in English*, p. 167. 'In a statute of Queen Anne, a particular kind of paper is called "Genoa Foolscap." The word foolscap is a corruption of the Italian "*foglio capo,*" a chief or full-sized sheet of paper.'—*Notes and Queries.*

Foot, a measure, was originally taken from the length of a man's foot. A word signifying a man's foot is used in almost all languages to denote a linear measure of ten to twelve inches.

Football was prohibited in Scotland by James II. in the year 1457, and again in 1481 by James IV. It was at one time illegal in England, as the following presentment (*temp.* Henry VIII.) will show:—'Item, they present that William Welton misbehaved himself in playing at football and other unlawful sports.'

Footmen. A century ago noblemen and gentlemen of large estate kept servants called 'running footmen,' whose duty it was to run in advance of their master's carriage, on long journeys, to secure changes of horses, meals, lodgings, &c. They carried tall canes or poles, such as are still carried by the footmen of some families at the present day. Fifty or sixty miles a day was no uncommon journey for a footman. The male attendants who waited at table were called 'serving men.'

Foppery in 1770. Mr. E. J. Wood, 'Curiosities of Clocks and Watches,' Bentley, 1866, p. 342, says, 'About the year 1770 it became the fashion among the dandies of that day to wear two watches, the chains and seals of which dangled on each side beneath their embroidered waistcoats.' The 'Universal Magazine' for 1777 thus alludes to the custom in a poetical 'Receipt to make a modern Fop':—

    Two tons of pride and impudence,
    One scruple next of modesty and sense,
    Two grains of truth. Of falsehood and deceit
    And insincerity a hundred weight.
    Infuse into the skull,—of flashy wit
    And empty nonsense—*quantum sufficit.*
    To make the composition quite complete,
    Throw in th' appearance of a grand estate,

> A lofty cane, a sword with silver hilt,
> A ring, *two watches*, and a snuffbox gilt,
> A gay, effeminate, embroidered vest,
> With suitable attire—*probatum est*.

Some of the Chinese at the present day carry two European watches; but they have the excuse, 'Suppose one make stop, the other walkee!'

Foreign Exchanges. Professor Jevons, in his invaluable work 'Money and the Mechanism of Exchange' (King and Co. 1876), gives the following clear account of the manner in which *Exchange* acts in settling mercantile transactions between foreign countries:—'England buys every year from America a great quantity of cotton, corn, pork, and many other articles. America, at the same time, buys from England, iron, linen, silk, and other manufactured goods. It would be obviously absurd that a double current of specie should be passing across the Atlantic Ocean in payment for these goods, when the intervention of a few paper acknowledgments of debt will enable the goods passing in one direction to pay for those going in the opposite direction. The American merchant who has shipped cotton to England can draw a bill upon the [English] consignee to an amount not exceeding the value of the cotton. Selling this bill in New York to a merchant who has imported iron from England to an equivalent amount, it will be transmitted by post to the English creditor, presented for acceptance to the English debtor, and one payment of cash on maturity will close the whole circle of transactions' (p. 301).

Fore Name or **Christian Name.** The first instance on record of a name given to a child by a minister of God is that of David's son, whom *he* called *Solomon*, but who was afterwards named by Nathan the prophet *Jedidiah* (2 Samuel xii. 25).

Forestall is to waylay a dealer and buy his goods before he can place them on the *stall* in the market.

Forgery, as applied to the falsification of written documents, is derived from the old French *forjuror*, and *forjur*, which imply 'falsehood in a court of justice,' or 'falsehood in legal matters.' The man who swore to the truth of a legal deed or instrument was a *forjur*, from which to the modern notion of a forger is an easy step. Forgery was punishable by death from A.D. 1634 to 1837. The last person hanged for forgery was Thomas Maynard, who was executed December 31st, 1829.

Forget-me-not. Henry IV. of England, before his accession assumed this flower as his emblem, with the motto '*Souviens de moi*' —'Remember me.' Hence the application to the flower of the name 'Forget me not.'

Forgiven. All the English words having this, or a similar, meaning imply some equivalent. 'Forgiven' is absolved, for (*something*) *given*. 'Pardon' has the same meaning; a person is forgiven—*par-donnée*. 'Condone,' again, is based upon the Latin *done*, to give; and 'absolve' means paid for, *ab-solvere*.

Forks were introduced into England in the sixteenth century. The custom of using them was brought from Italy. In the 'Travels of Thomas Coryate, of Odcombe near Yeovil,' 1611, he says, 'The Italians, and also most strangers that are commorant in Italie, doe alwaies at the meales use a little forke when they cut their meate. For while with their knife which they hold in one hand, they cut the meate out of the dishe, they fasten their forke, which they holde in their other hande, upon the same dishe.' Queen Elizabeth was the first English Sovereign who used a fork. Her nobles and people thought it a piece of great affectation on her part, and the example was only very scantily followed. So great was the prejudice against their use, even amongst educated people, that a bold divine of those days preached a sermon against the practice of using them, saying 'it was an insult to the Almighty not to touch one's meat with one's fingers.' Forks, however, came slowly into use; but even so late as the reign of George I. they were so little known that few inns provided them for the use of guests, so that 'it was customary in travelling to carry with them a portable knife and fork in a shagreen case.'

Forma pauperis. A poor person who has cause of legal action can sue *in formâ pauperis*—that is, as a pauper—by which he avoids payment of the court fees.

Forsooth. This was formerly used as a term of respect in addressing a lady or a mistress. Ben Jonson says, ' Carry not too much underthought betwixt yourself and them; nor your City mannerly word "*forsooth*," use it not too often in any case, but "Ay, madam," and "No, madam."' 'Our old English word "*forsooth*" has been changed for the French "madam."'—*Guardian*.

For the nonce. 'The old English phrase, *for than anes* (for then once) has become *for the nonce*.'—*De Vere, Studies in English*, p. 271.

Fortnight. A contraction of *fourteen nights*.

Forty stripes, save one. The Jews were forbidden by the Law of Moses to inflict more than forty stripes, and lest they should exceed that number, they generally gave fewer. It is thought that they used a whip with three thongs, and therefore could not strike more than thirteen times without exceeding the lawful number. This phrase is applied by a section of the Anglican Church to the Thirty-nine Articles.

Foster Father. This, in the Anglo-Saxon times, according to Verstegan, was written '*Fodster* father, or, as we now might write it, Foodster father, seeing it cometh of providing food and nourtriture for such children as are under his and his wife's charge to bring up.'—*Restitution*, &c., p. 257.

Foundling Hospital. The Foundling Hospital in London was established, in 1739, by Thomas Coram, a retired sea captain. It is no longer a *foundling* hospital in the ordinary sense of the word, but is a hospital or home for poor illegitimate children whose mothers are known and are believed to have been 'more sinned against than sinning.' One of the conditions of admission is that the mother ceases to have any control over, or even any future knowledge of, her unfortunate offspring.

Fourth Estate of the Realm. There is reason for believing that Carlyle originated this phrase. In 'Hero-Worship,' lect. v., he says, 'Burke said there were three estates in Parliament, but in the Reporters' Gallery yonder there sat a fourth estate, more important far than they all.'

Fowls. In Leviticus xi. 20 of the Authorized Version is the passage 'all fowls that creep, going upon all four.' In Ecclesiasticus xi. 3, as translated by Coverdale; in the 'Bishops' Bible'; and in the 'Geneva Bible,' is 'The bee is but a small beast among the fowles.' Both these passages are explained by the Authorized Translation of the latter text, which runs, 'The bee is little among such as fly'; proving that the word 'fowl' was formerly applied to any animal having the power of flight, including locusts, grasshoppers, and beetles, which were to be unclean to the Israelites, because they were such as 'creep, going upon all four.'

Foxglove. The foxglove, or *digitalis*, is said to have been originally brought from the Canary Islands. It is thought that foxglove is a corruption of 'folk's glove,' or 'fairies' glove.' The flower is called 'fairy bell' by the Irish, and 'fairy glove' by the Welsh. There is, however, reason to believe that 'foxglove' may be right. In Norway the name is *revhanskje*, foxglove; or *revbjella*, fox-bell, from *rev*, a fox.

Frail is probably a contraction of fragile, and had originally the same meaning, i.e. brittle or easily broken.

Frangipani. The popular perfume known by this name is so called after Mutio Frangipani, a Roman alchemist of great repute.

Franking Letters by Members of Parliament. The system of franking letters, which originated in 1660, was so much abused that, in 1763, a Commission of Enquiry was opened. The Commission reported that, amongst other matters sent free by post were 'fifteen couples of hounds; two maidservants going as laundresses; Dr. Crichton, carrying with him a cow, two bales of stockings, and a deal case with four flitches of bacon.' No wonder that the report states that 'the amount of postage which would have been payable on *letters* so franked is estimated at 170,000*l.*' Notwithstanding this enquiry, the privilege continued to be greatly abused, and in the early part of the nineteenth century it was customary for needy members of the Legislature to sell their signatures by the dozen. This practice was restricted in 1837 by stringent rules, and the privilege was finally abolished on the introduction of the penny post in 1840.

Franking Newspapers. In 'Bell's Weekly Messenger,' May 16, 1813, is an impudent advertisement, referring to a Monday edition of the paper, 'which,' it is stated, 'may then be had and sent free of postage to any person in the country by directing it to Lord Onslow at the person's residence for whom it is intended, in the usual manner of franked newspapers.' Lord Onslow, as a peer, was entitled to receive letters and newspapers free of charge. The Post-Office people could not, of course, say that Lord Onslow was not at the house to which the paper was sent.

Free Library. Manchester is entitled to the credit of the establishment of the 'first institution in the United Kingdom which combined a free library of reference, open to all comers, with a free library of circulation.' It was opened in 1853. The example has rapidly been followed, so that free libraries now exist in all the principal towns, and the smaller places are gradually establishing them. The Free Libraries Act of 1855 provides that all municipal boroughs; all districts having a Board of Improvement Commissioners; and all 'parishes, or two or more parishes conjointly, having a population of 5,000 persons,' shall have the option of establishing such a library by levying a rate of a penny in the pound upon the inhabitants of the district.

Freemason. This is a corruption of the French *frère-maçon*, brother-mason.

Freemasonry. Originally Freemasons were really connected with the building craft, and the members bound themselves together somewhat after the manner of the modern trades-unions, with a view to protect the interests of their trades. Their interference with the wages of labour caused considerable jealousy on the part of government, and at length, in 1423, an Act of Parliament was passed (3 Henry VI. c. 1), prohibiting 'the Chapiters and Congregations of Masons in tyled lodges,' under the penalty of being 'judged for felons, and punished by imprisonment and fine and ransom at the king's will.'

Freezing Point. The freezing point of any substance is the degree of heat at which it loses the liquid form and becomes solid. The identical degree of heat is also the 'fusing' point, that is, the degree of heat at which a solid becomes liquid. Thus the freezing point of water is said to be 32°, so that water reduced by the most infinitesimal amount below that point becomes ice, and ice raised by the minutest addition of heat above 32° becomes liquid. The principle may be applied to nearly all other substances; as, for instance, lard is fluid above 91°, and solid below that point. Tin is solid at 451°, but liquid on the least accession of heat; lead follows the same rule at 620°; zinc at 773°; copper at 1,926°, and cast iron at 2,786°.

French leave. This proverbial expression appears to have arisen from the ancient custom of French armies on their marches taking whatever they wished for or required without payment or any other consideration.

Friday. From *Freya, Freja, Friga*, the Northern Venus, wife of Odin.

Friday Street, London, was 'so-called of Fishmongers dwelling there and serving Friday's market.'—*Stow*.

Frill is a corruption of the word *furl*.

From Greenland's icy mountains. This celebrated hymn was composed at Wrexham in 1819. On Whitsunday in that year Dr. Shipley, Dean of St. Asaph and Vicar of Wrexham, preached a sermon in his church on behalf of the Society for the Propagation of the Gospel. Heber was son-in-law to Dr. Shipley and was on a visit. The doctor on the previous Saturday asked Heber to 'write something for them to sing in the morning,' and in a few minutes, without leaving the room, Heber produced the hymn now so well known all over the world. He was then in his thirty-sixth year, and was rector of Hodnet.

From pillar to post. This is a corruption of an old proverb signifying to go from bad to worse. The original was 'To go from post [*i.e.* whipping post] to *pillory*.'

From the sublime to the ridiculous. The great Napoleon is generally credited with having originated this *mot*. It occurs, however, in Paine's 'Age of Reason.' The passage is as follows:—'The sublime and the ridiculous are often so nearly related, that it is difficult to class them separately. One step above the sublime makes the ridiculous, and one step above the ridiculous makes the sublime again.'

Frump. The modern dictionaries define this as a cross-tempered, old-fashioned woman. This is just the reverse of its original signification, which, according to Bailey, was 'plump, fat, jolly.'

Fuchsia. This beautiful flower was brought from America in the sixteenth century by Leonard Fuchs, Professor of Botany at Tubingen, in Germany. The plant was named after him. Fuchs was born in Swabia in 1501, and died at Tubingen in 1565. The *Fuchsia fulgens* was brought from Mexico about 1830.

Fudge. In a 'Collection of some Papers of William Crouch' (8vo. 1712), Crouch, who was a Quaker, says that one Marshall informed him that 'In the year 1664, we were sentenced for banishment to Jamaica by Judges Hyde and Twysden, and our number was 55. We were put on board the ship "Black Eagle," the master's name was *Fudge*, by some called "Lying Fudge."' Isaac D'Israeli quotes from a pamphlet entitled 'Remarks upon the Navy' (1700), to show that the word originated in a man's name: 'There was, sir, in our time one Captain Fudge, commander of a merchantman, who, upon his return from a voyage, how ill fraught soever his ship was, always brought home his owner a good cargo of lies, so much that now aboard ship the sailors when they hear a great lie told, cry out, "You *fudge* it!"'

Fulfill. Literally, to *fill full*; and anciently so used. A good example of its former use is the prayer in the Liturgy, 'That we may be *fulfilled* with thy grace.'

Full-fig, applied to dress, is a cant phrase which probably arose in some humorous allusion to the fig-leaf costume adopted by Adam and Eve.

Fulsome. This word has a disagreeable meaning, and it had a disagreeable origin. It is a contraction of *foul*some.

Funeral. From the Latin *funus, funeris*, a funeral procession or funeral rites. 'It is an error to suppose that permitting a funeral procession to pass over private grounds creates a right of way. Funerals are exempt from tolls.'—*Wharton*.

Funeral Custom. The leading of the charger of the deceased at the funeral of a cavalry officer is a relic of the old custom of sacrificing a horse at the burial of a warrior. The last record of this custom being followed refers to the burial at Trèves in 1781 of General Kasimer, when the General's charger was killed by a hunting knife, and the dead animal thrown into the grave upon the coffin.

Funk. To be 'in a funk' is a common proverbial saying, signifying that a person is in a dilemma, causing some degree of fright or perturbation. In German *funke* is a spark, and in Walloon *fonk* is smoke. *In de fonk zün* is, literally, to be in the smoke; but metaphorically, it is exactly equivalent to the English phrase 'in a funk.'

Funnel is a purely Celtic word. The Welsh *ffynel*, airhole, shows its derivation clearly.

Furlough, i.e. leave of absence granted to a soldier. The word, in various forms, is common to all the Teutonic and Scandinavian dialects. In the Dutch it is *verlof*; in Danish *forlof*; in Swedish *förlof*, and in German *verlauben*.

Furniture. This word formerly included any kind of moveable property. A farm well stocked with animals was said to be *well furnished*.

Furze. *Fir* in all the old Northern languages was the general name for trees with needle-shaped leaves. Hence *fir*, or *firres*, was also applied to the *gorse*, which, although a plant altogether of different species, has sharp spines, or spikes, instead of flat leaves.

Fusileer. This is an old military term originally applied to a body of foot soldiers who were armed with *fusils*; that is, with muskets, which, before the invention of gunlocks, were fired by a lighted slow match or *fuse*.

Futile. This word originally meant *to pour out*. A '*futile*' person was a talkative blabber, whose words *ran out* without thought. Bacon, in his 6th Essay, speaks of 'Talkers and Futile persons,' and in the 20th says :—' One *futile* person, who maketh it his glory to tell, will do more hurt than many that know it their duty to conceal.' The Latin word is *futilis*, the meaning of which is, that which easily lets out.

G

G. In words derived from the Anglo-Saxon beginning with this letter, the initial is often used interchangeably with Y; thus *yard* and *garden* are both from the same root, signifying an enclosure *guarded* or *girded* by a fence.

Gab. We speak of a man having 'the gift of the gab' when he talks glibly without much reference to the sense of what he says. The word is from the Anglo-Saxon *gabban*, to prate.

Gad's Hill. The word *gad*, according to Cotgrave, signifies a vagabond. Ash defines *gad* as a club, or wedge. The Anglo-Saxon *gad* was 'a goad or wedge.' In Irish *gadh* is a dart, and *gad* is stealing. Cruden, in his 'History of Gravesend,' says :—' The name of this spot, like that of Shooter's Hill in the same line, was derived from the depredations of highwaymen and footpads; Gad's Hill had long been infested with robbers when it acquired an enduring notoriety from being selected by Shakespeare as the scene of a dramatic incident, probably suggested by frequent depredations there in his time.'

Gaffer. This word is generally thought to be a contraction of grandfather. Amongst the working population of Birmingham it is the general term for a master or employer, and wives speak of their husbands as 'my *gaffer*.'

Gale of Wind. This is a sea term for a continued storm of wind. Sailors describe the degrees of intensity of gales by the terms—a *fresh* gale; a *strong* gale; and a *heavy* gale. The last is sometimes called a *hard* gale, and occasionally a *whole* gale.

Gallon. The capacity of the imperial gallon is fixed by Act of Parliament at 10 lbs. avoirdupois of distilled water, weighed at the temperature of 62° Fahrenheit, the barometer standing at 30 inches. This is equivalent to $277\frac{1}{4}$ cubic inches (or, more exactly, 277·274 inches). The old English gallon, wine measure, was 231 cubic inches. Beer was measured by a gallon of 282 cubic inches. Both these are now abolished, the imperial measure being the only legal standard of capacity.

Gallop. This word is from the Anglo-Saxon *gehlopen*, to leap or jump.

Galloshes, or **Galloshoes,** are wooden shoes worn by French peasants. Spenser speaks of 'my galage grown fast to my heel.' From this our English word for an outer shoe has been derived.

Gallypot, or **Gallipot,** is the Dutch *gley pot*, clay pot; i.e. a pot of earthenware or burnt clay.

Galore. One often meets in literature with the Irish or Keltic word galore, usually as a synonym for plenty. The proper spelling is *go leor*; *leor* is an adjective, meaning sufficient; *go leor* is an Irish phrase formed of *go*, to, and *leor*, plenty; *go leor* is generally used in the sense of superabundance or over-sufficiency.

Gambler. This word has greatly changed in meaning. In Johnson's time the word 'gamester' signified what we now mean by the word 'gambler,' which Johnson says is 'a cant word, I suppose, for game or gamester.' He defines it thus :—' A knave whose practice it is to invite the unwary to game, and cheat them.' In Bailey's time the word had a still worse signification, for he tells us that a gambler is 'a guinea-dropper; one class of sharpers.' The Rev. John Earle, in his 'Philology of the English Tongue,' points out that nearly all our gambling terms are of Norman origin. He says (p. 56) :—' The rage for gambling which distinguished the habits of our Norman-French rulers is aptly commemorated in the fact that up to the present day the English terms for games of chance are of French extraction. *Dice* were seen in every hall, and were called by the same name as now. *Cards*, though of later invention, are still appropriately designated by a French name. The fashion of counting by *ace, deuce, tray, quart, cink, sis*, &c., is French—not modern French, but of the feudal age.' Chance and Hazard too are mentioned as gaming terms derived from the same source.

Gammon, in the sense of joking, nonsense, or 'chaff,' is from the Anglo-Saxon *gamian*, to make sport of.

Gamut. The *gamut*, or musical scale, consists of five parallel horizontal lines on which the musical notes are disposed. The gamut was invented, about the year 1025, by Guido Aretino, a monk of Tuscany, who was led to adopt it from his having at first used the five fingers or digits of his hand to demonstrate the progression of the sounds or notes. It was called *gamut* from the Greek letter, gamma, which Guido adopted as the name of the first note.

He afterwards used the syllables *do, re, mi, fa, sol, la, si*. These have, in modern music, given place to the first seven letters of the alphabet.

Gaol is the only word in English where the diphthong *ao* occurs.

Garble. The modern use of this word is erroneous. It is altogether wrong to speak of 'a garbled statement' in the sense of a mutilated or dishonest statement. The meaning of the word is to assort or arrange. Spices, drugs, &c. are 'garbled,' that is examined, to free them from impurities or improper admixtures. The City of London formerly employed officers called 'garblers' to inspect imported goods.

Gargle, Gargoyle, from the French *gargouiller*, a gurgling noise in the throat. Hence *gargouille*, the throat, and hence also the English 'gargoil,' or 'gargoyle,' which in Gothic architecture is applied to grotesque figures through the 'throats' of which spouts are turned, to throw off the water from the roofs.

Garlick. In the Gaelic, *luigh* meant a plant. The Welsh word for plant is *llys*, a corruption of *llych*, the same word as *luigh*. In English we have *leek*, and we have preserved the original word in several combinations, as char*lock*, hem*lock*, gar*lick*, &c. Garlick is *gar-leek*, that is, the '*spear* leek,' *gar* being Anglo-Saxon for a spear or weapon. The similarity of the seed spike of the plant to a spear with its slender staff is very obvious. See LEEK.

Garment is from the French *garnir*, to decorate or garnish. It was anciently written 'garnement,' as in Wicliff, 'a long garnement.'

Garret, the upper room of a house. This word comes to us from the French *garite*, which originally signified a lofty tower, built on the wall of a fortified town for the purposes of observation.

Garrick seems to have been originally a wine merchant. Horace Walpole says, 'All the run is now after Garrick, a wine merchant, who is turned player. The Duke of Argyll says he is superior to Betterton.'

Gas. The word gas, from the German *geist*, a ghost or spirit, was introduced by Van Helmont, a physician of Brussels, who employed the term to represent all the non-condensible airs; but his first application was to what he called the 'gas of water,' now known as hydrogen.

Gas Lighting. The first notice of the artificial production of an inflammable air from coal is in a letter from the Rev. Dr. John Clayton of Kildare to the Hon. Robert Boyle, published in the 'Philosophical Transactions' for 1739. In this letter Dr. Clayton states that he distilled coal in a close vessel and obtained abundance of gas, which he collected in bladders, and afterwards burnt for the amusement of his friends. As Boyle died in 1691, the letter must have been anterior to that date. Mr. Murdock, of Soho, near Birmingham, was the first to apply gas to the purpose of artificial lighting. His house and offices at Redruth were so lighted in 1792. The first public exhibition was in 1802, at the Soho Works of Boulton and Watt, near Birmingham, in which Murdock had an interest. A Mr. Winsor, in the year 1807, lighted up a portion of Pall Mall, and this was the first instance of gas being applied to street lighting.

Gate. The English word gate has two distinct origins; the Anglo-Saxon *geat*, meaning a passage through, and the Danish *gata*, a passage along, as a road or street. In the latter sense the word is used for the streets in Northern towns, as in Briggate, Leeds, Stonegate, and many others in York, Millgate in Manchester, and Cowgate in Edinburgh. From the Anglo-Saxon *geat* we obtain *gut*, and the nautical name for a narrow channel, as the Cattegat. From the same root is *gate*, the way through which a man passes into a field or other enclosure, and *gaiters*, which he wears when he passes through muddy places. The second syllable in Margate, Reigate, and other similar names is also from this root, signifying, as they do, gates or passages through ranges of hills or cliffs.

Gauge. The *u* in this word is not sounded in pronunciation. It is *gage*, not *gawge*.

Gaunt, from *want*. Sullivan says 'Nothing is more common than the substitution of *g* or *gu* for the Gothic *w*, as in *guard* from *ward*; *guaranty* from *warranty*; why not *gaunt* from *want*?'

Gauntlet. To run the gauntlet. The word gauntlet in this phrase is improperly used. The word should be *gauntelope*. Phillips, in his 'World of Words,' tells us that to 'run the *gauntlope* is a punishment among soldiers; the offender having to run, with his back naked, through the whole regiment, and to receive a lash from a switch from every soldier. It is derived from *Gant* [Ghent], a town of Flanders, where the punishment was invented, and the Dutch word *lope*, running.' Mr. Ingram, one of the survivors of the wreck of the 'Royal George,' who died a few years ago at Woodford in Gloucestershire, used to say that he had seen sailors run the gauntlope on board the king's ships, and that to prevent the runner from going too fast, the ship's corporal walked before him with his drawn cutlass under his arm, with the point backwards, and that he had seen a man get a scratch from the cutlass in trying to escape from the switches.

Gauze. First made at Gaza, in Palestine. Hence the name.—*Brand.*

Gavelkind. The law or custom of *gavelkind* divided a man's lands, after his death, in equal shares amongst his sons. The term *gavelkind* is one of the very few Saxon law terms that have survived. It is composed of the words *gif ael kynd*, 'give all children,' *kynd* meaning offspring. From this root *kynd* we get our word kindred.

Gawky, clumsy, from *awk*, the left hand, *awkward*, with the prefix *g*.

Gazette. Mr. Wedgwood ('Dictionary of Etymology') thinks it is an error to suppose that the original newspaper was so named from the *gazatta*, the small coin of Venice. The meaning of the word gazette, or gazetta, is derived from the *gazza*, a magpie, and *gazetta* means all sorts of idle chattering, like that of the magpie. Hence the word would be a fitting title for a paper circulating at Venice, and filled with the tittle-tattle of Venice, Rome, and Amsterdam. 'The value of the *gazetta* (the coin) was so small—less than a farthing of English money—that it never could have been the price either of a written or printed sheet.'

Gazetteer. This name for a geographical dictionary originated with Laurence Echard, who, having compiled a work of the kind, and thinking it would prove particularly useful to newspaper writers, called it the 'Gazetteer's or Newsman's Interpreter, being a Geographical Index.' It was first published in 1703. The fifteenth edition was published in 1741. When the 'Gazetteer's Interpreter' first became the 'Gazetteer' is not accurately known.

Generous. This word originally meant well-born, of illustrious descent, of good extraction. 'Let her not be poor, how *generous* soever, for a man can buy nothing in the market with gentility.'—*Lord Burleigh.*

Genius originally signified the tutelary god or demon that was supposed to preside at the birth and over the future destinies of every human being. Hence it was common to speak of a man's 'good genius' or 'evil genius' as urging him to good or evil deeds. From this original meaning may be traced the signification the word now bears, and which causes it to be applied as the highest eulogium that can be applied to intellectual endowments. In modern usage it has hitherto been the custom to apply the term *genius* almost exclusively to poets, painters, sculptors, musicians, and architects, as though there could be no genius at work in any other region than that of the fine arts. But as in its proper signification genius is the power which *creates* something that ministers to the pleasures of life, or diminishes its pains, the term should, in modern times, have a wider range of application. If Shakespeare, Raphael, Canova, Handel, and Wren are entitled to the appellation *genius*, it ought, in common fairness, to be conceded to Watt, to Stephenson, to Caxton, to Wheatstone, and to Rowland Hill, all of whom have been *creators*. In this wider sense, genius may be defined as the 'creative power;' talent, the power which 'sustains and developes.' Some have thought that genius is nothing but infinite capacity of painstaking. Carlyle seems to have first broached the idea. In 'Frederick the Great,' vol i. p. 407, he says, 'Genius, which means transcendent capacity for taking trouble.'

Gent. Thackeray by his pungent satire drove this word, as a contraction of *gentleman*, completely out of use. It is curious to find that Spenser, in two cases, uses it in reference to a lady. In the 'Faerie Queene,' I. ix. 6, we find—

> Well worthie impe! said then the *lady-gent*,
> And pupil fit for such a tutor's hand.

And, *Id. id.* st. 27—

> He loved, as was his lot, a *lady-gent*.

In both cases, the affix *gent* means of gentle birth, noble, of good rank. (For the meaning of 'impe,' see IMP.)

Gentleman. Verstegan's remarks upon this word are so quaint, that any abbreviation would interfere with their terse humour. They are therefore given verbatim:—'Our modern name of Gentleman is not rightly either English or French, but composed and made up of two distinct languages. For as elsewhere I have showed (see EARL) our ancient word *Ethel* signifieth noble or gentle, and were it *Ethelman*, it were a meer Teutonick word and anciently our own; and if it were Gentilhomme, then were it French; but now we take *gentle* from the French (though a little altred) and add unto it *man*, and so composing them together make it *Gentleman*. This manner of speech-mixing hath hapned upon the Norman Conquest, and in some other words now in our language is to be found very absurd and ridiculous, but for brevity, and as here being impertinent, I will pass them over.'—*Restitution of Decayed Intelligence*, edit. 1655, p. 257. The origin of the word was the Latin *gens*, which signified a known family or clan. The word *Gentile* or *gentilis*, among the Romans, had a similar meaning to that which we now give to 'gentleman.' In modern times a distinction is made between a 'gentleman by birth' and a gentleman by profession or social position. The families known as 'county families' are those of 'gentlemen by birth.'

Geranium, from a Greek word signifying a crane. So called from the shape of the capsule and beak, which resemble the head of a crane.—*Loudon*. The first red geranium seen in England is said to have been raised by a Mr. Davis in the King's Road, Chelsea, about the year 1822.—*Old and New London*, vol. v. p. 51.

German and English compared. The compound nature of the English language, as compared with the simplicity of the German, is nowhere more obvious than in German words beginning with the word *halb*, the equivalent of the English *half*. The German-English Dictionaries contain from two to three hundred such words, while of English words beginning with *half*, Dr. Worcester's great Dictionary contains but 68, while there are 34 commencing with the Greek *hemi*, 116 with the Latin *semi*, 42 with the French *demi*, and 10 with the Italian *mezzo*.

German Silver has no silver in its composition. It is a compound of copper, zinc, and nickel. The proportions of each metal vary according to the use to which the mixture has to be applied; but, speaking generally, it may be said to consist of 55 parts copper, 25 zinc, and 20 nickel. The metal called 'nickel silver' has less zinc and more nickel in its composition. It is harder and whiter than the German silver, and is admirably adapted as a base for electro-plating in such articles as forks and spoons.

Get. Professor Gibbs says, 'There is no word in the English language capable of performing so much labour in a clear, intelligible sense as the verb to *get*,' and Dr. Withers gives a specimen of its capabilities as follows :—' I *got* on horseback within ten minutes after I *got* your letter. When I *got* to Canterbury, I *got* a chaise for town; but I *got* wet through before I *got* to Canterbury, and I have *got* such a cold as I shall not be able to *get* rid of in a hurry.

I *got* to the Treasury about noon, but first of all I *got* shaved and dressed. I soon *got* into the secret of *getting* a memorial before the Board, but I could not *get* an answer then; however, I *got* intelligence from the messenger that I should, most likely, *get* one the next morning. As soon as I *got* back to my inn, I *got* my supper and *got* to bed. When I *got* up in the morning, I *got* my breakfast, and then *got* myself dressed that I might *get* out in time to *get* an answer to my memorial. As soon as I *got* it, I *got* into the chaise, and *got* to Canterbury by three, and about tea-time I *got* home. I have *got* nothing for you, and so adieu.'

Getting into a hole. This proverbial saying is said to arise from an accident which sometimes occurs in playing at golf, where, if a ball 'gets into a hole,' it is almost certain that the owner must lose the game.

Getting into a scrape.—'The deer are addicted, at certain seasons, to dig up the land with their fore feet, in holes, to the depth of a foot, or even of half a yard. These are called "scrapes." To tumble into one of these is sometimes done at the cost of a broken leg; hence a man who finds himself in an unpleasant position, from which extrication is difficult, is said to have "got into a scrape."'—*Newspaper Paragraph.* The Rev. H. T. Ellacombe, M.A., in 'Notes and Queries,' Feb. 14, 1880, says that in 1803 a woman was killed by a stag in Powderham Park, Devon. 'It was said that, when walking across the park, she attempted to cross the stag's *scrape*,' which he says is 'a ring which stags make in rutting season, and woe be to any who get within it.' He confirms his story by a copy of the parish register, which records that 'Frances Tucker (killed by a stag) was buried December 14th, 1803.'

Get money, &c. The common saying, 'Get money—honestly if you can—but get money,' is almost literally translated from one of the Satires of Horace, who says, *Rem facis:—recte si possis : si non, Rem facis.'*

Gherkin. This means 'little cucumber.' The German for cucumber is *gurcke*, and the Dutch *agurkje*; the termination 'kin' is Anglo-Saxon, and means small, or young.

Giant's Causeway. The Giant's Causeway was anciently believed to be the commencement of a mole or causeway to be constructed by giants across the Channel to Scotland. It is now known to be part of a plateau, many square miles in extent, and from 300 to 500 feet thick. This plateau is composed of basalt, a volcanic rock, which in cooling has crystallised into polygonal columns, varying from 15 to 24 inches in diameter, and so closely compacted, that the blade of a knife can with difficulty be inserted between them. The causeway is about 30 feet in width, and the portion exposed is about 200 feet in length.

Gibberish. The etymology of this word is uncertain. Johnson says, ' As it was anciently written *gebrish*, it is probably derived from the chymical cant, and originally implied the jargon of *Geber* and his tribe.' Geber was an alchemist, and, as Nares says, ' Considering the great prevalence of that affected science, and the early ridicule thrown upon it, it [Johnson's theory] is not improbable.'

Gibbet. The last gibbet erected in England was for George Cook, a bookbinder of Leicester, who was executed for the murder of Mr. Paas, a London commercial traveller. Cook's body was put on a gibbet 33 feet high, on Saturday, August 11, 1832, in Saffron Lane, Aylestone, near Leicester; but, owing to great disturbances which arose among the crowds of people who thronged the place every Sunday, it was soon afterwards taken down by order of the Secretary of State, and buried on the spot where the gibbet stood.

Gibbon seems to have had the title of his great book, the ' Decline and Fall of the Roman Empire' suggested by Thomson's lines :—

> The sage historic Muse
> Should next conduct us through the deeps of Time,
> Show us how Empire grew, *declined*, and *fell*.

Gibraltar is derived from *Gibel el Tarik*, 'the mountain of Tarik.' Tarik was the leader of the Saracens when they entered Spain in 711, and he first fortified the hill as a base of operations and a ready point of access from the Barbary coast. Gibraltar was taken by the English in 1704, and it was formally ceded to them in 1713. The Great Siege, by the Spaniards and French, lasted from July 1779 to February 1783, when it was abandoned as hopeless.

Gilly-flower. We get this name from the French *giroflée*. The French took it from the Italian *garafalo*, and the Italians from the Latin *caryophyllus*, a clove, the Roman name of the flower, given to it from its clove-like smell.

Gilpin. A Mr. William West, who was formerly a bookseller in London, and who died in the Charterhouse, November 17, 1854, at a great age, used to affirm that a Mr. Beyer, a linendraper, whose shop was at the corner of Paternoster Row and Cheapside, was the original of John Gilpin. Beyer died May 11, 1791, aged 98. Professor De Morgan, writing to 'Notes and Queries,' January 1860, mentions that a book had been seen by a friend of his on the fly-leaf of which was written ' To be left att Mr. John Gilpin's House att the Golden Anchor, in Cheapside, at ye corner of Bread Street, London.' The gentleman who saw the book was of opinion that this could not have been written after 1701. The same gentleman thought it very improbable that Beyer was the original, and adds that ' Beyer knew nothing about Gilpin till he read Cowper's ballad.' From other evidence it seems that 'John Gilpin,' whether that were his true name or not, must have lived in the seventeenth century, and that the story—as a story—was a very old one when Cowper wrote the ballad.

Gin. This name is derived from the Dutch *giniva*, which they have in turn derived from the French *genièvre*, juniper. Hollands gin is sometimes called 'Geneva,' but it is merely a corruption of *giniva*, having nothing in common with the name of the city of Geneva. Our ancestors had some curious slang names for this spirit. Bailey says, ' GENEVA, *genevre*, F. juniper, of the berries from which a compound spirit is drawn, called by several names, as " Pityre," " Royal Poverty," " White Tape," &c.'

Girl. The etymology of this word has been much disputed. Bailey ungallantly derives it from *garrula*, 'because they are addicted to Talkativeness.' Minshew from the Italian *girella*, a weather-cock. Skinner, with greater probability, thinks that, as the Anglo-Saxon word *ceorl* meant a man, so they might have had *ceorla* for a woman. Lye and Tyrwhit say that 'girl' was anciently used for young persons of either sex, and they decide for *ceorl* as the origin. Halliwell gives ' *Gerl*, A.-S., a young person of either sex.' But Webster says, ' It is most probably from the Low Latin, *gerula*, she who carries, applied to a young woman employed to tend children.'

Gist. The derivation of this word from the old French *giste*, a lodging-place, as given in the dictionaries, is by no means satisfactory; the *gist* of anything is its pith, narrow, or essence. May it not be derived from the German *geist*, a spirit ?

Given Name. In America the first name is called the *given* name, in contradistinction to the surname, which is inherited. It is thought to be a relic of Puritan scrupulousness : the Pilgrim Fathers objecting to apply the term *Christian* to any person not 'converted,' which of course an unconscious infant could not be. Jews, in courts of justice, are often thoughtlessly asked, 'What is your *Christian* name?' The proper question is, 'What is your *personal* name?'

Giving Quarter. This phrase originated in an agreement between the Dutch and Spaniards that the ransom of an officer or soldier should be one-quarter of his pay. Hence, to 'beg quarter' was to offer a quarter of their pay for their safety, and to refuse quarter was to decline that composition as a ransom.— *Notes to Assist the Memory* (Murray : London, 1825).

Gladiolus, the flower, from the Latin word *gladiolus*, a sword; so called from the sword-like shape of its leaves.

Glanders, the disease of the horse; so called because it is a disease of the *glands*. Old French *glandre*.

Glass. Two ingenious theories exist as to the origin of this name. One is that it comes from the Celtic word *glâs*, green or bluish-green, the colour of common window glass when seen edgeways. The other theory is that, as *crystal* comes from a Greek word signifying ice, so glass may come from the Latin *glacies*, also ice. The alleged accidental discovery of glass by some Phœnician merchants may be true, but it is equally true that the Egyptians understood the process of manufacturing glass some centuries before. It is mentioned by the name of *Bashna* as early as the 5th and 6th dynasty, and articles of glass are represented in the tombs of that period. In the 12th dynasty, or about 1800 years before Christ, that is about 100 years before Joseph was sold into Egypt, artists of the period painted on the interior walls of one of the tombs pictorial representations of the entire processes of making glass vessels. Windows of glass have been found in the ruins of Pompeii, showing that they must have been used before A.D. 79. Window glass was first brought to England from Italy by Biscop, the Abbot of Wearmouth, A.D. 676.

Glass-making. *Flint* glass—that is, the glass used for decanters, dishes, &c.—is a compound of sand, red lead, and pot-ash. However pure the sand may be, there is always a trace of iron in it, which gives a green shade to the glass. To destroy this objectionable colour, a small quantity of the black oxide of manganese is added, which oxidises the iron, and thus neutralises its influence. The adjustment of the proper quantity of manganese is an operation of great nicety, for an excess of half an ounce in a ton of glass-material will cause a perceptible pink shade in the finished goods. The rich blue colour, seen in smelling bottles and other ornamental glass articles, is given by the oxide of cobalt. So great and diffusive is the colouring power of this material that as much as will lie on a sixpenny piece will give a distinctly blue tinge to a ton of molten glass. The fine canary colour occasionally seen in glass is due to the presence of oxide of uranium; ruby colour is produced by oxide of gold; the finest amber colour by oxide of silver; pale blue, green, and a deep red, are the results of different oxides of copper.

Glass vessels cracking by heat. It is a mistake to suppose that glasses which crack when hot water is poured into them have not been annealed. What is called 'annealing' is a gradual cooling of a vessel after it has been shaped by the workman. If not annealed, the vessel would 'fly' to atoms within a few minutes after being made. The cause of 'flying' is, generally, inequality of thickness in different parts of the vessel. Glass is a slow conductor of heat, and where there is greater thickness in one part than another, the thin part will become expanded by sudden application of heat, while the thicker portions are still in a state of contraction. The struggle between the two forces splits the vessel to atoms. So, with a very thick glass, when hot water is suddenly poured into it, the surface of the *interior* of the vessel rapidly expands, while the *outside* remains contracted; this, of course, splits the vessel. The best glasses for hot water are of *equal substance throughout*, and the thinner the better. The gold refiners boil their strongest test acids in glass vessels, not much thicker than paper, which are made specially for the purpose.

Glorious uncertainty of the law. In 1756, soon after Lord Mansfield had over-ruled several ancient legal decisions, and introduced many innovations in the practice, Mr. Wilbraham, at a dinner of judges and counsel in Serjeants' Hall, gave as a toast 'The glorious uncertainty of law.' This was the origin of the phrase.

Glove. This word is of Keltic origin. In Gaelic *ceil* is to cover, the *c* being hard, and *lamh* is the hand. These two words in pronunciation would become *keillav* or *klav*, meaning a 'hand covering.' Our modern word glove is not far off its parent words in sound.

Goat and Compasses, a tavern sign. It has often been said that this is a corruption of the Puritan motto, 'God encompasseth us,' but this is probably a mistake. It is with far greater probability derived from the coat of arms of the Carpenters' Company, in the city of London, which are *azure*, a chevron *or*, between three goats heads erased, *argent*. Probably some one, ignorant of the chevron —which is a representation of two rafters meeting at the top— has mistaken it for a pair of compasses. The transition from the plural *goats* to the singular would be easy.

Godfathers. Anciently jurymen were jocularly nicknamed *godfathers*. In the 'Muses' Looking Glass,' printed in 'Dodsley's Old Plays,' a West-countryman is made to say, 'I had rather zee him remitted to the jail, and have his *twelve god vathers*, good men and true, condemn him to the gallows.'

This explains the obscure passage in the 'Merchant of Venice,' where Gratiano says :—

> In christening time thou shalt have two *godfathers*.
> Had I been judge, thou should'st have had *ten more*,
> To bring thee to the gallows,—not the font.

Godfrey's Cordial—the well-known nostrum, used by nurses —is of considerable antiquity In Reed's 'Weekly Journal,' February 17, 1722, is the following advertisement :—'To all retailers and others.—The General Cordial formerly sold by Mr. Thomas Godfrey of Hunsdon in Hertfordshire, deceas'd, is now prepar'd according to a receipt written by his own hand, and by him given to my Wife, his relation, is now sold by me *Tho. Humphreys*, of Ware, in the said county, Surgeon, or at John Humphreys, at the Hand and Sheers in Jewin Street, near Cripplegate, London. Also may be furnished with Arcanums or Vomits, and will be allowed the same for selling as formerly.'

God save the King. In the 'State Papers,' vol. i. p. 184, under the head, 'Flete taken by the Lord Admirall the 10th day of August, 1545,' is the following :—'The watch worde in the night shalbe thus, "God save King Henrye"; thother shal aunswer, "And long to raign over us."'

God save the King. There is every reason to believe that the *tune* of 'God save the King' was composed in the time of James I., by Dr. John Bull, but it was not by him used for a national hymn. One Anthony Young, organist of All Hallows, Barking, adapted it to a 'God save the King' for James II. at the time when the Prince of Orange was hovering over the coast, but it was not so used until the time of George II. A letter from Victor to Garrick, October, 1745, mentions that it was sung at both theatres nightly amid great applause. It is a singular coincidence that Young's daughter was married to Arne, who composed 'Rule Britannia.'

Mrs. Arne received a pension of 30*l*. a year. In 1789 Mrs. Henslowe, who was grand-daughter of Mrs. Arne, received 100*l*. from the government as 'the accumulated amount of a yearly pension of 30*l*. a year, awarded to Mrs. Arne as the eldest descendant of A. Young, the composer of 'God save the King.' 'God save the King' is almost a literal translation of a *cantique* sung by the Demoiselles de St. Cyr, when Louis XIV. attended morning prayer at that chapel. The words were by M. de Brion, and the music by the famous Sully:—

> Grand Dieu sauve le Roi!
> Grand Dieu venge le Roi!
> Vive le Roi!
> Que toujours glorieux,
> Louis victorieux!
> Voye ses ennemies—
> Toujours sommis!
> Grand Dieu sauve le Roi!
> Grand Dieu venge le Roi!
> Vive le Roi!

It appears to have been translated and adapted to the House of Hanover by Handel.—*Diary of Madame de Créquy.*

God save the mark. These words are connected with an old Irish superstition. If a person, on telling the story of some hurt or injury which another has received, should illustrate his narrative by touching the corresponding part of his own or his hearer's body, he averts the omen of similar injury by using as a sort of charm the words 'God save the mark.'

God tempers the wind to the shorn lamb. Sterne first used this phrase in English, by putting it into the mouth of Maria in the 'Sentimental Journey.' It is an adaptation of the French proverb, '*A brebis tondue Dieu mesure le vent.*'

Gog and Magog. In a description of the procession of Queen Elizabeth, 13th January, 1858, the day before her coronation, the writer says:—'From thence her Grace came to Temple barre, which was dressed finely with the two ymages of Gotmagot the Albione, and Corinæus the Britain, two gyantes, bigge in stature, furnished accordingly; which helde in theyre handes, even above the gate, a table whering was written in Latin verses theffet of all the pageantes which the citie before had erected.' Mr. Douce the antiquary thinks that these figures must have been brought from Guildhall for the occasion. The original giants were destroyed in the great fire of London; and the present figures were carved by Richard Saunders, and set up in Guildhall in 1708. The name of

Corinæus has evidently been dropped, and Gotmagot, being divided, has been made to do duty for both.

Going snacks. In Wadd's 'Memorabilia,' he gives a brief account of the plague in London, in which he states that the important office of body-searcher was held by a man named Snacks. During the height of the plague his business increased so fast that he gave to any one who would assist in the hazardous business half the profits. Thus those who joined him were said to 'go with Snacks,' and hence arose the expression *going snacks*, meaning dividing the spoil.

Go it blind. An Americanism meaning to act without due deliberation. It is derived from the game of Poker, where a player may if he chooses 'go it blind' by doubling the 'ante' before looking at his cards, and if the other players refuse to see his 'blind,' he wins the 'ante.'

Gold. Mr. Timbs, in 'Things Not generally Known,' states that all in the gold in the world, if melted into ingots, might be contained in a cellar 23 feet square, and 16 feet high.

Goldbeater's Skin is made from the large intestine of the ox, which undergoes a number of processes to free the outer membrane from grease and other impurities. It is then cut into pieces four inches square, one hundred of which are worth about 1*l*. Such is its tenacity and power of resistance, that it will resist the continuous blows of a hammer twelve pounds in weight for many months.

Gold chain an emblem of authority. The custom of investing persons with authority by placing a gold chain round their necks is of great antiquity. Pharaoh (Genesis xli. 42) put a gold chain about his [Joseph's] neck, when he set him 'over all the land of Egypt.'

Golden Fleece. In the mountains of the Caucasus are several torrents, which wash down minute particles of gold. The people place fleeces of wool in the waters to intercept and retain the gold. Hence the phrase.

Golden Square in London, immortalised by Dickens in 'Nicholas Nickleby,' was originally, according to Pennant, called 'Gelding Square,' from a tavern known as the 'Gelding,' which stood in the neighbourhood. The square was built before the Revolution of 1688. It is mentioned in an advertisement in the 'Gazette' of that year.

Gold Fish are natives of China, and were introduced into

England about the end of the seventeenth century. They are bred principally in ponds fed with the waste hot water from condensing steam-engines. The writer has seen a pond of this kind near Derby literally swarming with gold fish in all stages of growth.

Goliath. The height of Goliath, according to Samuel, was 'six cubits and a span.' Mr. Greaves gives the length of the cubit as 21 inches, and the span 9. This would make Goliath's height about 11 feet 3 inches.

Gone to the Devil. There was formerly a tavern next door to Child's Banking House in Fleet Street, near Temple Bar, known by the sign of the 'Devil and St. Dunstan.' It was much frequented by lawyers as a place for dining, &c., and was noted for the excellence of its liquors. It was familiarly called the 'Devil.' When a lawyer from the Temple went to dinner there, he usually put a notice on his door, 'Gone to the Devil.' Some who neglected their business, frequently had this notice exhibited, until at length 'Gone to the Devil' became synonymous with 'gone, or going, to ruin.'

Good. This word is frequently used in America as an adverb. It is not uncommon among the uneducated to hear such phrases as 'He can't read good,' 'It does not shoot good,' &c.

Good-bye is a contraction of 'God-be-with-you.' It was formerly the custom for monarchs to bless their subjects from their thrones, as the following passage from the 'Mirrour which Flatters not,' published by R. Thrale, 1629, will show. It is addressed to absolute kings and puissant sovereigns :—'You never seate yourselves upon these thrones of magnificence, but as it were to take leave of the assembly, continuing still to give your last *God-b'w'yes* like a man who is upon the point to depart.'

Good Hater. This phrase was first used by Dr. Johnson, who said of Bathurst, a physician, 'He was a man to my very heart's content. He hated a fool, and he hated a rogue, and he hated a Whig; he was a *very good hater*.'

Good wine needs no bush. The bush formerly hung out at the doors of taverns was always of ivy, probably in allusion to Bacchus, to whom the ivy bush was sacred. The old poets and dramatists have many allusions to the custom of hanging out a bush. In Lily's 'Euphues,' A. 3, we have, 'Things of greatest profit are set forth with least price. Where the wine is neat, there needeth no ivie-bush.' Allot, also, in his 'English Parnassus,' in a sonnet to the reader, says—

...has evidently been dropped, and Gotmagot, being divided, ... made to do duty for both.

...ing snacks. In Wedd's 'Memorabilia,' he gives a brief ... of the plague in London, in which he states that the im... office of body-searcher was held by a man named Snacks. ...ng the height of the plague his business increased so fast that ... to any one who would assist in the hazardous business ... the profits. Thus those who joined him were said to 'go with ...,' and hence arose the expression *going snacks*, meaning ...ing the spoil.

...o it blind. An Americanism, meaning to act without due ...eration. It is derived from a game of Poker, where a player ... if he chooses 'go it blind' by doubling the 'ante' before ...ng at his cards, and if the other players refuse to see his ...d,' he wins the 'ante.'

...old. Mr. Timbs, in 'Things Not generally Known,' states ... world melted into ingots, might be ... square and 16 feet high.

...Goldbeater's Skin is made from the large intestine of the ox, ... undergoes a number of processes to free the outer membrane ... grease and other impurities. It is then cut into pieces four ... square, one hundred of which are worth about 1*l*. Such is ... tenacity and power of resistance, that it will resist the con... blows of a hammer two pounds in weight for many ...

Gold chain an emblem of authority. The custom of invest... by placing a gold chain round their ... Pharaoh ... a gold ... neck when he set him 'over all the ...

Golden Fleece. In the mountains of the Caucasus are several ... minute particles of gold. The people ... fleeces of wool in the water to intercept and retain the gold.

Golden Square in London, immortalised by Dickens in 'Nicho...,' which was originally, according to Pennant, called 'Gelding ...,' from a tavern known as the 'Gelding,' which stood in the ..., was ... before the Revolution of ... The square was built ... mentioned in an advertisement in the 'Gazette' of ...

Gold Fish are natives of China, and were introduced into

GOOD WINE NEEDS NO BUSH.

...d about the end ... the seventeenth century. They are principally in ponds ...ed with the waste hot water from con... ...g steam-engines. ...he writer has seen a pond of this kind ...erby literally swar...ng with gold fish in all stages of growth.

...liath. The height ...f Goliath, according to Samuel, was ...ubits and a span.' Mr. Greaves gives the length of the ...is 21 inches, and t... span 9. This would make Goliath's ...about 11 feet 3 inc...s.

...ne to the Devil. ...ere was formerly a tavern next door to ...Banking House in Fleet Street, near Temple Bar, known ...sign of the 'Dev... and St. Dunstan.' It was much fre... ...d by lawyers as a ...ace for dining, &c., and was noted for ...ellence of its liquo... It was familiarly called the 'Devil.' ...a lawyer from the ...mple went to dinner there, he usually ...iotice on his door, '...ne to the Devil.' Some who neglected ...usiness, frequently ...d this notice exhibited, until at length ...to the Devil' becar... synonymous with 'gone, or going, to...

...od. This word is f...quently used in America as an adverb. ...ot uncommon amon... the uneducated to hear such phrases as ...in't read good,' 'It ...es not shoot good,' &c.

...od-bye is a contract ...on of 'God-be-with-you.' It was formerly ...stom for monarchs ...bless their subjects from their thrones, ...following passage ...om the 'Mirrour which Flatters not,' ...hed by R. Thrale, 629, will show. It is addressed to ...te kings and puissa...t sovereigns:—'You never seate your... ...upon these thrones o... magnificence, but as it were to take leave ...assembly, continuin... still to give your last *God-b'w'yes* like a ...ho is upon the poin... to depart.'

...od Hater. This ph...se was first used by Dr. Johnson, who ...Bathurst, a physici..., 'He was a man to my very heart's ...t. He hated a fool... ud he hated a rogue, and he hated a ...he was a *very goo... ater.*'

...d wine needs no b...h. The bush formerly hung out at the ...f taverns was alw...s of ivy, probably in allusion to Bac... ...o whom the ivy bus... was sacred. The old poets and drama... ...ve many allusions ... the custom of hanging out a bush. ...'s 'Euphues,' A. 3, ...e have, 'Things of greatest profit are ...h with least price. Where the wine is neat, there needeth ...bush.' Allot, also, i... his 'English Parnassus,' in a sonnet to ...der, says—

R

> *I hang no ivie out* to sell my wine;
> The nectar of good wits will sell itselfe.

The proverb means that where the wine sold was good, no bush or other sign was necessary. Customers would find their way to the place without. In the reign of Edward III. all the 'taverners' in the City of London were summoned to the Guildhall, and warned that no sign or *bush* would henceforward be allowed to 'extend over the King's highway beyond the length of seven feet.'

Goose. The tailor's smoothing iron. The plural of this is *gooses*.

Goose. The phrase 'To cook one's goose' probably owes its rise to a saying of a king of Sweden, which is thus related in an old chronicle :—'The Kyng of Swedland coming to a towne of his enemyes with very little company, his enemyes, to slyghte his forces, did hang out a goose for him to shoote, but perceiving before nyghte that these fewe soldiers had invaded and sette their chiefe houlds on fire, they demanded of him what his intent was, to whom he replyed, "To cook your goose!"'

Goose on Michaelmas Day. The custom of eating goose on the anniversary of the feast of St. Michael has been attributed to the circumstance that Queen Elizabeth was eating of this bird at dinner at the house of Sir Neville Umfreyville on September 29, 1588, when the news arrived of the destruction of the Spanish Armada. This story may possibly be true, but it was not the origin of the custom, for in the year 1470, one John De la Hay took of William Barnaby, lord of Lastres, in the county of Hereford, one parcel of the land of that demesne, rendering twentypence a year, and *one goose fit for the lord's dinner on the feast of St. Michael the Archangel.*' And that this was not an isolated case, but that the custom of dining upon goose at Michaelmas was in use before the defeat of the Armada, is quite clear from the following lines from the 'Posies of Gascoigne,' published in 1575 :—

> And when the tenants come to pay their quarter's rent,
> They bring some foule at Midsummer, a dish of fish at Lent,
> At Christmas time a capon ; *at Michaelmas a goose*;
> And somewhat else at New-year's tide, for fear their lease fly loose.

Goose and Gridiron. This well-known tavern sign is said to have originated in St. Paul's Churchyard in London. At the north-west corner there was a celebrated music-house, which had for its sign the Swan and Harp. It was turned into a tavern, and the landlord, 'to ridicule its former destiny, chose for its sign a goose striking the bars of a gridiron with its foot.'

Gooseberry. Mr. Fox Talbot gives the following remarkable account of the origin of this name:—'Gooseberries are called in German, *Johannis-beeren,* that is "John's berries," because they ripen about the feast of St. John. St. John is called in Holland *St. Jan,* and the fruit is there called *Jansbeeren.* Now this word has been—centuries ago—corrupted into *Gansbeeren,* of which our English word gooseberries is a literal translation; *Gans,* in German, signifying a goose.' We have *gander* for a male goose.

Gooseberry Fool is gooseberry *foulé,* from the French word *foulé,* crushed, or smashed.

Gore. The verb *gore,* to stab ('Gored with Mowbray's speare'—*Shakespeare*), has no affinity with the noun *gore,* blood. The first comes from the Gaelic *gaorr,* to pierce; the latter from the Anglo-Saxon *gor,* Welsh *gwyar,* clotted blood, mud, &c.

Gorse. Gorse is furze. The name is derived from the Welsh *gores, gorest,* waste land; hence *gorse* or *gorst,* the growth of waste land.

Gosling, the diminutive of goose, *gooseling;* as duckling is the diminutive of duck.

Gospel was anciently *Godspel,* of which Verstegan says:—'Godspel was the name in our ancient language of the sacred writings of the four Evangelists. *Spel* is as much as to say *a mystical speech,* an oracle, or hidden knowledge.'—*Restitution,* &c., p. 175. We retain some portion of this meaning of *spel;* we still speak of the magician's *spell.*

Gossamer. The threads of gossamer which are seen so abundantly in autumn, are supposed to be spun by young spiders, who are great consumers of water, in order that the dew which the gossamer films attract may serve them as drink.

Gossip is a corruption of *Godsib,* a sponsor. Our ancestors understood that at baptism a relationship or affinity was established, not only between the sponsors and the child for whom they undertook certain vows, but between themselves and the child's parents. *Sib* being an old Anglo-Saxon synonym for kin, they used to call each other *Godsib,* implying a relationship through God. This name became corrupted to *gossip,* in which form it is used by Shakespeare in the sense of 'sponsor.' In 'Henry VIII.,' act v. sc. 4, the King addresses the sponsors of the Princess Elizabeth as 'my noble gossips.' 'As the gossips, especially the two godmothers, were accustomed to meet at the house of the parents of their godchild and have a little chat together, such trivial chat came to be called gossipping, and the original meaning of the word has become entirely obsolete.'—*Dean Hoare.* Pepys, in his 'Diary,' under date May 20, 1666, says:— 'Lord's Day. With my wife to church. At noon dined nobly, ourselves alone. After dinner my wife and Mercer by coach to Greenwich to be *gossip* to Mrs. Daniel's child. My wife much pleased with the reception she had; and she was godmother, and did hold the child at the font, and it is called John.'

Gotham, Gothamites. The term *Gotham* is satirically applied to the City of New York, and its inhabitants are called 'Gothamites,' just as Londoners are called 'Cockneys.' 'Ye dandies of Gotham! I have seen fools and fops in forty different cities, but none to compare with you.'—*Dow's Sermons.* 'I intend to present you with some phases of outward life and manners,—such things as would strike or interest a stranger in our beloved *Gotham*, and in the places to which regular Gothamites—American Cockneys, so to speak—are wont to repair.'—*Fraser's Magazine*, '*Sketches of American Society.*'

Gothic Architecture. The name 'Gothic' was first applied to the English style of architecture by the Italians as a term of reproach. Fuller, in his 'Worthies,' says, 'Let the Italians deride our English and condemn them for *Gothish* buildings.'

Go to Bath, and get your head shaved. Formerly persons who showed symptoms of insanity were sent to drink the mineral waters at Bath. Shaving the head was always performed where insanity was suspected. The obvious meaning of the proverbial saying is, therefore, satirically, 'You are going mad; you had better "go to Bath, and get your head shaved."'

Go to grass. This is a common expression in America. It is equivalent to the English 'Be off!' or 'Get out!'

Got the mitten. This is an American phrase, used when a young man is discarded by a lady to whom he has been paying his addresses. Sam Slick ('Human Nature,' p. 90) says, 'There is a young lady I have set my heart on; though whether she is a-goin' to give me hern, or *give me the mitten*, I ain't quite satisfied.' This seems to be the only remaining use of the old English word *mittent* (Latin *mittens*, to send), which Johnson defines 'sending forth, emitting.' *Mittent* itself is obsolete, but it survives in the compound 'intermittent.'

Gourmand, Gourmet. Both French terms. A *gourmand* is a *glutton*, a greedy heavy feeder; one who looks more to the quantity than the quality of his food. A *gourmet*, on the contrary, is an epicure; one delicate in the choice of his food, looking more to quality than quantity.

Gracechurch Street, in London, was formerly called Grasschurch Street, from the Grass Market which was held there.

Grace-cup. Margaret Atheling, the English consort of Malcolm III. of Scotland, found the Scottish nobles rough and uncouth in manners, and did much in the endeavour to ameliorate them. One habit prevailed, even at the royal table. Each man, when his appetite was satisfied, rose and left without ceremony. Margaret, who had her English chaplain to say grace at table, promised all those who would remain until grace had been said, a draught *ad libitum*, from a large cup, filled with the choicest Rhenish wine. This was a temptation too acceptable to be resisted, and each person remained until the grace-cup had passed round. From this circumstance the grace-cup became an institution in barons' halls; and wherever a banquet was served, both in England and Scotland. The custom was general down to the time of the Reformation.

Grade. It seems incredible that this word, now so universally used, is not to be found in any dictionary earlier than Todd's 'Johnson,' which appeared in 1818. Todd inserts the word, but says, 'This word has been brought forward in some modern pamphlets, but it will hardly be adopted.' It was stigmatised by the 'British Critic' as an 'unauthorised Americanism'; but it has stood its ground, and is now firmly established as an English word.

Grain—the weight. The old English pound was equivalent to 'the weight of 7,680 grains of wheat, all taken from the middle of the ear.' This gives 480 to each of the 16 ounces of which the pound was composed. Although the standard is now entirely different, the fact that there are still 480 grains to the ounce Troy, and the ounce in Apothecaries' Weight, carries us back to the time of the Conquest, and shows us how the name *grain* originated.

Grain is a word used in the United States to signify a little, or a particle. For example, a man will say, 'I don't care a *grain*,' or 'push the candle a *grain* nearer to me.'—*Bartlett*.

Gramercy. This old-fashioned word is a corruption of the French *grand merci*, many thanks, e.g. :—

> Be it so, Titus, and *gramercy* too.
> *Titus Andronicus*, act i. last line.

Grampus, a common name for the whale, is a corruption of the French *grand poisson*, great fish.

Grandfather. A man may be his own grandfather. This seeming anomaly is provable thus :—A widower and his son marry; the father marries the daughter of a widow, and the son marries the young lady's mother, thereby becoming father (in law) to his own father, and consequently grandfather to his father's son; that is, himself.

Grange. The *grainage* was originally a place or building where rent and tithes, paid in *grain*, to the abbeys and monasteries were deposited. In the neighbourhood of Glastonbury some very fine Gothic tithe barns or *grainges*, built before the Reformation, are still in existence.

Granite, so called because composed of *grains* of various minerals firmly compacted together.

Grave. The noun *grave*, a place of burial, is from the old verb to *grave*, meaning to dig or excavate, as in Psalm vii. 16, 'He hath *graven* a pit.' In some parts of Yorkshire they *dig* with a mattock, and *grave* with a spade. The word engrave, and its compounds, come from the same root.

Grave. Our Anglo-Saxon forefathers had the beautiful word, *slapigrava* (literally *sleep grave*), to designate a grave, 'because,' as old Verstegan says, 'the dead body may be accounted as being asleep.'

Gravesend. This name signifies the end, or termination, of the jurisdiction of the Reeve, or governor. The old English term, *gerefa*, or *greve*, was the same as the word reeve, which we still retain in the words port-reeve and shire-reeve, or sheriff. Gravesend has been for ages looked upon as the commencement of the port of London, and the word Gravesend means the boundary or end of the jurisdiction of the Reeve of the port of London.

Graving Dock. Graves are the dregs at the bottom of a pot used for melting tallow. Ships, before the use of pitch or tar was introduced, had their hulls well *graved*, that is, greased with graves or impure tallow. To do this it was necessary that the hull should be dry. A *graving dock* was therefore a dock into which a ship could be floated, and the water afterwards drawn off, so that the graving process could go on. The name has been retained, although the practice is obsolete.

Gravy. In the New England States this word is always used for the syrup of tarts, &c., as 'the *gravy* of an apple pie.'

Gray's Elegy. The line in this elegy
>And waste its sweetness on the desert air

was copied from Churchill, who has
>Nor waste their sweetness in the desert air.

Lloyd also has
>Which else had wasted in the desert air.

The line
>And leaves the world to darkness and to me

is parodied in the 'Beggar's Petition':—
>And leave the world to wretchedness and me.

The 'Elegy' was published in the 'Magazine of Magazines' for January, 1751; the 'Petition,' which is by Moss, appeared in 1769.

Great cry and little wool. There are many variations of this proverbial saying, but the true one appears to be the Scottish one, 'Great cry and little woo, as the Soutar said when he clippit the sow'—*Soutar* is shoemaker; and the phrase doubtless arose in times when shoemakers were indebted for the bristles which form the flexible needles of their thread, to native swine. In modern times shoemakers' bristles come principally from Russia.

Greatest happiness of the greatest number. Jeremy Bentham says ('Liberty of the People,' 1821) that this phrase occurs in a 'pamphlet of Dr. Priestley's.'

Grecian Bend. This is not a new term. It was used in the 'Etonian' more than half a century ago, as the following extract shows :—'In person he was of the common size, with something of the *Grecian bend*, contracted doubtless from sedentary habits' (iii. 57).

Greek Characters. The first book printed in Greek characters was a *Greek grammar*, printed at Milan by Dionysius Paravisinus, in 1476.

Greek meeting Greek.
>When Greek joined Greek then was the tug of war.

This line is from Nat. Lee's 'Alexander the Great.'

Greengage Plum. The Rev. John Gage, brother of Sir Thomas Gage of Hengrave Hall, in the county of Suffolk, was a priest of a monastery near Fontainebleau, in France. On a visit to his brother he brought from the monastery garden, slips of this kind of tree, which, being grafted in the garden at Hengrave, soon spread over England.

Green Man and Still. The public-house sign, the 'Green Man,' originally meant a forester, or what we now call a gamekeeper. The 'Green Man and Still,' in Oxford Street, London, the sign of which has puzzled so many people, and which a Frenchman once translated ' *L'Homme verdant et tranquille*,' had a different origin. It meant a man who dealt in green herbs for distillation, and the ' still ' was the apparatus so much in use by our great-grandmothers for extracting the essences of herbs for various culinary and medicinal purposes. Fifty years ago, when the writer as a boy lived in the heart of Surrey, a ' still ' was commonly to be found in the possession of elderly people, and many a glass of home-made peppermint water has been given him as a protection against taking cold in foggy and damp weather.

Greensward. The word *sward* is an old Anglo-Saxon term for skin. The rind of bacon in the Midland counties is called the *sward*. Green *sward* is the green skin or covering of a lawn.

Greenwich. The first stone of the Observatory was laid in August, 1675, and in a year afterwards the building was handed over to Flamsteed the astronomer, from whom the hill on which the observatory stands was named Flamsteed Hill.

The magnificent elms which adorn Greenwich Park were planted in 1663. This is shown by Evelyn's ' Diary,' where, under date March 4, 1663, he says, ' This spring I planted the Home and West-field at Saye's Court with elmes; the same yeare they were planted in Greenwich Park.'

Greese, Degrees. In Lincoln there are some steps leading from the New Road towards the Minster Yard, which by a very curious corruption are called the *Grecian Stairs*. *Gree*, or *greese*, is an old English word for a step, and the now obsolete plural *en* being added, a flight of steps became *greesen*, which was the ancient name of these particular steps. When *greesen* ceased to be understood, the word *stairs* was added by way of explanation, and, by a very easy transition, *greesen* became ' Grecian.' In the verse Acts xxi. 40, our version has 'Paul stood on the *stairs*.' Wicliffe translates this, ' Paul stood on the *greezen*.' Shakespeare has the

word, but spells it differently. In 'Othello,' act i. sc. 3, he says :—
> Let me speak like yourself; and lay a sentence
> Which, as a *grize*, or step, may help these lovers
> Into your favour.

Johnson thinks it is contracted from *degree*, which seems probable, as Chaucer uses 'degree' in the sense of a step or stair, and we still use it metaphorically in a similar sense, as when we say of a man, 'He is rising in his profession step by step;' that is, by degrees. Latimer ('Sermons,' fol. 72), in mentioning Christ's refusal to throw himself from the pinnacle of the Temple, says, 'It is no time now to show any miracles. There is another way to goe down, by *greesing*.' Coryat, in his 'Travels,' vol. i. p. 31, says, 'As we go up towards the hall, there are three or four paire of staires, whereof one paire is passing faire, consisting of very many *greeses*.' And Thomas, in the 'History of Italy,' 1561, H. 22, speaks of 'certain skaffolds of borde, with *grices* or steppes one above another.'

Grenade. Grenade is the French name for a pomegranate. A *grenade* used in warfare is an iron shell filled with gunpowder and bits of iron like the seeds in a pomegranate.—*Wedgwood*.

Grenadiers. On June 29, 1678, Evelyn paid a visit to the encampment on Hounslow Heath, and made the following entry in his 'Diary':—'Now were brought into service a new sort of soldiers called *Grenadiers*, who were dextrous in throwing hand-grenades.' The name is now applied to the first company of a battalion of infantry, which is formed of the tallest and finest men of the regiment.

Gresham. *Grassheim* (*heim*, home) is one of the German names for the grasshopper. The grasshopper on the top of the Royal Exchange is therefore a rebus on the name of its founder.

Gretna Green Marriages. Gretna is a small village in the county of Dumfries, and but a short distance from the border between England and Scotland. A generation ago, run-away marriages were usually performed at this place according to the Scottish law, which then required no residence and no notice. Gretna was selected because it was the nearest point of Scotland that could be reached. It is commonly believed that a blacksmith performed the ceremony, but this was not the case when the writer visited the place some thirty years ago in search of information. The house where the marriages took place was originally a mansion, within a small park, but had been converted into an inn. A large and lofty apartment was fitted up as a kind of chapel, in which the innkeeper performed the simple ceremony, entered the names in a register, and gave the parties a formal certificate. These marriages, since the year 1856, are not valid, unless one of the contracting parties has resided in Scotland for twenty-one days before the marriage.

Greyhound. The Anglo-Saxon name was *grighound*; but the animal known in England at that time was probably allied to the Irish greyhound, an animal of great size and strength, having rough and coarse hair. The smooth-haired variety was originally brought from the East, but has been greatly improved by crossing with other varieties. The Arabian greyhound has a bushy tail. Bailey derives greyhound from the word grey, an old name for the badger; a *greyhound*, he says, is 'a dog that hunts the *grey*.' The word *grey* he defines thus:—'A wild beast called a badger.'

Grig. The proverbial saying, 'As merry as a grig,' refers to a small eel, so called, which is taken as a type of merriment from its perpetual wriggling, lively motion. The name has the same significance in other languages; *gringalet* in French is a merry grig, which in Low German (*Platt Deutsch*) is *wrickken* or *wrikkeln*, and with the nasal, becomes *wringen*—'*Sik wringen als ein wurm.*' See, however, MERRY AS A GRIG.

Grimace. From *grima*, the Anglo-Saxon word for mask. The ancient comic masks were so distorted, that any hideous, forbidding, or distorted expressions of the human face were likened to a *grima*; hence grimace.—*Fox Talbot*.

Grimalkin. A cat is called *grimalkin*, or more properly *Gray Malkin*, from the name of a fiend supposed to assume the form of a cat. Shakespeare makes the first witch in 'Macbeth' say—

I come, graymalkin.

Groat. The name of the silver groat was derived from the French word *gros*, it being, when first coined, the largest silver coin in existence.—*Old and New London*, vol. ii. p. 101.

Grocer originally meant a wholesale dealer, one who sold his goods *en grosse*, that is, in unbroken packages; but Minshew thinks it may have arisen to denote dealers in *grossis*, or figs, 'which they very considerably traded in.'

Grog. Admiral Edward Vernon, in the year 1745, ordered that the men under his command should no longer be allowed to drink undiluted rum. By his directions the spirit was mixed with water before being served out. This at first was greatly resented by the sailors, who christened the mixture 'grog,' in ridicule of the admiral, who was known as 'old grog,' from his custom of wearing *grogram* breeches.

Gross. The great (*gros*) hundred of twelve dozens.

Grosvenor Square. The aristocratic inhabitants of this square were the last to resist the innovation of gas-lighting. The square continued to be lighted by oil lamps down to 1842.

Groundlings. When plays were performed in inn yards, or in the early theatres that were built on the same plan, the spaces under the galleries were occupied by persons of the lower class, who were called the groundlings from their standing on the ground. They paid a penny each for admission. Ben Jonson ('Case is Altered') has, 'Give me the penny—give me the penny! I care not for the gentleman, let me have a *good ground.*' Shakespeare makes Hamlet caution his players not to rant, so as to

Split the ears of the *groundlings.*

Grouse. In the household regulations of Henry VIII. ('Archæologia,' vol. iii. p. 157) this name occurs under the form *grows*.

Gruel is from the French word *gruau*, oatmeal or groats.

Guano. The earliest mention of guano is in Acosta's 'Historia natural y moral de las Indias' (Seville, 1590). In an English translation by E. G., published in 1604, after mentioning *ilands* on the coast of Peru as being white with the dung of sea foule, the writer goes on:—'They goe with boates to these ilands, onely for the dung, for there is noe other profit in them. And this dung is so commodious and profitable, as it makes the earth yeeld abundance of fruite. They call this dung *guano*, whereof the vally hath taken the name, which they call *Limaguana* in the valleys of Peru, where they use this dung, and it is the most fertile of all that countrie.'

Guelder Rose (*Viburnum Opulus*), altered from *Elder* Rose. The earlier botanists considered it to be a species of elder. This plant and the elder are placed next to each other by Smith in the 'English Flora.' When in a wild state the flowers greatly resemble the flowers of the common elder; it is only when cultivated that they assume the ball-like appearance.

Guernsey. There is reason to believe that the name of this island was originally *Ger's-ey*, and that the name, as well as those of Jersey and Cherbourg, are derived from the same root. Camden says that *Ger, Jer,* and *Cher* are corrupted abbreviations of *Cæsar*.

There is a fort in Guernsey called *Jerbourg*, or Cæsar's-burg, which seems to support Camden's view. *Ey* in Jersey, Guernsey, and Alderney, is the ancient word for island, of which there are several forms; as *ea* in Chelsea and Battersea, *ey* in Putney, and *eyot* in numerous islets on the Thames.

Guernsey Lily. This flower is a native of Japan. The ship in which Kæmpfer, the Dutch botanist, was bringing specimens to Europe was wrecked on the coast of Guernsey, where some of the bulbs took root in the sandy soil. They were seen by a son of Governor Hatton, and by him sent to England, in the middle of the 17th century. From the place where they had accidentally been found they were called Guernsey lilies.

Guess, Well. The Americans, as is well known, use the word guess in the sense of to believe, to think, to imagine, to suppose, to fancy, and even to assert, as in the phrase, 'I guess I'll have a drink.' The word *well*, too, pronounced *wal*, is the universal expletive; for few sentences in speech are commenced with any other word. Both are admitted by good American writers to be unmitigated vulgarisms. Yet an American Shakespearian critic (Mr. Richard Grant White, M.A.), writing on the following passage from Richard III., act iv. sc. 4—

>STANLEY.—Richmond is on the seas.
>K. RICH.—There let him sink—and be the seas on him,
>   White-livered runagate;—what doth he there?
>STANLEY.—I know not, mighty sovereign, but by guess.
>K. RICH.—Well, as you guess?—

says:—'If there be two words for the use of which, more than any others, our English cousins twit us, they are "well" as an interrogative exclamation, and *guess*. Milton uses both, as Shakespeare also frequently does, and here we have them both in half a line. Like most of those words and phrases which it pleases John Bull to call "Americanisms," they are English of the purest and best, which have lived here, while they have died out in the mother country.' Well may the Rev. A. C. Geikie retort:—' To such "English of the purest and best" are we fast hastening, if some check is not put on the present tendencies of our colloquial speech, and the style adopted in our periodical literature.'—*Canadian Journal*, September, 1857.—

Chaucer uses 'guess':—

>This woful hande quod she
>Ys strong ynogh in swich a werke to me,
>For love shal me geve strengthe and hardyknesse,
>To make my wounde large ynogh I gesse.

and Richardson quotes from Phaer's 'Virgil'

<blockquote>Nor mortall like, ne like mankind, thy voice doth sound I guess.</blockquote>

Guildhall. The original Guildhall of London was built in 1411, and burnt down in the great fire of 1666. When rebuilt the interior of the porch and the walls of the great hall were retained, and they are the only remaining portions of the original building. The new roof was put up in 1865.

Guillotine. This is the name given to the instrument used in France for capital punishments. It is so called from Joseph Ignace Guillotin, by whom it was introduced into use in that country. Guillotin was a physician at Paris, and soon after the Revolution was sent as a deputy to the National Assembly. In 1790, in a discussion on the penal code, he proposed that decapitation—up to that time used only for nobles—should be the sole method of capital punishment, and he suggested the adoption of a machine used for the purpose in Italy, Scotland, and at Halifax in Yorkshire. The plan was adopted, and the machine received the name of guillotine. Guillotin neither invented the machine, nor did he, as is commonly asserted, perish by it. He was imprisoned during the 'Reign of Terror,' but was liberated in 1794. He afterwards founded the Academy of Medicine in Paris, and died in 1814, aged 76.—*Brand's Dictionary*, vol. ii. p. 75.

Guilt. 'To find *guilt* in a man is to find that he has been *beguiled* by the devil.'—*Trench*.

Guineas. When the guinea was originally coined, the intention was to make it current as a twenty-shilling piece; but, from an error in calculating the exact proportions of gold and silver, it never circulated for that value. Sir Isaac Newton fixed the value of the guinea, in relation to silver, at 20*s.* 8*d.*, and by his advice the Crown proclaimed that it should be current at 21*s.* The first guineas bore the figure of an elephant on the reverse, as an emblem of that part of Africa which furnished the gold and gave its name to the coin.

Gulf Stream. This important oceanic current derives its name from the Gulf of Mexico out of which it flows, between the coast of Florida on the one side, and Cuba on the other. It is about 50 miles wide, and it passes, at a rate of about five miles an hour, along the American coast until it reaches Newfoundland, when it turns and sweeps across the Atlantic. One portion of its volume passes eastwards towards the Azores, but the larger portion washes the shores of the British Islands and Norway, and finally passes away to northerly seas.

The waters of the Gulf Stream are of a deep indigo blue colour, and do not mix with the green sea waters on each side. The temperature of the stream in the Gulf from which it takes its name is 86° F., and after crossing the Atlantic and reaching the British Isles, it still retains so much heat as to modify and influence the climate. In Ireland this effect is so remarkable, that at a time when the north-eastern parts of the island have a temperature of 32° or 33°, the thermometer on the south-western coast stands at 50° or 51°. It is owing to the influence of the Gulf Stream that England and Scotland have a genial, moist, and pleasant climate, while Labrador, in the same parallel of latitude, is almost uninhabitable; and that at Lisbon frosts are unknown, while at Washington, in the same latitude, the river Potomac, a mile wide, is sometimes completely frozen over in a single night.

Gull. The verb *to gull* is a metaphorical allusion to the helplessness of a young bird (*gul*, yellow, from the colour of the down of an unfledged bird). The French use the word *niais*, a nestling, to signify one easily *gulled*. The Italians use the word *pippione*, a young pigeon, in the same sense. We have borrowed the latter, and use the word in the case of a *pidgeon*, one who has been duped at cards.

Gumption. This is a term used colloquially for shrewdness, common sense, or sagacity, as in the lines by Nicoll :—

> Sometimes I think it rank presumption
> In me to claim the muse's *gumption*.

The word comes from the old verb to *gawm*, i.e. to understand; as in the North, 'I dinna gawm ye,' 'I don't understand you.'

Gun, from the French *guigner*, to aim with one eye. This gave *guigneur*, one who aims with one eye. This passing into English as *gunner*, and having no signification in our language, took the meaning of one who works with *guns*, and so localised the word *gun*. No other language in Europe has the word gun or any modification of it.

The earliest mention of a gun is probably that in Chaucer's 'House of Fame':—

> Swift as a pellet out of a *gunne*,
> When fire is in the powder runne.—Book iii.

Gunpowder. The popular notion that Friar Bacon, or Bartholdus Schwartz, was the first who invented gunpowder is altogether erroneous. It was certainly known in China and India many centuries before the birth of either of these so-called inventors. Sir George Staunton says that in these countries 'the knowledge of gunpowder seems to be coeval with that of the most distant historic events.' It is recorded, moreover, that in the year 618 B.C., a cannon was employed in China bearing the inscription, 'I hurl death to the traitor, and extermination to the rebel.' There is unquestionable evidence, from the records of Lord Macartney's mission, that gunpowder was in use by the Chinese two or three centuries at least before the Christian era.

Gunter's Chain. This is the name of the chain, 66 feet long, used by land surveyors. Its convenience arises from the fact that 10 square chains make one acre. The chain is divided into 100 links, and thus 100,000 square links make an acre. See ACCORDING TO GUNTER.

Gutta-percha. This useful substance is the solidified sap of a Malayan tree called *percha* by the natives. The Latin word *gutta* was prefixed to the native name to signify that the sap exuded from the tree in *drops*. It was first brought to England and exhibited at the Society of Arts in 1843, by Dr. Montgomerie. As there are still people who pronounce *percha* as though written 'perker,' it is as well to state that, a few years after he had introduced it, Dr. Montgomerie wrote a letter to the *Times* in which he said that the word is pronounced by the natives of Singapore 'perch-a,' and that, if he had thought any doubt could have arisen, he should have spelt it in English, *pertsha*. Notwithstanding this clear statement, some of the cheaper dictionaries still give it the hard sound *perker*, which is altogether wrong. Articles made of this material were in use in England long before it was known of what substance they were made. This was particularly the case with drinking vessels called *mazer bowls*, the origin of which gave rise to great controversy, but which are now known to have been Malayan bowls made of gutta percha.

Gutted, in the sense of completely emptied and destroyed, came into use on the night James II. fled from London. Lord Macaulay says :—' The king's printing-house . . . . was, to use a coarse metaphor, which then for the first time came into fashion, completely *gutted*.'

H

H. The initial letter H is never mute in words of Anglo-Saxon origin. Whenever it is mute in English it is in the words derived from the French, in which language there is no true aspirate.

Habeas Corpus Act. This Act was passed in the reign of Charles II., May 27, 1679. Under its provisions any person confined in prison by any Court is entitled to a writ of *Habeas Corpus* to bring him before the Court of Queen's Bench or Common Pleas, which shall determine whether his committal be founded upon justice. 'There appears to be good reason to believe that the Habeas Corpus Act was passed by a mistake and a trick..... A division was taken upon the third reading in the House of Lords, on the very day of prorogation, and was carried affirmatively, or the Bill would have been lost. Bishop Burnet says :—" Lord Grey and Lord Norris [*qy.* Norreys?] were named to be the tellers. Lord Norris being a man subject to vapours, was not at all times attentive to what he was doing; so a very fat Lord coming in, Lord Grey counted him for ten as a jest at first, but seeing Lord Norris had not observed it, he went on with this misreckoning of ten; so that it was reported to the House, and declared that they who were for the Bill were the majority.' Incredible as this story would at first sight seem, it derives support from an entry in the manuscript journal of the Lords, that [shows that] the numbers in the division were fifty-seven and fifty-five, while the Journals record the presence of only a hundred and seven members on that day.'—*Christie's Life of the First Earl of Shaftesbury*, 1871.

Haberdasher. An ancient name for a neckcloth was *berdash*, probably from *beard*, and *tache*, a covering, band, or pocket—still used in *sabretache*. Chambers says :—' Berdash was a name formerly used in England for a certain kind of neckdress; and hence a person who made or sold such neckcloths was called a berdasher, from which is derived our word haberdasher.' Another authority says :—' Haberdashers were of two kinds. Those who sold small wares, as buttons, tapes, and other trifles, which might be included in the old Norman term, from which the name is derived, *hapertask*, that is, trumpery, things of small value. The other use of the word was " haberdasher of hats." The meaning is here not quite so clear, but it is probably from a material of which hats were made—*hapertas.* In the "Liber Albus," 225, is an item "Le charge de *Hapertas,* xiid."' In the 'Register of Burials' for the parish of Ware, Hertfordshire, is the following entry :—'1655, Apl. 22nd : Michaell Watkins, son of Robert W.; of Fanshawe Streate, London, Haberdasher of hatts,'

Hack. To 'hack' is to cut or chop. It was the term used for chopping off the spurs of a knight when he was to be degraded or baffled. (See BAFFLE.) When Mrs. Ford, in the 'Merry Wives of Windsor,' has read Sir John Falstaff's love-letter, she tells Mrs. Page that, 'if it were not for one trifling respect . . . . I could be knighted.' Mrs. Page replies, 'What?—thou liest!—Sir Alice Ford! these knights will *hack;* and so thou should'st not alter the article of thy gentry.' The meaning of which puzzling speech is, 'What? Even if you, being a female, were knighted, the other knights would hack off your spurs, and degrade you, so that you would still retain your present rank.'

Hackney. Spanish, *hacanea,* a large pony; Italian, *achanea;* French, *haquenée,* an ambling horse. In 'Rymer's MSS.,' v. p. 18, it is shown that an order was made (19 Rich. II., Jan. 5), setting forth that Reginald Shrewsbury and others, of Southwark, Dartford, Rochester, and other towns between London and Dover, were *hackney men,* and that the hire of a hackney from Southwark to Rochester was sixteen pence; but that in future it is to be twelve pence. The term 'hackney' here evidently means a saddle horse.

Hackney Coaches. The common opinion that the name originated in the London suburb of Hackney is an error; the name is derived from the French *coche à haquenée,* a vehicle drawn by a hired horse (*haquenée*). Hackney coaches were established in London, in 1634, by a Captain Bailey, who set up four. They increased so rapidly that their number was afterwards limited by law. In 'Stafford's Letters and Despatches,' vol. i. p. 227, is a copy of a letter from G. Garrard to the Lord Deputy of Ireland, April 1, 1634. The writer says, *inter alia,* 'Here is one Captain Bailey, he hath been a sea captain, but now lives on the land about this city, where he tries experiments. He hath erected, according to his ability, some four Hackney Coaches, put his men in a livery, and appointed them to stand at the May Pole in the Strand, giving them instructions at what rates to carry men into several parts of the Town. . . . . Everybody is much pleased with it. For whereas before, Coaches could not be had but at great rates, now a man may have one much cheaper.'

In the year 1660 the following proclamation was issued:—

'By the King.

'A Proclamation to restrain the Abuses of Hackney Coaches in the Cities of London and Westminster, and in the Suburbs thereof.

'CHARLES R.

'Whereas, the excessive number of Hackney Coaches and Coach Horses in and about the Cities of London and Westminster and the Suburbs thereof are found to be a common nuisance, to the Publique Damage of Our People, by reason of their rude and disorderly standing and passing to and fro, in and about our said Cities and Suburbs, the Streets and Highways being thereby pestred and made impassable, the Pavements broken up, and the Common Passages obstructed and become dangerous, Our Peace violated, and sundry other evils and mischiefs occasioned:

'We, taking into Our Princely consideration these apparent Inconveniences, and resolving that a speedy remedy be applied to meet with and redress them for the future, do by and with the advice of Our Privy Council publish Our Royal Will and Pleasure to be, and we do by this Our Proclamation expressly charge and command, That no Person or Persons, of what Estate, Degree, or Quality whatsoever, keeping or using any Hackney Coaches or Coach Horses, do from and after the sixth day of November next, permit or suffer the said Coaches and Horses, or any of them, to stand or remain in any the Streets or Passages in or about Our said Cities, either of London or Westminster, or the Suburbs belonging to either of them, to be there hired; but that they and every of them keep their said Coaches and Horses within their respective Coach-houses, Stables, and Yards (whither such Persons as desire to hire the same may resort for that purpose), upon pain of Our high displeasure, and such Forfeitures, Pains, and Penalties as may be inflicted for the Contempt of our Royal Commands in the Premises, whereof We shall expect a strict Accompt:

'And for the due execution of Our Pleasure herein, we do further Charge and Command the Lord Mayor and Aldermen of Our City of London, That they, in their severall Wards, and Our Justices of Peace within Our said Cities of London and Westminster, and the Liberties and Suburbs thereof, and all other Our Officers and Ministers of Justice to whom it appertaineth, do take especial care in their respective Limits that this Our Command be duly observed, and that they from time to time return the names of all those who shall wilfully offend in the Premises, to Our Privy Council, and to the end that they may be proceeded against by Indictments and Presentments for the Nuisance and otherwise according to the severity of the Law and Demerits of the Offenders.

'Given at Our Court, at Whitehall, the 18th day of October, in the 12th year of Our Reign.

'GOD SAVE THE KING.'

Haddock. There is a popular belief that the haddock was the fish from which St. Peter took the tribute money on the shore of Gennesaret, and that the dark spots behind the pectoral fins of the fish represent the marks made by Peter's finger and thumb. It is manifestly erroneous. The haddock is a marine fish, which has never been found even in the Mediterranean. Besides, the water of the Lake of Gennesaret is fresh, in which the haddock could not exist.

Hadrian's Wall, from Newcastle to Carlisle, has given names to many places on its route. From Wallsend (which see), passing westward, we find places named Benwell, Walbottle, Heddon-on-the-Wall, Welton, Wallhouses, Wall, Walwick, Wall Shiels, Walltown, Thorlwall, Birdoswald, Wallbours, Walton, Oldwall, Wall Knoll, Wallmill, Wallboy, Wallend, Wallfoot, and Wallhead.

Haft, the handle of a knife or similar implement. 'Haft, as of a knife, is properly only the participle perfect of "to have," that wherewith you have, or hold it.'—*Trench.*

Haggard. Haggard was the name applied to a hawk that could not be tamed.

Hair. The popular belief that the hair of persons labouring under great mental grief or terror undergoes change of colour seems to be unfounded. Under certain conditions of bodily health the colouring matter of the hair ceases to be supplied, and the hair may consequently become white or grey in a short time. In these cases, however, it is only the growing hair that has no colour; the hair as it gradually rises from the root is grey, while that which is outside the cuticle retains its original colour. No well-authenticated case of sudden change in the colour of the hair is mentioned in the 'Transactions of the Royal Society' extending over 200 years, where, if any such circumstance had occurred, it is almost certain it would have been recorded. The case of Marie Antoinette does not rest upon evidence sufficiently strong to warrant belief.

Hairdressers. 'At the coronation of George II. there were but two hairdressers in London. In 1795 there were 50,000 in England.'—*Walford, Old and New London*, vol. iv. p. 118.

Hair of the Dog. When a man is debilitated from the effects of the previous night's debauch, he is frequently counselled to take 'a hair of the dog that bit him,' the meaning being that he should take a little of the same kind of liquor that had upset him. The saying is a remnant of an old superstitious belief that the burnt hair of a dog was an antidote against the ill effects of intoxication.—*Timbs.* In a song of the date 1650 the following verse occurs:—

> If any so wise is, that sack he despises,
> Let him drink his small beer and be sober;
> And while we drink and sing, as if it were spring,
> He shall droop like the trees in October.
> But be sure overnight, if this dog do you bite,
> You may take it henceforth for a warning ;
> Soon as out of your bed, to settle your head,
> Take a hair of his tail in the morning.

Hair Powder. In 1795, according to the 'Hull Advertiser' of July 11th of that year, the number of persons in that town who took out hair-powder certificates was 'nearly one thousand.' The same authority states that 'London and the circumjacent counties of Middlesex, Surrey and Kent, have already produced for hair-powder licences no less than £100,000, one half the sum at which the aggregate of the tax throughout Great Britain was estimated.'

Hair standing on end. Dr. Andrews, of Beresford Chapel, Walworth, was called upon to attend Probert, the companion of Thurtell, the murderer, when he was under sentence of death for horse-stealing. For some days Probert was in a kind of stupor, but on the morning of execution his mind cleared. The Doctor said that, 'when the executioner put the cords to his wrists to bind his hands, his hair—long, lanky, weak, iron-grey hair—rose gradually, and stood perfectly upright, and so remained for some short time, and then as gradually fell down.' Probert was hanged June 20th, 1825. See Job iv. 13, 14, 15.

Halbert. The weapon so called derived its name from the Teutonic *hild*, battle, and *bard*, axe.

Half. 'Anciently "half" meant any part, and the expression "four halves" is old English.'—*Tyrrwhit*, quoted by *Dean Hoare, English Roots*, p. 87.

Half-faced Groat. This was a term of contempt or reproach which arose in the time of Henry VIII. Shakespeare uses it in

'King John,' i. 1, and also in '2 Hen. IV.' iii. 1, and in 'Robert, Earl of Huntingdon,' we have, 'Thou half-faced groat; you thick-cheeked chitty-face.' The allusion seems to be to the debased groats issued by Henry VIII., on which his head was represented in profile, whereas on those of full value, issued by Henry VII. and his predecessors, the king's head was represented with the full face.

Halfpennies and Farthings. Milner, in his 'History of Winchester,' speaking of Edward I. at Winchester, in 1279, says:— 'Before this time no pieces of less value than pennies were struck, and these [were] marked with a double cross on the reverse, by which means they might be divided into halfpennies and farthings [four things]. And whereas this mode of dividing the pieces gave occasion to great waste and frauds, the king now gave orders for the coining of 'halfpence and farthings.'—3rd edit. vol. i. p. 204. 'Anno 1280, 8 Edward I.: Where as before this time, the peny was wont to haue a double crosse, with a creast, in such sorte that the same might be easily broken in the midst, or into four quarters, and so to be made into halfe pence, or farthings, it was now ordeyned that pence, halfe pence and farthings shoulde be made rounde, wherevpon was made these Verses following:—

> Edward did smite round peny, halfepeny, farthing,
> The crosse passes the bond of all throughout the ring,
> The Kings side was his head, and his name written,
> The crosse side, what Citie it was in, coyned and smitten.
> To poore man, ne to priest, the peny frayses nothing,
> Men giue God aye the least, they feast him with a farthing.
> A thousand two hundred fourescore yeares and mo,
> On this money men wondred, when it first began to go.

At this time, twentie pence wayed an ounce of Troy weight, whereby the peny, halfepeny, and farthing, were of good quantitie.'

Hallelujah, a Hebrew word, signifying, 'Praise ye Jehovah.' The *j* in the word hallelujah stands for *i*, and is pronounced as *y*, thus, *Halleluyah*. It was used by the ancient Hebrews in their songs of praise. St. Jerome introduced it into Christian worship about A.D. 390.

Hallelujah Chorus. At the first performance of the 'Messiah in Westminster Abbey, the effect produced by this chorus upon the king (George II.), who was present, was such that he started to his feet, and remained standing until its conclusion. His example was followed by the entire congregation, and it has been customary ever since to stand during the performance of this chorus.

Hall Mark on Gold. The Hall marks on gold are, 1st, the maker's initials, 2nd, the assay mark, 3rd, the mark of the office where it is stamped, and 4th, the head of the Queen. The assay mark designates the fineness of the gold. Thus '9/375' signifies that $\frac{9}{24}$ths of the weight of the article are pure gold; '12/5' is 12 carats fine; '15/625' is 15 carats fine; a crown and the figures 18 is 18 carats fine, or three-quarters pure gold; and 'crown 22' is standard for the coin of the realm, and of this quality wedding rings are usually made. These figures may be relied on, and purchasers should inspect the Hall mark. 18-carat is the most usual quality in use for the better description of goods. Gold and silver watch-cases and jewellery, not being liable to duty, do not bear the Queen's head.

Hall Mark on Silver. Two qualities of silver are marked at the Assay Offices, the one contains 11 oz. 10 dwts. of pure silver to the lb. Troy; the other 11 oz. 2 dwts., which is the 'standard' for English coin. Each piece of silver manufactured has five marks. 1st, the initials of the maker; 2nd, the Queen's head; 3rd, a figure of Britannia for the finest, and a lion passant for 'standard'; 4th, the mark of the district office; and 5th, the date letter. The London district mark is a leopard's head, crowned; for York, three lions and a cross; for Exeter, a castle with three wings; for Chester, three wheatsheaves or a dagger; for Newcastle, three castles; for Birmingham, an anchor; for Sheffield, a crown; for Edinburgh, a castle and lion; for Glasgow, a tree, salmon, and ring; and for Dublin the figure of Hibernia. The date marks are letters, one for each year. The type of letter is varied every twenty years. Each office has its special form of date letter. The London marks from 1716 have been as follows:—

From 1716 to 1736 Roman capitals.
,, 1737 ,, 1756 Roman small letters.
,, 1757 ,, 1776 Old English capitals.
,, 1777 ,, 1796 Roman small letters.
,, 1797 ,, 1816 Roman capitals.
,, 1817 ,, 1836 Roman small letters.
,, 1837 ,, 1856 Old English capitals.
,, 1857 ,, 1877 Old English, small.
,, 1876, still in use, Roman capitals.

Halo. This word comes from the Anglo-Saxon *halig*, holy. From this root we get the verb to *hallow*, and the noun *halo*; the latter confined in its meaning at first to the 'glories' represented by artists around heads of saints and divine persons, but afterwards to the luminous circle occasionally seen around the sun or moon.

Halse, Halter. *Halse* was the Anglo-Saxon word for the neck.

It occurs in the 'Canterbury Tales,' 4,493 and 12,353. It is generally used by the old writers in the sense of hanging by the *halse*. Thus, in 'Gammer Gurton,' 'Dodsley's Plays,' ii. 64, we have :—

> A thievisher knave is not on live, more filching, no more false ;
> Many a truer man than he has hanged up by the *halse*.

Our word 'halter,' the name of the rope with which we hang criminals, was formerly written *halster*, from *halse*, the neck. Hence, too, the halter which fastens a horse by the neck.

Hamlet. This word is the diminutive of the Anglo-Saxon *ham*, a home. The word 'ham' was sometimes applied to a group of several houses belonging to one family or tribe. 'Hamlet' is a little ham; a small collection of houses.

Hammer-cloth, the cloth covering of the box or seat of the driver of a coach. So called because it covered a box containing a hammer and other tools, to be used in the case of a break down, in the days when roads were so badly made as to be dangerous to travellers. Hence also the 'box-seat,' the seat over the box. This is the generally accepted origin, but some writers derive it from 'hamper,' as in the following quotation :—'In old times it was customary with travellers to place in front of the carriage a hamper, containing provisions, over which a cloth, called a hamper-cloth, was thrown for concealment. This hamper served as a seat for the driver. An ornamental cloth is still thrown over the seat of the driver of a carriage, but its name has been corrupted to "hammer-cloth."'

Hammock. This was originally a North American Indian word. 'A great many Indians in canoes came to the ship to-day, for the purpose of bartering their cotton and *hamacas*, or nets, in which they sleep.'—*Columbus, First Voyage*, quoted in Webster. Sir Walter Raleigh mentions 'Cotton for the making of *hamacas*, which are Indian beds.'—*Discovery of Guiana*, 1596. 'The Brazilians call their beds *hamacas*.'—*Sir R. Hawkins's Voyage to South Sea*.

Hamper. Bailey derives this word from *hand-pannier*, that is, a basket to be carried by hand. Pannier is from *panis*, bread, and originally signified the baskets which bakers slung on each side of horses to carry round their bread for sale ; a hand-pannier would, therefore, of course, be a small basket. Although modern dictionary-writers have rejected this etymon, there is great probability that Bailey was right. Baskets slung on horses for general purposes were called 'dorsers' or 'dossers,' from the French *dossière*, the back strap of a horse.

Hampstead Heath. ' Down to the commencement of the eighteenth century the Parliamentary elections for the County of Middlesex were held on Hampstead Heath.'— *Old and New London*, vol. v., p. 454.

Hand (in measuring horses). A hand is four inches, the breadth of a man's hand when closed, or when he ' doubles his fist.'

Handel. On the 13th of February, 1726, 'George Frideric Handel' petitioned the House of Lords ' That he may be added to the Bill now pending, entituled, " An Act for Naturalising Loris Sechehaye."' This petition being granted, Handel attended at the House on the following day and took the oaths. His name was then added to the Bill, which received the Royal Assent on February 20, 1726. In the petition Handel states that he was ' born at Hall, in Saxony.'

' The Public Advertiser' of Friday, April 6, 1759, contained the following advertisement:—

' At the Theatre Royal, in Covent Garden, this day will be presented a Sacred Oratorio call'd THE MESSIAH. Being the last time of performing It this Season. Pit and Boxes to be laid together, and no Person to be admitted without tickets, which will be Delivered this Day, at the Office in the Theatre, at Half a Guinea each. First Gallery, 5s.; Upper Gallery, 3s. 6d. Galleries to be open'd at Half an Hour after Four o'clock. Pit and Boxes at Five. To begin at Half an Hour after Six.'

This was not only the last performance of the season; it was Handel's last appearance in public. He died on the following Friday, which was the anniversary of the first performance of the ' Messiah,' at Dublin, seventeen years before.

Handicap. It is singular that this word seems to have escaped the notice of most dictionary-makers. It is not in Bailey, Johnson, or Maunder. Mr. Earle says ('Philology,' p. 181), ' I have searched Richardson, Webster, and Latham in vain.' It is, however, in the later editions of both Worcester and Webster, where the various significations of the word are carefully recorded. In Nuttall's Dictionary, too, it is given, but explained only as ' a kind of race.'

The word, in modern usage, is applied to denote the endeavour to make competitors in a race or other sport who are unequal in point of speed or ability more fairly matched. In foot races this is done by allowing some of the athletes in a race a certain less distance to cover than those who are known to be swift runners have to accomplish. In horse-racing the practice is different; where the horses to run are of different ages, the weights they have to carry are proportioned, bags of shot being added to the harness of the more mature to make the handicap equal and fairly proportioned to the strength, or supposed speed, of the competing horses.

Handsome. This word originally had nothing to do with the meaning beautiful or good-looking. It meant simply that which was ready to the hand, handy. Afterwards it was applied to anyone who was handy or dexterous, so that a handsome man was one who was ready to turn his hand to anything.

Hand-writing. Dr. Parr, who wrote an illegible and almost undecipherable hand, was the author of the following:—' I would check the petty vanity of those who slight good penmanship, as below the notice of a scholar, by reminding them that Mr. Fox was distinguished by the clearness and firmness, Mr. Professor Porson by the correctness and elegance, and Sir William Jones by the ease and beauty of the characters they respectively employed.'

Handywork. This word is wrongly divided; it is not handywork in the sense of skilful or ingenious. It is the Anglo-Saxon *hand-geweorc*, hand-work.

Hang. This verb has two past participles, *hung* and *hanged*. The latter is always used in the case of suspension for the purpose of destroying life; as 'the man was hanged.' Formerly malefactors stood in a cart under the gallows with the rope round their necks until the signal was given; the cart was drawn away, and the criminal was left hanging. Earl Ferrers, who was hanged May 5, 1760, was the first executed by the drop. It is stated ('Remarkable Trials,' 1765, vol. ii. p. 347) that 'His arms were secured by a black sash, and the halter, which was a common one, was put round his neck. He then mounted a part of the scaffold eighteen inches above the rest, and the signal being given by the Sheriff, that part of the floor sunk under him to level with the rest, and he remained suspended in the air.' 'There is a very common, but most erroneous, belief that a woman, by marrying a man under the gallows, can save him from execution. It is not so.'— *Wharton.* ' In England great offenders are "hanged," but in the United States and Canada criminals are never hanged; they are all "*hung.*" In England beef is hung, gates are hung, and curtains are hung; but felons are hanged. In Canada felons, beef, gates, and curtains are all treated in the same way.'—*A. C. Geikie*, in the *Canadian Journal*, September 1857.

Hanging in chains, or gibbetting, was abolished by Act of Parliament, July 25, 1834. The practice was upheld in former times, in the case of murderers, for two reasons. First, that it might strike terror into other offenders; and, secondly, that it 'might afford a comfortable sight to the relations and friends of the deceased'! Whether the term 'deceased' referred to the murdered person, or to the murderer, the old writer from whom the above quotation is given does not condescend to say.

Hang up one's fiddle. To 'hang up one's fiddle' is an American proverb, meaning to desist, to give it up. Sam Slick says, 'When a man loses his temper, and ain't cool, he might as well hang up his fiddle'; and in 'Dow's Sermons,' p. 78, we find: 'If a man at forty-two is not in a fair way to get his share of the world's spoils, he might as well hang up his fiddle, and be content to dig his way through life as best he may.' In English literature the phrase is used in a totally different sense. To 'hang up one's fiddle with one's hat' is said of a man, who, while pleasant abroad, is churlish or stupid at home; e.g.:— 'May be so,' retorted the lady. 'Mr. N—— can be very agreeable when I am absent, and anywhere but at home; I always say he hangs his fiddle up with his hat. Did you ever hear the saying before, Mr. Gurney?' 'Once, I think, ma'am,' said I, with becoming gravity. 'Once!' said Nubley; 'a thousand times; it is in all the jest books.'—*Gilbert Gurney; Theodore Hook.*

Hanker (Dutch *hunkeren*). This word is probably a corruption of 'hunger.' It is always used in connection with the word 'after.' We hanker after something. Paley says, 'without hankering after something better.' The text (Matthew v. 6), 'Blessed are they which do hunger and thirst after righteousness,' shows the affinity, even if it does not establish the identity, of the two words 'hunger' and 'hanker.'

Hanks. The word 'hanks,' as applied to skeins of thread or worsted, is derived from the name of a Brabant manufacturer who came to England, on the invitation of Edward III., in 1391.

Hansard. This is the name by which the published authorised reports of the speeches in Parliament are known. The full title is

'Hansard's Parliamentary Debates.' The work was established by Luke Hansard, who was born at Norwich in 1752, and worked as a compositor for Hughes, the printer to the House of Commons. In 1800 Hansard succeeded to the business, which has since been carried on in his name.

Hansardise. This word was first used by Earl Derby in a debate (April 27, 1868) on the 'Life Peerage Bill,' when the noble Earl assured Lord Granville that, in referring a second time to his speech on life peerages in 1856, he 'had no desire to Hansardise the noble Earl.'

Hansom Cabs were so named from their inventor. Hansom was an architect at Birmingham and at Hinckley, in Leicestershire.

Hapsburg. The English manner of spelling this name—with a *p*—is incorrect; it should be Ha*b*sburg—with a *b*. Mr. Freeman, in his 'General Sketch of European History,' uses the *b*.

Harbinger, from the ancient word *har*, a message; whence har*bringer*, one who brings a message, a herald, or *avant courier;* and, hence, by the elision of the *r*, 'harbinger.'—*Fox Talbot.* Some authorities, however, think it was originally one sent on, in advance of his employer, when taking a journey, to secure that harbourage, or lodgings, should be in readiness.

Hardy. We have two distinct meanings to this word. One is derived from the French *hardi*, which means bold, audacious, &c., which we use in such phrases as 'He had the hardihood,' &c. The other meaning is from the Anglo-Saxon *heard*, hard; and we use it in such sentences as 'A hardy, weather-beaten sailor'; 'Take exercise to make you hardy,' &c.

First catch your Hare. This saying, attributed to Dr. Kitchener, but which is probably far older than his time, is, perhaps, a play upon an ancient word still in use in Norfolk and Suffolk. In those counties where the word *skatch* means to skin and dress an animal for cooking, the direction 'first *skatch* your hare' might be easily mistaken for the mythical phrase 'first *catch* your hare,' a saying which has been productive of so much merriment that it seems a pity to disturb it. There is, however, another theory, which is that the word used was 'case,' one meaning of which was formerly, according to Johnson, 'To strip off the covering; to take off the skin.' Shakespeare also uses the word in this sense in 'All's Well that Ends Well,' where he says, 'We'll make you some sport with the fox ere we case him.' The direction in the old Cookery Book would probably therefore be, 'First "case" your hare,' that is, 'first skin him.' Mrs. Glasse, in all the editions examined for the purposes of this work, uses the word 'cast.'

Hares. It was formerly a settled belief amongst country people that hares annually changed their sex; and this belief was countenanced by many respectable authorities. Even Sir Thomas Brown seems undecided about it. Fletcher, in the 'Faithful Shepherd,' iii. 1, has :—

> Snakes that cast their coats for new,
> Chameleons that alter hue,
> Hares that yearly sexes change.

And Butler has :—

> When wives their sexes change like hares.
> *Hudibras*, ii. ii.-v. 705.

Harmonious Blacksmith. This was not an original idea of Handel's. Chaucer, in his 'Boke of the Duchesse,' has the following lines (1161-5) :—

> Lamekys sone Tuballe,
> That founde out firste the art of songe,
> For as hys brothres hammers ronge,
> Upon hys anvelet uppe and downe
> Thereof he took the fyrst sowne.

Harrington. In the writings of the old dramatists there are constant allusions to a Harrington as a piece of money. A Harrington was a farthing; so called because Lord Harrington obtained from James I. a patent for making brass farthings. Ben Jonson, in 'The Devil is an Ass,' ii. 1, has :—

> I will not bate a Harrington o' the sum.

And in the 'Magnanimous Lady,' ii. 6 :—

> His wit he cannot so dispose by legacy,
> That they shall be a Harrington the better for it.

Harvest. We get this word from the Saxon *Hœrfest*, which Bailey thinks originally meant herb-feast.

Hat. Hats were first made by a Swiss, at Paris, in 1404. They were not made in England until 1510. There was a stamp duty upon hats from 1784 to 1811. 'The cocked hat survived till nearly the present century. It was superseded by the round one [the chimney-pot or flower-pot] during the French Revolution.'—*Leigh Hunt, Autobiography.* Silk hats were first introduced about 1820.

Hatbands, &c., at Funerals. Formerly the hood or capuchin, with its flowing *liripipe* or tippet, was the universal head-covering for both sexes. During the reign of Henry VI. the hood was superseded by the hat, but the tippet was retained, and was generally worn attached to the hat. Although for generations discarded in ordinary dress, the tippet, in the form of the hatband, still holds its place at funerals. And even now, when women attend funerals, they are attired in hoods of similar fashion to those worn five hundred years ago.

Hatch, in the names of places. Wherever this name occurs it signifies that there is, or was, a gate across a high road at the entrance to a common, to prevent the escape of cattle. There is one between Richmond and Kingston, at the entrance to Ham Common, and the house adjoining it is called the Hatch. In many places where the commons have been enclosed, the gate has disappeared, but its locality is still discoverable by the word 'hatch' being affixed to the name of the place.

Hate. Perhaps the finest definition of a word ever given is that of the word *hate*, by Chaucer, in the 'Persone's Tale':—

Hate is olde wrathe.

Haughty is from the French *haut*, high.

Hautboy. The wind instruments in an orchestra are, collectively, always spoken of as 'the wind'; those of brass, separately, as 'the brass'; and those of wood, as 'the wood.' As the oboe was formerly the acutest sounding, or highest wooden instrument for orchestral purposes, it probably, from this circumstance, received the French name *haut bois*, high wood; and, from this, the English name is a very easy transition.

Havoc is probably from the Celtic word, adopted by the Anglo-Saxons, *hafoc*, a hawk; a bird which sometimes causes great havoc in a poultry yard. The Welsh call out '*Hai hafog!*' when a cow or other animal is committing waste in a neighbour's field. So Shakespeare:—

Cry havoc! and let slip the dogs of war.

Haw was the Anglo-Saxon word for a ditch; hence 'ha-ha' for a fence in the centre of a haw or ditch.

Hayrick, Cornstack. Except that one is of hay, and the other of corn still in the straw, both these collections of farm produce are alike, yet one is universally called a rick and the other a stack. It was so in Swift's time, for he tells us that, on a time,

> An inundation
> O'erflowed a farmer's barn and stable;
> Whole ricks of hay, and stacks of corn,
> Were down the sudden current borne.

The dictionaries give the Anglo-Saxon *hreac* as the root-word, but that throws no light upon the origin of the word. Nares gives 'reck' as the original form of the word now spelled and spoken 'rick,' which he erroneously says is 'a stack of hay or corn.' An old Warwickshire farmer told the writer that a stack of hay is called a rick because it reeks, or throws off a quantity of warm vapour, when it is first built. There seems some feasibility in this. There is certainly some affinity between the two words.

Hazel Nut. The word 'hase,' in various forms, is general in the Northern languages for the husk, beard, or shell of fruit or grain. The Dutch say *hase noot*; the Norwegian, *hasl*; the Danish *hase*. In Provincial Danish *haas* and *haser* are used for the beard or husk of corn. In Bavaria *hosen* is the beard of corn. Hazel nut therefore means 'the bearded nut.'

Head of Oliver Cromwell. It is well known that the body of Cromwell was exhumed, and beheaded, and that the head was afterwards exposed on the top of Westminster Hall for more than twenty years. It was blown down on a stormy night, and was taken possession of by a soldier. Its subsequent fate is fully set out in a letter which appeared in the 'Times' of December 31, 1874, with the signature 'Senex.' It came, it appears, into the possession of a Mr. Wilkinson, a medical man, 'in whose family it still remains.' Another letter, which appeared in the 'Globe,' in September 1874, states that the head 'is now in the possession of Mr. Horace Wilkinson of Sevenoaks, Kent.'

Heads on London Bridge. The heads of persons beheaded for State offences were formerly exposed to view, on long poles, upon London Bridge. Cunningham ('Handbook of London') says that the last head so exhibited was that of Venner, the Fifth-Monarchy zealot, who was beheaded in the reign of Charles II.

'**Hear, hear!**' This is a Scriptural phrase. It occurs in 2 Samuel xx. 16: 'Then cried a wise woman out of the city: Hear, hear!' Lord Macaulay gives the following account of the rise of the exclamation in English usage:—'The King, therefore, on the fifth day after he had been proclaimed, went with royal state to the House of Lords, and took his seat on the throne. The Commons were called in, and he, with many gracious expressions, reminded his hearers of the perilous situation of the country, and exhorted them to take such steps as might prevent unnecessary delay in the transaction of public business. His speech was received by the gentlemen who crowded the bar with the deep hum by which our ancestors were wont to indicate approbation, and which was often heard in places more sacred than the Chamber of the Peers. As soon as he had retired, a Bill declaring the Convention or Parliament was laid on the table of the Lords and rapidly passed by them. In the Commons the debates were warm. The House resolved itself into a Committee, and so great was the excitement that, when the authority of the Speaker was withdrawn, it was hardly possible to preserve order. Sharp personalities were exchanged. The phrase "hear him," a phrase which had originally been used only to silence irregular noises, and to remind members of the duty of attending to the discussion, had, during some years, been gradually becoming what it now is; that is to say, a cry indicative, according to the tone, of admiration, acquiescence, indignation, or derision.'—*Hist. of Eng.* ch. xi. (1689).

Hearse. The hearse was formerly a framework for setting candles in, used at some offices of the Church, and particularly at funeral services, where hearses of great splendour were placed over the bodies of distinguished persons. Portable hearses, for the reception of coffins, and having covers with fittings for candles, were used to carry corpses from the house to the church, where the candles were lighted. They were the origin of modern hearses. 'The number of candles being the great distinction of the funeral, the name of the frame which bore them came to be used for the whole funeral obsequies, or for the cenotaph at whose head it was placed, and finally for the funeral carriage.'—*Wedgwood.*

Hearth. The earliest mention of a 'hearth' for a fire is in the 22nd verse of the 36th chapter of Jeremiah.

Heart of Grace, meaning to be of good pluck, or to have plenty of courage. The saying is derived from a hunting phrase; a stag in good condition being called a 'hart of grease.' A pun seems to have been intended in the first instance, but the joke is neither a very obvious nor a very lively one.

Heathens, dwellers upon heaths. 'The word heathen acquired its meaning from the fact that at the introduction of Christianity into Germany the wild dwellers on the heaths longest resisted the truth.'—*Trench.* See PAGAN.

Heaven, from the Anglo-Saxon *heafen*, raised, elevated. 'Heaven, or heaved up; to wit, the place which is elevated.'— *Verstegan*.

Height of St. Paul's. It is singular that there are scarcely two authorities which agree as to the height of St. Paul's Cathedral in London. 'Chambers's Encyclopædia' says 356 feet; 'London in 1880' (Bogue), 370 feet; Haydn's 'Dictionary of Dates,' 404 feet. For the purposes of this work application was made to the Surveyor of the Cathedral for the correct measurement. His assistant, Mr. George McDowell, in a letter dated September 25, 1880, says, 'Having personally measured the height of the building some years ago, I am in a position to give the required information. The height, externally, from the centre of the street on the south side is 365 feet. The level varies all round.'

Heirloom. This term is derived from the English word *heir* and the Anglo-Saxon *geloma* or *loma*, household stuff. In old times, when the clothing of a family was spun and woven at home, the loom was the most important article of furniture in a house, and eventually its name became representative of all, in the same sense as we now use 'furniture.' In Cheshire, to this day, the word 'loom' is used as descriptive of any article of furniture. From this use of the word comes its application to specific articles descending from father to son, and called 'heirlooms.'

Heir Presumptive is one who, if the ancestor should die immediately, would be his heir, but whose right of inheritance may be defeated by a nearer heir being born.

Heligoland is Holy-island-land.

Hell, from the Anglo-Saxon *helan*, to cover or conceal, originally meant the grave. 'The word *Halla*, the abode of death of the Northern nations, may be the origin of this word.'— *Bosworth*.

Hell and Tommy. In some parts of England it is very common for an angry man to threaten another that he will 'play hell and tommy' with him. It is thought that this is a corruption of 'Hal and Tommy,' and that the allusion is to Henry VIII. and his unscrupulous Minister, Thomas Cromwell, who seized and rifled the religious houses, and turned out their occupants to starve.

Helter-skelter. All the dictionaries, from Bailey to Worcester, have missed the true etymology of this phrase. The ordinary orthography has perhaps led them astray. It should be written 'helter-kelter.' Helter (perhaps a corruption of halter) is an old word for 'hang,' and kelter is found in all the dictionaries in the sense of 'order' or 'in a proper state.' Thus Barrow says, ' If the organs of prayer be out of kelter, how can we pray?' Helter-kelter is, therefore, literally 'hang-order'; and may mean, 'O hang order! let us do it, or let it remain as it is, in defiance of order,' i.e. *helter-kelter.*

Hence, Thence, Whence. Hence means *from here*; thence, *from there*; and whence, *from where*. This being so, it is obvious that the common phrases 'from hence,' 'from thence,' 'from whence,' are all incorrect. ' He departed from hence' is equivalent to saying 'He departed *from from* here,' because 'from' is included in the word 'hence.' This will perhaps be more apparent if we say, 'He remained hence,' which, of course, is an absurdity.

Herd. In English we have only one word 'herd' to express the meaning of two distinct ancient terms. A 'herd,' as of cattle, was formerly *hairda*, but a 'herd' who took care of them took his name from the verb *hyrdan*, to guard. In England we now only use this word in the compound shepherd, neatherd, swineherd, goatherd, &c. We have, however, another word from the same root, *hurdle*, i.e., the temporary fence by which sheep are guarded, or kept from danger by wandering.

Heresy, Schism. Schism comes from a Greek word signifying to 'split.' ' Schism ' is, strictly speaking, the renouncing allegiance to the ecclesiastical government under which one lives; whilst 'heresy' is the adopting opinions and practices contrary to its laws.—*Eden.* 'Heresy relates to errors in faith, and schism to those in worship or discipline.'—*Locke.* In an old print by Sebastian Brandt, in the 'Prophecies of Methodius,' 1449, a schism in the Church is represented by two men cutting up a miniature church with a saw.

Herodians. The sect so called in the New Testament was composed of Jews, who believed that Herod was the Messiah, because 'when the sceptre departed from Judah,' he was declared king by a decree of the Roman Senate.

Herring. 'The word herring is derived from the Anglo-Saxon *hær*, an army, to express their numbers.'—*Pennant.*

He who fights and runs away, &c. It is generally thought that these lines are in 'Hudibras,' and many wagers have been won and lost on the subject, but those who search will not find them there. Butler wrote—

>For those who fly may fight again,
>Which he can never do that's slain.

And in this shape the words appeared from 1678 to 1762, when Goldsmith published a work, the 'Art of Poetry on a New Plan,' where, paraphrasing Butler's couplet, he issued the following—

>For he who fights and runs away
>May live to fight another day;
>But he who is in battle slain
>Can never rise and fight again.

Both Butler and Goldsmith, however, were plagiarists, for in Newman's 'Church of the Fathers,' p. 215, is an extract from Tertullian, as follows:—'The Greek proverb is sometimes urged, "He who flees will fight another day," and Goldsmith's lines, almost verbatim, *e.g.*

>For he that fights and runs away
>May live to fight another day.

appear in "The Muses' Recreation," a volume of poems published in 1656, and written by Sir John Minness, Vice-Admiral to Charles I., and comptroller of the navy after the Restoration. He died 1670, and was buried in the church of All Hallows, Barking, where there is a monument to his memory.'

He who steals my purse, &c. Shakespeare probably got the idea upon which he founded these words from the 'Homily against Contention,' set forth in the time of Edward VI., from which the following is an extract:—' And many times there cometh less hurt of a thing than of a railing tongue, for the one taketh away a man's good name, the other taketh away his riches, which is of much less value and estimation than is his good name.'

Hey-day. Probably from the German *Heyda! Heysa!* exclamations of high spirits or active enjoyment.

Hey derry down. 'Blackwood's Magazine' (July 1878) says that this has been traced to a Druidical chant, *Hai down, ir, deri danno,* 'Come, let us hasten to the oaken grove.'

Hic jacet. A Latin phrase often seen on tombs. Its meaning is 'here lies,' or 'here he lies.'

High Church and Low Church. In Cromwell's time the inhabitants of the fenny parts of Cambridgeshire were almost entirely dissenters, and Cromwell's followers were originally chiefly from that district. The old parish churches were mostly on the adjoining hills. It is still common in the fens to hear the doctrines of the Church of England spoken of as *High doctrines,* alluding to the topographical position of the churches, in contrast to *Low,* or dissenters' doctrine, the religion of the fenny country.

High Court of Justice. This is no new term in English jurisprudence. There was a 'High Court of Justice,' which sat from the 20th to the 27th January, 1648-9, to try Charles I There was another which sat from the 10th of February to the 6th of March in the same year to try the Duke of Hamilton, the Earl of Holland, Lord Capel, &c. A third met on June 30th, 1654, for the trial of several cavaliers; and a fourth sat in Westminster Hall, 25th May, 1658, for the trial of Sir H. Slingsby and others, for high treason against the Commonwealth.

High faluten, probably a corruption of 'high flighting,' though it may be from the Dutch *verlooten,* a term originating in the Western States of America to signify high-flown, stilted, or bombastic language. The word is becoming domesticated in England, and has even crept into a 'Times' leader.

Himalaya Mountains. The name Himalaya is formed from two Sanscrit words, *hima,* snow, and *âlaya,* abode. The meaning is, therefore, 'the abode of snow,' which is singularly appropriate, as the summits, some of which are more than 23,000 feet in height, are perpetually covered with snow from the height of 16,000 to 17,000 feet.

Hinge. From the old English word *hing,* to hang. The hinges are the hooks or other contrivances upon which a door is hung.

Hippocras. The name of a drink formerly much used in England. It was made of equal parts of Canary and Lisbon wines, in which spices of various kinds were digested for a few days, after which the liquor was strained and sweetened with sugar.

History, Historian. The *h* is sounded in both these words, but we say *a* history, *an* historian. The reason is that in 'historian' the accent on the second syllable is so strong, that the sound of the first is scarcely perceptible.

Hobble-de-hoy. The derivation of this singular phrase is obscure. Tusser is the earliest authority for its use, and he writes it *Hobbard-de-hoy.* He is dividing man's life into apprenticeships of seven years each, and he says—

The first seven years bring up as a child,
The next to learning, for waxing too wild ;
The next keep under Sir Hobbard de Hoy,
The next a man, no longer a boy.

Hobby Horse. *Hobba* in the Icelandish language means a mare. The term 'hobby' was, a century ago, given to Irish or Scotch horses of rough and hardy breeds, some of which were kept in the Royal stables for odd jobs. In the 'London Chronicle' of December 7th, 1788, is the following, which gives the exact date of George the Third's first attack of mental derangement :—

'Kew, Friday night, Dec. 5, 1788, ¼ past 10 o'clock.

'Hurst, the *hobby* groom, is this moment sent as fast as possible to bring Mr. Dundas (the medical gentleman attending his Majesty) from Richmond.'
A 'hobby' was usually the favourite cob upon which gentlemen rode about their estates, and the word easily adapted itself to the meaning which it at presents holds in the language.

Hob or Nob. Nares says this is a corruption of the old *hab-nab*, from the Saxon *habben*, to have, and *nabban*, not to have; it was formerly used as an alternative, precisely as we now say 'give or take.' Shakespeare certainly uses it in this sense in 'Twelfth Night,' act iii. sc. 4, 'Hob-nob is his word, give 't or take 't.'

Hobson's choice—that or none. In the time of Charles I. one Hobson let horses to the students at Cambridge. He would never break his rule of letting the horses in strict rotation. Persons wanting a horse must take the one whose turn it was to go, or they could have none. Hence the saying, 'That or none.' Milton wrote Hobson's epitaph.

Hocus-pocus, Hoax. Mr. Wedgwood thinks that hocus-pocus is pure gibberish, and that it is most improbable that it is a corruption of *Hoc est corpus*. The modern word *hoax* is derived from hocus-pocus, but what hocus-pocus comes from is doubtful.

Hog. This word has become a general name for swine, but it formerly applied to the *age* only. Thus a wild boar of two years old was a *hog*, but when three years old was a *hog-steer*. A wether sheep until first shorn at the age of twelve months is a *hog*. A ewe two years old is a *hoggerel*, or *hogget*, and a colt of a year old was formerly called a *hogget*.

Hog. 'To go the whole hog.' This phrase probably arose in some gambling transaction. A *hog* is in slang phrase a crown-piece. Suppose one gambler to say, 'I'll go a shilling'; another, more bold, might say, 'I'll go half a crown'; and a third, still more venturesome, might add, 'I'll go *the whole hog*'; that is, 'I'll venture the entire crown.' Probably the word 'hog,' as applied to a piece of money, is from the Jewish name for a ducat—*hoger*. The phrase 'the whole hog' occurs in Cowper's 'Love of the World Reproved.' Mahomet, according to the poet, allowed his followers to eat pork, except one portion of the animal, which he did not specify, and consequently strict Mahommedans were debarred from eating any. Others, however, through one piece being forbidden,

> Thought it hard
> From *the whole hog* to be debarred;

and so, one taking a leg, another a shoulder, and so on—

> With sophistry their sauce they sweeten,
> Till quite from tail to snout 'tis eaten.

Hog-guessing. They have a peculiar sport in Long Island, in America, called Hog-guessing. A fat hog is 'put up,' as in a ballot or raffle, to be 'guessed for.' A number of chances at a fixed price each are sold, and each chance-holder has the right to make one guess at the weight of the animal. The hog is then put into the scale, and the chance-holder who has guessed nearest to the weight takes the hog as a prize.

Hogshead. It has been suggested that, as skins and hides formerly did duty as bottles and vessels for conveying wines and other liquors, that the *hogshead*, or *hogshide*, was originally a barrel of the same capacity as a liquid-containing vessel made of the skin or hide of a hog. Others think it may have been an *oxhide* from which the word was derived. As the Dutch and Scandinavians call this kind of cask by some equivalent of 'oxhead,' there is some probability that this may be the origin of the word.

Hoity-toity. In Selden's 'Table Talk' is the following passage:—'In Queen Elizabeth's time, gravity and state were kept up. In King James's time, things were pretty well; but in King Charles's time there has been nothing but Frenchmore and the cushion dance, *omnium gatherum*, tolly-polly, and *hoite-come-toite*.' The last phrase in modern French would be *haut comme toit*—'as high as the roof'; a pretty good equivalent for the slang 'hoity toity.'

Hold—of a ship. Corrupted by a very natural transition from the word *hull*.

Holland. This name is not heard of before the year 1064. Its derivation is uncertain, but there are two plausible theories. Some derive it from the old German *hol*, low, and *land*; but Dr. Bosworth thinks it comes from the Dutch *ollant*, trembling, which, he says, 'exactly suits the fenny and boggy soil which it designates.'

Hollyhock is the garden mallow (Anglo-Saxon *hoc*, mallow). It is called hollyhock or holyhock, from the Holy Land, where it is indigenous.

Holograph. 'A will, or deed, written wholly by the grantor's or testator's own hand.'—*Chambers.*

Holy. 'It is a curious thing that I remarked long ago, and have often turned in my head, that the old word for "holy" in the German language, *helig*, also means "healthy." And so *Heilbronn* means "holy-well," or "healthy-well." We have it in the Scotch "hale"; and, I suppose, our English word "whole"—with a "w"—all of one piece, without any hole in it—is the same word. I find that you could not get any better definition of what "holy" really is than "healthy"—completely healthy.'—*T. Carlyle.*

Holy Thursday was formerly called Shere Thursday. In the 'Liber Festivalis,' Caxton, 1483, the reason is thus given:—'It is also in Englysshe called Sherthoursday, for in olde fader's dayes the people wolde that day shere theyr hedes, and clyppe theyr berdes, and polle theyr hedes, and so make theym honest ayenst Ester day.'

'**Home, sweet Home.**' This popular ballad was written by John Howard Payne, an American dramatist, for the opera 'Clari, the Maid of Milan,' the music of which was by Balfe. Payne became U.S. Consul at Tunis, where he died in 1852.

Homœopathy. Milton, in the preface to 'Samson Agonistes,' makes a distinct reference to the principles upon which the modern system of homœopathy is founded. He says:—'So, in physic, things of melancholie hue and quality are used against melancholy, sour against sour, salt to remove salt humours,' &c.

Honey-moon. It was anciently the custom amongst the Northern nations of Europe for newly-married people to drink metheglin or mead—a kind of wine made from honey—for thirty days after marriage. Hence the term 'honey-moon,' or 'honey-month.'

Honi soit qui mal y pense. This is the ancient Norman-

French motto of the Knights of the Garter. It is generally interpreted, 'Evil be to him that evil thinks'; but it is more accurately 'Dishonoured be he who thinks evil of it'—that is, of the Garter.

By hook or by crook. In Marsh's Library, Dublin, is a manuscript entitled 'Annales Hiberniæ,' written in the seventeenth century by Dudley Loftus, a descendant of Adam Loftus, Archbishop of Armagh. The following extract gives a feasible account of the origin of this popular saying:—'1172. King Henry the 2nd landed in Ireland this year, on St. Luke's eve, at a place in the bay of Waterford, beyond the fort of Duncannon, on Munster syde, at a place called ye Crook over ag^t the tower of ye Hook; whence arose the proverbe to gayne a thing by Hook or by Crook; it being safe to gayne land in one of those places when the winde drives from the other.' There is, however, another more probable origin. Anciently the poor of a manor were allowed to go into the woods to gather dead wood. They were allowed to cut off dead branches with a bill*hook*, or to pull down by means of a *crook* any dead branches that otherwise would be above their reach. In the records of the town of Bodmin there is a document claiming for the burgesses of the town, under a concession of the Prior of Bodmin, 'to bear and carry away on their backs, and in no other way, the lop, crop, *hoop, crook*, and bag wood in the Prior's wood of Dunmeer.' Another part of the record calls this right 'a right with *hook* and *crook* to lop, crop, and carry away fuel, &c., in the same wood.' The date of the document is 1525.

Hookey Walker. 'Notes and Queries' says that the original Hookey Walker was John Walker, who was a clerk in the employ of Longman, Clementi & Co., Cheapside, London. He had a crooked or hooked nose, from which his nickname was derived. He was employed by the firm as a kind of spy upon his fellow-servants. Jack's reports of the malpractices going on were always met by so many preconcerted denials, that at last his reports were discredited and he was dismissed. In course of time any dubious statement in the City was received with the remark 'O! that's Hookey Walker,' and in that way the name of the old clerk has passed into a proverb. Another authority says the term is derived from the name of a London police magistrate of great acuteness and incredulity, who had a remarkably hooked nose. This peculiarity, it is said, also gave rise to the term 'beak,' as applied to magistrates generally.

Hooping Cough, or **Chin Cough.** There was formerly a current belief that the seat of this disease was in the spine, and the most popular remedy—Roche's Embrocation—is applied between the shoulders, or that part of the back which is called the *chine*. The name *chin-cough*, so common in country places, is probably a contraction of ' *chine*-cough,' as Bailey spells it. It may, however, be a corruption of an older Saxon word. The Germans have the verb *keichen*, signifying to gasp, to pant, or to breathe spasmodically. Our ancestors had a similar word, *kink*, which, Bailey says, ' is spoken of children when their breath is stopped through eager crying or coughing.'

Hop. The hop is mentioned by Pliny as one of the garden plants of the Romans, who ate the tender shoots as we eat asparagus. Those who have never tasted hop-shoots in this way will be surprised to find that they are really a delicious esculent. The tops of common stinging nettles are also excellent when cooked as spinach.

Hornpipe. The musical instrument called the horn was originally, as its name indicates, made from the horn of an ox or cow. Some were drilled with holes at regular distances, similar to those in a flute. These were called horn-pipes, and the ancient dance known as the hornpipe was so named from its having been originally danced to the music from one of these rude instruments.

Hors de combat, a French phrase, signifying completely disabled; incapable of further resistance in a contest or fight. It is pronounced *hor-de-com-ba*.

Horse-radish, &c. The prefix ' horse ' is very commonly applied to vegetables of a coarse or rank quality. Thus we have horse-radish, horse-bean, horse-vetch, horse-chestnut. The same prefix is also used in the case of some animals, as, horse-leech, horse-crab, horse-mussel, &c., in all of which there is a coarse resemblance to the animals bearing the simple name. The same word is likewise used to designate rough or uncouth habits or conduct, as, horse-play, horse-laugh, and so on. Probably the original word used was ' coarse,' which has been corrupted.

Hosanna. This is a Hebrew exclamation or prayer used by the Jews on day of the Feast of Tabernacles. Its literal meaning is ' Save now,' the words ' we beseech Thee ' being implied.

Hottentot. The early Dutch settlers at the Cape of Good Hope were much struck with the *click* which forms such a distinct feature of the Caffre languages, and which sounded to them like a perpetual repetition of the syllables *hot* and *tot*. From these sounds they gave the natives the name of Hott-en-tot; *en* in the Dutch language meaning 'and.'—*Proceeds. of Philological Society*, 1844.

Housebreaking is breaking into a house with a view to robbery, *by daylight*. Housebreaking *at night* is burglary. 'In the day-time there is no burglary.'—*Blackstone*.

Household. The English names of the different members of a household are, in their original signification, very expressive. 'Husband' is *house-bond*, which explains itself; 'wife' is *weaving one*, she who weaves for the house; 'son' is *cleaner*; 'daughter' is *milker*; and 'spinster' is *unmarried woman*, such as the sister of the husband or wife—one who spins.

House-leek is, properly, house-*leaf*. The German name is *hauslaub*.

House of Commons. In a printed copy of the Standing Orders of the House of Commons, dated May 17, 1614, it is—

'ORDERED—That this House shall sit every day at 7 o'clock in the morning, and enter into the great business at 8, and no new motion to be made after 12.

'ORDERED—That so soon as the clock strikes twelve, Mr. Speaker do go out of the Chair and the House shall rise; and that in going forth no member shall stir until Mr. Speaker do go before, and then all the rest shall follow. Whosoever shall go out of the House before Mr. Speaker shall forfeit 10s.'

In the year 1693 it was

'ORDERED—That no member of the House do presume to smoke tobacco in the gallery, or at the table of the House sitting at Committees.'—*Solicitor's Journal*.

The form of the proceedings of the House is intimated by the position which the Mace occupies at the time. Hatsell says:— 'When the Mace lies *upon* the table it is a "House;" when *under*, it is a "Committee;" when the Mace is *out* of the House, no business can be done; when *from* the table, and *upon* the Serjeant's shoulder, the Speaker alone manages.' The present mace dates from the time of the Restoration. It bears the initials C.R. The resolution ordering a new mace appears in the books in 1660.

'The table of the old House, which was saved from the fire of 1834, is now in the office of the Board of Works, Whitehall Place.'—*Old and New London*, vol. iii. p. 522.

Houses of Parliament. The embankment was commenced in 1837, the building in 1840. The Lords first sat in the new House, April 15, 1847; the Commons not until November 4th, 1852. The building covers 19 acres, and contains nearly 1,200 apartments.

How to deal with a Cucumber. Many physicians have been credited with the advice as to how to prepare a cucumber, ending with 'and then give it to the pigs.' 'An Antidote against Idolatry,' by Henry More, D.D. (1669, p. 104), has the following ' Prescript touching the safe eating of a pear,' which is attributed to 'that skilful, and famous physician, Dr. Butler':—' That we should first pare it very carefully, and then be sure to cut out, or scoup out all the coar of it, and, after that, fill the hollow with salt, and when this is done, cast it forth into the kennell.'

In the 'Beggar's Opera' is the following :—

> And when she's dead and furnished out,
> All painted fine and gay,
> As men should serve a cucumber—
> She flings herself away.

Hoyle on Whist. Edmund Hoyle, the author of the celebrated book on Games, was the Registrar of the Prerogative Court, in London. He died in Cavendish Square, London, in August, 1769, aged 97.

Huckster. In Hone's 'Everyday Book' (September 5) is an engraved figure of a man carrying on his back a small barrel containing fruit, underneath which is the title, '*A Huxter*,' of which Hone says, 'Randle Holme, in his heraldic language, says of this representation, "He beareth *gules* a man *passant*, his shirt or shift turned up to the shoulder, breeches and hose *azure*, cap and shoes *sable*, bearing on his back a bread basket full of fruit and herbs, and a staff in his left hand *or*. This may be termed either a gardener or a huxter . . . . this was a fit crest for the Company of Fruiterers or Huxters. This man was a costermonger in Nare's view of the term, for doubtless a huckster pitched his load in the market and sold it there; yet Holme does not give him that denomination; he merely calls him the *hutler* or *huxter*."' Huckster now means any petty dealer, and in the Midland counties a *huckster's* shop is what Londoners call a chandler's shop.

Hugger mugger. This is one of those duplicated phrases so common in the English language, of which it is difficult to trace the origin. Nearly every lexicographer has his guess at the origin of this one, but Johnson seems to hit upon the most probable etymon, though he says, 'I know not how to determine.' His theory is that it is a corruption of *hugger morcher*, a hug in the dark. *Morcher* is Danish for darkness, and is akin to our *murky*. The following extract from L'Estrange seems to favour this derivation : ' There's a distinction betwixt what's done openly and barefaced and a thing that's done in *hugger mugger* under a seal of secresy and concealment.'

Human Bones. The number of distinct bones in an adult human body is 254.

Human Stature. The following instances of extraordinary height are well authenticated :—

	ft.	in.
Duke John Frederick of Brunswick	8	6
One of the Prussian Guards	8	6
Gilly—a Swede—exhibited	8	0
O'Brien, the Irish giant, whose skeleton is in the College of Surgeons, London. His real name was Patrick Cotter. He died at Clifton, Bristol, 1806	8	4
Reichart, a German	8	3

Humble Bee. In many parts of England this insect is called dumble-door, which is a corruption of the French *double-doré*, or double-gilt, applied to the insect in reference to the rich yellow colour of some parts of his body.

Humble Pie is properly *umble* pie. The umbles of a deer correspond to the giblets of a goose. The venison pasty in feudal times was reserved for the lord and his principal guests. For those who sat 'below the salt,' pies were made of the inferior portions, and these were called ' umble pies.' Hence to eat ' umble pie ' was to occupy an inferior position.

Humbug. This word is generally supposed to have originated in the present century. It is however of much earlier origin. The title-page of the ' Universal Jester,' published before 1740, describes the book as a collection of ' clenchers, closers, bon-mots, and *humbug*.' The word is mentioned in the ' Connoisseur ' about 1755 as ' a new-coined expression.' In a letter from Mann to Walpole, in 1760, the writer, speaking of ' Tristram Shandy,' uses the word ' humbugging.' The following, taken from the ' Berwick Advertiser,' some twenty-five years ago, seems feasible. It is right to premise that the name ' Bogue ' is pronounced *bug* in that locality : —' It is not generally known that this word is of Scottish origin. There was in olden time a race called Bougue of that ilk in Berwickshire. A daughter of the family married a Hume. In progress of time the Bougue estate devolved on one George Hume, whose name was popularly pronounced "Hum o' the bug." Mr. Hume was inclined to the marvellous, and exalted himself, his wife, and all his ancestors on both sides. His tales did not however pass current, and at length, when any one in the neighbourhood made any extraordinary statement, the hearer would shrug his shoulders, and say it was just a "*hum o' the bug*." This was shortened into *humbug*, and the word soon spread itself over the whole kingdom.'

Whether this derivation be true or not, it is certain that the lands of 'Bougue,' still called '*bug*' by the country people, passed by marriage into the Hume family, in whose possession they still remain.

Another derivation is founded upon the following advertisement of a celebrated Dublin dancing-master which appeared in 'Dublin Freeman's Journal,' January 1777:—'To the Nobility. As Monsieur Humbog does not intend for the future teaching abroad after 4 o'clock, he, at the request of his scholars, has opened an academy for young ladies to practise minuets and cotillons. He does not admit any gentlemen, and his number of ladies is limited to thirty-two, and as Mr. Humbog is very conversant in the business of the toilet table, the ladies may depend upon being properly accommodated. Mr. Humbog having been solicited by several gentlemen, he intends likewise to open an academy for them, and begs that those who choose to become subscribers will be so good as to send him their addresses that he may have the honour of waiting upon them to inform them of his terms and days. Mr. Humbog has an afternoon school three times a week for little ladies and gentlemen not exceeding 14 years of age. Terms of his school are one guinea per month and one guinea entrance. Any ladies who are desirous of knowing the terms of his academy may be informed by appointing Mr. Humbog to call upon them, which he will do on the shortest notice. Capel Street, January 21, 1777.'

Hummums. This singular name is borne by a highly respectable hotel in Covent Garden. It is a corruption of the Persian word *humoun*, which means what we now call a Turkish bath. The old and new Hummums were originally established as baths of this character. They were known as 'sweating baths' or 'hot houses.' Ben Jonson, in the 'Puritan,' makes one of his characters say, 'Marry, it will take me much sweat; 'twere better to go to sixteen hot-houses.' The Hummums when first established were well supported, and respectably conducted, but they gradually declined in character, and were ultimately suppressed by authority in consequence of immoralities. The buildings were afterwards converted into hotels, which have borne for several generations the highest reputation.

Hundred. *Raed* is a term formerly used in counting by tens. Thus in Swedish *attraed* is eighty, *nyraed* is ninety, and *hundraed* a hundred. Sometimes the hundraed comprised twelve *raeds* instead of ten. This was called the *hundraed tolfraed* of twelve tens, or 120, corresponding to the 'long hundred' of modern commerce. The Gothic term *hund* seems an abbreviated form of some word signifying ten. The word *hund-seofon-tig* has come down to us; it means ten seven times or *seventy*.

Hunter's Moon. The lunation after the harvest moon is often called the 'hunter's moon.' Sportsmen do not hunt by moonlight. The obvious meaning, therefore, is 'hunter's *month*,' the crops being harvested, there is nothing to interfere with the sport of the hunter. Honeymoon is another example of the word moon being used to express month.

Hunting Cries. All these cries seem to have 'come in' with the Normans. 'Hoix' is corrupted from *Haut-ici*; 'hark forward' from *forbeur*—'à qui forbeur'; 'halloo' from *au loup*—'a wolf.'

Hurly-burly, Hulla-baloo. Words similar to these are in use in almost all languages to express confusion and uproar. Thus, French, *hurluburlu*; Champagne, *hustuburlu*; Platt-Deutsch, *huller de buller*; Swedish, *huller-om-buller*; Dutch, *holder de bolder*; Bohemian, *hala-balu*; Turkoman, *qualabálac'h*, &c. &c.

Hurrah. Probably a corruption of *Tur aie!* 'Thor, aid,' a battle-cry of the Norsemen.—*Wace.* The word is very generally now, and was formerly invariably, spelt *huzza.* The pronunciation in Pope's time, and even until living memory, was *hurray.* The following couplet, from the 'Rape of the Lock,' shows the current pronunciation at the time the poem was written:—

> One self-approving hour whole years outweighs
> Of stupid starers, and of loud huzzas.

Hurricane. This word does not appear in any English dictionary earlier than Phillips's, which was published in 1720. Dampier, however, who died in 1712, says, in the second volume of his 'Voyages,' ch. vi., 'I shall next speak of hurricanes. These are violent storms, raging chiefly among the Caribee Islands, though by relation Jamaica has of late years been much annoyed by them. They are expected in July, August, or September.' 'Hurricane' is a Carib word for a high wind, which being brought to Europe by seamen, is now incorporated with most of the European languages.

Hurry. A word formed from noises made by drivers of horses and mules, to urge their cattle to greater speed. In the Teutonic dialects it takes the form huri! In France and Italy arri! or harri! is the form. In Spain, arri! arri! is the cry of a muleteer, and, according to Halliwell, 'harrer' was the Anglo-Saxon word by which drivers urged their horses.

Hurst in English local names means a wood or grove. *Chiselhurst* is the chestnut grove; *Hazelhurst* is the hazel grove; *Midhurst* the middle grove, &c. &c.

Husband, from the Anglo-Saxon *hus,* a house, and *bonda,* a master of a family. 'I have no housebonde.'—*John* iv. 17, *Wycliff's Translation.*

Husbandman. A husbandman was formerly one who tilled his own land, in distinction from a farmer, who was a tenant. In the register of Barwell, Leicestershire, is an entry, '1655, Mr. Gregory Isham, attorney and husbandman, buried 7th October,' and in that of St. John's, Newcastle-on-Tyne, is 'Umphraye Hairope, husbandman, and Fortune Shafto, gentlewoman, married 20th January, 1599.'

Hussar. This word is derived from the Hungarian word *husz,* signifying twenty. At the time when the Turks were over-running Eastern Europe, every twenty houses were compelled to send, and to maintain in the field, one soldier, fully equipped. These men, to distinguish them from the regular army, were called 'hussars,' and they proved so valiant in the field, that the name became a synonym for dash and courage, and has been adopted in all the languages of Europe. The Hungarian cavalry claim that the name was given, because, in the Turkish wars, each man of them was a match for twenty.

Hussy. A corruption of the word housewife in a bad sense.

Hyde Park. This was originally the manor of Hyde, belonging to the Abbey of Westminster. It became Crown property at the dissolution of the monasteries in 1539. It contains about 400 acres.

Hyde Park Corner. Up to the year 1825 a turnpike stood at

Hyde Park Corner. In Hone's 'Every Day Book,' October 5th of that year, is a view of the old gate, as it appeared, when a few days before, the auctioneer stood, hammer in hand, disposing of the building materials of the 'toll houses, gates, rails, posts, inscription boards, and other material.' The 'tall house near the bun house at Chelsea, with lamp posts on the road, were likewise sold on the same day in seven lots.'—*Hone*.

Hydropathy. In a letter of Horace Walpole to Cole, dated June 5, 1755, he says :—' Dr. Heberden (as every physician to make himself talked of *will* set up some new hypothesis) pretends that a damp house, and even damp sheets, which have ever been considered fatal, are wholesome. At Malvern they certainly put patients into sheets just dipped in the spring.' This Dr. Heberden was one of the physicians in ordinary to George III.

Hy-jinks. This is often erroneously written 'High jinks,' as though it were synonymous with uproarious hilarity. Hy-jinks, as a note from Allan Ramsay shows, was a tipsy game, comprising dice, forfeits, and heavy drinking. Ramsay says :—' A covetous fellow may [by this game] save money and get himself as drunk as he can desire in less than an hour's time.'

I

I. It is thought that the practice of writing *y* at the end of a word instead of *i*, while the *i* is substituted when another syllable is added, as in duty, dutiful, may have arisen in the wish to please the eye by giving a sort of finish to the word, in the same way as in Roman numeration, where the final unit always had a tail given to it, as *iiij*.

I beg to say is a contraction of 'I beg *leave* to say.' The full phrase is not only more elegant, but is far more polite.

Iceberg. From the German *eis*, ice, and *berg*, a hill.

Iceland Dogs, Poodles. The dogs now called poodles seem to have come originally from Iceland. There are many allusions to these dogs in the works of dramatists and authors of two and three centuries ago. The following quotations are copied from Nares :—

But if I had brought little dogs from Iceland.
Preface to Sweetnum's Arraignment of Women.

> We have sholts or curs dailie brought out of Iceland.
> *Holingshed, Desc. of Brit.* p. 231.
>
> Hang hair like hemp or like the Isling curs.
> *Beaumont and Fletcher, Queen of Corinth*, iv. 1.
>
> So I might have my bellyful of that
> Her Island dog refuses.—*Massinger.*
>
> Our water dogs and Islands here are shorn,
> White hair of [by] women here is so much worn.
> *Drayton, Mooncalf*, p. 489.

The following seems conclusive as to these dogs being the original poodles:—' Use and custome hath intertained other dogges of an outlandishe kinde, but a few and the same beying of a pretty bygnesse; I mean *Iseland dogges*, curled and rough all over, which by reason of the lenght of their heare make showe neither of face nor of body. And yet these curres, forsoothe, because they are so strange, are greatly set by, esteemed, taken up, and made [much] of, many times in the roome of the gentle Spaniell or comforter.'—*Of English Dogges, &c.*, 1576.

Ich Dien. The popular belief that these words were the motto of the King of Bohemia who was slain by the Black Prince at Cressy does not rest upon any good authority. The three plumes were certainly not the crest of the King of Bohemia, which was an eagle's wing. Verstegan, with great probability, makes it purely Anglo-Saxon. '*Ic* or *Ich*,' he tells us, meant 'I, as I myself,' and he further says it was pronounced 'as we should do if it were written *Igh*, whereby it hath some aspiration.' '*Theyn*,' he informs us, was 'a chiefe, or very free servant; hereof cometh *Thiene*, to serve.' In a subsequent article he says, 'The Prince of Wales, the King of England's eldest son, is wont to use for his Poesie (after our ancient English speech), the words *Ic dien* for *Ich thian*, that is, I serve; where the reader is to remember that *d* and *th* was in our ancient language indifferently used.'—*Restitution of Decayed Intelligence*, edit. 1655, pp. 177–185. It is quite clear, however, that after the battle of Cressy, Edward the Black Prince adopted the plume and motto as a crest, and it has since been borne by the heirs to the Crown of England, as such. It is not exclusively confined to the Princes of Wales, and might have been adopted by the Duke of Clarence during that portion of the reign of George IV. during which the Duke was heir-presumptive to the throne. Probably the Black Prince, who was as modest as he was valiant, when he adopted the motto, had in mind the verse, Galatians iv. 1, 'The heir, as long as he is a child, differeth nothing from a servant.'

Idea, from a Greek word signifying *to see*. 'In the Platonic sense "ideas" were the patterns according to which the Deity created the World.'—*Hamilton*.

'This word *idea* is perhaps the worst case in the English language; in no other instance, perhaps, is a word so seldom used with any tolerable correctness; in none is the distance so immense between the sublimity of the word in its proper, and the triviality of it in its common and popular, use. How infinite the fall of the word, when this person has an "idea" that the train has started, and the other had no "idea" that the dinner would be so bad.'—*Trench*.

Idea. To make war for an idea. The Emperor Napoleon III. is generally credited with having originated this phrase, but in point of fact it was first used by Mazzini in a leading article of the 'Italia del Popolo,' published at Milan, July 27, 1848. It occurred in the following sentence:—' Wait not for the fiat of men who do not comprehend what it is to make war for an idea' (*che sia la guerra per un idea*).

Identity, from the Latin *idem*, the same. But identity and sameness have different meanings, the first applied principally to persons, the second to things. The *same* sound may be repeated, but the *identical* sound means a sound heard at some particular time, which cannot be reproduced or repeated.

Id est, Latin, *that is*. The initials of this phrase, the letters *i.e.*, are commonly met with. They are to be read as 'that is,' or 'that is to say.'

Idiot. The Greek word *idiotes* signified a private person as distinguished from those holding office, or sharing in the management of public business, and the English word idiot originally had the same meaning. 'Humility is a duty in great ones as well as *idiots*.'—*Bishop Taylor*. Its next meaning was that of a rude ignorant boor or rustic. It now signifies one born without understanding or mind, a *natural* fool. Idiocy should not be confounded with lunacy or insanity, both which terms are applied to the condition of persons whose minds are diseased. See IMBECILITY.

If the salt have lost his savour, &c. 'It is a common thing for rock salt when exposed to the sun in hot climates to lose its saline quality. Maundrel says, "Along one side of the Valley of Salt, viz. that towards Gibul, there is a small precipice about two men's length, occasioned by the taking away of the salt. I broke a piece off, that was exposed to the sun, rain, and air; though it had the sparks and particles of salt, yet it had perfectly lost its savour. The inner part, which was connected with the rock, retained its savour, as I found by proof." '—*Dr. Adam Clarke.*

Ignoramus Jury. This was formerly the title of the body now known as a Grand Jury, from the custom of their writing the Latin word '*ignoramus*,' meaning 'we do not know,' ' the evidence does not inform us,' on the back of a bill of indictment when they 'ignored' it. The words now used are 'no true bill.' In ' Collectanea Curiosa,' Oxford, 1781, p. 393, is a copy of a charge by Judge Allibon, at the Croydon Assizes, in 1688, in which the judge directs the jury thus :—' If you find that anything proceeds from envy and malice, and not of due prosecution, you may acquit the person that is so wrongfully prosecuted, and so justice is done between party and party, so an Ignoramus Jury may not be of no use.'

I.H.S. 'This was originally IHΣ, the first two and the last Greek letters of IHΣOYΣ, Jesus, but its origin was lost sight of, and the Latin letter S having been substituted for Σ it became I.H.S., and a Latin word was found for each initial. Hence *Iesus hominum salvator*, 'Jesus the Saviour of men.' Formerly it was customary to put the horizontal abbreviation mark over the letters, thus :— I.H.S. This mark was afterwards altered into a cross, and it became I ₦ S, as it now frequently appears in Roman Catholic publications. In this form it forms the initials of ' In hâc salis,' meaning ' In this [cross] salvation.'

A curious instance of ignorance as to the signification of the symbolic use of these letters occurred in 1860, when some thief managed to cut out the gold embroidered letters from the altarcloth of Mary-le-bone Church. The vestry were in full conclave on the question of the sacrilege, when a sage churchwarden observed that he did not approve of the Vicar (John Henry Spry) putting his initials on the cloth.

Ilk. This word, commonly used in Scotland and the north of England, has two distinct meanings, 'each' as in the phrase 'Ilk one of you'; and 'the same,' as in the phrase ' Mackenzie of that ilk,' where it means ' Mackenzie of Mackenzie,' the latter being the name of Mackenzie's ancestral estate. An improper use of the phrase has, however, become common in American newspapers, where, of that sort, of that party, of that class, &c., have given place to the incorrect expression ' of that ilk.'

Illusion. It is a common error to confound this word with delusion. Illusion refers to errors or deceptions of the senses;

delusion to deceptions, false hopes, or false impressions of the mind. An optical deception is an illusion. A false opinion that leads astray is a delusion.

Illustrated Newspapers. The 'Times' in the early part of the century gave occasional woodcuts. There were two in 1804 (February 15, August 11); two in 1807 (April 6 and 15); five in 1809, one of which, September 12, was a plan of Covent Garden Theatre, and another, October 26, a design for illumination at the Jubilee. The first number of the 'Illustrated News' appeared May 14th, 1842.

Imbecility differs from idiocy. In idiocy the mind is not developed; in imbecility it is imperfectly developed. Idiocy is absence of mental power; imbecility is feebleness of mental action. See IDIOT.

Imitation Pearls. These are hollow glass beads coloured by the pearly dust which falls from the scales of the little fish known as the bleak, when repeatedly agitated in water. This powder is kept in liquid ammonia until wanted for use. The price of the finest is sometimes as high as 5*l.* per ounce.

Immemorial. In English law, a custom or prescription is said to be immemorial when its existence can be proved from the time of the return of Richard I. from the Holy Land, A.D. 1189. This is called 'the period of legal memory,' or, 'whereof the memory of man runneth not to the contrary.'

Immigrant—opposed to 'emigrant.' Thus, a person leaving England to settle in Australia is an emigrant; but when he arrives in Australia he is an immigrant. An emigrant goes out; an immigrant comes in.

Immodest Words, &c. The two lines—

Immodest words admit of no defence,
For want of decency is want of sense.

are generally attributed to Pope. They are by Lord Roscommon, and occur in his 'Essay on Translated Verse.'

Imp. The word *imp* originally signified a child or progeny. In an old work, 'Pathway unto Prayer,' reprinted by the Parker Society, the following passage occurs (p. 187) :—' Let us pray for the preservation of the King's most excellent Majesty, and for the prosperous success of his beloved son, Edward, our Prince, *that most angelic imp*.' Spenser, in the 'Faery Queene,' has—

Ye sacred *imps* that on Parnassus dwell.

And another old writer—North—says, 'He took upon him to protect them from all, and not to suffer *so goodly an imp* to lose the good fruit of his youth.'

Implement means something to supply a want, and was formerly much wider in significance than it is now. It could even be applied to persons. In the 'Wild Goose Chase' (Beaumont and Fletcher) is the passage—

> Yet if she want an usher, such an *implement*,
> One that is thoroughly paced, a clean made gentleman,
> Can hold a hanging up with approbation,
> Plant his hat formally and wait with patience, &c.

Improve. This word originally meant to rebuke, to disapprove, to condemn. Neither the verb 'improve' nor the noun 'improvement' can be found in the Bible. Shakespeare uses the word 'improve' in the sense *to make use of*, and Milton uses it in the sense of *to increase*. The French word *improuver* has the exactly opposite meaning to the same word in modern English.

Inch is the Erse word for island. It is found as a prefix in the names of several islands of Scotland, as *Inchcomb*, *Inchkeith*, *Inchkenneth*, &c. Jamieson points out that the word still exists in the kindred dialects Welsh, Cornish, Breton, Irish, and Gaelic, with trifling variations.

Inclement. This word is now used only of the weather, but it was formerly used in reference to the actions of men. An inclement man was one devoid of clemency, pity, compassion, or mercy.

Incognito. This is an Italian word signifying unknown. It is generally contracted to *incog*. It denotes the disguise assumed by sovereigns or princes when they do not wish to be recognised. Sometimes this is done by assuming a fictitious name or title, and sometimes by travelling without retinue or other distinctive marks.

Incoherent. In its original sense it means anything which does not cohere, or is unconnected. Ansted speaks of 'incoherent strata.'

Indenture. A legal document or deed, the upper edge of which is *indented* or cut unevenly, so as to form a serrated or tooth-like edge. Formerly it was customary to write a deed and its copy both on one sheet of parchment, the division between them being cut in an irregular or indented line, so that when the two were compared, the projections on the one would correspond with the depressions in the other.

India-rubber. The earliest allusion to this substance is, probably, the following from the preface to Dr. Priestley's 'Familiar Introduction to the Theory and Practice of Perspective,' 1770, 8vo. :—'Since this work was printed off, I have seen a substance excellently adapted to the purpose of wiping from paper the marks of a black-lead pencil. It must, therefore, be of singular use to those who practise drawing. It is sold by Mr. Nairne, mathematical instrument maker, opposite the Royal Exchange. He sells a cubical piece of about half an inch for three shillings, and he says it will last several years.'

Indigo. This, as is well known, is a vegetal production, but it was for a long time believed in England to be a mineral, and letters patent were actually granted, December 23, 1705, for obtaining it from mines in the principality of Halberstadt. Bailey describes it as 'a blue stone brought out of India, used for dyeing, painting, &c.'

Indulge. 'If the matter of indulgence be a single thing, it has *with* before it, as, "He indulged himself *with* a glass of wine;" if it be a habit, it has *in*, as, "He indulged himself *in* shameful drunkenness."'—*Johnson.*

Inert, from the Latin *Iners, inertis*, idle, lazy. Inert is the opposite of alert (which see). Alert is wide-awake, active, lively. Inert is sleepy, sluggish, indolent. *Erto*, in Italian, is upright. *Inerto* may therefore be prostrate, indolent.

In esse. This is a Latin law term, applied to things actually existing, palpably and visibly. It is opposed to the term '*in posse*,' which means things which are not, but which may be.

Inexorable logic of facts. This phrase, which is supposed to have originated in Napoleon's proclamation from Milan, before the battle of Solferino, is really Mazzini's. It occurred in a leading article, published in 1849, which commences thus :—'*Nella genesi dei fatti la logica è inesorabile.*'

In extenso, a Latin phrase, signifying that the matter to which it refers is not abbreviated.

Infantry. This term was originally applied to a body of men collected by the *Infante* (heir apparent) of Spain for the purpose of rescuing his father from the Moors. The attempt being successful, the name was afterwards applied to foot-soldiers in general.—*Sullivan.*

Influence—originally the supposed directing power of the planets over man. Whenever the word 'influence' occurs in the earlier poets there is always some allusion to the planetary powers supposed to be exercised by the heavenly bodies over men.—*Trench.*

Influenza. This word seems to have originated about 1765 to 1770. In Foote's 'Lame Lover,' which was first acted in the latter year, Sir Luke Limp, who had promised to dine with Alderman Inkle, receives an invitation to dine with Sir Gregory Goose, upon which he instructs his man-servant as follows:—' George, give my compliments to Sir Gregory, and I'll certainly come and dire there. Order Joe to run to Alderman Inkle's, in Threadneedle Street; sorry can't wait upon him, but confined to bed two days with the new influenza.'

Informant, Informer. Both are from the Latin *informans,* to describe, but the first is always used in an innocent or good sense, the other generally in a bad one, as 'an odious informer.'

Infusions are vegetable extracts obtained by steeping in water *Decoctions* are obtained by boiling.

Ingenious, from the Latin *in,* in, and *gigno,* to beget. The word means having the inventive faculty. Ingenuous is from the Latin *ingenuus,* meaning fair, open, candid, sincere. The word ingenuous, and its compounds, is often improperly used by old writers for ingenious, as in the following passage from Locke:—
' If a child, when questioned, directly confess, you must commend his *ingenuity* and pardon the fault.' The word here should have been ingenuousness.

Ingot. Probably from the Anglo-Saxon *geotan,* to pour; whence *in-geotan,* to pour in, and *ingot,* that which has been poured in. The French *lingot* is the same word with the article *l'* prefixed.

Ingrain Colour. The term 'ingrain' is applied in commerce to fabrics dyed with a particularly durable or 'fast' shade of scarlet. The process of dyeing is so costly, that 'ingrain colours' are always quoted at an advance upon the price of 'common colours.' The origin of the term is of great antiquity. *Granum* in Latin signifies a seed, and it was early applied to all minute objects in the same way as we now say 'grains' of sand. The small insect *coccus* (see CARMINE) which produces the beautiful red dye is called in Latin *granum*, from its similarity to small seeds. This became *graine* in French, and grain in English. Grain, therefore, as a colouring matter is the dye from the *coccus*, or kermes insect, and 'ingrain' is an abbreviation of the phrase 'dyed in grain.' Shakespeare uses the phrase in 'The Comedy of Errors,' act. iii. sc. 2, where, in reply to an observation of Antipholus, 'That's a fault that water will mend,' Dromio replies, 'No, sir, 'tis *in grain*; Noah's flood could not do it.' The term is also to be found in 'Twelfth Night,' act i. sc. 5—

'Tis *in grain*, sir ; 'twill endure wind and weather.

Iniquity. This word was anciently, and far more properly, spelt inequity, with an *e*. We spell the kindred word inequitable with an *e*, why not this also?

Ink. The derivation of this word is given by B. H. C. in 'Notes and Queries,' series I. vol. xi. p. 283, as follows :—'Pancirollus says that kind of ink which was used by emperors alone, and forbidden to others, was called *encaustum*, from whence he derives the Italian *inchiostro*. From the same source we may derive the French *encre*, and the English *ink*.'

Inoculate, from the Latin *in*, in, and *oculus*, an eye. Its original meaning in English was the insertion, by a gardener, of the *eye* of a bud into the stock of another plant.

To plant, to bud, to graft, to *inoculate.—Dryden.*

In our midst. This is a vicious phrase which is common amongst preachers, who use it, there is no doubt, unthinkingly. The Bible has the phrase 'in the midst,' but the definite article *the* makes the scriptural phrase correct; Jesus was in 'the midst' of a certain number of people, that is, he was in the middle of a crowd. So also we may be in the 'midst' of a storm, but '*our* midst' means our *middle*, which is absurd. Enthusiastic preachers can say 'in the midst of us,' without any very great impropriety, but the term 'midst' had better be avoided altogether.

Inscription, Legend. In Numismatics, the legend is that which is written round the face of a coin, the inscription is that which is written across it. Thus, in the case of an English shilling, the legend comprehends all the words encircling the bust of the Queen, and the inscription consists of the words 'one shilling,' which are inscribed across the reverse.

Insect, from the Latin *in*, in, and *seco*, to cut. The allusion is to the apparent separation in insects of the head and thorax from the abdomen, by a deep incision or cut.

Insense, in the meaning of making a person comprehend, was formerly correct English. It is commonly used in that sense, at the present day, in Ireland, and in some of the Northern counties. Shakespeare, in 'Hen. VIII,' act v. sc. 1, makes Bishop Gardiner say :—

> Sir, (I may tell you) I think I have
> *Insensed* the Lords of the Council, that he is
> . . . . a pestilence
> That doth infect the land.

The word also occurs in this sense in a proclamation of Henry VIII. in 1530.—*Wilkins's Concilia*, iii. 740.

Insinuate. From the sinuous motion of a snake. 'The serpent sly, *insinuating.*'—*Milton.* The word was at one time used in a good sense. In the appendix to 'Lady Cowper's Diary' is a copy of a letter dated 'Newcastle, October 9th, 1715,' in which the writer says, 'Sir Charles Hotham's regiment is expected here upon their route to Berwick, but I hope, through the *insinuation* of Lord Scarborough, to keep them here till further orders from Government.' Insinuation here evidently meant friendly interposition.

Instinct in human beings is that natural law which operates for self-preservation or protection without the aid of reason. The infant instinctively carries everything to the mouth. The man closes his eye instinctively at the approach of anything which is likely to be dangerous. The cry of an infant, the wail of a feeble invalid, the groan of a wounded man, are all instinctive appeals for help. The desire in young people to associate with the opposite sex is an instinctive provision, designed by Providence for the continuance of the race.

Institution. This word is very much misused in America, as the following examples will show :—'The driving of vehicles is a great *institution* among us.'—*New York Herald.* 'Garotting, as an *institution*, may be said to be almost extinct in New York.'—*Tricks and Traps of New York*, p. 47. 'Woman cannot be classified as a mere appendage. She is an *institution.*'—*New York Tribune*, August 11, 1858. 'A very unwholesome object, the carcase of a large dog, has been suffered to lie in Ninth Street, near D., since Tuesday. A similar *institution* has occupied the site on the commons for some time past, filling the air with noxious odors.'—*Washington Evening Star*, July, 1858.

Instrument, Tool. An instrument and a tool are both implements, but when the words are used in a figurative sense to signify human agency, their meanings widely diverge. 'Instrument' is generally used in a good sense, 'tool' in a bad one, as, 'he was "instrumental" in doing a great deal of good'; 'He was a mere "tool" in the hands of the conspirators.'

Insult, from the Latin *in*, upon, and *salto*, to leap. Originally it meant to trample upon, also to leap or land upon an enemy's coast. 'An enemy is said to "insult" a coast when he suddenly appears upon it, and debarks with purpose to attack.'—*Stocqueler*.

Insurance, or **Assurance.** These words are really of the same meaning, but by usage the term 'assurance' is confined solely to risks depending upon human life, while 'insurance' is applied to risks connected with property. The practice of insuring houses, goods, and merchandise against fire began in London after the great fire of 1666. The Hand-in-Hand office commenced business in 1696. The Sun office was established in 1710.

Inter alia, a Latin phrase, signifying 'among other things.' Thus we say, 'In his speech on Reform, he alluded, *inter alia*, to the necessity for a wider distribution of the franchise.'

Interest of Money. In nearly all languages the word used to designate *interest* is one having the primary meaning of 'fruit,' 'offspring,' or 'increase.' Mr. Fox Talbot therefore ('English Etymologies,' p. 76) thinks that our word interest is a mere 'corruption of *incress* or *increase*, and that our ancestors lent and borrowed money at such and such a rate of *increase*.' (See Ezekiel xviii., v. 8, 13, 17.) The word 'interest' was first employed in this sense in an Act of Parliament (21 James I., 1623), where it was declared to signify 'lawful increase by the way of compensation for the use of money lent.' The 'lawful' rate was fixed at 8 per cent.

Interloper is from the Dutch *interlooper*, a smuggler (*loopen*, to run); one who enters, running (*looping*) between the customs officers.

In the neighbourhood of. This phrase is common in America in the sense of about, or near, in cases where there is no connection with locality. An example of its use is :—' The loss is computed at something in the neighbourhood of forty thousand dollars.'

In the straw. This expression, commonly used to signify that a lady of whom it is spoken has recently been delivered of a child, is derived from the fact that formerly all beds were stuffed with straw. In old books are frequent allusions to straw for beds. Even the luxurious Henry VIII. lay upon straw, for we read that 'there were directions for certain persons to examine every night the straw of the King's bed that no daggers might be concealed therein.'—*Brand.*

In the wrong box. George Lord Lyttelton was of rather a moody disposition, and of restless habits. He used to go to Vauxhall, and frequently said that he always 'got in the wrong box,' for the folks in those next to which he sat were always merry enough, but he felt dull and melancholy. In a printing office, when a letter is found in the compartment appointed for some other letter, it is said to be 'in the wrong box.'

Into, In. An Englishman, some years ago, gave the following as an example of the American use of these words :—' We get *in* a carriage, and have the rheumatism *into* our knees.'

Intoxicating. This word, in its present sense, was probably introduced into the English language by Milton, who says ('Tetrachordon,' 1644), 'If the importation of wine, and the use of all strong drink were forbid, it would both clean rid the possibility of committing that odious vice [drunkenness], and men might afterwards live happily and healthfully without the use of these intoxicating liquors.' The word 'intoxicate' is derived from the Latin *toxicum*, the poison in which arrows were dipped.

Intrepid is from Latin *intrepidus*, without trembling.

Intrinsic means inherent, or inborn. It was formerly used in the sense of 'intimate,' as in the following passage :—' He falls into *intrinsical* society with Sir John Graham.'

Innuendo is a sly hint or oblique allusion. It comes from the Latin *innuo*, to nod. The innuendo is sometimes conveyed by a wink. 'A wink is as good as a nod.'

Invalid. This word has two distinct meanings, which are intimated by accent. Where it is intended to signify something not valid it is pronounced in-val'-id, the accent being on the second syllable ; but when used in the sense of a weak or infirm person, the accent is on the third syllable, and it is pronounced in-val-eed'.

Invent, from the Latin *in*, upon, and *venio*, to come. It is often erroneously used as synonymous with discover. To 'invent' is to devise, or produce, something new, or not before made available. To 'discover' is to uncover, or make known, something that had hitherto existed, although hidden or unknown. Thus Watt 'invented' the steam-engine; Harvey 'discovered' the circulation of the blood.

Iodine, so named from the Greek *iōdēs*, violet-like, was first discovered by De Courtois, a saltpetre maker, at Paris, in 1812.

Iōta (three syllables). Iōta is the name of the ninth letter in the Greek alphabet. It is also the smallest; hence its application to anything very small, as to a jot, a tittle, a minute particle.

I.O.U. What is called an I.O.U. requires no stamp, as it is a mere acknowledgment of a debt, and cannot be sued upon as a bill. If, however, it specifies a day for payment it becomes a bill, and must be stamped. Although an I.O.U. cannot be sued upon, it can be used as *evidence* in an action for the debt.

Iowa, the name of one of the United States, is an Indian word signifying 'the best land,' or 'land of all others.' The name given to the river Ohio, which is also borne by one of the States, is supposed to be a corruption of the word *iowa*.

Ipse dixit, Latin, literally 'he said it himself.' In English it generally implies a doubt of the truth of a statement, as, 'There is only his *ipse dixit* to depend on, we must get further evidence.'

I remain, &c. This subscription should never be used in addressing a person by letter for the first time; the form should be, 'I am.' If the letter be answered, and a reply is afterwards sent, the form 'I am' would be tautological, and 'I remain' is therefore properly substituted.

Iron Bridges. The first iron bridge constructed in England is that over the Severn near Coalbrookdale, in Shropshire. It was designed by Mr. Pritchard in 1773, and was opened for traffic in 1779. Its span is 100 feet. The next iron bridge to be built was the one at Sunderland, designed, in 1792, by Burdon. It has a span of 200 feet. The centre arch of Southwark Bridge is 240 feet span.

Iron Railings of St. Paul's. The iron railings enclosing St. Paul's Cathedral in London were made of Kentish iron at Lamberhurst in that county. Queen Anne's son visited the ironworks, which thenceforth took the name of Gloucester Furnace, in his honour. The weight of the entire fencing, with the gates, &c., was 200 tons and 81 lbs., and the cost at 6*d*. the lb. was £11,202 0*s*. 6*d*.

Iron Ships and Sailing Vessels. The earliest notice of an iron sailing vessel is mentioned by Mr. Grantham, in his work on shipbuilding. He quotes from a publication bearing date July 28th, 1787, a description of an iron canal boat, built by a Mr. Wilkinson of Bradley Forge, near Bilston, which had arrived at Birmingham a few days before. In a letter written in 1872, Mr. J. E. Reed, the celebrated ship architect, in allusion to this canal boat, says, 'I had occasion a few years ago to look up the early history of iron shipbuilding, but did not discover any earlier instance than this of a really working commercial vessel built of iron.'

Isaac. This name signifies ' he will laugh.'

Isabel. This Christian name is a corruption of Elizabeth. It was first corrupted as a compliment to Queen Elizabeth, who was called Eliza*bella*. Afterwards the first syllable was dropped. In Spain, Isabel, or Isabella, is always used ; Elizabeth never.

Isinglass. A corrupted form of the German name of the sturgeon, *hausenblas*. Isinglass is made from the bladder of the sturgeon. It has probably received its English name from some improper association with the word *icing*, and the French *glace*, ice.

Island. This word seems to have been originally Anglo-Saxon, and signified an ' eye' of land. The Anglo-Saxons gave names to many localities from their supposed resemblance to parts of the human body, as a *head*land, a *neck* of land, a *tongue* of land, the *mouth* of a river, the *brow* of a hill, the *back* or *chine* of a hill, the *foot* of a hill, an *arm* of the sea, and so on. The word ' eye,' in various forms, as *ea*, *ey*, &c., was used to signify small islands. In the river Thames there are numerous islands known as eyots, aits, or aights. Battersea was once known as Peter's Eye, or Peter's island ; Chelsea was Cheles-eye, and Bermondsey was Bermonds-eye, all of them having been originally islands.

Isle of Man. The name has given rise to much speculation. The most probable derivation is from the Celtic *maen*, a stone or rock.

Isle of Skye. Bellot derives this name from the Irish word *skiach*, cloudy, or darkness.

Isle of Thanet. Lambarde thinks this is from the Saxon or old English word *thanet*, moist, watery, 'a name well suited to its situation.'

Isle of Wight. This name is probably tautological. In the Gothic, *we* is holy, and *ight*, *igt*, or *igot* is island. We retain *eyot* in the same sense. If this derivation is correct, the words 'isle of' are surplusage, the word 'Wight' signifying holy island.

Isolated. This word, the proper pronunciation of which is iz-o-lated, seems to be derived from the Italian word *isola*, an island. It does not appear to have been in use in the early part of the last century, for Bolingbroke says:—'The events we are witnesses of in the course of the longest life, appear to us very often original, unprepared, single and *unrelative*, if I may use such a word for want of a better in English. In French I would say *Isolés*.'

Isthmus, from a Greek word, signifying a neck.

It, Its. Professor De Vere ('Studies in English,' London, 1867) says, 'The earliest case of *it* being used as a possessive pronoun occurs in the year 1548, in the Bible, where we find, 'The loue and deuotion towardes God also hath *it* infancie, and hath *it* commyng forward in growth of age' (p. 252). Ben Jonson has *its*, though he does not mention the word in his grammar. Shakespeare has *its* several times, but Mommsen did not discover the word in any earlier edition than 1623. Milton only has *its* twice ('Par. Lost,' i. 254, and iv. 813). Dean Trench points out that, 'if there had been no other reason for concluding that Chatterton's poems—which it was pretended were written by a monk in the eleventh century—were forgeries, the use of the word 'its,' in the line 'Life and its goods I scorn,' would have proved it, inasmuch as the word did not come into use until several hundred years after the assumed date of the work.' It is twice used in the Psalms:—Psalm 1. 3, 'bringeth forth *its* fruit abundantly,' and Psalm lxxx. 10, 'set *its* roots so fast.'

Italics are letters formed after the Roman model, but sloping towards the right, used to emphasize words or sentences. They were first used about A.D. 1500, by Manutius, a Venetian printer, who dedicated them to the Italian States. Hence the name. The first book printed in Italics was an edition of Virgil, printed at Venice, by Aldus, in 1501. There is a copy in the British Museum.

Italian Opera. The following extract refers to the introduction into England of Italian opera:—'At that time (1650) tragedies and comedies being esteemed very scandalous by the Presbyterians, and therefore by them silenced, William Davenport contrived a way to set up an Italian opera, to be performed by declamations and music. This Italian opera began in Rutland House, in Charter House Yard, May 23, 1656, and afterwards translated to the Cockpit in Drury Lane, and delighting the eye and ear exceedingly well, was much frequented for many years.'— *Wood's Athenæ Oxon*, vol. iii. pp. 805-6.

It is easier for a camel, &c. Lady Duff Gordon, writing from Cairo, says, 'Yesterday I saw a camel go through the *eye of a needle*, i.e., the low arched door of an enclosure. He must kneel and bow his head to go through, and thus the rich man must humble himself.'—*Wood's Bible Animals*, p. 243. Lord Nugent, in his 'Travels,' tells us that when at Hebron, he was directed to 'go out by the needle's eye, that is, by the small side gate of the city.'

Ivanhoe, Waverley. Sir Walter Scott took his title 'Ivanhoe' from the manor of that name in Buckinghamshire, and 'Waverley' from Waverley Abbey, near Farnham. There seems to have been no other reason for the choice than a fanciful liking for the names.

Ivory, from the Sanscrit word *ibha*, an elephant.

Ivy. As the Welsh name is *eiddew*, the Gaelic *eidhean*, and the Anglo-Saxon, *ifig*, the plant evidently has its name from the Gaelic *eid*, to clothe. The name 'the plant that clothes' is singularly appropriate.

J

J. This letter was first distinguished from *I* by the Dutch in the sixteenth century. It was first printed as a separate letter by Giles Beys, at Paris in 1550.

Jack-a-napes. Sharon Turner, in his 'History of England,' vol. iii. p. 80, says that in the British Museum (Vesp. B. 16) is a ballad of the date 1450, referring to the Duke of Suffolk and his friends in most offensive terms. 'It designates the Duke of Suffolk by the cant term of "Jacknapes," and is perhaps the earliest instance we have of the abusive application of the word jack-a-napes. Our lexicographers derive this word from Jack and ape, but the ballad shows that 'napes' was a term of derision signifying a knave, and is, therefore, probably the Saxon *cnapa*, which bore also this meaning. If this be so, it will explain why our third-figured card is called 'Jack' and also 'knave,' and proves that *Jack-a-napes* meant Jack the knave. There is some doubt, however, whether Mr. Turner is right in deriving *napes* from *cnapa*, for in a tract the term 'Yack-an-napes' is used in reference to a buffoon or mummer. The writer of this tract says that 'it is better to hunt the bull, here, hurt, or any other thynge like to suceur the powre with the mette than to here Sir Jhon Singyl Sowle stombil a prayer of mattens in Laten, slynge holy water, curse holy brede, and to play a caste lyke *Yack-an-napes* in a foles cotte.'

Jack and Gill. Anciently a 'Jack' was a pitcher made of waxed leather, and a 'gill' was, as now, a metallic measure of capacity. The probable origin of the old versicle, 'Jack and Gill went up the hill,' &c., is that it is a humorous personification of the two vessels, which some one had unfortunately accidentally upset.

Jackass, the donkey. The word has an Eastern origin. *Jackhsh*, in Arabic, means 'one who extends his ears.' When Dr. Wolff, the father of the present Sir Henry Drummond Wolff, was a missionary in Bokhara, he was startled by being called, in contempt, '*Wolff Jackhsh*,' which he, without hesitation, put down as the original of the English term for the donkey.

Jacket. A Jack anciently was a horseman's defensive upper garment. It was usually quilted internally, and covered outside with stout leather. A jack is well described in Lily's 'Euphues and his England,' Ff. 2, b: 'Jackes quilted and covered over with leather fustian or canvas, over thicke plates of iron, that are sowed to the same.' Our modern jacket is a garment of the same shape, but being made to be worn in peaceable times, it is made of lighter and thinner material, and has no 'plates of yron' to ward off unfriendly arrows.

Jack Ketch. All London criminals condemned to death were formerly executed at Tyburn, which was then quite out of town. The manor of Tyburn was held by a family named Jaquett. The surname was probably the origin of the term 'Jack Ketch,' as applied to a common hangman.

Jack Sprat could eat no fat, &c. Howell, in his 'Proverbs,' 1659, gives this in a different form from the modern one. He says, 'Archdeacon Pratt would eat no fatt.' In Le Neve's 'Fast Eccl. Ang.', out of many thousand names, there is only one Archdeacon Pratt. His name was John, and he was archdeacon of St.

David's from 1557 to his death in 1607. It would appear that he was the original Jack Sprat of the old nursery saying.

Jasmine, or **Jessamine.** This plant is a native of Persia, and was first brought to England about A.D. 1500. The yellow variety came from India in 1656.

January. So named by the Romans from Janus, one of their deities. The name was given to the first month, because Janus was thought to preside over the beginnings of all matters.

Javelin. In Spanish, *Jabalé* is a wild boar, and *Jabalína* is a spear used in hunting wild boars. Our English word 'javelin' comes, by an easy transition, from the latter.

Jaw. The ancient spelling was 'jowe' 'Thi jowes.'—*Reliq. Antiq.* p. 157. The word jowl has an allied meaning. The smoke-dried half of a pig's face is called a 'chawl' in many parts of England.

Jehovah. The Jews holds this word in such peculiar veneration, that they never pronounce it, even when reading their sacred books, but always substitute for it the word *Adonai*, or Lord, nor will they write the word in perfect Hebrew characters. Hence they have left the word imperfectly written over the altar-piece in the synagogue in St. Helen's Place, in London, making it to resemble that word, but in reality to signify the Beloved.—*Brand's Dictionary*, vol. ii. p. 264.

Jejune. This is a word frequently employed by literary critics to denote writings which are flat, dry, or uninteresting, as 'a jejune narrative.' The word comes from *jejunum* (from the Latin *jejunus*, empty). The 'jejunum' is a portion of the small intestine next to the 'duodenum,' and is so called because it is generally found empty after death.

Jelly, from the Latin *gelo*, to congeal.

Je ne sais quoi, French, literally 'I know not what.' It is a very significant phrase. It is sometimes used to express that indescribable something that either makes one like or dislike a person. Thus we say, 'There was a *je ne sais quoi* about him that was very charming,' or that 'made me dislike him at once.'

Jeopardy. Johnson marks this word as obsolete.

Jephthah's Daughter. The commonly received notion that the life of Jephthah's daughter was sacrificed in pursuance of his vow is not warranted by the sacred text. All that is meant is that whoever, or whatever, came forth to meet Jephthah should be 'consecrated' to God. The vow was kept by the daughter being dedicated to a life of perpetual virginity. This is obvious from the verse, Judges xi. 37, where she asks for two months in which to 'bewail her virginity,' and by v. 39, where we are told that, 'according to his vow,' she 'knew no man,' which was in consonance with a 'custom or statute (*chok*) in Israel.'

Jericho. 'Gone to Jericho.' In the manor of Blackmore, about seven miles from Chelmsford, King Henry VIII. had a house which had been a priory, to which he frequently retired when he desired to be free from disturbance. To this place the name Jericho was given as a disguise, so that when anyone enquired for the King when he was indulging himself in animal pleasures in Essex, it was customary to say he was 'gone to Jericho.' In a letter from the Rev. W. Callandar, vicar of Blackmore, dated October 21, 1880, the compiler of this book is informed that the place still 'habitually goes by the name of the "Jericho estate," or the "Blackmore Priory."' There is a brooklet running through the village, which, Mr. Callandar says, 'I have heard called "the Jordan."' There seems evidence that the phrase was used in the time of Henry VIII., but it is not quite clear that it originated in the circumstances stated. It may have been originally a rebuke to young upstarts, in allusion to the verse, 2 Samuel x. 5, 'Tarry at Jericho until your beards be grown.'

Jeroboam of Claret. In the works of Walter Scott this phrase frequently occurs. It is understood to mean a large bottle, but the exact contents are not known. Mr. John Hall, writing to 'Notes and Queries,' January 17, 1880, says, '*A magnum* [of claret] was [?contained] two bottles,' a *tappit hen*, four bottles ; a *jeroboam*, six bottles.'

Jersey is contracted from 'Czar's-ey,' that is, 'Cæsar's ey,' or island (*ey*, an island).

Jerusalem. This name means 'foundation of peace.' It is derived from the Hebrew *yaráh*, a foundation, and *shalaim*, or *shalem*, peace, perfect, whole.—*Charnock*.

Jerusalem Artichokes. This name is an absurd corruption of the Italian name of the plant *Girasole Articiocco*, the sunflower artichoke. It is a native of Peru, and was introduced into Europe by the Italians, who gave it the name from the resemblance of its stem and leaves to those of the sunflower, or girasole.

'**Jerusalem, my happy home.**' This beautiful hymn is found in a thin quarto in the British Museum, lettered on the back '*Queen*

Elizabeth,' and numbered 15225. The probability is that it was written by a Roman Catholic priest who suffered in the persecutions in the reign of Elizabeth or James I.

Jesebel. The J in this letter is a misprint for I. The name is *Isabel.—Adam Clarke.*

Jet takes its name from a river of Lycia, from the banks of which it was first obtained. In the time of Pliny the name of the river was *Gages*, and the pieces of jet obtained from thence were called *Gagates*, afterwards contracted into *gagat*, and finally to *jet*. It is sometimes called black amber.

Jeu de mot, Jeu d'esprit. Both are French expressions. A *jeu de mot* is a play on words; a *jeu d'esprit* is a play of wit, a witty remark or retort.

Jewel. This word is derived from the Italian *giola*, joy; whence *gioiello*, a jewel, that which gives pleasure.

Jew's Harp. Perhaps 'jaw's harp'; though it may be from the French *jeu-harpe*, toy-harp. Beaumont and Fletcher call it 'jew-trump,' probably from another French compound, *jeu-trompe*; *trompe*, a trumpet.

Jig. This word originally meant what we now call a comic song. Thus Hamlet, sarcastically, when Polonius objects to the players, says 'He's for a jig, or a tale of bawdry, or he sleeps.' In the 'Harleian Collection of Old Ballads' are many under the title of jigs, as 'A Northerne *Jige*, called Daintie, come thou to me'; 'A merry newe *Jigge*, or the pleasant wooing betwixt Kit and Pegge,' &c. In the 'Fatal Contract,' by Hemmings,

    We'll hear your *jigg*.
    How is your ballad titled?

and in 'Hamlet,' iii. 2, Ophelia says to Hamlet, 'You are merry, my lord.' *Ham.* 'Who, I?' *Oph.* 'Ay, my lord.' *Ham.* 'O! your only jig-maker.'

Joe Miller, who has given his name to so many jokes and jests, was a comic actor in London, and was in great request amongst the tavern frequenters of his day, as a sayer of witty things. He was born in London in 1684 and died in 1738. A tombstone to his memory stands in the churchyard of St. Clement Danes, in the Strand. The compiler of the 'Jest Book' which goes by his name was John Mottley, a playwright of no great celebrity, who brought out 'Joe Miller's Jest Book,' about a year after the jester was dead. Mottley died in 1750.

John. The *h* in this name is a remnant of its ancient form, Johannes. It was first contracted to Johan, and afterwards the *a* was dropped. The custom of writing Jno. for John seems to be an ancient one, and is thus explained by the editor of 'Notes and Queries,' June 1864 :—' Our forefathers wrote Jhon oftener than John, and the *h* in former days frequently assumed the form of *n*. Jhon contracted into Jho. or Jho., and writing the *h* as *n* becomes Jno, or Jn°.'

John Bull. This well-known phrase, applied collectively to the English nation, first appeared in a satire called 'The History of John Bull,' which is generally attributed to Swift, but which was written by Dr. Arbuthnot. The French in this work are personified as *Lewis Baboon*; the Dutch as *Nicholas Frog*, &c.

John Dory. The origin of the name of this fish is generally attributed to the French *jaune doré*, yellow golden fish. This is obviously incorrect, as the fish is neither golden nor yellow. Besides, the French name of the fish is *poisson de Saint Pierre*, or 'St. Peter's Fish,' from a tradition that this is the fish from which St. Peter took the tribute-money. A writer in the 'Cornhill Magazine' says that the name of the fish in Spain is *Janitore*, so named because St. Peter is the 'janitore,' or doorkeeper, of Heaven. If this be correct, the transition to the English 'John Dory' seems obvious and easy.

John of Gaunt. This should be written John of *Ghent*, he havnig been born in that Flemish city. 'Gaunt' was the vulgar English pronunciation of the name at the time. It was spelt 'Gaunt' by Heylin in his 'Cosmography,' 1703; but in Moll's 'Geographicus,' 1713, it is given correctly—'Ghent.'

John o'Groat's House. This was a house built about 1489 by a Dutchman from Groot in Holland, and hence called *John of Groot*, upon Duncan's Bay Head, the most northerly point in Great Britain. It has long since disappeared, but 'From the Land's End to John o'Groat's house' is still a proverbial expression for 'from one end of Britain to the other.' The house was probably built for the accommodation of travellers crossing the ferry to the Orkneys. The name Groat or Groot is constantly cropping up in deeds dated from 1488 to 1741, when Malcolm Groat sold his 'lands in Dungansby, with the ferry house,' to William Sinclair of Freswick. There are still persons of the name of Grot or Groat in the neighbourhood, 'but a small green knoll is now all that remains of John o'Groat's house.'

Jolly. The dictionaries derive this word from the Latin *jovialis*, from which we get the cognate word 'jovial.' This may be correct, but Bishop Stillingfleet does not think so. In his 'Origines Britannicæ' (edit. 1837, p. 342), he says that anciently 'the feast of the new year was observed with more than ordinary *jollity*; thence, as Olaus Wormius and Scheffer observe, they reckoned their age by so many *Iôlas*; and Snorro Sturleson describes this new year's feast just as Buchanan sets out the British Saturnalia, by "feasting and sending presents or new year's gifts to one another." Thence some think the name of this feast was taken from *Iôla*, which in the Gothic language signifies " to make merry." ' Whatever its origin, there is ancient authority for its use in the modern *slangy* fashion. In Spenser's ' Shepherd's Calendar,' he makes Diggon say :—

> In deede thy bull is a bold bigge cur,
> And could make a *jolly hole* in their fur.

Others have suggested that it is the French word *joli*, pretty, and that it was once used in English in the same sense as we now say ' pretty good,' or ' pretty fair.' A commentator on the Scriptures (Trapp), writing in 1656, says, ' All was *jolly quiet* at Ephesus before St. Paul came thither.'

Jolly Nose. In the half-forgotten drama founded upon Harrison Ainsworth's ' Jack Sheppard,' Paul Bedford, as Blueskin, used to sing a song, the opening lines of which were :—

> Jolly nose, the bright rubies which garnish thy tip
> Were dug from the mines of Canary.

This is evidently founded upon an old French song by Olivier Basselin :—

> Beau nez dont les rubis ont coûté mainte pipe
> De vin blanc et clairet.

Jordan. The Hebrew name is *yardên*, which Robinson translates ' the flowing,' ' the river '; ' like the German Rhein from *rinnen*.'

Jot, meaning a small particle, is from *iota*, the smallest letter in the Greek alphabet. The word probably arose when the letters *i* and *j* were used indiscriminately.

Journal. This word does not contain a single letter of its Latin root, *Dies*. It has passed through many changes; thus :— *dies, diurnus, giorno* (Italian), *jour* (French) *journal*. Its strict meaning is, of course, a daily record; yet it is often applied as a title to weekly newspapers and other publications. Even such accomplished men as the Messrs. Chambers of Edinburgh publish a weekly periodical which they call Chambers's 'Journal.'

Journey. 'A day's journey [in Scripture] is 33 miles, 172 paces, and 4 feet. A Sabbath day's journey is 600 paces.'—*Bailey.* A Roman *pace* was about 5 feet, so that the 'Sabbath day's journey' was 1,000 yards.

Journeyman. A journeyman is one who works for daily wages; from the French *journée*, or day's work.

Jovial. At one time it was thought that every man was born under the influence of some planet, which was supposed to govern his habit or disposition through life. Thus a 'jovial' person was one who was influenced by *Jove* or Jupiter, and was supposed to be continuously happy or joyful. *Mar*tial persons were so called from Mars; *Saturn*ine from Saturn; *Mercur*ial from Mercury; and a lunatic was one under the influence of *Luna*, the moon.

Jubilee. This word comes from the Hebrew *yobel*, a horn. Its application to the peculiar institution known amongst the ancient Jews as the Yobel or Jubilee comes from the fact that the commencement of the Year of Jubilee was proclaimed on the Day of Atonement—the 10th of the 7th month—by the sound of a peculiar horn called the *yobel*. It is a current error that the Jubilee occurred every 49th year. The 49th year *expired* before the *Yobel* commenced.

Judas-coloured Hair. It has long been a current belief that Judas Iscariot had red hair and beard, though there was probably nothing but the popular dislike of the colour to justify the opinion. The old dramatists and poets have frequent allusions to the subject. Shakespeare, in 'As You Like it,' makes Rosalind say, 'His hair is of the dissembling colour,' to which Celia replies, 'Something browner than *Judas's*' (act iii. sc. 4). Middleton, in the 'Chaste Maid of Cheapside,' 1620, makes one of his characters, speaking of a gilt Apostle spoon, say, 'Sure that was Judas with the *red beard.*' Dryden, in 'Amboyna,' has 'There's treachery in that *Judas-coloured* beard,' and in his celebrated epigram on Jacob Tonson describes him as having ' two left legs and Judas-coloured hair.' The national dislike to red hair has been conjectured to have originated in the aversion English people felt to the red-haired Danes. It is curious that Cain is also credited with having had a red beard. In the 'Merry Wives of Windsor,' Shakespeare makes Simple speak of Slender as having a 'yellow beard, a Cinacoloured beard.' It is but fair, however, to say that this may mean *cane*-coloured.

Judges' Circuit. These circuits are of great antiquity. In 1 Samuel vii. 16, we are told that Samuel 'went from year to year, on circuit, to Bethel, and Gilgal and Mispeh, and judged Israel in all these places.'

Judge Jeffreys. The chair in which the infamous Judge Jeffreys sat at the Bloody Assize is still preserved in the Town Hall of Dorchester.

July. This month is generally believed to have been so named in honour of Julius Cæsar. There is good reason, however, for believing that it bore a similar name (Jule), before Julius Cæsar was born, and that the name was derived from *huil*, a wheel (see YULE), the symbol of the summer solstice. There is no doubt that the name *Jule*, being already in use in some parts of the empire, induced the courtiers at Rome to suggest that the name *Julius*, which so closely resembled it, should supersede *Quintilis* in all; and that the same reason induced the Roman Senate to adopt the idea. See AUGUST.

Jumble. This word is marked in the Dictionaries as 'of unknown etymology.' In 'The Lady's Cabinet, enlarged and opened,' by Lord Ruthven, 1667, there is 'A Recipe to make jumbols.' These were cakes made of such a *jumble* of materials that the name may have become a synonym for a heterogeneous mixture. Jumbols are still made at Market Bosworth. They are of this shape :— ∞.

June, the sixth month. By some the name is supposed to be derived from Junius, the Roman Emperor. By others it is thought to come from Juno, the consort of Jupiter, and queen of Heaven.

Jury. During the Saxon heptarchy, juries of six Welsh and six Anglo-Saxon freemen were appointed to try causes between Welsh and Saxon disputants. Alfred the Great in 886 established juries on their present basis. Juries for the trial of aliens are, according to English law, composed of six Englishmen and six foreigners.

The Scottish juries consist of fifteen men, and the majority pronounce the verdict. In England the jury consists of twelve men, and the finding of a verdict must be unanimous. It is erroneously believed that a surgeon or a butcher cannot be sworn as a juryman. Both are liable to serve.—*Wharton.*

Justices of the Quorum. Formerly it was the custom of the

Crown to select in each county certain justices, generally such as had some knowledge of law, who were called 'justices of the quorum,' whose presence was necessary when certain business had to be done. This selection caused great jealousy, and the stringency of the rules concerning it were modified by statutes of George II. and III. Recently the Crown has made all justices 'justices of the quorum,' so that the distinction no longer exists.

K

Kaleidoscope. This interesting toy was invented by Dr. Brewster (afterwards Sir David), in April 1818. He intended to patent it, but having inadvertently shown it to a London optician, he was forestalled, and missed the opportunity of acquiring a large fortune. It was computed that in three months a quarter of a million were sold.

Kean. 'Henry Carey, musical composer and poet, was the illegitimate son of George Savile, Marquis of Halifax, and left a son, George Savile Carey, whose daughter married Edmund Kean, an architect. The issue of this marriage was Edmund Kean, the celebrated actor.'—*Notes and Queries.*

Keel-haul. To keel-haul a sailor is to punish him by fastening him to a rope, and hauling or drawing him completely under the *keel* or bottom of a ship, from one side of the vessel to the other.

Kent. This is probably derived from the ancient British word *cant*, a corner, because, says Camden, 'England at this place stretcheth out itself in a corner to the north-east.'

Kentish Fire. This term is applied to a peculiar kind of cheering at public meetings, produced by clapping the hands together rapidly, to a kind of musical rhythm. It was first used at the meetings held in Kent, about 1828 and 1829, for the purpose of opposing the passing of the Catholic Relief Bill.

Kentish Town. In 'Domesday Book' this district is mentioned under the name of 'the manor of Cantelowes, or Kennestoune, the manor comprising "four miles of land."' The entry goes on to say that 'there is plenty of timber in the hedgerows, good pasture for cattle, a running brook, and two 20*d*. rents.' The rents payable altogether to 'the Canons of St. Paul's' were forty shillings a year.

Kerchief is properly a covering for the head. It comes from *cur*, to cover, *chef*, the head. In Scotland a *curch* is a covering for the head. The words *handkerchief* and, still worse, *pocket-handkerchief* are verbal monstrosities. The verb *cur* is found in *cur*few and in *cur*tain, in both of which it has the meaning of covering.

Kernel, of a nut, &c., is a corrupted form of the word *corn*.

Kerseymere, Kersey. Kerseymere is a fine description of woollen cloth much in use for making riding breeches. It is generally of a drab colour, and is principally made in the West of England. The name is a corruption of Cashmere. Kersey is a different fabric. It is a coarse, thick material made of long wool, and is usually ribbed. The name is a corruption of *Jersey*, whence it originally came.

Kettle. The Anglo-Saxon kettle (*cytel*) was very different to a modern 'tea-kettle.' It was more like the three-legged 'pots' in which gipsies boil their food. Boiling and broiling seem to have been the principal methods used by the early Anglo-Saxons in cooking their food. The proverbial 'pretty kettle of fish' probably originated in the misfortune of some early Saxon cook, who, by overboiling the fish, spoiled the whole 'cytel' full.

Kew. The name of this place has undergone many transitions. In a court roll of the manor of Richmond, in the reign of Henry VII., it is written Kayhough, and in subsequent entries it is varied to Kayhowe, Kayhoo, Keyhowe, Keye, Kayo, and Kewe. The name is probably derived from the word *quay*, a landing place.

Khedive. This word, according to the best authorities in Persian, means Prince. The proper pronunciation is said to be *Keddiffe*.

Kibe. Lord Byron, in 'Childe Harold,' canto i. st. 67, in speaking of a rapid succession of pleasures, says,

> Devices quaint, and frolics ever new,
> Tread on each other's *kibes*,

which is an unfortunate mistake. Byron evidently thought kibe was another name for the heel, but it happens to mean an ulcerated or broken chilblain, a signification which knocks all the poetry out of his couplet.

Kickshaws. Tit-bits to eat, not to satisfy hunger, but to gratify the palate. This is not from the French *quelque-chose*. More probably it is from the Dutch *kiesen*, to choose; *kiesch*, nice in eating; *kies-kawen*, to eat in a picking-and-choosing manner. From this latter the transition is easy.

Kidnap. In the gipsy slang, *kid* is a child, and to *nab* is to steal—hence kidnapper, or more properly *kidnabber*.

Kilderkin. In the Dutch, *kinder* means a child, or the young of anything, and a *kinderkin* is a small barrel, equal in capacity to half of a barrel of 36 gallons. An early use of the word in English is found in Dr. Simpson's 'Notes on St. Peter's Cheap,' where the following entry from 'Machyn's Diary' is quoted:—'1447. It. payde the xxvj daye of Maye, for chese at the drynking of Stodell Kyldirkyn ale xv*d*.'

Kilkenny Cats. Everybody has heard of the two cats of Kilkenny that fought till nothing was left but their tails. Strange as the tale seems, there is a substratum of fact upon which it is founded. During the Rebellion in Ireland in 1803, Kilkenny was garrisoned by a troop of Hessian soldiers who amused themselves in barracks by tying two cats together by their tails and throwing them across a clothes line to fight. The officers hearing of the cruel practice, resolved to stop it, and deputed one of their number to watch. The soldiers, on their part, set a man to watch for the coming officer. One day the sentinel neglected his duty, and the heavy tramp of the officer was heard ascending the stairs. One of the troopers seizing a sword cut the tails in two as the animals hung across the line. The two cats escaped, minus their tails, through the open window, and when the officer enquired the meaning of the two bleeding tails being left in the room, he was coolly told that two cats had been fighting and had devoured each other, all but the tails.

Kilt, Filibeg. The word *kilt* is Gothic, and is used in England and the Lowlands of Scotland to designate the peculiar petticoat worn by the Scotch. The Highlanders use the Gaelic name *filibeg* to denote the identical garment.

Kin as a diminutive. This word, generally signifying small of its kind, is an English affix to nouns, which has originated many words and names, in some of which the relationship to the original is not very apparent. Thus we have *finnikin*, from fine; *napkin*, from nappe, a cloth; *pumpkin*, from pompe, a gourd; *griskin*, from gris, a pig; *slammikin*, from schlamm, dirt or mud; and *firkin*, from feowr, or vier, the fourth part. Others are more obvious, as *lambkin, mannikin, ladikin,* or *lakin,* from lady; *girkin,* from gurche, a cucumber, &c.

Kinder. (The *i* long, as in kind.) This is a word in very common use in America in the sense of 'in a manner,' 'as it were,' &c. Good examples of its use are the following quotations from 'Major Downny':—'A *kinder* notion jist then began to get into my head.' 'At that the landlord and the officer looked *kinder* thunderstruck.' In Surrey, fifty years ago, the villagers, in attempting to describe something they had seen, but did not thoroughly understand, would use the phrase 'a kind of.' This was invariably pronounced 'a kind er,' the *i* being long. The writer remembers a boy who had seen a white peacock saying, 'It was a *kinder* peacock, on'y it was white.' The American word may have originated from this use of the phrase *a kind of*, which is perfectly applicable in both the cases quoted above.

King is from the Anglo-Saxon *cyning,* which comes from the root *can,* power, or *ken,* knowledge.—*Camden.*

King's Bench (Court of). Anciently the sovereign presided in this court personally, sitting on a high bench, with the judges on a lower bench in front. In the king's absence the judges were supreme.

King Charles's Statue at Charing Cross was modelled by Herbert le Sœur, a Frenchman. It was commissioned by the Earl of Arundel, and was cast 'near Covent Garden Church, in the year 1639.' It was set up just before the difficulties between Charles and the Parliament. After the king was beheaded, the statue was sold to Rivers, a brazier in Holborn, for the purposes of being broken up. Rivers, however, kept the statue entire, but made a fortune in selling to Royalists knives and forks, with handles which he asserted were made of the metal of the statue. After the Restoration, the statue again came to light, and was set up in its present position in 1674. The sword is a modern one; the original was stolen about 1838.

King's Cross. The origin of this name is given in 'Notes and Queries' (July 1861), as follows:—Up to the accession of George IV., the spot now so called was known as Battle Bridge, and was a notorious spot, habited by thieves and other bad characters. In 1821 some speculators having acquired some freehold land, put up a large number of houses, but owing to the evil reputation of the locality, they would not let. The result was that a change of name was resolved on. St. George's Cross was suggested by one,

Boadicea's cross by another, but a Mr. Bray, who was the largest freeholder, suggested King's Cross, which was adopted. A few years ago a stuccoed statue of the king stood on a huge pedestal in the middle of the road, but 'Punch' ridiculed it so persistently, that it was eventually taken down.

King's English. From the time of the Conquest to the fourteenth century, the language of England was in a very unsettled condition. The Norman and the Saxon elements were struggling for mastery. Latin seems to have been used in formal written documents, while French was the spoken language of the Court and the nobility. Saxon was spoken universally by the lower orders, and even this varied so greatly, that the people of the south could scarcely understand those of the north. The language of the Court could not, of course, be comprehended by the people, who only knew Saxon, and so a language suitable for proclamations and edicts was gradually formed, and, to distinguish it from mere dialects, it was called 'the King's English.' Chaucer and Gower at this time were much about the Court, and learnt this style of speech, and they are the first writers who adopted the English language as an entity. 'Piers Plowman' is in a dialect; Wycliff's 'Bible Version' is in a dialect; but Chaucer and Gower wrote in a speech which is thenceforward recognised as the 'English language,' and which before their time is hardly found.—*Earle, Philology of the English Tongue*, p. 68.

King's Evil. The following advertisement appears in the 'Public Intelligencer,' in 1664 :—'WHITEHALL, May 14, 1664. His Sacred Majesty having declared it to be his Royal will and purpose to continue the healing of his People for the Evil during the month of May, and then to give over till Michaelmas next, I am commanded to give notice thereof, that the people may not come up to Town in the interim and lose their labour.'

King's Highway. 'When there were many jurisdictions in this country, which were practically independent of the Crown, the border-lands of the counties, and likewise the highways, appertained to the royal jurisdiction. That is to say, a crime committed on the highway was as if committed in the king's own personal domain, and fell to his courts to judge. The highways were emphatically under the King's Peace, and hence they came to be spoken of as the King's Highways.'—*Rev. J. Earle, Philology*, p. 68.

Kings of Scotland. 'The Scottish kings appear to have been anciently regarded as members of the English parliament; and there are instances among the Tower Records of the issuing of writs to summon their attendance at Westminster.'—*Brayley's Londoniana.*

Kissing goes by choosing. As *kiesen* is the Dutch word for choosing, this proverbial saying originated in a pun.

Kiss it and make it well. Sir John Lubbock, after giving instances of the almost universal custom among barbarous nations of sorcerers pretending to cure internal or other diseases by sucking the part affected, says, 'We find, all over the world, this primitive cure by sucking out the evil, which perhaps, even with ourselves, lingers among nurses and children in the universal nursery remedy of "kiss it and make it well."'—*Origin of Civilization,* p. 20.

Kiss the mistress. The line in 'Troilus and Cressida,' iii. 2, where Shakespeare says, 'Rub on, and *kiss the mistress*,' has often been misunderstood. It is in allusion to the game of bowls. The white ball now called the 'jack' was formerly known as 'the mistress'; the term 'kiss' is still used when one ball gently touches another in the play. To 'kiss the mistress' meant, therefore, to touch the white ball gently.

Kit-cat. This was the name of a club founded at Westminster in 1703, by Addison, Steele, and others. The name was taken from that of Christopher Kat, a pastrycook, at whose house the club met. The members had their portraits painted of uniform dimensions, which particular size has been known ever since as 'kit-cat.'

Kite. The falcon known as the kite is remarkable for its power of remaining in mid air without apparent motion of its wings. This peculiarity seems to have suggested its name as that of the boy's favourite toy, the kite.

Kith and Kin. Kith is from the Anglo-Saxon *cuth,* or *cyth,* known, acquainted with; 'Ne *cuth* mon, ne *cunnes* mon' ('Reliq. Antiq.' p. 4); that is, neither *kithman* (acquaintance) nor *kinsman* (relative). '*Kith and kin*' may be paraphrased by 'friends and relatives.'

Knap. The 'knap' of a hill is the top or head of it. The word is probably the Welsh *cnap,* which has the same meaning. Browne ('Shepherd's Pipe,' Ecl. i.), has:—

Hark on *knap* of yonder hill,
Some sweet shepherd tunes his quill.

There is a hill in the parish of Woking, Surrey, called *Knap* Hill. The word knap was also formerly used in the sense of snap, as in the Prayer-book version of Psalm xlvi. v. 9, 'He breaketh the bow, and *knappeth* the spear in sunder.'

Knapsack. The meaning of this word is literally a provision bag. In the German and Dutch languages the word *knappen* signifies to gnaw, bite, or nibble, and is often used in the sense of eating. '*Wir haben nichts zu knappen*' means 'we have nothing to eat.'

Knave. A knave was anciently the name applied to a man servant. In some of the earlier translations of the Scriptures the Epistles commence 'Paul, a *knave* of Jesus Christ.' The word was also used to designate one of the male sex, as in Wycliff's translation of the Bible, where the verse Rev. xii. 5 is rendered 'and sche bare a *knave* child.'

Kneel. This word is formed from *knee*; to *kneel* is to rest upon the knee.

Kneeling after a Play. It was anciently the custom, after a play or epilogue was finished, for the players to assemble on the stage, and kneel in prayer for their patrons; the Royal companies invariably praying for the King and Queen. Many allusions to this custom are found in the old dramatists. Shakespeare has only one. The Epilogue to '2 Henry IV.,' spoken by a dancer, ends as follows:—'My tongue is weary; when my legs are too, I will bid you good night, and so *kneel down before you*, but indeed to pray for the queen.' In 'Lusty Juventis' ('Origin of Drama,' i. 163), we have:—

> Now let us make our supplications together,
> For the prosperous state of our noble and vertuous king,
> That in his godly procedynges he may stil perséver,
> Which seketh the glory of God above al other thing, &c.

At the end of the 'Disobedient Child' (black letter, no date) are the following directions quoted by Nares:—'Heere the rest of the players come in, and kneele downe all togyther, eche of them saying one of these verses, &c.' And in 'Clitus's Whimsies' (1631), p. 57, is the following:—'Which he performes with as much zeale as an actor after the ende of a play, when he prayes for his Majestie, the lords of the most honourable privie councell, and all that love the king.' Up to a very recent period the playbills of the Patent Theatres always bore the prayer, 'Vivant Rex et Regina.'

Kneepan. The second syllable of this word is evidently

corrupted from the Anglo-Saxon word *ban,* a bone. The proper form of the word is *kneeban,* or kneebone.

Knell, Knoll. 'Knell is derived both from Welsh and Saxon, and these more remotely from *Nola,* which in Low Latin signified a bell; church bells having been first used by St. Paulinus, Bishop of Nola, in Campania, whence such a bell was also called Campana.'—*Nares.* A curious instance of the occurrence of the two words, knell and knoll, in one line occurs in 'Macbeth' (v. 7):

> Had I as many sons as I have hairs,
> I would not wish them to a fairer death.
> And so his *knell* was *knolled.*

Knighthood. Up to the reign of George IV. there was a clause in the patent of every baronet, giving his eldest son the right, upon attaining his majority, to claim knighthood. This right is, of course, still in force in the case of baronetcies existing before that period, but from about 1820 the clause has been omitted, so that in recent baronetcies there is no such right attaching to the position of the eldest son of a baronet. A claim of knighthood on behalf of the eldest son of a baronet, created *ante* 1820, was made and allowed in 1874.

Knock-kneed. It is a singular fact that this very expressive term has not found its way into the dictionaries.

Knowledge. This word is often improperly used in the sense of wisdom. Cowper shows the difference of meaning in the following lines:—

> Knowledge and Wisdom, far from being one,
> Have ofttimes no connection. Knowledge dwells
> In heads replete with thoughts of other men;
> Wisdom in minds attentive to their own.
> Knowledge is proud that he has learned so much,
> Wisdom is humble that he knows no more.

Knowledge is power. Lord Lytton, in 'My Novel,' says that no such sentence or thought as this is to be found in Lord Bacon's works. The great novelist was wrong. It occurs in Bacon's treatise 'De Heresibus,' and is in Latin, '*Nam et ipsa scientia potestas est.*' The sentence means, not that knowledge confers power, but that the capacity to know may be termed a power. The expression is perhaps founded on the passage, 'A wise man is strong' (Proverbs xxiv. 5).

Knuckle under. The word 'knuckle' anciently meant any joint of the body, and was commonly applied to the knee. It is now retained in this sense only in the phrase 'a *knuckle* of veal.' Hence to 'knuckle under' meant to *kneel and crave pardon.*

'Knock under' is merely a corrupt contraction of '*knuckle* under.' Both phrases signify submission, and are stated by Johnson to refer to the old custom of striking the under side of a table with the knuckles in admission of having been beaten in an argument.

L

La Belle Sauvage, Ludgate Hill. Numerous conjectures have been made as to the origin of this inn sign. It has now been conclusively settled that the original sign was 'The Bell in the Hoop,' or 'Savage's Inn.' This is proved by a paper read by Mr. Lysons before the Society of Antiquaries, and published in the 'Archæologia,' in 1815 (xviii. pp. 197, 198). Mr. Lysons met with its origin in the 'Clause Roll,' dated February 5th, 31 Henry VI. (1453), wherein John French gave to his mother, Joan French, widow, 'Savages Inn, otherwise called the Bell in the Hoop,' in the parish of St. Bride. In 1568 John Craythorne gave the reversion of the 'Belle Savage' to the Cutlers' Company for ever, on certain conditions, and a portrait of Mrs. Craythorne, accompanied by her conveyancer, presenting the deed to the master and wardens of the company, still hangs in the Cutlers' Hall.

Labrador. The Portuguese discoverers gave the name '*Terra laborador*,' 'cultivable land,' to this inhospitable country. The name has since been contracted to 'Labrador.' Although it is in the same latitude as England, the thermometer sinks in winter to 30 degrees below zero.

Laburnum. This beautiful tree was formerly known in England as 'peascod tree,' but the Latin name *Laburnum*, under which name the tree is mentioned by Pliny, has completely superseded its old designation.

Lac. This is an Indian word, signifying the number 100,000. It is seldom or never used, except in reference to money; the phrase 'a lac of rupees' being almost the only form in which the word is met with. The value of English money in a lac of rupees is about £12,000.

Lace-making. Beckman says that lace-making was invented in the year 1561 at St. Annaberg, in Saxony, by Barbara Uttmann. 'Tradition ascribes the first establishment of lace manufacture in England to some refugees from Flanders, who settled in the village of Cranfield, in the west of the county of Bedford, adjoining Buckinghamshire.'—*Fairholt.*

Lack, Want, and **Need,** all signify to be destitute of, but they vary in degree. 'A man without superfluities *lacks* them; without conveniences, *wants* them; without necessaries, *needs* them.'

Ladies and Gentlemen. Englishmen are thought by their continental neighbours to be very deficient in politeness, yet in addressing an audience we at least set them an example in gallantry. We say 'ladies and gentlemen,' the French say '*Messieurs et mesdames*,' and the Germans '*Meine herren und damen.*'

Ladies' Privilege in Leap Year. 'The ladies' leap year privilege took its origin in the following manner:—By an ancient act of the Scottish Parliament, passed about the year 1228, it was "ordonit that during ye reign of her maist blessit maiestie, Margeret, ilka maiden, ladee of baith high and lowe estait, shall hae libertie to speak ye man she likes. Gif he refuses to tak hir to bee his wyf, he schale be mulct in the sum of ane hundridty pundis, or less, as his estait may bee, except and alwais, gif he can make it appeare that he is betrothit to anither woman, then he schal be free."'—*Illustrated Almanack*, 1865.

Ladies' Saddles. Mr. Wright, in his 'Domestic Manners of the Middle Ages,' gives several illustrations from ancient drawings, showing ladies on horseback, both astride and sideways. Mr. Wright is of opinion that ladies 'were taught to ride both ways, the side saddle being considered the most courtly, while it was thought safer to ride astride in the chase.' In the earlier illustrations of riding sideways, the ladies seem to be seated on a kind of pillion, the legs hanging down side by side, but in one of the fourteenth century, taken from a MS. in the French National Library, two ladies are represented riding in the modern style, except that they are seated on the 'off' side, and the left leg is raised over the pommel in a very awkward manner. That it was no uncommon thing for ladies to ride astride may be inferred from Chaucer's description of the Wife of Bath, whom he describes as wearing a *pair* of spurs.

And on hire feet a *paire* of spores, scharpe.
Canterbury Tales, i. 471.

Lady, Sympathy, &c. These words, and a few others, are exceptions to the general rule, that where singular words terminate in the single vowel *y*, the plural is *ies*. The reason for the exception is that anciently these words terminated in *ie*, lady being spelt *ladie*, and that, although the spelling of the singular has been altered, the plural has remained untouched.

Lager-beer. German, from *lager*, a bed. The German beer is so called from being kept in barrels a long time on the 'lager,' or frame, before it is considered fit for use.

Lake, Loch, Lough. A lake in England is a sheet of water having no inlet from the sea. A *loch* in Scotland is either an inland lake, or an arm of the sea nearly land-locked. The word *lough* in Ireland has the same significance as the Scottish word 'loch.' Both the *ch* and the *gh* are heavy gutturals, and both words are pronounced as the German *ch* in *Ich dien*.

Lambeth. In a charter of Edward the Confessor, A.D. 1062, this place is called Lambe-hithe. Its probable derivation is from the Anglo-Saxon *lam*, mud, and *hyth*, a haven or port. Its name, in that case, would mean the 'muddy landing-place.'

Lamb's Conduit Street. An old English Herbal, speaking of winter rocket or cress, says, 'It groweth of its own accord in gardens and fields by the wayside in divers places, and particularly in the next pasture to the Conduit Head behind Gray's Inn, that brings water to Mr. Lamb's Conduit in Holborn.' 'The conduit was taken down in 1746.'—*Cunningham*.

Lamb's-Wool. The feast of apple gathering was called by the Anglo-Saxons *la maes abhal*, which, being pronounced *lammas ool*, was the origin of the name of the drink used on these occasions, which was compounded of the pulp of roasted apples, mixed with hot ale, spices, and sugar. In all the older dictionaries the word is defined as 'ale and roasted apples.' It was a favourite drink two or three centuries ago, and there are many allusions to it in old writers. Gerard, the Herbalist, gives the receipt for preparing a similar drink with water, as follows:—'The pulpe of the rosted apples, in number foure, or five, according to the greatnesse of the apples (especially the pomewater), mixed in a wine quarte of faire water, laboured together, untill it comes to be as apples and ale, which we call Lambes wooll.'—*Johnson's edit.* p. 1460.

> Now crowne the bowle,
> With gentle lambe's wooll,
> Add sugar, and nutmegs, and ginger.—*Herrick*, p. 376.
>
> A cupp of lambs wool they dranke unto him then.
> *Percy's Reliques*, iii. p. 184.

A correspondent of the 'Gentleman's Magazine' says that in his boyhood it was customary to roast apples on a string until they dropped into a large bowl of spiced ale, and this was the true composition of the drink called lamb's-wool.

Lame Duck is a Stock Exchange term for a member who has made default on settlement day. The names of defaulters are posted on a black board in the room where the members transact their buying and selling.

Land o' Cakes. This phrase was first applied to Scotland by Burns in 1789, in his poem, 'Captain Grose's Peregrinations through Scotland,' which commences with the couplet—

> Hear, *Land-o'-cakes* and brither Scots,
> Frae Maidenkirk to Johnny Groat's.

'Maidenkirk' is an inversion of the name of the most southerly parish of Scotland, Kirkmaiden.

Land of Green Ginger. This is the strange name of a street in the town of Hull, and has given rise to many conjectures. Some manuscripts discovered a few years ago mention that, in the year 1685, Sir Willoughby Hickman was a candidate for the representation of the borough in Parliament. He came to Hull by way of the Humber, and on arriving 'one of Jonas Gould's coaches was taken to the waterside to meet him, and in he got, and the men pulled it right away to the George Inn, at the corner of the land of *Moses Greenhinger*, the boat builder in Whitefriars Gate.' The boat-builder's name has been strangely metamorphosed.

Lanes in the City of London. 'Fyefoot Lane' was originally, according to Stow, '*Five-foot Lane*,' from its being but five feet in width. 'Duck's-foot Lane' was formerly '*Duke's Foot Lane*,' it being a private footway of the Duke of Suffolk, who lived at the Manor House in the parish of St. Laurence Poultney.

Lapsus linguæ, a Latin phrase, meaning literally 'a slip of the tongue.' It is generally applied in this country to an imprudent remark or admission dropped in the course of an ordinary conversation.

Lares and Penates were the household gods of the Romans. The *Lares* (singular *Lar*) were supposed to be the protectors of the property of the household, whilst the *Penates* were believed to have power over events, and to be controllers of fate or destiny. Some suppose that no family had more than one *Lar*; but *Penates* are always mentioned in the plural number. The words are divided into syllables and pronounced as follows:—La-rees, Pe-na-tees.

Large Parishes. Some of the English parishes are of enormous size, as the following examples will show:—

		Statute acres.
Lancaster, Lancashire	which contains	106,395
Aysgarth, Yorkshire	,,	80,000
Kendal, Westmoreland		68,360
Halifax, Yorkshire		58,880
Lydford, Devon		57,600
Rochdale, Lancashire	,,	57,600
Falstone, Northumberland	,,	56,960
Prestbury, Cheshire	,,	56,320

Larking. 'Skylarking' is a term much used by sailors for games or tricks upon each other in the rigging and tops of ships. Skylarking thence became a general term for mischievous frolicking, and has been abbreviated to *larking*.

Larva, from the Latin *larva*, a mask; applied to an insect in the grub condition, because its true form is, as it were, masked.—*Brand*.

Lash. To lash a person is to beat him with a leathern whip, or with a strap. Hounds were formerly fastened together in threes by leather straps, which were called leashes, and the dogs, being sometimes beaten with these straps, were said to be 'leashed,' hence 'leashed' came to mean beaten with a strap. In Lyly's 'Midas' (act iv. sc. 2) we find, 'If I catch you in the forest, thou shalt be *leashed*.' From this the transition to *lash* is easy. We do not 'lash' a person with a stick; that is '*thrashing*' him.

Lass. The feminine of *lad*, laddess, abbreviated into *lass*.

Launch. The verb 'to launch' a boat or ship is from the French *lancer*, to rush. The noun 'launch,' a boat, is from the Spanish *lancha*, a long boat.

Latin and Greek Primitives. Dr. Angus tells us that 'One hundred and fifty-four Greek and Latin primitives [or roots] yield nearly 13,000 [English] words.'—*Handbook of the English Tongue*, p. 46.

Lavender, from the Italian *lavanda*, a washing. The name is applied to the plant because its dried flowers are put away with newly-washed linen to perfume it. Vossius says the Romans used the flowers to perfume the water in which they bathed (*lavo*).

Laverock is the old English name for the lark. Izaak Walton spells it 'Leverock' in the 'Angler's Wish':—

Here see the blackbird feed her young,
Or the *leverock* build her nest.—*Edit*. 1815, p. 200.

Law. Mr. Sheldon Amos, in his excellent work, 'The Science of Law,' says that *a law* is 'A command proceeding from the supreme political authority of a State, and addressed to the persons who are the subjects of that authority.'

Law of Gravitation. Shakespeare evidently understood the law of gravitation, although he lived before Newton. In 'Troilus and Cressida,' act iv. sc. 2, it is thus alluded to :—

> The strong base and building of my love
> Is as the very centre of the earth,
> Drawing all things to it.

Leadenhall Market. Leadenhall is a corruption of Leather Hall, from a large market for leather which formerly existed there. There are still some remains of the leather market.

Leading Articles in Newspapers were first adopted by the 'Leeds Mercury.' They commenced in 1801.

Leading Questions are questions put by counsel to a witness in such a way as to lead to, or suggest, the answer desired. Leading questions are not allowed to be put by the counsel who 'calls' the witness. He must not ask, for instance, 'Did he wear a black coat?' The question must be, 'What colour was his coat?' or in some similar form. Leading questions are permitted in cross-examination.

'**Lead, kindly Light.**' This beautiful hymn was written by Dr. Newman, in 1833, while becalmed in an orange boat in the Straits of Bonifacio. It first appeared in the 'British Magazine,' and afterwards in 'The Lyra Apostolica' (Mozley, Derby, 1836, p. 28).

Lead Pencils. What are called 'black lead pencils' have no lead in their composition. They received their name from the leaden plummets which were used for ruling faint lines on paper, before the discovery of the mines of graphite in Cumberland.

Leaf. Anything flat and thin is called a '*leaf*,' from its resemblance to the leaves of plants. Thus we say a *leaf* of paper; 'turn over *leaf*'; the *leaf* of a table; gold-*leaf*, &c.

Leap in the dark. In the debates on the Reform Bill in 1868, the late Lord Derby applied this phrase to the proposed legislation. It was, however, not original; it has been traced to a song in the 'British Museum Collection' (H. 1601, p. 62), where it occurs in the line :

> All you that must take a leap in the dark.

Thomas Hobbes on his death-bed (1679) is reported to have said, 'I am taking a frightful leap into the dark,' which is not unlike the exclamation of Rabelais in his last illness, 'I am going to the Great Perhaps.'

Leap Year is a year of 366 days. Every fourth year is a leap year, except such years as complete centuries, and whose numbers, after suppressing the two ciphers, are not divisible by four. Thus the years 1700 and 1800 were not leap years, and 1900 will not be, although 1896 and 1904 will. The year 2000, being divisible by four, will be a leap year. 'Leap year' is a singularly inappropriate name. We do not 'leap over' or 'omit' a day; on the contrary, we thrust one in. See BISSEXTILE.

Leases for 99 years. Leases were formerly granted for 100 years; lessees frequently granted under-leases, in which they reserved the reversion of the last year to enable them to recover rents by distress. 'Careless and ignorant practitioners followed these forms of demise in cases where the reason for them did not exist, until terms of 99 years grew into a custom.' Another reason may probably have been the restriction of corporations, or ecclesiastical persons, from demising lands for terms longer than 100 years. This would lead naturally to demises whose durations were just within the prohibited period. 'A lease for more than ninety-nine years does not, as is commonly believed, constitute a freehold.'—*Wharton.*

Leash. As applied to game means *three.* The name is derived from the French word *laisse*, a strap or thong. Formerly hounds were strapped together, and led by *threes*, three hounds so bound being called 'a leash.' From the hounds the transition to the game was easy, so that 'a leash of hares' has come to mean three, although the term has nothing whatever in common with the word from which it is taken.

Leasing. Leasing, from the Anglo-Saxon *leasung*, false, is an old English word for lying. In Psalm iv. 2 we have 'How long will ye love vanity or seek after *leasing*?' In 'Twelfth Night,' act i. sc. 5, Shakespeare has 'Now Mercury endue thee with *leasing*, for thou speakest well of fools.' And Spenser, in the 'Faery Queene,' l. vi. 48, says, 'But that false pilgrim which that *leasing* told.' This word is not to be confounded with *leasing*, gleaning, which comes from lea, a field; nor with another old English word, *leese*, to lose, used in Wycliff's translation of Matthew ix. 29, 'He that findeth his life shall *leese* it.' This is from the Anglo-Saxon *leasan*, to lose. Wycliff has still another *leese*, which comes from the Latin *læsus*, to hurt—'The princes of the people sought to leese him.'

Leathern Bottles. Castor oil is imported from India in bottles made of buffalo hide. They are called *duppers* or dubbers. Each dupper contains about 80 lbs.

Leave. To take leave. In old French and English the phrase to 'ask leave,' or 'take leave,' was always completed by the words 'to go.' 'It is a modern barbarism which has dropped the significant last words, and put in the absurd "my."' A modern Greek, in quitting the presence of a superior, asks permission to leave, saying, 'I ask your leave.' The same custom prevails in Ceylon; a Cingalese gentleman, either in his own language or in English, always says, ' I take *your* leave,' which, whether clearer in expression or no, is at any rate more polite.

Leave some for manners. This is often used as a direction to children in eating. The same advice will be found in the Apocrypha, Ecclesiasticus xxxi. 17.

Leden. This is an old English word derived from the Anglo-Saxon *læden*, which the dictionaries define as 'language,' and usually explain by saying that it originally meant 'Latin.' Nares, in his 'Glossary,' gives the same definition, and quotes instances of its use by Chaucer, Spenser, Fairfax and Drayton. Chaucer writes :—

> Through which she understode well every thing
> That any *foule* may in his *leden* faine,
> And couthe he answer in his *leden* again.—*Cant. Tales,* 10749.

Spenser has :—
> And could the *ledden* of the gods unfold.
> *Faery Queene,* iv. xi. 19.

Fairfax, in his 'Translation of Tasso,' says:—
> A wondrous bird among the rest there flew,
> That in plain speech sung love-lays loud and shrill,
> Her *leden* was like human language true.—xvi. 13.

And Drayton, 'Polyolbion,' xii. p. 905, says :—
> The *ledden* of the birds most perfectly she knew.

Nares, in reference to these quotations, says, 'It is observable that all of these, except Spenser, apply it to the *speech of birds*, of which Chaucer sets them the example.' But Nares, having got hold of the derivation from the word Latin, did not see that the poets were on the right track, and that all the dictionary makers had been wrong. We have no example of the use of the verb to lede, but it is quite clear, by analogy, that *lede* was identical with the German *lied*, which is defined as 'warbling, singing, song, air'; and that *leden*, in English, meant simply the *songs of birds*. In fact, 'leden, is exactly what Mendelssohn meant when he named his exquisite collection of wordless airs *Lieder ohne Wörte*, 'songs without words.' The attempt to derive 'leden' from the word Latin, simply from an accidental resemblance in form, is absurd and ridiculous.

Ledge, or **Lege**. All monosyllables ending in *ege* are spelt with the *d*, as pledge, sledge, &c. In words of more than one syllable the *d* is omitted, with the exception of knowledge and 'acknowle*d*ge.'

Ledger-fishing. From the Saxon *licgan*, to lie. In ledger-fishing a weight is attached to the line, about four feet from the bait. The weight lies still, but the bait sways from side to side with the motion of the stream. Izaak Walton says, 'That I call a *ledger bait* which is made to *lie* or rest in one certain place.'—*Complete Angler*, i. 8.

Lee, of a ship. The 'lee side' of a ship is that which *lies*, or is inclined downwards when driven by the force of the wind. The Dutch phrase expresses this meaning clearly; it is *de lij zijde*, the *lie* side.

Left, in the sense of departed. It is common to write, 'Thomas *left* this morning.' This is incorrect, unless the name of the place which is *left* be added or indicated. 'Thomas left *here*,' or 'Thomas left *Oxford*,' are correct forms.

Left Hand. 'The *left* hand is that which is *leaved*, *leav'd*, *left*, or which we are taught to *leave* out of use when one hand only is employed.'—*Horne Tooke, Diversions of Purley*.

Left in the lurch. This is a metaphor derived from the gaming-table. A *lurch* is where one player makes every point, before his opponent makes one. The word in French is *lourche*; in German *lurtsch*; and in Italian *lurcio*.

Legal Tender. The tender of a larger sum than the amount due is a legal tender, but the creditor cannot be compelled to give change. Thus, in the possible case of a debt of 96*l*. which, under some penalty, the debtor is bound to pay by noon of a certain day, if he tenders to the creditor ten Bank of England 10*l*. notes a minute before twelve o'clock of the appointed day, it is a legal tender of the amount due; but, if the creditor should refuse to give change, the debtor, not having time to procure smaller money, must either submit to lose the 4*l*. of excess, or become liable to the penalty for default of due payment. The Coinage Act (33 Vic. cap. 10) declares that a tender of money in payment 'shall be a legal tender in the case of gold coins for a payment of any amount; in the case of silver coins, for a payment of an amount not exceeding 40*s*., but for no greater amount; in the case of bronze coins, for a payment of an amount not exceeding 1s., but for no greater amount.' 'If a debtor tender to his creditor the amount due in legal tender money, and it be refused, the debt is not thereby cancelled; the creditor may sue for it afterwards, but the costs of the action will be thrown upon him.'—*Jevon.*

Legem pone is a proverbial expression for ready money, often met with in old writers. In Ozell's 'Rebelais' we find, 'They were all at our service for the *legem pone*'; and in Minshull's 'Essayes in Prison,' p. 26, we have :—'But in this, there is nothing to be abated; all their speech is *legem pone*.' The origin is curious. The portion of Psalm cxix. appointed for the 25th day of the month has the title 'Legem pone,' being the first words in the Latin version. These words occurring in the service on the great pay day, March 25th, were associated with payment, and became a general synonym for prompt cash. From this use of the words also arose another proverbial expression, 'Post the pony,' meaning put down the money.

Leek, Onion, Garlic. The leek seems to have been the only plant of the Allium tribe known in England in pre-Saxon times, and it is probably from the fondness of the Keltic tribes for this esculent that their descendants, the Welsh, still retain it as an emblem of their nationality. The *leac*, or *leak*, was also an important table vegetable amongst the Anglo-Saxons, for they called their gardens 'leek gardens'(*leac-tun*), and the gardener was a 'leek-ward' (*leac-weard*). As other species of the same tribe were introduced, they also were called leeks, with a prefix denoting some peculiarity. Thus garlic was anciently *gar-leac*, the leek with a spear (*gar*), from the spear-like stem and head of the seed vessel; and onion was *enne-leac*, or one-leek, from its not throwing off side bulbs. See GARLIC.

Leighton Buzzard. The latter word in this name was formerly written 'Beau desart,' from the Norman *beau*, fair, or beautiful, and *desart*, woody.

Lely. The family name of Sir Peter Lely was *Van der Vaas*. Sir Peter's grandfather was a Dutch perfumer, whose 'sign' was a *vase* of lilies. Sir Peter's father ran away and entered the British army. He discarded his proper patronymic, and adopted his father's shop sign, Lilly, or Lely, as a surname.

Lent. The Anglo-Saxon name for the month of March was *Lenet-monat*, length month, from the rapid lengthening of the days in March. The word Lent is a contraction of the name of the month. The forty days' fast, now so called, was instituted by Pope Telesphorus, A.D. 130. It was first observed in England about the year 640.

Leopard. The leopard was anciently believed to be a mongrel of the male panther or '*pard*,' and a lioness; hence the double name *leo*, or *lion-pard*. The error descended to modern times. Fuller, in 'A Pisgah Sight of Palestine,' vol. i. p. 195, says, ' Leopards and mules are properly no creatures.' The leopard has long been known to be a distinct species of the genus *Felis*.

Leprosy. This was formerly called in England the ' linenless disease,' which phrase, according to Mr. William Howitt ('Northern Heights of London'), ' denotes the true cause of leprosy—the wearing of woollen garments next the skin; for through wearing these garments till saturated with perspiration the skin becomes diseased.' Formerly leprosy was very prevalent in this country, but since the introduction of linen and cotton garments, and more frequent washing, it has almost disappeared.

Less, Lesser. ' Less ' is generally used as the comparative of *much*, while ' lesser' is generally contrasted with great. Less means 'not so much '; lesser means ' not so large.'

Let. There are two distinct and opposite meanings to this word; to *permit* and to *hinder*. ' Let me go ' is an example of the first. This comes from the Anglo-Saxon *lætan*. The second meaning is retained in the law phrase ' without *let* or hindrance,' and is used in Romans i. 18—' Oftentimes I purposed to come unto you, but was *let* hitherto.' This use of the word comes from the Anglo-Saxon *lettan*.

Letter-writing. Up to the commencement of the reign of Edward I., all letters, even of the most private nature, were written in Latin. About the time of Edward's accession, French, which had been the spoken language of the Court from the time of the Conquest, began to be used in written correspondence. In the reign of Edward III., the English language, in pursuance of an Act of Parliament, was made the language of legislation. The oldest known private letter in English is one written to Sir John Pelham by his wife in 1399.

Lettuce. The name of this plant in the Latin is *lactuca*, from *lac*, milk. It was so named from the milky sap which exudes when the stem of the plant is cut. It was introduced into England from Holland about the year 1520.

Levant. ' Levant ' means simply the east, though it is generally confined in its use to the eastern parts of the Mediterranean, as the coasts of Egypt, Syria, and Asia Minor. The word is Italian, and signifies *rising*, alluding to the sun rising in the east.

Lewd. 'That *lewd*, which meant at one time no more than *lay*, or unlearned (the lewd people the lay people), should come to signify the sinful, the vicious, is not a little worthy of note.'—*Trench*. The Caxton Society published a 'Romance of Englische of the begynnyng of the world, and of al that a *lewed* man hath need for to knawe for hele of soul.'

Lewes. The name of this Sussex town 'is derived from the old French *Les ewes*, the waters, as expressive of its state when the levels north and south of the town were flooded for the greater part of the year.'—*Rowe*. Mr. Churnock, however, thinks it 'comes from the Anglo-Saxon *hlœw*, a word expressive of the gradual ascent which the eastern termination of the Down makes from the river, joined to the old British name of the stream *Isca*, or *Ise*, whence *hlœw-ise*, *hlœw-ese*, *Lewes*.'

Lias. The word 'lias,' as applied to lime, is merely a provincial pronunciation of the word *layers*, in allusion to the occurrence of the limestone in strata or layers, between the oölite and the new red sandstone.

Libel, from the Latin *libellus*, a little book; generally used in the sense of pasquinade, lampoon, &c. Libel may be defined as published slander. It is punishable under the criminal law by fine and imprisonment, and the defendant cannot plead the truth of his statements in justification, because he is not to be punished for the falsehood, but for the provocation. In an action for damages in a civil court, he may however plead, in defence, that his statement is true. The communication of libellous matter to *one person* has been held to be a publication. 'Written or printed slanders are libels.'—*Bouvier*. Lord Ellenborough was the author of the legal maxim, 'The greater the truth the greater the libel.' He used the words at a trial, adding, 'If the language used was true, the person would suffer more than if it was false.'

Liberals. This word, as applied to a political party, is said to be derived from the name of 'The Liberal,' a periodical of advanced views on politics and religion, which Lord Byron and some of his friends established about the year 1815.

£. This symbol for a pound sterling is a contraction of the Latin word *libra*, a pound. The contraction was originally to the letters *lib.*, the usual mark of abbreviation, a dash or line over the letters, being used to signify the contracted form of the word. In dotting the *i* a careless or rapid writer would sometimes, as many modern writers do, make the dot more or less in the form of a dash or short line. Thus *lib.* came to have two strokes or dashes, one for the abbreviation, and the other to represent the dot of the *i*. By and by the *i* was dropped as unnecessary, and the word stood as *lb.*, but the two strokes were retained. This was found to interfere with the ℔, the symbol used for a pound weight, which had only one dash for the abbreviation, and so the *b* was omitted where the mark meant money. The two dashes or strokes were, however, perpetuated, and the £ with its crosses is now known all over the world as the symbol of an English pound sterling.

Library, from the Latin *libraria*, a bookseller's shop. It is derived from *liber*, the thin coat of the inner bark of the Egyptian plant *papyrus*, which was the material upon which the ancient Greeks and Romans wrote their books. The word paper is also derived from *papyrus*.

Licgan, Lecgan. These are two Anglo-Saxon terms, from which are derived a large number of English words; as lie, lay, layer, lair, belay, outlay, relay, law (*laid* down), lea, ley, ledge, ledger (the book that *lies* on the desk), low, lower, lowlands, &c.

Lich was the Anglo-Saxon word for a dead body. 'Lichfield in Staffordshire hath that name of the *Liches* (more rightly to be pronounced *Lighes*), to wit, dead bodies of such as were slain there.'—*Verstegan*. Lichgate is a covered gateway to a churchyard, where a corpse brought for burial was detained under shelter, while the priest was fetched to commence the funeral service.

Lie in lavender. To lie in lavender was anciently to lie in pawn. The following quotations show the former use of the phrase:—' But the poore gentleman paies so deere for the *lavender* it is laid up in, that if it lies long at a broker's house, he seemes to buy his apparel twice.'—*Greene's Imp. Harl. Misc.* v. 405. 'And a black satten of his own to go before her in; which suit, for the more sweet'ning, now *lies in lavender.*'—*Ben Jonson, Every Man Out of his Humour*, act iii. sc. 3.

Lieutenant. The usual pronunciation of this word—leftenant —probably arose from the custom of printing the letter *u* as a *v*. In the 'Colonial Records,' relating to New York, the word is invariably spelt lie*v*tenant. The earliest known use of the word is in 'Chevy Chase,' which Professor Skeat reproduces in his 'Specimens of English Literature,' 1871, i. 122. The passage in which it occurs is as follows:—' That dougheti duglas, *lyff-tenant* of the marches, he lay slean chyviat within.' Professor Skeat thinks the date 'probably after 1460.'

Lightning Conductors. Professor Silliman says that lightning conductors cannot be relied on unless they terminate in some part where the earth is permanently wet. He advises, therefore, that the conductor should terminate in the water of a well, or in some other water that never fails. The Professor's own house was struck, although he had lightning conductors, but he found that they terminated in dry soil a few inches below the surface.

Like angels' visits, few and far between. A line in Campbell's 'Pleasures of Hope.' Blair, in the 'Grave,' has:
> Like those of angels, *short* and far between.

Both writers, however, appear to have borrowed from John Norris, who died in 1711. In his poem 'Transient Delights' is the line—
> Like angels' visits, short and bright.

Lilac. In the south of Scotland this flowering tree is called the *lily-aik*, or lily-oak. The word lilac is generally thought to be Persian; if so, the similarity is very curious.

Limber. The 'limber' of a cannon or howitzer has the same relation to the gun as a tender has to a locomotive engine; it carries the ammunition, and the necessary moveable furniture. In action it is removed from the gun, so as to be out of the way of the working gunners. To 'limber up' and retreat or pursue is the work of but a few moments.

Limbo. To be in limbo is now used as equivalent to being in gaol. Formerly it was used to denote a place fabled as being on the borders of hell, and the word was sometimes used to denote hell itself. Shakespeare seems to use it in this latter sense in the line—
> As far from hell as Limbo is from bliss.

Limehouse. The name of this suburb seems to have originated from a lime warehouse formerly existing there. Pepys, in his 'Diary' (9th October, 1661), says, 'By coach to Captain Marshe's at Limehouse, to a house that hath been their ancestors' for this 250 years, close by the *Lime-house* which gives the name to the place.' In 'An Account of Millwall,' published in 1853, the writer says the limehouse is there to this day, and he adds, 'these limekilns must have existed for 450 years.'

Linch-pin. A *linch-pin* is a pin placed through an opening at the end of an axle-tree, to prevent the wheel from sliding off. None of the modern dictionaries give any etymology, but Bailey suggests *link-pin*, which seems reasonable. Worcester defines the verb *to link*, thus :—' To join or connect by something which serves as a bond of connection; to connect; to conjoin; to unite; to bind; to tie.'

Lincoln. An old proverb says 'The Devil looks over Lincoln.' 'The tower of Lincoln Cathedral is the highest in England, and when the spire was standing on it, it must, if in proportion, have exceeded that of Old St. Paul's, which was 525 feet. The monks are said to have been so proud of this structure that they thought the devil looked upon it with an envious eye, whence the proverb of a man who looks insidious and malignant, 'He looks as the devil did over Lincoln' ('Parl. Gazetteer,' vol. iii. p. 118). A more probable theory is that the proverb originated in the circumstance that a small figure of the devil stands on the top of Lincoln College at Oxford.

Lincolnshire Bagpipes. In the 'First Part of Henry IV.,' act i. sc. 2, Shakespeare makes Falstaff speak of 'The drone of a Lincolnshire bagpipe.' Some commentators on Shakespeare have endeavoured to prove from this passage that Lincolnshire was colonised by immigrants from Scotland. They are wrong; the phrase has no reference to the musical instruments known as *bagpipes*, but applies to the croaking of the innumerable frogs which flourish in the fenny portions of that county.

Lincoln's Inn is so named from an Earl of Lincoln who had a mansion on the site. It became an Inn of Court in 1310. Inigo Jones laid out the fine square called Lincoln's Inn Fields in 1620. It is thought by some to occupy the same space as the great pyramid of Egypt, but this is an error. The pyramid is 764 feet square; the square of Lincoln's Inn is 821 by 625 feet. There was formerly a theatre in Lincoln's Inn Fields. It was pulled down in 1848.

Ling is an old Anglo-Saxon termination signifying immaturity, and in nearly all the cases in which it is now used, it implies something either small or young. Thus darling is '*little* dear,' whilst yearling, firstling, duckling, gosling, stripling, and foundling, all convey the notion of tender age.

Lingua Franca is not, as might be supposed, the language of France. It is a dialect of corrupt Italian, mixed with many words of modern Greek and other languages, which is spoken on both coasts of the Mediterranean Sea.

Liquor. The verb 'to liquor' is commonly thought to be of American origin, yet we are told, in 'Atheniæ Oxonienses,' that an

Irish singer, named Quin, so pleased Oliver Cromwell at Oxford, that Oliver, who loved a good voice and instrumental music well, heard him with great delight, and *liquored* him with sack, saying: "Mr. Quin, you have done very well; what can I do for you? &c."'

Lissome. This contraction of the word *lithesome*, in the sense of supple or flexible, which until lately has had but a local use, is now, on the authority of Tennyson, admitted into the dictionaries.

Lithography (literally, writing on stone) was invented by a German named Sennefelder about 1796. It was introduced into England about the year 1800, but did not come into general use until 1817. Mr. Ackermann, of the Strand, first popularised it.

Little Britain. This London locality is so named from its having been the site of the mansion of the Duke of Bretagne or Brittany, in the time of Edward II.

Liturgy in Greek and formerly in English meant any public work or service. It is now confined in its use to the public service of worship and prayer.

Liverpool. There is some reason for believing that this name signifies simply the pool where small trading vessels *livered*, or delivered, their cargoes. To 'liver' a ship, in Eastern Scotland, is to discharge her cargo. 'Unlivery' in Admiralty law means the same thing.

Livery. This word was formerly of much wider significance than now. In the case of servants it comprised meat, drink, lodging, and a part, at least, of the clothing. In reference to visitors, to whom it was also applied, it meant all their meat and drink, which latter was rather bountifully served both by day and night. The following extract from an account of a feast given by Cardinal Wolsey at Hampton Court gives an illustration of this use of the word, and affords a curious insight into the manners of the times. Two hundred and eighty chambers were fitted up for the guests, and 'Every chamber had a basin and an ewer of syluer, a great *livery pot* of sylver, and some gilt; yea and some chambers had two *livery pots* with wine and beere, a boule, a goblet, and a pot of sylver to drink in, both for wine and beere; a sylver candlestick both white and plaine, having on it two sizes, and a staff torche of waxe, a fine manchet, and a cheat loaf.'

Spenser tells us the meaning of the word in his time, as follows:—'What *livery* is, we by common use in England know well enough, namely, that is, allowance of horse meat, as to keep horses at *livery*, the which word, I guess, is derived from *livering* or *delivering* forth their nightly food. So in great houses the livery is said to be served up for all night, that is their evening allowance of drink. And the *livery* is also the upper weed which a servant man weareth, so called, as I suppose, for that it was *delivered* and taken from him at pleasure.'

Llan. This prefix to the name of a locality occurs in upwards of 450 places in Wales. The word is Celtic, and signifies an enclosure. It afterwards came to mean a sacred enclosure, or churchyard. Where it now occurs, it is generally the prefix of the name of the saint to whom the church of the place is dedicated.

Lloyd's. The institution known by this name in connection with marine insurance originated A.D. 1710, in a coffee-house kept by one Lloyd, in Abchurch Lane. It was removed to the Royal Exchange in 1774.

LL. Whisky. This is a particular 'brand' of whisky, blended by Messrs. Kinahan of Dublin. It is so named from the fact that the Duke of Richmond, who was Lord Lieutenant of Ireland 1807-13, having been supplied with a small quantity, desired Messrs. Kinahan to reserve for him all they had of that kind. The cask was accordingly marked 'LL.', and under that designation the same quality of whisky has been popular ever since.

Llyn in Welsh local names means a lake, or pool, as *Llyn Glas*, the blue pool; *Llyn Coch*, the red pool, &c.

Loafer. 'An old Dutchman settled at New York and acquired a large fortune. He had an only daughter, and a young American fell in love with her. The father forbad him the house, but the daughter encouraged him. Whenever the old merchant saw the lover about the premises, he used to say to his daughter, 'There is that "*lofer*" of yours, the idle, good for nothing, &c.,' and so an idle man, hanging about, came to be called a "lofer;" how the letter *a* got into the word is not known.' This originally appeared in 'Notes and Queries,' but has been adopted by Bartlett in his 'Dictionary of Americanisms.'

Lobster. The word 'lobster' as applied to soldiers is of very old date. In Clarendon's 'History of the Rebellion,' iii. 91, edit. 1849, it is stated that in 1643, 'Sir William Waller received from London a fresh regiment of 500 horse under the command of Sir Arthur Haslerig, which were so prodigiously armed that they were called by the King's party "the regiment of *lobsters*," because of their bright iron shells with which they were covered; being perfect cuirassiers, and were the first seen so armed, on either side.'

Local Names. Names of places were originally descriptive *words* applicable to the locality, whether hilly, flat, mountainous, on the banks of rivers, woody, or bare. To these general features, prefixes or affixes were added by the settlers to denote circumstances connected with the nature of the settlement. These compound appellations, or their separate roots, much disguised in the lapse of ages, may generally be traced in the modern names of places.

In the article 'NAMES OF RIVERS' (which see), it is shown that nearly all river names are *Celtic*. This is true also of the names originally given to all remarkable natural features, as hills, valleys, plains, woods, morasses, rocks, waterfalls, and so on.

They are commonly monosyllables, as *pen* or *ben*, a hill or mountain; *dun*, a hill fortress; *dol*, a plain; *bryn*, a ridge; *rhos*, a moor; *craig*, a rock; *tor*, a projecting rock; *ard*, high or great; *cwm*, a valley, or cup-shaped depression; *llwch*, a lake or morass; *tre*, a place or dwelling; *llan*, an enclosure; *man*, a district, and *nant*, a valley. These and others enter into a large number of names. In fact, as Mr. Taylor says ('Words and Places,' p. 256), 'Over the whole land almost every river name is Celtic, most of the shire names contain Celtic roots, and a sprinkling of names of hills, valleys, and fortresses bears witness that the Celt was the aboriginal possessor of the soil.' When the Anglo-Saxons overran the country, they gave names of their own to their settlements, or added something to the Celtic names already existing. Most of these affixes have the meaning of enclosure or dwelling. The following are to be found—sometimes disguised by alterations of spelling—in many modern names. Wherever they are so found they are indicative of Anglo-Saxon origin:—ton, ham, wick, stead, set, worth, hay, cote, sal, fold.

Danish and Norwegian affixes came later. The following are all Norse affixes, and have the same general meaning as the Anglo-Saxon words just quoted:—Byr, by, thorp, loft, thwaite, will, garth, beck, haugh, nith, tan, dale, fell, and holm. Where these words form part of a name, it is evidence that the place was a Danish settlement.

In Celtic compound words the noun is generally placed first; the *adjective following*. The word *dun*, for instance, means a hill fortress, and we find it in such names as Dunmow, Dunstable, Dunkeld, and Dunleary. When the Saxons came they frequently retained the word *dun* in its original sense, but removing the Celtic adjectival suffix, placed an adjective of their own, according to the genius of their language, *before the noun*, and in this way obtained the names Huntingdon, Farringdon, Croydon, Clarendon, and numerous others.

Ford, in the names of the many hundreds of places in which it occurs, always signifies a passage (ford) across a stream. *Gate* always means passage, as in *Reigate,* the passage through the Surrey hills. Gatton in the same locality is Gatetown. Ramsgate, Margate, Sandgate, Westgate, and Kingsgate are all near passages through the Kentish cliffs.

Bury as a suffix always means an enclosed or fortified camp. The word seems to have been used in this sense by Celts, Saxons, and Danes. There are hundreds of names of English places having this termination. In one county alone, *Wiltshire,* Camden enumerates no fewer than thirty-two as follows:—Chisbury, Boadbury, Abury, Yanesbury, Ambresbury, Selbury, Sidbury, Badbury, Wanbury, Woodbury, Barbury, Oldbury, Rybury, Westbury, Battlesbury, Avesbury, Heytesbury, Scratchbury, Waldsbury, Bilbury, Winklebury, Cliselbury, Clerebury, Whichbury, Frippsbury, Ogbury, Malmesbury, Salisbury, Ramesbury, Titsbury, and Marlbury or Marlboro'.

The Romans have left few traces of their rule in the names of places. The great roads—*strata*—which they left, gave the root of the Anglo-Saxon *street,* and this word, or some of its corruptions, is found in the names of many places lying on the lines these roads took. Such names as Stretton, Stratton, Streatham, Streatley, Streetley, Stretford, Stratford, Ardwick-le-Street, and Chester-le-Street, are only found on the lines of some of the Roman roads.

The Latin name *castra,* in some of its many modifications in modern names, always denotes the site of a Roman station. The Saxons, in adopting the word, altered it to *chester,* and the Anglians and Danes to *caster,* whilst in Mercia, which, although Anglian, was greatly modified by Saxon elements, the intermediate word *cester* is adopted. Thus in Essex, Kent, Sussex, and Wessex we have Colchester, Rochester, Chichester, and Winchester; in East Anglia and in Danish districts, Tadcaster, Lancaster, Caistor, Doncaster, Brancaster, and Alcaster; whilst in Mercia we find the *h* dropped, and a tendency to still further elision, as in Leicester, Worcester, Gloucester, Bicester and Towcester, in all of which *cester* is *in pronunciation* abbreviated to *ster.*

Towards the Welsh frontier *castra* is still further contracted, and appears in the form *caer,* which, in the Celtic fashion of placing the noun first, becomes a prefix; hence the names Caerleon, Caergai, Caergwyle, Caersws, Caerwent, Caerphilly, and Caerwis.

Many names are compounds of two or three roots from as many separate languages. The original settlers gave the place a name descriptive of its features. In process of time this name lost its significance as a *word*, and as language changed by conquest another *word* was added, also descriptive, and this process of super-addition can be traced, giving rise to some curious compounds. 'In the name Wansbeckwater, for instance, we first find *wan*, which is a slightly corrupted form of the Welsh *afon*; the *s* is probably a vestige of the Gaelic *uisge*; the Teutonic *beck* was added by the Anglian colonists, and the English word *water* was suffixed when the meaning of *Wansbeck* had become obscure, and *Wansbeckwater*, or Riverwaterriverwater is the curious agglomeration which has resulted.'—*Words and Places*, p. 222.

In the name of Brindon Hill we have first the Cymric *bryn*, a hill, then the Celto-Saxon *dun*, which is almost synonymous, and finally the English word *hill*, so that the name is compounded of the word hill repeated three times in different languages. Pendlehill, in Lancashire, is compounded also of three synonymous words, the Cymric *pen*, the Norse *holl*, and the English *hill*.

Notwithstanding the length to which this article has extended, the subject has, as it were, only been skimmed over. Sufficient, however, it is hoped, has been cited to show how interesting is the study of the origins of local names. Those who desire to study the subject thoroughly will find Mr. Taylor's work ('Words and Places') an invaluable guide and a most interesting book.

Locate. This verb, in the sense of selecting public lands for allotment to settlers in a new country, is generally thought to be a pure Americanism. The earliest known use of the word is, however, English. It occurs in a speech made by Burke in the House of Commons, in 1774, part of which runs thus:—'A peer, who, I think, does not always vote in the majority, made a sort of proposition for an address to the king, that no more lands be *located* in America.'

Locofoco. Lucifer matches are called in America 'locofocoes.' The origin of the term is thus given by Mr. Bartlett, in his 'Glossary':—In 1834, John Marck opened a store in Park Row, New York, and drew public attention to two novelties. One was champagne wine drawn like soda-water from a 'fountain'; the other was a self-lighting cigar, with a match composition on the end. These he called 'Locofoco cigars.' The mode of getting at the name is obvious. The word 'locomotive' was then rather new as applied to an engine on a railroad, and the common notion was that it meant *self-moving*; hence, as these cigars were self-firing, this queer name was coined. His patent for 'self-igniting cigars' bears date April 16th, 1834. The name as applied to a political party in America originated in 1835, at a stormy political meeting at Tammany Hall. During the confusion, the gaslights were suddenly turned out. 'The Equal Rights' party, having received information that such would be the course of their opponents, had provided themselves with *locofoco* matches and candles, and the hall was re-lighted in a moment. The 'Courier and Enquirer' newspaper dubbed the anti-monopolists who used the matches with the name of 'Locofoco,' which the Democratic party has borne ever since.—Hammond, *Political History of New York*, vol. ii. p. 491.

Locomotive Engine. The first practical application of the steam-engine as a locomotive power took place in 1804, on a railroad at Merthyr Tydvil in South Wales. The engine was constructed by Messrs. Trevithick and Vivian, under a patent obtained by them two years previously. This engine in several respects resembled in its form and structure those which have since been used for a like purpose.—*Brand's Dictionary*, vol. ii. p. 387.

Locum tenens, a Latin phrase; literally, 'holding the place.' It is exactly equivalent to the French *lieutenant*, and is generally applied to one temporarily occupying the place or doing the duty of another. See LIEUTENANT.

Locusts and Wild Honey. The 'locusts' on which we are told John the Baptist fed were probably not the insects so called, but the leguminous fruit of the Carob-tree (*Ceratonia siliquia*), the dried pods of which are the 'locust beans' sold in the shops as food for cattle. The Carob-tree is sometimes called the Honey-tree, from the sweet pulp contained in its pods while they are fresh.

Lollard. A name given to the followers of Wycliff by the priests, 'who thereby intimated that these Wycliffites who had dared to read and interpret the Bible for themselves were "lollards," *i.e.* spouters, talkative, uneducated men.' The Lollards' Tower in Lambeth Palace has an apartment in which eight 'Lollards' were imprisoned. It is a room about fifteen feet by eleven, and there are still eight massive iron rings in the walls, to which the men were chained. Probably the word is a corruption of *lolium*, an old name for tares. Gregory XI., in one of his bulls against Wycliff, urges his clergy to endeavour to extirpate this *lolium.*

London. The origin of this name cannot be ascertained with any certainty. Its most probable derivation is from *Llyn-Din,* the 'town on the lake.' It was the capital of the Saxon kingdom of Essex, and was known in the time of the Heptarchy as *Lundenceaster.*

London City Wall. The City wall commenced at a fort near the Tower, passed along by the Minories to the Old Gate (Aldgate), then by Bishopsgate and Aldermanbury Postern to Cripplegate; thence passing the Barbican to Aldersgate, and from thence by Newgate and Ludgate to the Thames, where it was completed by another fort. Its length was somewhat more than a mile, and the space enclosed about 640 acres.

Long Acre. Mr. Rimbault says that 'Long Acre, in Henry VIII.'s time, was an open field called "The Elms," from a line of those trees growing upon it, as shown in Aggas's plan. It was next called "Leven Acres," and since 1612, from the length of a certain slip of ground then first used as a pathway, "*Long Acre.*"'—*Notes and Queries,* December 1864.

Long-bow. The long-bow was a powerful bow used by soldiers before the introduction of gunpowder. 'To draw the long-bow' was formerly a term applied when one boasted of his skill or strength as an archer, not always truthfully, but as a vain-glorious soldier might after the wars. It is now applied, in general terms, to notorious liars, who are said to 'draw the long bow.'

Long Vacation. The Long Vacation is a relic of Norman usages in the English Courts. The time of the long vacation in Normandy was adapted to the season of the vintage, and the same period was fixed in England by the Normans, and has remained unaltered to the present day.

Long Words. The Sanscrit is said to include one word of a hundred and fifty-two syllables. Aristophanes made one, for a special purpose, of seventy-seven; and the Germans have some words frightful to look at from their length. The English is, from its terse and concise nature, free from these monstrosities; but even in English we are sometimes startled by huge compounds, such as Miss Burney's 'the-sudden-at-the-moment-though-from-lingering-illness-often-previously-expected death of Mr. Burney's wife.'—*De Vere.*

Looked. In such phrases as 'Miss Jones looked beautifully';

'The trees looked splendidly'; 'Everything was well arranged, and the park looked magnificently,' the adverbial form is improper. The verb 'to look' in all these cases is strictly neuter, and means 'to appear,' 'to be,' 'to seem.' It does not mean looking 'with' the eye, but appearing 'to' the eye; and consequently the formation of the sentences is ungrammatical. Their absurdity will be clearly seen by using other verbs; as, Miss Jones *is* beautifully; the trees *are* splendidly; the park *seemed* magnificently.

Loom is from the Anglo-Saxon *geloma*, utensils, and formerly signified any domestic utensil. We still retain this meaning in the word heir-*loom*. The word has been stated to be derived from the name of Sir Thomas Lomb, who put up the first machine for weaving raw silk, in Derby, 1725. This, however, must be erroneous, for Matthew Prior, who died in 1721, has the line :—

A thousand maidens ply the purple *loom*.

See HEIR-LOOM.

Loose, and Unloose. Johnson says that unloose is 'a word perhaps barbarous and ungrammatical, the particle prefixed implying negation.' The two forms have, however, been in use from the Anglo-Saxon times, the original words having been *lesan* and *unlesan*, both meaning the same.

Loot. This is an East Indian word signifying plunder, robbery, pillage, &c. It was introduced into the English language at the time of the Mutiny, 1857-8.

Lorcha. This is the Chinese name for a peculiar kind of sailing vessel. Mr. Cobden, February 26, 1856, said, in the House of Commons, 'Lorcha is a name which the Chinese derived from the Portuguese, at their settlement at Macao on the mouth of the Canton river, opposite to where Hong-Kong lies. The word merely means that it is built after the European model.' The Chinese word is probably a corruption of the Portuguese *laucha*, a launch or pinnace.

Lord. In the English Bible, the word 'Lord,' when printed in capital letters—thus, LORD—means Jehovah, or God. When printed in ordinary type, it means simply a lord or master.

Lord, Lady. Lord is derived from the Anglo-Saxon *hlaf* and *ord*; but etymologists disagree as to the meaning of *hlaf*. Some think that *hlaf* or *laf* is loaf, and *ord*, origin or source, making *hlaford*, one who is the origin of or *affords* bread for his household.

Others adopt Horne Tooke's opinion that *hlaf* is the past participle of *hlifian*, to lift, and as *ord* is source or origin, that *hlaford* means high-born, or of exalted [lifted] origin. The same difference of opinion exists with respect to the word lady, one party thinking it is *hlafdian*, the dispenser of bread, the other, following Horne Tooke, that it is from *hlifian*, one *lifted*, or raised, to the rank of her husband or lord. Although the bread-dispensing origin has been generally adopted from the time of Verstegan (1605), it is now giving way in favour of Horne Tooke's far more probable derivation. See LOAF.

Lord Byron's First Letter. In the library of Trinity College is the original letter of which the following is a copy. It is written in a schoolboy's hand, upon pencil lines partially obliterated :—

'DEAR MADAM,

My Mamma being unable to write herself desires I will let you know that the potatoes are now ready and you are welcome to them whenever you please.

She begs you will ask Mrs. Parkyns if she would wish the poney to go round by Nottingham, or to go home the nearest way, as it is *now* quite well, but too small to carry me.

I have sent a young Rabbit which I beg Miss Frances will accept off [sic] and which I promised to send before. My Mamma desires her best compliments to you all, in which I join. I am,

Dear Aunt,

Yours sincerely,

Newstead Abbey, Nov. 8. 1798. 'BYRON.

I hope you will excuse all blunders, as it is the first letter I ever wrote.'

Lord Mayor of London. The first Mayor of London was Henry Fitz Alwhyn, who was appointed in 1189, and held office during twenty-four years. The prefix 'Right Honourable' and the title 'Lord Mayor' were granted by Edward III., in 1354. The first 'Lord Mayor' was Thomas Legge, ancestor of the Earl of Dartmouth; the first show was in 1453. The Lord Mayor is not a Privy Councillor, although he is always styled Right Honourable. He is, however, always summoned to the Privy Council held on the death of the Sovereign. In the City he takes precedence of all others except the Sovereign, not even excepting the Prince of Wales. He has the right of private audience of the Sovereign.

Lord Mayor of York. York is the only city in England, besides London, whose Mayor is called *Lord* Mayor. The title was conferred by Richard II., in 1389. On the occasion of a visit to York in that year, the King took his sword from his side, and handed it to William de Selby, the Mayor, to carry before him, at the same time calling him 'Lord' Mayor. By ancient, and indeed immemorial, custom, the wives of the Lord Mayors of York are not only entitled 'Lady' during their husband's tenure of office, but are privileged to retain that title before their surnames during life. There is a old couplet current which says:—

> The Mayor is a Lord for a year and a day,
> But his wife is a Lady for ever and aye.

The custom of retaining the title is not in modern times usually kept up.

Lord's Prayer. In this beautiful prayer the words are nearly all of Anglo-Saxon origin. In the first edition (1611) of the Authorised Version of the Bible the words *debts* and *debters* stood where we now find 'trespasses' and 'trespass.' Before that alteration there was but one word of Latin origin in the prayer—*temptation*; there are now, of course, three. It will be well if in course of time some word will be hit upon which will restore to us the simple grandeur of the pure Anglo-Saxon 'forgyf ús úre *gyltas*, swa swa we forgifath úrum *gyltendum*.'

Losing a ship for a hap'orth of tar. This phrase does not apply to a ship at all. It refers to *sheep*, which word is generally pronounced 'ship' by rustics. The reference is to marking a sheep with its owner's initials in hot tar. To lose a sheep through its not being marked is losing it for the want of a hap'orth of tar.

Lottery. The earliest known lottery was drawn at Bruges, February 24th, 1446. The last State lottery in England was drawn on the 18th of October, 1826, at Coopers' Hall, in Basinghall Street.

Low Dresses. 'Queen Isabella of Bavaria, as remarkable for her gallantry as the fairness of her complexion, introduced the fashion of leaving the shoulders and part of the neck uncovered.' *I. D'Israeli, Curiosities of Lit.*, vol. i. p. 29.

Lowther Arcade. This Arcade was named after Lord Lowther, who was Chief Commissioner of Woods and Forests at the time when the extensive alterations took place at Charing Cross, and the Arcade was built.

Loyalty. 'The word loyalty, which is derived from the French *loi*, law, expresses properly that fidelity which one owes according to *law*, and does not necessarily include that attachment to the royal person which, happily, we in England have been able further to throw into the word.'—*Trench.*

Lucifer Matches. Mr. Isaac Holden, in his evidence before the Patent Committee in London, said that he was in the habit of rising at four o'clock in the morning to commence his studies, and that he found it tedious and troublesome to obtain a light by the then ordinary method with tinder, flint, and steel. Like other chemists, he knew the explosive material for producing instantaneous light, but he found it difficult to communicate that light to wood. In a fortunate moment the idea of placing sulphur next the wood occurred to him, which he tried satisfactorily, and soon after exhibited the experiment in a lecture at a large school. 'One of the pupils communicated the result of the experiment to his father, a London chemist, and in a short time lucifer matches were in general use.'—*Notes and Queries*, January 1872. This was about the year 1833. What were called phosphorus boxes were obtainable a few years before that date, but they were very costly and uncertain in use. Before that time fire was produced by striking sparks from steel with a flint stone. The sparks fell upon tinder or partially burnt linen rags, and flame was obtained by touching the ignited tinder with matches tipped with sulphur. 'Lucifer' is one of the names applied to Satan. It is singularly applicable to its modern use as a name for matches. It is derived from the Latin *lux, lucis*, light, and *fero*, to bring.

Lucubration is from the Latin *lucubratio*. However loosely this word may be used by modern writers, its literal meaning is study by candlelight, or a writing or composition prepared by night. What a man writes or thinks in the daytime is not a 'lucubration.'

Lukewarm. The prefix 'luke' in this word is derived from a Celtic root which is variously spelt *lieh, liegh, leath, leth*. It signifies half or partly. In Welsh llug-dwym and llug-oer both mean lukewarm, but the *form* of the first is 'half-warm' and of the second 'half-cold' (*twym*, hot, *oer*, cold).

Lumber. The Lombards were the original pawnbrokers, and the apartment where the pledges were kept was the *Lombard* or *Lumber*-room. Hence miscellaneous articles of furniture and clothing placed together in a lump or heap are called lumber.—*Trench.*

Mr. Wedgwood, however, in his 'Dictionary of English Etymology,' ridicules the derivation of the word from 'lumbar,' a pawnbroker's shop or warehouse, and contends that it is from a root signifying *impediment*, anything that hinders, and creates noise and heaviness. He quotes Cowper's 'John Gilpin':—

> The postboy's horse right glad to miss
> The *lumbering* of the wheels.

From which he argues that lumber is anything which makes one stumble or is an impediment to free motion. Probably both derivations are right. There are evidently two words 'lumber' alike in spelling and sound, but of totally different signification. A man or horse may have a heavy lumbering gait, and so far Mr. Wedgwood is unquestionably right; but this does not appear to have any affinity with the word lumber as applied to a lot of old-fashioned and disused furniture or other matters stowed away in a garret.

Luncheon. 'Instead of "luncheon," or "lunch," our country people in Hampshire, as in many other parts, always use the form *nuncheon* or *nuntion*. In Howell's "Vocabulary" (1659), and in Cotgrave's "French and Spanish Dictionary," both words occur; *nuncheon* or *nuncion*, the afternoon repast, and *lunchion*, a big piece, i.e. of bread; both give the old French *caribot* as the equivalent of *luncheon*, which word has this meaning. It is clear that in this sense of *lump*, or *big piece*, Gay uses *luncheon*.'—*Trench*.

Luscious, corrupted from 'delicious,' which in old times was shortened to ''licious.'

> Good drynk thereto, *lycyus* and fine.—*Reliq. Antiq.* p. 30.

Lutestring. A fashionable kind of silk is known by this name, but improperly so. The correct name is 'lustring,' in allusion to the *lustre* or glossy appearance of its surface.

Luther's Hymn. The original source of the so-called 'Luther's Hymn'—'Great God! what do I see and hear?'—is Jacobi's translation of Ringualdi's German hymn on the Last Judgment—''Tis sure that awful time will come.'—*Jacobi's Psalmodia Germanica*, 1722.

Lynch-law. This term is said to be derived from the name of a Virginian farmer, who, having caught a thief, instead of delivering him to the officers of the law, tied him to a tree and flogged him with his own hands.—*Brand*. The word is now in common use in America as a term for the rough justice of a mob, substituted for the regular operations of law.

Lyrical Poetry was, among the ancients, poetry to be sung to the accompaniment of the lyre or harp. In modern usage the term 'lyrical' is confined to songs relating to feelings or emotions, as distinct from descriptive songs. For instance, 'The Bay of Biscay' is a song, but not a 'lyric,' whilst Burns's 'Highland Mary' is one of the most exquisite of modern purely 'lyrical' poems.

M

Macadamised Roads were devised by an Ayrshire road surveyor named MacAdam, who adopted them first in that county, and from whom they received their name. He published an essay on the subject in 1819. He was appointed surveyor-general of the metropolitan roads in 1827, and received a Government grant of 10,000*l*. for his discovery.

Macaulay's 'History of England.' It is not generally known that there have been two distinct persons named Macaulay, who have each written a History of England. The first was Mrs. Catherine Macaulay, the wife of a London physician, who published between 1763 and 1771 'The History of England from the Accession of James I. to the Elevation of the House of Hanover.' The History was published in five quarto volumes, and was very popular, owing perhaps to its violently republican tone. It is now little thought of. Of Lord Macaulay's History it is needless to speak.

Macaulay's New Zealander. Perhaps no passage of Macaulay's writings has been so frequently quoted or alluded to as that in which he pictures some future traveller from New Zealand sitting on a broken arch of London Bridge, sketching the ruins of St. Paul's. Consciously, or unconsciously, the sentence is a reproduction of similar passages by two previous writers, Walpole and Mrs. Barbauld. In a letter written by Horace Walpole to Sir Horace Mann, November 24, 1774, is the following passage:—
'The next Augustine Age will dawn on the other side of the Atlantic. There will perhaps be a Thucydides at Boston, a Xenophon at New York; and, in time, a Virgil at Mexico, and a Newton at Peru. At last some curious traveller from Lima will visit England, and give a description of the ruins of St. Paul's.'
'Mrs. Barbauld wrote a poem in heroic rhyme, which she entitled

"1811." In it she prophesies that at some future day a traveller from the antipodes will, from a broken arch on Blackfriars Bridge, contemplate the ruins of St. Paul's.'—*Old and New London,* vol. v. p. 488.

Macduff. There was an ancient law in force in Scotland, by the provisions of which any person who could prove kindred with the Macduffs, the Earls of Fife, no matter how remote, enjoyed immunity from punishment for the crime of homicide. Macduff's Cross stood on the boundary between Fife and Strathearn, and any homicide who could establish clanship, and could reach this cross before capture, was 'free of the slaughter committed by him,' but had to pay to his chief 'nine kye and a kolpindash' (nine cows and a calf).

Mackerel. 'Mackled' is an old English word for spotted or speckled, hence 'mackerel' is the name of the speckled fish, and hence also the phrase 'a mackerel sky.'

Madam. 'The title of "Madam" is given in Charleston and the South of the United States generally to a mother whose son has married. The daughter-in-law then becomes "Mrs." By this means they avoid the inelegant phraseology of "old Mrs. A.," or the Scotch "Mrs. A., senior." '—*Sir Charles Lyell, Second Visit,* ch. ix.

Mad as a hatter. In the Anglo-Saxon the word 'mad' was used as a synonym for violent, furious, angry, or venomous. In some parts of England, and in the United States particularly, it is still used in this sense. *Atter* was the Anglo-Saxon name for an adder, or viper. The proverbial saying has therefore probably no reference to hat-makers, but merely means 'as venomous as an adder.' The Germans call the viper *Natter.*

Mad as a March hare. 'March hare is *marsh* hare. Hares are wilder in marshes than elsewhere, because of their greater flatness, and the absence of hedges and cover.'—*Apophthegmes of Erasmus,* 1542, reprint, p. 266.

Maen, in local Welsh names, means a stone; as in *Pen-maen-mawr,* which means the large—*mawr,* stone—*maen,* at the summit of a hill or mountain—*pen.*

Magazine. The original idea of a magazine to be periodically published was that it should be a receptacle for selections from the newspapers, which were to be received as into a storehouse or *magazine,* and thus redeemed from the ephemeral destiny to which the remaining matters of the public journals were condemned.

Thus the earlier volumes of the 'Gentleman's Magazine,' which originated in 1731, are full of chronicles of homely and simple matters, which, not being recorded elsewhere, are now a mine of wealth to those fond of research. The word magazine is a slightly altered form of the Arabic *maghazin*, or storehouse.

Magnet. 'The word magnet is derived from the name of the city of Magnesia, in Asia Minor, where the properties of the loadstone are said to have been discovered.' So far one authority; another derives it from the name of 'Magnes, a shepherd, who is said to have discovered the magnetic power through being detained on Mount Ida by the magnetism of the mountain attracting the nails in his shoes, so that he was unable to move from the spot.'

Magnolia. This beautiful flower was so named after Pierre Magnol, who was Professor of Botany at Montpellier in the seventeenth century.

Magpie. This is an abbreviation of the old name *magot-pie*. Nares thinks magot came from the French *magot*, a monkey, because the bird chatters and plays droll tricks like a monkey.—*Glossary*, p. 304. Shakespeare has:—

> Augurs and understood relations have
> By *magot-pies* and choughs and rooks brought forth
> The secret'st man of blood.—*Macbeth*, iii. 4.

Minshew and Cotgrave have it ' maggatapie.'

Mahogany. The 'Gentleman's Magazine,' September 1874, says that this wood was first brought as ballast by a West Indian captain named Gibbons, who gave some to his brother, a physician in Covent Garden. The first to use it was Woollaston, a cabinet maker in Long Acre, who made a bureau for Dr. Gibbons, which, being seen and admired by the Duchess of Buckingham, brought the new wood into fashion.

Maiden Assize formerly meant an assize where no criminal was left for execution. The judges were entitled to white gloves on these occasions. The phrase, in modern times, has come to signify an assize, or a session, where there are no prisoners to try.

Maidstone was anciently called *Medwegston*, the town on the Medway.

Mail Coaches. Up to 1784 the mails were carried by post-boys on horseback at an average speed of four to five miles an hour. On the 2nd of August in that year the first journey of a mail coach was made from London to Bristol. The change was so beneficial that the new system became general, and remained in vogue until the introduction of railways. At the present day the drivers of mail carts are forbidden to carry passengers, and the vehicles are by law required to be made with no seat, except that for the driver. Before the introduction of railways, two hundred horses were necessary to perform the journey of the mail from London to Edinburgh, the time required being forty-three hours, and relays of horses being required at every eight miles. See MALE.

Main-brace. The main-brace is the rope by which the mainsail of a ship is placed in position. To splice it is to join it when broken or repair it when injured. Hence the expression 'to splice the main-brace' is proverbial amongst seamen for taking a drink of strong liquor to strengthen or fit them for extra exertion, or to enable them to bear up against exposure to cold or wet weather.

Majesty. This title was assumed by Henry VIII., but it does not appear to have superseded the earlier titles borne by English kings. Froude (vol. iii. p. 53) quotes, from a letter written on behalf of Henry by Starkey to Cardinal Pole, the following passage, in which the three titles 'Grace,' 'Highness,' and 'Majesty' are all used to designate Henry:—'*His Grace* supposed his benefits not forgotten, and Pole's love towards *his Highness* not utterly quenched. *His Majesty* was one that forgave and forgot displeasure both at once.'

Make the Door. Shakespeare ('As You Like It,' iv. 1) has 'Make the doors upon a woman's wit, and it will out at the casement'; and in the 'Comedy of Errors' (iii. 1), 'Why, at this hour the doors are made against you.' The expression 'make the door,' though incomprehensible to a Londoner, is always used in Warwickshire and Staffordshire in the sense of fasten it. Many Anglo-Saxon words and phrases are retained in the Midlands. For example, before retiring for the night the mistress of a house will sometimes give directions to the servant to 'make the door, dout [do out] the candle, and rake the fire'; the latter operation being performed by putting thereon a lump of coal sufficiently large to keep burning till the morning.

Making a Bed. Mr. Wright, in his 'Domestic Manners of the Middle Ages,' says that in the fourteenth century 'People had few spare chambers, especially furnished ones, and in the simplicity of mediæval manners guests were obliged either to sleep in the same room as the family, or more usually in the hall, where beds were made for them on the floor or on the benches. " Making a bed " was a phrase true in its literal sense, and the bed when made consisted of a heap of straw with a sheet or two thrown over it.'

Malakoff. The Malakoff, near Sebastopol, which was so hotly contested in the Crimean war, was so called from the name of an innkeeper who built a liquor shop on the hill, in 1831. His house was 'Malakoff's inn,' and the suburb which arose also received the name, which has since become historical.

Male. This word formerly meant a bag or portmanteau in which travellers on horseback carried their luggage. The male was usually fastened to the crupper-strap. Chaucer mentions that one of his Pilgrims had one, but that it contained so little luggage that he had doubled it (*tweyfold*) :—

> A male tweyfold on his croper lay,
> It seemed that he caried litel away.

Bailey says that the word male was derived from a Greek word for a fleece, because these bags were made of wool. He defines it to be 'a sack or budget to carry letters, &c., in on a journey.' This may have been the origin of the mail bag of the Post Office.

Malmsey. This wine was so called from its having originally been made at Malvasia, in the Morea. It is a strong and fine-flavoured sweet wine made in Madeira of grapes which have been allowed to shrivel on the vine. It is of a deep golden hue, and contains about 16 to 17 per cent. of alcohol.—*Brand.*

Malvern. This name is not from *moel-y-barn*, the bare hill of council; but from *moel-hafren*, the bare hill by the Hafren—now the Severn.

Mammoth. Probably a corruption of Behemoth (Job xl. 15).

Manchester. This name is derived from the Celtic *maen*, a stone or rock, and the Anglo-Saxon *ceastre* or *chester*, a castle or fortification. The name signifies ' the fortified rock.'

Mandamus is a writ issuing from the Court of Queen's Bench, commanding (*mandamus*) some public body, or inferior Court, to do something which they have refused or neglected to perform.

Mandarin. This is not a Chinese term. It was first applied by the Portuguese to Chinese officials, and from them spread over

Europe, under the belief that it was a native word. It is from the Portuguese *mandar*, to hold authority, to govern; mediæval Latin, *mandaria*, dominion.

Mangel Wurzel, from the German *mangel*, scarcity, and *wurzel*, a root. So called because formerly used as a substitute for bread in times of scarcity.—*Baird*.

Manna. Dr. Adam Clarke, in reference to the word *manna* in the verse Exodus xvi. 15, says, ' This is a most strange and unfortunate translation of the original *man-hu*, which literally signifies " What is this ? " for, says the text, " they knew not what it was," and therefore they could not give it a name.'

Man-of-war is a phrase applied to a line of battle ship, contrary to the usual rule in the English language by which all ships are feminine. It probably arose in the following manner :—' Men of war ' were heavy armed soldiers. A ship full of them would be called a ' man-of-war ship.' In process of time the word ' ship ' was discarded as unnecessary, and there remained the phrase 'a man-of-war.'—*Talbot*.

Mansard Roofs are so named from their inventor, Francis Mansart, a French architect of the seventeenth century. Mansard roofs are constructed with a break, or shoulder, in the slope, so that each side consists of two distinct slopes or planes, the lower of which is much steeper than the upper. This arrangements gives more space in the roof for living rooms than where only one slope exists.

Mansion House. The architect of the Mansion House was named Dance. The first stone was laid by Perry, who was Lord Mayor in 1739. The first to inhabit it was Sir Crisp Gascoigne, who was Lord Mayor in 1753. It was built on the site of an old market called the Stocks Market. This market was removed, in 1737, to Farringdon Street, and from that time was called the Fleet Market. The old Mansion House in Cheapside, near Bucklersbury, is now occupied as a toy-warehouse.

Mantel-piece. The original use of mantel-pieces is thus described in the ' Memoirs of the Life and Adventures of Colonel Maceroni, late Aide-de-Camp to Joachim Murat, King of Naples,' London, 1838 :—' Around the spacious cupola over the Italian fire-places is a ledge to which are affixed pegs on which the postillions hung their wet clothes to dry. We call the shelves over our fire-places " mantel-pieces," but we no longer hang our mantles upon them to dry. In some of the old palaces of Rome I have seen mantelpieces applied to a similar purpose.'

Man Traps and Spring Guns. In the early part of the present century it was customary in lonely parts of the country to set traps and guns around dwelling-houses to deter burglars. The inscription, 'Man traps set on these grounds,' much defaced, may even now occasionally be met with. An Act of Parliament in 1827 (7 & 8 Geo. IV. c. 18) made the setting of such engines a misdemeanour.

Manure. This word was formerly of very wide significance. Derived from the French *manœuvrer*, it originally meant any kind of manual labour, but was particularly applied to the cultivation of the soil. Richardson, in his Dictionary, quotes from Smith:—
' The commonwealth or policy of England is governed, administered, and *manured* by three sorts of people.'

'**Man wants but little,**' &c. Young, in his ' Night Thoughts,' Night IV., says :—
>Man wants but little, nor that little long.

Goldsmith, two generations later, has :—
>Man wants but little here below,
>Nor wants that little long.—*Edwin and Angelina.*

Maps are said to have been introduced into England in the year 1489 by Bartholomew, the brother of Christopher Columbus.

Marabou Feathers are the delicate white feathers from beneath the wing of the Marabou stork (*Leptoptilus marabou*), a native of West Africa.

Marauder. Between Aachen [Aix-la-Chapelle] and Cologne there is a very extensive wood, in which is a château called *Merode*, formerly quite concealed from the road by the forest. At one time its owner was a brigand, and he and his retainers were known as *meroders*. It is probable that the word marauder is corrupted from the name of the place of their abode. Some, however, derive it from the French *maraud*, a tom-cat.

Marbles. These boyish playthings had their origin in an imitation of bowls. ' Bowls' were formerly made of marble, and other smooth and hard stones ; hence the name ' marbles ' for the juvenile imitation.

March. The verb 'to march' is probably derived from the Celtic *marc*, Welch *march*, a horse. To march, if this derivation be correct, was originally to ride on horseback.

Marigold. The French call this flower *souci*, which is a curious name for so cheerful, bright-looking a flower. It was, however, in old French, spelled *soulsi*, which throws light on its derivation. It is abbreviated from its full name *solsequieum*, the sun-follower.

Mariner's Compass. The invention of the compass is generally attributed to Flavio Gioïa, an Italian, in the year 1302. There is reason, however, for believing that it was in use at least a century before. A French poet, named Guyot de Provins, in a satirical poem written in 1205, in speaking of the Pope, uses words to the following effect :—' I wish he resembled the star which never moves. The mariners take it for their guide, observe it carefully, and direct their way by it. They call it the polar star. They have a contrivance which never deceives them through the qualities of the magnet. They stick the needle into a straw, which they put into water, the straw causing it to swim. Then the point turns directly towards the star with such certainty that it will never fail, and no mariner will have any doubt of it.' Mr. T. Wright has also discovered a manuscript by Neckham, of the date 1217, showing that the compass, with the needle moving on a pivot, as at present, was in common use at that period. The Chinese claim that they were acquainted with the properties of the compass in the year 2634 B.C. They certainly used it at sea A.D. 300, long before it was known in Europe. It is thought to have been made known in Europe by Marco Polo, on his return from Cathay in the thirteenth century.

Mark % for Per Cent. Many speculations have been made as to the origin of this mark, but none seems to be so feasible as the following. If it be granted that the figures '00' designate *centum* or hundred, which they certainly do, as the figures 1, 2, and 3 placed before them only signify the number of hundreds, as 1 hundred, 2 hundreds, and so on; and if it be remembered that one of the meanings of *per* is 'through,' then the diagonal line drawn *through* or between the two ciphers will give us the exact meaning of the symbol %—a line drawn *through*, or 'per,' '00' (centum).

Marmalade. This word, which means quince jam, comes to us from the Portuguese *marmelada*, from *marmelo*, a quince. The modern conserve called marmalade is not necessarily made from quinces, as the name suggests, but is also made from oranges, apricots, greengage plums, and other luscious fruits.

A A

Marriage. Formerly marriages took place at the doors of churches. Chaucer, in 'The Wife of Bath,' says,—

> She was a worthy woman all her live,
> Husbands at the church dore she had five.

A manuscript quoted in 'The History of Shrewsbury,' 1779, says 'the Pride of the Clergy and the Bigotry of the Laity were such that both rich and poor were married at the church doors.' An Act of Parliament in the reign of Edward VI. first authorized the solemnization of marriages within the body of the church, 'standing no longer as formerly at the door.' Before the passing of the Act of George II. the law relating to marriages in England was the old law of Christendom, the simple contract law, as it is now in Scotland. An 'Encyclopædia' published in 1744, speaking of marriages without the sanction of the Church, says, 'But marriages without this sanction are not therefore null and void, but are only esteemed irregular.' 'When it is vulgarly said that first cousins may marry, but second cousins cannot, probably this arose by confounding the canon and the civil law; for first cousins may marry by the civil law, and second cousins cannot by the canon law; but now, by statute, it is clear that both first and second cousins may marry.'—*Burn*.

Marry. This word, used as an expletive, was probably derived from the ancient practice of swearing by the Virgin Mary. In Foxe's 'Martyrs,' in the examination of John Careles, the term appears in the original form, 'Yea, *Mary*! you say truth.'

Marrying a Woman in her Shift. 'There is a popular belief that a man who marries a woman in debt, absolves himself from all liability if he take her from the hands of the priest clothed only in her shift. It is a vulgar error.'—*Wharton*.

Marseillaise Hymn. Both the words and the music of this celebrated piece were composed by Rouget de Lisle, a French officer of Engineers. It was first produced at the House of Baron Dietrich, in Strasburg, in 1792, under the name of the '*Chant du Départ de l'Armée du Rhin.*' It received its present name from the circumstance of a body of troops from Marseilles singing it with great energy as they marched into Paris, where it was, till then, unknown.

Marsh. From the Gaelic *mar*, or *mare*, a pool; whence marish, or mar'sh, watery or swampy.

Martello Tower. These towers, so familiar to visitors to the

Kentish and Sussex coasts, received their name from a fort in *Mortella* (Myrtle) Bay, Corsica, which, after a most determined resistance, was captured by the British in 1794.

Martinet, a severe disciplinarian. From Colonel *Martinet*, a French military officer in the time of Louis XIV.—*Voltaire.*

Mary-le-bone. The parish of St. Marylebone derives its name from the ancient village of Tyborne, which was situated on the east bank of a brook or bourn, which passed, under various names, from Hampstead to the Thames. When the ancient church of Tyburn was pulled down, the new one was erected on another spot near the brook, and the church received the title of 'St. *Mary at the Bourne.*' From this the present name has been derived. The seal of the parish bears a figure of St. Mary with a stream running beneath her feet.—*Smith's Account of St. Mary le bone*, 1833. The parish of Marylebone is more than twice the size of the City of London, and its population is larger than that of either of the great cities of Madrid, Moscow, Naples, or St. Petersburg.

Marylebone Church. The interior of this church was depicted by Hogarth in 'The Rake's Progress' as the scene of the marriage.

Master Humphrey's Clock. Opposite the principal hotel in the town of Barnard Castle there formerly resided a clockmaker named Humphrey. Dickens stayed at Barnard Castle for some time when collecting materials for 'Nicholas Nickleby,' and became rather intimate with the clockmaker. A large clock-face surmounted the shop window, and this suggested the title for Dickens's next work. Dr. Rogers, in a letter to 'Notes and Queries' in 1870, says that, in a conversation he had with Humphrey, 'the worthy horologist entered into particulars, and said, "My clock suggested to Mr. Dickens the title of his book of that name, and I have a letter from him stating this, and a copy of the book inscribed with his own name.'

Masterly inactivity. This phrase was first used by Sir James Mackintosh in 'Vindiciæ Gallicæ,' p. 91. The words are, 'The Commons, faithful to their system, remained in a wise and masterly inactivity, which tacitly reproached the arrogant assumption of the nobles, whilst it left no pretext to calumniate their own conduct.'

Mastiff. Marrwood, in his 'Lawes of the Forest,' published in

1598, says, 'In the old British speech they doe call him a masethefe, from maze, or amaze, and thief.' It is but right to say that this derivation is not looked upon with much favour by critics.

Math is the modern form of the Anglo-Saxon *mœth*, a mowing. It is now only used in the term aftermath, a second crop of grass cut for hay. Aftermath is, literally, 'after-mowing.'

Maudlin. 'The corrupt appellation of Magdalen, who is drawn by painters with swollen eyes and disordered look.'—*Johnson*. Magdalen College at Oxford is usually called 'Maudlin,' which makes this etymology the more probable.—*Sullivan*.

Maundy Thursday. This is a Roman Catholic festival, and in that church the name originated. The epistle in the Mass of Maundy Thursday is taken from 1 Cor. xi. In the 24th verse are these words: 'Take, eat;' in Latin, '*Accipite et manducate*.' This is believed to be the original of *Maundy*, and the word was certainly used to signify the Last Supper of the Lord. Sir Thomas More, in his 'Answer to the first parte of the poysoned booke which a nameless hereticke hath named the Supper of the Lord,' says, 'In hys seconde parte he treateth of the *maundye* of Christ with hys Apostles upon the *Sheare* Thursday, wherein our Saviour actually dyd institute the blessed Sacrament,' &c.

Mausoleum. This word is derived from the tomb erected at Halicarnassus to Maüsolus, king of Caria, in the year 353 B.C., by his widow Artemisia. It was esteemed one of the wonders of the world. The site has recently been excavated, and many fragments of sculpture—including portions of the statue of Mausolus—have been placed in the British Museum.

Mauther. In Norfolk and Suffolk this word is used by the country people to signify a girl. It is sometimes spelt *modder*, and in speech is occasionally contracted to *mor*, which supports Spelman's view, that Mauther is from the Danish word *moer*. In Ben Jonson's 'Alchemist' (iv. 7), Kastril says to his sister, 'Away; you talk like a foolish *mauther*.' By some of the dictionaries it is erroneously put as a mere vulgarism for 'mother.' This, however, is shown to be wrong by the following quotation from Fraunce's 'Ivychurch,' A 4, *b* :—

> What? will Phillis then consume her youth as an ankresse
> Scorning daintie Venus? Will Phillis still be a *modder*,
> And not care to be called by the dear sweate name of mother?

Bloomfield uses it ('Rural Tales,' 1802, p. 5) where Richard says to Kate,—

> When once a giggling *mauther* you,
> And I a red-faced chubby boy.

Mayduke Cherries are so called from the corrupted name of the place from which they were originally brought—*Medoc* in France.

Mayfair. The district of London which bears this name is so called from a pleasure fair formerly held in the neighbourhood. In the 'Gentleman's Magazine,' April, 1816, a Mr. Sharp gives an interesting account of the fair as he remembered it fifty years before. Duck-hunting, prize-fighting, donkey-racing, bull-baiting, and other brutal practices were among the chief amusements.

Mayor. 'This honourable name of office in the chief and most famous city of our realm is divers waies written. Some write it "major," some "mayor," and some "Maire." And because *major* in Latin signifieth greater or bigger, some, not looking any further, will needs from thence make it Major. But seeing the names of Sheriff and Alderman cannot be drawn from the Latin, why should it be thought that mayor cometh from *major*? Certain it is that as the other names of offices are not derived from the Latin, no more is this. For the etymology thereof we are to note that in our own English to *may* signifieth to have might or power; so a *mayor* is as much as to say a *haver* [possessor] of might, one that hath, and may use, authority.'—*Verstegan's 'Restitution of Decayed Intelligence,'* edit. 1655, p. 254.

Mead. Mead, metheglin, and hydromel were three distinct drinks made from honey. In an old work, 'The Closet of the eminent learned Sir Kenelm Digby, Knt., opened,' 3rd edit., 1677, there are many receipts for making each. *Mead* appears to have been made from honey, water, spices, and bitter herbs. *Metheglin* was composed of honey, water, spices, and sweet herbs—sometimes twenty to forty varieties. *Hydromel* was a compound of honey and water, with a little ginger, cloves, and rosemary, fermented with ale yeast. The compiler of the present work has frequently seen mead made, and has often tasted it. The process of making was this: after the honey had been drained from the comb, the latter was scalded to dissolve any honey that might still adhere. The wax being strained away, the sweetened liquor was strengthened by additional honey until a fresh egg floating in it would show a disc the size of half a crown. This was the test for strength. The liquor was then put into casks with a little yeast, and when fermentation was over, it was corked up.

Mealy-mouthed. A phrase used to denote persons who are habitually soft-spoken, and who, even when provoked, are incapable of harsh or strong expressions. It is generally applied to hypocritical or affected delicacy of speech. The old manner of writing it was meal-mouthed. All the dictionaries derive it from the word 'meal.' Nares says, 'Applied to one whose words are fine and soft as meal, as Minshew well explains it.' It is with far greater probability derived from the Latin *mel* (old English *mell*), honey. From a *mel-y* mouth may well come 'honied' words. Shakespeare has 'honey-mouthed.'

Mean and Means. 'Mean,' without the *s*, is an adjective; as 'He is a very mean man.' 'Means,' with the *s*, is a noun singular, and therefore the phrase 'By this means' is perfectly grammatical. Dr. Campbell, in his 'Philosophy of Rhetoric,' says, 'No person of taste will, I presume, venture so far to violate the present usage, and consequently to shock the ears of the generality of readers, as to say, "By this mean;" "By that mean."'

Meander means winding, as of a stream. The word comes from Meander, a river in Phrygia, noted for its serpentine course. It has three syllables—me-an-der.

Measles. This word originally meant leprosy. It comes from the French *meseau*, or *mesel*, a leper. Chaucer uses *meselrie* for leprosy.

Medal. 'The Roman "medals" were their current coin. When an action deserved to be recorded on a coin, it was stamped and issued out of the mint. "*Medallions*" in respect of the other coins were the same as modern medals in respect of modern money.'—*Addison.*

Mediterranean Sea, from the Latin *medius*, middle, and *terra*, land. So named by the ancients from its being almost encircled by the lands of Europe, Asia, and Africa.

Meeting-house. This term for a place of worship originated with the Puritans in America. In Elliot's 'History of New England' it is stated that 'the religious services of the Plymouth Church were held in the fort, upon the roof or deck of which were mounted the great guns; and it was in 1648 that a meeting-house was built. They held that a church was a body of Christians, and the place where they met was a "meeting-house," and so they called it by that name' (vol. i. p. 131).

Melancholy, from two Greek words signifying *black bile.* The ancients supposed melancholy to arise from a redundancy of black bile—hence the name.

Melody, from a Greek word for a tune to which lyric poetry might be set. A melody is an arrangement for one voice or instrument. Harmony is the concord of several.

Members of Parliament for the City of London have the privilege, on the opening of a new Parliament, of sitting on the right hand, immediately next to the Speaker's chair, in the House of Commons. These are the seats usually occupied by the members of the Cabinet.

Men, Mans. It is singular that there are few persons who are conscious that both these plurals of the word 'man' are in daily use. We say *men,* hors*emen,* country*men,* &c.; but we always say Ger*mans* and Nor*mans*.

Men of Kent and Kentish Men. This distinction is as old as the time of Augustine, who established the bishopric of Rochester. The men of the eastern diocese of Canterbury retained the name of 'Men of Kent.' Those who were included in the West Kentish diocese of Rochester adopted the title 'Kentish men.'

Men of Straw. 'We have all heard of a race of men who used in former days to ply about our own courts of law, and who from their manner of making known their occupation (*i.e.* by a straw in one of their shoes) were recognised by the name of "straw shoes." An advocate or lawyer, who wanted a convenient witness, knew by these signs where to find one, and the colloquy between the parties was brief. "Don't you remember?" said the advocate. (The party looked at the fee, and gave no sign; but the fee increased, and the powers of memory increased with it.) "To be sure I do." "Then come into court and swear it." And straw shoes went into court and swore it.'—*Quarterly Review,* xxxiii. 344.

Mensce. Our ancestors used this word to signify a human being in the abstract. Verstegan says, very sensibly, that 'it is a word of necessary use; as, for example, a man beholding some living thing afar off in the field, not well discerning what it is, will say it is either a man or a beast. Now it may be a woman or child, and so not a man, and so he should speak more properly in saying it is either a *mensce* or a beast,' &c.—*Restitution of Decayed Intelligence,* p. 180.

Merchant Princes. This term originated in the verse Isa. xxiii. 8 : 'Tyre, whose merchants are princes.'

Mercurial. A mercurial person is supposed to derive his restless disposition from the influence of the planet Mercury, which, according to astrologers, was in the ascendant at his birth.

Merino. This is a Spanish word, signifying 'moving from one feeding-ground or pasture to another.' It is applied to a migratory breed of sheep, the wool of which is of remarkably fine texture.

Merrie England. The word 'merrie' in this phrase did not originally mean cheerful or gay, as is commonly supposed. It was anciently *mere*, probably from an Anglo-Saxon adjective meaning excellent, illustrious, famous, or renowned. Hence 'merry men,' in the address of a chief to his followers, meaning not men of mirth, but of renown. Spenser uses the word 'merry' in the sense of excellent or agreeable in the couplet,—

> Then eke my feeble bark awhile may stay,
> Till *merry* wind and weather call her thence away.

Merry Andrew. This name was first applied to a facetious physician named Andrew Borde, who was one of the Court physicians in the time of Henry VIII.

Merry as a Grig. A grig is a grasshopper. The cricket and the grasshopper are in most countries taken as types of a careless, happy existence. We have the related saying, 'Merry as a cricket'; and Tennyson, in 'The Brook,' speaks of—

> High-elbowed *grigs*, that leap in summer grass.

See, however, GRIG.

Mess, as applied to soldiers dining together. This use of the word is derived from the ancient custom of arranging the guests at dinners and great feasts in companies of four, which were called messes. From this custom the word mess came to mean a set of four in other matters. In 'Love's Labour's Lost,' act iv. sc. 3, Biron says, 'I confess that you three fools lacked *me*, fool, to make up the mess'; that is, four. Latimer, in his fifth sermon, says, ' Avarice is the mother ; she brings forth bribe-taking ; and bribe-taking [brings forth] perverting of judgment; there lackes a *fourth* thynge to make upp the *messe*.'

Metaphor, from two Greek words, signifying to 'carry over,' is a figure of speech in which a comparison is implied but not expressed, as 'the *silver* moon.' A 'simile' has the comparison distinctly shown, as ' the moon is bright as silver.'

Methodist. This epithet is not, as is generally supposed, of modern origin. There was a sect called 'Methodists,' founded some thirty or forty years before the Christian era. It lasted more than three hundred years. Many of them were eminent physicians. The name was revived in Cromwell's time, by John Spencer, librarian of Zion College in the City of London, who published a book, in which he employs the word as one commonly in use to designate a certain class of religionists. He asks, 'Where are now our Anabaptists, and plain pack-stuff *Methodists*, who esteem all flowers of rhetoric in sermons no better than stinking weeds?' *Gale, also, in his 'Court of the Gentiles,' published in 1678, speaks of a religious sect called 'the New Methodists'; and Dr. Calamy, in 'The Ejected Ministers,' says that those who stood up for God were called 'Methodists.' This was two generations before Wesley founded the sect now known as 'Wesleyan Methodists.'

Methylated Spirit is a mixture of alcohol, usually called spirits of wine, with ten per cent. of wood spirit or naphtha. The wood spirit renders it unfit for drinking purposes, and as the mixture pays only a small duty, it can be sold for manufacturing purposes —such as making varnishes—at a much lower price than the pure alcohol, whilst it answers the purpose equally well.

Metropolitan Bridges. The toll for passing over bridges within the metropolitan districts was finally abolished on Saturday, June 26, 1880, by the freeing of the bridges at Wandsworth, Putney, and Hammersmith.

Mews. Strictly, cages for birds, but now used to designate stables. 'On the north side of Charing Cross stand the Royal Stables, called, from the original use of the building on their site, the "Mews;" having been used for keeping the king's falcons at least from the time of Richard II.'—*Pennant*.

Mezzotint Engraving was invented by Louis von Siegen, a Dutch artist of German extraction, whose first work was dedicated, in August 1642, to the Landgrave (William VI.) of Hesse Cassel. The invention, on the authority of Evelyn ('Sculptura,' 1662), has been generally attributed to Prince Rupert, but this is proved by an original letter of Siegen's, which is in existence, to be altogether an error. Prince Rupert, there is no doubt, was an accomplished artist in mezzotint, but he was not the inventor. 'Mezzotinto engraving consists in scratching, by means of a tool called a "cradle," the whole surface of the plate uniformly, so that an impression taken from it in that state would be entirely black; then tracing the drawing, and scraping and burnishing up the strongest lights until the desired effect is produced.'—*Fairholt.*

Middlesex is the middle country of the Saxons, in distinction from Sussex (South-sex), Essex (East-sex), and Wessex (West-sex). The latter extended from Berkshire to the east of Cornwall.

Middling Interest. This is the American equivalent of the English term 'middle class.' 'They have felt that they belonged to the *middling interest*, and have resolved to stay there, and not cope with the rich.'—*Connecticut Courant.*

Midwife. Bailey derives this from *mede-wife*, which, he says, means 'a woman of merit or worth.' In this he has evidently followed Verstegan, who says, 'a woman of mede, or merit, deserving recompense.' 'The derivation of midwife is uncertain, but when we find it spelt *meedwife* in Wycliff's Bible it leaves hardly a doubt that it is the *wife* or woman who acts for a *meed*, or reward.'—*Trench.*

Mignonette is a native of the north of Africa. It was introduced into England by Lord Bateman, in 1752. It had been cultivated in the Royal Gardens at Paris for a year or two before that date. The name is French, and signifies 'Little darling.'

Mile. The word 'mile' is corrupted from the Latin *mille*, a thousand. The Roman mile was a thousand paces (*mille passus*), each pace being 5 Roman feet, equal to about 58 English inches. The Roman mile was 1614 English yards in length. The present English statute mile was instituted in the time of Elizabeth, and is defined as 'eight furlongs of 40 perches of $16\frac{1}{2}$ feet each,' which is 1,760 yards.

Miles's Boy. Many an improbable story and dubious anecdote has been fathered upon 'Miles's boy' during the last half-century by people who have little thought that 'Miles's boy' had once a real existence. Mr. Robins, in his 'History of Paddington' (1853), tells us that, at the beginning of this century, Mr. Miles, his pair-horse coach, and his redoubtable boy, were the only appointed agents of communication between Paddington and the City. The fares were 2*s.* and 3*s.*, the journey occupying more than three hours; and, to beguile the time at resting-places, 'Miles's boy (who presumably acted as a sort of 'guard' to the coach) told tales and played on the fiddle.

Military Terms. Nearly all our military terms and designations are derived from the Normans. These designations are marshal, general, colonel, major, captain, adjutant, cornet, lieutenant, ensign, officer, sergeant, corporal, and soldier. The military terms are siege, manœuvre, trench, tactics, march, invasion, assault, escalade, encampment, column, battery, fortification, battalion, bombardment, reconnaissance, enfilade, escarpment, army, regiment, company, military, artillery, militia, cavalry, infantry, volunteer, grenadier, commissariat, &c., &c. These are in strong contrast to the SEA TERMS (which see), nearly all of which are pure Anglo-Saxon.

Milk (Dr. Johnson tripping). Dr. Johnson gives us an example of the use of the word *milk* in the following passage:—

> I fear thy nature;
> It is too full o' the milk of human kindness
> To catch the nearest way;

which he erroneously quotes as from 'Shakespeare—"King Lear."' He has been followed implicitly by other dictionary makers (*vide* Dr. Todd, 1827). The passage really occurs in 'Macbeth,' act i. sc. 5.

Milled Money was invented by Antoine Brucher, in France, and was first struck in England about 1553. Elizabeth issued milled money from 1562 to 1572, after which it was disused until 1623. About 1662 it became permanently established. Milled sixpences were at one time so rare that they were kept as counters. Sir W. Davenant speaks of—

> A few *milled sixpences* with which
> My purser keeps account.—*News from Plim.*

Milliner. A milliner was originally a man, and was so called, probably, from *Milan*, whence he imported female finery. Shakespeare ('1 Henry IV.,' i. 3) has 'He was perfumed like a milliner'; and Ben Jonson ('Every Man in his Humour,' i. 3) settles the question of the sex of the original milliners in the words, 'To conceal such real ornaments as these, and shadow their glory, as a *milliner's wife* does her wrought stomacher with a smoky lawn or a black cyprus.'

Million of Facts. In the introduction to this celebrated work of Sir Richard Phillips, it is stated that the volume contains far more than a million of *facts*. A correspondent of 'Notes and

Queries' (January 23, 1875) points out that the volume contains only 403,650 *words.*

Milord Anglais. This French phrase has been greatly ridiculed in England. The 'milord,' however, is but the Celtic word *milwr*, still in use in Brittany in the sense of a gentleman, a cavalier. It is pronounced *milôr*. It is allied to the Latin *miles,* a knight or soldier.

Mines. The deepest mine in the world is the rock-salt bore hole at Spesenberg, near Berlin, which is 4,175 feet in depth. It is not, however, quite perpendicular. The deepest perpendicular shaft is that of Adalbert, at Prisbram, in Bohemia, which is 3,280 feet. The deepest British mine is Dunhill Colliery, near Wigan, which is 2,824 feet. The deepest boring in the world is the Artesian well at Potsdam, Missouri, in the United States, which is 5,500 feet, or 220 feet beyond a mile.—*Times*, Jan. 17, 1881.

Miniature. This word has nothing in common with the word minute, small. It comes to us from the Italian *miniatura*, which was formed from the Latin *minium*, red-lead. The word was applied to small paintings from the practice of ornamenting the margins of books and manuscripts with pictures highly coloured with minium and vermilion.

Minim, from the Latin *minimus*, the least. The minim, in the very old musical notation, was the shortest note, though now one of the longest. The old musical notes were the 'long,' the 'brief' [Latin *brevis*, short], the 'semi-brief,' and the 'minim.' The long and the brief are now practically obsolete, though the latter, now called *breve*, is occasionally met with in chants and other Church music. Crotchets, quavers, &c., have been subsequently adopted to mark more minute divisions and subdivisions of musical time.

Ministry. 'The "Ministry" is, in fact, a committee of the leading members of the two Houses. It is nominated by the Crown, but it consists exclusively of statesmen whose opinions on the pressing questions of the time agree in the main with the opinions of the majority of the House of Commons.'—*Macaulay.*

Miniver, the fur. This is a corruption of the French *menu vair*, which, Cotgrave says, is 'the furre of ermines mixed or spotted with the furre of the weesel called *Gris*.'

Minnow. 'The *minnow* is the smallest British fish, of the order *Cyprinidæ*, and is chiefly remarkable for the circumstance that in spawning each female is attended by two males.'—*Brand's Dict.*, vol. ii. p. 345. This statement must be taken *cum grano salis*.

Minster, in the names of English places, always signifies the site of a monastery or abbey; as Bedminster, Axminster, Leominster, &c.

Mint. The locality known as 'The Mint,' in the Borough of Southwark, was originally the site of a palace of Charles Brandon, Duke of Suffolk. This came into the hands of Henry VIII., who established there a place for coining money.

Mint Sauce. Eating mint sauce with lamb is probably a remnant of the custom of eating bitter herbs with the paschal lamb. It is a custom unknown on the Continent, and peculiarly English.

Minutes, Engross. The 'minutes' of any proceeding are so called because formerly taken down in minute characters, preparatory to being engrossed, that is, written in large (*gros*) characters for preservation or record.

Minx. A minx is a female puppy.—*Crabb*.

Mischievous. 'Old authors, and the modern vulgar, accent the second syllable of this word instead of the first.'—*Smart*.

Misery formerly meant avarice, and to be miserable was to be avaricious. We still retain the root-word in the term miser. 'The man who enslaves himself to his money is proclaimed in our very language to be a *miser*, or a miserable man.'—*Trench*. 'Our language, by a peculiar significance of dialect, calls the covetous man the *miserable* man.'—*South*.

Miss. 'With respect to the use of this title when two or more persons of the same name are spoken of or addressed, there is a good deal of diversity. Some give the plural form to the name, as "The Miss Smiths;" others to the title, as "The Misses Smith." In favour of the first may be cited Boswell, Northcote, Malone, Goldsmith, De Quincey, and Wilberforce. The latter form is preferred by Bishop Horne, Sir E. Brydges, Charles Lamb, Southey, and Sir R. Peel.'—*Grant*. The easiest way out of the difficulty appears to be to *speak* of 'the Miss Smiths,' but in addressing them in correspondence to *write* 'To the Misses Smith.' Arnold in his Grammar says, 'With respect to the Miss Thompsons or the

Misses Thompson, I am decidedly for the *Miss Thompsons*. No one would think of speaking as we are told to write.'

Mississippi. The name of this great river is a slightly corrupted form of the original Indian name *Miche Sepi*, Great River, or literally Father of Waters. It is the longest river in the world; its length, from its mouths in the Gulf of Mexico to the source of the Missouri, being upwards of 4,500 miles.

Miss Nancy. Applied to young men of affected speech and demeanour, and who ape superiority, walk gingerly, and dress effeminately. The allusion is to Miss Anna Oldfield, an actress who died in 1730. Her vanity was such that she desired on her death-bed that her remains should be laid 'in state, dressed in a very fine Brussels lace head-dress, a holland shift with tucker and double ruffles of the same lace, new kid gloves, &c., &c.' Pope alludes to her in the lines—

> Odious! in woollen? 'twould a saint provoke,
> Were the last words that poor Narcissa spoke.

Mistake, Mistaken. To mistake is to misjudge, to misapprehend, to misconceive, to misunderstand. Therefore if any one tells me something that he clearly states, but which I do not clearly understand, it is he who is mistaken, not I; because it is he who is misunderstood. I mistake his meaning, but he is mistaken, for what he tells me is not properly taken, or received into my mind. Yet in ordinary conversation the word 'mistaken' is used just in the contrary sense. If I tell a man that a sovereign is equivalent to twenty-one shillings, and he tells me that I am 'mistaken,' he uses an incorrect term. I am not 'mistaken,' because he understands what I say; but I 'mistake,' or 'make a mistake,' because a sovereign is only equal in value to twenty shillings.

Mister. At a time when men were generally called by their Christian and surnames only, the word *Mister* was probably applied as a sort of title to those who had learned a *mystery* or trade, and who would perhaps be looked upon as of higher rank or position than mere labourers or husbandmen. The question so often met with in old writers, 'What *mister* wight is that?' meaning, what is that man's employment and consequent condition in life? seems to favour this view. Smart, however, seems to think that Mister was adopted, or at least promoted, for the sake of analogy with 'mistress'; 'for mistress, among our old writers, often had the form of mastress in order to suit with master, which was then used where we now find "mister."' And Walker says, 'The same process of change which has "corrupted master into mister, has, when it is a title of civility only, contracted mistress into missis. Thus '*Mrs.*' Montague, '*Mrs.*' Carter, &c., are pronounced '*Missis*' Montague, '*Missis*' Carter, &c. To pronounce the word as it is written would in these cases appear quaint and pedantic."' A curious instance of the incongruous way in which the titles Mister and Esquire are sometimes used, occurred at the time when the Corporation of Stratford-on-Avon resolved to present the freedom of that town to Garrick. Their resolution declares that this was done 'through love and regard to the memory of the immortal Mr. William Shakespear, and as an acknowledgment of the extraordinary merits of his most distinguished representative, David Garrick, Esquire.'

Mistletoe. The Anglo-Saxon name for this shrub was *misteltan*. *Tan*, being another form of the old word *tine*, the prong of a fork, is suggestive of the fork-like shoots of the plant. *Mistel* may probably have something in connexion with the old Saxon word *mist*, dung; as it is known that the plant is propagated by the seeds being deposited within openings of the bark of trees, in the ordure of the missel-thrush. In this case the name, freely translated, becomes 'dung-sown-fork-plant.' This of course is merely speculative. But whatever may be the meaning of 'missel' or 'mistel,' its occurrence in the names both of the bird and the plant is presumptive proof of some analogy.

Mistranslation of 2 Sam. viii. 4. Our version says that 'David houghed all the chariot horses.' There is no such cruelty mentioned in the original. The Hebrew, '*Vayaker David eth col harechab*,' means 'And David disjointed all the chariots.' It is, however, stated that he reserved one hundred of the 'chariots'; not the horses for them, as in our version.

Mrs. Glasse's Cookery Book. In an old 'Biographical Dictionary,' the following paragraph attributes the authorship of this book to Sir John Hill, the author of the 'System of Botany,' &c.:— 'On his outset in London, he (Astley the painter) lived in St. James's Street, where Dr. Hill followed him and wrote that book which, except the Bible, has had the greatest sale in the language, the "Cookery of Mrs. Glasse."' As Sir John was a scribbler and a quack, it is possible, and indeed probable, that he *revised* the book. The writer of this book gives in the fourth edition (1751) her autograph 'H. Glasse,' and annexes her name and address in an advertisement as follows:—'Hannah Glasse, Habit maker to Her Royal Highness the Princess of Wales, in Tavistock Street,

Covent Garden.' The advertisement announces that she makes and sells 'all sorts of riding habits, josephs, great-coats, horsemen's coats, bed gowns, night gowns, and robe de shambers (*sic*), &c., after the neatest manners. Likewise Parliament, Judges', and Councillors' robes; also all sorts of childbed linning (*sic*), &c., and all sorts of masquerade dresses.' The business does not appear to have prospered, for in the 'Gentleman's Magazine,' the list of 'b-kr-pts' for May, 1754, contains the following entry:—'Hannah Glasse of St. Paul's, Covent Garden, Warehouse Keeper.'

Mitrailleuse. In 'Luttrell's Diary,' under date January 8, 1689-90, it is mentioned that preparations are being vigorously pushed forward for an expedition to Ireland; and among other matters to be sent forward are '4 of the new-invented wheel-engines, which discharge 150 musquet barrels at once, and turning the wheel as many more.' In the 'Life of Monmouth,' by Roberts, ii. 46, it is stated that there is a machine in the Arsenal of Vienna, bearing date 1678, by which fifty muskets could be discharged in any direction, and at any angle, by the application of a single match.

Mitre. 'The two horns of the mitre are generally taken to be an allusion to the cloven tongues as of fire which rested on each of the apostles on the day of Pentecost.—*Hook*.

Mixed Races. In America—where, from the constitution of society, admixtures of species are very frequent—the various gradations are designated by specific names, a few of the more important of which are as follow:—

FATHER	MOTHER	MALE OFFSPRING	FEMALE
White	Negro	Mulatto	Mulatta
White	Mulatta	Cuarteron	Cuarterona
White	Cuarterona	Quintero	Quintera
White	Quintera	White	White
White	Indian	Mestizo	Mestiza
Negro	Indian	Zambo	Zambu
White	Chinese	Chino-blanco	
Negro	Chinese	Zambo-chino	
Mulatto	Chinese	Chino	

Mob. This word arose in the reign of Charles II. A writer of that period, speaking of the 'Green Ribbon Club,' says, 'I may note that the rabble first changed their title, and were called "the mob" in the assemblies of this Club. It was their beast of burden, and called first "*mobile vulgus*," but fell naturally into the contraction of one syllable, and ever since is become proper English.'

Modern, from the Latin *modo,* just now, lately. It was formerly used in a different sense to that now in use. In the 'Proceedings of the Council' (vol. i. p. 191) Henry III., in the fourth year of the reign of his successor, is called '*Rex Henricus modernus,*' that is, the late or the last King Henry.

Moel in Welsh local names means a mountain.

Molasses (singular). This word is generally used as exactly synonymous with treacle. The two substances are much alike, but 'molasses' comes from sugar in the process of making, treacle in the process of refining.—*Worcester.* See TREACLE.

Monastery, Convent. A monastery is the actual building inhabited by the monks, who themselves compose the convent presided over by the abbot or prior. The latter word comes from the Latin *conventus* (*con,* together, and *venire,* to come), which signifies an assembly. Monastery is therefore the house, and convent the religious community inhabiting it.

Money was so called from its having first been coined in the temple of Juno *Moneta* at Rome.—*Brand.* As a proof of the altered value of money, it may be mentioned that Latimer in the reign of Edward VI. mentions, as a proof of his father's prosperity, that, although only a yeoman, he gave his daughters five pounds each as a marriage portion.

Monkey, from *mon,* a common countrified pronunciation of the word *man,* and *kin,* a diminutive. The word means *mannikin,* or little man. The word monkey, in the common phrase 'to put his monkey up,' is probably the Welsh *mwng,* the mane. Angry animals erect the mane. *Mwnci* means a horse-collar.

Mont Blanc. The first successful ascent to the summit of Mont Blanc was made in August 1786 by a gentleman named Paccard, and a guide whose name was Jacques Balmat.

Month. By the Act 13 Vict. c. 21, it is enacted that the word month is in all future Acts to mean calendar month.

Monument. The monument on Fish Street Hill, London, is the loftiest isolated column in the world. It was built by Wren, 1671. It is 202 feet in height, including the pedestal of 40 feet. The gallery is approached by a winding stair of 345 steps of black marble. It was built to commemorate the great fire of London (1666), which broke out within a short distance of its site.

Monumental Brasses. The earliest record of a monumental brass relates to that of Simon de Beauchamp, who died at the beginning of the thirteenth century. This brass has, however, disappeared. The earliest existing is that of Sir John d'Abernon, who died in 1277 and was buried at Stoke d'Abernon in Surrey.

Moon. Herschel thought it probable that there is a second moon or satellite to the earth. Speaking of the August and November meteors, he said :—'There is reason to believe that one of these bodies has become attached to the earth as a permanent satellite, revolving about it in three hours and twenty minutes, at the distance of 5,000 miles from its surface.'

Moot Point. A *moot point* in law is a point unsettled, undecided, and so left to be debated or discussed. Ben Jonson says ('Disc.' vol. vii. p. 84), 'There is a difference between *mooting* and pleading, between fencing and fighting.' Mootings were formerly held as trials of forensic skill in the Inns of Court, and were, according to the old writers, mental tournaments, or trials of skill, of no mean order. Overbury, in his 'Characters,' K. 4, has : 'By the time that he [an Inns-of-Court man] hath heard one mooting, and seene two playes, he thinks as basely of the universitie, as a young Sophister doth of the grammar schoole.' The word is probably connected with the old Saxon word *mote* or *gemot*, a meeting, as in *wardmote* (still in use) a ward meeting ; *burgmote*, a town's meeting ; and *witenagemote*, a meeting of the wise, the name of the Anglo-Saxon Parliaments. As these motes were held to discuss weighty matters, there seems good reason to believe that the word moot may be derived from *mote*, a meeting.

Morganatic Marriages are common in Germany between royal personages and ladies of inferior rank. The man in these marriages gives the left hand instead of the right. Such unions do not confer rank upon the wife or her offspring ; and the children, although legitimate, have no claim to inherit the property of the father, nor to higher rank than the mother originally possessed. Dr. W. Bell ('Notes and Queries,' 3rd S. No. 116) says:—
'For morganatic the best, in fact the only, solution is to be found in the derivation of the word. In the arid deserts of Arabia the parched traveller is mocked by optical delusions of running streams and green meadows ; these the Italians call *Fata Morgana*, the delusions of the *Morgana*. Something thus delusive is a morganatic marriage. For though it involves no immorality, and has always the full sanction of the Church, it is, as regards the wife and children, an illusion and a make-believe.'

Morsel meant originally a small bite or bit of anything. The word comes from the Latin *morsus*, a bite. The Italian word *morso* means both morsel and the bit of a horse's bridle.

Mortar (the building cement). This word is derived from the Latin *mortarium*, the vessel in which, according to the elder Pliny (xxxvi. 55), *arenatum*, or sanded cement, was made. We retain the original use of the word in the name of the vessel in which an apothecary mixes his drugs. In an account of the charges for repairing the spire of Newark Church in the year 1571, the following items appear:—

'Item, 6 Strike of malte to make worte to blende with the lyme and temper the same.
'Item, 7 quarter lyme.
'Item, Three hundreth and a halfe eggs to temper the same lyme with.'

In old receipt-books lime mixed with white of egg is recommended as a good cement. Possibly these ingredients afford some clue to the manner of producing the ancient mortar, which is well known to have been of excellent quality.

Mortgage, from the French *mort*, dead, and *gage*, a pledge. 'According to Littleton, Coke, and others, a mortgage is so called (dead pledge) because in case of non-payment of the debt at the time limited, the land was for ever *dead* and gone from the mortgagor, and in case of payment it became *dead* as to the mortgagee.'— *Burrell*.

Mosaic. Moses directed the breastplate of the high priest to be divided into twelve squares, each of a different colour; hence inlaid work of different coloured stones is called mosaic work.

Mosey. This word is not in the dictionaries, but is in frequent use in the Midland Counties to express the condition of a turnip when the interior has become dry and fibrous, or of an apple when it is withered and juiceless. It is equivalent to the term *woolly*, which is used in a similar sense in the Southern Counties. Grose has 'mosey' in his 'Glossary.'

Moses represented by Artists. Most of the mediæval artists who represented Moses painted him with horns upon his head. This arose from a mistranslation of the Hebrew word *karan*, which in the Vulgate was translated *cornuta*, or horned, but which really meant rays of light darting out, in the manner in which the sun was formerly represented in the rude woodcuts of early almanacs. Our translation, 'his face shone,' does not give the full force of the original.

Mosquitoes do not take their name from that of the Mosquito Coast. The word is the diminutive of the Spanish word *mosca*, a fly. Mosquitoes were formerly so troublesome in England that in sleeping places nets were necessary to keep them from attacking the sleepers. In 'Archæologia,' xliii. 240, we are told that at the dissolution of the Cistercian Abbey of Sawtree, the inventory shows that in ' The Newe Chamber' there was 'a beadstead with a net for knatts.' 'Gnat' is the English name for the insect known in hot climates as the 'mosquito.'

Mother Carey's Chickens. This is a term applied by sailors to flocks of the stormy petrel. Mother Carey is 'Mother dear' (*mater cara*), and the term signifies the Virgin Mary, who is the patroness of sailors. Roman Catholic sailors believe that the Virgin Mary gives notice to seamen of approaching storms by sending flocks of the stormy petrel to warn them.

Mothering Sunday. The ancient Romans celebrated on the Ides of March a festival in honour of the Mother of the Gods, the people bringing offerings which became the property of the priests. From this practice arose the Roman Catholic custom of attending the mother church on Mid-Lent Sunday with presents for the Church. In time these presents were looked upon as dues, and they were the origin of the Easter offerings. Mid-Lent or Mothering Sunday is still celebrated in the Midland Counties by apprentices and servants visiting their parents on that day.

Mountebank. Quack doctors formerly vended their nostrums in markets and fairs, where, mounted on benches (*bench*, bank), they harangued the people in similar 'patter' to that used by the modern Cheap Jacks who vend hardware. The term was applied to them from their mounting the bank or bench to display their eloquence and sell their nostrums.

Mourning. The custom of wearing black as symbolic of mourning arose from the circumstance that Anne, the queen of Charles VIII. of France, on the death of that king in 1498, surrounded her coat of arms with black in token of her widowhood, and clothed herself in black, in opposition to the then prevalent habit, which was for widows to mourn in white.

Moving the previous question. Sometimes a question arises in the House of Commons which the Government or the Opposition do not wish to pass, and yet do not like to vote against. The difficulty is got rid of by what is called 'moving the previous question.' When the Speaker rises to put the original question to the vote, some member interposes by moving 'that this question be *now* put,' which, if negatived, disposes of the matter altogether, no vote being taken upon its merits. It is customary in these cases for the mover and seconder to vote against their own proposal.

Mow. This word now signifies to cut down with a scythe. Formerly it meant a stack of corn. Thus a field of barley was 'cut down ready for mowing,' that is, stacking. A stack of barley is still called a barley *mow*.

Muff, as applied to a stupid person. This use of the word is probably from the Dutch *mof*, a clown or boor, applied generally by the Netherlanders to a German, and particularly to a Westphalian. Marlowe uses the word in this sense in the following sentence: 'Sclavonians, Almains, Rutters [German horsemen], Muffs, and Danes.'

Muffin. Probably from the Old French *mou-pain*, soft bread. This in rapid pronunciation would easily be corrupted into mouffin, or muffin.

Muggy, as applied to the weather, is from one of the Welsh words—*mwcan*, a cloud of fog; *mwg*, smoke; or *mwygl*, tepid, sultry; most likely from the last.

Mulatto, from the Spanish *mulo*, a mule. 'The offspring of parents, of whom one is white and the other a negro.'—*Dunglinson*.

Mule. The mule is a hybrid animal produced between a mare and a male ass. The offspring of a horse and a female ass is called a hinny.

Mulled Ale. The word 'mulled' is derived from the Old Norman *molda*, to commit to mould or earth, to bury. The ale given at funerals was always warmed, and was called *mold ale*, or *molde ale*, that is, funeral ale. In Scotland a funeral banquet is still called *mulde-mete*. The transition of the meaning of the adjective from 'funeral' to 'being warmed' is easy and natural.

Multitude. A *multitude* is a large number collectively; a *crowd* or *throng* is a collection of persons or animals pressing upon each other; a *rabble* is a tumultuous assemblage; a *swarm* is a large collection of persons, animals, or insects. In the 'Boke of St. Albans,' 1496, Dame Juliana Barnes tells us that we should say 'a *congregation* of people; a *host* of men; a *fellowship* of yeomen; and a *bevy* of ladies. We must speak of a *herd* of deer, swans, cranes, or wrens; a *sedge* of herons; a *muster* of peacocks; a *watch* of nightingales; a *flight* of doves; a *clattering* of choughs; a *pride* of lions; a *slewth* of bears; a *skulk* of foxes; a *skull* of friars; a *pontificality* of priests; and a *superfluity* of nuns.' To this we may add a *shoal* or *school* of fishes; a *flock* of sheep; a *covey* of partridges; a *pack* of grouse; a *stud* of mares; a *team* of oxen; a *brood* of chickens; a *mute* of hounds; a *litter* of pigs; a *regiment* of soldiers; a *gang* of slaves; a *crew* of sailors; the *Society* of Friends; the *House* of Commons; a *bench* of magistrates, &c., &c.

Multitude. In law, ten or more persons constitute a multitude.—*Wharton.*

Multum in parvo (Latin), much in little; a great deal in a few words.

Mummy. This word is derived from the name of a plant, *amomum,* because an ointment made from it was used in embalming. D'Israeli calls *amomum* 'a perfume' (' Cur. of Lit.' p. 499). Bailey defines *amomum* to be 'certain grains of a purple colour, spicy smell, and biting taste; the fruit of a tree in the East Indies.'

Munchausen's Travels. In the 'Gentleman's Magazine' for January 1857 is a paper proving that this book was written by Mr. Raspe, a German, who was keeper of the stores at Dolcoath Mine, Cornwall.

Murphy's Almanac. In the edition of this almanac for the year 1838, the compiler foretold that on January 20 in that year the weather would be 'Fair, prob. lowest deg. of winter temp.' Strange to say, that day was the coldest known in the present century, the thermometer falling considerably below zero. The prediction was a lucky one for Murphy; the almanac went rapidly through several editions, realising a profit of upwards of 3,000*l.* in a month or two.

Muscat, Muscatel. 'The term *muscat* applied to particular kinds of grape is not derived from the perfumed or musky flavour of those varieties, but from the berries attracting flies (*muscæ*).'— *Loudon.*

Museum, from a Greek word signifying a place dedicated to the Muses.

Mushroom. We get the word mushroom from the French *mousseron,* but we apply the name to a different species of fungus

The French *mousseron* grows in forests among the moss (*mousse*). Our mushroom is called in France *champignon*, from its growing in fields (*champs*).

Musical Notes. The earliest printed musical notes are found in a book, 'Collectorium super Magnificat,' printed at Esslingen in Wirtemberg by Gerson, in 1473.

Musket. Musket is the name of the male young of the sparrow-hawk. It is derived from the Latin *musca*, fly. 'As the invention of firearms took place at a time when hawking was in high fashion, some of the new weapons were named after those birds, probably from the idea of their fetching their prey from on high. *Musket* has thus become the established name for one sort of gun.'—*Nares*.

Muslin. It is said that muslin was first made at Moussul in Mesopotamia, whence the name. The Arabic name of the town is *Mousöl*, and the fabric is called *mousöliyy*. Mr. Fox Talbot, however, thinks the derivation from the name of the city of Moussul incorrect. He says that 'the ordinary pronunciation of the word *Moslem*, a Mahometan, is *Muslim*, and that the material of which the Moslem dress is composed—a light cotton fabric—gave us the slightly corrupted word *muslin*.' 'The first muslin was imported into England in 1670.'—*Brand*.

Mussulman. The plural of this word is often incorrectly written Mussulmen; it should be Mussul*mans*. Byron jestingly wrote 'Mussulwoman,' but a correspondent of the 'New York Daily Times' (November 6, 1851), seriously wrote, 'The Turkish Sultan has just sent me one of his sons, Master Abdul Hamid, a little Mussul*boy* of nine years, to be educated at Paris.' This little 'Mussulboy' is now (1881) Sultan of Turkey.

Mustard. Mr. Fox Talbot derives this word from *nasturtium*. The Romans called all cruciferous plants of hot biting qualities by this name. The Spaniards, converting the *n* into *m*, called the plant *mastuerzo*, which, quickly pronounced, would be *mastordo*, from which the transition to 'mustard' is easy. The Latin word *nasturtium*, according to Varro, is *quasi nasi tortium*, or nose-torment. This shows that it was some plant affecting the nose by its acridity. Supposing the nasturtium to be indigenous to England, and its British name to have been formed on analogous principles, it would probably be 'nose wort,' which would be certainly a very descriptive name, and would be easily transformed to 'mustard.' The nasturtium above mentioned is not the plant now so called (the *tropeolum* of Linneaus), which is of

Peruvian origin, and a totally different kind of plant. Mr. Earle, in his 'Philology of the English Tongue,' p. 290, differs altogether from Mr. Fox Talbot, and gives the following as a probable derivation of the word mustard:—'It is said that the first depôt for the sale of *sinapis* was at Dijon, and that the jars containing it were marked with the local motto, *Moult me tarde,* which in French of the fifteenth century meant " I am very impatient," and that to the condensation of this motto we have the word "mustard," which is an Anglicism of the French *moutarde*.' 'The English Cyclopædia' differs from both, and says the name is 'from *mustum ardens,* in allusion to its hot and biting character.'

Mutual Friend. In a communication to ' Notes and Queries,' January 5, 1850, Dr. Kennedy, the then learned master of Shrewsbury Grammar School, shows that this expression is absurd and incorrect. ' The word mutual,' he says, ' equals reciprocal, and can only be used *of that which passes between two, from each to each.* The word is correctly used in such expressions as mutual love, mutual reproaches, and the like, but when we speak of a third as having equal relations to two others, we properly use the adjective " common." " Mutual esteem " means the esteem we both feel for each other. " Common esteem " means the esteem we both feel for some other person or persons.'

My eye and Betty Martin. The origin of this phrase is generally attributed to the mistake of a sailor, who, going into a Roman Catholic church, heard the words of a Latin prayer commencing *O mihi Beate Martine,* which he converted into 'O my eye, Betty Martin.' This story is most improbable, for there is no such public formulary in existence in the Roman Church, and, supposing there were, the pronunciation would be ' O mēhē beātay martenay,' which has not the slightest resemblance to the other phrase. The following very much more probable origin was told to the boys at Shrewsbury School by Dr. Butler (afterwards Bishop of Lichfield) when he was head-master :—A number of gipsies were taken before a magistrate by a constable, who complained principally of a woman named Betty Martin. After he had given his evidence the woman rushed excitedly to him in court and gave him a tremendous blow in the face, saying that what he had been telling the magistrate was 'all my eye.' The man's eye was fearfully discoloured by the blow, and ever after he was teased by the populace calling after him ' My eye and Betty Martin.' Cuthbert Bede, however, states in 'Notes and Queries,' December 17, 1859, that he has found the phrase in an old black-letter volume, without date, entitled, 'The Ryghte Tragycall Historie of Master Thomas Thumbe.' This shows that the phrase has been in use for something like three hundred years, but throws no light on its origin.

My Lord Tappes. One of the old plays in 'Dodsley's Collection' is entitled 'Lingua.' In this play the following passage occurs: 'Of great denomination, he may be *my Lord Tappes* for his large titles.'—*Reed's edit.* vol. v. p. 202. Nares says, 'Who this personage was remains to be discovered.' In the margin of a copy of the first edition of Nares (1822), the compiler of this book found the following note, written in pencil : ' *My Lord Tappes* is a burlesque dignitary at Turbick Fair, Cambridge. He is decorated with spigots and fossets, or taps, and takes a toll of the ale sellers.' The note has apparently been written many years, and is evidently the writing of a very old man.

My mother bids me bind my hair. This exquisite lyric was written by Anne, the wife of John Hunter the anatomist, about the year 1791. It was first published in a volume of her songs in the year 1802. The words were originally set to an air of Pleydell's, and they then began with what is now the second stanza—

'Tis sad to think the days are gone.

My stars and garters! This old lady's expletive was formerly much commoner than now. It is clearly an allusion to the star and garter of the order of knighthood, which is, of course, highly prized. Hence, when an old lady swore by her stars and garters, it is fair to presume that she swore by the most prized of her possessions.

Mystery. In ordinary indentures of apprenticeship, the master binds himself to teach the apprentice his 'art, trade, and *mystery*.' In this sense the word is probably derived from the old French *mestier*, a trade, or it may have been corrupted from 'mastery'— that is, the boy is to be taught until he has become the *master* of his craft or business. See MISTER.

N

Nab. This word is inserted as a law term in Wharton's 'Law Lexicon.' The definition given is 'to catch unexpectedly ; to seize without warning.'

Nacker. This word in the East of England means a harness-maker. It is not in Johnson, but Worcester gives it, and it is in Grose's 'Glossary.'

Naked Eye. This expression was first used by Galileo, in a letter written March 1610, describing his invention of the telescope. He says, after describing the mechanism of the new instrument: 'Bringing the eye near the concave glass, I saw the objects, large and near enough. They appeared three times nearer and nine times larger than if seen with the *naked eye.*' Probably the phrase was suggested by the passage Heb. iv. 13, which in the English version is rendered 'Naked and opened to the eyes.'

Namby-pamby, i.e. finical, affected. 'Another of Addison's favourite companions was Ambrose Phillips, a good Whig and a middling poet, who had the honour of bringing into fashion a species of composition which has been called after his name, *Namby-pamby.*'—*Macaulay.*

Names of Animals. The English names of domestic animals are nearly all Anglo-Saxon monosyllables, as, for instance, cat, dog, pup, horse, mare, hound, hog, sow, pig, sheep, cow, ox, bull, ram, ewe, lamb, calf, colt, foal, ass, drake, duck, cock, hen, chick, goose, swan, &c. The names of wild beasts, on the contrary, are nearly all of Norman introduction, as lion, tiger, elephant, leopard, panther, &c. It is singular, too, that, although we have retained the Saxon names for living domestic animals, we use the Norman names for their flesh when killed, as beef, mutton, veal, pork, &c.

Names of Places in America. According to the United States Official Postal Guide there are in that country 12 towns named Boston, 25 Springfields, 20 Brooklyns (besides 2 Brooklins and 3 Brooklines), 4 Baltimores, 17 Buffaloes, 17 Burlingtons, 7 Charlestowns and 20 Charlestons, 5 Chicagoes, 8 Cincinnatis, 12 Clevelands, 21 Columbuses, 25 Daytons, 5 Detroits, 17 Lowells, 8 Memphises, 17 Nashvilles, 9 Pittsburgs, 7 Philadelphias, 15 Portlands, 14 Quincys, 22 Richmonds, 5 St. Louis, 12 St. Pauls, 7 Toledos, 30 Washingtons, 13 Wilmingtons, and 28 Williamsburghs.

Names of the Popes. The custom of each Pope taking a fresh name on his assuming the pontificate originated A.D. 687 with Pope Sergius, whose original name signified Swine-snout.

Naming Dogs. Many of our favourite names for dogs show a Spanish origin, and no doubt came in with the spaniel. Sancho is

Spanish, as we all know; Ponto is from *punta*, the Spanish word for pointer; Pero is the Spanish *perro*, a dog; and Tray is the Spanish *trae*, fetch, or bring.

Nankeen Cloth. Fifty years ago nankeen cloth was imported from China in enormous quantities. It was used for men's summer trousers, ladies' dresses, and for children's clothing, and was greatly prized because its peculiar buff colour was remarkably permanent. Many experiments were made with a view to discover the dye used by the Chinese, but it was at last ascertained that the cloth was produced from a coloured variety of cotton. Cotton cloth dyed 'nankeen colour' is now exported to China in larger quantities than the true nankeen was formerly imported.

Nant in the names of Welsh localities means a valley, a ravine formed by running water, a mountain torrent, as *Nant-Gwyrfai*, the vale of fresh water; *Nant Frangon*, the beaver's hollow, &c.

Nape of the Neck. Bailey, in his Dictionary, says, 'So called from the soft short hair growing there like the *nap* of cloth.'

Napkin, from the French *nappe*, a table-cloth. 'Napkin, the diminutive of *nappe* in its modern sense, was the badge of the office of the butler in great houses.'—*Nares*.

Napoleon III. When spoken of, without reference to his imperial rank, this personage is generally called 'Louis Napoleon.' This is erroneous. His name in full was Charles Napoleon Louis, and before his elevation to the throne he invariably signed 'Napoléon Louis,' and not Louis Napoléon.

Napoleon's return from Elba. Napoleon escaped from Elba on March 1, 1815, reaching Paris on the 20th. His progress was marked by some strange alterations in the tone of the French newspapers. On March 9 the 'Journal des Débats' spoke of him as 'the poltroon of 1814'; on the 15th occurs the sentence, 'Scourge of generations, thou shalt reign no more.' On the 16th he is described as 'a Robespierre on horseback'; on the 19th as 'the adventurer from the island of Corsica'; but on the 21st the tone is changed, and we are told that 'THE EMPEROR has pursued his triumphal course,' and 'THE EMPEROR has found no other enemies than the miserable libels which were vainly scattered in his path to impede his progress.'

Nasty. This word was originally written *nasky*, probably in allusion to the filthy habits of the pig. In Finnish *naski* is a pig; in Danish *snaskè* is to eat like a pig; and in Swedish *snaskig* is filthy.

Natal. This name was given to the country by its discoverer, Vasco da Gama, a Portuguese, from the fact of his having first seen it on Christmas Day—*Christi dies natalis.*

Nation. The word 'nation' is used in America as an adjective to express immense, enormous, very, extremely, a great deal, &c. Sam Slick says, 'You colony chaps are a *nation* sight too well off'; and in 'Yankee Doodle' this verse occurs:—

> And every time they shoot it off,
> It takes a horn of powder;
> And makes a noise like father's gun,
> Only a *nation* louder.

Mr. Bartlett, in his 'Glossary,' says the word 'is a *corruption* of damnation.' He probably meant to write 'a contraction.'

Nation of Shopkeepers. Napoleon I. is generally credited with having first applied this sneering phrase to the English people. It was, however, used by Barère in the French Convention, June 18, 1794, in a speech in which he asserted that Howe had been defeated in the famous battle of June 1, and said, 'Let Pitt, then, boast of his victory to his nation of shopkeepers' (*sa nation boutiquière*).

National Debt. The British National Debt dates from 1690. In 1697 it amounted to 5 millions sterling. By 1702 it had grown to 14 millions. Twelve years later it was 54 millions. By 1763 it had mounted up to 139 millions, and by the end of the war with Napoleon it had reached the enormous sum of 867 millions.

National Gallery. The National Gallery was instituted in 1824, the first purchase being the thirty-eight pictures forming the Angerstein Collection at a cost of 57,000*l.* They were exhibited in Pall Mall in May 1824. Sir George Beaumont, two years later, gave fifteen choice works by the Old Masters, and in the same year the Rev. W. H. Carr bequeathed thirty others. These three collections were the nucleus of the present magnificent collections at Charing Cross and South Kensington. The National Portrait Gallery was established in February 1857.

Naturalist. A *naturalist* two hundred years ago was a denier of revealed truth; he is now an investigator, and often a pious one, of nature and its laws; yet the word has remained true to its etymology all the while.—*Trench.* The first naturalist of whom we have any account was Solomon, who 'spake of trees, from the cedar tree that is in Lebanon even unto the hyssop that springeth out of the wall: he spake also of beasts, and of fowl, and of creeping things, and of fishes' (1 Kings iv. 33).

Naughty. This word is from the Anglo-Saxon *ne aught*, not anything; from this 'not worth anything,' and from that to *worthless* or bad, are natural transitions. *Be naught* was formerly a mild sort of execration, which has given place to *be hanged* and even to stronger terms. A singular use of the word naughty in the sense of worthless occurs in Jeremiah xxiv. 2, *naughty figs*.

Nautical Phrases. A ship cruises *in* any particular sea or ocean, as *in* the Baltic, *in* the Atlantic, *in* the Mediterranean, &c. She cruises *off* any cape or town, as *off* the Lizard, *off* Ushant, &c. She cruises *on* a coast, as *on* the coast of Africa, *on* the coast of Brasil, &c. Thus a seaman, speaking of the Channel Fleet, might say it 'had been cruising *in* the Channel, principally *off* the Bill, but that it was now *on* the coast of Ireland.'

Navel, Nave. The word navel was until a comparatively recent period used in the sense of centre, or middle. Thus in Fuller's 'Observations of the Shires' (*Collectanea Curiosa*, Oxford, 1781, vol. i. p. 223), Northamptonshire is described as 'being seated almost in the *navel* of England. This gives a clue to the origin of the word nave. The *nave* of a church, according to Ayliffe, is the middle, being the part between the side aisles or wings. The *nave* of a wheel, again, is the middle into which the end of the axle-tree is inserted, and from which the spokes radiate.

Navigable Canals in England. Although from the time of Henry I., 1134, when the Trent was joined to the Witham, down to 1715, when the Kennet was made navigable to Reading, many cuttings and improvements were made in the existing natural rivers and streams to make them available for navigation, no *canals* in the present sense of the word were made until after 1750—the Bridgewater being commenced in 1759. The earliest known mention of this scheme is contained in a newspaper article of the date 1737, of which the following is a copy:—'We have taken notice, in a late paper, of an ingenious contrivance for the general advantage of commerce, which, considering its extensive view, we venture to reprint, viz., that there is now in the hands of a gentleman of the county of York a plan for the improvement of navigation by carrying it on in small currents of water from one town to another without the assistance of locks, and may communicate with the next adjacent rivers already navigable, which will greatly increase the trade thereof. The vessels for this purpose are calculated to carry twenty tons weight, managed by two men only, and will, with the utmost probability, render the conveyance of coal, stone, timber, lime, &c. much cheaper than by land, and nearly in the same time,' &c. &c.

Navvy. This name, now applied to persons employed as labourers in the construction of railways and other heavy earthworks, is a contraction of the word navigator. It originated when such persons were occupied in forming navigable canals, and the name, although no longer applicable, is still retained.

Near Side and Off Side. The left side of a horse is called his 'near' side, and the right side his 'off' side. The terms are derived from the times when the driver of the horses in a vehicle walked by their side. In order that his right hand might be instantly available in case of need, he always walked on the left of his horses. The *near* side of a horse was therefore that nearest his driver, and the *off* side that furthest off.

Nebuchadnezzar. In Russian the compound word Ne-Bochad-ne-Tzar signifies 'There is no God but the Czar.'—*Notes and Queries*, July 21, 1877.

Neck-verse. Formerly any person in holy orders accused of felony or other indictable offence, and brought before a secular judge, could plead the *privilegium clericale,* or the benefit of clergy, in bar of the judge's jurisdiction. This exception was pretended to be derived from the text, 'Touch not mine anointed, and do my prophets no harm.' In course of time the privilege was extended to all who could read, they being considered to be 'capable of becoming clerks' or clergy. The test as to whether the accused could read or not was applied in open court by the book of Psalms being put into his hands for him to read a verse. If the bishop's commissary, who was always present on these occasions, was satisfied with the reading, he said 'legit,' upon which the accused was slightly burned or branded in the palm of the hand and discharged, but if the commissary said 'non legit,' the prisoner was punished as other felons. The test verse was usually the first of the fifty-first Psalm, and this verse was known as the neck-verse, because if he could read it the prisoner saved his neck, that is, was not hanged. There are many allusions in the old dramatists to this custom, as

> Within forty feet of the gallows, conning his *neck-verse.*
> *Jew of Malta, Dodsley,* viii. 368.

> Twang it perfectly,
> As you would read your *neck-verse*.
> *Massinger, Guard.* iv. 1.

An old song has the following :—

> If a monk had been taken
> For stealing of bacon.
> For burglary, murder, or rape,
> If he could but rehearse
> (Well prompt) his *neck-verse*,
> He never could fail to escape.—*British Apollo*, 1710.

Nectarine. The nectarine and the peach are both Persian fruits, bearing Persian names. *Nectarine* is a Persian word signifying 'the best,' and it was applied to this fruit to signify that it was 'the best' kind of peach. It has nothing to do with the word *nectar*. Nectarines were introduced into England by the Dutch about 1560.

Née, a French word meaning *born*. It is used to designate the maiden name of a married lady—as, Madame Philipon, *née* Roland.

Needle. The art of making needles was introduced into this country in 1566 by Elias Grouse, a German, who taught the art to the English.

Needle in a bottle of hay. 'Bottle of hay is the Breton *botel-foenn*; French *botel, boiteau*, the diminutive of *botte*, a bunch or bundle; *botte de foin*, a wisp of hay; Gaelic *boiteal*, a bundle of hay or straw.'—*Wedgwood*.

Needs must when the Devil drives. This proverb is of considerable antiquity. In 'Johan the Husbande, Tyb his Wyfe, and Syr Jhan the Priest,' printed by Rastall 1533, it is mentioned as a proverb then current in the following couplet :

> There is a proverbe which trewe now preveth,
> He must nedes go that the dyvell dryveth.

Shakespeare uses it in 'All's Well that Ends Well,' act i. sc. 3, where the clown says :

> He must needs go that the devil drives.

Negus. The mixture of wine, sugar, and hot water was named negus from Colonel Francis Negus, who was Commissioner for executing the office of Master of the Horse in the reign of George I. A writer in the 'Gentleman's Magazine,' February 1799, p. 119, says :—' Negus is a family name, and that the said liquor took its name from an individual of that family the following relation will, I think, ascertain [? determine]. It is now nearly thirty years ago that, being on a visit to a friend at Frome in

Somersetshire, I accompanied my friend to the house of a clergyman of the name of Potter. The house was decorated with many paintings, chiefly family portraits, amongst which I was particularly pleased with that of a gentleman in military dress which appeared by the style to have been taken in or about the reign of Queen Anne. In answer to my enquiries concerning the original of the portrait, Mrs. Potter informed me that it was a Colonel Negus, an uncle of her husband's, and that from this gentleman the liquor usually so called had its name, it being his usual beverage. When in company with his junior officers he used to invite them to join him by saying, "Come, boys, join with me; taste my liquor." Hence it soon became fashionable in the regiment, and the officers in compliment to their Colonel called it negus.'

Neighbour. *Boor*, from the Anglo-Saxon, is a rustic or countryman, and *neah* is nigh. Neighbour is *nigh-boor*, the boor who dwells near.

Nelson's Last Signal. The exact words of Nelson's celebrated signal at Trafalgar are given below with the symbols by which they were transmitted.

Symbol	253	269	863	261	471	958	220	370	4	21	19	24
	England	expects	that	every	man	will	do	his	d	u	t	y

Nem. Con. An abbreviation of the Latin phrase *nemine contradicente*, no one contradicting. Thus we say, 'The resolution was passed *nem. con.*' that is, unanimously.

Nemo me impune lacessit. This is the motto of the Order of the Thistle. It was first used on the coins of James VI. of Scotland. It means 'None shall insult me with impunity.'

Nephew. This word originally meant a grandchild, and is used in that sense by Spenser, Shakespeare, Hooker, and Ben Jonson. It is also so used in 1 Timothy v. 4, 'If a woman have children or nephews,' the latter word, in the original, meaning descendants. Niece follows the same rule, being derived from the Latin *neptis*, a granddaughter. Holland says that niece is 'a descendant, male or female.' (Since this work was in the hands of the printer, the Revised New Testament has been published, in which the word 'nephews' in the text quoted is replaced by 'grandchildren.')

Ne plus ultra (Latin); literally, 'nothing more beyond.' Used in England as a synonym for perfection. Thus we say, 'He has achieved the *ne plus ultra*. No one can go further in the direction in which he has been so successful.'

Nesh. This is an Old English word, derived from the Anglo-Saxon *nese*, meaning delicate, tender, soft. It is still used in the Midland Counties, where it is said that a horse is *nesh* when he refuses his food, and Chinese pigs have to be kept very warm 'because they are so *nesh*.' Dickens tried hard to revive the use of the word, but his example has not been generally followed, although there is no other English word that is so expressive of constitutional tenderness or delicacy.

Ness. This affix to the names of places always signifies a jutting-out, or promontory. The word is the Anglo-Saxon term for nose (*nœse*). In Scandinavia it takes the form *naes*, as in Lindesnaes. In France it is *nez*, as in Grisnez, and in Scotland *ness*, as in Inverness and Caithness. In England the termination is also *ness*, as in Dungeness, Sheerness, Shoeburyness, &c.

Never buy a pig in a poke. It is said that some wags at Northampton Market put a cat in a bag, or poke, and sold it to a countryman as a pig. Upon going to a tavern to 'have a drink' over the bargain, the buyer opened the bag, and of course the cat jumped out. This is stated to be the origin of the proverb 'You should never buy a pig in a poke,' and also of 'You have let the cat out of the bag.' The word *poke* is still used for sack in the south of England.

News. This word is commonly believed to be formed of the initial letters of the names of the four cardinal points. If, however, this be the case, it is difficult to understand how the synonymous foreign words, *nova* and *nouvelles*, which are spelt in a totally different manner, can mean the same thing. But it is not necessary to go out of our language to refute the N E W S theory. The word news was formerly spelt 'newes,' and as this contained five letters, it completely negatives the suggestion that the word was derived from the four letters on a weathercock. It was probably derived from the German *das neue* in the nominative case and neuter gender. The German phrase *Was giebt neues?* is the exact equivalent of the English 'What is the news?'

Newspapers. The following are the dates of the establishment of the leading daily newspapers:—

Public Ledger	. 1759	Standard	.	. 1827
Morning Post	. 1781	Daily News	.	. 1846
Times	. 1788	Daily Telegraph	.	. 1855
Morning Advertiser	. 1794	Pall Mall Gazette	.	. 1865
Globe	. 1803			

Newspapers in America. 'It is the general belief that the first American newspaper was the "Boston News Letter," first published in 1704. There is, however, a single copy of a Boston paper of the date September 25, 1690, in the State Paper Office in London.'—*Notes and Queries*, February 7, 1857.

Newspaper Leaders. When a newspaper editor sends his writings to the printer, directions are added as to the type he wishes to be used, as 'brevier,' 'brevier, leads,' 'bourgeois,' or 'bourgeois, leads,' the addition 'leads' denoting that the matter is to be set up in type of the size indicated, with strips of lead between the lines to keep them wider apart than usual. The editor's comments on passing events, being always 'leaded,' are in the printing-office called 'leaders,' which was formerly pronounced ledders. The term 'leading article' arose from a misapprehension of the original word.

Newspaper Stamps. Up to the year 1712 newspapers were entirely free from Stamp Duty. A Bill had been brought into Parliament in 1701 imposing a penny stamp, but it did not pass into law. In 1712 a halfpenny stamp was imposed upon every half-sheet, and a penny for a whole sheet. This impost was fatal to many papers, and their discontinuance was humorously described by Addison as the 'fall of the leaf.' These duties, however, were shortly afterwards repealed, but were reimposed in 1725. In 1761 the stamp was made a penny, irrespective of size; in 1776 it was advanced to $1\frac{1}{2}d.$; in 1787 to $2d.$; in 1794 to $2\frac{1}{2}d.$; in 1797 to $3\frac{1}{2}d.$; and in 1815 to $4d.$ In 1836 the duty was reduced to a penny for a sheet of given size, and a halfpenny additional for supplements. In 1855 the Stamp Duty was abolished, except in cases where copies were required to be sent free through the post. This was discontinued in 1870, when halfpenny wrappers and stamps were substituted. The duty of $1s.\ 6d.$ for each advertisement, however short or long, was abolished in 1853.

Newt, the name of a lizard. Probably a corruption of 'an ewt.' The names *ewt, evet, effet,* and *efete* are common names for the reptile in different parts of England.

New Testament. The earliest specimen of the Scriptures printed in English is a fragment in the British Museum of Tyndale's translation of the New Testament, the printing of which, by Quentell, he was superintending at Cologne in 1529 when he was driven from that city. This fragment is all that is known to remain of an edition of 3,000 copies.—*Power.*

New Version. The 'New Version' of the Psalms was introduced in consequence of an order of William III., December 3, 1696.

New Year's Day. Up to the 24th George II. the *legal* year commenced March 25, but the natural and historical year commenced as now on January 1. Legal documents before 1750, relating to events occurring between January 1 and March 25, bore double dates, as 171$\frac{6}{7}$ or 1716-7. The latter of the two dates corresponds to our present computation. The 1st of January has been 'New Year's Day' in Scotland from the year 1599.

New York. The city of New York is built on the island of Manhattan, which is 13½ miles long by about 1½ mile wide. It contains 22 square miles of surface. The entire island was bought in 1621, in fee simple, from an Iroquois chief, by the Dutch for twenty-four dollars, or something less than 5*l.* of our money. This purchase was at the rate of about twelve acres for a penny. Some choice City central lots have recently been sold at the rate of 200,000*l.* an acre. The city was first called *Nieuw Amsterdam*, and in 1652 contained about a thousand inhabitants. It was seized by the British under Colonel Nichols in 1664, and was by him re-named New York, a name which was afterwards extended to the whole province. The British held it until the conclusion of the War of Independence, finally evacuating it on November 25, 1783. It is now the third city in the civilised world in point of population, and is second only to London in commercial importance.

New York Shilling, or York shilling, is the old Spanish *real*, or one-eighth of a dollar. It is about equivalent in value to sixpence, English. In the Southern States it is called a 'bit.'

Next. This word has in Scotland a different signification to that which it bears in England. The words in the Common Prayer Book, 'on Sunday next,' signify to an Englishman the Sunday next or nearest. In Scotland, that day is 'Sunday first,' and the words 'Sunday next' mean 'the Sunday next following Sunday first'; i.e. the second Sunday.

Niagara. This name is a compound of two Indian words, *Niag hera*, 'hark to the thunder!'

Nice originally meant foolish, from the Latin *nescius*, ignorant. Chaucer has—

> For he was *nyce* and knowth no wisdome;

and he uses 'nice fare' for foolish to do. To be 'over-nice' still means to be foolishly particular, and 'more nice than wise' also carries the original meaning. Archdeacon Hoare, however, derives the word from the French *niais*, simple; and speaks of 'That stupid vulgarism by which we use the word *nice* to denote almost every mode of approbation for almost every variety of quality; and from sheer poverty of thought, or fear of saying anything definite, wrap up everything indiscriminately in this characterless domino—speaking in the same breath of a nice cheesecake, a nice tragedy, a nice oyster, a nice child, a nice man, a nice tree, a nice sermon, and a nice country; as if a universal *niaiserie* (for nice seems originally to have been only *niais*) had whelmed the whole island. This vulgarism has already taken, even in the lower classes, and one hears ploughboys speaking of nice weather and sailors of a nice sea.' Another meaning of *nice* is over-fastidiousness, or affectation of purity and delicacy, often employed by the most vicious people. It is in this sense that Swift said, 'A nice man is a man of nasty ideas.'

Niche. The concave recesses in a wall for the reception of statuary, &c. are so called from the Italian word *nicchia*, a shell; the archivolts being often formed like shells.

Nickname. Several derivations of this word have been suggested, the most probable being an *eke* name, or an additional name. Johnson thought it came from the French *non de nique*, a term of contempt. Worcester suggests from *nick*, to suit. Camden says, 'From nicknames or *nurse*-names come Bill for William, Nat for Nathaniel, &c.' Another derivation is from Old Nick, Satan, the διάβολος, or false accuser, who slanders people and gives them contemptuous epithets. Shakespeare uses the word in a different sense altogether, e.g. 'You *nickname* virtue, vice.'

Nicotine. This word is derived from the name of John Nicot, who introduced tobacco into France in 1560.

Night. Under the Poaching Act (9 Geo. IV. c. 69), night legally commences at the expiration of the first hour after sunset, and concludes at the beginning of the last hour before sunrise.

Nightingale. We derive this name from the Anglo-Saxon *nihtegale—niht*, night, and *galan*, to sing.

Nightmare. Nightmare is still called in remote country districts 'witch-riding.' The name is a remnant of Scandinavian mythology. '*Mara* was, in the Runic theology, a spectre of the night which seized men in their sleep and suddenly deprived them of speech and motion.'—*Brand's Popular Antiquities*, vol. iii. p. 279.

Nine days' wonder. This phrase is thought to have originated in some reference to the nine days during which Lady Jane Grey was styled Queen of England. Another authority attributes it to the nine days after birth during which a puppy remains blind. There is an old proverb given in Bohn's 'Handbook of Proverbs,' ' A wonder lasts nine days, and then the puppy's eyes are open.'

Nine-pins. This game was formerly illegal. In Bailey's Dictionary the word *closhe* stands as follows: ' Closhe (Old Statutes), the game at nine-pins; forbidden by statute anno 17 Edw. IV.' The prohibition was afterwards withdrawn, and the game became very popular. The name *skittles* seems to have been introduced as another name for the game about the beginning of the eighteenth century. Poor Robin, in his ' Almanack ' for 1695, says :—

People to Moorfields flock in sholes,
At *nine-pins* and at pigeon-holes
The country lasses pastime make.

In the Almanack for 1707 the word *skittles* is substituted, the term 'nine-pins' being discarded. The game of nine-pins was formerly very popular as a gambling game in the United States, and in some of the States was prohibited by law. With their usual ingenuity the Americans evaded this law by adding another pin and calling the game 'ten-pins,' under which name it is one of the most popular games in the States. The slang phrase 'right as ninepence' is a corruption of ' right as nine-*pins*.' The nine pins of the popular game are placed with great *nicety* so as to form rows of three in each direction.

Nine tailors make a man. In North's 'Church Bells of Leicestershire,' the author, in speaking of tolling for the dead, says : ' These tolls are called "tellers," and it has been suggested that the old saying " Nine tailors make a man " is a corruption of " Nine tellers mark a man," meaning that three times three tolls or tellers are struck on the passing bell for a man.' At Wimbledon it is still the custom to strike three times three for an adult male and three times two for a female on the tenor bell ; but for children under twelve the treble bell is used, and the strokes are twice three for a male, and twice two for a female.

Nineteenth Century. The first century began on January 1, A.D. 1, and the hundred years making the entire century ended December 31, A.D. 100. The second century commenced on the following day, viz. January 1, 101. The eighteenth century therefore ended December 31, 1800, and the nineteenth commenced January 1, 1801.

Nippant. This is an American adjective meaning impudent or impertinent, which might with utility find a place in English dictionaries. We already have the verb *to nip*, in the sense of to satirise. Ascham has, ' Soothing such as be present; *nipping* any that is absent.' We have ' flippant,' why not adopt ' nippant ' ?

Nisi Prius, the literal meaning of which is *unless before,* is the name given to the sittings of a court for the trial of civil causes. Formerly causes were tried in London by juries from the counties where the actions arose. In summoning these juries the jurors were required to attend in London at a certain time, ' *nisi prius justiciarii ad assisas. capiendas venerint*'—that is, *unless before* [that time] the judges shall come into the county in question.

Noah's Ark. Bishop Wilkins, taking the cubit at 22 inches, calculated that the ark was 547 feet long, 91 broad, and 54 high. Its capacity, according to the same authority, was 72,625 tons. The ' Great Eastern ' is 694 feet long and 83 broad.

Nob. At the Universities the sons of the nobility, after their signatures in the college books, inscribe the words '*fil. nob.*' son of a noble. Hence all young nobles were called *nobs,* and the word, although slang at first, is gradually making its way into the language as genuine.

No Cards. In a lecture at Cambridge, March 7, 1868, Mr. S. C. Whiteley stated that the first advertisement of a marriage in which these words occurred appeared in the ' Times ' of November 19, 1862.

No great shakes. This proverbial expression probably arose in an allusion to shaking walnut trees to dislodge the fruit. Where there is a scanty crop of walnuts, there will be ' no great shakes.'

For the nonce. There is perhaps no phrase in the English language concerning the origin of which there have been so many conjectures. Tyrwhitt and Rittson suppose it to be corrupted from the Latin *pro nunc.* Jamieson derives it from the Gothic *naennas.* Wright says it was anciently 'for the nones.' Gifford traces it from the Anglo Saxon in the following stages : ' a ones, an anes, for the ones, for the nanes, for the nones, for the nonce.' Perhaps, after all, the phrase may have arisen in a clerical error, some careless scribe prefixing an *n* to the word ' once.' The expression 'for the once ' would thus become ' for the nonce,' which, as now used, has the precise meaning of ' for the once ' or for this once.

Nonconformists. This name arose and was applied in 1662 to the 2,000 ministers of the Established Church who resigned their benefices rather than ' conform ' to the statute ' for the uniformity of public prayers and administration of the Sacraments.'

Non est. This is an abbreviation of the Latin phrase *non est inventus*, he has not been found. Thus we say of a person who has absconded, He is *non est*.

Non nobis, Domine. ' Not unto us, O Lord,' &c. is the first verse of the 115th Psalm. The music to the words—sung as a grace at public dinners—was composed by W. Bird in 1618.

Non sequitur (Latin), it does not follow, as, ' Your conclusion is a *non sequitur*, it is not warranted by the premisses.'

Nook. This word is from the Gaelic *nuic*, a corner.

Noon. Most writers have supposed this word to be derived from *nona*, nine. An almanack printed at Antwerp in 1530 spells the word 'none,' and this suggests that the word originally meant *none*, nothing. After the clock had struck twelve the cycle was complete, and there was *nothing to count*. At the expiration of the first hour *one* could be counted, in another hour *two*, and so on. Is it not probable, therefore, that none, or as we call it, noon, originally meant the time when none, or nothing, could be named as the hour of the day? Of course the reader will see that this is mere speculation.

No one is a hero to his valet. This saying is generally attributed to Montaigne, but Madame Cornuel, who died in 1694, wrote : ' Il n'y a pas de grand homme pour son valet de chambre.' Montaigne's words are : ' Peu d'hommes ont esté admirés par leurs domestiques.'

Norfolk is the shire of the North folk. It was originally written Northfolke. ' The [river] Wantsume riseth in Northfolke at Galesend in Holt Hundred.'—*Harr., Descr. of Brit.* xii. 1.

Norfolk Biffins. The word ' biffin ' is a corruption of the name *beaufin*, a celebrated Norfolk variety of the apple. These apples are dried in ovens, and, being packed in boxes, are sent to every part of the country.

Nose. There is a curious association between the letters *sn* and the nose. The following words, commencing with those two consonants, have all some connection with that organ :—Snout, snar, sneeze, snast, snore, snub, snite (to blow the nose), snarl, snuffy, snort, sneer (originally to turn up the nose), sniff, snigger, snuff, snift, snuffle, snooze, snub, snaffle, snivel, &c.

Notary Public, generally contracted to *notary*, is an officer of the law whose chief function is to act as a legal witness of some formal act. The certificate of a notary is accepted in all the courts of the civilised world as good evidence of any fact which he certifies.

Notes of Admiration and Interrogation. The mark ! is the two letters I and O placed one above the other, ¡, *io* in Latin means joy. The mark ? was originally compounded of Q and O, thus, ?; they are the first and last letters of *questio*, the Latin word for question.

Not lost, but gone before. These words are quoted in a collection of epitaphs by Pettigrew, published by Lackington early in the nineteenth century. The tomb on which they occur is that of Mary Angell, widow, who died at Stepney 1693, aged seventy-two. The inscription runs thus :—

> To say an angel here interred doth lye
> May be thought strange, for angels never dye,
> Indeed some fell from heav'n to hell;
> Are lost and rise no more.
> This only fell from death to earth,
> Not lost, but gone before.
> Her dust lodged here, her soul, perfect in grace,
> 'Mongst saints and angels now hath took its place.

Not worth a rap. Probably from the letters forming the heading of Indian money columns in account-books, R. A. P., meaning rupees, annas, and pice. In Indian accounts these letters are used precisely in the same manner as our £ s. d. See RAP.

Not worth a rush. 'It was probably the custom of strewing rushes on the floor that gave rise to this phrase for any thing of no value. Being scattered so profusely and trodden to pieces without reserve, they were, of course, singly of very little value.'—*Nares.* The following quotation from Lyly supports this view :—' But bee not pinned alwayes on her sleeves; strangers have *green rushes*, when daily guests are *not worth a rush.*'—*Sappho and Phaon*, ii. 4.

Nought, naught. In the Scriptures, the word nought (spelled with the *o*) always means *nothing*. In 2 Kings ii. 19, ' the water is naught' (spelled with the *a*), the meaning is *bad*. In Jer. xxiv. 2, the same original is translated naughty—'*naughty* figs,' that is, *bad* figs. See NAUGHTY.

Noun, from the Latin *nomen*, a name. A noun is the name of any thing. See THINGS.

NUMERALS. 393

Nous. Although generally applied ludicrously, this word is a pure Greek term for mind or understanding.

Nous verrons (French), we shall see.

Noyeau. The name of this cordial is from *noyau*, the kernel of a peach-stone or nut. In Languedoc *noualh* is a kernel; and in Welsh *cnewyll* is a cherry-stone or plum-stone.

Nucleus, from the Latin *nux, nucis*, a nut; thus a *nut* is the *nucleus* of a future hazel-tree.

Nugget. Some have attempted to show that this is a Persian word signifying *ready cash*. The word, however, is Scottish, and signifies a lump, as a *nugget* of bread, a *nugget* of sugar, &c.

Number of Separate Parts in a Watch. Mr. E. J. Wood, in his 'Curiosities of Clocks and Watches,' says that 'a good three-quarter plate watch as usually made requires no fewer than one hundred and thirty-eight distinct pieces in its frame, train, escapement, potence, fusees, arbors, clicks, ratchets, and other nicely contrived and adjusted constituents. To these must be added the chain of six hundred and thirty pieces, thus swelling the contents of a common detached lever watch to seven hundred and sixty-eight separate pieces' (p. 370).

Number of the Stars. Sir William Herschel, after some very elaborate investigations and calculations, estimated the total number of stars within the celestial vault at something more than twenty millions. Mr. Chacornac thinks this estimate too small, and is of opinion that seventy-seven millions are comprised within the first thirteen magnitudes.

Numbering of Houses. In 1760 names were first put on doors, and in 1764 houses were numbered. The first houses numbered were those in New Burleigh Street; the next those in Lincoln's Inn Fields.—*Haunted London*, p. 458.

Numerals. All the English names of numerals from 1 to 999,999 are Anglo-Saxon. The word million we get through the French from the Latin. Similarly, the names of all the ordinals up to the same point are Anglo-Saxon except the word 'second,' which is of French origin. This singular exception arose from the fact that in the Anglo-Saxon there was no ordinal corresponding to the number two, its place being filled with the word 'other'; they accordingly counted 'first,' 'other,' 'third,' &c. The word 'second' is from the Latin *sequor*, to follow, from its following the first.

Nurse, from the Anglo-Saxon *norice*, meaning one who nourishes.

Nutmeg, from the French *noix muscade*, scented nut. The nutmeg is the fruit of the tree *Myristaca moschata*, a native of the Molucca Islands and of Central Africa.

O

Oaf, a simpleton, a blockhead, an idiot. Formerly supposed to be a changeling, the true infant being removed by fairies, and an oaf, aulf, or elf substituted. Drayton says:

> Some silly doating brainless calf,
> Will say the fairy left this *aulf*
> And took away the other.

In the remote parts of Worcestershire the clown at a circus is still called the *oaf*. Not long since the writer heard a native of that county give a verbal description of rope-dancing, one of the incidents of which was that 'the *oaf* cum an' choaked 'is fit'—that is, the clown came and chalked the feet of the dancer.

Oaks. The celebrated race at Epsom called the Oaks was founded in 1779 by the twelfth Earl of Derby, who owned an estate in the neighbourhood called Lambert's Oaks.

Oat. This word is seldom used except in the plural, and is the only English grain of which we can speak in the singular without the intervention of another noun. Thus we say 'an oat,' 'a grain of wheat.'

Obiit. A Latin word often seen on tombs. It signifies he, or she, died. It is a word of three syllables, *o-bi-it*.

Oblige. Formerly this word was pronounced *obleege*. The compiler has heard it so pronounced by the late Earl Russell and the great Duke of Wellington. Pope adopted that pronunciation in the lines

> Dreading even fools, by flatterers besieged,
> And so obliging that he ne'er obliged.

Obsequious. This word was formerly used only in reference to funeral *obsequies*. Shakespeare has many examples of the word applied in this sense. It does not seem formerly to have conveyed any idea of cringing or insincerity. Thus in 'Hamlet,' act i. sc. 2 :

> And the survivor bound
> In filial obligation for some term
> To do obsequious sorrow.

And in 'Richard III.,' act i. sc. 2 :

> While I awhile obsequiously lament
> Th' untimely fall of virtuous Lancaster.

And again in the Thirty-first Sonnet :

> How many a holy and obsequious tear
> Hath dear religious love stolen from mine eye
> As interest of the dead.

Observation. The habit of observation is the most fruitful source of knowledge. Herschel defines it as 'passive experience.'

Obsolete. Many words marked obsolete by Johnson have since come again into use; *jeopardise* is one word so marked. Dryden, who was born in 1631, speaking of Spenser, who died in 1599, says, 'Notwithstanding his *obsolete* language he is still intelligible.'

Obverse. The obverse of a coin or medal is that side of it which contains the principal device. Thus the obverse of an English coin is that which contains the head of the king or queen in relief.

Obvious. This word has considerably changed in signification. Its original meaning is *opposed in front,* open to attack, exposed, liable. Milton says, ' Obvious to dispute.'

O dear me! This is probably a corruption of the Spanish '*Ah de mi!*' Woe is me! the burden of a song very popular in England temp. James I. But the Italians frequently use a similar expression, '*Dio mio,*' My God, which, spoken rapidly, sounds exactly like ' Dear me!'

Of. Simple as this preposition appears, it requires care in its use, or it may express in some cases exactly the opposite of the writer's intention. In the sentence 'the fear of the enemy,' it may mean the fear felt by the enemy, or the fear felt lest the power or strength of the enemy should be too great to be overcome.

Offend, from the Latin *ob,* against, and *fendo,* to strike. ' To offend originally signified to infringe, that is, to stumble or hit dangerously upon somewhat lying across our way, so as thereby to be cast down, or at least to be disordered in our posture and stopt in our progress.'—*Barrow.*

Officious did not always have the meaning of improper interference. An old lady not long ago told a clergyman that her friends had been very 'officious'; she meant attentive.

Off the hooks. A gate is usually hung with hinges that turn upon hooks driven into the gate-post. If the gate should by any accident get 'off the hooks,' it is of course useless for a time. Hence any one temporarily indisposed and unfitted for duty is metaphorically said to be 'off the hooks.'

Oid. With the exception of void, avoid, and devoid, all English words with the termination *oid* are from the Greek, and the last three letters form two syllables. Thus *aneroid* should be pronounced an-e-ro-id, *rhomboid* rhom-bo-id, and so on.

O Jiminy! This, which was a common interjectional remark in the last generation, and is not yet quite extinct, is a corruption of '*O Gemini*,' a Latin invocation to the divine brothers Castor and Pollux.

O.K. These letters in America signify 'all right.' Their use, it is said, originated with old Jacob Astor, the millionaire of New York. He was looked upon in commercial circles as a man of great information and sound judgment, and was a sort of general referee as to the solvency or standing of other traders. If a note of enquiry as to any particular trader's position came, the answer to which he intended to be satisfactory, he was accustomed to write across the note the letters 'O.K.,' and return it to the writer. The letters O.K. he supposed to be the initials of 'all correct,' and in this sense they are now universally current in the States.

Old Cities. 'The names of five of the oldest cities of the world, Damascus, Hebron, Gaza, Sidon, and Hamath, are still pronounced by the inhabitants exactly in the same manner as was the case thirty or perhaps forty centuries ago.'—*Taylor, Words and Places.*

Old Curiosity Shop. 'The church which Dickens described and Cattermole drew, in connection with the story of Little Nell, and in which the poor child was laid to rest, is the parish church of Tong, in Shropshire.'—*Building News*, September 13, 1871.

Old Dominion. Virginia in the United States is familiarly known as the 'Old Dominion.' It is perhaps so called from its having been the only part of America which was nominally included in the English royal title, and whose arms were quartered on the royal shield. Spenser, as it may be remembered, dedicated the 'Faerie Queene' to Elizabeth, by the title of 'Elizabeth by the grace of God Queen of England, France, and Ireland, *and of Virginia*, Defender of the Faith,' &c.

Old Harry. A slang name for the Devil. It is a corruption of the words 'Old Hairy.'

Old Hundredth Psalm. There is a curious error, probably originating in a misprint, in the ordinary metrical version of this Psalm. The words of the Authorised Version, 'We are his people, and the sheep of his pasture,' are rendered:—

> We are his *flock*, he doth us feed,
> And for his sheep he doth us take.

Here the word 'flock' is evidently a mistake for 'folk.' In Scott's edition of the Psalms (Edinburgh, 1765), and in the 'Bay Psalm Book,' the words adopted are:—

> His *folk* and pasture sheep are we.

But the question as to the original words of the poet, whose version is still used, is settled by reference to the earliest known edition, 'The Whole Booke of Psalmes, Printed by John Daye, liuing over Aldersgate, 1578'; where the words are:

> We are his *folke*, he dothe usse feede,
> And for his sheepe he dothe usse take.

There is another discrepancy between the original version and that now in use. The original reading in the first verse was, 'Him serve with *mirth*,' which is certainly nearer 'Serve the Lord with gladness' than 'Him serve with *fear*.' The 'Scotch Psalm Book' (1865) has the word 'mirth'; and Tate and Brady have 'Glad homage pay with awful mirth.'

Old Inn. There is, or was until recently, a tavern at the foot of Shude Hill, in Manchester, known as 'The Seven Stars,' which the records in Lancaster Castle prove to have been a licensed tavern for about 530 years. This is probably the oldest inn in England.

Old maids leading apes in hell. In a rare tract in the library of Peterborough Cathedral, 'The Passionate Morrice,' 1593, the word *ape* is used in the sense of an unsuccessful wooer. Now, as old maids are supposed to become so from refusing offers, there seems some reason why they should 'lead apes in hell,' although the late Mr. Dyce used to say the phrase 'never could be explained.'

Old man eloquent. This epithet, so often applied to Mr.

Gladstone, is from Milton's fifth Sonnet, which was addressed to Lady Margaret Ley. The lines in which it occurs are:—

> Till sad the breaking of that parliament
> Broke him, as that dishonest victory
> At Chæronea, fatal to liberty,
> Kill'd with report that *old man eloquent.*

Old Nick. This term is from the name of a Scandinavian demon, Nikr, who haunts mines. The name of the metal nickel comes from a legend amongst the miners that the hardness of the ore is attributable to the malevolence of Nikr.

Old Phrases still in common use. Sherlocke's 'Hatcher of Heresies,'. printed at Antwerp 1565, contains the following phrases which are still in use:—

> Differ as much as chalk and cheese.
> As plain as a pike-staff.
> The ignorant sort believe that the moon is made of green cheese.
> They have made no bones at it.
> Proud as peacocks.
> It is but a tale of a tub.
> It is not worth a straw.
> Neither by fair nor foul means.
> Choppings and changings.
> Melancthon hath turned his coat.
> Made such a stir as though he would have thrown the house out of the window.
> Such a brazen face, &c. &c.

Old Scratch. This term is from *Skratti*, a Scandinavian word for demons. Weird and lonely rocks in little frequented spots in Norway are called *Skrattaskar*, from their being thought to be haunted by Skratti.

Old Tom (applied to gin). One of the partners in 'Hodge's' distillery at Millbank was Thomas Chamberlain, familiarly known in the distillery as Old Tom. His department was the superintendence of the distilling operations. One of the employés of the firm, a man named Norris, left their service and opened a 'gin palace' in Great Russell Street, Covent Garden, and he—out of respect to his old master—christened a cordial of Hodge's make 'Old Tom,' a name which is now general for a fine quality of gin.

Oliver Cromwell. The parish registers of St. Giles's, Cripplegate, record that on August 22, 1620, Oliver Cromwell and Elizabeth Bourchier were married at that church. Cromwell was then in his twenty-first year.

Olla podrida, a term naturalised in England for a medley or odd assortment of anything, is a Spanish phrase, the literal meaning of which is *putrid pot*. It is applied in Spain to a dish of mixed vegetables and remains of flesh meat, and is akin to what the Scotch call *hotch-potch*, and the French *pot-pourri*.

Omnibus. Mr. C. Knight, in his 'Volume of Varieties' (p. 178), says: 'The omnibus was tried about 1800 with four horses and six wheels; but we refused to accept it in any shape till we imported the fashion from Paris in 1830.' Mr. John Ellerby, of Leamington, has a copy of a large coloured print, 'A View of London from Blackfriars,' taken in 1796, in which an omnibus of the exact shape now in use is represented passing over Blackfriars Bridge. Haydn, in his 'Dictionary of Dates,' says: 'The idea of such conveyances is ascribed to Pascal, about 1662, when similar carriages were started, but soon discontinued. They were revived in Paris April 11, 1828, and introduced into London by a coach proprietor named Shillibeer. The first omnibus started from Paddington to the Bank of England on Saturday, July 4, 1829.' The original of the name may be found in the following extract from the 'Revue de Brétagne et de Vendée':—'A certain M. Baudry established in 1827 hot baths in a suburb of Nantes. As customers did not come in sufficient numbers, he resolved, as the best means for attracting them, to send at fixed hours a long car to the centre of the town. This car was known at first as the *Voiture des bains de Richebourg*, but a friend of Baudry's suggested, as a shorter and more convenient designation, the word *omnibus*, which had already obtained a certain vogue because a grocer of the town named Omnés had painted over his shop entrance the words '*Omnes Omnibus.*' Baudry established, shortly afterwards, lines of omnibuses at Bordeaux and Paris, but the rigorous winter of 1829, which rendered the streets very difficult and forage very dear, caused him to die of grief. The omnibus, however, survived both the bad winter and its founder.'

One half the world knows not how the other lives. This proverbial saying seems to have originated with Bishop Hall. It occurs in 'Holy Observations,' No. XVII., ed. 1837.

One step from the sublime to the ridiculous. This saying is generally attributed to Napoleon. It is, however, to be found in the works of the notorious Tom Paine, before Napoleon's time. Paine says: 'The sublime and the ridiculous are often so nearly related that it is difficult to class them separately. One step above the sublime makes the ridiculous, and one step above the ridiculous makes the sublime again.'

On hand. This phrase in England is confined to the language of commerce. A corn merchant may say he 'has no oats on hand,' or a fishmonger when applied to for salmon may say he has none on hand. The Americans give the phrase a far wider significance, as the following extract from the 'New York Express' will show: 'The anti-Sabbath meeting, so long talked of, has at length taken place in Boston. About three hundred females were *on hand*.'

On the nail. To pay on the nail—that is, at once. On the Bristol Exchange are four bronze pillars having expanded tops like tables; they are called nails. On these 'nails' the earnest money of bargains was formerly paid by merchants at the time the bargain was made. Hence to pay on the nail became synonymous with paying ready money.

On the street. The Americans, like the Scotch, say '*on* the street,' instead of the absurd English phrase '*in* the street.' We say 'on the road,' 'on the way,' 'on the path,' &c.; why therefore '*in* the street'? The phrase is even more absurd in the saying, 'He's out *in* the street.'

On tick. This is not a modern phrase. In 'The Diary of Abraham de la Pryme,' published by the Surtees Society, the following passage occurs under date 1696: 'Here is very little or no new monney comes yet down amongst us, so that we scarce know how to subsist. Every one runs *upon tick*, and those that had no credit a year ago has (*sic*) credit enough now.' In a 'Letter of Dean Prideaux of Norwich, written from Oxford, May 1661,' is the following:—The Mermaid Tavern is lately broke, and our Christchurch men bear the blame of it, our *ticks*, as the noise of the town will have it, amounting to 1,500*l*.

Onus probandi. These Latin words mean 'the burden of proof.' In law and in ordinary life, where A. makes a statement, which B. disputes, the *onus probandi* lies upon A., who has to *prove* what he asserts.

Opal, from the Sclavonic. In the Polish language *palać* is to glow, to blaze, and *opalać* is to burn on all sides. In the Servian, *opaliti* is to shoot, to give fire. These are words all of which are singularly applicable to the iridescent glowing rays of the opal.

Opera. The simple and original meaning of this word is *work*. It comes from the same root as the verb 'to operate.'

Opposite. Opposite and contrary are often used as if there were no essential difference between them, and yet there is a most essential one. For example, a man may be at once prudent and bold, although these are *opposites*, but he cannot be at once prudent and rash, for these are *contraries*. Sweet and sour are *opposites*; sweet and bitter are *contraries*.—*Trench*.

Optimist. An optimist is one who believes that everything in the universe, being the work of a perfect Being, is the best that could be devised or created, and that events, being controlled by the same almighty hand, will ultimately be for the benefit of mankind.

Oranges. The sweet orange was first brought from China to Europe by the Portuguese in 1547. The identical parent tree is said to be still in existence at Lisbon.

Orator. This word, in the sense of *one who prays for*, was commonly used by bishops and the clergy generally two centuries ago as a part of the subscription of a letter. Thus in a letter of Archbishop Sancroft to the Princess Mary of Orange, afterwards queen, dated 'Lambhith Palace, Nov. 3, 1687,' the archbishop subscribes himself 'Your m. devoted faithfull servant and daily *orator* at the throne of Grace, W. C.' ('Collectanea Curiosa,' Oxford, 1781, p. 302.)

Oratorio. The first oratorio performed in England was Handel's 'Esther,' which was produced at the Opera House, Haymarket, in 1732.

Orchard. This word is from the Anglo-Saxon *ortgeard*, or *wortgeard*, a yard or *gearden* where worts or vegetables were grown.

Order of the Garter. It has been frequently stated that this knightly order had its origin in the accidental dropping, by the Countess of Salisbury, of her garter, which the king (Edward III.) picked up and presented to her with the words which have since become the motto of the order, *Honi soit qui mal y pense*—evil be to him who thinks evil of it. This is now thought to be incorrect. At the battle of Cressy, 1346, the king's garter was used as a standard, and the order was afterwards instituted, 1349, to celebrate the victories gained by the Black Prince. Wharton, in the 'Law Lexicon,' says, 'This military order of knighthood is said to have been first instituted by Richard I. at the siege of Acre, when he caused twenty-six knights, who had firmly stood by him, to wear thongs of blue leather about their legs.' Brand states that 'it is the custom in Normandy for a bride to bestow her

garter on some young man as a favour, or sometimes it is taken
from her. In "Aylet's Poems," 1654, is a copy of verses, "On sight
of a most honourable Lady's Wedding Garter." I am of opinion
that the origin of the "Order of the Garter" is to be traced to this
nuptial custom, anciently common to both court and country. . . .
These garters, it should seem, were anciently worn as trophies in
the hats.'—*Popular Antiquities*, edit. 1870, vol. ii. p. 78.

Ordinary. An *ordinary* in English law is a judge in *his own
right*, and not by delegation from others. It is confined in practice to the ecclesiastical law. A bishop is an ordinary in his
diocese; an archbishop in his province. The following passage from
Hamilton shows some of the various meanings attached to this
word :—' Two persons rose very early, as was their *ordinary* habit.
Their means were only *ordinary*. They were much shocked at the
spectacle of an execution which they were compelled to pass just
as the *ordinary* of the jail was bidding farewell to the prisoner.
The next scene was more pleasant, for they saw a review precisely
as the regiments were marching past the general in *ordinary* time.
They finished their walk at an excellent *ordinary*, where there
was a very sumptuous entertainment.'

Ordnance formerly meant only the arrangement or preparation
of the artillery in the sense of the French *ordonner*. In the
'English Chronicles,' published by the Camden Society, we read,
'The *ordenaunce* of [*i.e.* the arrangements for] the kinge's guns
avayled not, for that day was so grete rayne that the gonnes lay depe
in the water, and so were queyet and could not be schott' (p. 97).

Organic Disease is so called in cases where the *structure* of the
organ affected has become altered, as in induration or hardening of
the liver. *Functional* diseases are those in which the *functions* of
an organ are deranged in their operation, as when the liver secretes
viscid or unhealthy bile.

Oriel. An oriel window differs from a bay window, though
both may be alike in shape. A bay window rises immediately
from the ground, and even if the bay be carried two or three
storeys high, with windows on each, they are all called bay
windows. An oriel, on the contrary, is one which projects from
the face of the wall, *supported on brackets or corbels*.

Origin of Coinage. 'The mode in which the invention [of
coinage] happened is sufficiently evident. Seals were formerly
employed in very early times, as we learn from the Egyptian
paintings and the stamped bricks of Nineveh. Being employed
to signify possession, or to ratify contracts, they came to indicate

authority. When a ruler first undertook to certify the weight of pieces of metal, he naturally employed his seal to make the fact known, just as, at Goldsmiths' Hall, a small punch is used to certify the fineness of plate. In the earliest forms of coinage there were no attempts at so fashioning the metal that its weight could not be altered without destroying the stamp or design. The earliest coins struck, both in Lydia and the Peloponnesus, were stamped on one side only.'—*Prof. Jevons, Money, &c.,* p. 56.

Origin of Essences. ' The perfume of flowers often consists of oils and ethers which the chemist can compound artificially in his laboratory. Singularly enough, they are generally derived from substances of intensely disgusting odour. A peculiar fetid oil, termed fusel oil, is formed in making brandy and whiskey. This fusel oil, distilled with sulphuric acid and acetate of potash, gives the oil of pears. The oil of apples is made from fusel oil, sulphuric acid, and bichromate of potash. Oil of pineapples is produced by making a soap with butter, and distilling it with alcohol and sulphuric acid. The artificial oil of bitter almonds is prepared by the action of nitric acid on the fetid oil of gas tar. Many a fair forehead is damped with *eau de millefleurs,* without knowing that its essential ingredient is derived from the drainage of cowhouses.'— *Dr. Lyon Playfair.*

Ormolu. This word refers to a kind of brass closely resembling gold in appearance. The name is derived from the French *or,* gold, and *moulu,* to grind to powder. The genuine *ormolu* was made by grinding a fine quality of brass to an impalpable powder, with which the surface of objects was covered. It is now only a fine description of brass, brought by chemical processes to resemble the colour of gold. The mixture which produces brass of such fine colour is 75 parts of pure copper, and 25 parts of spelter.

Orpheus. This name is commonly but erroneously pronounced *or-phe-us;* it should be pronounced as though written *or-fuce.* All *Greek* proper names ending in *eus* follow the same rule; but if *eus* is only a Latinised form of the Greek *eos,* as in Timotheus (Timotheos), Rom. xvi. 21, *eus* is a dissyllable, the name being pronounced Ti-mo-the-us.

Orrery. This name is applied to an instrument invented by George Graham for representing the orbits and motions of the bodies composing the solar system. The Earl of Orrery, about the year 1715, bought one which had been made by a person named Rowley, and Dean Swift gave it the name of Orrery in the earl's honour. Sir John Herschel ('Astronomy,' Cab. Cycl., p. 287) says, 'As to getting correct notions on the subject [the magnitudes and distances of the planets] by drawing circles on paper, or, still worse, from those very childish toys called *orreries*, it is out of the question.'

Orthography of the Early Printers. The early printers were ignorant of the modern method of making printed lines of equal length by using spaces of different widths. They, therefore, were in the habit of shortening or lengthening words by omitting or adding letters to a word, according to the exigencies of space. Thus, in an old black-letter Bible, the word 'hot' is spelt *whot, hote,* and *hot,* according as larger or smaller spaces had to be filled with the word. In the same copy of the Scriptures the words *ye* and *we* are spelt in Judg. xiii. 13 with a single *e*, but in verse 15 of the same chapter both words are spelt with two, *yee* and *wee,* for no other reason than that the length of the line required additional letters. A more striking example is to be seen in the printing of Isa. xlii. 17, in an edition of 1611, part of which is printed thus :—

17   They shall bee turned back they shalbe greatly ashamed that trust.

These examples show that little dependence can be placed upon early books as authorities for the current orthography of the period.

Osborne House takes its name from one of the family of the Fitz Osbornes, lords of the Isle of Wight, whose principal residence was Carisbrooke Castle.

Ostend. At first sight the name of this city would appear to mean its situation upon the East (*ost*, east) end of the great canal which goes thence to Bruges and Ghent ; but as it is at the west end, we are driven to the conclusion that what is now 'ost' was originally 'ouest,' the French word for west.

O tempora ! O mores ! Latin. Literally, 'O the times ! O the manners !' Generally used in England deprecatingly, as, ' How the times have changed for the worse ! How the manners of the people have become degraded !'

Other-some. This compound word was in general use in the county of Surrey fifty years ago. A labourer digging potatoes would say, ' Some are pretty tidy, and *other-some* are just as bad.' It is not unknown in literature ; Parnell, in the 'Fairy Tale,' has

Some wind and tumble like an ape,
And *other-some* transmute their shape
In Edwin's wondering eyes.

It also occurs in the New Testament, Acts xvii. 18 : ' Other some, He seemeth to be a setter forth of strange gods.'

Otium cum dignitate, Latin. Literally, 'ease with dignity.' Thus we say of a person who has retired from the active pursuits of life, he enjoys his *otium cum dignitate.* 'Dignitate' is a word of four syllables, dig-ni-ta-te.

Over his Signature. This form of expression is becoming common in America. Mr. E. S. Gould, an American writer, thus stigmatises it :—' No well-educated man could have originated such a preposterous conceit as the phrase " *over* his signature; " yet many well-educated men permit themselves to follow the example that ignorance has placed before them. The words over and under have various meanings besides the designation of mere locality. The terms " under oath," " under hand and seal," " under arms," " under compulsion," " under the sanction of," " under his own signature,' are fully established and authorised forms of expression, which have nothing to do with the *relative position* of the things indicated; they are idiomatic.'—*Good English*, New York, 1867.

Over the Left. This expression, which is usually thought to be modern slang, is really sanctioned by the usage of 200 years. ' What the Protestant religion gets by lives and fortunes spent in the service of a Popish successor will be *over the left shoulder.'— Julian the Apostate*, 1682. In the records of the County Court at Hartford, Connecticut, it is stated than on September 4, 1705, one James Steel brought an action against Beevel Waters, in which judgment was given for the plaintiff. On departing from court the said Waters addressing the court said, ' God bless you, over the left shoulder.' At the next sitting of the court Waters was fined 5*l.* for contempt of court, against which he appealed. Pending the hearing, the court asked counsel of the ministers of two Hartford churches as to the meaning of the phrase, and those gentlemen decided, ' 1st, that the words were prophane'; and secondly, ' that they carry great contempt in them, ariseing to the degree of an imprecation or curse.' This opinion, which is still in existence, is signed 'T. Woodbridge' and 'T. Buckingham,' and is dated March 7, 1705-6. The judgment was held to be good.

Oxford Street was originally Oxford Road, or the road to Oxford. Pennant, who lived to 1798, remembered Oxford Street as ' a deep hollow road, full of sloughs, with here and there a ragged house, the lurking-place of cut-throats.'

Oyer and Terminer. The ancient Norman name given to the

commission, by virtue of which the Judges of Assize are empowered to *hear* and *determine* treasons, felonies, &c.

O yes! This phrase, repeated thrice, is the opening call for attention by the crier of a court of justice, before reading the commission or proclamation. It is derived from the Norman-French *oyez*, 'hear ye.'

Oz. (for ounce). The z in this abbreviation is an example of the use of the letter by the early printers, instead of the terminal contraction mark 3, for which they had no type. The error has been perpetuated, as in the cases of 'Boz' and 'Viz' (which see).

Ozokerit. A few years ago this word stared one in the face from every wall, and from the most prominent places in all newspapers and periodicals. It was the advertisement of a new candle, but nobody, or at any rate very few, knew its meaning. It afterwards became known that Ozokerit was no new word, it having been fully explained in a German work in 1841. It is derived from Greek roots signifying '*I smell of wax.*' The material is a kind of mineral wax, which when properly prepared makes candles of exquisite beauty. The mineral is found at Urpeth, near Newcastle, Durham, and at various places in Austria and Moldavia.

P

Pace, as a measure of length. The modern acceptation of the term *pace* is the distance, when the legs are extended in walking, between the heel of one foot and that of the other. The marching *pace* in the British army is 30 inches. In 'double-quick,' or running, the pace is 36 inches. With the Romans, the single extension of the legs was a step (*gradus*), and their *pace* (*passus*) was the interval between the mark of one heel and the second mark of the same heel. This was equivalent to 4·84 feet; the fifth of this space was a Roman foot.

Pacha, or **Pasha,** the name applied to civil or military officers of high rank in the Ottoman Empire, is from two Persian words, *pa*, foot, and *shah*, ruler: it signifies the support of the ruler.

Pacific Ocean. Magellan, after entering this ocean, in 1520, by the straits which still bear his name, sailed for three months and twenty days towards the north-west without discovering land. The weather was so fair, and the winds so favourable, during his voyage that he named it the *Pacific*, or peaceful; a name it still retains.

Padding the Hoof. *Pad* is Sanskrit for *foot*, and the word is used in many parts of the country to signify a narrow walk or *foot*way. It is, perhaps, another form of the word *path*. *Padding* seems to have been used at one time to signify walking. If, as Horne Tooke tells us, a road is that on which we *ride*, is not a path that on which we *pad*?

Paddle your own Canoe. This expressive phrase seems to have first appeared in a poem published in 'Harper's Magazine' (New York, May 1854). The following stanzas give a fair example of the whole:—

> Voyager upon life's sea,
> To yourself be true;
> And, whate'er your lot may be,
> *Paddle your own canoe.*
>
> *   *   *   *
>
> Leave to Heaven, in humble trust,
> All you will to do;
> But if you would succeed, you must
> *Paddle your own canoe.*

Paddock. This word is supposed by some to be from *pad*, a pony for riding, and *dock*, a receptacle. It is, however, more probably a corruption of *parroc*, a park or enclosure. See PARK.

Paddy is not a corruption of *Patrick*. It is from St. Palladius, the precursor of St. Patrick.—*Didot's Nouvelle Biographie Générale*.

Pagan, from the Latin *pagus*, a hamlet or village. '*Pagani* signifies dwellers in hamlets and villages. *Pagans,* or villagers, came to be applied to all the remaining votaries of the old and decaying superstitions, inasmuch as far the greater number were of this class.'—*Trench*.

Paging of Books. The earliest known printed book in which the pages are numbered is 'A Sermon on the Presentation of the Virgin Mary,' printed at Cologne in 1470.—*Typ. Gaz.*, 1831, p. 66.

Painful. 'Fuller, our Church historian, having occasion to speak of some famous divine who had lately died, exclaims, "O the *painfulness* of his preaching!" The words are not a record of the pain which he caused to others, but of the pains which he bestowed himself; and I believe if we had more painful preachers in the old sense of the word, that is who took pains themselves, we should have fewer *painful* ones in the modern sense, who cause pain to others.'—*Trench.*

> Robin redbreast *painfully*
> Did cover them with leaves.—*Children in the Wood.*

Pair off is the phrase used to signify that two members of the House of Commons, of opposite political opinions, have agreed to absent themselves from voting for a certain period. By 'pairing' in this way they neutralise each other's absence. The 'Whips' of the House generally manage to find 'pairs' when, from ill-health or family reasons, members desire to be temporarily absent from Parliamentary duties. The custom of *pairing* in the House of Commons originated in Cromwell's time.

Pal is the Gipsy word for brother.

Palaver is a corruption of the Spanish word *palabras*, words. Shakespeare makes Dogberry ('Much Ado about Nothing,' iii. 5) say, 'Comparisons are odorous; *palábras*, neighbour Verges.'

Palimpsest is a name derived from the Greek, and applied to parchment, papyrus, or other writing material from which a first writing has been wholly or partially obliterated for the purpose of the page being written upon a second time. The custom of so re-using old manuscripts was very general among the ancient Romans, and many valuable works have been found over written with matter of inferior interest. Dr. Barrett, of Trinity College, Dublin, about the beginning of the present century, published 'Fragments of the Gospel of St. Matthew,' recovered in this way, and the result was that the subject rose at once in interest and importance. Since his day Mai, Blume, Mone, and Pertz have carried the matter out with great success.

Pall Mall. This is a corruption of the French name of a game, *pale maille*, which was somewhat similar to the modern croquet. Cunningham says it was 'a game wherein a round ball was struck through a high arch of iron (standing at either end of an alley), which he that can do at the fewest blows, or at the number agreed on, wins. The game was heretofore used in the long alley near St. James's, and [was] vulgarly called Pell Mell.' Hence the name now applied to the palatial street which skirts that portion of St. James's Park where the game was played.

Palmer. 'A *palmer*, opposed to a pilgrim, was one who made it his sole business to visit different holy shrines, travelling incessantly, and subsisting by charity; whereas the *pilgrim* retired to his usual home and occupations when he had paid his devotions at the particular spot which was the object of his pilgrimage.'—*Sir W. Scott.*

Palming. The proverbial expression *palming anything upon you*, comes from palming the dice in gaming, which is thus described by an old writer:—'Having the box in his hand, he nimbly takes up both the dice as they are thrown within the hollow of his hand, and puts but one into the box, reserving the other in the *palm*, and observing with a quick eye what side was upward, he accordingly conforms the next throw to his purpose, delivering that in the box, and the other in his hand, smoothly together.'—*Memoirs of Gamesters*, 1714, p. 27.

Palsy is the old English name for paralysis.

paltry. The dictionary makers have made a great many guesses at the origin of this word; but, after giving all their theories in detail, Dr. Worcester comes to the conclusion that the word is 'of uncertain origin.' Yet in his own work, a few pages on, he has '*Pelter, n.*, a sordid wretch, a pinch-penny, *Huloet*'; and '*Pelting, a.*, mean, paltry, pitiful, *Shak.*' Shakespeare speaks of 'low farms, poor *pelting* villages,' &c., in 'Lear' (ii. 3); and Beaumont and Fletcher have the alliterative line—

Your penny-pot poets are such *pelting* thieves.—*Bloody Br.*, iii. 2.

Paltry, therefore, is an adjective probably derived from the obsolete verb to *pelt*, the vowel being changed from *e* to *a*. Dr. Todd thinks that *pelt* and its derivatives were originally spelt with an *a*, which, if correct, settles the matter.

Pamphlet. This term is probably from the French *par un filet*, by a thread. It signifies a small book merely *stitched* together.

Pane (of glass) is a contraction of the word *panel*.

Panic. Pan, a general in the army which Bacchus led into India, being surrounded by an opposing army while encamped in a rocky valley, caused his men in the middle of the night to set up a simultaneous shout. The hills echoing the sound, so increased its volume that the enemy took flight and fled. Unreasoning and groundless fears hence take the name of *panic.*—*Potter.*

Pannier, from the Latin *panis*, bread. Originally baskets suspended on each side of a horse in which *bread* was carried for the supply of armies in the field. Fanyer Alley, in London, was so named from its being the standing-place for bakers with their *panniers*, when bread was sold in markets only, and there were no bakers' shops. In this alley there is a stone figure of a boy sitting on a basket. The pedestal is dated 1688, and has the following inscription :—

> When you have sought
> The citie round,
> Yet still this is
> The highest ground.

In the 'Illustrated London News,' December 13, 1856, it is said, 'A baker's boy seated on his panyer, or bread-basket (from *panis*, bread), indicates the site of the old market of the Stratford bakers, held in St. Martin's-le-Grand as early as the fourteenth century. A sign of the panyer, whether of the baker himself or his basket, appears to have existed in Stow's time.'

Pansy. Mr. Fox Talbot derives pansy from *panacea*, a name signifying *all-heal*, given by the Greeks to a plant which was considered a cure for all diseases and sorrows. Its other English name, *heart's-ease*, shows that the theory that the plant is a cure for sorrow was common to both countries.

Pantaloons. *Trousers*, abbreviated by the Americans to '*pants*,' from *Pantaleon*, the patron saint of Venice. 'Originally a baptismal name very frequent among the Venetians, and hence applied to them as a common name, and afterwards as a term of derision, as referring to a part of their dress that then distinguished the Venetians, namely, breeches and stockings that were all of a piece.'—*Smart*.

Pantomime. This word, among the ancient Romans, from whom we derive it, denoted a person, not a spectacle. The original pantomimes were performers who acted, not by speaking, but wholly by gestures, movements, and posturings. They are supposed to have first appeared in Rome about 350 to 400 years before Christ. They invariably wore masks, so that no facial expression was possible, but such was the perfection to which the art was carried, that it was said that the pantomime could interpret passion and action better than the poets themselves. As Roman morals became corrupted, so the pantomimic representations became more gross, until at last actresses appeared in a state of absolute nudity. The early Christians, and even pagan writers, denounced these exhibitions as opposed alike to decency and morality. Pantomimes were first produced upon the English stage by John Rich, who, under the name of Lun, produced one annually from 1717 until his death in 1761.

Pantry. A place where *bread* is kept—a *panary*, from *panis*, bread.

Paper. The earliest mention of linen rags as a material for making paper occurs in an account written by an Arabian physician, *Abdollatiph*, of a visit he made to Egypt, A.D. 1200, in which he states that the linen cloth 'found in the catacombs, and used to envelop mummies, was sold to the scribes to make paper for shopkeepers.' The oldest known piece of linen paper in existence is in the monastery of Goss, in Upper Styria. It is a mandate of Frederic II., Emperor of the Romans, and is dated 1242. Power ('Handy Book about Books') says that 'a charter on paper of the year 1239 is in existence, but Montfaucon could find nothing later [? earlier] than 1270' (p. 27). Haydn ascribes the first manufacture of paper in England to Speilman, and gives the date 1590 as that of the erection of the first paper mill. There is, however, in the 'Land Revenue Records,' mention of one which appears to have been in operation before that date. The entry is as follows:— 'Fencliften, co. Cambridge. Lease of a Water Mill, *called Paper Mills*, late of the Bishopric of Ely, to John Grange, dated 14th July, 1591 (34th Elizabeth).' The earliest allusion to papermaking in England occurs in an entry in the privy purse expenses of Henry VII., dated May 25, 1498, published in the 'Excerpta Historica,' 'For a rewarde geven at the paper mylne 16s. 8d.' This 'paper mylne' is supposed to have been erected at Stevenage in Hertfordshire, by John Tate. Nicholls, in his 'Progresses of Queen Elizabeth,' has reprinted a poem dated 1588, entitled 'A description and playne Discourse of Paper, and the whole Benefits that Paper brings, with Rehearsall and setting foorth in Verse a Paper Myll built near Darthford by an high Germaine called Master Spilman, Jeweller to the Queene's Majestie, 1588.' The 'myll' appears to have been of some magnitude, for we read that—

> Six hundred men are set to work by him
> That else might starve, or seek abroad their bread,
> Who now live well, and go full brave and trim,
> And who may boast they are with paper fed.

See SIZES OF PAPER.

Paper Knives. An early—perhaps the earliest—mention of paper knives occurs in Swift's Works (ed. 1755, vi. 182):—'I said to Lord Bolingbroke that the clerks in his office used a sort of ivory knife with a blunt edge to divide a sheet of paper, which never failed to cut it even, only requiring a strong hand; whereas if they should make use of a sharp penknife, the sharpness would make it often go out of the crease and disfigure the paper.'

Par. This is a Latin term signifying *equal*. It is usually employed to denote the market value of a public security or stock. Thus, if 100*l*. stock in a railway company will sell on the Stock Exchange for 105*l*. it is said to be 'above par'; but if it is worth no more on the market than 95*l*., it is said to be 'below par.'

Parable. This word was formerly used in England to signify *easily procured*. In this sense it comes from the Latin *parabilis*. In the sense of a fable or similitude it is derived through the Latin *parabola* from the Greek, and according to Trench it 'is a fictitious but probable narrative taken from the affairs of ordinary life to illustrate some higher and less known truth. It differs from the *fable*, moving as it does in a spiritual world, and never transgressing the actual order of things natural; from the *myth*, there being in the latter an unconscious blending of the deeper meaning with the outward symbol, the two remaining separate and separable in the parable; from the *proverb*, inasmuch as it is longer carried out, and not merely accidentally and occasionally, but necessarily figurative; from the *allegory*, comparing, as it does, one thing *with* another, at the same time preserving them apart as an inner and an outer, not transferring, as does the *allegory*, the properties, and qualities, and relations of one *to* the other.'

Paraffin was so named from the Latin words *parum*, little, and *affinis*, kin, because it had *little affinity* with any other known substance.

Parapet, Battlement. The upper edge of a wall which rises above the roof of a building, if straight, is a *parapet*; if indented, it is a *battlement*.

Paraphernalia. This word, which means goods in a wife's disposal independently of her husband, is gradually getting into use to denote *insignia*, as of Odd Fellows, teetotalers, and other bodies. Its use in this sense is to be regretted, but as it has crept into the later dictionaries there seems no help for it.

Paraphrase is a free, loose, and somewhat diffused translation, in which sense is followed rather than diction. Metaphrase is a strict following of an author's words, rendering them literally into another language.

Parasite. Bailey gives a very scornful definition of this word.

He says a parasite is 'a smell-feast, a trencher-friend, a flattering spunge.'—*Dictionary*.

Parbleu! This is a French interjection which the dictionaries translate as equivalent to zounds. It is a softening of the profane expression *Par Dieu*.

Parcel. Strictly speaking this word should not be used in the sense of a bundle or package. Its true meaning is *a portion of*. The following illustrations seem strange to modern ears:—

> Two *parcels* of the white of an egg.—*Arbuthnot*.

> That I would all my pilgrimage dilate,
> Whereof by *parcels* she had something heard.
>   *Shakespeare*, *Othello*, Act. i. sc. 3.

Parchment. Parchment is so called because it was invented at Pergamos, by King Eumenes, when paper, which was made in Egypt only, was prohibited by Ptolemy to be transported from that country.—*Wharton*.

Pare. To pare is to cut off the rind of a fruit, to peel is to pull it off. We *pare* an apple and *peel* an orange.

Parish Churches. The largest parish church in England is that of St. Nicholas, Yarmouth, the area of which in superficial feet is 23,085; St. Michael's, Coventry, is five feet less, being 23,080; Boston Church is 22,270; St. Nicholas, Newcastle, 20,110; Holy Trinity, Hull, 20,036; and St. Saviour's, Southwark, 18,200.

Parishes. Camden says that England was first divided into parishes by Honorius, Archbishop of Canterbury, A.D. 636.

Park. The word park in various forms is common to most of the languages of Europe. In the Anglo-Saxon it was written *peorroc*, and occasionally *parruc*. In German, Icelandic, and Dutch, it is spelt, as in English, *park*. In the Welsh it is *parc*; in the Scottish, *parroc*; in Italian, *parco*; in Spanish and Portuguese, *parque*; and in French, *parc*. It appears to have been originally a Greek word, and to have been adopted into the Latin, where it sometimes occurs in the form *parcus*. In all these languages it has, as it formerly had in English, the meaning simply of an enclosure; a place 'fenced round about,' or protected. In military phraseology it is still employed in this sense; thus, a 'park of artillery' is the *encampment* assigned to the artillery, and a 'park of provisions' is the place allotted to the sutlers attached to an army. The modern meaning of the word in English is narrowed to the ornamental grounds surrounding a mansion. It is not so limited in any other language. In Scotland the ornamental grounds, such as in England are called the park, are always called the 'policy.' Busbey Park, Richmond Park, Greenwich Park, and others of similar character were originally called *parks* because they were *enclosures* in which deer and other game were confined for sporting purposes. The park of Sutton Coldfield, near Birmingham, is an uncultivated enclosure of between 2,000 and 3,000 acres, which has been known as Sutton *Park* for more than a thousand years. It is the property of the inhabitants, and is much used by Birmingham people as a place of public recreation. The park at Woburn contains 3,500 acres, and is supposed to be the largest in England. The boundary wall is twelve miles in length.

Parliament. This word is derived from the French *parlement*, from *parler*, to speak. Blackstone says the word was first applied to general assemblies of the States under Louis VII. in France about the middle of the twelfth century. The first English parliament met on the 22nd of January, 1265. The writs are still extant, which directed the sheriff of each county to elect and return to this parliament two knights for each county, two citizens for each city, and two burgesses for every borough or burgh in the country. The shortest English parliament was that of 1399, which deposed Richard II.; it sat but one day. The longest met November 3, 1640, and was dissolved by Cromwell, April 20, 1653. It is known as the 'Long Parliament.'

Parlour, from *parler*, to speak. The original parlour was the French *parloir*, the room in a nunnery where the nuns were allowed to speak through a grating to visitors.

Parole. Officers, when prisoners of war, are sometimes released 'on parole,' that is, on their word of honour (parole) to abide by certain imposed conditions, the most stringent of which is generally that they will not fight again during the then existing war. To break parole is considered infamous in all civilised countries; and such is the high sense of honour among military men, that very few cases of breach of parole are recorded.

Parrot. The name of this bird is derived from *Pierrot*, the French familiar term for Peter, in the same way as the *robin* is so named from Robert. The *daw* on the same principle is called *jackdaw*, from Jack.

Partisan. This was formerly the name for a halberd or pike, and it seems to have been applied to soldiers armed with such weapons. In an account (printed in 1660) of the execution of Charles I. is the following:—'From thence [the Cabinet Chamber, Whitehall], about one o'clock, he was accompanied by Dr. Juxon and Col. Tomlinson, and other officers formerly [*qy.* formally?] appointed to attend him, and the private guard of *partisans,* with musketeers on each side,' &c.

Party. The use of this word in the sense of person is of considerable antiquity. In a work, 'The Practice of Piety,' published in 1638, the following words occur (fol. 663):—' When the sick *party* is departing, let the faithfull that are present kneel down and commend his soul to God.' It is also used in the sense of person in Burton's 'Anatomy of Melancholy,' published in 1621. Shakespeare says ('Tempest,' iii. 2), ' How shall this be compast? Canst thou bring me to the *party?*' Bacon has ' The imagination of the *party* to be cured is not needful to concur.' And Davies says, 'If the jury found that the *party* slain was of English race, it had been adjudged felony.'

Pasquinade. Satirical writings are so called from *Pasquin,* a Roman cobbler in the sixteenth century, opposite whose house was the statue of an ancient gladiator. Against the pedestal of this statue it was the custom to affix satirical placards, many of which were thought to be the productions of *Pasquin,* and were thence called *pasquinata.*

Passover. The derivation of this word from *pass* and *over,* as given in Exod. xii. 27, is obviously incorrect. The word was in use in Northern Europe centuries before the present Authorized Version was published. In Hebrew the word for the passover was *pascha,* a word having no affinity with the English word *pass,* and certainly the English word *over* has no connection whatever with it. Our word ' passover' was originally the Teutonic *Passofer,* or *Pasch-opfer,* a term meaning 'paschal sacrifice,' or ' paschal offering.' The Anglo-Saxon word for a sacrifice was *opfer,* and the modern German *opfer* means a victim. The erroneous derivation from *pass* and *over* is more apparent when we consider that we are commanded to ' *eat* the passover' and to ' *kill* the passover;' and are told (2 Chron. xxxv. 13) that ' they *roasted* the passover,' none of which phrases would have the least propriety if the derivation given in Exodus is to be followed, or unless the sacrifice were an *opfer* or victim.

Pastern (Low Latin *pastorium*) is a shackle for horses when pasturing, to prevent them straying. Hence the joint of the horse's leg, to which the shackle is attached, is called the *pastern joint*.

Pastime. 'Amusements and pleasures do not really satisfy the mind and fill it with the sense of abiding and satisfying joy. They are only *pastimes*; they serve only, as the word expresses, to *pass* away the *time*, to prevent it from weighing an intolerable burden on men's hands.'—*Trench.*

Patent. The word 'patent' means open, as opposed to concealed. 'Letters patent' are open letters addressed by the Crown to all the subjects of the realm. They have the seal of the sovereign pendent at the bottom. It is a curious fact that, although it is illegal to mark the word 'patent' upon any article not the subject of an existing patent, there is no penalty or punishment attached to such a breach of the law.

Pater Noster. These are two Latin words signifying Our Father. They are used in the Catholic Church as the name of the Lord's Prayer, and are the first two words in the Vulgate version of the Lord's Prayer.

Pathetical. This word is used two or three times by Shakespeare in the sense of hypocritical; *e.g.*, 'I will think you the most *pathetical* break-promise, and the most hollow lover.'—*As You Like It*, act iv. sc. 1.

Patois. This word comes to us through the French from the Latin *patrius*, ancestral. It means the dialect which *descends from one generation* to another in rude unlettered districts.—*Brand.*

Pattens. This name was evidently derived from the French, who still use the word *patin* for a skate, which is of similar construction to a *patten*.

Paul before Agrippa. The verse Acts xxvi. 28, where Agrippa says, 'Almost thou persuadest me to be a Christian,' is translated by Dean Alford, 'Lightly art thou persuading thyself that thou canst make me a Christian.' In the revised edition (1881) it is rendered, 'With but little persuasion thou wouldest fain make me a Christian.'

Paul's Chain. A street near St. Paul's Cathedral in London was so named, because near the spot where it opens into the churchyard a chain was drawn across the roadway to hinder vehicles from passing at the time of Divine service, lest the noise should disturb the worshippers.

Pawn (at chess). Perhaps from the Spanish, where *peone* is a foot-soldier, and where 'peone' is also used at chess to signify what we call a pawn.

Pawnbroker's Sign. The three balls so well known as the pawnbroker's sign were originally the arms of the Medici family, the earliest and most important of the money-lenders of Lombardy. The three balls were first used in England by the agent of that family, and were afterwards copied by others. They represent three gilded pills; and were used by the Medici in allusion to the profession of medicine, in which that family was eminent, and from which they derived their name.

Payment of Members of Parliament. John Strange, the Member for Dunwich in the reign of Edward II., agreed with the burgesses of that borough in 1463 to take his wages in red herrings.—*Johnson's Life of Coke* (Colburn, 1837).

Pea Jacket is from the Dutch word *pije*, a coarse thick cloth or felt.

Pearl Barley. A corruption of peeled barley—i.e. barley deprived of its outer shell or husk.

Pease. This, which is generally thought to be the correct plural of the word *pea*, is really a singular noun, the true plural of which is *peasen* or peason. Thus Tusser, in his 'Five Hundred Points of Good Husbandry,' says, in his directions for the month of February:

> Sow peason and beanes in the wane of the moone,
> Who soweth them sooner, he soweth too soone.

In modern usage 'pease' is generally used for an indefinite quantity in number or bulk, and peas to designate two or more individual seeds. 'Peas, number, as two peas. Pease, quantity, as a bushel of pease.'—*Chambers's Dictionary*.

Ped, Pedlar. Ped is an old word for a basket. In the 'Original Glossary to Spenser' (v. 16) we find 'A haske is a *wicker ped* wherein they used to carrie fish.' *Ped* is still in use in Norfolk as the name of a basket. There is little doubt that *pedlar* is derived from *ped*, in allusion to the basket in which pedlars carry their wares.

Pedant had originally the meaning of *schoolmaster*. Shakespeare speaks of

> A pedant that keeps a school in the church.—*Twelfth Night*, iii. 8.

Pedigree. Formerly a genealogical tree was represented as issuing from the prostrate figure of a man. This was exactly in accordance with the meaning of the word pedigree, which is from the Latin *pes*, a foot, also the stem of a tree, through the French *pied*, which has the same signification. The terminal portion of the word is from the Latin *gradus*, which, by various transitions through *gré*, *gráo*, *grado*, arrives at the French *degrés*. The entire word, therefore, is *pied-de-grés*, a stem of degrees or a stem of lineage, which is exactly its present signification.

Peelers, Bobbies. These names for policemen were given to them by the populace in ridicule of the founder of the force, Sir Robert Peel.

Peers of the Realm. The word peer is usually thought to be derived from the Latin *par*, equal. This origin is unsatisfactory; first, because the 'peers' are not equal, but are of many degrees; and secondly, because it is obvious that no monarch establishing an order of dignity would adopt so common a term as 'equals among themselves.' The word is with far greater probability derived from the Norman *pier* or *père*, father. The senators of Rome were called the *patres conscripti*; and if, in paraphrasing *Senatus populusque Romanus*, we use the word *patres* instead of *senatus*, we get almost the exact equivalent of the wording of early Anglo-Norman enactments, which were made '*per comen assent des piers et du People de roilme*'—that is, 'by the common assent of the fathers and the people of the realm.' Peerages are created by 'Royal Letters Patent,' but there are some exceptions. The possession of the Castle of Arundel was declared by Act of Parliament (2 Hen. VI.) to confer the title of Earl of Arundel without creation. The earldom of Abergavenny is held by the Neville family in right of the tenure of the ruined castle near that place. The anomaly in the latter case has been got rid of by the present holder having been created a marquis.

Peg. 'To take one down a peg' is in allusion to the lowering a ship's flag, which is regulated by the pegs to which the line is fastened on deck. The higher a ship's colours are raised in saluting, the greater the honour. Hence, to take [the colours] down a peg is to lower the dignity. *A peg too low.*—Formerly tankards were marked inside by pegs at graduated distances for equally dividing the contents. Hence 'a peg too low' means that a man is so low-spirited that he must drink down to another 'peg' to revive him. See PIN.

Peggie is not a diminutive of Margaret; it is merely the Danish word for girl, *pigé*. Similarly Mag, Maggie, Madge, Meg are merely forms of the German *Magd*, a maid.

Pelican. The notion that a pelican feeds her young upon her own blood originated in the fact that the pelican has a receptacle under its bill in which she macerates the food intended for her young. In feeding them the bag is pressed against the breast, and the macerated food is ejected into the open mouths of the young.

Pen. This is a contraction of *penna*, the Latin name for the tubular part of a feather. When the ancients adopted quills instead of reeds for writing instruments, they naturally used the name *pennæ* to designate them.

Peninsula, from the Latin *pene*, almost, and *insula*, an island: almost an island.

Pennant. When Van Tromp, the Dutch admiral, appeared with his fleet on the coasts of England, he hoisted a broom on the topmast of his ship, as indicative of his intention to sweep the ships of England from the sea. The English admiral, in retaliation, hoisted a horsewhip at his masthead, to indicate that he intended to chastise the Dutchman. The pennant, which symbolises the horsewhip, has ever since been the distinguishing mark of English ships of war.

Penny. The 'penny' mentioned in the New Testament was the Roman *denarius*. It was a silver coin weighing about the eighth of an ounce. It was worth about sevenpence-halfpenny of our money. From Matthew xx. 2 we learn that it was the ordinary pay of a labourer for a day's work. The silver penny of the Anglo-Saxons was the first coin struck in England. Until the time of Edward I. pennies were deeply indented, so that they might be easily divided into *half*-pence and *fourth*-ings—the latter name has been corrupted into farthing. Penny has two plurals; *pennies* when the number of coins is referred to; *pence* when the aggregate amount is spoken of, as twelve pence.

Penny Daily Newspaper. The first penny daily newspaper was 'The Bulletin,' which was published at Glasgow before the penny stamp was abolished. In fact, the earlier numbers bore the penny stamp. The experiment was a failure, for the paper only lived a few weeks.

Penny Royal (*Mentha pulegium*). The prefix 'penny' is a corruption. The old name of the plant in English was *pulial royal*, from *polium*, a sweet-scented herb. The correct modern English name is *poly-royal*.

Pennyworth. This word—sometimes with the adjective good, as 'a good pennyworth'—was formerly used in the sense in which we now say 'a bargain.' The following is a copy of a newspaper advertisement, A.D. 1725:—'To be sold, a Pennyworth. A handsome crane-neck Town Chariot with springs, a whole Fore-glass, lined with crimson castog. Inquire, Cooper, Coachman, New Bond Street Mews.'

Pentecost is from a Greek word signifying *fiftieth*. It was applied to the Jewish festival because it was held on the *fiftieth* day after the feast of unleavened bread.

Pent-house, the old English name for a projecting roof over a shop front, is a corruption of the Italian *pentice* or *pendice*, a roof. Fairfax, in his 'Translation of Tasso,' uses the original word:

<blockquote>And o'er their heads an iron pendice vast (xi. 33).</blockquote>

Pentonville was so named in 1773, from the name of the owner of the estate on which it was built—Henry Penton, M.P. for Winchester, and one of the Lords of the Admiralty. He died in 1812.

Pepys. This charming, gossiping diarist was buried on June 4, 1703, in the Church of All Hallows, Barking, in a vault which he had built in 1664 to receive the remains of his brother. Samuel Pepys's wife had been buried in the vault in the lifetime of her husband.

Père-la-Chaise. The Parisian cemetery so named is the site of a great monastery founded by Louis XIV., of which the Père la Chaise, a favourite confessor of that luxurious monarch, was the first superior. He died in 1709. After the Revolution the grounds were laid out for a cemetery, which was first used May 1804.

Perforating Postage Stamps. The machine for perforating postage stamps was invented and patented by Mr. Henry Archer in 1847. The authorities would for a long time have nothing to do with the plan, but Mr. G. F. Muntz, then M.P. for Birmingham, brought the matter forward so frequently, and with so much pertinacity, that on August 5, 1853, the House of Commons voted 4,000*l.* for the purchase of the patent rights, and the perforated stamps soon afterwards were issued to the public.

Perfume. This word is derived from the Latin *per*, from, and *fumus*, smoke. The first *perfumes* were wood or aromatic gums which in burning gave off agreeable odours.

Perhaps it was right, &c.
> Perhaps it was right to dissemble your love,
> But why did you kick me downstairs?

These lines were first published anonymously in 'An Asylum for Fugitive Pieces,' 1785, vol. i. p. 15. J. P. Kemble afterwards introduced them in a play, 'The Panel' (act i. sc. 1), in the year 1788.

Periodicals. The earliest periodical in England was the 'Philosophical Transactions of the Royal Society,' which first appeared in 1665. The first magazine—properly so called—was 'The Gentleman's Journal or Monthly Miscellany,' established in 1692. 'The Gentleman's Magazine,' which still survives, was started by Cave in 1731. The earliest of the reviews was 'The Monthly Review,' which appeared in 1749. In 1756 Smollett founded 'The Critical Review.' The modern style of criticism dates from 1802, when 'The Edinburgh Review' appeared.

Periwinkle, from *petty*, small, and *wincle*, an Anglo-Saxon generic word for shell-fish. Sometimes, particularly in London, erroneously called pennywinkles.

Perry, an early English Engineer. In the church of Spalding, Lincolnshire, is a tomb to the memory of John Perry, who was 'several years comptroller of the maritime works to the Czar Peter, and on his return home was employed by ye Parliament to stop Dagenham breach, which he effected, and thereby preserved the navigation of the river of Thames, and rescued many private familys from ruin.' He died February 1732.

Person. The Latin *persona*, of which the word person is the Anglicised form, meant originally a mask. From that it came to mean the person wearing the mask, and finally to denote any distinct sentient being.

Perspective. This word comes from the Latin *perspicere*, to look through; and it was formerly, with great propriety, confined in meaning to telescopes and microscopes. The word is now improperly applied to 'the delineation of objects on a plane surface, as in pictorial art.' This ought to be called *prospective*. The Italians use the correct term; they say '*prospettiva.*'

Pert is a contraction of *malapert*, an almost obsolete word, signifying ill-bred, impudent, saucy.

Pestle and Mortar. The pestle was anciently the leg-bone of an animal. In an old Bill of Fare, quoted by Wright ('Domestic

Manners of the Middle Ages,' p. 349), '*pestles* (legs) of pork' are quoted as being served in the first course. Johnson also has 'pestle of pork,' and Worcester defines pestle, *inter alia*, as 'the leg, or the bone of the leg, of an animal.'

Petard. The petard was a half-cone of thick iron filled with powder and ball and firmly fastened to a plank. The plank was provided with hooks and other appliances to permit of its being attached to the gate of a fortification or other obstruction. The duty of the engineers was to attach the petard, ignite the slow match, and escape as quickly as possible. When the explosion took place a column of soldiers charged through the breach while the defenders were still in confusion. If the engineer were tardy in escaping, or the match proved to be faulty, the explosion might occur prematurely, in which case the engineer might be 'hoist with his own petard.'

Petroleum. Literally, rock oil, from the Latin *petra*, a rock, and *oleum*, oil. Petroline is refined petroleum.

Pettifogger. To *fog*, Nares tells us, was 'to hunt in a servile manner,' hence pettifogger. A soldier says to a lawyer, in reproach,

> Wer't not for us, thou swad (quoth he),
> Where wouldst thou *fog* to catch a fee?
> *Dryden, Miscellanies*, iii. 340.

From this definition it would appear that a pettifogging lawyer was one who touted, fogged, or hunted for small matters in the purlieus of courts.

Petty Wales, in Thames Street, London, is believed to have been so called because Prince Hal kept his noisy court there.

Petunia. This plant is a species of tobacco. The name is derived from *petum* or *petun*, an old name for tobacco.—*Fox Talbot.*

Pews. The earliest known mention of pews is in the will of John Rocke, citizen and haberdasher of London, dated December 11, 1488, in which he desires that he may be buried in the church of St. Michael in the Querne, 'at my pew's end.' Other early pews are mentioned by Whitaker in his 'History of Whally,' 1801. He describes a pew which belongs to the manor of Upton as 'of ancient and massy wainscote, long prior to the Reformation. The pew next it, which is much more modern, will yet prove the falsehood of the commonly received opinion that before that period the naves of our parish churches were like those of cathedrals, or only fitted up with forms. This latter is a magnificent old pew, belonging to the manor of Read, with this inscription in black letter: "*Factum est per Rogerum Nowell, Armigerum, Anno Dn̄i MCCCCCXXXIIII.*"' Pew rents, it appears, were payable before the Reformation. Bishop Bale, in his 'Image of bothe Churches,' printed in 1550, has the following passage : ' All shrynes, images, church stoles, and pewes that are welle payde for.' There is plenty of evidence that long before the Reformation pews were luxuriously fitted up. In 1631 Bishop Corbet said, 'I am verily persuaded that but for the pulpit and the pews (I do not now mean the altar and the font for the two sacraments, but for the pulpit and stools as you call them), many churches had been down that stand. Stately pews are now become tabernacles with rings and curtains to them. There wants nothing but beds to hear the word of God on ; we have casements, locks and keys, and cushions—I had almost said bolsters and pillows—and for those we love the Church. I will not guess at what is done within them ; who sits, stands, or lies asleep, at prayers, communion, &c.; but this I dare say, they are either to hide some vice or to proclaim one, to hide disorder or to proclaim pride.'—*Corbet's Poems*, edit. 1807. In St. Margaret's accounts ('History of Pues,' p. 33, Camden Society, 1843) is the following droll item : ' 1611. Item Paid to Goodwyfe Wells for salt to destroy the fleas in the Churchwarden's pew, 6*d*.'

' By the general law, and of common right, all the pews in the parish church are the common property of [the inhabitants of] the parish, who are all entitled to be seated orderly and conveniently so as best to provide for the accommodation of all. The distribution of seats rests *with the churchwardens*, as the officers, and subject to the control of the Ordinary. Neither the minister nor the vestry have any right whatever to interfere with the churchwardens in seating and arranging the parishioners, as is often erroneously supposed.'—*Sir J. Nichols* (2 *Addams*, 425).

Phaëton. This is a most unfortunate word. It is generally printed phæton, which is wrong, and it is called by some *phe-a-ton*, and by others *phayton*. The proper pronunciation is pha-e-ton.

Pharisees. The Pharisees arose in Judea about 140 B.C. They affected great piety, imposed on themselves lengthened fasts and other mortifications, and made great show of praying and other outward signs of religion. They believed in future states of reward or punishment, and held the Sadducees in great contempt. (See Professor Mozley's ' University Sermons.')

Pharmaceutical. The question as to whether the *c* in this word should be hard or soft can hardly yet be said to be settled.

Some of the courts decided a few years ago that it should be soft, but the general opinion seems now to be that Sir Frederic Pollock was right in holding that the sound is properly hard, 'because its sound is not governed by the silent *e* which immediately follows, but by the sound of the letter *u*.' As *ceutic* is Greek, like *ceramic*, which is now spelt with *k*, there can be no doubt whatever that the hard sound is correct.

Philippic. The name Philippic was originally applied to the three orations of Demosthenes against Philip of Macedon. It was afterwards applied to Cicero's orations against Mark Antony. The word is now employed proverbially to designate any severe or violent invective, written or spoken.

Phiz, from the old French *vis*, the face, from which we get visage. *Vis-à-vis* is face to face.

Phœnix Park, Dublin. The Irish name was *Fionn-Uisge*, meaning spring of fair water. This was changed to Phœnix Park by the celebrated Earl of Chesterfield when he was Lord Lieutenant of Ireland, about the year 1745.

Physician. 'The practice of physicians is so much altered of late years that even in Dr. Mead's time (who died 1754) no physician visited the ward of any hospital, nor ever saw the greater number of his patients. The business was conducted by consultations held at the physician's house with the apothecaries who related the patients' cases. Dr. Mead used to go into the City to Batsson's Coffee-house, and meet all the apothecaries and prescribe.'—*Diary and Correspondence of Lord Colchester*, vol. i. p. 25; date, January 1796. This does not quite agree with the following quotation from Howell, who, writing in 1660, says of physicians' fees: 'Nor are the fees which belong to that profession anything considerable; where doctors of physic use to attend a patient with their mules and foot-cloths in a kind of state, yet they receive but *two shillings* for their fee, for all their gravity and pains.'—*Parley of Beasts*, p. 73. The fee was raised in the course of the next forty years, for we are told that, 'To a graduate in physic, his due is about 10*s*., though he commonly expects or demands 20*s*. Those that are only licensed physicians, their fee is no more than 6*s*. 9*d*., though they commonly demand 10*s*. A surgeon's journey is 12*d*. a mile, be his journey far or near. Ten groats to set a bone broke or out of joint, and for letting of blood, 1*s*. The cutting off or amputation of any limb is 5*l*., but there is no settled price for the cure.'—*Levamen Infirmi*, 1700. Physicians' prescriptions are written in Latin throughout Europe, the reason being that a prescription may be understood by any dispenser in whatever country a patient may be travelling or residing. The phrase 'physician's bill' in the writings of the old authors does not mean *account*; it denotes a physician's *prescription*.

Pianofortes were invented by Schröder of Dresden in 1717. Square pianofortes were first made in Saxony about 1760. The earliest known mention of this instrument in England is in a play-bill announcing a performance at Covent Garden Theatre, May 16, 1767, for the benefit of Miss Brickler. The play was the 'Beggar's Opera,' in which Miss B. played Polly. The bill announces that at the 'end of act i. Miss Brickler will sing a favourite song from Judith, accompanied by Mr. Dibdin on a new instrument called *pianoforte*.'

Piazza. This Italian word (pronounced pe-ăt-za) has nothing to do with arcades or arches, as is commonly thought. It is merely the French word *place*, or what we call a 'square.' The Spanish equivalent is *plaza*.

Pibroch, Gaelic *piobairechd,* the pipe summons. This word does not mean, as Lord Byron and other writers have thought, the bagpipe of the Highlanders. It signifies a strain of music or tune, peculiar to a clan, by which its members are summoned, and to the strains of which, *played on the bagpipe alone*, they were formerly led by their chieftains to fights, or to which they danced at their festivities. Each clan had its special *pibroch*, which was scrupulously adhered to by its pipers, and was played on all great occasions. The pibrochs are supposed to be of very great antiquity.

Piccadilly. This has been thought to be a corruption of Peaked Hill. There is a hill near Ivingho in Bucks which is called indifferently Peaked Hill and Piccadilly, and there is a lofty plateau near Aberystwith known as Piccadilly, near which is a tavern known by the same name. It has been suggested that the street in London may have been so called from its being higher ground than Westminster, but there is greater probability that the street was so named from an article of dress called a 'pickadil,' which word is thus defined in an old dictionary: 'Pickadil, the hem about the skirt of a garment, also the extremity or utmost part of anything. Whence a great gaming-house, built by one Higgins, a taylor, famous for making those kinds of skirts in fashion, is called Pickadilly.'—*New World of Words.* In 1615, when the king was expected to visit Cambridge, the Vice-Chancellor of the University issued an order against wearing *pickadells* or *pickadilloes*. A satirical poem of the time thus alludes to this order—

> But leave it, scholar, leave it, and take it not in snuff [*i.e.* dudgeon],
> For he who wears no *pickadel*, by law may wear a ruff.—*Camb. Mag.*

Pickle. It is erroneously believed by many that this word is derived from the name of William Beukels of Bierfleet, the inventor of pickled herrings. The real origin is the Dutch word *pekel*, brine.

Picnic. This is a corruption of the French *pique-nique*. In its native country it signifies an entertainment in which each person contributes to the general supply of the table. It is not in France, as with us, confined to out-of-door entertainments. The 'Literary World,' August 1, 1879, gives the following as an extract from a French newspaper: 'Pique-nique of Saint Henri.—The list of subscribers at fifteen francs a head will be closed at four o'clock. Evening dress and white ties are *de rigueur*. They will sit down to table at eight o'clock.'

Pie is a contracted form of pastie, the old name, probably from the word being written p^{ie}.

Piebald is a term applied to a black and white horse. It is from *pie*, the magpie, and *bald*. Originally it signified a horse deprived artifically of the hair on certain portions of his body, so as to become like a magpie, black and white. Where the colour alternating with the white is bay, roan, brown, or chestnut, the proper appellation is skewbald.

Piecemeal. The affix *meal* in this word is the only relic of the use of the word in the sense of a piece or fragment. It comes from the Anglo-Saxon root *mæl*, which, except in this phrase, is now confined to the meaning of a meal or repast. The Anglo-Saxons had *thusan mælum*, in a thousand parts. Meal in the sense of flour is from a different root, being the modern form of the Anglo-Saxon *melew*, *melo*, or *melu*, ground corn.

Piedmont, now a part of the Kingdom of Italy, is so named from its position at the foot of the Alps. *Piè-di-monte*, foot of mountain.

Pier, a landing place. The ordinary derivation of this word from the French *pierre*, a stone, is incorrect. The word is from *pyr*, or *pyre*, a beacon. It was customary in olden times to keep a light burning at landing places, to guide seamen who might be desirous to land. In the Danish the word *pyr* is defined as 'a pier or lantern by the shore side.' In Swedish the word is *fyr*, and the authorities collect *fyr-penningar*, or pier-dues. The pier was, therefore, originally the 'light at the jetty' or landing place, and the word was gradually transferred to the whole structure. The word 'pier,' in the sense of a support of a bridge, is probably with correctness derived from *pierre*, a stone.

'Pig and Whistle.' This familiar tavern sign is, according to Professor Max Müller, derived from *Piga, waes-hael*, a Danish salutation to the Virgin Mary.

Pig-iron. The ingots of iron known as 'pigs' are so called from their supposed resemblance when first made to a litter of pigs in the act of sucking. When the iron is produced from the ore, the red-hot semi-fluid metal runs from the furnace down a straight channel, having at intervals lateral branches about four feet long into which the metal gradually flows, finally filling up the main channel and the offshoots. In this state it resembles a huge double-sided comb, and is called by the workmen the 'sow and pigs.' When broken up into ingots it is known by the term 'pig-iron,' and on the market is spoken of and dealt in as 'pigs.'

Pilgrim's Progress. This well-known allegory was written in Bedford Gaol by a tinker named John Bunyan, who was imprisoned there from 1660 to 1672. The first part was published A.D. 1678.

Pillory. The pillory was a scaffold upon which persons convicted of certain crimes were exposed to public view. The spectators were permitted to pelt persons standing in the pillory with rotten eggs and filth of any kind. The last person who 'stood in the pillory' in England was Peter John Bossy, who, on June 24, 1830, stood in the pillory in the Old Bailey, London, for one hour. He had been convicted of perjury, and was sentenced to seven years' transportation as well as to this exposure in the pillory. An Act of Parliament in 1837 abolished pillories throughout the kingdom. A pillory is still preserved in the church of Rye, in Sussex.

'Pilot that weathered the storm.' This well-known political song in praise of William Pitt was written by George Canning in the year 1802 for a convivial party in the City of London.—*Cleland, Life of William Pitt,* 1807.

Pimlico took its name from one Ben Pimlico, a tavern keeper, who removed from Hoxton and opened a tavern between Westminster and Chelsea.

Pin. The word 'pin' was sometimes used instead of peg to note the projections inside drinking tankards. Hence it became proverbial to say 'in a merry pin':

> The calender right glad to find
> His friend in merry pin.—*Cowper.*

See PEG.

Pin Money. In the 'Everyday Book,' in an article on New Year's Gifts, Hone says : ' Pins were acceptable New Year's Gifts to the ladies instead of the wooden skewers they used till the end of the fourteenth century. Sometimes they received a compensation in money, and hence allowances for their separate use are still called *pin money*.' Pins are mentioned in a statute of 1483. They were brought from France for the use of Queen Catherine Howard in 1540, and were made in England three years later.

Pinchbeck. The mixture of metals so called took its name from the inventor, Christopher Pinchbeck, a celebrated clockmaker in London in the early part of the eighteenth century. The following is from an old book :—' Mr. Xtopher Pinchbeck had a curious secret of a metal which resembled gold in colour and ductibility. Y^e secret is communicated to his son.'

Pineapple. The correct name of this fruit is *anana*, under which name it is mentioned in Thomson's 'Seasons.' The similarity in shape to the cone of the pine no doubt suggested the name 'pineapple.' Dr. Trench mentions a curious mistake arising out of this name, made by the French newspaper the 'Journal des Débats.' In giving an account of a banquet at the Mansion House in London, the paper made some very uncomplimentary remarks on the voracity of the English, who could wind up a Lord Mayor's dinner with fir-cones for dessert !

Pines and Firs. Trees of these classes cannot be propagated by cuttings, nor do they throw up shoots from the roots when cut down. They can only be propagated by the seeds which are contained in the fir-cones or pine-apples.

Pink-eyed. This term is often met with in old writers. Coles, in his 'Latin Dictionary,' translates *ocellæ*, ' Maids with little eyes, pink-eyed girls.' Shakespeare has :—

> Come, thou monarch of the vine,
> Plumpy Bacchus with *pink eyne*,
> In thy vats our cares be drowned.
> *Ant. and Cleo.* act ii. sc. 7.

The term has nothing to do with the colour which is now called pink. It simply means that the eyes are small and narrow in the opening. Old Laneham, in a letter from Kenilworth at the time of Elizabeth's visit, speaks of 'the beare with pink nyez leering after his enmiez approach.'

Pint and Pound 'were originally the same word, but for the sake of convenience usage has introduced a distinction. The pint no longer contains an exact pound of water, but a pound and a quarter. Wine was anciently measured by the pound in Germany; and the Romans sold liquids by the *libra*, or pound.'—*Fox Talbot*.

Pippin. The name 'pippin' applied to an apple signifies that the particular variety was raised from a seed or pip. As in the case of new varieties of flowers and shrubs raised from seed, the new plant is called a 'seedling,' so varieties of the genus *pyrus* raised from pips are called 'pippins.' The prefixes to the names have usually some reference to the place of origin or the name of the raiser.

Pistol. Pistols were first brought into England from Pistoja, a town in Italy, in 1526.

Pit. The name 'pit,' applied to the space in theatres between the boxes and the stage, is an abbreviation of the word *cockpit*. At one time these spaces were used for cock-fighting. The following lines are conclusive:

Let but Beatrice
And Benedict be seen: Lo, in a trice
The *cockpit*, galleries, boxes, are all full.

Pith Hats. These hats, so useful in hot weather, are not of modern invention. In the diary of Albert Dürer (1520–21) is an entry stating that 'Thomasin has given me a plaited hat of elder-pith' (*Hist. of the Life of Albrecht Dürer*, &c., p. 269).

'**Pity the sorrows of a poor old man.**' The well-known lyric of which this is the first line was written by the Rev. Thomas Moss of Trentham, and was first published in a volume of 'Poems' in the year 1769.

Placard. This word formerly meant a licence. In the statute Hen. VIII. c. ix., it is enacted, *inter alia*, that 'If any person sue [i.e. apply] for any "placard" to have common gaming in his house, contrary to this statute, that then it shall be contained in the same placard what game shall be used in the same house, and what persons shall play thereat, and every placard to the contrary to be void.'

Places of Worship. This term did not always bear its present meaning of a house of prayer. In Fenn's 'Paston Letters' (vol. ii. p. 333, edit. 1778) is a letter from Margery Paston to her husband, dated December 24, 1484, in which she tells him that she had sent her son 'to my Lady Morley to have knowledge of what sports were used in her house at Christmas, . . . and she said that there were none disguisings, nor harpings, nor luting, nor singing, nor none loud disports; but playing at the tables, and chess, and cards.' She also says that she had sent another son 'to the Lady Stapleton, and she said according to my Lady Morley's saying in that, and as she had seen in places of worship where she had been,' &c. By 'places of worship' Mistress Paston meant the houses of worshipful people, as lords, knights, and justices of the peace.

Plaid and Tartan. Plaid (pronounced plade, not plad) is the garment; tartan is the peculiar pattern denoting the clan to which the wearer of the plaid belongs. The editor of 'Popular Ballads' says in the glossary to his work, 'This word in the Gaelic, or in any other language of which I have any knowledge, means anything broad and flat, and when applied to a plaid or blanket signifies simply a broad, plain, unformed piece of cloth.' Tennant says, 'Their brechan or plaid consists of twelve or thirteen yards of narrow stuff wrapped round the middle, and reaches to the knees.' The word has no reference whatever to the chequered pattern which the fabric generally bears.

Plancher, an Old English word for a floor. Johnson marks it as obsolete, but it is still used in Norfolk. Lord Bacon, speaking of various kinds of wood, says, 'Some are for planchers, as deal; some for tables,' &c. The name of a popular toy, 'planchette,' is from the same root, and means a small plank or board.

Planets. The planets may easily be distinguished from other stars by the fact that they do not twinkle.

Plant Growth. If, early in the morning of a day that is likely to be hot and sunny, a mark is made on the training stick of a hop or scarlet bean plant, exactly opposite the top of the shoot, and this mark be examined at night, it will be found that the plant has not grown during the day. If, however, it be again examined the next morning, it will be seen that it has considerably advanced; this advance being always in proportion to the light and heat of the previous day.

Plantagenet. This royal name was first adopted by the Counts of Anjou, and it is said to have been assumed by the first Count of that name from his having caused himself to be scourged with branches of broom (*planta genesta*) as penance for some crime he had committed. Henry II. of England, whose father was Geoffrey, Count of Anjou, was the first Plantagenet who filled the English throne.

Plaster of Paris is so called from having been originally obtained from Montmartre in the vicinity of Paris.

Plate. This word, as applied to silver spoons, forks, &c., comes to us from the Spanish word *plata*, silver.

Plateau. This word was introduced into the English language in 1807. The editor of the 'Annual Register' for that year described the battle of Eylau, and in doing so mentioned a flattish hill, which he said 'in French military phraseology is called a *plateau*.' Lest this should be misunderstood, he inserted a footnote to state that the word meant a platform.

Platform. The American use of this word in the sense of a political plan, scheme, or design is justified by ancient use in England. In Lyly's 'Alex. and Camp.,' act v. sc. 4, Apelles is asked, 'What peece of work have you now in hand?' to which he replies, 'None in hand, if it like your Majestie, but I am devising a platforme in my head.' And in the 'Discovery of the New World,' quoted by Nares, 'To procure himself a pardon went and discovered the whole platforme of the conspiracie.' A very early example occurs in the following title of a tract in the Library of Queen's College, Cambridge: 'A Survey of the pretended Holy Discipline, faithfully gathered by way of Historical Narration out of the Works and Writings of the principal favourers of that Platforme, 4to. London, 1593.' Another example is in Patrick's 'Parable of the Pilgrim,' published in 1687, p. 206, where, speaking of persons changing their sect, the writer says, 'He can soon quit the way wherein he was, and become religious, after the manner of this novel platform.'

Playbills. In the 'Register of the Stationers' Company,' under date October 30, 1587, is the following entry: 'John Charlewood. Lycenced to him by the whole consent of thassistantes [the assistants] the onelye ympryntinge of all manner of Billes for players, iis. vid.' Mr. Payne Collier thinks that playbills must have been printed before this date, but this is the first entry of any exclusive right to print them.

Plead. The Americans always use 'pled' as the past participle of the verb to plead. They spell it 'plead,' but it is universally pronounced 'pled.' As plead is a regular verb, they are unquestionably wrong, but they can cite Spenser as an authority, e.g.:

<blockquote>
With him . . . . came
Many grave persons that against her <i>pled</i>.—<i>Faerie Queene</i>.
</blockquote>

Please the pigs. This proverbial expression, ludicrous as it is in its present shape, had its origin in a deep religious feeling. It was formerly 'please the pyx.' The pyx was the box which contained the consecrated wafer, and was held in the greatest veneration as the symbol of the Almighty. The phrase, therefore, 'If it please the pyx' was equivalent to 'If it shall please God,' or in modern form 'D.V.,' i.e. *Deo volente,* or God being willing.

Pleiades. The remarkable group of stars in the second sign of the Zodiac known to astronomers by this name, and which is such an interesting object in the heavens on clear nights, is popularly known as *the seven stars,* and is believed to consist of seven. In reality there are but six. The erroneous belief dates from the time of the Greek mythology. The *Pleiades* were the seven daughters of Atlas and Pleione, who were translated into stars. They had all married, but only one, Sterope, had married a mortal, and it was believed that she had since hidden herself, from shame that she alone was not the wife of a god.

Plough-tail. Probably originally 'plough's stail,' from the Anglo-Saxon *stail,* a handle. In Warwickshire, and especially in Birmingham, the handles of brooms and mops are universally called 'stails'—'broom's stail,' 'mop's stail,' &c. &c.

Plumper. In the 'Ladies' Dictionary,' 1694, is the following: 'A plumper is a fine, thin, light ball, which old ladies that have lost their side teeth hold in their mouths to plump out their cheeks, which else would hang like leathern bags.'

Plunder. This word, in different forms, is common to all the Northern Continental nations of Europe, but was not known in England until the period immediately preceding the civil wars— 1630 to 1640. Fuller says it was introduced by the soldiers who had been sent to the assistance of Gustavus Adolphus, King of Sweden. In the Swedish language it is *plundra.* The word 'plunder' in the Southern and Western States of America is used as a general term for personal luggage, baggage of travellers, goods, furniture, &c.—e.g. 'Help yourself, stranger,' added the landlord, 'while I tote your *plunder* into the other room' (Hoffman, 'Winter in the West,' letter 33). The Canadians use the word 'booty' in the same sense.

Plural. 'In law the plural form of a noun may sometimes be taken to mean only one ; as, supposing a man to devise to another all his property, providing he (the testator) died without children; and he died leaving one child, the devise would not take effect.'— *Bouvier.*

Poacher. This word is derived from the French *poche*, a pocket or bag. A poacher is one who unlawfully kills and pockets another man's game.

Pocket. 'Poke' is an old name for a bag or sack, which survives in the proverb 'to buy a pig in a poke'; *et* is a common diminutive, so that pocket is etymologically poke-et, or *little bag.*

Pocket-handkerchief. This is one of the most curious compounds in the language. The first form of the word was kerchief, from the French *couvre-chef*, a covering for the head. By prefixing the word 'hand,' we get 'handkerchief,' a covering for the head held in the hand; but when we use the term pocket-handkerchief we speak of a covering for the head which is held in the hand and is contained in the pocket!

Poet Laureate. The earliest Court Poet of whom any record is preserved was Martin Henry de Avrinces, who in the time of Henry III., 1256-7, was paid 6*d.* per day as ' the king's versifier.' Poet Laureate was formerly a regular degree in our universities, the graduate being *laurea donatus.* Caxton, in the preface to ' The Boke of Eneydos,' 1490, says, ' I praye Master John Skelton, lately created poete laureate in the unyversitie of Oxford,' &c. Perhaps the best account of Poets Laureate is in the ' History of Poetry,' vol. ii. p. 228-230, by Warton, who was himself a Poet Laureate.

Poetry. This word had its root in the Greek *poieo*, to create, but its equivalent *poiesis* was applied by the Greeks to imaginative productions expressed in language. The word has not necessarily any connection with rhyme or metre. The books of Ruth and Job are examples of the highest poetry, though both are presented to us in prose form. Coleridge thought that poetry was ' not the proper antithesis to prose, but to science. Poetry is opposed to science, and prose to metre.'

Pohead. In the northern counties a tadpole is called a pohead. In the same locality the same name is given to musical notes, from their similarity to tadpoles. 'To play by the poheads' is therefore to play according to the musical notes.'—*Grose.*

Polar Star. The polar star is the last in the tail of the constellation called the Little Bear. It never sets to the inhabitants of the Northern hemisphere, and is therefore an invaluable guide to seamen.

Polemic, from a Greek word signifying *warlike.* Its original English meaning was simply controversial; but 'at present by popular usage it has some fantastic connection with controversial theology.'—*De Quincey.*

Police. The Metropolitan Police Force was established by Act of Parliament June 19, 1829. It commenced duty September 29 of the same year. From being organised by Mr., afterwards Sir Robert, Peel, the members were nicknamed Bobbies, a designation which appears likely to become permanent.

Policy. 'A pleasure ground about a gentleman's estate; alterations made in a town for the purpose of improving its appearance.'—*Jamieson.* Its use in either of these cases is confined to Scotland.

Polished Shoes. About the beginning of the seventeenth century the wearing of polished shoes was greatly ridiculed. Frequent allusions to it appear in the literature of the period. Ben Jonson, in 'Every Man in his Humour,' makes Kitely say:

> Mock me all over,
> From my flat cap unto my shining shoes.—Act. ii. sc. 1.

And in Shirley's 'Doubtful Heir,' he has:

> I have no mind to woollen stockings now
> And shoes that shine.

Polka. This dance is not of modern introduction. In Sir John Davis's poem on dancing, 'The Orchestra,' published in 1596, the polka is clearly indicated in the following lines:—

> Yet there is one, the most delightful kind,
> A lofty jumping, or a leaping round,
> Where arm in arm two dancers are entwined,
> And whirl themselves, with strict embracements bound;
> And still their feet an anapæst do sound,
> An anapæst is all their music's song,
> Whose first two feet are short, and third is long.

Pollard. This is the name applied to trees whose whole upper portion has been cut away (*polled*) to within ten or fifteen feet of the ground, leaving the stem to shoot out fresh branches. The new branches are never equal in size to the original, and when frequently polled the tree itself forms a large lump or head which is scarred and covered with numerous excrescences. When the pollard is finally cut down, the head is of great value for veneers, as the peculiar markings of the grain form surfaces of great beauty. Pollard oak furniture is highly prized.

Polony. The bloated-looking sausages seen in the shop windows in low localities in London are called *polonies*. The name is a corruption of *Bologna*, a town in Italy celebrated for its sausages.

Poltroon. From the Latin *pollice truncato*, deprived of the thumb; it having been a common practice among the Romans to cut off a thumb to avoid serving in the wars. Hence our word poltroon for a coward.

Pomade was originally made by boiling very ripe apples in fat. By this process the pleasant odour of the fruit was communicated; and the name pomade—from *pomum*, an apple—originated. The word pomatum comes from the same root.

Pompey's Pillar at Alexandria. This name is altogether a misnomer. The inscription on the base shows that it was erected by Publius, Prefect of Egypt, A.D. 296, in honour of the Emperor Diocletian. It is a monolith of red granite, 73 feet long and about 10 feet diameter. It stands upon a pedestal, and has a Corinthian capital. The total height is 98 feet 9 inches.

Pond is from *ponned*, ponded or impounded:

> The citizens are like *ponned* pikes, the lesser feed the great.
> *Alb. Engl.*, p. 135.

Pont. A relic of the Roman occupation of Britain survives in the Welsh word *pont* for a bridge. It is a contraction of the Latin *pons pontis*, which has the same meaning. So far as can be ascertained, the ancient Britons had no native word for a bridge, and consequently adopted the name given by the Romans to the structures they introduced into Britain. The Welsh retain the word, which enters into many of their local names of places, as *Pont-y-glyn*, the bridge of the glen; *Pont-y-Mynach*, the bridge over the Mynach, &c.

Pontiff, from the Latin *pontifex*, a name given by the ancient Romans to a high priest, from *pons*, a bridge, and *facio*, to make, because the first bridge over the Tiber was constructed by the chief priest. Milton uses a compound of the word in the sense of bridge-building—' By wondrous art pontifical.'

Pony. This word is of modern adoption in English. It does not appear in the first edition of Bailey's Dictionary, but is inserted in the second, published in 1736, the definition being 'a little Scotch horse.' The 'Gentleman's Magazine,' 1789, says the word is derived from the French *puisné*.

Pope's Ode is evidently founded on Flatman's 'Thought of Death'; indeed the language in some portions is very closely imitated. For instance, Flatman says:

> Methinks I hear some gentle spirit say,
> Be not fearful, come away;

which evidently suggested Pope's

> Hark! they whisper, angels say,
> Sister spirit, come away.

Then Flatman has:

> Fainting, gasping, trembling, flying,
> Panting, groaning, speechless, dying;

which no doubt inspired Pope's much finer couplet:

> Trembling, hoping, lingering, flying,
> Oh, the pain, the bliss of dying.

It is but fair to add that Pope never claimed that the ode was entirely original. In sending the manuscript to Steele to be set to music, he says, 'I had in my head not only the verses of Adrian, but the fine fragment of Sappho, &c.' No doubt he intended that the '&c.' should cover his indebtedness to Flatman.

Population of London. The population of London in 1881 exceeds by nearly a million the estimate of that of all England at the accession of Henry VII.

Population of the World. According to a calculation recently (1880) made by Dr. Behm and Professor Wagner, the population of the world is 1,455,923,500, divided in the following way:— Europe, 315,929,000; Asia, 838,704,000; Africa, 205,679,000; America, 95,495,500; Australia and Polynesia, 4,031,000; Polar regions, 82,000. According to this estimate, it will be seen that the population of Asia is two hundred and twelve millions more than that of all the rest of the world, the Asiatics numbering ten out of every fourteen human beings.

P's and Q's—' Mind your p's and q's.' There are two different origins assigned to this expression. The one is that it arose from the custom of chalking up behind alehouse doors the debts due from customers, in which the number of pints or quarts they owed for were made by strokes opposite the letters 'P' and 'Q.'

Charles Knight, the editor of the 'Penny Cyclopædia,' thinks it originated in a printing office. The p's and the q's in small Roman type are so much alike that they are always puzzling to a printer's apprentice. '"Mind your p's and q's" means, Do not be deceived by apparent resemblances; learn to discriminate between things essentially distinct, but which *look* the same; be observant, be cautious.'

Porcelain. This name was given to China ware from a supposed resemblance of its surface to that of the univalve shell called *porcellana*. The shell was so named from the shape of its outer surface, which was thought to resemble the back of a pig (*porcella*).

Porch. A contraction of portico.

Porcupine, from the Italian *porco-spinoso*; Venetian, *porco-spin*, the spiny pig. In English the name of the hedgehog was *porpin*, and then *porpentine*, as used by Shakespeare. The word is rendered *porcupine* in all the modern editions, but the line ought to run :

Like quills upon the fretful *porpentine.*

Porpoise, from the French *porc*, a hog, and *poisson*, fish—hog-fish. It is curious that while we call the animal by a French name, the French have adopted an Anglo-Saxon or German one, *mere-swine*—sea-pig. Spenser derives the English name from the Latin direct, instead of through the French, and writes:

Stinking scales and *porc-pisces.*

This is nearer to the correct English pronunciation, which has always been 'porpeese'; not por*poyse*.

Porringer. A vessel for holding or making porridge or pottage; it is called 'pottinger' in the West of England.

Portcullis. *Coulisse* in French is anything that slides or slips up and down; portcullis is *porte-coulisse*, the gate-slide.

Porter. The earliest mention of porter as a beverage is probably the following in Nicholas Amherst's 'Terræ Filius' for May 22, 1721 :—' We had rather dine at a cook's shop upon beef, cabbage, and *porter* than tug at an oar or rot in a dark, stinking dungeon.' In the following quotation the date should evidently be 1720 :—' Before the year 1730 the malt liquors in use in London were ale, beer, and twopenny, and it was customary to call for a pint or tankard of half-and-half, i.e. half of ale and half of beer. In course of time it also became the practice to ask for a pint of "three-thirds," i.e. one-third of ale, beer, and twopenny. To avoid trouble, one Harwood, a brewer, made a liquor which combined the flavours of all three, which he called entire, or "entire butt beer," meaning that it was entirely from one butt. Being much relished by porters and other hard-working men, it obtained the name of 'porter.' It was first retailed at the "Blue Last," Curtain Road, Shoreditch.'—*Leigh.*

Portrait. Sir Joshua Reynolds in one of his lectures laid down the true canon of portrait-painting as follows: 'In portraits the grace, and we may add the likeness, consists more in taking the general air than in observing the exact similitude of every feature.'

Post, from the Latin *positus*, placed. 'How various are the senses in which the word post is employed! Post office; post haste; a post standing in the ground; a military post; an official post; to post a ledger. Yet, when once on the right track, nothing is easier than to bring all these uses of post to a common centre. Post is the Latin *positus*, that which is placed. The piece is placed in the ground and becomes a post; a military station is a post, for a man is placed in it; to travel post is to have relays of horses placed at intervals so that no delay can occur; the post office is that which availed itself at first of this mode of communication; to post a ledger is to place or register its several items.'—*Trench.*

Postage of Newspapers. Before the introduction of the penny postage, newspapers were carried free, in consideration of the stamp duty of fourpence per copy to which they were liable. Up to the year 1825 they were supposed to be franked by a member of Parliament, but this custom had degenerated into the habit of any sender of a paper himself writing the name of some member, whether with his cognizance or not. This infamous and immoral system was abolished by an Order in Council, June 1825.

Post and Pan Houses, the name by which half-timbered houses are known in some parts of England. Halliwell says: 'A post and pan house is one formed of uprights and cross-pieces of timber which are not plastered over, but generally blackened, as many old cottages are in various parts of England.' The timber in these structures is represented in the word post. The Anglo-Saxon word pan, or *pane*, a piece or portion, refers to the filled-up interstices. We still use the word in the phrase 'a pane of glass.' ' The knight showed me a pane of the wall, and said, "Sir, see you yonder part of the wall, which is newer than all the remnant?"'—*Berners.* See PANE.

POTATOES. 439

Postal Business in 1635. In a 'Project for Accelerating Letters,' issued in 1635, it is stated that 'if anie of his Ma^{ts} subjects shall write to Madrill (*sic*) in Spain, hee shall recieve answer sooner and surer than hee shall out of Scotland or Ireland. The letters now being carried by carriers or foot post 16 or 18 miles a day, it is full two monthes before any answer [comes] from Scotland or Ireland to London.'

Post Office. The post office as a national institution was founded in 1660. The letters were carried by mounted messengers. In 1784 the coaches went from London to Bath in seventeen hours, while the post took forty for the same journey. In that year, on the suggestion of Mr. Palmer, the manager of the Bath Theatre, mail coaches were established on all the principal roads. The first, carrying the Bristol mail, started August 2, 1784. Rowland Hill in 1837 suggested penny postage, which came into operation January 10, 1840. The building which was the General Post Office from about 1690 to 1829 is the present Lombard Street branch. On September 23, 1829, the office on the east side of St. Martin's-le-Grand was first opened for business.

Post Office Orders. In 1791 Lackington, the well-known bookseller, wrote as follows : 'Many in the country found it difficult to remit small sums that were under bankers' notes, which difficulty is now done away, as the postmasters receive small sums of money and give drafts for the same on the post office in London.'—*Notes and Queries*, October 3, 1874.

P.S. These letters are an abbreviation of the Latin phrase *post scriptum*, written afterwards. In English the word 'postscript' has become a noun, the words written at the bottom of a letter, with the prefix P.S., being spoken of as 'the postscript.'

Posy, a contraction of poesy. 'Posy originally meant verses presented with a nosegay or bunch of flowers, and hence the term came to be applied to the flowers themselves.'—*Sullivan*.

Potatoes. The potatoes mentioned by Shakespeare and his contemporaries, as in the 'Merry Wives of Windsor,' act v. sc. 5, where Falstaff says, 'Let the sky rain potatoes,' were not the esculent roots now found upon every dinner-table, but were *batatas*, the tuberous roots of *batatas edulis*, or the sweet potato. They were formerly imported into England by way of Spain, and sold as a delicacy before the present potatoes were known. They were looked upon as having a stimulating effect upon human desires and passions. Hence Falstaff's allusion. Our word potato is derived from the Spanish *batata*. The balance of testimony attributes the introduction into England of the plant now called the potato to Sir Walter Raleigh, or to some of the colonists whom he had settled in Virginia. An old English botanist—Gerarde—mentions in his 'Herbal,' published in 1597, that he had planted the potato in his garden in 1590, and that it flourished as well there as in its native soil, Virginia, from whence he received it. It did not come into general cultivation, however, for nearly two centuries afterwards. Mr. Wright Hill, father of Sir Rowland Hill of the Post Office, says in his autobiography: 'About the year 1750 my uncle, having heard of potatoes, procured some and planted them in his garden. At harvest time he gathered some of the balls from the top, and, of course, found them uneatable. He left the stems to wither until he wished to re-till the garden, when he found, to his utter astonishment, under the ground a most excellent crop.' A member of the well-known family of the Howards of Bedford, who resided at Cardington near that town, brought them into general culture about the year 1765.

Pottle. 'Pottle' is the name of a measure containing two quarts, or half a gallon. A 'pottle' of strawberries was originally two quarts. *Tempora mutantur!*

Potwalloper. Before the Reform Act of 1832 the members of Parliament for certain boroughs in England were elected by the 'potwallopers'—that is, by all those residents who boiled a pot, which of course meant all householders. This franchise was abolished by the Act just mentioned, and the word has gone out of use in England. The Americans, however, with characteristic humour, have adopted the word, applying it as a name for a scullerymaid. A woman who cleans, scours, or wallops the cooking pots or vessels is with them a 'potwalloper.'

Poultry. From *poule*, the French name for the domestic hen. Hence also pullet, from *poulet*, a little hen.

Pounce. The claws of an eagle or a falcon are called pounces. Hence to pounce upon anything is, literally, to seize it by the claws.

Pound. An imperial pound weight contains 7,000 grains *troy*. A pound troy contains 5,760 grains *troy*.

Pound Weight of Silver. Up to the time of Henry VIII. the Anglo-Saxon pound—called also the *Tower* pound—was in use for gold and silver. It was three-quarters of an ounce less than the pound troy which superseded it.

				s.	*d.*
A Tower pound of silver in	1066	was coined into	20	0
,,	,,	1346	,,	22	6
,,	,,	1412	,,	30	0
,,	,,	1464	,,	37	6
,,	,,	1560	,,	56	3
,,	,,	1601	,,	58	1½

Prairie. The name given to the vast fertile plains of America by the early French settlers is their native French word *prairie*, meadow or pasture land.

Prayer-book. When the prayers in this book were first compiled, the authors, in their anxiety to adapt it to all capacities, used in many cases two nouns or two verbs of synonymous meaning, so that at least one of the two might be understood. Thus we have 'pray and beseech'; 'acknowledge and confess'; 'sins and wickedness'; 'goodness and mercy'; 'dissemble nor cloak'; 'assemble and meet together'; 'requisite and necessary'; 'erred and strayed'; 'pardoneth and absolveth'; and many others.— *G. F. Graham.*

Prebend or **Prebendary.** The word 'prebend' is often erroneously used to signify the person holding the office. A prebendary is a person holding a prebendal stall or office, which is usually called his prebend.

Precedent. A precedent was formerly a rough draft or previous copy of a writing. Thus Shakespeare ('King John,' act v. sc. 2) makes the Dauphin say:

> My lord Melun, let this be copied out,
> And keep it safe for our remembrance;
> Return the precedent to these lords again.

Predecessor. 'The word predecessor is applied to a body politic or corporate in the same sense as ancestor is applied to a natural person.'—*Burrill.*

Predicament. This word is generally used in a wrong sense. Thus we commonly hear that 'So-and-so, by doing certain things, has placed himself in an awkward predicament,' the latter word being used instead of position, condition, or circumstance. This use is utterly wrong. Bailey says a predicament is 'a certain class, or determinate series, or order, in which simple terms or words are ranged.' Johnson, following Harris, says it is 'a class or arrangement of beings or substances ranged according to their natures; called also categorema, or category.' The nearest approach to accuracy in the modern use of the term is that a man may occupy a bad position *in a predicament* or a category.

Perhaps the error originated in a misunderstanding of Shakespeare's passage—

> The offender's life lies in the mercy
> Of the duke only, 'gainst all other voice;
> In which *predicament* I say thou stand'st.

By which it may fairly be assumed that Shakespeare meant, 'Your name is in the *predicament*, or list, of persons whose lives are at the mercy of the duke.'

Prefixes to Proper Names signifying descent or sonship are common in many languages, as the Norman *Fitz*, the Scotch *Mac*, the Welsh *Ap*, the Irish *O'*, the Arabic *Ben*, and the Russian *witch* or *vitch*. The latter, however, is an affix.

Prejudice. This word is commonly used in a bad sense, as, 'I have a prejudice against him.' Yet the word means simply a judgment formed beforehand, which may be favourable or otherwise. It is quite correct to say 'I am prejudiced in his favour.'

Premises. This word, the literal meaning of which in law is 'statements previously made,' is now commonly used as signifying a house and its surroundings. In this sense it had a singular origin. In a legal deed of conveyance it was customary, at the commencement of the document, to give a formal description, at great length, of the property to which the deed related. When in the same deed it was necessary again to refer to the property, the words '*the premises*,' in the sense of 'that which has been already described,' saved useless repetition and were well understood. By some extraordinary change, the phrase 'the premises' came to signify, not the description of the property, but the property itself, and in this sense the word has now become incorporated with the English language, and has been used in Acts of Parliament. None of the dictionaries consulted for the purposes of this work have any reference to this misuse of the word. (See Jacob's 'Law Dictionary.')

Preposterous is from the Latin *præ*, before, and *posterus*, after. It means putting before that which should be behind. It is exactly equivalent to the saying, 'the cart before the horse.'

Presently. This word originally meant that something was to take effect after some future event had happened. Lord Coke uses it in this sense in the words 'to take effect presently after the decease of her husband.' In England it now means in a short time, almost immediately; but in Scotland it signifies 'now' or 'at present,' as in the sentence ' Presently in the occupation of Donald Nicol.'

Prestige. This is a French word which has become naturalised in English within the last fifty years. Trench says it 'manifestly supplies a want in our language; it expresses something which no single word in English could express, which could only be expressed by a circumlocution, being "that moral influence which past successes as the pledge of and promise of future ones breeds."'

Pretentious. This word, 'the adjective of pretence, supplies a real need in our language. In a very little time multitudes will use it quite unconscious that it is not older, nor perhaps so old, as they are themselves.'—*Trench*, 1851.

Pretext. 'Pretext and pretence both imply intention to deceive; pretext covers the thing done, pretence covers the thing to be done; pretext conceals motive, pretence conceals purpose.'—*Worcester*.

Pretty. This word implies some drawback, as beauty without dignity, pleasing without being striking, elegance without elevation. Pretty means agreeable to the eye, yet wanting in something which would satisfy the canons of good taste.

Prevent. This word has completely changed in meaning within the last two centuries. It is from the Latin *præ*, before, and *venio*, to go or come, and meant originally to precede. Thus we have in the Prayer-book, '*Prevent* us, O Lord, in all our doings'; in the Bible (Psalm cxix. 14), 'I *prevented* the dawning of the morning'; and in that glorious work of Izaak Walton's, 'The Compleat Angler,' 'I will have nothing to hinder me in the morning, for I will *prevent* the sun rising.'

Prices at Theatres. Nares, in his 'Glossary,' gives a number of extracts, showing the prices anciently paid for admission to the old playhouses. The highest price appears to have been a shilling, for which the gay gallants of former days might have a stool on the stage—

> The private stage's audience, the twelvepenny stool, gentlemen.
> *Decker's Roaring Girl, Dodsley,* vi. 31.

Or they might for the same money have a seat in the best box or room—'But I say any man that hath wit may censure, if he sit in the twelvepenny room.'—*Malcontent, Dodsley,* iv. 12. These were the best places. Sir Thomas Overbury has, 'If he have but twelve pence in his purse, he will give it for the best room at a playhouse.' But there were cheaper places—'Your groundling and your gallery commoner buyes his sport by the penny' ('Gul's Hornbook,' chap. vi. p. 27)—and there was the twopenny gallery— 'One of them is a nip, I took him once at the twopenny gallery at the Fortune' ('Roaring Girl,' Dodsley, vi. 113). But there were also the contingent expenses; as Prynne says, 'Many there are who, according to their severall qualities, spend 2d., 3d., 4d., 6d., 12d., 18d., 2s., and sometimes four and five shillings at a playhouse day by day, if coach-hire, boate-hire, tobacco, wine, beere, and such-like vaine expenses be caste into the reckoning.'

Price of Books before the Invention of Printing. In the year 1274 the price of a Bible in nine volumes, 'fairly written,' with a glossary or commentary, was fifty marks, or 33l., and in 1433 the cost of transcribing the works of Nicholas de Lira, to be chained in the library of the *Grey Friars, London*, was 66l. 13s. 4d. This shows the enormous cost of books before the discovery of printing, for if we take the money of those times to be twenty times its present value, the Bible must have been worth 660l., and De Lira 1,333l. 6s. 8d. The pay of a labouring man in 1272 was 1½d. a day.—*Brand's Dict.*, vol. iii. p. 63.

Price of Provisions in Ireland, 1742. 'The Dublin News Letter,' May 8, 1742, says: 'We hear from Derry [Londonderry] that provisions there are as cheap as they were ever known, there being twenty pounds of meal for ninepence, twenty ounces of butter for twopence-halfpenny, eighteen eggs for a penny, and potatoes for threepence per bushel.'

Prickle. A prickle belongs to the bark, and peels off with it, as in the rose. A spine or thorn grows from the wood.

Pride 'makes us esteem ourselves, vanity makes us desire the esteem of others.'—*Blair*. Sometimes a man is 'too proud to be vain.'—*Dean Swift*.

Prig. In England this word is a slang term for a thief, and to prig is to steal. In Scotland it means to cheapen, to try to get an abatement in the price. A Scotchman who had announced his intention of *prigging* a hat which he had seen in a London shop window was brought before a magistrate for loitering in front of the shop with the intent to commit a felony.

Primâ facie (Latin). Literally 'on the first face.' In English composition the words signify 'at the first glance.' Thus, of a man charged with a crime a magistrate may say, 'There is a strong *primâ facie* case, but I do not consider the evidence sufficiently strong to warrant a conviction.'

Primary and Secondary Colours. The primary colours, from which all others are derived, are red, blue, and yellow. When all these are mixed in equal strength and proportion, the result is black, but any two of them, when mixed, produce what is termed a secondary colour. Thus red and blue produce *violet*; red and yellow, *orange*; blue and yellow, *green*. The contrasting colour of any primary is the secondary of the other two; thus red is contrasted by green; blue is contrasted by orange; and yellow is contrasted by violet. The union of any primary with its opposite secondary, as red with green, destroys both, and produces a dark grey or black.

Primary Colours in Flowers. There seems reason for believing that the three primary colours are never found in any one class of flowers. Nature seems to have limited them to two. A blue rose or a blue dahlia is never seen. The nearest approach hitherto observed is in the case of the hyacinth, where blue and yellow are common, and where different shades of pink, verging almost to crimson, are met with; but these shades have all a slight tinge of blue in them, which makes them very unlike to the true primary red. This circumstance is worthy the attention of floriculturists. It is merely mentioned here tentatively.

Prime Minister. The term 'Prime Minister' seems to have originated in banter. It was first applied in this spirit to Sir Robert Walpole. On February 11, 1712, that statesman is reported to have said in the House of Commons, 'Having invested me with a kind of mock dignity and styled me a "Prime Minister," they [the Opposition] impute to me an unpardonable abuse of the chimerical authority which they only created and conferred.'

Primrose was anciently written 'pryme rolles,' in which form we find it in old books and MSS. 'It is called pryme rolles of pryme tyme, because it beareth the first flower in pryme time.' Chaucer writes it 'primirole.' 'This common little plant affords an extraordinary example of blundering. Primirole is an abbreviation of the French *primeverole*, Italian *primeverola*, diminutive of *prima vera* from *flor de prima vera*, the first spring flower. *Primirole*, as an outlandish unintelligible word, was soon familiarised into prime rolles, and then into primrose. The rightful claimant of the name, strange to say, is the daisy.'—*Prior, Names of British Plants.*

Prince of Wales. The title of Prince of Wales originated with Edward I. After he had subdued the Welsh, he promised them, if they submitted without further opposition, to give them a Prince who was born amongst them, and who could speak no other language. Upon their acquiescence he bestowed the title of Prince of Wales upon his son Edward, then an infant, born in Wales, and unable to speak any language. From that time the title has always been conferred upon the eldest son of the sovereign.

Printing Machine. Townsend says that the first sheet printed by machinery, ever published, was the Sheet H of the number of the 'Annual Register' for April 1811. This does not appear to have been printed by steam power. The 'Times' newspaper of Tuesday, November 29, 1814, in its 'leader' says:—'Our journal of this day presents to the public the practical result of the greatest improvement connected with printing since the discovery of the art itself. The reader of this paragraph now holds in his hand one of the many thousand impressions of the "Times" newspaper which were taken off last night by a mechanical apparatus. A system of machinery, almost organic, has been devised and arranged which, while it relieves the human frame of its most laborious efforts in printing, far exceeds all human powers in rapidity and despatch. That the magnitude of the invention may be justly appreciated by its effects, we shall inform the public that, after the letters are placed by the compositors, and enclosed in what is called the forme, little more remains for man to do than to attend upon and watch this unconscious agent in its operations. The machine is then merely supplied with paper; itself places the forme, inks it, adjusts the paper to the forme newly inked, stamps the sheet, and gives it forth to the hands of the attendant, at the same time withdrawing the forme for a fresh coat of ink, which itself again distributes, to meet the ensuing sheet now advancing for impression; and the whole of these complicated acts is performed with such a velocity and simultaneousness of movement that no less than eleven hundred sheets are impressed in one hour.' The first book printed by steam was Dr. Elliotson's edition of 'Blumenbach's Physiology' which was published in 1817.

Printing on China and Earthenware. 'It is usually said that printing on china was invented by Dr. Wall of Worcester; but we believe it to have been first done from copper plates by Sadler, in Harrington Street, Liverpool, where Wedgwood sent his to be printed.'—*Fairholt.*

Probate of a Will. Exhibiting a will before the properly appointed officer, and obtaining an office or proved copy, is called obtaining probate. The original will is retained in the registry of the court, and the executors act on the authority of the proved copy. Any person, on payment of a shilling, can see an official copy of the will at the registry office.

Proctor. Over the door of Watts's Hospital at Rochester, celebrated by Dickens in the 'Seven Poor Travellers,' is an inscription setting forth that travellers, 'not being rogues or proctors,' can have for one night only 'lodging, entertainment, and fourpence each.' Many have been the conjectures as to why such respectable persons as the lawyers of the ecclesiastical courts should be associated with rogues in the disqualification mentioned, and much wit has been indulged in at the expense of the legal gentlemen in question. All this trouble might have been avoided if it had been known that a 'proctor' was 'a person appointed to beg or collect alms for lepers, or bedridden persons.' An Act of Edward I. sanctioned the employment of such persons; but by another Act (39 Elizabeth) 'proctors or patent gatherers for . . . . hospitals' were declared rogues and vagabonds. The term proctor is now altogether obsolete, as the designation borne till lately by ecclesiastical lawyers has been abolished by Act of Parliament.

Profane, from the Latin *pro*, before or in the precincts of, and *fanum*, a temple.

Prog is the English form of the Danish *prakker*, from the verb *prakke*, to beg. In Dutch *pragcher* is a beggar. Prog is therefore the collection of scraps which a beggar collects.

Programme, from the Greek word *programma*, meaning a law proposed to be adopted by the Athenian senate, but which was exposed upon a tablet for inspection before being proposed to the general assembly of the people for confirmation as law.

Progress, as a verb. This is generally looked upon as an Americanism, but it is used by Shakespeare and Milton:—

> Let me wipe off this honourable dew
> That silently doth *progress* on thy cheeks.
> *K. John*, act v. sc. 2.

'In supereminence of beatific vision, *progressing* the dateless and irrevoluble circle of eternity.'—*Milton's Reformation in England.*

Pronounce. In some parts of America, particularly in Nantucket, they use this word in the sense of perform, prove, turn out, fulfil expectations, &c.; e.g. 'How does your new horse *pronounce*?'

Proof. There are two, almost contradictory, senses in which this word can be properly used. A proof may be a trial, as a printer's proof or the trial of a gun at a proof-house; or it may signify the evidence which renders a truth certain or that which leaves no room for doubt. 'Proof and evidence are constantly used (in law) as synonymous, and are sometimes so treated in the books. Properly speaking, however, evidence is only the medium of proof; proof is the effect of evidence.'—*Burrill.*

Proportion of Cash Payments. The proportion of actual cash, and even of bank notes, used in large mercantile transactions is so small as to appear utterly insignificant. In the 'Statistical Journal' for September 1865 Sir John Lubbock published some particulars concerning the business of his bank during the last few days of 1864. Transactions to the amount of 23,000,000*l.* were effected by the use of coin and documents in the following proportions:—

	Per cent.
Cheques and Bills passed through the Clearing House	70·8
Cheques and Bills not cleared	23·3
Bank of England notes	5·0
Coin	·6
Country bank notes	·3
	100·0

The sums of money paid in by town customers amounted to 19,000,000*l.*, and when analysed gave the following results:—

	Per cent.
Cheques and Bills	96·8
Bank of England notes	2·2
Country bank notes	·4
Coin	·6
	100·0

Propriety originally had the meaning which we now attach to the word property. Clarendon says, 'They compounded with Sir Nicholas Crispe for his propriety in the fort and castle.'

Prose is the antithesis of verse or metre, not of poetry. **Poetry,** according to Hogg, is 'impassioned prose.' There is often much poetry in prose, but prose cannot exist in verse, although much verse is prosaic in the sense of being dull.

Pro tempore. This is a Latin phrase, meaning—for the time; temporarily; for the present; until something is permanently settled. It is pronounced pro tem-po-re.

Protestant. The word is derived from the Protest sent by the Convention of the States of Bohemia and Moravia to the Council of Constance. The original document is in possession of the College of Edinburgh, who acquired it in 1657. A copy of the Protest is in Maitland's 'History of Edinburgh,' pp. 371-72.

Proven. In the Scottish criminal law the jury can return a verdict of 'not proven,' which legally acquits the prisoner. Morally it is not so complete a clearance as a verdict of not guilty. 'There is a mighty difference between not proven and disproven.'—*Chalmers.*

Proverbs. Proverbs are short sententious sayings, generally embodying some frugal or prudent maxim. They have been variously defined by men of all ages. Thus Aristotle says they are 'remnants which on account of their shortness and correctness have been saved out of the wreck and ruins of ancient philosophy.' Agricola describes them as 'short sentences, into which, as in rules, the ancients have compressed life.' Cervantes, with his usual terseness, describes them as 'short sentences drawn from long experience.' Howell says their characteristic qualities are 'sense, salt, and shortness.' Lord Bacon calls them 'the genius, wit, and spirit of a nation'; and Earl Russell called them 'the wisdom of many and the wit of one.' In 1 Kings iv. 32, we are told that Solomon 'spake three thousand proverbs.' Most of these must have been lost, for all that are now attributed to him are about six hundred and fifty. Of the 'thousand and five' songs mentioned in the same verse we have only the book of Canticles and the 123rd Psalm.

Prude is a French word signifying prudent or virtuous; *prud'homme* being a man of courage and probity. In English prude is always used in a low sense, meaning an over-scrupulous woman, one who hypocritically affects coyness and superior delicacy of manners or speech.

Prune. Birds are said to prune their feathers when they clean and adjust them with the beak. It is sometimes written preen.

Pruning, Lopping. A tree is pruned by being deprived of some of its branches in order to give greater vitality to the remainder. Thus an apple tree is pruned so that the branches that are left may be more fruitful. Lopping is where the branches are cut off to be sold. In the south of England elm trees are regularly lopped, leaving the tree at certain times little more than a central shaft with the 'crop' at the top. When timber trees are sold for the purpose of felling, the purchaser bargains to take them with or without the 'lop and crop' as may be agreed upon.

Pryze. To pryze or prize is a verb used by English mechanics for lifting or raising with a lever, as 'Let us prize it.' It is perhaps a contraction of uprise or upraise. The Americans have coined a noun from the verb; with them a lever is a pry.

Psalms. The Psalms in the Prayer-book were translated in 1539. Those in the Authorised Version of the Bible in the year 1611.

Psalm CV. 28. The Prayer-book and the authorised edition of the Bible give directly contradictory readings of a portion of this verse. The first has, 'And they were not obedient unto his word.' The Bible has, 'And they rebelled not against his word.' The explanation is that Tyndale and Coverdale, the translators of the Prayer-book version, understood the words to apply to the Egyptians, while the later translators rendered them as applicable to Moses and Aaron. The Prayer-book version is probably correct.

Publican. The term publican, which in the New Testament is nearly always used in connection with sinners—'publicans and sinners'—meant a low and unscrupulous class of persons who paid a certain sum to the Roman Government for the privilege of collecting the taxes in certain defined districts. They were of the most degraded class, and their extortions and cruelties made them most unpopular. We have no word in our language to express the combined loathing, fear, and hatred with which the publicans were regarded in the time of our Saviour.

Public-house Signs. Hotten's 'History of Signboards' mentions the 'Three Crowns and Sugar-loaf' at Kidderminster, and says it was 'the grocers' sign.' The house in question is at Franche, two miles from Kidderminster, and its sign represents three golden crowns and a sugar-loaf, but there is little doubt that originally it meant the Papal tiara, a triple-crowned mitre, which, to the rustic mind, would doubtless suggest the name by which the house is now known.

Publishment. In the 'Laws of Massachusetts' the publication of the banns of marriage is called the 'publishment.' In one of the statutes it is ordered that 'Any persons desiring to be joined in marriage shall have such their intention published .... or posted up by the clerk of each town, and a certificate of such publishment .... shall be produced as aforesaid previous to their marriage.'

Pudding-time. Formerly all English dinners commenced with pudding, as they still do in remote districts. Hence pudding-time meant dinner-time. A foreigner who in the seventeenth century visited England and published his experiences in French at the Hague, in 1698, speaks enthusiastically of English puddings. 'Oh,' says he, ' oh, what an excellent thing is an English pudding ! To come at pudding-time is a proverbial phrase, meaning to come at the happiest moment in the world. Make a pudding for an Englishman and you will regale him, be he where he will.'

Puisne, i.e. junior (from the French; literally *since born*), is only applied in its original sense to the junior judges. It is in all other senses degraded to puny, which signifies immature, ill-grown, ill-developed, or misshapen.

Pullen. This is an Old English name for poultry, still used in the north. The word is often met with in old writers, as in Beaumont and Fletcher's 'Scornful Lady,' act v. sc. 2, 'She can do pretty well in the pastry, and knows how pullen should be crammed.' The word seems to be the Norman *poule*, a hen, and the Old English plural terminal *en*, *poulen* being equivalent to poules or hens. We still have the diminutive pullet, a small hen.

Pulpit. In the 'New World of Words,' a dictionary issued in 1696, a pulpit is defined to be 'the place upon which the comedians acted.' The Latins called their stage *pulpitum*.

Pumpernickel is the rye bread used by the Westphalian peasants, which in some other parts of Germany is considered a great delicacy. The loaves are sometimes 60 lbs. in weight. The name is said to have originated in the saying of a French cavalry soldier, who rejected the bread with disgust, saying it was only *bon pour Nicolas*—that is, fit or good for Nicholas, his horse.

Punch (the liquor). 'At Nerule (near Goa) is made the best arack or *Nepa di Goa*, with which the English on this coast make that enervating liquor called *paunch* (which is Indostan for five) from five ingredients.'—*Frayer's Travels to the East Indies*, 1672.

Punch formerly meant anything thick and short. Pepys says : 'I did hear them call their child Punch, which pleased me mightily, that word having become a word of common use for everything that is thick and short.' A Suffolk Punch is a short thickset cart-horse. A puncheon is a wide cask, and modifications of the word are common all over Europe to signify a cask or barrel.

Punch. This popular periodical, according to Mr. Blanchard, originated in an idea of Mr. William Last, a printer in Crane Court, who proposed to Mr. Henry Mayhew that they should jointly start a comic paper. Mayhew mentioned Mark Lemon as likely to be of great service, and they called upon him to propose it. Lemon fell in with the idea, and at a meeting at the 'Edinburgh Castle' Lemon drew up the prospectus. The name fixed upon was 'The Funny Dog with Comic Tales.' At a subsequent meeting at Last's office, some one mentioned Punch, and there was a joke about the Lemon in it. Mayhew caught the idea, and called out instantly, 'A good thought; we'll call it " Punch."' The new name was adopted by acclamation, and the first number appeared in July 1841. Although popular at first, it was soon in difficulties, at which time it was bought by Bradbury and Evans, and has continued its marvellously successful career ever since. The late Henry Mayhew told the compiler of this book, in the year 1845 that he originated not only the paper itself, but its name.

Punch and Judy. There is little doubt that the origin of Punch and Judy is to be found in some early mystery play, and that the characters originally represented Pontius Pilate and Judas. Some, however, have derived Judy from Giudei, the Jews. It was introduced into England about 1666 by an Italian, who erected a booth near Charing Cross for its performance. The parish books of St. Martin's-in-the-Fields, which contain the name of every householder from the time of Queen Elizabeth, show that a rental was paid to the Overseers for the land on which the booth was erected. The entry in the book credits the money as received from 'Punchinello.' Mr. J. Payne Collier wrote a history of Punch and Judy.

Punctuation. Points or stops are said to have been first used by Aristophanes, the Greek grammarian; but the modern system of punctuation was devised by Aldo Manucci (Manutius), a learned printer, who lived at Venice in the fifteenth and sixteenth centuries. Timperley says that the colon (:) was first used, but sparingly, in a black-letter edition (1550) of Bale's 'Actes of English Votaries,' but in Elyot's 'Governor' (1580) it is frequently used. He also says that the note of admiration (!) was first used in Edward VI.'s Catechism.

Punjab or Punjaub. This great Indian territory derives its name from two Persian words, signifying five rivers. The five affluents of the Indus which give rise to the name are the Jhelum, the Chenab, the Ravi, the Beas, and the Sutlej.

Punning. Dr. Johnson, it seems, was not the author of the saying, 'He who would make a pun would pick a pocket.' In the 'Public Advertiser' newspaper, January 12, 1779, is the following account of the origin of the saying :—'The aversion which Dennis bore to a pun is well known. Purcell and Congreve going into a tavern, by chance met Dennis. After a glass or two had passed, Purcell, having some private business with Congreve, wanted Dennis out of the room, and, knowing no way more effectual than punning, began to pull the bell. No one appearing in answer, he put his hand under the table, and looking full at Dennis said, "I think this table is like the tavern." "How so?" said Dennis. "Why," said Purcell, "because there's never a *drawer* in it." [1] The witticism had the desired effect, for Dennis started up and left the room, saying that any man who would make such an execrable pun would *pick his pocket.*'

Punt. The name of this convenient boat for angling is derived from the Latin word *pons*, a bridge. The French originated the name *pontoon*, which now in most European languages signifies flat-bottomed vessels used for making temporary bridges for military purposes. Our word punt is a contraction of pontoon, which vessel it resembles in its shape.

Pupil. The original meaning of this word is a fatherless child, either boy or girl.

Puppy originally meant a puppet or doll. The French still say *poupée* for a doll. The Dutch have *pop* for the same purpose, and in the Magyar language *buba* is a doll. It is in this sense that a young, conceited, over-dressed young man is called puppy. The term here has nothing to do with a young dog.

[1] 'Drawer' in those days was equivalent to the modern term 'waiter.'

Purchase. This word was anciently of wider significance than now. It was frequently used in the sense of acquire, and even to signify strong desire. Shakespeare has, 'Your accent is something finer than you could purchase in so remote a dwelling.' Berners tells us that 'Duke John of Brabant purchased greatly that the Earl of Flanders should have his daughter in marriage'; and the Scottish metrical version of Psalm lxxxiv. 3 runs thus :—

> Behold the sparrow findeth out
> A home wherein to rest,
> The swallow also for herself
> Hath purchased a nest.

Ben Jonson, in his play of 'The Fox,' makes Volpone say, 'I glory more in the cunning purchase [i.e. acquisition] of my wealth than in the glad possession of it.' In Beaumont and Fletcher's 'Coxcomb,' Dorothy, meditating a theft, says, 'I'll be hanged before I stir, without some purchase.'

Puritans. This was the name by which dissenters from the Church of England were known in the time of Elizabeth and the first two Stuarts. Fuller tells us that the name was first applied to them about the year 1564.

Purity. 'Purity is the feminine, truth the masculine of honour. By the ancients courage was regarded as the main part of virtue; by us, though I hope we are not less brave, purity is so regarded now.'—*Hare*.

Purlieu, land formerly part of a royal forest, but separated from it by roads or walks for perambulation (*pourallée*), and made *pure* or free from the laws of the forest.—*Burrill, London Ency*.

Purveyor. Recently it has become common for retailers to style themselves 'purveyors.' A fishmonger, ashamed of the good old word 'monger,' is now a 'purveyor of fish'! and a butcher is a 'purveyor of meat'! This use of the word is incorrect. A purveyor is strictly an officer who under the law of purvey had the right of buying provisions for the king's household at prices fixed by himself, and also of impressing the carriages and horses of subjects to do the king's business on the public roads. A purveyor, therefore, is one who *buys* for the king, not a seller to the public. The only portion of the law of purvey now in use is the right of the Crown to billet soldiers upon innkeepers, who are compelled by law to supply food and lodgings for soldiers and their horses at rates of pay fixed by the State.

Puss. This common term, used in England when calling a cat, or when fondling or caressing one, is the ancient Gaelic and modern Irish name for the animal, who in those languages would be called 'a *puss*.' In England the hare is often called 'puss.' The origin of the application of the name to so different an animal from that to which it legitimately belonged carries us back nearly to the time of the Norman Conquest. At that time, and for two or three generations afterwards, the fashionable language among the upper classes in England was a mixture of Latin and Norman-French. Amongst those who spoke pure Latin, the hare was called by its Latin name, *lepus*, which was perfectly correct. Others, probably, who spoke a jumble of both languages, took the word to be Norman, and, supposing the first syllable to be the article *le*, converted *lepus* into *le puss*.

Putting in the Stocks. Fifty years ago there were few hamlets or villages without a pair of stocks, in which minor offenders, such as drunkards or abusive persons, were sometimes condemned to sit for three, six, nine, or twelve hours, according to the gravity of the offence of which they had been guilty. These stocks were strongly fixed to the earth, and consisted of a framework of wood opening horizontally, and having apertures for the ankles of offenders, who sat on a stool with their legs through the openings, the framework being securely locked. The 'Leeds Mercury' for April 14, 1860, mentions that on the previous Thursday one John Gambles, of Stanningly (Pudsey), sat in the stocks from two to eight o'clock, having been convicted of Sunday gambling. This was probably the last occasion of the use of this ancient instrument of punishment.

Putting Sweet Herbs in Linen Presses. The custom of putting lavender and other scented herbs into linen presses and other places containing clothing is an old one. In Genesis xxvii. 27, we are told that Isaac, when old and blind, 'smelled the smell of [Jacob's] raiment,' which he compared to 'the smell of a field which the Lord hath blessed.' Rebecca had evidently perfumed the clothes of her favourite son with sweet-smelling herbs.

Pyramids. The great pyramid of Cheops, near Cairo, in Egypt, is 763 feet square, so that it covers a space of nearly 13 acres. Its height is 480 feet, or 115 feet higher than the cross of St. Paul's Cathedral in London. Sir William Tite says that it consumed nearly ninety millions of cubic feet of stone, and could not be built in the present day for less than thirty millions sterling. But even this vast structure is outdone in its area by the pyramid of Cholula in Mexico, whose sides are 1,423 feet, or nearly double the length of those of the pyramid of Cheops. The form, however, being truncated, the height is only 127 feet. On its summit stood the temple of Quetzalcoatl, the God of the Air. The base of the pyramid covers an area of nearly 50 acres.

Q

Q. The name of this letter is said to be derived from the French word *queue*, a tail; its form being that of the letter O with a tail.

Quack Doctor. A corruption of the term 'quake doctor,' or ague doctor. The ague being known as the quake, and in fenny countries being generally treated by ignorant persons, who professed to *charm* away the disease, the term 'quake doctor' arose, which has been corrupted into quack doctor.

Quad is a contraction of quadrangle. In some of the colleges at Oxford the students, when guilty of minor offences, are for a certain specified time not allowed to leave the college precincts. They may not pass beyond the quad or quadrangle. Hence to be 'in quad' is equivalent to being a prisoner.

Quadrille. A game at cards similar to whist was formerly known by this name. It was played with forty cards only, the tens, nines and eights being thrown out. It was a popular game about the time of the accession of George III.

Quadrilles. The popular dance so called was introduced into England by the Duke of Devonshire in 1813. The first quadrille danced at Almack's was in 1815. Captain Gronow has recorded the names of those who danced the first set. They were Lady Jersey, Lady Harriet Butler, Lady Susan Ryder, and Miss Montgomery. Their partners were the Count St. Aldegonde, Mr. Montgomery, Mr. Montague, and Charles Standish.

Quaint. This word, which is now limited to the meaning of odd, curious, or unusual, had a very wide range of signification three or four centuries ago. 'Whatever things were agreeable, elegant, clever, neat, trim, gracious, pretty, amiable, taking, affable, proper, spruce, handsome, happy, knowing, dodgy, cunning, artful, gentle, prudent, wise, or discreet, were included under this comprehensive word.'—*Earle, Philology of the English Tongue*, p. 343. Thus Shakespeare, in 'Much Ado about Nothing':

> But for a fine, *quaint*, excellent fashion, yours is worth ten of it.—Act iii. sc. 4.
>
> More *quaint*, more pleasing.—*Taming of the Shrew*, act iv. sc. 3.

And .

> 'Tis vile, unless it be *quaintly* ordered.—*Merchant of Venice*, act ii. sc. 4.

Quakers. This name was originally applied by a Derby magistrate to the members of the Society of Friends, because George Fox, the founder, admonished him and those present to tremble at the name of the Lord.—*Haydn*.

Quality. The common people, particularly in Ireland, speak of the upper classes as 'the quality.' Almost all our titles of respect come from qualities, as majesty, highness, excellency, worship (worthship), grace, honour, &c.

Quandary, a puzzle or perplexity, is a corrupted form of the French *Qu'en dirai-je?*—What shall I say of it?

Quarrel. This word was formerly used in the sense of a reason for, an excuse. Lord Bacon says: 'Wives are young men's mistresses, companions for middle age, and old men's nurses. So as a man may have a quarrel to marry when he will.'— *Essay VIII.* Holinshed has, 'He thought he had a good quarrel to attack him.'

Quarry. 'The excavation from which stone is extracted is termed a quarry, because there stones are quadrated (French *quarré*), squared or formed into rectangular blocks.'—*Tomlinson*.

Quarry, as applied to game, or anything else pursued. This word, there is no doubt, was at first the Norman-French *curee*, which signifies the offal portions of the slain deer, &c. given to the hounds. The meaning it bears now—the living object of pursuit— seems to have originated with Spenser, who, in the 'Faery Queene,' says (vi. 2, 20):

> Whilst they together for the quarry strove.

Quarry. This is a name given to the small diamond-shaped panes of glass, formerly in general use for windows. As Jean Quarré was the first to obtain a patent for making window-glass in England (temp. 2 Eliz., A.D. 1567), it seems probable that these panes of glass were called after his name. It may be, however, that they were anciently called 'quarries' from the Latin *quadro*, a square. The name is now confined to panes of a lozenge or diamond shape.

Quart, from the Latin *quartus,* a fourth. A quart is the fourth part of a gallon.

Quarter (in war). To give quarter to a prisoner is to send him to the rear to be lodged and fed by the captors. To refuse quarter is to dispatch the prisoner without mercy.

Quartern Loaf. A quartern loaf is one made from the fourth part (quarter) of a peck of flour.

Quassia, a plant possessing medicinal virtues, was so named from a negro Quassy, who first made it known to Europeans.

Queen. 'It seems that *cwene* or *quen,* the original of the word "queen," was used as a term of equality, applied indifferently to either sex. In the "Norman Chronicle" the historian speaks of the duke and his quens, meaning peers. A collection of verses written by Charles of Anjou and his courtiers is mentioned in a book of the thirteenth century as the songs of the quens of Anjou. A poem of the twelfth century, in detailing the war cries of the French provinces, says:
> And the *quens* of Thibaut
> "Champagne and passavant" cry.'

Chambers's Journal, Sept. 1845.

Queen Anne's Bounty. This is the name given to a fund for the augmentation of the incomes of the poorer clergy of England. It is created out of the 'first fruits' and 'tenths' of all livings, formerly exacted by the Pope, but by Henry VIII. annexed to the Crown. The first fruits are the entire profits of a living for one year after the incumbent is presented to it, and the tenths are a tithe of the subsequent income. These, however, are calculated on the profits of the living in the time of Henry VIII., and bear but a small proportion to the present value. By the Statutes 2 and 3 Anne, c. 11, a Corporation was formed to whom this income was granted for ' the augmentation of the maintenance of the poor clergy.' The present income is about 14,000*l.* a year, from which grants are made to assist in building new parsonage houses, or by making special grants of 200*l.* in cases where offers of private benefactions are made towards additional endowments on the condition of 200*l.* being added from this fund. The Corporation is composed almost entirely of *ex officio* members, such as the archbishops, bishops, privy councillors, judges, &c. They make an annual return to Parliament of their income and expenditure.

Queen Victoria's Baptismal Names. In the 'Greville Memoirs,' published 1874, it is stated that the Duke of Kent—the

Queen's father—wished his daughter's name to be 'Alexandrina Georgiana'; the first in compliment to the Emperor of Russia, who was the sponsor; but the Prince Regent objected, stating that the name Georgiana could be second to none in this country.

Queer. This word has been thought to have originated in the practice of an early trader, who in a list of his customers placed the word *quære* (enquire) opposite the names of those of whose solvency he was not certain. The word is certainly used in a similar sense to this day. A man who is thought to be in difficulties is said to be 'in Queer Street.' The word may, however, come from the German *quer*, which means cross, athwart, crooked.

Q in the Corner. Properly 'queue in the corner.' The *queue* is the seal affixed to legal documents in France. They were so called because they were formerly attached to a loop or *tail* (French *queue*) which depended from the parchment. The seal is now placed in a corner of the deed itself, but is still called the *queue*. The 'Q in the corner' is therefore the most important part, as it ratifies the whole contents of the document.

Quick. The ancient and primary meaning of this word is life or living. Thus in 1 Timothy iv. 1, 'Who shall judge the quick and the dead;' and in 1 Cor. xv. 36, 'That which thou sowest is not quickened, except it die.' So again in Chaucer we have, 'Not fully quick nor fully dead they were.' We speak of 'cutting to the quick' and of a quickset hedge, meaning a living, growing hedge, in contradistinction to a fence made of hewn timber, or other material not having life.

Quid of Tobacco. The word *cuid* is pure Gaelic for a portion; some think this is the origin of quid. Others, however, think that it is from cud. Ruminants chew the cud, sailors chew a quid.

Quid pro quo (Latin). Literally, what for what. In English usage, a consideration. Thus one may say, 'He lent me his horse; I will send him a brace of pheasants as a *quid pro quo*.'

Quid rides? This is a Latin expression meaning 'Why do you laugh?' It is pronounced 'quid ri-dees.' There is an old tale told of Mr. Lundy Foot, the celebrated Dublin tobacconist, who, it is said, having made a fortune, was desirous of a coat of arms and a motto for the panels of his carriage. Some wag suggested 'Quid rides?' for the motto, giving Foot the Latin pronunciation and meaning, and it was adopted. When the carriage appeared in the streets, the people read the motto as though it were English; and the association of 'Quid,' a tobacconist, riding in a carriage, created shouts of laughter, which Foot attributed to the Latin meaning, quite unconscious of the double signification of the words. Professor De Morgan, however, in 'Notes and Queries,' March 1862, say this is wrong, and gives, on the authority of a venerable friend of his, the true origin of the story as follows:—One Peter Brandon was a London tobacco broker of the last century who became rich and gouty, and bought an old carriage, which he had newly painted. He was asked by the painter for his arms. Brandon loved a joke and cared nothing for heraldry, so he determined to have some symbol of his business painted on the panel, but was at a loss for a motto. One Harry Callender suggested *Quid rides?* which was adopted. Professor De Morgan says that his informant had seen the carriage as a hackney coach plying in Cheapside, still having a shield bearing a sample of tobacco and the motto. His father had known Brandon, and he himself remembered Callender, who died within the present century.

Quill Pens. At first pens were made of reeds, and reeds are still used for the purpose in some parts of the East. The earliest notice of quills is in a passage of Isidore, who died A.D. 636. He mentions as writing materials reeds and feathers. In a Latin poem by Adelmus, who died 709, allusion is made to writing with a pelican's quill. Beckmann tells us that Mabillon saw a MS. of the Gospels written in the ninth century, in which the Evangelists were represented with quill pens in their hands. Soon after this period reeds seem to have been discarded in favour of quills.

Quinsy. A dangerous swelling of the throat, arising from inflammation of the tonsils. It is derived from two Greek words signifying to throttle a dog.

Quintain. 'A sport yet in use at marriages in Shropshire and elsewhere, in which they run a tilt on horseback with poles against a thick post fixed in the ground, and he who breaks most poles has the prize, formerly a peacock, now a garland.'—*Bailey's Dictionary*, edit. 1757. A quintain was set up at the Eyre Arms, St. John's Wood, London, in 1838, by the Earl of Eglintoun. It was in the shape of a man, and was used for practice by those who were to figure at the celebrated tournament at Eglintoun Castle in 1839. Louis Napoleon, afterwards Emperor, was one of those who used the quintain.

Quintal. This is an old word signifying a hundredweight. An English quintal is 112 lbs. In some countries the quintal is 100 lbs. only. The word is used by Defoe in 'Robinson Crusoe.'

Quits. This term, used to signify that money matters between two persons are finally adjusted, is probably derived from an old term used in the Royal Exchequer when a matter was balanced or settled. The auditor, after giving a statement of the manner in which an account was adjusted, and mentioning the balance which was paid, concluded by writing, 'which sum was paid in the King's Exchequer on the day above mentioned, as by the tallie thereof remayninge may appeare, and so here quyte.'

Quit Rent. Blackstone says that 'a quit rent is usually a very small rent paid by the tenants of manors in token of subjection, and by the payment of which the tenant goes quiet and free.' In ancient records the quit rent is called 'white rent,' because it was paid in silver money, and to distinguish it from corn rent, which is a chief rent, and was generally paid in kind.

Qui vive? is the challenge of a French military sentinel. Literally it is 'Who lives?' but it is equivalent to the English 'Who goes there?' To be on the *qui-vive* means, therefore, to be on the alert, or to keep a sharp look-out as a sentinel does.

Quiz. This word and all its derivatives originated in a joke. Daly, the manager of a Dublin theatre, wagered that a word of no meaning should be the common talk and wonder of the city in twenty-four hours. Within that time the letters q u i z were chalked or posted on all the walls of Dublin, with an effect that won the wager.—*Smart.*

Quod, for saith. This is really the Old English *quoth.* In the Anglo-Saxon quoth was written *quoð,* the ð being an Anglo-Saxon character for *th.* The early printers, having no type for ð, used a *d* instead as being the nearest in shape, and so *quoð,* which really meant and was sounded as quoth, became quod.

Q.V. These letters are a contraction of the Latin phrase *quod vide,* 'which see.' The letters *q.v.* are often used in cyclopædias, &c. in referring from one word to another—for example, in an article on the partridge, the writer may say, 'The partridge is a species of game (*q.v.*)'

Quoits. A game similar to quoits was known to the ancient Greeks, with whom throwing the *discus* was a favourite amusement. It was played at the Olympic games nearly 1,500 years before the Christian era. The *discus,* however, was solid, not annular like a modern quoit, and the object in the game was to throw the heaviest *discus* to the greatest distance. It was a game of strength rather than skill. The original of the modern quoit was a horseshoe. In some districts the quoit is still called the 'shoe.'

Quondam. This Anglicised Latin word signifies formerly, anciently, heretofore. 'My quondam schoolfellow' means my schoolfellow years ago. Dryden has 'My quondam barber,' meaning a barber he formerly employed. Its best English equivalent is the compound 'sometime'—thus, 'Richard Whittington, sometime mayor of this city.' In French they use the phrase *ci-devant*, as 'Louis Napoleon, *ci-devant* Emperor of the French.'

R

Rabbi. The modern Jewish Rabbi is in no way a priest in the sense of the Old Testament. He belongs hereditarily to no priestly family, and all that is necessary is that a candidate for the office should prove to the satisfaction of a college of Rabbis that he is well versed in the oral and written law in all its bearings. He then receives from them the degree of *morenu*, or teacher. The office of Rabbi carries with it no authority except as to the interpretation of a few ritual points. He is simply the teacher of the young, delivers sermons, and assists at marriages and divorces.

Rabbit. Coney is the Old English name for this animal, and the name for a young coney was rabbit. The latter word has superseded coney, and is now generic for coneys of any age.

Race. This word, when used in the sense of nationality, lineage, &c., is identical with the Spanish *raiz*, a root; its origin is the Latin *radix*. The French use the same word as ourselves, *race*. There is, however, a Mœso-Gothic word *raz*, a house, which may be its origin. We say 'the house of Israel,' 'the house of Hanover,' &c.

Race of Ginger is a root. Race is derived from the Spanish *raiz*, a root.

Radical. This word, as applied to a political party, came into use in 1818, when Hunt, Cartwright, and others sought to obtain a *radical* reform in Parliament.

Ragamuffin. Johnson says, 'From rag, and I know not what else.' In Dr. Whittaker's edition of 'Piers Plowman,' Ragamofin is said to be 'one of the demons in hell.'

Railway. 'Nearly two centuries before the introduction of the locomotive steam-engine, the colliers of the North of England made use of wooden rails for the purpose of reducing the labour of drawing coals from the pit's mouth to the place of shipment.'—*Tomlinson.* The word railway first appears in print in the 'Term Reports,' 1798, in a report of an appeal against a poor-rate made 'on a piece or parcel of land situate at Wallsend, and leading from a colliery there to the river Tyne,' in which it is stated that 'the appellants .... put and placed sleepers, or dormant timbers, below the surface of the soil, and to the sleepers, or dormant timbers, they affixed rail ways, or waggon ways.' The words rail and ways are printed separately, and the alternate words 'waggon ways' seem to show that the term was a new one at the time. The term railway as one word first appears in the title of an Act of Parliament in 1801. It runs as follows: 'An Act for making a Railway from the Town of Wandsworth to the Town of Croydon, &c.' This was a railway on which trucks of coal and heavy goods were drawn by horses from the Thames. A similar railway formerly ran by the side of the coach road from Gloucester to Cheltenham, and another from Stratford-on-Avon to Moreton-in-the-Marsh. The first railway constructed for locomotive power was the 'Stockton and Darlington,' which was opened September 27, 1825. The Liverpool and Manchester was opened September 15, 1830. The first locomotive engine, made by George Stephenson in 1824, travelled at the rate of six miles an hour. In 1829 Stephenson produced the Rocket, which travelled nineteen miles in the hour.

Railway, Railroad. The Americans never use the word 'railway'; with them it is always 'railroad.' They say railroad track, railroad depôt, and railroad car for the English equivalents railway, railway station, and railway carriage.

Railway Grease. The yellow compound used for lubricating the axles of railway carriages is really a kind of soap; a certain proportion of soda being mixed with the fats and oils, principally of vegetal origin, of which it is composed, with a view of preventing the too rapid melting which would ensue but for this slight saponification.

Railway Mania and the 'Times.' In the autumn of 1845 the whole country went mad upon the subject of railway construction. Fresh schemes were projected daily, and the 'Times' newspaper came out as three whole sheets daily, the greater part of which were filled with railway advertisements. The advertisement receipts for nine weeks were as follows:—

	£	s.	d.		£	s.	d.
September 6	2,839	14	0	October 11	6,543	17	0
,, 13	3,783	12	0	,, 18	6,687	4	0
,, 20	3,935	7	6	,, 25	6,025	14	6
,, 27	4,692	7	0	November 1	3,230	3	6
October 4	6,318	14	0				

During the whole of the time these magnificent sums were rolling into the 'Times'' treasury, the leading articles day after day denounced the infatuation and foretold the inevitable result. This continued until the crash came, which resulted in a falling off in one week of one-half the 'Times'' receipts from this source. The independence of the English press never had more glorious manifestation.

Railway Tunnels. The St. Gothard tunnel is 16,280 yards long; the Mont Cenis, 13,364; the Stanedge, between Manchester and Leeds, 5,430; and the Woodhead, between Manchester and Sheffield, 5,300.

'Rainbow' in Fleet Street. This celebrated tavern was the second coffee-house started in London. It was opened in 1656 by a barber named Farr.

Rainfall. The average rainfall in different countries, and even in different parts of the same country, varies considerably. Thus the western parts of Great Britain have a rainfall nearly double that of Norfolk and Lincolnshire, whilst in western mountainous districts the fall is sometimes prodigious. On December 5, 1863, $12\frac{1}{2}$ inches fell at Portree, in the island of Skye, in thirteen hours; and on November 27, 1845, there fell at Seathwaite, in Borrowdale, nearly $6\frac{3}{4}$ inches. But these enormous falls have been exceeded on the Continent. At Joyeuse, in France, 31 inches fell in twenty-two hours, at Geneva 30 inches in twenty-four hours, and at Gibraltar 33 inches in twenty-six hours. The enormous weight of the water which descends from the clouds, even in dry districts such as London, can scarcely be believed. In round numbers, every inch of rainfall represents 100 tons per acre, and, as the average fall in London is 24 inches, the yearly fall *per acre* is 2,400 tons. The area of what is called 'London' is upwards of 78,000 acres, so that the weight of rain that falls yearly within the metropolitan district is more than 187 millions of tons. This, taking the population at the extreme figure of five millions, would give more than 37 tons of water per annum for every person, man, woman, and child, within the district. In round numbers this comes to about 30 gallons a day for each. The heaviest annual rainfall in the world is on the Khasia Hills, in Bengal, where it is seldom less than 600 inches.

Raining cats and dogs. 'The male blossoms of the willow tree, which are used on Palm Sunday to represent the branches of palm, are called "cats and dogs" in many parts of the country. They increase in size rapidly after a few warm April showers, and the belief formerly prevailed that the rain brought them. Hence the saying to "rain cats and dogs."'—*Notes and Queries.* It may, however, be from the French *catadoupe,* a waterfall.

Rake, in the sense of a libertine, is, according to Richardson, 'a contraction of *rakel,* which is a corruption of *rekeles,* or reckless.' Milton spells the word rakel 'rakehell,' and it was so used by many old writers. Rakehell is probably a corruption of the French *racaille,* a word signifying the dregs and offal of society.

>   And far away amid their rakehell bands
>   They spied a lady left all succourless.—*Francis Quarles.*

There is still another probable origin. The Old English *rakel* or *rackyl* meant impetuous, unbridled, or passionate.

Ralph Allen, in the year 1720, made a contract with the Post Office for improving the system of 'cross-posts,' for the exclusive use of which system he agreed to pay 6,000*l.* a year. It was so successful that Allen made a fortune of about half a million. It is mentioned here to show the origin of a line of poetry which has almost become proverbial. Pope says:

>   Let humble Allen, with an awkward shame,
>   Do good by stealth, and blush to find it fame.

Ramage. This word, if used at all now, is made identical with rummage, which, according to Worcester, means 'to make a search by turning things over.' Swift uses rummage in this sense when he says, 'I have often rummaged for old books in Little Britain and Duck Lane.' 'Ramage,' however, in its primitive meaning has no such signification. It means the song of birds. It comes from the French *ramage,* of which the primary meaning is a collection of branches (*rames*), and the secondary the wild notes that are sung amongst the branches. Drummond of Hawthornden, in his 'Address to my Lute,' has:

>   When immelodious winds but made thee more,
>   And birds on thee their ramage did bestow.

Ramage is also a term in falconry. Latham says, 'Ramage is when a hawk is wilde, coy, or disdainfull to the man, and contrary to be reclamed.'—*Words of Art Explained.* Chaucer and Donne both use *ramage* in the sense of wild.

Ramble. This word is derived from the Latin *perambulo,* to wander about.

H H

Ramsgate. The Isle of Thanet was called in the British tongue 'Ruim.' The gaps in the chalk hills in Kent are all called 'gates.' Ramsgate, therefore, is the gate leading to Ruim—Ruimsgate.

Random is a corruption of randon, which means something done without method or settled purpose, and seems to convey the notion of the erratic course taken by a torrent rushing along where there is no defined watercourse.

Rank and File. A body of soldiers standing side by side is called a 'rank.' A body standing one behind another is called a 'file.' The strength of a body of soldiers is reckoned by its rank and file, the officers, commissioned and non-commissioned, being considered supernumeraries having merely directive functions.

Ransack. In nearly all the Northern languages there are words of similar structure to this, all of which signify searching or scrutinising. The old Gothic form was *rann saich.* The Swedish *Ransaker skrifterna* is 'Search the Scriptures.'

Rap. In the early part of the last century large numbers of counterfeit halfpence were current in Ireland, and were known as 'raps.' Their use as coin was forbidden by proclamation, May 5, 1737. The slang phrase 'not worth a rap' therefore means not worth even a bad halfpenny.

Rappee, the name of a coarse kind of snuff, is from the French *râpe,* a rasp, which was formerly used to reduce the stalks and veins of the tobacco-leaf to powder. The French name is '*tabac râpé.*'

Rara avis (Latin); literally, a rare bird; but in English applied to anything very uncommon.

Rascal. A *rascal* is literally a deer unfit for hunting. Ascham, in his 'Scholemaster,' gives the following quaint illustration of this use of the word:—'A father that doth let loose his son to all experiences is most like a fond [foolish] hunter that letteth slip a whelp to the whole herd; twenty to one he shall fall upon a rascal and let go the fair game' (p. 61). Dr. Johnson says that the original meaning of rascal was 'a lean worthless deer.' 'Piers Plowman' says, 'rascally or refuse whereof it be.' Palgrave says, 'rascall, refuse beasts.' In the Norman, Dutch, Spanish, and Italian there are verbs similar in formation which mean to scrape, and *rask* is a noun which means offal, or what is scraped off.

From this, again, comes the French *racaille*, scum, offal, dregs, outcasts or sweepings of society.

Raspberry. The modern name is a contraction of raspis-berry, the ancient name. Herrick spells it 'respass'; Gerard describes it under the name of 'rappisbush, or hindberrie'; and Langham, in his 'Garden of Health,' says, 'It were good to keep some of the juice of "raspis-berries" in some wooden vessel, and to make of it, as it were, "raspis wine,"' p. 522. An old name for the raspberry was 'hindberry" (German *himbeere*). The bilberry was called hartberry (Anglo-Saxon *heortbeorg*), from the stag or hart; and the raspberry was called hindberry from the female of the same species.

Ratafia (the liqueur). 'It is so called from the custom of drinking such liquors at the ratification of an agreement.'—*Tomlinson.*

Raven, Ravener. There are many words retained in the Authorised Version of the Scriptures that are never met with elsewhere. Such are the words 'raven' and 'ravener,' in the sense of robbing and robber. In Genesis xlix. 27 we have, 'Benjamin shall raven as a wolf'; in Ezekiel xxii. 25 we read of a 'roaring lion ravening the prey'; and in Psalm xxii. 13, David likens his enemies to a 'ravening and roaring lion.' We still, however, retain the word 'ravenous.'

Raw Lobsters. As lobster is a sobriquet for a soldier whose coatee is red, so at their first establishment about fifty years ago policemen were sarcastically called raw lobsters, from the blue colour of their uniform. The name was first given by the 'Weekly Dispatch' newspaper, which for years tried in vain to 'write down' the new force. A *raw* lobster is dark blue, and turns red by being boiled.

Raze comes from the Spanish *raiz*, a root or foundation. To 'raze' anything is to root it up, to destroy it from its foundations.

Razor. The earliest mention of a 'barber's razor' is in the first verse of the fifth chapter of Ezekiel.

Real Jam. This slang expression seems to have been first used in America. It occurs in 'Sam Slick,' which was published more than forty years ago. There must have been a charming climate in Paradise. The temperature was perfect; and connubial bliss, I allot, was *real jam* up.'—*Human Nature,* p. 273.

Reaping Machines were used nearly two thousand years ago. Pliny the Elder describes one that he saw in Gaul in the first century of our era. He says: 'In the extensive fields in the lowlands of Gaul machines with projecting teeth on the edge are driven through the standing corn by an ox yoked in a reverse position; in this manner the ears are torn off and fall into the van.' From this it would appear that the ancient machine was a low cart, into the shafts of which an ox was fastened in such a way as to drive the cart in front of him. In what we should call the back of the cart, but which really went first, a sort of close-fitting comb was fitted horizontally, the interstices of which, although allowing the straw to pass, were too small for the ears, which were therefore torn off, and were gradually forced backwards into the body of the cart. Of course this process left the stalks or straws standing where they grew. A machine of similar construction is used at the present day in Australia, but the Australian machine thrashes and winnows the corn at the same time.

Rebec. The rebec was a musical instrument having three catgut strings, and was played with a bow. It was introduced into Spain by the Moors, and was common in England two or three centuries ago.—*Nares.*

> And all that day to the rebec gay
> They frolicked with gladsome swains.
> Song, *The Brave Old Oak.*

Recherché. This French word, now in such common use, means—much sought after, choice, uncommon.

Receipt, Recipe. A 'receipt' is a written or printed direction for *mixing or compounding* certain materials with a view to the production of something; it may be an article of food, a compound for personal or household use, or a medicine. The word 'recipe' is only properly used medically, and it means *directions for taking*. The symbol ℞ in a physician's prescription means recipe, 'take'; a similarly formed character formerly represented *Jupiter*. In the 'Physical Dictionary,' by Blanchard, published 1715, is the following: '℞. Take, which also represents Jupiter's arms, as if physicians would first of all invoke the Deity. 'Tis marked thus at the beginning of a prescription, ♃.' The present form ℞ seems to be a compound of the two forms; the cross-stroke in the tail evidently representing a similar stroke in the older form ♃.

Recorder. The first Recorder of London was Jeffrey de Norton, who was elected A.D. 1298 at a salary of 10*l.* per annum. The present Recorder's salary is understood to be 2,500*l.*

Red Coats in Hunting are said to have been established by Henry II., who made fox-hunting a royal sport, and enjoined by mandate all those who took part in the sport to wear the royal livery.

Red-letter Day, a holiday, a fortunate day. Formerly the saints' days kept in the English Church, the king's birthday, the anniversary of his accession, King Charles's day, the 5th of November, &c. were kept as holidays at the Transfer Office of the Bank of England, and the days on which they occurred were printed in the almanacs with red ink.

Red Sea. The English name 'Red Sea' is a translation of the name 'Sea of Edom' (*Edom*, red).

Red Snow. Paradoxical as it may appear, there is such a thing as red snow. It was observed by the ancients, and is mentioned by Aristotle. Saussure observed it in the Alps in 1760, and Captain Ross found it extending over a range of cliffs on the shores of Baffin's Bay for a length of eight miles and a depth of twelve feet. It is caused by the presence of innumerable plants belonging to the order *Algæ*, to which Sir William Hooper gave the name *palmella nivalis*. 'The red snow plant, in its mature state, consists of brilliant globules, like fine garnets, seated on, but not immersed in, a gelatinous mass.'—*Chamb. Ency.*

Redstart. The Old English word 'start,' from the Anglo-Saxon *steort*, means, according to Todd, 'a long handle; a tail, as of a plough.' This gives the etymology of the name of the pretty bird, the redstart. A 'redstart' is a bird with a red tail.

Red Tape. The use of red tape for tying up papers is of considerable antiquity. An advertisement in the 'Public Intelligencer,' December 6, 1658, offers a reward for the restoration of 'a little bundle of papers tied with a red tape which were lost on Friday last was a sevennight between Worcester House and Lincoln's Inn.' The term seems to have been first satirically applied to official routine by Sydney Smith. Speaking of Sir J Mackintosh he says, 'What a man *that* would be, had he a particle of gall, or the least knowledge of the value of red tape! As Curran said of Grattan, " he would have governed the world."'

Reduce, from the Latin *re*, back, and *duco*, to lead. It meant originally to bring back. Bishop Taylor says, 'A good man will go a little out of his road to *reduce* the wandering traveller.'

Reductio ad absurdum. This is a Latin term denoting an argument which proves, not the thing asserted, but the absurdity of that which contradicts it.

Reesty Bacon. Grose says that 'reesty' means rancid, and that it is 'vulgarly pronounced in the south rusty, as rusty bacon,' but he also gives 'reusty.' Worcester says 'reasty' is 'a corruption of rusty.' Bishop Hall uses the word 'reezed' to express the rancidity of old bacon. The yellow colour of smoke-dried bacon, so much like the rust of iron, favours the view that the word should be rusty, but all the older writers use 'reasty.'

Refectory. This is an old name for the apartment in a monastery in which the monks took their meals. In America it signifies a public eating-house or restaurant.

Regalia. One scarcely ever takes up a newspaper containing an account of processions of teetotallers or Oddfellows without being told that the members wore their 'regalia.' Of course the word means *royal* adornments. The term 'insignia' so exactly expresses the meaning in the case of 'lodges' or 'orders' that it seems strange that the word regalia should be gradually ousting it from use.

Regalia in the Tower. The origin of exhibiting the regalia in the Tower is thus related in 'Archæologia,' xxii. 122 :—'He (the Master and Treasurer of the Jewel-house) hath a particular servant in the Tower, intrusted with that great treasure, to whom (because Sir Gilbert Talbot was retrenched in all the perquisites and profits of his place, and not able to allow him a competent salary) his Majesty doth tacitly allow him that he shall show the Regalia to strangers, which furnished him with so plentiful a livelyhood that Sr Gilbert Talbot, upon the death of his servant there, had an offer made to him of 500 old broad pieces of gold for the place, yet he first gave it to old Mr. Edwards freely, whom Blud murthered when he attempted to steal the Crown Globe and Scepter.' Dated May 20, 1680.

Regatta. The word in the Venetian dialect originally denoted a race among the gondoliers, which took place annually with great solemnity. The word is now applied to both rowing and sailing matches indiscriminately.

Regent's Park. This park was originally attached to a palace of Queen Elizabeth which stood near the north end of the Tottenham Court Road. About the year 1600 the greater portion of the land was let on long leases. When these fell in, at the commencement of the present century, the present park was formed under the direction of Mr. Nash, and was named after George IV., then Prince Regent.

Registration of Birth. 'There is no obligation to give a child any name whatever at the time of registration, as the Schedule for Registration of Births states that the first column in reference to the child is to be filled up with the name *if given.*'—*Notes and Queries,* October 29, 1864.

Regret. This word is used in America as a noun. If a lady finds that she cannot accept an invitation she says, 'I must send a regret'—meaning a note regretting that she is compelled to decline.

Regulating Clocks. If a clock goes too fast, lengthen the pendulum; if too slow, shorten it. If the screw or nut of the pendulum is below the weight or 'bob,' turn it to the right if the clock be slow, and to the left if it be fast. If the 'nut' is above the 'bob,' these motions must be reversed.

Reigate is probably from the Anglo-Saxon *rig*, a ridge, and *gate*, a way. This corresponds exactly to its position near an opening or gate through the rig or ridge of the Surrey hills. The town was not called Reigate until about a century after the compilation of Domesday Book.

Reindeer. This word is thought by some to be from the German *renn Thier*. *Renn* is from the verb *rennen*, to run, and *Thier* is a general term for any wild animal. The Anglo-Saxon word *deor* was applicable to any wild quadruped. Johnson spells it raindeer, but does not seem very confident; but Professor Skeat, in 'Notes and Queries,' May 1, 1880, traces the origin to the Lapp word *reino*, pasture, and says that *reindeer* is a compound, half Lapp and half Scandinavian, the meaning of which is *pastured* or *domesticated* deer. The Professor concludes his paper by saying, 'I consider this puzzle as solved.'

Relay (of horses or dogs). This is not laying on a fresh lot of animals, but releasing those that are exhausted. In French '*chevaux de relais* means horses placed at certain places on a road for the ease of those one hath already rid hard on' (Roquef).

Relief (in art). Sculptured works are said to be in relief when the figures project, or stand out from the background or plane to which they are attached. The word comes from the Italian *rilievo* (pronounced reelyavo). There are three degrees of relief: bàs-relief (*basso-rilievo*), in which the figures project but little from the background, as in the figures upon ordinary coins; demi-relief (*mezzo-rilievo*), in which the figures project about one-half their natural proportions; and high relief (*alto-rilievo*), in which the figures project entirely, being only attached here and there to the background.

Religious. A religious person, in the Roman Catholic sense of the word, is one who has taken monastic vows.

Relish, from the French *relécher*, to taste anew. '"A relish of" is actual taste, "a relish for" is disposition to taste.'—*Smart.*

Re-marriage of Widows of Peers. 'If a woman, noble in her own right, marries a commoner, she still remains noble and shall be tried by her peers; but if she be only noble by marriage, then by a second marriage with a commoner she loses her dignity, for as by marriage it is gained, by marriage it is also lost.'—*Blackstone, Commentaries*, i. 12. Thus, if a lady chooses to take her second husband's name, she cannot add to it her first husband's title. For example, Mr. Hanbury Lennox married Lady Strangford, who chooses to be called Mrs. Hanbury Lennox. So again Mr. Whately, the eminent barrister, married Lady Henry Churchill, but she chose to retain the title of Lady Henry Churchill, rather than be called Mrs. Whately, after her second marriage.

Renaissance. This is a French term signifying a new birth. It is applied to the revival of classical art by Raphael. The style of the Renaissance is akin to what is termed Elizabethan.

Rennet (the apple). This is a corrupted form of the Old English word *renate*, to be born again or to be revived. Old Fuller says ('The Holy State'), 'When a pippin is planted [grafted] on a pippin stock the fruit growing thence is called a "renate," a most delicious fruit, as being both by sire and dam well descended.'

Reply, from the Latin *replico*, to turn back, is often used erroneously in the sense of answer. It means something following an answer—e.g. (1) A. writes a letter, to which (2) B. sends an answer asking for further information. A. (3) replies; and if it be necessary to carry the correspondence further, B. (4) responds or rejoins.

Request. One old meaning of this word—'to go again in quest of'—does not appear in modern dictionaries. 'To request,' in old hunting phrase, was to put hounds again upon a scent which they had lost.

Requiem (in music), a funereal composition. So called from the first word of a prayer in a Roman Catholic mass for the dead, *Requiem æternum dona iis, Domine*' (Give eternal rest to them, O. Lord).—*Brand*.

Reredos is from the French *arrière*, behind, and *dos*, back—*arrière-dos* meaning something behind or at the back of (a sacramental table or altar).

Resentment meant originally gratitude, or, more correctly, 'a grateful sense.' In Walker's 'History of the Eucharist' is the following passage :—'We need not now travel so far as Asia or Greece for instances to inhaunse our due resentments of God's benefits.' In the 'Life of Dean Comber,' of Durham, a letter is quoted, dated May 1681, which is subscribed, 'Thy truly pitying and love-resenting friend and brother.' Burrow says, 'How much more should we resent such a testimony of God's favour?' and Dr. Beach, of Salisbury, writing to Bishop Burnet, says, 'And I cannot but deeply resent your obliging readiness to relieve me,' &c.

Restive, applied to a horse, is from the verb to resist—thus 'resistive,' with the middle syllable omitted, becomes 'restive.'

Retiracy. In America they say of a man who has made his fortune that 'he has secured a retiracy'—i.e. sufficient to retire upon.

Revalenta Arabica is the meal produced by grinding lentils. The names 'Revalenta' and 'Ervalenta' are corrupted forms of the botanic name of the lentil plant, *Ervum lens*.

Revenue. In the reign of Henry V. the revenue of the kingdom was seventy-six thousand pounds. It is now about the same number of millions of pounds.

Reverend. This is a title borne by the deacons and priests of the Churches of England and Rome. In the English Church Deans are called 'Very Reverend,' Bishops 'Right Reverend,' and Archbishops 'Most Reverend.' The title Reverend was formerly very generally assumed by the ministers of dissenting churches, but within the last quarter of a century many of the younger ministers have ceased to use or to sanction it. In addressing letters to clergymen it is a very common practice to omit the definite article 'the.' All such letters should be fully inscribed, 'The Rev. William Smith,' and so forth. No one would think of addressing a letter to 'Venerable Archdeacon Jones,' 'Right Hon. Lord

Chancellor,' or 'Lord Mayor of London,' without **prefixing** the word 'the'; and yet it is quite common to see letters addressed 'Rev. W. Jones.'

Review. The first Review published was the 'Journal des Sçavans,' No. 1 of which appeared in Paris on January 5, 1665. It was published weekly, each number containing from twelve to sixteen small pages. The first book reviewed was an edition of 'Victor Viténsis and Vigelius Tapsensis,' African bishops of the fifth century. The critique was written by Father Chiflet, a Jesuit. The 'Edinburgh Review' was commenced in 1802; the 'Quarterly Review' in 1812.

Reward. The etymology of this word gives no clue to its present meaning, which arose in a mistake. It is composed of two Old English words, *rear*, behind, and *ward*, to guard. The verse, Isaiah lviii. 5, in the Authorised Version gives us the clue to the origin. It runs, 'Then shall thy light break forth as the morning, and thine health shall break forth speedily; and thy righteousness shall go before thee [that is, shall be thy vanguard]; the glory of the Lord shall be thy rereward [or rearguard].' In the absence of any true etymon of the word 'reward' it is fair to presume that the last word in the verse quoted has been interpreted in the sense of recompense, and so the present contracted word 'reward' has arisen, but with an entirely different meaning. According to Grose, this word is used in a very singular sense in the North. In his 'Glossary' he has, 'Reward, or Good Reward, a ruddy countenance.'

Rhubarb was first introduced into England in 1534, in which year 'the eccentric physician Andrew Boorde sent to Mr. Vicar-General Cromwell " the seedes of reuberbe, the which came out of Barbary."'—*Ellis's Original Letters*, vol. ii. p. 301. In Queen Elizabeth's time the broad leaves of rhubarb were used as a potherb. It was not until the early part of the present century that the leaf-stalks were used for tarts, &c.

Rhyme may be either male or female. A male rhyme is one in which the final syllables only agree, as strain, complain; a female rhyme is one in which the two final syllables agree, the last being short, as motion, ocean.

Rhythm in poetry (Greek, Latinized *rhythmus*) means the regularity with which the accents follow each other, producing musical cadence. Its use is not confined to poetry, but refers to any action repeated at regular intervals. The ticking of a clock is rhythmic;

the step in dancing should be rhythmic, following the time of the music. 'No English word better expresses *rhythmus* than the word time as used in music.'

Rib. There are twenty-four ribs in the human body. The common belief that a woman has one more rib than a man is erroneous.

Ribald. Verstegan derives this word from *Rabod,* who was a heathen King of Friesland in the seventh century. 'The missionary Bishop Wipan instructed him in Christianity, and he agreed to be baptized. While standing in the water he asked the bishop where all his forefathers were, to which the bishop replied that, as they died without knowledge of the true God, they were in hell. "Then," replied the king, "I would rather go to hell with them, than with your few Christians to heaven," and went out of the water "unchristened."' From this impious speech 'his very name became so odious through his wickedness that it grew to be a title of reproach and shame, and hath so continued ever since.'— *Restitution, &c.,* p. 263.

Ribbon. Formerly spelt ribband; that is, a band which encircled the waist, enclosing or binding the ribs. Drapers designate the various widths of ribbons by the expressions 'twopenny,' 'fourpenny,' 'sixpenny,' and so on up to 'thirtypenny.' These names have nothing whatever to do with the price at which the ribbon is sold, but originally represented the width of so many of the thick old pennies placed face to face. Thus 'twopenny' was the width of the thickness of two pennies; sixpenny of six pennies, and so on.

Rice-paper. What is called rice-paper is made from the pith of *Aralia papyrifera,* a plant closely allied to the ivy. The paper called india-paper, used for proofs of engraving, is made from the inner bark of the bamboo.

Riddle, a coarse iron sieve. From the Anglo-Saxon *hreddan,* to free or to rid. The word would be more appropriately spelt ridder.

Ride. Some modern writers erroneously confine the meaning of this word to riding on horseback. The word from its etymology has stronger claims to be used exclusively in the sense of riding in a carriage or vehicle. By the Romans and the old Gauls the word *rheda* meant a calash or chariot. In Iceland the word *reid* signifies a carriage. In High German *reita* has the same meaning. The Anglo-Saxon *ridan,* the Dutch *ryden,* the German *reiten,* the Danish *ride,* the Swedish *rida,* and the Icelandic *reida* have the double meaning of being carried or drawn, as opposed to walking. Bailey says the verb to ride means 'to go on horseback; in a coach, wagon, &c.'; Johnson defines it 'to travel on horseback or in a vehicle'; Richardson and Todd both mention vehicles in their definitions. The 'Quarterly Review' stigmatises the use of the word 'ride,' when employed in the sense of being carried in a vehicle, as an Americanism, and says 'it has been for a hundred years a noted vulgarism in England'; and this in spite of the fact that all the best dictionaries, as shown above, define the word 'ride' so as to include conveyance in a vehicle. To confine its use to riding on horseback is a modern affectation, neither justified by sense nor authority. People do not 'drive' in an omnibus, nor in a cab; the coachman 'drives,' and they 'ride' as Jehu did (2 Kings ix. 16, and x. 16). Addison, whose authority no one will dispute, says:

> Calm and serene he drives the furious blast,
> And, pleased th' Almighty's orders to perform,
> Rides in the whirlwind and directs the storm.

Dr. Johnson, in his 'Tour,' says that he and Boswell were satisfied with each other, whether 'riding in the chaise' or sitting in the inn. Macaulay has, 'The richest inhabitants exhibited their wealth, not by riding in gilded carriages,' &c.

Riding, one of the three divisions of the county of York. Originally *thrithing*, a third part (Norwegian *tridjimg*, a third part). The word is misapplied in the case of the county of Tipperary, which has only two divisions.

Riff-raff. To rife and to raff had the signification of clearing everything out; scraping, raking, sweeping everything away. Hence the noun raff—refuse, scraping—and, intensifying by repetition, riff-raff, the scum, refuse, dregs, and sweepings of society (Swedish *rifwa*, to scrape; German *raffen*, to rake together). The term, riff-raff is of great antiquity. The following is from the works of Robert de Brunné, who lived in the fourteenth century:

> Ne costom no seruise of thing that he forgaf
> That neither he no hise suld chalange rif no raf.

And the words occur again in the historical play 'Lord Thomas Cromwell,' quarto 1602:

> There's legions now of beggars on the earth
> That their original did spring from kings;
> And many monarchs now, whose fathers were
> The riff-raff of their age.—Act i. sc. 2.

Rifle. The name rifle, applied to a fire-arm, is from the German verb *reifeln,* to flute or form small grooves or channels.

Right, when used as an adjective, is sometimes opposed to the meaning of the same word when used as a noun. Thus we may say a man has a right to destroy the produce of his fields, but it would not be right to do so.—*Whewell.*

Right Honourable. This title is always applied to a 'lord,' whether he be so by right or by courtesy. The reason why commoners who are members of the Privy Council are 'Right Honourable' is that the general title of that body is '*Lords* of H.M. Privy Council.'

Right smart. American for a good many, large, plenty, &c., e.g. 'a right smart chunk of bacon.'—*Olmsted's Texas,* p. 301. 'I sold right smart of eggs this summer.'—*Mrs. Stowe, Dred,* vol. ii. p. 157. 'She had right smart of life in her.'—*Dred.* vol. i. p. 209.

Rights and Lefts. Shakespeare has a passage which shows that the shoes called 'rights and lefts' were known in his day. He describes a smith as

> Standing on slippers, which his nimble haste
> Had falsely thrust upon contrary feet.

Ring one's own Bell. A slang phrase, the equivalent of 'to be one's own trumpeter.'

Rink. This word is applied in Scotland to the piece of ice cleared for the game of curling. The Scottish emigrants carried the word to Canada, where it soon became extended in meaning so as to include ice for skating. When rolling skates were invented, the word 'rink' naturally suggested itself as the most appropriate for the levelled surface on which the new process of skating was carried on.

R. I. P. These letters, often seen at the end of announcements of death, or on tombs, are an abbreviation of the Latin words *Requiescat in pace,* May he [or she] rest in peace.

Rip, a bad horse. Nares thinks this is derived from *rippar* or *ripier,* one who sells fish. Formerly dealers in fish rode across country on horseback, and they were noted for the screwish character of their horseflesh. Beaumont and Fletcher have—

> Where now you're faine
> To hire a rippar's mare.—*Noble Gent.* v. 1.

Ri-tooral-looral. Dr. Mackay ('Blackwood,' July 1878), says that 'this vile trash contains two Gaelic words. "Tooral" may be derived from *turail*, slow, and "looral" from *luthrail*, quick, a musical composition to which the Druidical priests accommodated their steps in a musical procession.'

Rival, from the Latin *rivus*, a brook. Rivals were originally persons holding property on opposite sides of a brook, both of whom claimed the exclusive right to the stream.

River. The Americans always put the name before the word river, as Hudson River, Merrimac River, Charles River, &c., but the English always put river first, as the River Thames, the River Trent, &c. &c.

Rivers. The Rev. Isaac Taylor, in 'Words and Places,' says, 'There is, in fact, hardly a Celtic word meaning stream, current, brook, channel, water, or flood, which does not enter largely into the river names of Europe.' He also gives five Celtic roots, *avon*, *dwr* or *ter*, *uisge* or *wisk*, *rhe* or *rhin*, and *don* or *dan*, all of which mean water, and are to be found in 'the names of almost all the larger rivers of Europe, and those of a very great number of the smaller streams.' A few examples of each are given, but the lists might be indefinitely extended. The names, as will be seen, have in many cases become much distorted by alterations in orthography:—AVON.—Afon, Evan, Ife, Ann, Aun, Auney, Eweny, Eveneny, Inney, Aney, Awe, Ehen, Avonborn, Avenbanna, Avenbui, Avenmore, and many others in the United Kingdom and on the Continent. DWR is still the Welsh word for water. From this root we have rivers named Dour, Dore, Duir, Thur, Doro, Durra, Dairan, Durarwater, Deargan, Durbeck, Glasdur, Calder, Adder, Adur, Adar, Noder, Lodore, Derwent, Darwen, Derwen, Darent, and Dart, all of which are in Great Britain. On the Continent we find in France Durance, Dordogne, and Adour; in Spain Douro, Duraton, and Duerna; in Italy Torre, Turia, and Termus; in Germany Oder, Durbach, and Durrenbronne. UISGE.—The Gaelic word for water is *uisge*, from which we get *usquebaugh*, whisky; in Welsh *uisge* becomes *wysg*, a current. This word, subject to many changes in spelling, is found in the names of a great number of rivers and streams, as Esk, Esky, Esker, Eskle, Ease, Ewes, Exe, Ex, Iz, Ise, Isis, Isca, Ouse, Ousel, Use, Ousebourn, Usk, Ux, Wysg, Wisk, Wissey, and many others. RHE.—This word in the Gaelic is *rea*, rapid; in the Welsh *rhe*, swift, *rheda*, to run, *rhin*, that which runs. In England we have rapid rivers named Rea, Rye, Rey, Ray, Rhee, Rhea, Wrey, Roy,

Roe, Rue, Eryn, Roden, and Ribble. On the Continent we find Rhine, Rhone, Rega, Regen, Regge, Riga, Rha, and Rheno.

Don.—This is an obsolete Gaelic name for water. It is found in the names of many rivers in Europe. In the British Isles are Don, Dean, Dane, Dun, Tone, Eden, Tyne, Teane, Teign, Tian, Teyn, Tynet, and Bandon. Continental names are Danube, Danastris, Danaster (Dneister), Danasper (Dneiper), Don, Donetz, Adonis, Aredon, Derdon (Dwrdon), Madon, Verdon, Odon, Roscodon, and many others. In addition to these, which may be called noun names, there are many derived from Celtic adjectives, as from *garw*, rough. From this root come Gara, Garry, Yare, Garway, Garnere, Garnar, Yarro, Yarrow, Yair, Garve, and Gareloch. From *all*, white, we get *Al-ain*, White Avon, and hence Allen, Ellen, Auln, Aulne, Aln, Allan, Alan, Allwen, Elwyn, Ilen, and Ain. From the Gaelic *ban*, which also means white, we get Banna, Banon (*ban afon*), Bana, Ben, Bann, Bane, Bain, Bandon, Banney, Bainac, and Bannockburn. Other river names are derived from *clevn*, smooth, as Leven, Lane, Lain, and Lune. From *tam*, spreading, quiet, we get Tame, Thames, Tamar, Tema, Taw, Tay, and Tave. From *cam*, crooked, we derive Cam, Camil, Camlad, Cambeck, Camlin, and Camon. Many other groups of names might be traced, but enough has been quoted to show the extent of the subject, and to prove that the Celtic races at one time were spread over nearly the whole of Europe. The names given are all single, but many of them are repeated in many localities; the name Avon, for instance, is applied to more than twenty different streams. In fact, as Mr. Taylor, in his interesting book, from which these names have been gleaned, says, 'It is a curious fact that a unique river name is hardly to be found. Any given name may immediately be associated with some dozen or half-dozen names nearly identical in form and meaning, collected from all parts of Europe.'—*Words and Places*, p. 229.

Rix-dollar is a name for a silver coin of different values in various countries. It is a corruption of the German term *reichsthaler*, dollar of the empire.

Roam. Dr. Johnson says, 'It is imagined to come from the pretences of vagrants, who always said they were going to Rome.' The Italian word *romeo* means a pilgrim going to Rome.—*Talbot*.

Roan Leather. Morocco leather was anciently made in Morocco of goat skins. An imitation of it was made in England of sheepskins, prepared in a peculiar manner with sumach, and called 'roan' from the similarity of its colour to that of a roan horse. Roan can now be had of any colour.

Roast Beef. The vaunted 'Roast Beef of Old England' seems to have been almost an unknown dish to our ancestors in the fourteenth and fifteenth centuries. Mr. Wright, in his 'Domestic Manners of the Middle Ages,' pp. 349–358, gives a number of bills of fare of that period, some of which are of the most luxurious and profuse character, but the 'national dish,' the 'Roast Beef of Old England,' does not appear in any one of them.

Robbing Peter to pay Paul. In the year 1550, several estates belonging to Westminster Abbey were granted for the repair and sustenance of St. Paul's Cathedral. As Westminster Abbey is dedicated to St. Peter, the taking the Abbey funds for the benefit of St. Paul's gave rise to the proverbial saying.

Robert is Red-beard, from *ru* or *ro*, red, and *bert* or *bart*, a beard. Dr. R. S. Maitland gives no fewer than two hundred different methods of spelling this name. Rupert and Robert are identical, and were used occasionally for the same person.

Rob Roy. The 'Gentleman's Magazine' for 1735 contains the following notice in the obituary :—'Jany. 2. Rob Roy, the famous Scots Highlander.'

Robust, from the Latin *robur*, the oak, 'strong as an oak.'

Rock. In most parts of America a stone, however small, is called a 'rock.' The following are singular instances of its use :— 'Mr. M. had to carry rocks in his pocket to prevent the wind from blowin' him away.'—*Major Jones's Travels*. 'I see Arch Cooney walk down to the creek bottom, and then he began pickin' up rocks and slingin' 'em at the dogs.'—*Mike Hooter, by a Missourian*. 'On one occasion they threw a rock in at the window, hitting Mrs. Clem on the shoulder.'—*Jonesborough (Tennessee) Whig*.

Rocket. The phrase, 'He went up like a rocket, and fell like the stick,' was first used by Tom Paine in reference to the great orator Burke.

Rodentia, from the Latin *rodens*, gnawing. A class of quadrupeds, which includes rats, mice, rabbits, &c., characterised by their front teeth having enamel only on the outer surface, so that the back being rapidly worn away, leaves the front sharp and chisel-shaped, enabling them to gnaw their way through timber or even harder substances.

Rodomontade. Rodomonte is a blustering, boasting hero in the 'Orlando Furioso' of Ariosto. Hence 'rodomontade'—empty, noisy rant, vainglorious boasting. Mr. Moon ('The Dean's English,' p. 153) says, 'The word takes its origin from one of Boyardo's heroes, *Rodomonte*, a king of Algiers.'

Rogue in grain. This is a metaphor derived from an irremovable dye, INGRAIN (which see). It has nothing to do with dealings in grain or corn.

Roller Skates. In a periodical of the date 1823 is the following paragraph:—' SKATING.—A skate has just been invented with the design of rendering this amusement independent of the frost. It is like the common skate, but instead of one iron it has two, with a set of very small brass or iron wheels let in between, which, easily revolving, enable the wearer to run along with great rapidity on any hard level substance, and, indeed, to perform, though with less force or nicety, all the evolutions of skating. A patent has been obtained for the invention, and it is now practically exhibited at the old tennis court in Windmill Street.'

Romance. The Latin language ceased to be spoken in France about the ninth century, and was succeeded by a mixture of the language of the Franks and bad Latin, which was called the Romance language or dialect. Most of the early tales of chivalry being written in that language were called 'Romances.' Hence the name given to marvellous and half-fabulous stories or poems.

Roman Occupation of England. When the Romans, after an occupation of England for three or four hundred years, finally retired in the beginning of the fifth century, they left a few traces of their language grafted on to the Old Celtic tongue. The termination 'cester' or 'chester,' which the Saxons found in use here to signify a fortified place, and which they adopted in the names of so many places, is unquestionably the Latin *castrum* slightly disguised, which they must have picked up from the ancient British. So also the word street, from *strata*, and mil, or mile, from *millia*, a thousand, the Roman mile being a thousand paces. Other such words are—orchard, from the Latin *hortus*; pear, from the Latin *pyrus*; wall, from the Roman *vallum*; dish, from *discus*, and many others in which the Celtic and the Latin are strangely mixed. These hybrid words carry proofs of their origin in the fact that they are found alone in the English language, and are not to be discovered in any other dialects of the Celtic.

Roman Type. Roman type was first used in printing by Sweynheim and Pannartz, at Rome, in the year 1467. Up to that time all the printers had used black letter.

Roofing Slates. The names applied to the various sizes of roofing slates are very curious, being all founded upon feminine titles. Thus, slates 16 inches long by 8 wide are called *ladies*, *countesses* are 18 inches by 10, *princesses* 22 by 12, and *queens* 26 by 14. These names were given to slates by General Warburton, the proprietor of one of the largest North Wales slate quarries, about a century ago.

Rosemary, from the Latin *ros*, dew, and *marinus*, the sea. 'The gray bushes mantled with dewdrops on the rocky coasts of France and Italy justify the singular name which has been given to this plant.'—*Lindley.*

Roses. Roses were first brought to England from Holland in 1522. It is known that the moss rose was grown in this country before 1700. The China and Japan roses were brought from the East about 1790.

Ross, either as a name of a place by itself, or as a portion of a name, nearly always means a headland. It is a Celtic word, and is frequent in Scotland, as in Rosslyn, Culross, Rossberg, Ardrossan, &c. In the case of Roseness in Orkney, each syllable signifies a headland, Rose being Celtic, and ness being Teutonic. In Cornwall and Wales, however, there is another word, *rhos*, a moor, which is sometimes found in names, as in Rosshall, Rusholme, &c.

Rostrum, from the Latin *rodo*, to gnaw; literally, the beak of a bird. The Romans applied the term to the front or bow of a ship, where sharp irons were fixed for the purpose of attacking other vessels. In the Roman Forum the stage from which orators addressed the people was called the rostrum from its being adorned with *rostra*, or beaks of enemy's ships taken in war, which were exhibited as trophies.—*Worcester.*

Rothschild. The founder of this family was Meyer Anselm, who was a money-lender in Frankfort, the sign of his house being a red shield (in German *roth schild*). In 1806 the Landgrave of Hesse, during the occupation of Germany, entrusted Anselm with specie to the amount of about a quarter of a million of British money. With this money Anselm traded and made a large fortune. On the fall of Napoleon Anselm repaid the 250,000*l.* His sons took the name of Rothschild from their father's sign, and his descendants are now the greatest capitalists in Europe.

Rotten Row. The name of the fashionable ride in Hyde Park is supposed to be a corruption of the French phrase '*route du Roi*,' the King's road.

Roué, a name now applied to profligate or dissolute persons, is the French term for one broken on the wheel, which before the French Revolution was the punishment for the highest crimes. The word in its present sense is said to have originated with Philip of Orleans, Regent of France.

Rough and Ready. At the battle of Waterloo Colonel Rough was selected by the Duke of Wellington to perform some service requiring energy and promptitude. 'Rough and Ready,' said the Duke when the Colonel cheerfully undertook the duty; and the Colonel thenceforth adopted the words as a motto, which is still borne by his family.

Rough-hew.
> There's a divinity that shapes our ends,
> Rough-hew them how we will.

'Dr. Farmer informed Mr. Steevens that the phrase as used by Shakespeare is technical. A woolman, butcher, and dealer in skewers lately observed to him—Dr. Farmer—that his nephew, an idle lad, could only assist him in making them [skewers]; he could *rough-hew* them, but he could not *shape their ends*.'—*Todd.*

Rough or Ruffian. Charles Dickens ('All the Year Round,' October 10, 1868) said, 'I entertain so strong an objection to the euphonious softening of ruffian into rough, which has lately become popular, that I restore the right reading to the heading of this paper.' The paper was 'The Ruffian, by the Uncommercial Traveller.'

Roundhead. This was a term of contempt applied to the Puritans in the time of Charles I., from their custom of cutting their hair close to the head; the Royalist party wearing theirs in ringlets.

Round Peg and Square Hole. This witty saying in reference to misplaced talent is certainly earlier than the time of Sydney Smith, who is generally considered its author from his having used it in his 'Lectures Delivered at the Royal Institution,' 1824–26. His words are:—'If you choose to represent the various parts of life by holes upon a table of different shapes, some circular, some triangular, some square, some oblong, and the persons acting these parts by bits of wood of similar shapes, we shall generally find that the triangular person has got into the square hole, the oblong into the triangular, and a square person has squeezed himself into a round hole.'

Routine, from the French *route*, a road—hence *routine*, the ordinary beaten track, regular course, or custom.

Rover meant originally a pirate. It comes from the Dutch *roover*, a robber, from *rooven*, to rob. In Danish *röverskip* is a pirate ship.

Rowan. This is the Scottish name for the mountain ash (*Pyrus aucuparia*). It is looked upon in Scotland as having some power over witches and their evil spells. Johnstone says:

>   Roän-tree and red thread
>   Haud the witches a' in dread.

Rowland for an Oliver. 'Rowland and Oliver were two of the most famous in the list of Charlemagne's twelve peers, and their exploits are recorded so ridiculously and extravagantly by the old romancers that from thence arose that saying amongst our plain and sensible ancestors of giving one "a Rowland for an Oliver," to signify the matching of one incredible lie with another.'— *Warburton.*

Royal Academy. Hogarth may be considered the founder of this institution. He established in 1739 the Society of Incorporated Artists. The first exhibition was held in 1760. In 1768 the Royal Academy was established by charter, and Joshua Reynolds, who was knighted on the occasion, was the first president appointed. The first exhibition was in 1769. In 1771 there was another at Old Somerset House. From 1780 to 1838 the annual exhibitions were held in the present Somerset House. From that time to the year 1868 they were held at the National Gallery. The present magnificent galleries at Burlington House were first opened in May 1869.

Royal Arms in Churches. There is reason to believe that, shortly after the restoration of Charles II. in 1660, an Order in Council was issued commanding the setting up of the royal arms in all parochial churches. It is believed that no copy of this Order is in existence, but an entry in the registry of the parish of Warrington alludes to it in these terms :—' Whereas it is generally enjoined by the great Counsell of England that in all churches thorow out the Kingdom of England his Maiestie's armes shalbe sett upp,' &c. &c. A couple of years later Bishop Hackett, of Lichfield, in his 'Articles of Enquiry' for that diocese, asks,

'And are the king's arms set up?' The royal arms appear to have been first set up in churches about 1550. Elizabeth's are very general, but during the Commonwealth many were pulled down or defaced. Hence the necessity for the injunction of Charles II.

Royal Assent refused. The last occasion upon which the royal assent was refused to a Bill in Parliament was on March 11, 1707, when Queen Anne declined to sanction the Militia of Scotland Bill. Her Majesty was present, and on the title of the Bill being read by the Clerk of the Parliament, the Clerk of the Crown pronounced the Queen's pleasure with regard to the Bill in the ancient form of words, '*La Reine s'avisera.*'

Royal Exchange. The first Royal Exchange in London was opened by Queen Elizabeth, January 23, 1571. It was destroyed by the Great Fire in 1666. Charles II. laid the first stone of the second October 23, 1667; it was opened about three years afterwards, and was burnt January 10, 1838. The present building was commenced in 1842, and opened by the Queen October 28, 1844. It is generally believed that the grasshopper on the spire of the Royal Exchange is the identical emblem that surmounted the steeple of the building burnt down in 1838. In 'Notes and Queries,' January 19, 1861, is the following copy of an advertisement, taken by a correspondent from a then recent number of 'The Builder,' which seems to show that the general belief is unfounded:—' The original Grasshopper and Stone Statues from the Royal Exchange, &c., Mr. Frederick Indermans will sell by Auction on the premises, Kent Place, Old Kent Road,' &c. &c.

Royal Humane Society. This society was founded in London in 1774 for the recovery of persons apparently dead from drowning. It has been instrumental in saving many hundreds of lives.

Royal Signatures. Seton ('Gossip about Letters') thinks that Richard II. was the first English monarch to sign his name. The earliest document bearing his signature is dated 1386. The earliest royal holograph letter known is one written by Henry V. when Prince of Wales.

Royal State Coach. The state coach in which her Majesty rode to her coronation, and which has since been occasionally used on the occasions of opening Parliament, was designed for George III. by Sir William Chambers. Its cost was about 8,000*l*. The panels were painted by Cipriani.

Rubicon. This was the name of a small river separating Italy from Gaul, which Roman generals were forbidden to pass. Julius Cæsar did so with his army in the year 49 B.C., thereby causing a deadly civil war. Hence to 'pass the Rubicon' is proverbial for a rash and irretrievable act.

Rubric (Latin *rubrica*, red earth). The modern use of this word comes from the practice among the monks of the middle ages of writing with *red* ink the directions prefixed to the several prayers and offices in the missals. This plan was also adopted by the early printers of the English Prayer-book. In process of time the origin of the word rubric was forgotten, and it came to signify the directions themselves. It is now used whether the directions be printed in red or in black.

Rue. The Anglo-Saxon name for this plant was *rūd*. Probably from the resemblance of this name to the word rood, or holy cross, the plant received the designation 'herb of grace.'

Rule Britannia. 'This song was written by Mr. Thomson for the "Masque of Alfred," which was first performed August 1, 1740, at a private performance at Cliefden House, near Maidenhead, then the residence of Frederic, Prince of Wales. The music was composed by Mr. Arne.'—*London Daily Post*, August 2, 1740. The following advertisement appeared in the 'General Advertiser,' February 25, 1751. It refers to an entirely new version of the 'Masque of Alfred' which had just been brought out by Garrick :— 'As Mr. Arne originally composed the musick in the "Masque of Alfred," and the town may probably on that account imagine the musick as now performed to be all his production, he is advised by his friends to inform the Publick that but two of his songs are in that performance, viz. the first song, beginning "O Peace, thou fairest child of Heav'n," and the ode in honour of Great Britain, beginning "When Britain first at Heav'n's command," with the chorus "Rule Britannia, rule the waves," &c.' Some of the *words* are taken from Handel's works; notably the opening line, which is copied verbatim from Mirah's song in 'Saul,' 'See with what a scornful air.'

Rule Nisi. A *rule nisi* is an order of a court of justice to take effect at a given period, 'unless before' that time some reason shall be shown to the contrary; failing which the rule is 'made absolute.' See NISI PRIUS.

Rule of the Road. The ancient rule of the road—i.e. that horses and vehicles should keep to the left—has been pretty generally adopted by the railways. There is, however, one notable exception. Between Charing Cross and Cannon Street stations in London the system is reversed, all the trains running on the right hand track.

Rule of Thumb. This phrase signifies anything done without proper *formulæ*, or accurate measurement. It is said to have arisen from the practice in Yorkshire of determining the heat of the liquor in brewing, so as to regulate the fermentation, by dipping the thumb into the vat. Ale so brewed is called thumb-brewed.

Rule the roast. To 'rule the roast' is, no doubt, a corruption of 'rule the roost.' The strongest or most courageous cock in a poultry-yard becomes master, and rules over all the others which roost in the same shed. 'Geate you nowe up into your pulpittes like bragginge cocks on the rowst, flappe your winges and crowe out aloude.'—*Jewell.*

Rum (the adjective). In 'Literary Anecdotes,' V. 471, there is the following suggestion as to the derivation. The booksellers in the last century traded with the West Indies, furnishing books to the planters and receiving payment in consignments of rum. They were in the habit of putting by for their West Indian customers things that did not sell in England, and the books thus put aside were called 'rum books.' Professor De Morgan thought this 'the most probable derivation.'

Rum (the alcoholic spirit). Many speculations have been made as to the origin of this word. The most probable derivation is from the Scottish vernacular word *rum*, which as an adjective signifies in Lothian anything that is excellent of its kind. Rum is allowable to the Jews during the Passover, when beer—from suspicion of leaven—is forbidden. During the Passover the public-houses in Houndsditch, Whitechapel, and the neighbourhood sell to the Jews rum drawn from casks specially sealed by the Rabbi, and their shop windows are placarded with intimations that they do so 'by permission of the Rabbi.'

Rum-bud is the American name for the peculiar redness of the nose of drunkards, known in England as grog-blossom.

Ruminant, from the Latin *ruminans*, to chew the cud. 'The name "ruminant" indicates the singular faculty possessed by these animals of masticating their food a second time—which they return into the mouth after a previous deglutition—a power which is the result of the structure of their stomachs, four of which they always have. Of these stomachs the first three are so disposed that the aliment can enter at the will of the animal into any one of the three, because the œsophagus terminates at the point of communication. The fourth stomach is the true organ of digestion, analogous to the simple stomach of ordinary animals.'—*Cuvier*.

Rummage. This word means properly stowing the contents of a ship. 'And that the masters of the ships do look well to the romaging, for they might bring awaye a great deale more than they do if they would take paine in the romaging.'—*Hackluyt*. Modernly 'to rummage' is to thoroughly search amongst things stowed away in a given receptacle.

Rump and Dozen. This was a favourite form of wager with our forefathers. A legal definition of its meaning was given in the King's Bench, *tempo* Lord Mansfield. An action, 'Hussey *v.* Cricket' (Campbell's 'Nisi Prius Cases,' iii. 168), was brought upon a wager of a rump and dozen, made upon the question as to which —plaintiff or defendant—was the older. The question as to whether the action was maintainable was argued before the full court, Mansfield, C.J., presiding. In giving judgment Mr. Justice Heath said:—'I am sorry this action has been brought, but I do not doubt that it is maintainable. Wagers are generally legal, and there is nothing to take this wager out of the common rule. We know very well privately that a rump and dozen is what the witnesses stated, *viz.* a good dinner and wine, in which I can discover no illegality.'

Russia. The title Czar was assumed by Ivan the Great in 1482; that of 'Czar of all the Russias' by Alexei Mikailowitch in 1654, after the conquest of Little Russia and the acquisition of Smolensk. The phrase at first included Great Russia or Muscovy, White Russia, and Little Russia, but it now comprises the whole of the Russian dominions, and the title 'All the Russias' is the official designation of the empire. Peter the Great was the first to take the title of Emperor. This is the political title, but in Russia it is little used, the Emperor being universally called 'Czar,' which is pronounced as though written Tzar.

Russia Leather. The peculiar and agreeable odour of Russia leather is derived from the birch-bark used in tanning it. This odour repels moths and other insects, and makes it invaluable for bookbinding, as a few books bound in Russia leather in a library will protect the remainder from insect attacks.

Russian Matting. The matting used by gardeners for protecting plants from frost, and for tying up plants, is made from the inner bark of the lime tree (*Tilia Europœa*). It contains a large quantity of tannin, which preserves it from decay when exposed to variations of weather.

S

Sabaoth. 'Lord God of *Sabaoth*' is, Lord God of *Armies*, the Lord of *Hosts*.

Sabbath Day's Journey. A Sabbath day's journey, according to Dr. Adam Clarke, was $7\frac{1}{2}$ *furlongs*, or about 1,650 yards. The Rabbins fix it at 2,000 *cubits*, which is about 1,350 yards. Josephus says that the Mount of Olives was five *stadia*, or 625 paces, from Jerusalem, which would make the allowable Sabbath day's journey about 1,050 yards.—*Calmet*.

Sack (a bag). Dr. Johnson says, 'It is observable of this word that it is found in all languages, and it is therefore conceived to be antediluvian.'

Sack (the wine). This wine—so dear to Sir John Falstaff—was imported from the Canary Islands, from whence small quantities are still brought. It derived its name from having been brought down from the mountains in goat-skins, bags, or *sacks*. 'Sherris sack,' which was brought from Xeres, was probably akin to modern sherry. It was inferior in strength to that brought from the Canaries.

Sackbut, a musical instrument, now called a trombone. The name is derived from the Spanish *sacar*, to draw, and *buche*, the stomach, 'because the breath is *drawn* up with great force from the *stomach*' (Worcester), that word having formerly included what is now known as the chest. An ancient sackbut was found in the ruins of Pompeii. It resembled the modern trombone, which was copied from it by the Italians. Two sackbuts are represented in the 'Coronation Procession of James II.,' by Edward Sandford, 1689.

Sad. The earliest use of this word in English seems to have been in the sense of firm, settled, steady. Wycliff says, a *sad* stone, meaning a stone firmly set. Chaucer says, 'O stormy people *unsad* [i.e. unsettled] and ever untrue.' In the Sanscrit the word 'sad' means to be sick. Bread which is 'heavy' is said to be 'sad,' i.e. firm.

Sadder and wiser man. This phrase is from the 'Ancient Mariner':

> A sadder and a wiser man
> He rose the morrow morn.

Saddles. Originally riders appear to have had no covering for the horse's back. Xenophon says that the hair on a horse's back should be combed down, as the animal will then be less hurt by the rider. The earliest known reference to saddles is in an order of the Emperor Theodosius, A.D. 385, in which persons who wished to ride post-horses were forbidden to use saddles of a greater weight than 60 lbs. The long wooden seats seen in farmhouse and public-house kitchens, elsewhere called *settles*, are in the north of England known as *sadles*. *Sadle* is an old Anglo-Saxon term for seat, and is probably the origin of saddle.

Sadducees. This Jewish sect originated with Sadoc about the year 263 B.C. They believed that the soul and the body perish simultaneously, and that consequently there will be no resurrection.

Sadler's Wells. This well-known place of amusement was so called from a medicinal well, called Holy Well, which formerly existed on the spot. The well was stopped at the time of the Reformation, and was forgotten until it was rediscovered by a Mr. Sadler in 1683. The first theatre was built in 1765.

St. Andrew Undershaft. This church received its distinctive name from the circumstance that a 'shaft' or maypole, which was much loftier than the church itself, was annually raised in its immediate vicinity. The maypole, during the intervals between one May-day and another, was kept upon hooks over the doors of a row of houses in *Shaft* Alley in Lime Street. The maypole was not set up after the 'Evil May-day' in 1517, the riotings then almost putting an end to May-day rejoicing in London, as the following extract shows:—'These great Mayings, and Maygames made by the governours and masters of this city, with the triumphant setting up of a great shafte (a principall maypole in Cornehill, before the Church of St. Andrew), therefore called Vndershafte, by meane of that insurrection of youths against aliens on May-day, 1517, the ŏ [*octave*, that is, 8th year] of Henry VIII., have not been so freely used as before.'—*Standish's Spital Sermon.*

St. Bride's, Fleet Street. The houses on the south side of Fleet Street were formerly continuous, so that St. Bride's Church was shut out from view. On Sunday, November 14, 1824, a fire took place which burnt three or four houses in Fleet Street to the ground, thus affording a fine view of this superb work of Wren's. Advantage was taken of the accident to make the present opening; the present offices of 'Punch' and the bookseller's shop opposite being built on the site of the fire.

St. Catherine Cree. Cree is an abbreviation of the French manner of pronouncing the word Christ. The church in London so called was formerly known as ' St. Catherine's Christ Church.'

St. Cecilia. Towards the end of the seventeenth century an annual musical festival in honour of St. Cecilia was held in Stationers' Hall. The special attraction on these occasions was an ode by some popular poet set to music by a composer of note. Dryden wrote two odes for these festivals; the first (1687) 'The Ode for St. Cecilia's Day,' the second (1697) 'Alexander's Feast.'

St. Dunstan's Church. When old St. Dunstan's Church in Fleet Street was pulled down in 1830, the celebrated clock and the figures of boys with pole-axes which had struck the hours upon the bell for more than 160 years were sold to Lord Hertford, who re-erected them in the grounds of Dunstan Villa in the Regent's Park, where both the clock and the figures still remain in perfect working order.

St. James's Park. In Hall's 'Chronicles,' reprint 1809, p. 786, it is shown that Henry VIII. formed this park in 1531-32. The old chronicler says :—' Ye haue hearde before how the Kynge had purchased the Bysshop of Yorkes place, whych was a fayre Bysshopes house, but not meete for a Kynge ; wherefore the Kynge purchased all the medowes about saynt James, and all the whole house of s. James, and there made a fayre mansion and a parke, and buylded many costly and commodious houses for great pleasure.'

St. Leger. The great race known by this name was instituted in the year 1776 by the late Lieut.-General Anthony St. Leger, of Park Hill, near Doncaster. It was not, however, so named for two or three years afterwards, when, at the suggestion of the Marquis of Rockingham at a dinner at the Red Lion Inn at Doncaster, the name was adopted in compliment to the gentleman by whom the race was established. The origin of the race is often wrongly attributed to Major-General *John* St. Leger, the companion of George IV. when Prince of Wales. *Anthony* held Park Hill till his death in 1786 ; *John* died in India in 1799.

St. Pancras. Old St. Pancras Church is said to be the last parochial church in England in which mass was said and service performed according to the Roman Catholic ritual.

St. Paul's Cathedral. The first stone of the present edifice was laid June 21, 1675. The choir was opened for public worship December 2, 1697. The building was completed in 1710. Wren himself, though in his 78th year, assisted in laying the last stone. The old ball and cross were replaced by new ones in 1821, when the present ball and cross were put up by Mr. Cockerell. Their predecessors were exhibited for some years at the Coliseum in the Regent's Park, where the compiler saw them in 1834. The State entrance gates, and about 150 feet of the fencing, which formerly enclosed the space fronting the western façade of St. Paul's Cathedral, were sold by auction for a small sum in 1876 to Messrs. Davies of Vauxhall, who afterwards offered the whole 'for the lump sum of 150*l.*' They, as well as the remaining portion of the fence, were cast in 1710 from Sussex iron, and are supposed to be the last known specimen of the iron made in that county. The first burial within St. Paul's Cathedral was fittingly that of its builder, Sir Christopher Wren. He died in 1723, and is buried in the extreme east of the crypt. The earliest statue erected was that of Howard the philanthropist.

St. Paul's Clock. The clock of St. Paul's is thus described in Wood's 'Curiosities of Clocks and Watches' (Bentley, 1866):—
'The present clock at St. Paul's is remarkable for the magnitude of its wheels and the fineness of its works. It was made by Lang Bradley in 1708, at a cost of 300*l.* It has two dial plates, one south and the other west. Each is between fifty and sixty feet in circumference. The hour numerals are a little over two feet in height. The minute-strokes of the dial are about eight inches in length. The minute hands are about eight or nine feet long, and weigh seventy-five pounds each; and the hour hands are between five and six feet long, and weigh forty-four pounds each. Its beat is two seconds—that is, a dead beat of thirty to the minute instead of sixty. The clock goes eight days, and strikes the hour on the great bell, which is suspended about forty feet from the floor. The hammer lies on the outside brim of the bell, weighs one hundred and forty-five pounds, is drawn by a wire at the back part of the clockwork, and falls again by its own weight upon the bell. The clapper weighs one hundred and eighty pounds. The diameter of the bell is ten feet, its weight is five tons, two hundredweights, and it is inscribed "Richard Phelps made me, 1716." The pendulum

is sixteen feet long, and its *bob* weighs one hundred and eighty pounds, but it is suspended by a spring no thicker than a shilling.'—P. 22.

St. Paul's School. This school was founded by Dean Colet in 1509 for the free education of 153 poor scholars. The number is said to have been selected in reference to the miraculous draft of fishes (John xxi.), the net of St. Peter containing 'an hundred and fifty and three.'—*Knight's London*.

Saints' Days. The *vigil* or *eve* of a feast or saint's day is the day before it occurs. The *morrow* of a feast is the day after. The *octave* is the eighth day after.

Salary, from the Latin *salarium*, literally salt money, from *sal*, salt, which was a part of the pay of Roman soldiers.—*Worcester*. The ancient Romans allowed the soldiery so much salt *per diem*. When this was commuted to a money payment, it was still called by the same name.

Salic Law, under which females cannot succeed to a crown, was one of the laws of the Salian Franks, who settled in Gaul under their king, Pharamond, at the beginning of the fifth century.

Sales by Candle. A couple of centuries ago it was customary to sell by 'inch of candle.' A lot being 'put up' by the auctioneer, any bids were valid until the candle went out, when the last bidder was declared the purchaser. Upon this custom, Pepys, who was Secretary to the Admiralty, made the following curious entry in his 'Diary,' September 3, 1662:—'After dinner we met and sold the *Weymouth, Successe*, and *Fellowshippe* bulkes; where pleasant to see how backward men are at first to bid, and yet when the candle is going out how they bawl, and dispute afterwards who bid the most. And here I observed one man cunninger than the rest, that was sure to be the last man and to carry it, and enquiring the reason he told me that just as the flame goes out the smoke descends, which is a thing I never observed before, and by that he do know the instant when to bid last.'

Salmon. The greatest known weight of a single fish of this species is 83 lbs. The fish that attained this weight was a female which came into the possession of Mr. Groves, fishmonger, Bond Street, London, in the season of 1821. It is described as being short for its weight, but of unusual depth and thickness. The flesh is said to have been of excellent quality and fine colour. In 1376 (50 Edw. III.) a petition was presented to the Crown, praying that no salmon should be allowed to be taken in the

Thames 'between Gravesend and Henley in winter—that is to say, between the Feast of the Finding of the Cross and the Epiphany.' 'Wednesday, 7th.—Two of the greatest draughts of salmon were caught in the Thames below Richmond that have been known some years, one net having 35 large salmon in it, and another 22, which lowered the price of salmon at Billingsgate from 1s. to 6d. per lb.'—*Gentleman's Magazine,* June 1749.

Salt. Before the year 1823 salt was subject to a duty of 15s. a bushel, the actual value of the salt being about 6d. The retail price was from 4d. to 6d. per lb. In that year the duty was reduced to 2s. the bushel, and in 1825 it was abolished. From that time the price has been gradually reduced, until at the present time salt can be bought retail at less than a farthing the pound.

Salt. The position above or below the salt denoted the rank or estimation of guests at a dinner-table. 'At the ancient long dinner-table a large *salt*-holder was placed in the middle. Those sitting at the upper end, being *above the salt,* were the superior guests; the others, or inferiors, were *below the salt.*'—*Halliwell.*

Salt Cellar. This English word is an etymological curiosity. The term 'cellar' is a corruption of the French *salière,* a salt-holder. The word salt-cellar is literally a 'salt-salt-holder.'

Salt Works. The earliest salt works in England were at Droitwich in Worcestershire, which was the Roman town of Salinæ. The earliest *written* record of the Droitwich Salt Works is dated A.D. 816, when Kenulph, King of Mercia, gave ten houses in Wich (Droitwich), with salt furnaces (*Salinæ*), to the Church of Worcester.

Salute. This word, which is from the Latin *salus,* health, originally meant to greet a person with congratulations or enquiries having reference to his health.

Salve. This Latin word is often seen woven into the surface of door mats, or inscribed on encaustic tiles at the entrance of a house. It means 'Hail! Welcome!' It is pronounced *sal-ve,* two syllables. *Salve,* ointment, has the same derivation, but is a monosyllable.

Sample. This word is an abbreviation of the word *example*; it is from the Latin *ex,* from, and *amplus,* much.

Sanscrit (from the Hindu *sanscritu,* polished), the learned language of Hindustan and of the Brahmins, which was current at the time of Solomon. It is the parent of most modern languages. It contains the roots of Greek, Latin, Celtic, Slavonic, and German, and as it contains no exotic terms must be one of the primitive tongues.

Sans Culottes, a French term literally meaning 'without breeches.' It was applied to the revolutionists in 1791, not because they wore no lower garments, but because they wore trousers instead of breeches. The term was at first applied as a reproach, but was afterwards adopted by the party as a proud designation.

Sandwiches are so called from an Earl of Sandwich who introduced them about a century ago. Dr. Brewster says he 'passed whole days in gambling, bidding the waiter bring him for refreshment a piece of meat between two pieces of bread, which he ate without stopping from play.'

Sappers and Miners. The word sapper is from the Italian *zappare*, to dig.

Sappy. There are two words originally spelt thus in English. One is derived from the Anglo-Saxon *sæpig*, meaning full of sap, juicy, succulent; the other is from a Greek word signifying to become rotten. It is now generally spelt and pronounced *sāpy*, and is used in the senses of flabby, musty, tainted, unsavoury, tasteless, flat—as, 'the ale is quite *sāpy*,' 'a *sāpy* orange.'

Saracen. There are at least half a dozen different opinions as to the derivation of this word. Du Cange thinks it is from *Sarah*, Abraham's wife; Hottinger, from the Arabic *saraca*, to steal; Forster, from *sahra*, a desert. The 'Penny Cyclopædia' says it is certainly from the Arabic *Sharkeyn*, the Eastern people.

Sarcophagus was a name applied by the Greeks to a species of stone found at Assos in Troas, which the ancients believed to have the property of consuming human remains. Hence the name, which signifies flesh eater, and hence also the use of this kind of stone as receptacles for the dead. It was believed that a body buried in a coffin made of this kind of stone would be, with the exception of the teeth, entirely consumed in forty days. The name sarcophagus is now applied to stone coffins without reference to the kind of stone employed for making them.

Sardines. The *true* sardines (*Clupea sardina*) of the Mediterranean Sea are fish of the same genus with the herring and the pilchard. The fish imported from the west of France, and sold in England in such large quantities as sardines, are sprats.

Sardonic, applied to grinning, or laughing sarcastically or malignantly. 'Sardinia is free from all kinds of poisonous and deadly herbs excepting one, which resembles parsley, and which it is said causes those who eat of it to die laughing. From this circumstance Homer first, and others after him, call laughter which conceals some noxious design *sardonic.*'—*Taylor.*

Sash Windows. Formerly all windows opened by means of what were called casements. Sash windows came into use after the Great Fire of London; even in Queen Anne's time they were not common. In the 'Tatler,' May 27, 1710, a house in Devonshire Square, Bishopsgate, is advertised to be 'lett,' one of the recommendations of which is that it is 'sashed with thirty sash lights.' The word 'sash' is from the French *chassis,* a groove, or anything that slides in a groove. The following extract from Lister's 'Journey to Paris,' 1699, seems to show that these windows were of English invention:—'At De Lorge, we had the good fortune to find the marshall himself. He showed us his great *sash windows;* how easily they might be lifted up and down and stood at any height, which contrivance, he said, he had out of England by a small model brought on purpose from thence, there being nothing of this *poise* in France before.'

Satin. This word, and the fabric to which it is applied as a name, are both of Chinese origin. The nearest approach which ordinary type will enable us to make to the Chinese pronunciation of the word is sz-tün.

Saturday Half-holiday. The Saturday half-holiday movement is a revival of a very ancient custom. King Edgar (A.D. 958) ordained that there should be cessation of labour from Saturday noon until daylight on Monday. William of Scotland (A.D. 1203) in Council determined that Saturday after the twelfth hour 'should be kept holy.' In an old work, 'Dives and Pauper,' 1493, is the following:—'*Dives.*—Howe longe owythe the haliday to be kept and halowyd? *Pauper.*—From even to even. Nathelesse summe begynne sonner. . . . But that men use in Saturdaies to ryng holy at mid-day compellith nat men anon to halowe, but warnythe them of the halidaye folowynge.' In 'Divers Crab Tree Lectures,' 1639, p. 126, quoted in Brand's 'Popular Antiquities,' are the following homely lines:—

> You know that Munday is Sundayes brother;
> Tuesday is such another

> Wednesday you must go to church and pray;
> Thursday is half holiday;
> On Friday it is too late to begin to spin;
> The Saturday is half-holiday agen.

An unrepealed law of King Canute establishes the Saturday half-holiday in these words:—' Healde mon ælus Sunnandages freolsunge fram Saternesdages none oð Monandages lihtinge' (Let every Sunday's feast be held from Saturday's noon to Monday's dawn).—*Thorpe's Laws of England; Laws of Cnut*, i. 14.

Saturnine. A relic of astrology. When men believed that the planets had their influence upon human actions and character, each person was supposed to be governed by that of the star that was in the 'ascendant' at the time of his birth. Thus a saturnine man was one whose grave and stern habits were supposed to be derived from Saturn, his governing planet.

Saucer. The name saucer is now only applied to the hollow dish in which a teacup is placed. Anciently it was used to denote a vessel for holding sauces at a dinner. In the time of Cromwell an English illustrated edition of the 'Janua Linguarum' of Comenius was published, in which full details of the customs of the dinnertable are given. In this curious work we are told that 'messes are brought in platters; a pie in a plate. The carver breaketh up the good cheer and divideth it. Sauces are set amongst rostemete in *sawsers*.' 'Sauces' at that time meant the ordinary cooked vegetables.

Saucy. Lexicographers usually derive this word from the Latin *salsus*, salt, pungent, sharp. Mr. Fox Talbot thinks that as the Latin *supercilium*, from which we get supercilious, means an eyebrow, so our word 'saucy' may have been derived from the French *sourcil*, which also means an eyebrow.

Savings Banks were originally suggested by Jeremy Bentham in 1797, but Priscilla Wakefield established the first at Tottenham in 1803.

Saws 'were invented by Dædalus.'—*Pliny.* Apollodorus, however, ascribes their introduction to Talus, who, having found the jawbone of a snake, employed it to cut through a piece of wood, and then formed an instrument of iron of the same shape. Saw-mills are known to have been in use in Madeira as early as A.D. 1420, and at Breslau seven years later. They became general in England about the close of the eighteenth century.

Saxon English. Nowhere perhaps is the native force and vigour of the Anglo-Saxon element in the English language so clearly shown as in the twenty-seventh verse of the seventh chapter of Matthew: 'And the rain descended and the floods came, and the winds blew, and beat upon that house, and it fell, and great was the fall thereof.' Here, except the word 'descended,' which was evidently inserted to avoid the repetition of the verb 'fell,' every word is pure Saxon. Now take the account of the same occurrence as given by the translators of the evangelist Luke: 'Against which the stream did beat vehemently, and immediately it fell, and the ruin of that house was great' (vi. 49). The contrast is greatly in favour of the former version, which is almost as familiar as a proverb, while the latter account seems quite strange and outlandish.

Saxon Names for Parts of the Body. The names by which we distinguish the different parts of the human body are mostly of Saxon origin. Body itself is Saxon, signifying bode or abode, which is in keeping with *sarvol-hus*, or soul-house, another name the Saxons had for the body. Head was formerly *heved*, which means heaved up or raised above the other members. Eye is from *augyan*, to point out. Nose is from *ness*, a prominence; we use *ness* in such compounds as Sheerness, Shoeburyness, &c., which are promontories. Skull and shoulder are both from *scylan*, to divide; the skull because it consists of many divisions, the shoulder because at that point the arms divide from the body. Mouth is from *matgan*, to eat. Jaw is that with which a man chaws, or chews. Ear is from *eren*, to take or receive as sounds. Cheek is compounded of *chew* and *eke*, repetition. Tongue comes from *thingan*, to speak; and hand from *hentan*, to take. Nostril is from *nose thrill*, thrill meaning bored, as with an auger. Knee and knuckle are from *nicken*, to bend; finger from *fingan*, to take; foot from *fettian*, to carry; leg from *leggan*, to support; thigh is from *thick*, from its being the thickest part of the leg; sinew is *sine*, strength; joints are *joinings*; toe is from *tean*, to expand; and wrist is that with which we *wrest* or *wrestle*.

Saxon Roots of Modern Words. Some Anglo-Saxon words of simple meaning have been very prolific of English terms. Take *pyndan*, for instance, which meant to shut up or confine. From this we get *pound*, the place in which stray cattle are shut up; *pond*, in which water is confined within a narrow space; *pin*, in the sense in which it is used by Hooker when he says 'to *pin* the word of God in so narrow room'; *pinder*, the officer who impounds cattle; *pen*, an enclosure for sheep; *bin*, a chest for corn; *bound*, in the sense in which Shakespeare uses it in the line 'Now am I cabined, cribbed, confined, *bound in*'; and *binding*, which shuts in the leaves of a book.

Scamp, from the Latin *ex*, from, and *campus*, the field [of battle]. Literally, one who basely deserts his colours in time of war.

Scarlet. The original root of this word is supposed to be the Latin *carnis*, flesh. Hence Italian *scarlatino*, flesh-coloured, which in Venetian was *scarlatin*, a mixture of red and white. From *scarlatin*, a pale red, came eventually *scarlato*, full red, and from thence the English scarlet.

Scaramouch, a reproachful term used by boys, is derived from the Italian word *scarramuccia*. The name was given to a character in an Italian comedy, who was represented as a military poltroon and braggadocio. The character was always absurdly dressed, and Scaramouch always received a most severe and inglorious drubbing at the hands of the other characters.

Scarlet, Crimson. In the Old French these words were employed as adjectives, and were applied to various colours to signify fast, durable, deep. *Bleu cramoisi* meant deep blue; *écarlate noir*, deep black; and in Foulque's 'Fitz Warren,' p. 70, we have, '*e se vestirent de un escarlet vert*' ('and dressed in deep green').

Scavenger. 'The *scavage*, or skewage, was originally a duty paid on the inspection of customable goods brought for sale within the City of London. The scavengers or scavagers were the inspectors to whom the goods were actually shown. Afterwards the inspection of the streets seems to have been committed to the same officers.'—*Wedgwood*.

Scavenger's Daughter. This is the name by which an ancient instrument of torture shown in the Tower of London is known. The name is a corruption of that of the inventor. In 1604 a Committee of the House of Commons reported that 'they found in the Tower an engine of torture devised by Mr. Skevington, sometime Lieutenant of the Tower, called "Skevington's daughter."' Skevington was Lieutenant in the reign of Henry VIII.

Scent. The *c* in this word is an absurdity. The word comes to us from the French *sentir*, to smell. The letter *c* does not qualify the sound, and it ought to be expunged from the word.

Schedule. The authorities are much divided in opinion as to whether the proper pronunciation of this word should be sked-yule, sked-ul, shed-yule, shed-ul, sed-jule, sed-yule, or sed-ul; but the generally accepted modern pronunciation is *sed-yule*.

Schiedam is the town in Holland which has given its name to Hollands gin. It is situated on the river Schie, about four miles west of Rotterdam. There are something like 300 distilleries in the place, and 'the town is so much engaged in manufacturing gin and the preparatory processes that the air and water smell and taste of it.'

Schoolmaster abroad. This phrase originated in a speech of Lord Brougham's. The passage in which it occurred is subjoined:—
'Let the soldier be abroad if he will; he can do nothing in this age. There is another personage abroad, a person less imposing—in the eyes of some, perhaps, insignificant. *The schoolmaster is abroad!* and I trust to him, armed with his primer, against the soldier in full military array.'

Schooner. A schooner is a small sailing vessel; its name comes from the Dutch word *schoon*, beautiful. 'The first vessel of this kind is said to have been built at Gloucester in Massachusetts by Captain Andrew Robinson about the year 1714. The name was given to it from the following circumstance: 'When the vessel, which was masted and rigged as schooners are now, was going off the stocks, a bystander—using the word *schoon* as a verb—said, "O, how she *schoons*." The owner instantly replied, "A *schooner* let her be called"; and from that time this class of vessels has gone by that name.'—*Essex Memorial*, 1836.

Science, Art. Science is from the Latin *sciens*, knowing. 'The object of science is knowledge; the objects of art are works. In art truth is the means to an end; in science it is the only end. Science teaches us to know, art to do. Hence the practical arts are not to be classed among the sciences.'—*Whewell*.

Score. To score was to cut notches on a stick to denote numbers. The *number* of runs gained in a game of cricket is still, from this custom, called the *score*. Its application to the number 'twenty,' according to Tooke, arose from the custom of avoiding large numbers by cutting off the tally when twenty notches had been made. These tallies were afterwards reckoned as so many *scores*. In a poem on cricket in the 'Gentleman's Magazine,' 1756, is the following line:

    And squint-eyed prejudice computes the *score*.

See TALLY.

Scorn is probably the Danish word *skarn*, dirt, mud, mire. Pelting with mud is a natural expression of scorn. The Danes use the word *skarn* metaphorically as well as literally. '*Skarn-stykke*' is an act of malice or scorn.

Scotched Collops. In cookery books and on bills of fare we are constantly meeting with this term, spelt '*Scots* collops' or '*Scotch* collops.' The dish, however, has not a Scottish origin. The collops, or slices of flesh, before being cooked are 'scotched,' which means, according to Worcester, that they are 'cut with shallow incisions, or in a slight manner.' 'Scotched' in this sense is the word used by Shakespeare in the celebrated line :
We've scotched the snake, not killed it.

Scot-free. The word 'scot' in this term is the Anglo-Saxon *sceat*, a part or portion of tribute or taxation. The word is in use in most of the Northern languages in the sense of treasure, tribute, or wealth. In English it survives only in the legal phrase 'paying *scot* and lot' and in 'scot-free,' which means free from payment. The word 'shot' in the common saying 'paying the shot' seems allied.

Scotland Yard. Mr. Newton, in his 'London in the Olden Time,' says, 'This property was given by the Saxon King Edgar to Kenneth III., King of Scotland, for his residence, upon his annual visit to London to do homage for his kingdom to the Crown of England.' The last of the Scottish royal family to reside here was Margaret, Queen of James IV., who took up her abode here after the death of her husband at the battle of Flodden Field.

Scott's 'Waverley.' Sir Richard Phillips says in his 'Million of Facts': 'Scott's "Waverley" was offered anonymously to the editor of this volume. The price asked for it was refused. It then appeared as W. Scott's; but in a few days the name and placards were withdrawn, and the author was said to be unknown.'—C. 648, ed. 1842.

Scottish Marriage Law. 'Not long ago Lord Deas, in delivering a judgment from the bench in Scotland, used these words to describe the state of the Scottish law of marriage :—" Consent makes marriage. No form or ceremony, civil or religious; no notice before, or publication after; no cohabitation, no writing, no witnesses even, are essential to the constitution of this, the most important contract which two persons can enter into." '—*Man and Wife, by Wilkie Collins.*

Scraping an acquaintance. Dr. Doran, in the 'Gentleman's Magazine' (N.S. xxxix. 230), says :—'There is an anecdote connected with Hadrian, and the custom of bathing, from which is derived the proverbial saying of " scraping an acquaintance." The

Emperor, entering a bath, saw an old soldier scraping himself with a tile. He recognised the man as a former comrade, and pitying his condition that he had nothing better than a tile for a flesh-brush, he ordered the veteran to be presented with a considerable sum of money and a costly set of bathing garments. Thereupon all the old soldiers of the imperial army became anxious to claim fellowship with the Emperor. As Hadrian entered the bath the day after that on which he had rewarded his former comrade, he observed dozens of old soldiers scraping themselves with tiles. He understood the intent, but wittily evaded it, saying, " Scrape yourselves, gentlemen, you will not scrape acquaintance with me."'

Scrap, from the verb 'to scrape,' anything scraped off as comparatively useless. The word *scrap*-book should be properly *scrip*-book.

Scratch-cradle, or Cat's Cradle. This name is a corruption of *cratch-cradle*; *cratch* is an Old English name for a rack in which hay is placed for cattle. Wycliff's translation of Luke ii. 7 is, 'She bare her first-born and laid him in a *cratch*.' The scratch-cradle produced by children with a piece of twine is not unlike a modern *cratch* in which hay is placed in a fold-yard for cattle to eat.

Screw Propellers. The first *successful* application of the screw propeller to navigation was made on the ship 'Archimedes,' built in London, 1836, under a patent granted to F. P. Smith and J. Ericsson.

Scribe. The word 'scribe' in the New Testament means lawyer. Matthew, in telling (xxii. 35) of one who asked Christ which was the great Commandment, says he was a lawyer; whereas Mark, in relating the same circumstance (xii. 28), calls him 'one of the scribes.' In the Old Testament the word 'scribe' is used for a public notary or secretary. This agrees with the original meaning of the word, which is transcriber, one who copies or transcribes.

Sea Anemone. The first known mention of the marine anemone occurs in a description of the island of St. Lucia, published in 1764.

Seakale is indigenous in Dorset and Devon. It was first sent to the London market by the Rev. J. Frewen, who was incumbent of Sidbury, near Sidmouth, A.D. 1707-13. The Rev. Abraham Channing, Rector of Pentridge, Dorset, 1750-80, was the first to cultivate seakale in his garden, but he used it in the unbleached condition.

Sealing Wax. The earliest application of sealing wax to its present purpose appears to have been made about the year 1553. The first printed account of it, according to Berzelius, appeared in 1563. The oldest known impression of a seal upon ordinary sealing wax is that found by M. Roos on a letter written from London, August 3, 1554, to the Rheingrave Phillip Francis von Daun by his agent in England, Herr Gerrard Mann. The colour is dark red, it is very shining, and the impression bears the writer's initials.—*Beckmann.*

Sea Terms. It is curious that while nearly all our military terms are derived from the Norman, those connected with a seafaring life are mostly Anglo-Saxon or Dutch. Such are ship, boat, punt, boom, bowsprit, helm, stern, bow, mast, spar, sail, hold, lading, hatchway, rope, tar, hawser, wheel, porthole, keel, tack, ladder, hull, shrouds, dock, rudder, yard, skipper, skiff, mate, sailor, boatswain, coxswain, steward, steersman, crew, luff, thwart, leeward, aft, abaft, taut, deck, reef, ebb, flow, neap, full, rig, board, trim, knot, and many others. See MILITARY TERMS.

Second (of time). Among the Romans the sixtieth part of an hour was called *scrupulum*. This corresponded exactly to our minute. The sixtieth part of the 'scrupulum' was called *scrupulum secundum*, and this corresponded to our 'second,' and is the origin of the English word.

Secret. This word has many relatives which are almost synonymous, but which have distinct shades of meaning. The following examples will show their different significations: 'Secret enemy, hidden plot, concealed intention, clandestine marriage, covert allusion, latent motive, occult science, unknown circumstances, private reason, retired situation.'—*Worcester.*

Secular (Latin *secularis*), from *seculum*, an age. The word *seculum* originally meant a generation, but its meaning expanded until it embraced the ideas of an age, a century, &c. It was also used to denote the manners of an age. Hence Christian writers came to employ it in the sense of 'the world' as opposed to 'the Church,' and the term *secular* clergy was used to distinguish those priests who moved in the world amongst their people from the regular clergy, or those who belonged to monastic orders and lived under rule. By degrees the word has now come to denote things temporal and worldly as opposed to matters ecclesiastical or spiritual.

Sedan Chairs, so named from the town of Sedan, where they were first used. They were enclosed chairs, something like the body of a modern brougham, but wide enough for only one occupant. A long pole passed through square staples on each side, thus forming a pair of shafts before and behind, by means of which the passenger was carried by two men. A patent was sealed in 1634, granting to Sir Francis Duncombe the sole privilege of using and letting sedan chairs in England for fourteen years. They soon became fashionable, and were in use for two hundred years. The last the compiler remembers to have seen was used by Miss Linwood, celebrated for her magnificent pictures in needlework, one of which she bequeathed to the Queen. She spent her later years at Leicester, and her sedan chair was frequently seen in the streets of that town about 1840. She died March 2, 1845, in her ninetieth year. The Rev. W. K. R. Bedford, of Sutton Coldfield, writes to the compiler, 'Ladies went to balls in a sedan at Southwell, Notts, in 1849-50.'

Sedge, from the Anglo-Saxon *sæcg*, a little sword, in allusion to the shape of the leaves.

See. The *see* of a bishop is properly his *seat* or throne, but the word is generally used to express the extent of his jurisdiction.

See and its synonyms. 'We *see* all objects before our eyes; we *look at* those which excite our curiosity; we *behold* such as cause our admiration; we *view* or *inspect* those we are desirous of examining.'—*Trusler.*

Seedy. This cant phrase is supposed to be of very recent introduction. It was, however, used more than a century ago, e.g., 'Little Flanigan here is a little *seedy.*'—*Goldsmith.*

Seidlitz Water is a natural mineral water rising from a spring in the village of Seidlitz, in Bohemia. Its principal constituents are the sulphates of magnesia and soda, and carbonic acid. The powders sold as 'seidlitz powders' are potassa tartrate and bicarbonate of soda, which are neutralised in water by finely-powdered tartaric acid.

Selah. This word, which occurs so frequently in the Book of Psalms, is usually believed to be a direction to the musicians who chanted the Psalms in the Temple. Mattheson, the great musical critic, wrote a book on the subject, in which, after rejecting a number of theories, he came to the conclusion that it is equivalent to the modern 'da capo,' and is a direction that the air or song is to be repeated from the commencement to the part where the word is placed. If this be so, the custom of reading the word as though it were a part of the text is of course incorrect.

Selling a Wife. ' It is a popular error that a husband can get rid of a wife by selling her in an open market-place with a halter round her neck. Such an act ought to be severely punished by the local magistrate.'—*Wharton.*

Selling Mackerel on Sundays. By a statute of 10 Will. III., it is made lawful to sell these fish on Sundays 'before or after divine service.'

Seltzer or Selters Water. The natural seltzer or selters water rises at the village of Lower Selters in the Duchy of Nassau. It contains a large amount of free carbonic acid, combined with the carbonates of magnesia, lime, and soda, and is a wholesome and agreeable beverage.

Selvage in cloth is *self-edge*—that is, it is self-edged, and therefore does not require hemming or edging.

Semaphores were telegraphs similiar to the modern railway signal-posts. They consisted of a mast with two or more arms, each of which could be made to project on either side of the mast, and at any required angle. By the combinations thus formed, any message might be sent in clear weather. The last message sent in England by semaphore was despatched from London to Portsmouth December 31, 1847. From that date the electric telegraph has superseded it.

Sentinel, or Sentry. From the Old French *sente*, a path, from which is derived the modern *sentinelle*, the path of a soldier on guard. From this comes the English ' to keep sentry,' and eventually the name was transferred to the man employed to keep the sentry—that is, to keep to the appointed track or beat.

Sepia is prepared from a secretion found in a vessel called the inkbag of the cuttle-fish. It is black, and is the basis of Indian ink. When dissolved in a solution of caustic potash it becomes brown, and this being precipitated is the sepia of commerce.

Sepoy is a corruption of the Indian word *sipahi*, a soldier. The word itself is derived from *sip*, a bow and arrow, the ancient equipment of an Indian warrior. The word now denotes an Indian soldier in the British service in India.

Seraph. A seraph is an angel. The English plural is seraphs, the Hebrew is seraphim, without the *s*. The expression (Isaiah vi. 6) 'one of the seraphims' is incorrect in both languages. See CHERUBIM.

Serenade (Spanish *serenata*). The original signification of this word was music performed out of doors on a serene evening.

Serene. This word was formerly used to express the cold damp chill which sometimes comes on after sunset. Thus Ben Jonson, in 'The Fox,' ii. 6, has—

> Some serene blast me, or dire lightning strike
> This my offending face.

See ALL SERENE.

Serif. The little strokes at the top and bottom of the Roman capital letter I and the corresponding marks on other letters are called *serifs*. The 'block' letters A F T, &c. are known by printers as 'sans serif' letters.

Serjeant. When this word is used as the title of a barrister it should be spelled with a *j*, but when applied to a non-commissioned officer in the army it is properly spelled sergeant, the letter *g* being substituted for *j*. The *er* in this word was formerly, in common with most cases of the *e* followed by *r*, sounded as *ar* in March. Fifty years ago it was customary to say m*a*rchant, s*a*rvant, s*a*rvice, cl*a*rk, H*a*rtfordshire, B*a*rkshire, D*a*rbyshire, &c., but modern usage is in favour of *er*, and the sound *ar* is now seldom used except in proper names or titles—as the Earl of D*a*rby, the Earl of B*a*rkeley.

Serpents do not sting, nor is it their forked tongue that is their instrument of offence. The teeth or fangs are the real weapons of all the venomous serpents.

Set-off. In English commerce, where two persons are each selling to the other, and one claims payment in cash, the other may deduct the amount of the goods he has supplied. This is called a 'set-off.' In America the term 'off-set' is always used in similar cases.

Seven Dials. 'The Seven Dials in London is a place where seven streets branch off—viz. 1, Great Earl Street; 2, Little Earl Street; 3, Great St. Andrew's Street; 4, Little St. Andrew's Street; 5, Great White Lion Street; 6, Little White Lion Street; 7, Queen Street. The long cross stone which stood in the middle centre was seven square at the top, and a dial on each square, which stone I saw standing in the year 1770, but was put down in the year 1777.'—*A History of the Shire of Renfrew.* Paisley, 1782. The column is now standing at Weybridge in Surrey, as a monument to the Duchess of York.

Seven Senses. It is common to hear country people say of another 'He has taken leave of his seven senses.' In the apocryphal Ecclesiasticus (xvii. 5) is a verse which seems to justify the phrase—'They received the use of the five operations of the Lord, and in the sixth place He imparted them understanding, and in the seventh, speech, an interpreter of the cogitations thereof.'

Several. The original meaning of 'several' was that which is *severed*, or *separate*. Beaumont and Fletcher have 'be *several* at meat and lodging'; and in 2 Kings xv. 5 we are told that Azariah King of Judah was a leper, and 'dwelt in a *several* house.'

Sewing Machine. 'Mr. J. Stone, Rue de la Pepinière, Paris, obtained in February 1805 a *brevet d'invention*, or patent, for "a machine for joining the sides of segments of all flexible matters," which he asserts will be particularly serviceable in preparing clothing for the army and navy. It is supposed that one man may do as much work with this machine as one hundred persons with the needle.'—*Athenœum*.

Shade and Shadow. These words, although closely allied, are not identical in meaning. The side of an object which is farthest from the light is in 'shade,' and the object casts its 'shadow,' or a representation of its form, upon those portions of surrounding objects whose light it intercepts.

Shades. This is now a common name for vaults or other places where wines or other liquors are on sale. The name originated at Brighton. In 1816 a Mr. Savage, who had acquired the premises in Steine Lane formerly occupied by the Old Bank, converted them into a drinking and smoking shop. Mrs. Fitzherbert at that time lived exactly opposite, and Savage was fearful of annoying her by placing any inscription in front of his house designating its new character. It struck him, however, that as Mrs. Fitzherbert's house, which was south of his, was so tall as to prevent the sun from shining on his premises, he would adopt the word 'Shades,' which he accordingly placed over the door where the word 'Bank' had before appeared. The name 'took,' and a large business was secured. Numbers of other publicans, in London and elsewhere, adopted the name 'Shades,' which is now fully established in the language as a synonym for wine vaults.

Shagreen is the dried skin of an animal made rough by pressing small seeds into its substance while still soft.

Shakespeare. The well-known lines,

> He who filches from me my good name, &c.

appear to be founded on the following passage in the 'Homily against Contention and Brawling,' published in the time of Edward VI.: 'Many times there cometh less hurt of a thief than of a railing tongue: for the one taketh away a man's good name, the other taketh but his riches, which is of much less value and estimation.' In 'Richard III.,' act ii. sc. 3, is the line

> Woe to the land that's governed by a child.

This is evidently taken from Ecclesiastes x. 16—

> Woe to thee, O land, when thy king is a child.

Shakespeare and Cervantes. It is a singular coincidence that these two great imaginative writers should have died on the same day, April 23, 1616. Shakespeare died at Stratford-on-Avon, aged fifty-two; Cervantes at Madrid, aged sixty-nine.

Shakespeare and Dryden. Shakespeare wrote ('Measure for Measure'):

> Ay; but to die! and *go we know not where*.

Dryden ('Aurengzebe') has:

> Death by itself is nothing; but we fear
> To be we know not what, to *go we know not where*.

Shall and Will, the two signs of the future tense in the English language, are often erroneously applied, particularly by the Irish and Scotch, who frequently make the mistake attributed to the foreigner who, afraid of falling into a river, called out, 'I *will* fall in, and nobody *shall* help me.' The word 'shall' in the first person foretells something, as, 'I shall be married to-morrow'; in the second and third it implies a threat or promise, as, 'He shall do as I tell him,' 'They shall have a holiday.' In the case of the word 'will,' it is the first person that threatens or promises, as, 'I will knock him down'; and the second or third that foretells, as, 'He will die'; 'They will travel by railway.'

Shamefaced was originally shame*fast*, formed after the manner of steadfast. It was printed 'shamefast' in the early Bibles (1 Tim. ii. 9).

Shamrock. The original shamrock of Ireland was not the tre foil, but the common wood-sorrel (*Oxalis acetosella*), which also has leaves with three divisions.

Shanks's Pony. 'To ride on Shanks's pony' is to walk, 'shanks' meaning the legs. 'To go by Walker's omnibus' or 'Walker's 'bus' has the same signification.

Shape. The Old English word *sceap*, from which we get *shape*, meant a thing created. Verstegan says, ' Our Old English Christian ancestors said "Sceapor [Shaper] of Heofen and Eorth"; of the word sceap we have derived our word shape, which we now onely take for the form or fashion.'—*Restitution*, ed. 1655, p. 174.

Sharp-shins. This proverbial term for an acute, keen-witted person, has nothing to do with 'shins.' It comes from the German *scharf*, sharp, and *sinn*, wit, mind, sense. *Scharf-sinn* in German is the exact equivalent of the English 'Sharp-shins.'

Shawm. This was the name of an ancient musical instrument, which Nares says resembled a hautboy. Drayton ('Polyolbion,' iv. p. 736) has:

> Even from the shrillest shawm unto the cornamute.

It also occurs in the Prayer-book version of the 98th Psalm: 'With trumpets also and *shawms*.' The authorised version has, 'With trumpets and *sound of cornet*.'

Sheep. The Normans introduced the name 'mouton' into England as a name for sheep, but the old Anglo-Saxon name for the living animal still prevails. For three or four centuries, however, the Norman name was applied to what are now called 'wethers,' that is, castrated rams. In the will of the Earl of Salisbury, the natural son of Henry II., he leaves towards the building of a monastery a thousand 'sheep' and three hundred 'muttons'; and in an old inventory, *temp.* 1337, of property belonging to a priory it is mentioned that there were in store 140 'muttons,' each worth 10*d*., and 100 'sheep,' each worth 8*d*.

Shekel. A Jewish *shekel* was about ten pennyweights troy. Its value in silver was about 2*s*. 6*d*.; in gold, 1*l*. 17*s*.

Sheridan. When Sheridan, on being found found drunk by the watchmen, declared his name to be Wilberforce, he was a plagiarist, as he often was in other things. Almadovar, the Spanish ambassador, was arrested in 1778 for being mixed up in a disreputable row in a low neighbourhood in London. On being asked who he was, he replied, 'I am the ambassador from Venice.' As the Venetian ambassador was a solemn and severely 'proper' person, he was greatly scandalised. Sheridan, drunk as he was evidently remembered the story and made ready use of it.

Sheriff is a corruption of *shire reeve*, the governor of a shire or county. There were sheriffs of London before the Conquest. William I. first nominated them for counties in 1079. 'The sheriff is, during his year of office, the first man in his county, and is superior in rank to any nobleman therein.'—*Wharton.*

Sheriffs of London. The two sheriffs of the City of London are said to make the one sheriff of Middlesex. The reason is said to be that in a charter of King John which relates both to the city and county, the word 'sheriffs' in the plural is used, but that in a charter of Henry I. which relates only to Middlesex but one person is named. The duties of the two offices are entirely distinct, and are performed by separate deputies.

Sherry. This name is a corruption of the name of the place, Xeres, from which it was first imported. The ancient name by which this wine was known in England was sack, a name inseparably connected with that of Sir John Falstaff.

Shibboleth, the test word which the Ephraimites could not pronounce, has two meanings—an ear of corn and a stream of water. It was used in the latter sense by the Giliadites with some propriety at the fords or passages over the Jordan, itself a stream of water.

Shilling. Great diversity of opinion exists as to the origin of the word shilling. Bailey and others think it was so called because originally it bore the arms of the sovereign on a *shield.* The weight of authority is, however, in favour of its derivation from *scylan,* to divide, because the earlier coins were made with deep indented crosses, so that they might easily be divided into two or four, in the same manner as pennies could be divided into halfpennies and fourthings, or farthings. See FARTHING.

Ship. The etymology of this word shows that, in its origin, a ship was something *shaped,* and this proves that the word arose when a *ship* was nothing more than the trunk of a tree scooped out and shaped to enable it to glide smoothly and safely through the water. From the primitive ship of our ancestors to the 'Great Eastern'—as long, as wide, and as lofty as a good-sized street—is a change indeed! The length of this enormous vessel is 692 feet, the breadth 83 feet, and the height 60 feet.

Ships of War. In the French wars from 1793 to 1814, the English navy took or destroyed 207 ships of the line, 12 fifty-gun ships, 339 frigates, and 556 sloops and other vessels—a total of 1,114 vessels in twenty-one years!

Shire, County. The word *shire* signifies something *sheared* or cut off. All the counties except Cambridgeshire whose names have this affix were originally portions of larger territories, provinces, or kingdoms, from which they have been *shorn*. The counties of Kent, Essex, Sussex, Surrey, Middlesex, Suffolk, and Norfolk still retain their ancient boundaries. They are therefore not called 'shires.' The word is not always synonymous with county. There are two districts within the county of Yorkshire which are called 'shires'—Richmondshire in the North Riding, and Hallamshire in the West. The town of Sheffield is in the district of Hallamshire.

Shoe at Weddings. Urquhart in his 'Pillars of Hercules' says: 'At a Jewish marriage I was standing by the bridegroom when the bride entered. As she crossed the threshold he stooped and struck her with the heel [of a shoe] on the nape of the neck. I at once saw the interpretation of the passage of Scripture respecting the transfer of the shoe to another in case the brother-in-law did not exercise his privilege. The slipper in the East, being taken off indoors, is at hand to administer correction, and is here used to signify the obedience of the wife and the supremacy of the husband. The Highland custom is to strike for good-luck, as they say, with an old shoe. Little do they suspect the meaning implied.' See BRIDAL CUSTOM.

Shoes. Westmacott, speaking of the bronze recumbent figure of Edward III. in Westminster Abbey, says, 'Among the careful details it will be observed the shoes are rights and lefts, erroneously believed to be a very modern fashion of shoemaking.'

Shoeing of Horses. It is not clearly known whether the Romans shod their horses, or, if they did, whether they used iron shoes. The earliest definite knowledge on the subject is that the custom of shoeing horses was introduced into England by William the Conqueror, who gave the town of Northampton to Henry de Ferrers, and conferred upon him that surname (*fer*, iron) because he was intrusted with the inspection of the farriers. The Ferrers family still have for their arms six horseshoes.

Shoreditch is a corruption of the name of Soerdich, a family who were lords of the manor in the time of Edward III. Stow says, '*Soerditch*, so called more than 400 years since, as I can prove by record.' This carries the name back to A.D. 1200, and utterly upsets the theory that it derived its name from Jane Shore.

Shot in the locker. Lockers are compartments in ships of war for the reception of the shot. They are placed at the base of the mainmast, so that the weight of their contents may help to steady the motion of the ship. When a sailor, to express being without money, says he 'hasn't a shot in the locker,' it is equivalent to saying that he is like a ship which has expended all her ammunition.

Shot in the neck. To say in America that a person is 'shot in the neck' is equivalent to saying that he is drunk.

Shoulder-blade. The word blade in this term is the German *blatt*, a leaf, alluding to its flat broad surface. See BLADE.

Shovel. Probably from the word 'to shove.' In Gloucestershire a pitchfork is called a shove-pick. The word shovel was probably originally *shover*.

Shrapnel. The shells so called which are used in warfare were named after their inventor, General Shrapnel.

Shrewd. To beshrew or shrew persons was formerly to curse them, and 'shrew' was constantly used as an oath. Thus in the 'Winter's Tale' (act i. sc. 2) we have 'Shrew my heart!' and in 'Cymbeline' (act ii. sc. 3) 'Shrew me!' From this verb came the adjective 'shrewd,' meaning malicious, spiteful, venomous. A shrewd turn meant a malicious injury, and to be accounted shrewd was to be thought capable of diabolical wickedness. Shakespeare mentions the word shrewd in this sense in a passage which has puzzled many. In 'Henry VIII.' (act v. sc. 2) the King, addressing Cranmer after his reconciliation with Gardiner, says:—

> The common voice I see is verified
> Of thee, which says, 'Do my lord of Canterbury
> A *shrewd turn*, and he's your friend for life.'

Foxe, in the 'Book of Martyrs,' alludes to this quarrel and reconciliation, and adduces it as a proof of Cranmer's mild and forgiving temper. The word shrewd has now lost nearly all its bad significance, but it still conveys the impression that shrewdness is not always allied with honour and honesty. The term 'sagacity,' which is almost synonymous, is free from the implied want of conscientiousness contained in the word shrewd.

Shrewsbury is a corruption of the Anglo-Saxon *Scrobbesbyrig*—Shrub-borough.

Shrub and **Sherbet** are both derived from the Oriental word *sherab*, a sort of wine or liquor.

Shunt. The verb to shunt, as applied to the shifting of railway carriages from one line of rails to another, is generally thought to be of modern origin. It is, however, an Old English word. In a rare old ballad, mentioned in Strype's 'Life of Cranmer,' the word 'shunted' occurs. The writer is describing how, hearing the sound of the worship of a congregation of the Reformed faith, he was alarmed and hid himself—

> Then I drew me down into a dale wheras the dumb deer
> Did shiver for a shower but I *shunted* from a freyke.

In Sewell's 'English and Dutch Dictionary,' 1766, the Dutch word 'schuiven' is defined as follows—' To *shunt* (a country word for to shove)'; and in Surrey it is common to hear in a school, when one boy has pushed the elbow of another while writing, and so caused distortion of a letter or word, 'Please, sir, Smith shunted me.' It probably was first applied in its present meaning by some railway employé. It is a common word in Lancashire, signifying to shift, to move. Thus it is said of a thing that requires moving, 'Shunt it a bit that way,' or 'Shunt it at the other end.'

Sick. The Americans retain the use of this word in the sense in which it is employed in the English Prayer-book, 'All *sick* persons'; and in the Bible, 'The whole need not a physician, but they that are *sick*.' In the modern English signification of the word, Americans use the term vomit or some of its compounds.

Side-saddle. 'Queen Anne, wife of Richard II., first taught English women to ride on side-saddles, when, as heretofore, they rid astride.'—*Remains concerning Britain*, 1614.

Sidesman. 'A sidesman is an assistant churchwarden. The word is a corruption of synods-man.'—*Dr. Hook.*

Sidewalk. The Americans use this term for a footpath or pavement.

Siege. This French word, meaning *seat*, was formerly much used in England in the same sense. Shakespeare, in 'Measure for Measure' (act iv. sc. 2), speaks of the 'very *siege* of justice.' Spenser ('Faerie Queene,' II. ii. 39) has:

> Drawing to him the eies of all around
> From lofty *siege* began these words to sownd.

Siege is still used by glass makers as the name of the platform or seat in their furnaces upon which the melting-pots stand.

Sierra. This is a Spanish word signifying a saw. Its application to ranges of mountains, whose peaks, rising in succession, as do those of the Sierra Nevada, resemble the teeth of a saw, is peculiarly picturesque and poetical.

Siesta. This Spanish term for a nap in the daytime has become completely naturalised in England. The Spanish nap is usually taken about noon, which in their reckoning is the *sixth hour* (*sesta*). Hence in Spanish *sestéar* is to take the mid-day nap; and *sesteador* is the room appropriated to the purpose, usually on the north side of the house.

Signature in Printing. This term refers to the system of placing letters at the bottom of the first page of each sheet of a book to simplify the arrangement of the various sheets in forming a volume. The letters J, V, and W are not used, those letters having been introduced since the first use of *signatures*. The first sheet of matter in a book usually has the signature B, A being reserved for title, preface, &c. After the alphabet is exhausted, printers begin it again, generally as A A, A *a*, or A 2. If a third series is required A 3 is used, and so on as far as it may be necessary to go. Some printers in using the second alphabet put the figure before the letter, as 2 A.

Signing with a ×. Persons who cannot write their names are required to use as a substitute the *sign* of the cross (×). Anciently kings and nobles used the same *sign*, but not ignorantly, as it was used by those who could, as well as by those who could not write, as a symbol that the person making it pledged himself by his Christian faith to the truth of the matter to which he affixed it. Hence, although people now *write* or *subscribe* their names, they are still said to *sign*.

Sile. In some old cookery books we are told to 'soil the milk before using it.' This at first sight appears to be a curious direction. If, however, we use the correct modern orthography of the first word, we shall find that we are to 'sile' it; that is, to pass it through a fine sile or sieve in order that it shall be freed from hairs or other impurities.

Silhouettes, the cheap profile portraits which were so much in vogue before the introduction of photography, were so called after Étienne de Silhouette, the French Finance Minister in 1759. His extreme parsimony in all matters of finance was caricatured on all sides, and any cheap mode or fashion was sarcastically called by his name. About that time these profiles were produced by projecting, by means of the light of a candle, the shadow of a face, which was traced while the sitter was in position. These, because they were cheap, were called, in ridicule of the Minister, 'Silhouettes,' and the name has been retained ever since.

Silk Mercer. The word mercer in this term is another form of the word merchant.

Silkworms. The first silkworms seen in Europe were brought from China, in the year 552 of our era, by two Persian monks who had gone thither as Christian missionaries, and who managed to secrete a number of the eggs in a cane and to escape with them to Constantinople. From these few eggs have sprung all the successive generations of the insect which has supplied silk to Europe from that period to the present day.

Silly. This word has become completely changed in its signification. It is the modern form of the Anglo-Saxon word *sælig*, or blessed. One of the early English poets calls the infant Saviour, 'This harmless *silly* babe.' The word gradually changed; its meaning was first altered to *innocent*, then to *simple* in the best sense, and finally to its present signification. In Scotland it means sickly or weakly.

Silver Plating. Horace Walpole, in a letter to Mr. Montagu, dated September 1, 1760, says: 'As I went to Lord Strafford's I passed through Sheffield. . . . One man there has discovered the art of plating copper with silver. I bought a pair of candlesticks for two guineas that are quite pretty.'

Simon Pure. In Mrs. Centlivre's comedy, 'A Bold Stroke for a Wife,' there is a *real* and a *pretended* Simon Pure. In act v. sc. 1, they are both figuring at the same time in the house of Obadiah Prim.

Simon the Cellarer. On the title-page of this celebrated song, published by Addison and Hodson in 1847, it is stated that the words are by W. H. Bellamy, Esq., and the music by J. L. Hatton. The latter used to sing it at concerts.

Simple, from the Latin *sine*, without, and *plica*, a fold. 'Simple' implies want of knowledge; 'silly' or 'foolish' implies want of sense. We say a simple child, a silly speech, a foolish person.

Simplon. The Simplon is a road over the Alps, constructed by Napoleon in 1801-7. It occupied thirty to forty thousand men for six years in its construction.

Simulation 'is a pretence of what is not, and dissimulation a concealment of what is.'—*Sir R. Steele.*

Sine die (pronounced si-ne di-e) is a Latin term, literally meaning *without a day*. In English a postponement or adjournment 'sine die' means that no day is fixed for the resumption of the subject or for reassembling.

Sine quâ non (pronounced si-ne kwa non) is a Latin phrase; literally, *without which not*. It is used to signify some indispensable condition, as, Breathing is a *sine quâ non* of living.

Sing Old Rose and burn the Bellows. 'Old Rose' was evidently a popular song in days long gone by, for dear old Izaak Walton makes one of his characters say, 'Let's sing Old Rose'; but why 'burn the bellows'? A writer in 'Notes and Queries' suggests that the words are probably *et burn libellos*, from a jovial University version of 'Dulce Domum' (*libellos*, books).

Singular. This word formerly had the meaning of being alone. Wycliff's translation of Mark iv. 10 is, 'When he was *singular*.'

Sinister. This word means on the *left*, or to the *left*. Shakespeare says, 'His *sinister* cheek.' In heraldry 'sinister' is the left side of a shield. As the shield is supposed to be carried in front of the person who bears it, the sinister side is that which covers the bearer's left side. A 'bend sinister' is a *band* passing diagonally across the shield, from the top on the right to the base on the left, *as seen by a spectator*. It is supposed to have been used as a mark of illegitimacy, and its diminutive, a bâton sinister, was actually so used, as in the case of several of Charles II.'s children. Hence, 'He bears the bend sinister' is another way of expressing 'He is illegitimate.'

Sir. The title 'Sir' was formerly prefixed to the name of every person in holy orders. '*Dominus*, the academical title of Bachelors of Arts, was usually rendered by "Sir" in English, so that a Bachelor who in the books stood *Dominus* Brown was in conversation called *Sir* Brown. . . . As most clerical persons had taken that first degree, it became usual to call them "Sir."'— *Nares*.

Sirloin, properly written *surloin*, is from the French *surlonge*; *sur*, upon or above, and *longe*. loin. Dr. Johnson was the first lexicographer who spelt it with the letter *i*. He was probably misled by the tradition of the loin of beef having been knighted by James I. Mr. Roby, in his 'Traditions of Lancashire,' says that when James I. was entertained at Hoghton Tower, near Blackburn, 'he was more witty in his speech than usual. Some of his sayings have been recorded, and amongst the rest the well-known quibble, which has been the origin of an absurd mistake, still current through the country, respecting the surloin. The occasion was thus:—Whilst he sat at meat, casting his eyes upon a noble surloin at the lower end of the table, he called out, "Bring hither that surloin, sirrah, for 'tis worthy of a more honourable post, being, as I may say, not *sur*loin, but *sir*loin, the noblest joint of all," which ridiculous and desperate pun raised the wisdom and reputation of England's Solomon to the highest.' In 'Queen Elizabeth's Progresses,' one of the items mentioned under date March 31, 1573, is a 'sorloyne of byf, vi*s*.'

Sir Matthew Wood. The first baronetcy conferred by Queen Victoria was given in 1837 to Matthew Wood, who had been Lord Mayor of London in 1816 and 1817. It was understood that the baronetcy was bestowed as an acknowledgment of his exertions in favour of Queen Caroline, the unfortunate Queen of George IV.

Six and eightpence. The lawyers' fees 3*s*. 4*d*. and 6*s*. 8*d*. were fixed when money was reckoned by pounds, marks, and nobles—6*s*. 8*d*. is a noble, or the third of a pound; 3*s*. 4*d*. is half a noble, or the sixth of a pound. The noble was so called because it was made of gold, the noble metal. The half-noble was generally spoken of as 'ten groats.' Thus, in 'All's Well,' act ii. sc. 2, Shakespeare has—

As fit as *ten groats* is for the hand of an attorney.

Sixes and sevens. This phrase is of considerable antiquity. Shakespeare and Bacon use it, and their example has been followed by Arbuthnot and Swift. Many speculations as to its origin have been made. Some have thought it an allusion to Job's troubles (Job v. 19); others think it is in some way connected with six working days out of the seven days in a week; and the editor of 'Notes and Queries' connects it with the proverbially unlucky number thirteen. Nares (p. 467) thinks it was originally 'taken from the game of tables or backgammon, in which to leave single men exposed to the throws of *six* or *seven* is to leave them negligently, and under the greatest hazard, since there are more chances for throwing those numbers than for any other.'

Sizar. A *sizar* is a student at Cambridge or Dublin who is admitted upon lower terms of cost than others. A 'size' is the portion of food allotted to such students. Hence the name.

Sizes of Painters' Canvas. Certain sizes of canvas are kept by artists' colourmen ready for use. The most usual sizes are *kit-cat*, which is 36 inches by 28; *three-quarters*, 30 by 25; *half-length*, 50 by 40; *Bishop's half-length*, 56 by 45; *Bishop's whole length*, 94 by 58.

Sizes of Paper.

Drawing and Writing Papers	Length	Breadth	Printing Papers	Length	Breadth
	In.	In.		In.	In.
Emperor	66	47	Imperial	30	22
Antiquarian	53	31	Double Crown	30	20
Double Elephant	40	26¾	Super-royal	28	20
Atlas	34	26	Double Foolscap	27	17
Colombier	34½	23½	Royal	25	20
Imperial	30	22	Demy	22½	17¾
Elephant	28	23			
Super-royal	27	19			
Royal	24	19	Cartridge Papers		
Medium	22	17½	Double Demy	35½	22½
Demy	20	15½	Imperial	30	22
Large Post	20¾	16½	Double Crown	30	20
Copy	20	13	Elephant	28	23
Post	18¾	15¼	Cartridge	26	21½
Foolscap	17	13½	Royal	25	20
Pott	15	12½	Demy	22½	17¾
Double Demy	35½	22½	Copy	20	16½

Skedaddle. This word is generally thought to be an Americanism, but it has been long commonly used in Scotland in the sense of spilling, as, 'You will *skedaddle* that milk.' The American use of the word has, however, classical authority; the Greek word *skedannumi* means 'to retire tumultuously,' which is very near to the significance of the American phrase 'to skedaddle.'

Skirmish. Verstegan throws some light upon the disputed etymology of this word. He says in his 'Anglo-Saxon Glossary,' ' *Scrumebre,* or *scrimbre,* a fencer; *scirmung,* fencing or defending. Our word *scirmish,* which we have from the French, cometh originally here-hence.'—*Restitution, &c.* p. 182.

Skull or **Scull** is an Old English word for a drinking-cup, a bowl or dish. The Scotch have a word, *skoll,* and the Danish, *skaal,* of the same meaning. Our Anglo-Saxon forefathers are often described—by writers not acquainted with the ancient use of the word—as almost demoniacal because they drank out of *skulls.* The word 'scullery' is from this root; a scullery is a place where 'sculls,' that is, dishes, bowls, &c., are washed. A 'scullion' is one who washes or cleans these vessels.

Sky. Originally. the word sky meant a cloud. Chaucer says :—

> And let a certain winde goe
> That blew so hideously and hie
> That it ne lefte not a *skie*
> In all the *welkin* long and brode.

'Sky' is the present Swedish word for cloud. But see WELKIN.

Slade. A slade is a wooded valley, from the Anglo-Saxon *slæd*. Drayton uses the word frequently in his 'Polyolbion.' At page 938 of xiv. he has—

> Down the deeper *slades*;

and in ii. p. 690—

> And satyrs, that in *slades* and gloomy dimbles dwell.

A beautifully wooded glade in the park at Sutton Coldfield in Warwickshire is called 'Gum Slade.' It is said to be the place from which Shakespeare drew his pictures of sylvan scenery for the 'Midsummer Night's Dream.'

Slander is *spoken* defamatory matter, in contradistinction to libel, which must be *written or printed.*

> Slanderous tongues, and libellous pens.

Slave. The word is derived from the *Slavi*, or Sclavonians, who were reduced to servitude by the Germans. Gibbon says, 'The national appellation of the *Slaves* has been degraded by chance or malice from the signification of glory (*slava, laus, gloria*) to that of servitude.' The term, in its modern sense of a captive servant, came into use first in the eighth century.

Slavery in England. Up to the year 1772 slaves were bought and sold openly in England. One Matthew Dyer in 1756 advertised 'Silver Padlocks for Dogs and Blacks'; and the 'London Advertiser' of that year contains the following :—'To be sold, a Negro Boy, about 14 years old, warranted free from any distemper, and has had those fatal to that colour; has been used two years to all kinds of Household work and to wait at Table; his price is 25*l.*, and would not be sold but the person he belongs to is leaving off business. Apply to the Bar of the George Coffee-house in Chancery Lane, over against the gate.' In a manuscript diary kept by Sir John Phillips of Picton Castle, the fifth baronet, are the following entries :—'1761, Nov. 8—Went to Norbiton with Capt. Parr and Lieut. Rees, taking with me a black boy from Senegal, given me by Capt. Parr. Dec. 6—Dr. Phillips christened my black boy Cæsar; gave his gossips [sponsors] 7*s.* 6*d.*' On May 4, 1763, one John Rice was hanged at Tyburn for forgery. In an account of his execution published at the time it is said, 'A commission of bankruptcy was taken out against Rice, his effects were sold by auction, and among the rest his negro boy.' The 'Stamford Mercury' of November 30, 1771, records that 'at a late sale of a gentleman's effects at Richmond, a negro boy was put up and sold for 32*l.*,' and adds, 'A shocking instance in a free country.' This was probably the last sale of the kind in England. In 1772 a judgment of the Court of King's Bench decided that slavery could not exist *in England.* The act for the manumission of West Indian slavery, on payment of 20,000,000*l.* to the slaveholders, was passed on August 28, 1833, by the first Reformed Parliament. The total abolition of slavery in the United States was officially announced December 18, 1865.

Sleeve. 'To laugh in one's sleeve is to laugh unperceived or secretly, as behind the sleeve when it was worn long and pendent.'—*South.* 'To pin or hang on a sleeve is an allusion to the custom of wearing a token of faith or of love on the sleeve, and swearing to maintain it.'—*Hooker.*

Sling. A sling is an American drink composed of equal parts of spirit and water. A *rum sling* is, accordingly, half rum and half water. Probably the original of sling was the diminutive ' ling,' as in duckling. A *ginling* would in that case mean a small or weakened glass of gin. This, it is but right to say, is altogether conjectural.

Smart Chance. Smart chance, smart piece, smart sprinkle, are American provincialisms implying a good deal or a large quantity. It is an Old English form of speech. In the villages round Guildford in Surrey, fifty years ago, a 'smart lot' was the usual expression for a good many. A 'smart lot of apples' and similar phrases were very common, and may possibly still survive.

Smith. Verstegan ('Restitution,' &c. p. 183) has, 'SMITHE, to smite : hereof cometh our name of a smith, because he *smitheth* or *smiteth* with a hammer. Before we had the [word] carpenter from the French, a carpenter in our language was also called a smith, for that be smiteth both with his ax and his hammer, and for distinction the one was called a wood smith and the other an iron smith, which is nothing improper.' Verstegan was right ; the term smith is properly applied to all such artificers as use a hammer. A few instances are goldsmith, silversmith, coppersmith, tinsmith, whitesmith, locksmith, anchorsmith, and the typical smith, the blacksmith. The surname Smith is, of course, derived from the occupation of the original holders of the name. See SURNAMES.

Smithfield is a corruption of *Smooth*field. Smithfield in London has been a market for seven hundred years. FitzStephen, in the twelfth century, describes it as a 'plain field where every Friday there is a celebrated rendezvous of fine horses brought thither to be sold.'

Smollett's History. Smollett says in his 'History of England' that the Ancient Britons 'sowed no corn, and lived in cottages thatched with straw.' Query—Where did they get the straw?

Smyth (as a surname). Anciently many persons used the double *i* in spelling the name of Smith. The double *i*, as may still be seen in physicians' prescriptions, was written *ij*. This form, in time, having the dots omitted, became the *y* as we see it in Smyth or Smythe.

Snapdragon. The name of this game, so popular at Christmas-time, is probably derived from the German *schnappes*, ardent spirit, and *drache*, dragon.

Sneak. This word is allied to snake. A sneaking fellow is called 'a snake in the grass.' The word, in the sense of creeping slily, prying, pilfering, &c., is common to all the Northern languages of Europe. In the Anglo-Saxon it was *snican*, to creep; in the Old Norse *snikja*, to spunge or seek meanly after entertainment; in the Swiss *schnaken*, to creep; in the Gaelic *snaig*, to crawl, to sneak; in the Irish *snaighim*, to crawl; and in the Danish *snage*, to snuff about, to rummage. In all these languages the meaning expressed is exactly equivalent to the English slang term, *an area sneak*, one who sneaks around houses to see what he can pick up, honestly or otherwise.

Sneezing. The custom of saying 'God bless you!' to one who sneezes, takes its rise from the plague of sneezing in the year 558, when persons, apparently in good health, were suddenly attacked by fits of sneezing which proved fatal.

Snip, cutting with scissors or shears. This word is never used for cutting with one blade, as with a knife. It is probably derived from the Anglo-Saxon *snippe* or *snibbe*, the bill of a bird.

Snob (see NOB). In some of the college lists those who are not of noble birth are entered as *s. nob.*, that is, *sine nobilitate*. The word *snob*, which Thackeray has grafted on the English language, probably thus originated.

Snooks. This surname is a corruption of Sevenoaks. Messrs. Sharp and Harrison, of Southampton, solicitors, have or had in their possession some deeds belonging to a family named Snooks, in which the name is variously spelt, from 'Sevenokes,' through 'S'nokes' and 'Snokes,' to the present orthography.

Snow. Sir James Hogg, the Chairman of the Metropolitan Board of Works, stated in the House of Commons that the weight of the snow which fell on January 18, 1881, in the metropolitan area was 8¾ millions of tons. This is more than two tons for each inhabitant in the district.

Snow-covered Mountains. The names of the principal mountains in the world are nearly all suggestive or descriptive of their snow-covered summits. 'The names of Snowdon, Ben Nevis, Mont Blanc, the Sierra Nevada in Spain, Snafell in Iceland and in the Isle of Man, the Sneeuw Bergen at the Cape of Good Hope, the Sneehatten in Norway, Sneekoppe in Bohemia, and the Weisshorn, the Weissmies, and the Tête Blanche in Switzerland, as well as the more archaic or more obscure names of Lebanon, of Caucasus, and of the Himalayas, are appellations descriptive in various languages of the characteristic snowy covering of their lofty summits.'—*Taylor's Words and Places.* London, 1864.

Snuffers are first mentioned in Exodus xxv. 38, which in the early editions of the Bible is rendered: 'The snuffers and snuffedishes thereof shalbe of pure golde.'

Soap. Pliny mentions soap, and states that it was first discovered by the Gauls. It is also mentioned in Jeremiah ii. 22: 'For though thou wash thee with natron, and take thee much sope, yet thine iniquity is marked before me.'

Soap-bubble. 'The gorgeous tints of colour seen in the soap-bubble are due to the interference of rays of light reflected from its inner and outward surfaces. The thickness of the soap-bubble is the 600,000th part of an inch.'—*Young.*

Sock and Buskin. Sock was the name given to the shoes formerly worn by comedians. Buskins were high-heeled shoes worn by tragedians, to give them an appearance of greater height—

> Great Fletcher never treads in *buskins* here,
> Nor greater Jonson dares in *socks* appear.—*Dryden.*

Sodor and Man. The Isle of Man and the Hebrides were formerly parts of the kingdom of Norway. The Hebrides were then called by the Norsemen the '*Sudrejar*,' or the Southern Islands. There was a Bishop of Man, and another of the *Sudrejar*, which became united in the eleventh century. The name '*Sodor*' is the modern equivalent for the ancient *Sudrejar*, but the islands have long been without a bishop except in name.—*J. Taylor.*

Soft Sawder. This is a corruption of the term *soft solder*, which is a cheap imitation of real solder, used in the manufacture of low-priced articles of metal, which are afterwards electroplated and sold as 'plated' goods. Hence 'soft sawder' means deception or 'humbug.'

Soil. 'To take soil' was a hunting term formerly in use to signify the hunted game taking to the water. It is in frequent use by the old poets, as the following examples will show :—

> The stately deer
> Doth beat the brooks and ponds for sweet refreshing *soil*.
> *Drayton, Polyolbion,* xiii. p. 917.

> As when a chaséd hind her course doth bend
> To seek by *soil* to find some ease or good.—*Fairfax, Tasso,* vi. 109.

> Fida went down the dale to seeke the hind,
> And found her *taking soyle* within the flood.
> *Browne, British Pastorals,* i. 84.

Solan Goose is the 'Solent' goose, so called from Solent, an ancient name for the whole of the English Channel, which these birds formerly frequented in enormous numbers.

Solicit. This word originally meant to disturb or disquiet. Milton says: '*Solicit* not thy thoughts.' The word afterwards signified to seek to acquire, or to try to obtain. Gibbon says: 'To *solicit* by labour what might be ravished by arms was esteemed unworthy of the German spirit.'

Solidarity. This word was introduced into English by Kossuth. The French equivalent, *solidarité*, appeared for the first time in a speech of Cazotte, in which he foretold the downfall of the French monarchy and the decapitation of Louis XVI.

Somersault. This word should never be spelled or pronounced as though it were written *somerset*. It comes from the Latin *supra*, above, and *saltus*, a leap.

So much to boot. Verstegan says this is 'bote,' but he adds 'we now write it boot. It is a yeelding of amends or supplying a defect.'—*Restitution,* p. 164, edit. 1655.

Son of St. Louis, ascend to Heaven. This phrase is generally believed to have been used by the Abbé Edgeworth, the confessor of Louis XVI., at the instant the axe fell which deprived that ill-fated monarch of his head. The Abbé always said he did not use the words, and it is now known that the phrase was invented for him by the editor of 'Le Républicain Français.'

'**Song of the Shirt.**' The fine line in this immortal poem,

> It is not linen you're wearing out, but human creatures' lives,

appears to have been suggested by a speech of Maggie Mucklebackit in the 'Antiquary,' ch. xi.: 'It's no fish ye're buying; it's men's lives.'

Sooth. This word, as a noun, originally meant truth, verity, reality. Words of 'sooth' meant truthful words; and a 'soothsayer' was one who spoke truthfully. The adjective 'sooth' came by degrees to mean pleasant, kindly, trustworthy; and the verb *to soothe* in its modern sense was finally retained, while both the noun and the adjective have become obsolete. Chaucer uses the word *soote* in the sense of sweet.

Sorry, Sorrow. These two words are not related. Sorry is the Anglo-Saxon *sárig*, from *sár*, a sore or wound. Sorrow is the Anglo-Saxon *sorh*, the German *sorge*, care, anxiety, grief.

Sorter is a slang expression not uncommon among the lower classes in America. It is sometimes used in connection with KINDER (which see), as 'kinder sorter,' which, translated into ordinary English, means 'a kind of sort of,' e.g. 'They had with them a long-legged chap, a *kinder sorter* lawyer'; meaning they had some one with them who had a little knowledge of law, and who was, consequently, looked upon as a *kind of*, or *sort of*, lawyer.

Southernwood (*Artemisia abrotanum*), sometimes called 'old man.' The name southernwood is a corruption of the Old English name *suthe-wort*, or soothing-wort, the name given to it from its supposed soothing or soporific qualities.

Sovereign. The root of this word is the Latin *supremus*, which itself is derived from *supra*, above. The Italians changed the *p* into *v*, and the word *supra* in their language became *sovra*. Our word is compounded of the Italian *sovra*, and the Latin *regno*, to govern. The name 'sovereign' was first applied to a coin in the reign of Henry VIII., who issued a gold coin so called in which the King was represented in the royal robes. The name was afterwards in abeyance until 1817, when it was revived and applied to the coin, value 20s., which in that year superseded the guinea.

Sow, Sew. The erroneous expression *sewn* is often heard, and is even occasionally seen in print. The past participle of the verb to sow (seed) is *sown*, but the past participle of the verb to sew (cloth) is, properly, *sewed*.

Soy is made by the Japanese from a kind of bean similar in shape to the kidney bean. They are first softened by boiling, then mixed with an equal quantity of wheat or barley roughly ground. The mixture is then covered up and put for twenty-four hours into a warm place to ferment. Then salt, equal in quantity to the other ingredients, is added; water is poured over it, and it is stirred daily for two months, after which the liquor is poured off, strained, and preserved in casks for use or export.

Spade. 'Call a spade a spade.'—This saying is not of modern origin. Burton, in the preface to his 'Anatomy of Melancholy,' says, 'I drink no wine at all, which so much improves our modern wits; a loose, plain, rude writer, *I call a spade a spade*, I respect *matter*, not words.' The phrase is also used by Richard Baxter in his 'Narrative,' 1696.

Span. A *span* of horses in America is a pair of horses, alike in size and colour, used to draw a carriage. It is the height of ambition with American gentlemen to possess horses that *span* well— that is, agree in size, colour, and action. The origin of the term is not known; there is nothing analogous in English dictionaries or glossaries.

Spaniel. The breed of dogs so called came from *Hispaniola* in the West Indies; hence the name.

Sparables, sometimes written 'sperables,' are small thick nails driven into the soles and heels of boots and shoes to prevent too rapid wear. They were formerly made of cast iron, and were of the shape of an elongated pyramid, growing gradually thicker from the point. They are now cut from sheet iron, and although they grow *wider* from the point, they are of the same *thickness* throughout. The etymology is so obvious that it is strange that the dictionary-makers have missed it. This word is really *sparrow-bill*, and it is derived from the similarity of the shape of the cast-iron originals to the bill or beak of the sparrow.

Spare the rod and spoil the child. This saying is frequently erroneously attributed to Solomon. It is, however, from 'Hudibras,' and is to be found in Part II. canto. 1, verse 45. What Solomon really did say was, 'He that spareth the rod hateth his son' (Proverbs xiii. 24).

Sparrow. The bird called sparrow in the English translation of the Bible is a species of thrush; the English sparrow is not known in the East.

Sparse. This word has been said to be an Americanism, but it is not so. It is an Old English word, and is to be found as a verb in the past tense in 'Sternhold and Hopkins' Psalms,' A.D. 1611. The 10th verse of the 44th Psalm is paraphrased thus:—

> Thou mad'st us fly before our foes
> And so were over-trod,
> Our enemies rob'd and spoyl'd our goods
> When we were *spars't* abroad.

This evidently points to the word *disperse* (which in country places is usually pronounced as though written disparse) as the origin of *sparse*. Anything dispersed or scattered would of course be *sparsely* localised.

Speak by the Card. *Card* was the original name for the mariner's compass. Shakespeare ('Macbeth' i. 3) has—

> All the quarters that they know
> I' the shipman's *card*.

Hence to 'speak by the card' meant to speak with absolute correctness, true to a single point.

Speaker's Eye. The rule in the House of Commons is that the member whose rising to address the House is first observed by the Speaker shall be allowed precedence. At all other times the members are known by the names of the places they represent, as 'the right honourable member for Derby,' &c., but when called upon by the Speaker he names them, as 'Mr. Gladstone,' &c. The custom of leaving the Speaker to call on the members originated on November 26, 1640, when, a number of members rising together, 'the confusion became intolerable.' At last 'the House determined for Mr. White, and the Speaker's eye was adjudged to be evermore the rule.'

Specie, probably from *pecie*, gold or silver coined into *pieces* of uniform weight and form. The word *pecie* is used in the Exchequer Records, e.g., 'Sex *pecie* ponderum de plumbo' (i. 137).

Specific Names for Tea. Hyson means 'before the rain,' or 'flourishing spring'; Young Hyson is merely surplusage; Bohea is the name of the hills among which it is grown; Pekoe means 'white hair,' or the down of tender leaves; Souchong, small plant; Twankay is the name of a river in the region where it is grown; Congo, which is misspelt Congou, means labour, and is expressive of the extra care taken in its preparation.

Spectacles. An early, perhaps the earliest, mention of spectacles, or, in the language of that time, 'a spectacle,' occurs in Chaucer, where the Wife of Bath says—

> Povert [poverty] ful often when a man is lowe
> Maketh himself his God, and eke himself to knowe
> Povert *a spectacle* is, as thinketh me,
> Through which he may his verray frendes se.

Speech. 'Speech is silver, silence is golden.'—This is a Dutch proverb, 'Spreken is zilver, zwijgen is goud.' 'Speech was given to man to disguise his thoughts.'—Talleyrand usually gets credit for the authorship of this *bon mot*; it is really by Voltaire.

Speed of Ships at Sea. The speed of a ship at sea is reckoned by *knots*, each knot being a geographical mile. Six geographical miles are about equal to seven statute English miles, so that a ship making twelve 'knots' an hour is actually travelling at the rate of fourteen statute miles. The speed is ascertained by means of the log-line, which is a cord knotted at equal distances of 51 feet; 120 of these lengths are equal to a geographical mile. At one end of this line the 'log,' which is a piece of flat, light wood, generally triangular in shape, weighted along one edge, is attached, much in the same way as a boy fastens his kite to the string, so that it floats vertically, with its flat surface presented to the ship. When thrown overboard, and the line allowed to pass over the stern freely, the log meets with so little resistance that theoretically it remains stationary. The number of knots in the cord being equal to the number of half-minutes in an hour, it follows that as many 'knots' of the line as pass over the stern of the vessel every half-minute, so many geographical miles or *knots* are being 'made' by the ship in an hour.

Spencer, the name applied to a coat without tails, arose in reference to a former Earl Spencer, who wore one to decide a wager that he would make such a garment fashionable. He won his bet, for spencers as outer coverings over the coat were universally adopted.

Sperate, from the Latin *spero, speratus,* to hope. This is an excellent word, though but little used. It means to hope reasonably. It is the exact opposite of desperate.

Spermaceti is a crystalline fat found in the head of the sperm whale (*Cetodon macrocephalus*). It differs from ordinary fats in not containing glycerine, and in solidifying in semi-transparent crystals of pearly whiteness.

Spic and span new (Dutch *spikspelderniew*, fresh from the hands of the workman, chip and splinter new; German *span*, chip, splinter, fragment). The term was originally applied to a boat. Spike or spic is a nail, and span—pronounced spaun or spawn—is a chip thrown off in shaping timber to form a boat. The full meaning therefore is, 'Every nail and every chip of timber in this boat is entirely new, it is spike-and-spaun new.'

Spider. This insect is so named from spinning his web, the letter *n* being dropped. In Dutch the name is *spin*; in German *spinne*; in Swedish *spinnel*; and in Old English *spither*. Such is the size of the spiders in Ceylon that Sir James E. Tennent says 'their webs, stretched from tree to tree, are so strong as to cause a painful check across the face when moving quickly against them, and more than once in riding I have had my hat lifted off by a single thread.'

Spilling the Salt. The popular belief that it is unlucky to spill the salt probably originated from Leonardo da Vinci's picture of the Last Supper, in which Judas Iscariot is represented as spilling the salt. Or Da Vinci may have so painted it to embody in his picture a then popular superstition. A gift of bread and salt was a token of friendship; salt was a sign of amity, so spilling a man's salt may have betokened enmity.

Spinach is from the Arabic word *Hispanach*, the Spanish plant. The first known mention of spinach is in Turner's 'Herbal,' published in 1568, where it is said to be 'an herb lately found, and not much in use.' 'It is a singular fact that the water drained from spinach after being boiled is capable of making as good match-paper [touch-paper] as that made by a solution of nitre.'—*Brand's Dict.*, vol. iii., p. 535.

Spinney, from the Latin *spina*, a thorn or prickle. It is applied to small woods or thickets from their being generally full of thorns and brambles.

Spinning. The earliest known mention of spinning is in Exodus xxxvi. 25, 'And all the women that were wise-hearted did spin with their hands.'

Spinster. 'Formerly it was a rule that a young woman should never be married till she had spun herself a set of body, table, and bed linen. From this custom all unmarried women were called spinsters, an appellation they still retain in all deeds and law proceedings.'—*Pulleyn*. This requires qualification. Spinster is only properly applied to unmarried females *not of gentle rank*. Lord Coke says, 'If a gentlewoman be termed "spinster" she may abate the writ'; yet, *per contra*, heralds compel ladies entitled to armorial bearings, if unmarried, to carry them on a lozenge or *spindle*-shaped shield.

Spire. This word is derived from the name of the sharp seed-leaf of corn that springs from the ground. The word is common in all the Northern languages in the sense of a sharp-pointed shoot of a plant or tree. Chaucer says, 'Out of this ground must come the spire.' Palgrave mentions a 'spyre of corne,' and says 'I spyer [aspire] as corne dothe.' Halliwell gives the meanings—*inter alia*—bud, shoot, sprout. In the Danish *spire* is to germinate, to sprout. The Norwegian word is *spir, spira*, to shoot up, to spring forth.

Spire (of a church). The word spire formerly had the meaning of *summit*. Shakespeare says, 'the spire and top of praises.' In this sense it was used by early builders to designate the roof of the tower of a church. A 'spire' even now is merely a lengthened or heightened roof. See STEEPLE.

Spitchcock (in cooking, as to spitchcock an eel). A fowl killed, cut up, and broiled immediately on an emergency, was called a *spatchcock*, from the word *despatch*. Hence anything cut up and broiled rapidly was said to be *spatch*cooked. This has been corrupted into *spitch*cocked.

Splendid comes from the Latin *splendeo*, to shine. It is often applied in a ridiculous manner, as 'a *splendid* leg of mutton,' '*splendid* oysters,' &c.

Spoil. This word has been greatly changed in its ordinary application. Originally it meant to deprive of, or to steal, and in this sense it is still used in warfare; the goods of an enemy which are seized being still called the *spoil*. It is also so used in Matthew xii. 29, 'How can one enter into the house of a strong man and *spoil* [i.e. steal] his goods?' It is now almost limited in meaning to damaging or rendering useless.

Spoke in his wheel. To 'put a spoke in his wheel' is to thwart or hinder a man in his design. Richardson thinks it meant to put a spike in the nave so as to prevent the wheel from turning. A more probable derivation refers it to a time when wheels were made of solid discs of wood without radiating bars. Such wheels are still in use on Dartmoor for vehicles called 'three-wheeled buts.' There are no shafts, and consequently the horse has no check on the vehicle in descending hills. To remedy this, the front wheel of the three has some holes bored through it, and the speed is checked by putting a stout bar of wood, locally called a *spoke*, through one of the holes, thus effectually blocking it. Mr. Cobden totally misunderstood the meaning of the word. Writing in 1852 as to W. J. Fox's candidature for Oldham, he says, 'If I can put a spoke in Fox's wheel, when in Lancashire, I shall be right glad to do so.'—*Life of Sir Joshua Walmsley.*

Spontaneous Combustion. Liebig, in his 'Familiar Letters on Chemistry,' asserted that 'spontaneous combustion is absolutely impossible, the human frame containing 75 or 80 per cent. of water; and as flesh, when saturated with alcohol, is not consumed upon the application of a light, the alcohol burning off first, the causes assigned to account for the spontaneous ignition are, *à priori*, extremely improbable.'

Spooney. Probably from the custom of nicknaming the lowest junior optime in the mathematical examination at Cambridge University the 'spoon,' and presenting him with a wooden spoon. In archery matches the one who has the lowest score is also rewarded with a spoon of horn or wood.

Spoonful. The plural of this word is *spoonfuls*, and must never be called or written *spoonsfull*.

Spouse. Sir John Stoddart says, 'The English word spouse has been represented as synonymous with a married person, either husband or wife, whereas in truth it signifies a person betrothed but not married. The word comes from the Latin *spondeo*, to promise solemnly.'

S. P. Q. R. These letters, often seen in representations of ancient Roman life, were inscribed on the military standards of the Roman Empire. They are the abbreviated form of the Latin words *Senatus populusque Romanus*, and they mean 'The Senate and the people of Rome.'

Spread Eagle Style of Oratory. A term for a kind of speaking common among American politicians, which is thus defined by a writer in the 'North American Review' for November 1858:—
'A compound of exaggeration, effrontery, bombast, and extravagance, mixed metaphors, platitudes, defiant threats thrown at the world, and irreverent appeals flung at the Almighty.'

Spree. Mr. Wedgwood, in his 'Dictionary of English Etymology,' derives this word from *spry*, nimble, active, alert. It is more probably a contraction of the French *esprit*, spirited; in the same way in which the boys at Westminster School call anything jolly, 'skee,' which they get from the French *exquis*.

Spring Mattrasses were first introduced about the beginning of the nineteenth century. Mr. Crabb Robinson, writing from Marburg in 1802, says, 'I lay on a sofa of *metal rings covered with hair*, the most elastic of couches, and to me quite a novelty.'

Sprite was formerly written *spright*. We still retain this form in the derivative sprightly.

Spruce (as applied to dress). Formerly Spruce meant Prussian, and a Spruce man was a man dressed in the Prussian fashion. 'After them came Sir Edward Hayward, then admiral, and with him Sir Thomas Parre, in doublets of crimson velvet, laced on the breast with chains of silver, and over that short cloaks of crimson satin, and on their heads hats after dancers' fashion, with feathers in them. They were apparelled after the fashion of Prussia, or *Spruce.*'—*Hall.*

Spruce Fir. Pruce was the ancient English name for Prussia, and Spruce meant Prussian. The variety of fir called the *spruce* was originally brought from Prussia; hence the name.

Spry. An American word signifying active, nimble, lively, cheerful, and good-humoured, all combined in one person. The word is very expressive—' Spry as a cricket.'

Squad, a contraction of the word squadron.

Squash, a sort of pumpkin. The American Indians called this plant *ascutaquash*. The settlers adopted only the latter part of the name.

Squirrel. The name of this pretty little animal is derived from the Greek *skiouros*, which is a very descriptive term. It is literally shade-tail.

Stabat Mater. A hymn on the Crucifixion, in Latin, commencing with these words, which signify 'The Mother stood.'

Stage Directions. O. P. means the side of the stage opposite prompter. P. S. means prompter's side.

Stairs. Verstegan tells us that the Anglo-Saxon word *astigha* meant mounting up or climbing, and he gives it as the origin of 'steghers, now stayers,' which is the old form of our word stairs. Up to the time of Elizabeth 'staircases' were constructed on a circular plan round a central axis or newel. They were generally inclosed in turrets or towers (cases) at the angle of buildings.

Square or straight 'flights' of stairs were introduced with Elizabethan architecture.

Stalking-horse. Wild ducks and other aquatic birds take flight upon the sight of man, but take no notice of the approach of a horse. It is therefore customary in the fenny countries to train horses to *stalk*—that is, to walk quietly by the margins of the haunts of the wildfowl, the sportsman walking by their side in such a manner as to be out of the sight of the game. When sufficiently near, he shoots beneath the horse's neck. Metaphorically, a stalking-horse is one who lends himself to others to hide villainy or deceit. The word is occasionally used to signify a disguise put on for evil purposes. Thus—

> A fellow who makes religion his *stalking-horse*,
> He breeds a plague.—*Malcontent, Dodsley,* iv. 79.

Stalwart. This word has a curious origin; it comes from the Anglo-Saxon *stealan*, to steal, and its original form was *stalworth*, that which is worth stealing.

> His *stalworth* steed the champion stout bestrode.—*Fairfax*.

Standing in another's shoes. In an article On Legal Usages amongst the Ancient Northmen, in 'Bayley's Graphic Illustrator,' London, 1834, it is said that 'The right of adoption obtained, one form of it consisted in making the adopted put on the shoes of the adopter. It has been asked whether our phrase of "standing in his shoes" may not owe its origin to this custom.'

Staple in the names of English places always means market, as Dunstable, Whitstable, Barnstaple, &c.

Star-spangled Banner. This term was first applied to the flag of the United States in a poem written by Francis S. Key on the morning after the British attack on Fort McHenry at Baltimore in 1812. The bombardment, which took place during the night, was witnessed by Mr. Key, who with some friends watched with intense anxiety for the return of day. At length the light came, and they saw the American flag still flying from the fort, the attack having failed. In the excitement of the moment he wrote the poem in which the phrase occurs—

> Oh! say, can you see by the dawn's early light
> What so proudly we hailed at the twilight's last gleaming,
> Whose broad stripes and bright stars through the perilous fight,
> O'er the ramparts we watch'd, were so gallantly streaming?
> And the rocket's red glare, the bombs bursting in air,
> Gave proof through the night that our flag was still there;
> Oh! say, does that *star-spangled banner* yet wave
> O'er the land of the free and the home of the brave?

Starch is from the German *starke*, strength, stiffness. We nave the same root in the English stark, stiff with cold, or in death. Starch was first used in England in 1553. It was introduced by a Mrs. Dinghein, a Flemish woman.

Starvation. This word is probably the only one in the English language having an Anglo-Saxon root and a Latin termination. It is not to be found in any of the early dictionaries, and is believed to have been first used by a Mr. Dundas in a debate in the House of Commons on an American question in the year 1775. Horace Walpole says the words used were, 'I shall not wait for the advent of *starvation* from Edinburgh to settle my judgment.'

Starve (Anglo-Saxon *steorfan*). This word originally signified to *die* or *perish* from any cause. Chaucer says the Trojans 'starved' through the strategem of the wooden horse. He also applies the word to the death of Christ upon the Cross. In the South of England it is confined in use to those who die of hunger, but in the North such people are said to be *clemmed*, and one who perishes of cold is said to be *starved*.

Statue of Queen Elizabeth. The statue of Queen Elizabeth, which stands over a doorway of St. Dunstan's Church in Fleet Street, formerly adorned the City gateway, Ludgate, where it escaped injury in the Great Fire. It was placed in its present position about the year 1838.

Steam Navigation. In 1736 Jonathan Hulls took out a patent for a machine for carrying vessels against wind and tide or in a calm. In 1778 Thomas Paine, in America, proposed this application of steam power. In 1789 Symington made a voyage in a steam vessel on the Forth and Clyde Canal, but with little success. He was more fortunate in another attempt in 1802. Soon after this Fulton went to America, where in 1807 he started a steam vessel on the Hudson River, which was absolutely successful, and was followed soon after by hundreds of imitations. The first steam vessel which crossed the Atlantic was the 'Savannah,' of 350 tons, which came from New York to Liverpool in 1819. The 'United Service Journal,' 1830, says: 'The first adoption of steam in the conveyance of the foreign post-office mail has taken place. H.M. steam vessel "Meteor," Lieut. W. H. Symons, left Falmouth on the 5th of February for the Mediterranean. We look upon this as an era in steam navigation which bids fair to introduce its more general adoption for the purposes of government.' The first steam collier arrived in the Thames from Newcastle in September 1852. She ran the distance in forty-eight hours, consumed 28 tons of coal on the voyage, brought 600 tons as cargo, which she discharged in one day, starting on the return voyage the same night.

Steel Pens. In the Diary of Byrom, the inventor of stenography ('Remains,' vol. i. 59), is a letter to his sister, dated August 1723, in which he says, 'Alas! alas! I cannot meet with a steel pen no manner of where. I believe I have asked at 375 places; but that which I have is at your service.' In the Fourth Report of the Royal Commission of Historical Manuscripts (Her Majesty's Stationery Office) a letter is mentioned of the date 1766 which refers to ' the excellent invention of steel pens.' Steel pens did not come into general use until 1829.

Steeplechase. 'The name and the practice of steeplechasing are said to have originated in a party of unsuccessful fox-hunters on their return home agreeing to try a race towards the steeple of a village church, the first who could touch the church with his whip to be the winner.'—*Chambers*.

Steeple, Tower, Spire, Turret. These terms are all applied to a high structure raised above the main edifice. The word *steeple* is *applicable to all the forms*. A *tower* is a square steeple; a *spire* is an elongated covering for a tower, and is really nothing more than an extremely elevated and tapering form of roof. A turret or towerette is a smaller spire, generally placed at an angle of a tower, and forming a roof for a winding staircase.

Stentor. This was the name of a herald mentioned by Homer, whose voice was as powerful as the united voices of fifty men; hence *stentorian*, signifying loudly sounding, powerful.

Step-father. This word, as well as the cognate step-mother step-son, step-daughter are all derived from the Anglo-Saxon *steop*, bereaved. The terms son-*in-law*,' ' mother-*in-law*,' &c. have been incorrectly used in this sense by Dickens and other writers. The form ' in law ' is properly used to designate persons who are connected by the marriage of descendants; not to those who are related by the marriage of parents.

Stepney was St. Stephen's Hithe (hithe, a small harbour). The ' Church Times,' November 25, 1870, says : ' It is curious that all persons born at sea should be parishioners of Stepney.' This belief is altogether erroneous. The question arose in the Court of King's Bench in 1813, and Lord Ellenborough directed the Overseers of

Stepney to indict a Chester magistrate, who had sent a pauper born at sea to Stepney for support under the belief that Stepney was his legal settlement.

Stereotype Printing. William Ged, a printer in Edinburgh, was the inventor of stereotype printing. The first book so printed was an edition of Sallust, published in 1739, and reprinted from the same plates in 1744. In the library of the Literary and Philosophical Society of Newcastle-upon-Tyne is a copy of a book entitled 'Translation of the Report made to the Philotechnic Society of Paris respecting Julius Griffiths, Esq., an English Traveller, by Joseph Lavallee, London. *Stereotyped* and Printed by A. Wilson, Duke Street, Lincoln's Inn Fields, 1804.' The work is dedicated to the Right Honourable the Earl of Buchan. On the fly-leaf in manuscript is, 'To the Literary Society at Newcastle, this early specimen of Stereotype in Britain, from their Ob. hble. Servt. Buchan.' Below this, in a different handwriting, is, 'N.B.—This was the first work stereotyped according to the process of Lord Stanhope, the first book printed at a Stanhope Press, and the first book printed upon machine-made Paper.'

Sterling. This word, according to Camden, is a corruption of the word *easterling*, and was originally applied to money from East Germany, which was greatly esteemed for its purity. In the reign of Richard I. it was usual to stipulate that payment should be made in *nummi easterling*.

Stern, severe. Abbreviated from *austern*, which was the Old English form of austere—

> But who is yond,
> That looketh with sic an *austern* face?—*Percy's Reliques.*

Sterne. Sterne's celebrated words in his 'Sentimental Journey,' 'God tempers the wind to the shorn lamb,' are evidently borrowed from Herbert, who in ' Jacula Prudentum ' (1640), says, ' To a close-shorn sheep God gives wind by measure.'

Steward. A steward is the Anglo-Saxon *stiward*, from *sti*, a house, and *ward*, a guardian or regulator.

Stewing in their own gravy. This historical phrase, applied by Bismarck to the French, was not new, though it may in his case have been original. In the ' London Spy,' published 1716, is a description of a hot-air bath at the Hummums in Covent Garden, in which the writer says, ' He relieved us out of our purgatory, and carried us to our dressing-rooms, which gave us much refreshment after we had been *stewing in our own gravy.*'

Stigmatise, to brand with a mark of infamy by means of a hot iron. Slaves and criminals were formerly branded, or *stigmatised*. A brand mark was called a *stigma*.

Stile. The Anglo-Saxon word *astigha* meant to mount up or climb. Verstegan says that from *astigha* we get ' *stighel*, now of us pronounced stile.'

Still waters run deep. The original of this saying is in ' Hen. VI.,' pt. ii. act iii. sc. 1—

Smooth runs the water where the brook is deep.

Stilton Cheese. This cheese was originally made near Melton Mowbray, in Leicestershire. Its name arose from the fact that it was first brought into notice at a celebrated inn on the great north road, in the parish of Stilton.

Stimulate is from the Latin *stimulus*, a goad or spur; our English word stimulus has the same derivation.

Stink was not originally used to denote disagreeable odours. The Anglo-Saxon *stenc* meant fragrance; *blostman stences* meant fragrant blossoms. In the Old High German *er stinchet suozo* was 'he smells sweet.'

Stingy. This word appears to have originated in the early part of the eighteenth century. It is included in a ' Dictionary of the Terms, Ancient and Modern, of the Canting Crew,' 1710, and is defined as ' covetous, close-fisted, sneaking.' Sir Thomas Brown says, 'I rather think it to be a newly-coined word.' It is probably a corruption of the old Lincolnshire word *skingy*, which is used in the same sense. There was an Anglo-Saxon word *skinch*, to give short measure, to pinch, pare, nip, or to squeeze out in driblets.

Stirrups. The Anglo-Saxon word *astigha* meant to mount up. Verstegan says, ' From *astigha* we derive many words of mounting upwards, as *stigh ropes*, which we now pronounce *stirops*, being first devised with cords and ropes before they were made with leather and iron fastened to it.' ' Stirrups were first used in the fifth century.'—*Haydn*.

Stiver. A stiver is a Dutch coin of the value of one penny. Stivers are also coined at the Royal Mint in London for circulation in the colony of British Guiana. These British stivers are handsome coins, having the bust of the Queen on the obverse, and the words ' one stiver ' within a wreath on the reverse.

Stock. 'In what an almost infinity of senses the word *stock* is employed, We have live *stock*; *stock*-in-trade; the village *stocks*; the *stock* of a gun; the *stock* dove; the *stocks* on which ships are built; the *stock* which goes round the neck; the family *stock*; the *stocks* or public funds in which money is invested; and other *stocks* besides these. What point in common can we find between them all? This—they are all derived from, and were originally the past participle of, *to stick*, which, as it now makes *stuck*, made formerly *stock*, and they cohere in the idea of *fixedness* which is common to them all. Thus the *stock* of a gun is that in which the barrel is fixed; the village *stocks* are those in which the feet are fastened; the *stock*-in-trade is the fixed capital; and so too the *stock* on the farm, although the fixed capital has there taken the shape of horses and cattle; in the *stocks* or public funds money *sticks* fast, inasmuch as those who place it there cannot withdraw the capital, but receive only the interest; the *stock* of a tree is fast set in the ground, and from this use of the word it is transferred to a family; the *stock* or stirps is that from which it grows, and out of which it unfolds itself. And here we may bring in the *stock* dove, as being the *stock* or stirps of the domestic kinds.'—*Trench.*

Stock Exchange. A newspaper of July 15, 1773, has the following paragraph:—'Yesterday the brokers and others at "New Jonathan's" came to a resolution that, instead of its being called "New Jonathan's," it should be called "The Stock Exchange," which is to be wrote over the door. The brokers then collected sixpence each and christened the house with punch.' 'On the Stock Exchange there are two distinct classes, viz. the brokers and the jobbers. It is the business of the brokers to receive orders from merchants, bankers, or private individuals. The jobbers hold themselves ready to act upon the orders received by the brokers. For instance, if a broker has to do business in 5,000*l*. Consols (the market price being about 90), the jobber offers to buy his 5,000*l*. at 90, or to sell him that amount at $90\frac{1}{8}$, without being aware whether the broker wishes to buy or sell; thus taking upon himself the risk of selling that which he does not possess, or of buying that which he does not intend to keep, his only object being to undo his bargain at a difference of $\frac{1}{8}$ per cent. or even less, with another broker who may have to effect an operation the very reverse of the other, which $\frac{1}{8}$ or even $\frac{1}{16}$ constitutes his profit.'—*Times.*

Stockings. Originally the clothing of the lower part of a man's body was a single garment called *hose*. For convenience sake this garment was afterwards divided at the knee, forming knee-breeches, or, as they were originally called, *upper-stocks* and *nether-stocks*, or stockings. The word hosier perpetuates the ancient name, and the word *hose* is always used by dealers to mean stockings. 'Knit stockings were first brought into England by William Rider in 1564, from Italy. Wove stockings were first devised by William Lee, of St. John's College, Cambridge, in 1599.'—*Bailey's Dictionary.*

Stockjobber. Macaulay says that this word was first used in London about the year 1688.

Stock, lock, and barrel. This expression is proverbial in the Midland Counties of England in the sense of *the whole*, or *complete in every part*. It no doubt originated in Birmingham amongst the gun-makers, where it meant all the parts belonging to a gun. Mr. Bartlett inserts it in his 'Glossary' as an Americanism, but it has been in use in Birmingham for more than a century. It is used comprehensively, as in the case of a man giving up farming, who advertised his stock as 'Horses, cows, sheep, pigs, poultry, carts, ploughs, harrows, and every thing about the place, *stock, lock, and barrel.*'

Stocks. The stocks as a means of punishment are nearly obsolete, but they are still to be seen in some remote villages. A moveable set is in existence at Lichfield, where they have been used within a very few years as a punishment for drunkards. They are kept at the town hall, and when in use are placed in front of that building so that the offender may be seen, a policeman being in attendance to preserve order.

Stoic. This comes from a Greek word signifying a *porch*, in allusion to the *portico* where Zeno, the founder of the *Stoics*, and his successors taught their disciples the peculiar tenets of the Stoical philosophy.

Stoke in the names of places signifies a wood—for example, Stoke Newington means the *new* village or town (*ton*, a house or collection of houses) built by the side of a wood. It is on record that in the time of the Commonwealth there were still upwards of seventy-five acres of woodland in the parish. Some authorities, however, derive the name Stoke from a stockaded place, or a place where a *weir* crosses a stream.

Stole. An undress robe formerly worn by the Kings of England was so called. The first Lord of the Bedchamber in the Royal Household is still called the *Groom of the Stole.*

Stone Jug. This is not so absurd a name for a gaol as many suppose. The Greek word κέραμος signifies both an earthen jug and a gaol. Homer uses it in both senses (Iliad, v. 387 and ix. 469).

Stool of Repentance. The stool so called was an elevated seat on which persons stood in Scottish churches who had been guilty of certain offences against chastity.—*L'Estrange.*

Stopping. Newspaper writers often use this word improperly, as when they say 'Sims Reeves has arrived, and is *stopping* at the Royal Hotel.' Stopping cannot be a continuous act like going; when a man *stops* he terminates the previous action. The absurdity is apparent if the question be asked, 'When will Sims Reeves *stop* "stopping" at the Royal Hotel?'

Stop, traveller! It was a custom among the Romans to bury their warriors near to some military way, and to erect monuments over their bodies. The inscriptions usually commenced with the words *Siste viator,* 'Stop, traveller'; appropriate enough in their case, but singularly out of place in a modern cemetery, which few 'travellers' ever visit.

Storey of a House, plural *storeys* (often improperly written story and stories), was originally *stagery*, which in times when the *g* and the *y* were used interchangeably, was often spelt *stayery*, the *a* having the broad sound as in straw; from this the transition to the present form was easy.

Storey's Gate. This gate was named from Edward Storey, keeper of the volary or aviary to Charles II.

Story. This pretty word is a contraction of *history.*

Stove. The word *stove* as employed in London to denote an open fireplace is a misnomer. *Stove* is the Anglo-Saxon *stofa*, which means a chamber or room, and the word, slightly modified, is so used in all the Northern countries of Europe. It should be confined in English use to a *closed chamber* in which fuel is burned. The open fireplace is a *grate*, and is so called almost everywhere north of London.

Straight and **Strait.** These two words are often confounded. The first is confined in its meaning to anything *not crooked.* Strait, without the *gh*, is more comprehensive, meaning narrow, confined, close, constrained, rigid, strict, difficult, &c. &c., as 'Strait is the gate,' meaning *narrow*; '*straitened* circumstances,' 'the *straitest* (i.e. the strictest) sect of our religion' (Acts xxvi. 5).

Strain at a gnat and swallow a camel. This should be 'strain *out*.' The allusion is to straining wine lest insects should be inadvertently swallowed. The revised version has the word 'out,' Mat. xxiii. 24.

Strand means the shore of a river or sea. The street in London is so called from its following the line of the shore of the Thames, which formerly flowed much nearer to it than now. 'Westminster and London were a mile asunder in 1603, when the houses were thatched and there were mud walls in the Strand.' —*Howel's Londinopolis.*

Stranger. 'The most singular formation in our language is, undoubtedly, that the word *stranger* should come to us from the Latin preposition *e*, out of, from. *E*, for the sake of euphony, often changes into *ex*. It is further prolonged into *extra*, now familiar to every ear. Our English adjective now arises, *extraneous*. It passes into French, changing the *x* into *s*, and becomes *estranger*, and returns to us as *stranger*, one who comes from without.'— *R. W. Hamilton.*

Strap (from strip). The first straps were narrow lengths of soft bark *stripped* from the branches of a tree. The word rope was probably formed in a similar manner from bands *ripped* from trees in the same way.

Strat, Streat, Strett, Street. Either of these words occurring in an English local name indicates that the place of whose name it forms a part is situated on one of the old Roman roads. There are numerous examples, as Stratford, Streatham, Streetley, Stretton, &c.

Strawberry, probably more correctly *stray*berry, from the runners which *stray* from the parent plant and establish themselves independently.

Streak of Silver Sea. This phrase was first applied to the Channel in an article in the 'Edinburgh Review,' October 1870.

Streets in London named after Flowers. The autumnal crocus, or meadow saffron, from its flowering before the leaves appear, is called 'naked boy.' Hence probably the various 'Naked Boy Courts' in the older parts of London. The dark red wallflower is known in some parts of England as 'bleeding heart.'

Hence probably 'Bleeding Heart Yard,' immortalised by Dickens in 'Little Dorrit.'

Street Lamps. 'It is worthy of note that the high road between London and Kensington was the first place where oil lamps with glazed lights were placed, for the convenience of the Court as they travelled backwards and forwards to St. James's and Whitehall. This was about the year 1694.'—*Old and New London*, vol. v. p. 204.

Strew. This word originally meant spreading straw.

Strike. This word is used in some parts of England to designate a measure of four pecks, *level*, i.e. where all above the rim or level is *struck* off. The same vessel, when used for measuring potatoes, apples, &c., which are heaped up, is called a bushel. A *strike* of barley, a *bushel* of pears.

Stringent, from the Latin *stringo*, to draw tight. The words string and astringent are both from the same root.

Stronghold. This word is printed in three different ways, as stronghold, strong-hold, and strong hold. All three are supported by good authority, but the first, when the word is used in the sense of a fortress, is the most usual.

Strontium (the metal) is so called from Strontian in Argyleshire, where the oxide was first found.

Structure is a contraction of the old word *constructure*, something that is constructed.

Stubborn, from *stub*, the butt or root of a tree which has been felled, which is *stubborn*, or hard to be moved. Stubble is a diminutive plural of the word stub, meaning a number of small stubs, as roots of corn, left after the harvest has been cut.

Stucco, a composition *stuck* upon brick walls to make them resemble stone.

Stultify. To stultify formerly meant to declare to be insane. Bouvier says, ' It is a general rule in the English law that a man shall not be permitted to stultify himself—that is, he shall not be allowed to plead his insanity to avoid a contract.'

Style. This word, when used to designate the peculiar style of an author, is in allusion to the *stylus* used by the Romans as a pencil, with which they wrote on waxen tablets.

Style of Cousin by the Crown. ' In writs, commissions, and other formal instruments, the king, when he mentions any peer of the degree of an earl, usually styles him " trusty and well-beloved cousin"; an appellation as old as the time of Henry IV., who being, either by his wife, his mother, or his sisters, actually related or allied to every earl in the kingdom, artfully and constantly acknowledged the connexion in all his letters and other public acts; from whence the usage has descended to his successors, though the reason has long ago failed.'—*Blackstone, Commentaries,* i. 398.

Sublime Porte. The origin of this phrase to designate the Ottoman Government is to be found in the Eastern custom of making the gates of king's palaces the places for the administration of justice. The *Sublime Porte*, or Lofty Gate, is the principal gate of the Seraglio at Constantinople, and is the place from which the *Hatti scheriffs*, or imperial edicts, are issued.

Submit, from the Latin *sub*, under, and *mitto*, to send. The word in English meant originally to send or put lower, to let down, to sink. Dryden says:

> Sometimes the hill *submits* itself awhile
> In small descents which do its height beguile.

Subpœna (Latin), literally ' under penalty.' A *subpœna* is a writ issuing from some court of law commanding the appearance of the person upon whom it is served before a judicial officer, under a penalty in case of disobedience. *Subpœna ad testificandum* is the common process when the person is required to come and testify, or give evidence. *Subpœna duces tecum* is of the same nature, but contains a clause requiring the person served to bring with him certain books, letters, or other documents specified.

Subscribe, from the Latin *sub*, under, and *scribo*, to write. A man *sub*scribes or writes his name *under* any document which he wishes to attest by his signature. Subscribers to a fund usually promise in writing to contribute the sum placed opposite their signature. The royal sign-manual is always *super*scribed—that is, written *above* the matter to which it refers.

Subtle, Subtile. These words are often confounded with each other both in speech and writing. Subtle means sly, cunning, crafty, acute, keen—as *subtle* (i.e. crafty) designs, *subtle* (i.e. acute) reasoning, &c. *Subtile* is used to express tenuity, fineness, not dense, as

> The *subtile* dew in air begins to soar.—*Dryden.*
> A much *subtiler* medium than air.—*Newton.*

In the works of the old dramatists the word subtle is often used in the sense of smooth, particularly as applied to the smoothness of a bowling-green. Shakespeare has

> Like a bowl upon a *subtle* ground,
> I've tumbled past the throw.—*Coriol.*, act v. sc. 2.

And Ben Jonson in 'Chloridia' has 'Six of the nine acres is counted the *subtlest* bowling ground in all Tartary.'

Succeed is from the Latin *sub*, under, and *cedo*, to go. It was formerly used in England in that sense. Dryden says:

> Or will you to the cooler shade *succeed*?

Succinct, from the Latin *succinctus*, girt up, meant originally having the clothes drawn up to disengage the legs.

> His habit fit for speed *succinct*.—*Milton*.

Sucking the monkey. This well-known cant phrase is thus explained by Grose—'to suck or draw wine or any other liquor privately out of a cask by means of a straw or small tube.'

Suffolk, the shire of the South folk (Anglo-Saxon *suth-folc*).

> Elfride had a kosyn, that king was of Schelde,
> *Northfolke* and *Southfolke* of Elfride he held.

Sugar. This word, almost in its English form, is common to most civilised languages, ancient and modern. In Greek and Latin it is *sacchar*; in Sanskrit *sarkara*; in Persian *scharkar*; in Arabic *soccar*; in Spanish *azucar*; in Italian *zuccehro*; in French *sucre*, and in German *zucker*.

Sugar Candy was originally sugar from Candia.

Suggest. Formerly used in the sense of tempt. Thus Shakespeare ('All's Well that Ends Well,' act iv. sc. 5), 'There's my purse; I give thee not this to *suggest* thee from thy master's service.'

Suicide. 'Up to the middle of the seventeenth century our good writers use " self-homicide," never suicide. The coming up of "suicide" is marked by this passage in Phillips's "New World of Words," 1671, dedication : " Nor less to be exploded is the word *suicide*, which may as well seem to participate of *sus*, a sow, as of the pronoun *sui*." '—*Dr. Trench.*

Suit of Hair. In the Middle and Southern States of America the hair of the head is always called a *suit* of hair. Dr. J. S. Cartwright, of New Orleans, in describing a 'strong-minded woman,' says, *inter alia*, 'She had a thick *suit* of black hair, and although she had reached her fortieth year it had not begun to turn grey, so active was her capillary circulation.'—*Boston Med. and Surg. Journal*, October 18, 1854. 'The face of this gentleman was strikingly marked by a *suit* of enormous black whiskers that flowed together and united under his chin.'—*Margaret*, p. 289.

Sulphur Showers, so called, are showers of yellow pollen from pine forests, often carried by the wind to enormous distances.

Sultry is a contraction of the older word *sweltry*, from the verb *to swelt*. 'The knights swelt for lack of shade.'—*Chaucer*.

Sumptuary Laws were laws for restraining the expenditure in apparel, food, or otherwise. 'That which causes expense is sumptuous; that which regulates expense is sumptuary.'—*Worcester*.

Sunday Newspapers. The first Sunday newspaper published in England was the 'British Gazette and Sunday Monitor,' the first number of which is dated March 26, 1780. It continued to be published until 1829.

Sundial. The earliest known mention of the sundial is in 2 Kings xx. 9-11.

Sunflower. The Anglo-Saxon name for the sunflower was *sol-sœce*, the sun-follower. It is curious that the plant should have two etymologies so much alike as flower and follower. It should be noted that the ancient sunflower was the *marigold*; the tall plants now called sunflowers are of American origin. See MARIGOLD.

Sun-up, Sun-down are Americanisms for sunrise and sunset. 'One would think that such a horse as that might get over a good deal of ground atwixt *sun-up* and *sun-down*.'—*Cooper's Last of the Mohicans*, p. 50.

Supercargo. The supercargo of a merchant ship is an officer having charge of the mercantile transactions of the vessel, selling the merchandise and purchasing returning cargoes, &c. He has nothing to do with the navigation, or with the discipline of the ship or crew.

Supplant meant formerly *to trip up*. It comes from the Latin *sub*, under, and *planta*, the sole of the foot.

Supplicate is from the Latin *supplex*, humbly begging. 'Supplex is probably derived from the *open palms* being held up—the root *plec* signifying "an open surface," and *sub* in composition frequently meaning "up."'—*English Journal of Education*.

Sure. One of the former meanings of this word was *affianced*, or *betrothed*. 'The king was *sure* to Dame Elizabeth Lucy.'—*Sir T. More*.

Sure as eggs is eggs. Professor De Morgan thinks this merely 'a corruption of the logician's announcement of identity, "X is X."'

Surly. From the Anglo-Saxon *sur*, sour, and *lic*, like, *sour-like*.

Surnames. In early times the names given by parents to their offspring were usually descriptive of some peculiarity already existing, or which it was hoped might become characteristic. This was the custom among all nations of which we have any record. The names of Jews, Greeks, and Romans were invariably of this character. Thus Eve means life-giving; Jacob signifies a supplanter; David is well-beloved; and Lazarus means one destitute of help. In the Greek, Alexander is a helper; Hector, a stout defender; and Charity signifies love or beauty. In Latin, Augustus means grand or venerable; Clement is mild-tempered; and Felix is happy. So also in English names, whether of Celtic, Anglo-Saxon, Danish, or Norman origin. Thus Cadwallader is valiant; Griffith, great faith; and Llewellyn, lion-like; Alfred is all peace; Bernard, bear's-heart; Edward, happy keeper; Gilbert, bright; and Richard, powerful.

These names were all *personal* names, having nothing in common with the names of others. In this respect they corresponded to the English Christian or Christened name of modern times, and to the *forename* of other countries. As population, however, increased, it was discovered that something more was required to distinguish between two or more persons named alike or similarly. Hence arose the practice of giving a supplementary name, or adding something to the proper name. These additions were called super- or sur-names, the first syllable of the latter word being spelled with the letter *u*. These surnames were not transmissible from father to son, and were changeable at the will of the owner. Nor was a man confined to one surname. Lord Coke says, 'It is requisite that special heed be taken of the name of baptism, for a man cannot have two names of baptism as [though] he may have divers surnames.' In 'Domesday Book' there is the case of the Earl of Clare, who had five surnames besides his title. He was known as Richard Fitzgilbert, from his father's name; Richard de Tonbridge, from an estate there; Richard de Clare, from his estate in Suffolk; Richard Benfeld, and Richard de Benefacta.

Much learned discussion has taken place among etymologists as to whether surname should be spelt with the letter *u* or with *i*. The compiler of this book thinks that *surname* and *sirname* are distinct words, differing both in their origin and signification.

The word surname, with the *u*, comes to us from the Roman custom of adding some descriptive epithet to the personal name. These 'super' or 'sur' names were not a portion of the name itself, and were not written on the same line, but above it, between the lines. They were called in Latin *supranomina*, or *over-names*, and they were generally of a complimentary nature. Good English examples of these *supranomina* are Richard *Cœur-de-Lion*, and John Howard *the Philanthropist*. When the French copied the practice they translated the term into their own tongue, making it *surnom*. This the Normans introduced into England, where it was corrupted into our present word *surname*, which Dr. Johnson says is 'a name which a man has *over* and *above* the Christian name.' In England these surnames were almost confined to rich men. We are told by Dr. Trench that 'There never was a time when every baptized man had not a Christian name in which his personality before God was recognised,' . . . yet 'only a few had surnames [because] only a few had any importance or significance in temporal things.'

After a time, as population increased, additions, somewhat analogous to these *over*-names, came to be adopted, to fix more completely and accurately the identity of any particular man. At the present time such is the density of population that even the Christian name and the family name are not sufficient in formal legal documents. A 'description' is now added—a name and description being something in this form: 'John Smith, of the City of London, merchant,' or 'Thomas Jones, of Birmingham, in the County of Warwick, labourer.' The following curious examples of the old descriptive names are taken from an old deed in the Record Office of the time of Edward III.:—Swetchild, Portebrief, Walkelate, Scorchbeefe, Thonderlonde, Ryghtwise, Personfisher, Falldew, Gooseflesh, Wetebody, Garlekmonger, Fowkesbailiff, Newehosband, Howeshort, Shepester, Spilewyn, and Buryman. From other sources three others, which are very curious, are added: William Felon (Record Office, Fines 374, A.D. 1321), John Makelyse (Assize Roll, Wilts, 1321), and William le Devel (Gaol Delivery Roll, 11th, Edward III.)

To obviate to some extent the inconvenience of this system of nomenclature, which gave no clue to family or connection, men began to add their father's name to their own in some way. The most obvious plan was that adopted by the ancient Jews—David, the son of Jesse; Joshua, the son of Nun, and so on. This plan when first adopted in England soon beame general, and gave rise to many hundreds of modern surnames. With this custom came in the now universal use of *sir*names, spelt with the letter *i*. It is no longer a *sur-* or *over-*name, but a *sir-* or *sire-*name—that is, *the name derived from the sire* or father. These sirenames were soon adopted by the whole population as collective or family names; the various members of each family being distinguished as heretofore by their baptismal or personal names.

The custom of using the sirename appears, however, to have been in use by the Celtic and Gaelic tribes of Scotland, Ireland, and Wales, before its adoption by their Anglo-Saxon neighbours. The distinction between father and son was marked by a prefix. In the Highlands of Scotland the word *Mac*, which signifies 'son of,' was universally adopted. Hence we have *Macdonald*, son of Donald; *Mackenzie*, son of Kenneth; *Macarthy*, son of Arthur, and many others, each of which originally was a compound of a Christian name with the prefix *Mac*. The late Lord Stair made a collection of names with this prefix, which he printed under the title of 'Seven Hundred Specimens of Celtic Aristocracy.' With two appendices, the later editions of the book contained nearly twelve hundred names beginning with *Mac*.

The northern parts of Ireland were peopled mainly by emigrants from Scotland, who took with them the prefix 'Mac,' but altered the manner of writing it by omitting the *a*, and making it 'Mc,' a form which is now usually held to be a distinctive mark of the Irish nativity or descent of those who bear it. The *Erse*, or aboriginal inhabitants, adopted the letter *O* as a prefix, as O'Brien, a descendant of Brian. This is thought by some to be merely a contraction of the word *of*, but it is more probably the Celtic word *oy*, which means a grandson. It is very curious to observe that, generally speaking, the Mc's are Protestants, and the O's, as the O'Connells, O'Conors, O'Neils, and so on, are Catholics.

In Wales the prefix signifying 'son of' is *ap*, a word apparently having no connection with the others, but really closely allied to them. The word was originally spelt with an *m*, making it *Map*, which was obviously another form of *Mac*. The *m* was dropped some centuries ago, leaving the prefix *ap*, as at present. This enters into the composition of almost as many names as the Highland Mac, but is not so persistent in form. *Ap Howel, Ap Roger, Ap Richard* are the full forms of names which have become modernised into Powel, Prodger, and Pritchard. To the same origin may be traced a very great number of names beginning with *P* or *B*, such as Pumphry, Parry, Probert, Pugh, Bevan, Barry, and Bowen.

Then there are an enormous number of Welsh names consisting

of the father's name in the genitive case, the word 'son' being understood. Thus David's son became *Davis*; Harry's son *Harris*; John's son *Jones*; Evan's son *Evans*; Hugh's son *Hughes*, and so on. Some curious cases of confusion have arisen from the Welsh practice of sometimes using the Welsh and sometimes the English form of their names. *Evan*, for instance, is the Welsh form of the English name *John*. A few years ago a witness was examined at the Hereford Assizes who gave the name of John Jones. In cross-examination he was asked if he had always gone by that name. He said he had. He was next asked if he was ever known as Evan Evans. To this question he also gave an affirmative reply. The judge lifted his eyebrows with astonishment at the apparent prevarication, but it was explained to him by a Welsh barrister that the witness had answered truthfully, and that he might, according to Welsh usage, call himself John Jones, Evan Jones, John Evans, or Evan Evans, without any real change of name.

In England the sturdy and independent spirit of the people would be bound by no general rules in the formation of surnames. Each man followed his own inclination as to the method of joining his father's name to his own, and it is accordingly difficult sometimes to trace to their origin names which are known to have been formed in this way. The number of this class of surnames is far greater than may be thought. From the Christian name *Peter*, for example, we get Peterson, Piers, Pearson, Perkins, and Perkinson; from *Richard*, Richards, Richardson, Dicks, Dickson, Dixon, Dickenson, Dickens; and from *William*, Williams, Williamson, Wilson, Wilkins, Wilkes, Wilkinson, Wilcox, and Billson.

But our forefathers did not always have things quite their own way, even in the matter of surnames. Some of the ladies even in those remote days 'went in' for women's rights, and insisted upon *their* names being transmitted to posterity through their offspring. In this way, from the name *Margaret*, we get the surnames Margetson, Margetts, Megson, Pegson, Peggison, and many others; while Anson, Bettison, Bridgetson, Mollison, Rachelson, and Nelson attest their maternal derivation.

Another large number of names is compounded of the word signifying the occupation of the father with the affix 'son.' Thus the son of a smith was called Smithson; Wrightson was the son of a 'wright' or artificer; Clarkson is the son of a clerk or clergyman; Cookson of a cook, and so on through the long list of employments or occupations.

Another large group of surnames is derived from the localities in or near to which the originators of the names resided, and which are frequently found spelled exactly in the same way as the name of the place where they originated. Others are derived from general terms denoting some particular feature of a locality, as a river, a wood, a hill or mountain, a brook, a heath, a homestead, a cliff, and so forth. Such names as Poole, Rivers, Dell, Forest, Bridge, Hill, Ridge, Orchard, Peak, Shore, Heath, Field, Lake, Lea, Lane, Hedge will readily occur to every reader; but there are others not quite so obvious. Such are Attwood, which was originally At-the-wood, Bytheway, Underwood, Underhill, Bridgefoot, Millhouse, Byford, and Woodhouse. Some of these root words have been prolific of changes; thus *ley* means a field, and from this we not only get Lee, Lea, Leigh, Leeson, Leighton, &c., but also all ending in *ley*, as Bromley, Bromleigh, Cranley, Tapley, and many more.

The third great group of names is derived from the occupations of the original owners. This includes the familiar name Smith, respecting which the Registrar-General tells us that there are more than a quarter of million of persons in England known by that name. The term 'a quarter of a million' does not convey to the mind an adequate idea of the enormous number it represents; but it will be more fully appreciated when it is stated that the number of Smiths in England is equal to the entire population—men, women, and children—of the fifteen county towns Canterbury, Guildford, Hertford, Chelmsford, Chichester, Winchester, Ipswich, Bedford, Buckingham, Reading, Salisbury, Oxford, Warwick, Northampton, and Lincoln. Nor are the Smiths confined to England; there are almost as many Schmidts in Germany, while in the United States the Smiths and the Schmidts form a large proportion of the population. In this group there are thousands of names, including nearly every trade, business, or profession, and all the subdivisions of each. The following will suggest many others:—Baker, Butcher, Grocer, Brewer, Draper, Painter, Dairyman, Tailor, Turner, Sawyer, Sadler, and so on. Then from titles we get Duke, Prince, Earl, Baron, Lord, Knight, and Squire; and from the clergy we have Pope, Bishop, Rector, Vicar, Parson, Priest, Deacon; and their subordinates, Churchwarden, Clerk, Singer, Sexton, and Bellringer.

The next great group of names is derived from bodily or mental characteristics. This comprises an enormous number of surnames, some of which are very unpleasant, such as Bald, Blear, Bony, Coward, Grim, Dowdy, Meager, Pert, Vaine, Tricky, &c. But these are counterbalanced by Faithful, Faultless, Able, Handsome, Hearty Noble, Gallant, Luckey, Sterling, and Wealthy. Others, very desirable for ladies, are Innocent, Blythe, Constant, Tidy, Good, Lively, Handy, Meek, True, Trusty, and, best of all, Well-beloved!

These four groups comprise the greater number of English surnames. The Registrar-General's figures show that of the names derived from parentage there are in England 242,000 Jones's and 160,000 Williams's. From localities there are 65,000 Woods and 64,000 Halls. From occupations, 254,000 Smiths and 125,000 Taylors. From personal characteristics, 105,000 Browns and 54,000 Whites. These four groups, however, do not exhaust the list, which is estimated by the Registrar-General to consist of more than 40,000 distinct surnames; but practical investigations, based upon lists of names copied *seriatim* from Street Directories, show that something like 90 per cent. of all names may be classified under these four heads.

The difficulty, however, in tracing all surnames back to their origin is very great, as may be estimated from the following transformations which one name has undergone in two or three generations. The statement is copied from an American newspaper:—
'A Scotchman named Feyerstone settled among some Germans in the western part of the State of New York. They translated his name, by the sound, into Feuerstein. On his return to an English neighbourhood his new acquaintances discovered that Feuerstein in German meant Flint in English. They retranslated his name, and his family name became Flint. One of the grandsons settled on the Arcadian coast of the Mississippi, and, with the common fate of his family, his name of Flint became translated by the French into Pierre-à-fusil, which means gun-flint. His son went north, and the last transformation was a retranslation, and Pierre-à-fusil became Peter Gun.'

It was decided by Sir Joseph Jekyll, Master of the Rolls in 1717, and has been upheld ever since, that there is nothing in law 'to prevent any one from assuming any sirname he or she may think fit.'

Surrender is corrupted from the French verb *se rendre*, to yield oneself.

Surtout, from the French *sur*, over, *tout*, all. The name is now generally used to designate a frockcoat, but it is strictly an overcoat.

Suspectable, a word that ought to come more into use. At present the word *suspicious* has to do duty for the 'tendency to suspect' and for being 'liable to be suspected.' *Suspectable* should displace 'suspicious' in the latter sense.

Sutton. There are many Suttons in England. The name means *South-town* or *South-dwelling*. Norton, Easton, Weston are in like manner derived from the names of the other cardinal points.

Swamp. A swamp differs from a bog and a marsh in producing trees and shrubs, while the latter produce only herbage, plants, and mosses.—*Farming Encyclopædia.*

Swans. The male swan is called the cobswan, the female the penswan. The young are called cygnets, from the Latin *cygnus*, a swan. Swans were introduced into England by Richard Cœur-de-Lion, who brought them from Cyprus. They live to a great age. There was one well known as 'Old Jack' on the ornamental waters in St. James Park which was known to have been hatched in the garden of old Buckingham House in 1770. Old Jack was killed in 1840, in a fight with a flock of Polish geese which had taken possession of the waters, and which Jack attempted to drive away.

Swan with Two Necks. This, which is a favourite tavern sign in London and elsewhere, is a corruption of the phrase 'a swan with two *nicks*.' It is well known that the swans upon the River Thames are the property of the Crown or of some of the City of London Companies. Each set of proprietors has a distinctive mark, by which all their birds are distinguished. The royal swans are marked by five *nicks*, or marks cut in the bill of the birds when young. The mark of the Vintners' Company is two *nicks*. Hence, as the vintners were generally tavern-keepers, the swan with two nicks became a usual sign. In modern days the word has been corrupted into necks, and the sign-painters, not being content to paint the birds with two necks, have generally given them two heads as well. There is, however, some probability in the conjecture that, as the spread eagle with two heads arose from an attempt to combine the eagles of the Eastern and Western Empires, so the swan with two necks might be a combination of the Plantagenet and Bolum badges, or some other swan cognisances. See DOUBLE-HEADED EAGLE.

Sward is an Old English name for skin. We retain it in the compound *greensward*. The skin of bacon or ham is called the *sward*, though it is often pronounced *sword*, and even *soord*.

Sweat. This word is almost banished from polite speech, but it has a distinct meaning from the word *perspire*, which has superseded it. A person *perspires* naturally through the pores of the skin, as in sleep. Exertion or great heat makes him *sweat*. Natural or *insensible* perspiration is invisible; sweat stands in visible drops upon the skin.

Sweetheart. The earliest known use of this term is by Chaucer ('Troilus and Creseide,' book iii. line 1,173). The words are

O swete herte mine Creseide.

Sweetness and light. This favourite phrase of the modern school of culture is not original. It is taken from Dean Swift's 'Battle of the Books.' The passage in which it occurs is as follows :—' The difference is that instead of dirt and poison we have rather chose to fill our hives with honey and wax, thus furnishing mankind with the two noblest of things, which are *sweetness and light.*'

Swine. There is a prevailing notion that this word is the plural of *sow*. It is not so, however. *Swine* is both singular and plural. Shakespeare has

O monstrous beast, how like *a swine* he lies.

The word in this respect follows the usage in the cases of deer and sheep.

Sworn brothers 'in the Old English law were persons who by mutual oath covenanted to share each other's fortunes.'—*Burrill*.

Sybarite, ' an inhabitant of *Sybaris*, a city on the Gulf of Tarentum, whose inhabitants were proverbially effeminate and luxurious; hence, metaphorically, an effeminate voluptuary.'—*Worcester*.

Sycophant. The original meaning of this word in the Greek and in English was 'a common informer, a false accuser.'—*Trench*. The literal meaning is 'the false, or pretended fig.'

Sydney. The capital of New South Wales was so named after Lord Sydney, who was Secretary for the Colonies in 1788, when the city was founded by Governor Phillip. Port *Phillip* perpetuates the name of the founder.

Syllable. The longest syllable in English is the word *strength*.—*Ency. Brit.*

Sylph. Penny-a-liners, and others who go into raptures over what they call *sylph-like forms*, will be surprised to find that the original meaning of *sylph* is 'a kind of grub.'

Syncopë (three syllables). The primary meaning of this word is 'the omission of a letter or syllable in the middle of a word, as e'en for even, ne'er for never, med'cine for medicine.'—*Johnson.* Besides this and its meaning of 'a fainting fit,' it signifies a sudden cessation, as in the following lines from Cowper:

> Revelry and dance and show
> Suffer a syncope and solemn pause.—*Worcester.*

Syncope (fainting). There is evidently some connection of this word with our 'sun-stroke.' Sun-stroke is in French *coup-de-soleil*, but in the early Frankish dialects this would probably be *sun-coup*, which is very close to syncope in spelling, though not in sound. Mr. Fox Talbot supports this view of the origin of the word at great length in his 'English Etymologies.'

Synonyme, or **Synonym**. Authorities differ as to the orthography of this word, as well as to its exact signification. The best definition is that of Worcester, who says a synonyme is 'one of two or more words in the same language which have the same or a similar signification, or which have a shade of difference, yet with sufficient resemblance of meaning to make them liable to be confounded together.' The word does not appear in Johnson's Dictionary, although he used the word in the sentence, 'Many words cannot be explained by *synonymes,* because the idea signified by them has not more than one application.'

Syringa, the name of a flowering shrub. The name is from a Greek word signifying *a tube or pipe.* It was first applied to the plant on account of its wood being used for the manufacture of Turkish pipes.—*English Cyclopædia.*

T

Tabinet. This once fashionable fabric for ladies' dresses was so named from a French refugee named Tabinet, who made the material in Dublin.

Table Knives. Mr. Wright ('Domestic Manners of the Middle Ages'), speaking of the dinner-tables of the fifteenth century, says in explanation of a drawing of a dinner party of the period, 'It will be seen that the "nappe" [table-cloth] is duly laid, and upon it are seen the salt-cellar, the bread (round cakes), and the cups for wine. Knives are wanting, and the plates seldom appear on the table. This, no doubt, arose from the common practice at that time of people carrying their own knives with them in a sheath attached to the girdle. In the "Rules for Behaviour at Table," written by Lydgate, the guest is told to "bring no knyves unskoured to the table," which can only mean that he is to keep his own knife, that is, the one he carries with him, clean.'

Taboo is a word borrowed from the Polynesian islanders, and naturalised in England. It is, however, as often used in a wrong as in a right sense. The word means *sacred, inviolable, holy*. To declare a thing *tabooed* is to shield it from profane, and to dedicate it to holy purposes. Yet we find vegetarians 'tabooing' flesh meat, and teetotallers placing fermented liquors under 'taboo,' with the most sublime contempt for the meaning of the word.

Tabor. This ancient musical instrument was a small one-ended drum, with a handle projecting from the frame, by which it was held by the left hand while it was beaten with one drumstick held in the right. From a drawing of the fourteenth century now in the British Museum (MS. Reg. 10 E. IV.) the tabor appears to have been from twelve to fifteen inches in diameter, and not unlike a modern stewpan in shape, except that the handle was at a right angle with the frame.

Tadmor in the Desert still bears the name given to it by its builder, Solomon (2 Chron. viii. 4).

Tadpole, from the Anglo-Saxon *tade*, a toad, and *fole*, a colt or foal. The entire word signifies the foal or young of a toad or frog.

Tag, rag, and bobtail. This proverbial saying is doubtless an old hunting expression to signify a herd of deer. In Prescott's 'Philip the Second,' quoted by Strype and Holingshead, is the following : 'They hunted the deer, and were so greedy of their destruction that they killed them rag and tag with hands and swords.' The word 'tegg' or 'tag' signifies, according to Bailey, 'a doe in the second year of her age.' 'Rag,' the same writer defines as 'a herd of young colts,' but other old writers have 'ræg' to signify a herd of deer at rutting time. 'Bobtail' means a fawn just after it has been weaned. 'Tag' and 'bobtail' are used in the same sense when speaking of sheep, but 'rag' does not seem known in this connection. The complete original sense of the phrase ' tag, rag, and bobtail ' seems to have been a collection of sheep or deer, of all sorts, mixed indiscriminately.

Taking a sight. This is the schoolboy's name for the act which Ingoldsby describes in the lines—

> The Sacristan he said no word to indicate a doubt,
> But he put his thumb unto his nose, and he spread his fingers out.

It is by no means a modern practice. In Rabelais (book ii. chap. 19) we read, ' Panurge suddenly lifted up in the air his right hand and put the thumb thereof into the nostril of the same side, holding his four fingers straight out.' Marryat, in his ' Jutland,' says, ' Some of the old coins found in Denmark represent the god Thor, and what do you imagine he is doing? Why, applying his thumb to the end of his nose, with his four fingers extended in the air.'

Taking one's ease in one's inn. Nares, in his ' Glossary,' says that the word inn in this proverbial saying did not mean hostelry, but one's own house, and that the proverb is akin in signification to the maxim ' Every man's house is his castle.' He says that ' when the word *inne* began to change its meaning, and to be used to signify a house of public entertainment,' the proverb was erroneously ' applied in the latter sense ' (p. 506). The word inn in the Anglo-Saxon language signified a chamber. Spenser seems to use it in this sense in the lines—

> Now day is spent,
> Therefore with me you may take up your *inn*.—*Faerie Queene*.

Taking time by the forelock. ' Time is painted with a lock before, and bald behind; signifying thereby that we must take time by the *forelock*; for when it is once past there is no recalling it.'—*Swift*.

Tale.
> And every shepherd tells his tale
> Under the hawthorn in the vale.

These lines of Milton's have generally been interpreted in the sense of love-making, the shepherd being supposed to be telling his tale of love to some blushing damsel. This is altogether erroneous. What Milton meant was that the shepherd counted his flock to see if they *tallied* with the proper number there should be in the flock. Dryden also uses the word in this sense in the line—

> She takes the *tale* of all the lambs.

Talent. A talent of silver was worth about 387*l*. ; a talent of gold about 5,550*l*.

Talented. The use of this word has been censured, and it has been styled a vile Americanism. The word, however, is an old one which has recently been revived and seems likely to hold its position. It is formed on the same principle as gifted, bigoted, lettered, learned, &c. Abbott, who was Archbishop of Canterbury in the reign of James I., says—

> One *talented* but as a common person.

The word has been much abused. Coleridge, writing in 1832, says, ' I regret to see that vile and barbarous vocable *talented* stealing out of the newspapers into the leading reviews and most respectable publications of the day. Why not shillinged, farthinged, tenpenced, &c. ?'—*Table Talk* (Murray, 1836). John Sterling, too, quoted by Carlyle in his ' Life of Sterling,' writes, 'Talented, a mere newspaper and hustings word, invented, I believe, by O'Connell.'

Tall. This word should only be applied to something that grows, as a tall man, a tall tree, tall soldier, &c. We should say a high building, a lofty steeple, an elevated mountain.—*Worcester*. The word tall was formerly used in the sense of valiant, brave. Thus in ' Henry V.,' act ii. sc. 1 :—

> Give me thy fist, thy forefoot to me give,
> Thy spirits are most *tall*.

And in Beaumont and Fletcher's ' Humorous Lieutenant,' i. 4 :—

> We fought like honest and *tall* men.

Tally was the name given to the notched sticks which were formerly used in England for keeping the accounts in the Exchequer. They were square rods of hazel or willow, inscribed on one side with notches indicating the sum for which the tally was an acknowledgment, and on two other sides with the same sum in Roman characters, with the name of the payer and the date of the transaction. Different kinds of notches stood for pence, shillings, pounds, and larger amounts. When a transaction was complete, the tally recording it was split lengthwise, so that each section contained a half of each notch and one of the written sides. One of these halves was handed to the payer as his receipt; the other was retained as a record in the Exchequer. In case of dispute the two halves were brought together, and if correct the notches on one would correspond to those on the other, in which case they were said to *tally*. We have retained the word, although we have long abandoned the practice. The use of tallies in the Exchequer was abolished by Act of Parliament, 23 Geo. III. The old tallies were ordered to be destroyed by the Act 4 and 5 Will. IV. c. 15. In burning them in 1834, the flues of the furnaces in which they were being consumed became over-heated, and led to the fire which destroyed the Houses of Parliament.

Tally-ho. One authority says this is a corruption of the Norman-French *tolleaux*; another derives it from *taillishors*, out of the coppice; and a third says it is the French hunting cry, *au taillis*, to the coppice, which being often repeated gives the same sound as tally-ho. See HUNTING CRIES.

Tallymen are travelling drapers, who call at the houses of their customers and sell their goods on a system of weekly payments. The name *tallyman* occurs in Bailey's Dictionary, first published about 1720. The name is derived from the accounts being kept by *tally*. See TALLY.

Tamarinds. The name of the tree which produces this fruit is compounded of the Arabic *tamar*, a date, and *Indus*, the native country of the tree. The name, therefore, means Indian date.

Tandem. 'This equipage derives its name from the Latin word *tandem*, at length. It means one horse preceding the other. It is a cognomen far-fetched, but it is accounted for by saying it is of University origin.'—*Pulleyn*.

Tankard. None of the dictionaries that have been consulted in the preparation of this book give any other meaning to this word than that of a drinking vessel with a lid. There is, however, an older meaning. The vessels in which water was fetched from the ancient conduits were called 'tankards,' and those who fetched the water were tankard-bearers. The term often occurs in Reed's edition of 'Dodsley's Old Plays,' of which the following are examples:—

Wilt thou bear tankards, and may'st bear arms.
Eastward Hoe, vol. iv. p. 207.

' As soon as I heard the messenger say my father must speak with me, I left my *tankard* to guard the conduit and away came I.'—*Four Prentices of London*, vol. vi. p. 459. Ben Jonson also uses it : ' To talk of your turn in this company, and to me alone, like a *tankard-bearer* at a conduit! Fie!'—*Every Man in his Humour*, act i. sc. 2. The term was probably derived from the tank into which the water from the conduits flowed, and from which it had to be dipped by those who required it.

Tansy. The common tansy of the gardens is closely allied to the yellow flower called everlastings by the English and *immortelles* by the French. The Greek name for the everlasting was *athanasia*, which signifies immortality. Our name tansy is corrupted from the Greek.

Tantalise. This word originated in the fable of Tantalus, who, according to Greek mythology, though afflicted with constant thirst, was placed in water up to his chin, but was in some way rendered unable to reach to drink it.

Tapis is the French word for *carpet*, but it is applied also to a covering for a table. Hence to be on the tapis is to be on the table for discussion.

Tares. The word which, in the Authorised Version of the Scriptures, is translated 'tares' is supposed to have been the red poppy or cockle. The plant was known to the Anglo-Saxons by the name '*cœcel*,' and in the Saxon Scriptures this word is used in Matthew xiii. 25, where in the Authorised Version we have 'tares.' Cockle is the old Celtic name of the red poppy (*Agrostemma githago*).

Tariff. This word comes from the Moorish name (*Tarifa*) of a fortress which stands upon a promontory of Spain, commanding the entrance to the Mediterranean Sea. When the Moors had possession, they levied duties at certain fixed rates upon all merchandise passing in or out of the straits. These duties, from the name of the place where they were levied, were called *tarifa*, or *tariff*, from whence we have acquired the word.—*Trench.*

Tarpaulin is a *tarred palling*, from the word *pall*, a cover ; as a funeral pall.

Tarring and Feathering. Richard Cœur-de-Lion seems to have originated tarring and feathering. Hoveden, quoted by Dr. Hook in his 'Lives of the Archbishops of Canterbury,' says that Richard, when he sailed for the Holy Land, made sundry laws for the regulation of his fleet, one of which enacted that 'a robber who shall be convicted of theft shall have his head cropped after the manner of a champion, and boiling pitch shall be poured thereon, and then the feathers of a cushion shall be shaken out upon him, so that he may be known, and at the first land at which the ships shall touch he shall be set on shore.'

Tarshish. The Tarshish of the Scriptures is supposed to be identical with Tartessus, a city and emporium of the Phœnicians, near the mouth of the Guadalquivir.

Tartan Plaid. The chequered cloth which English people call 'plaid' is known as 'tartan' by the Scotch. The origin of the name is supposed to be French. *Tiretaine* in French is a mixed fabric of linen and worsted similar to our linsey-woolsey. A *plaid* is a long, rather narrow, fringed piece of *tartan* cloth, worn by the Scotch as a sort of outer wrapper for the protection of the neck, throat, and chest in bad weather. The use of the word plaid in the English sense is just as reasonable as though the name *coat collar* were applied to velvet—the name of one of the uses of the *material* being wrongly applied to the material itself. See PLAID.

Taste. 'We may consider taste, therefore, to be a settled habit of discerning faults and excellences in a moment—the mind's independent expression of approval or aversion.'—*Pleasures of Literature*, 1851. 'The innate perception of fitness which we call taste.'—*Edwards*.

Tattoo, the beat of drum at night calling soldiers to their quarters. This word comes from the Dutch word *tap-too*, signifying the time when taps or ginshops are closed.

Tavern, Tabernacle. It is singular that both these words are derived from the same root. They both originate in the Latin *taberna*, a tent, hut, or booth.

Taverns. In the reign of Edward III. only three taverns were allowed in London. By an Act of Edward VI., 1552, forty taverns were permitted in London, eight in York, six in Bristol, four in Norwich, Hull, Exeter, Gloucester, Chester, Canterbury, Cambridge, and Newcastle, and three in Westminster, Lincoln, Shrewsbury, Salisbury, Hereford, Worcester, Southampton, Ipswich, Winchester, Oxford, and Colchester.

Tawdry, the name given to cheap finery, is a vulgar corruption of 'St. Audrey,' meaning 'St. Ethelreda.' The allusion is to laces and similar articles sold at the fairs of St. Ethelreda.

Taylor, or Tailor. Women's gowns and other articles of female dress were formerly made by men, who were called 'women's taylors.' Thus in the 'Taming of the Shrew' the *taylor* brings Catherine her dress, upon which Petruchio says:

> Come, *taylor*, let us see these ornaments;
> Lay forth the gown.—Act iv. sc. 3.

In Beaumont and Fletcher's 'Two Noble Kinsmen,' act iv. sc. 1, there is the following dialogue:—

    D. Are you a taylor?
    B. Yes.
    D. Where is my wedding gown?
    B. I'll bring it to-morrow.

Tea was first brought to Europe by the Dutch in 1610. It was first introduced into England about 1650. Pepys, in his Diary, under date September 26, 1661, says, 'I sent for a cup of *tea*, a China drink of which I had never drunk before.' In 1667 the East India Company imported 100 lbs. There are two principal varieties of the tea plant. The first, *Thea bohea*, is cultivated in what is known as the black tea country, which is the district adjacent to Canton. The second variety, *Thea viridis*, is grown in the northern, or what are called the green tea districts of China. It was at one time thought that all black teas were the produce of *Thea bohea*, and all greens that of *Thea viridis*. It is now known that both kinds are produced from each variety of the plant, and that their differences in colour and flavour arise from differences in drying and manipulation. Black tea, being dried slowly, loses its colour and some of its active properties. Green tea is dried quickly, retaining its colour and some of the volatile qualities that are lost in the slow process. In green tea the central woody vein of each leaf is removed, it being weak in extractive matter; in the black tea this vein remains. A pound of green tea, therefore, contains more strength than an equal quantity of the black kinds. The earliest known tradesman's advertisement in England appears in a copy of the 'Mercurius Politicus' of September 30, 1658. It is as follows:—'That Excellent and by all Physitians approved *China* Drink called by the Chineans *Tcha*, by other Nations *Tay* alias *Tee*, is sold at the *Sultaness Head Cophee House*, in *Sweeting's* Rents by the Royal Exchange, London.'

Tea-caddy. This is a corruption of the Chinese word *catty*, the name given to small packages in which the Chinese make up the finer kinds of teas. The Chinese catty is also a specific weight equal to 1½ lb. avoirdupois.

Teaching, Instructing, Informing, Educating. These words have their distinct meanings, not always, perhaps, present to the minds of those who use them. *Teaching* is the lowest and simplest in its signification. We may *teach* a dog or a horse, but we cannot go further with either. We teach a child to speak and to walk, and then he is fit to receive *instruction*. The word *instruc-*

tion implies understanding, such as a child does not possess until he has been taught something. *Information,* again, differs from instruction, inasmuch as information can be obtained upon many subjects from observation alone; but instruction may elicit new truths from the information the pupil has thus acquired. *Education* is more comprehensive than all the others, and includes them all. It *educes* or draws out the latent faculties of the mind, leaving it in a condition where it requires no further teaching, but is in a state in which it desires to *learn* for itself and is eager to obtain further information. At this stage the mind begins to be self-acting, and the knowledge it has acquired is gradually developed into wisdom.

Te Deum. This magnificent hymn of praise is so called from its first words in Latin, *Te Deum laudamus,* 'We praise Thee, as God!' It is supposed to have been composed by St. Augustine in the fourth century. Considerable controversy has arisen as to the genuineness of the canticles affirming the doctrine of the Trinity.

Teetotal. The origin of this word is ascribed to the stammering utterance of the word *total* by one Richard Turner, a plasterer's labourer at Preston in Lancashire. He was much given to holding forth in the Lancashire dialect at meetings of the temperance societies, and at one, in the midst of a philippic against what he called 'hawf measures,' he said, 'I'll hev nowt to do with this moderation-botheration pledge—I'll be reet down *tee-tee-total* for ever and ever.' 'Well done, Dick!' said the chairman, 'that shall be the name of our new pledge'; and the name it became, and still is. The phrase, although no doubt original on Dicky's part, was not, it appears, altogether new. It was merely an admirable application to a new purpose of an old word. In Sir James Spence's 'Tour in Ireland,' published in 1829, he speaks of the word 'teetotally' as an adverb in every-day use by the working classes. It has lately been discovered by Mr. O'Callaghan ('House and Home,' September 1879) that it is the Irish word *ttodhail* which by the English-speaking Irish is pronounced 'teetotal.' *Ttodhail,* it seems, has been a dictionary word for centuries. The meaning is entire destruction, or total annihilation.

Telegram. The 'Albany (United States) Evening Journal' of April 6, 1852, has the following paragraph: 'A friend desires us to give notice that he will ask leave at some convenient time to introduce a new word into the vocabulary. It is *telegram,* instead of telegraphic despatch or telegraphic communication. The word is formed according to the strictest laws of the language from which its root comes. *Telegraph* means to write from a distance; *telegram* the writing itself, executed from a distance.' The new word was first *used* in the 'Daily American Telegraph,' published at Washington, April 27, 1852. In July 1859 it appeared for the first time in England, the 'Illustrated London News' having a 'telegram' from Napoleon to Eugénie which announced that peace had been concluded.

Telegraph. The 'deflective electro-magnetic telegraph' was patented in England by Cooke and Wheatstone, June 12, 1837.

Telephone. In July 1835 M. Soudré exhibited at the King's Theatre in London an invention which he called the *telephone*. Leigh Hunt gave a full description of it in the 'London Journal.' The last paragraph said: 'His more moderate view of applying it to telegraphic communication seems better founded, though even that seems beset at the very threshold by the awkward necessity of securing a fair wind from the weather office.'

Telescope. Sir David Brewster has 'no doubt that this invaluable instrument was *invented* by Roger Bacon or Baptista Porta.' It is generally believed that the first telescope was *made* by Zachary Janssen, a maker of spectacles, at Middelburg in 1590.

Teller (of a bank). Bouvier says that in this sense the word takes its meaning from *tallier*, one who kept a *tally*, as it is his duty to make his accounts *tally* or agree. See TALE, and TALLY.

Temperature. The 'mean' or average temperatures of various localities in England have been published by the Meteorological Society. Ventnor stands the highest, with a mean temperature for the year of 51·5°; Greenwich is 49·5°; Bedford, 49·3°; Derby, 48·8°; Manchester, 48°; Scarborough, 47°; Berwick, 46·8°; and Shetland, 45·3°. The winter temperature in the west is higher than in more eastern places. Thus the average for the winter months is in Truro 45°; Ventnor, 42·2°; Liverpool, 40·6°; while in Greenwich it is 37·9°; Nottingham, 37·3°; and York, 37·1°.

Temple. The two Inns of Court are thus called because anciently they were occupied by the Knights Templars. They are called 'Inner' and 'Middle' Temple, in relation to Essex House, which was part of the property of the Knights Templars, and was called 'Outer' because it was outside the City walls.

Temple Bar. The first stone of Temple Bar was laid in 1670, during the mayoralty of Sir Samuel Stirling. It was concluded in 1672, in which year Sir George Waterman was the first Lord Mayor who passed officially beneath the arch. The process of demolition commenced December 10, 1877, during the mayoralty of Sir Thomas Owden.

Temple of Solomon. Mr. Timbs, in 'Notabilia,' p. 192, makes a calculation of the treasure provided by David for the building of the Temple. Reckoning the talent of gold at 5,075*l*., and the talent of silver at 355*l*. 10*s*., he makes the total contributed by David and his chiefs and princes amount to the enormous total of 907,782,176*l*. sterling, a sum more than equal to the entire income of the British empire for eleven years! Mr. Timbs has doubtless made some error in his calculations. It was not a large building, being only about 150 feet long and 105 wide.

Ten. Jäkel says this word is from the Old German *thai*, the, and *hend*, the hands; meaning both hands, or ten fingers, being held up to express the number.

Ten Commandments. The Commandments are not numerically distinguished in the Bible, and the number—ten—is not equally divided as to their respective references to God and man. The first four relate to sacred duties, and the other six to secular, or our duties to our neighbours.

Tenement is a building occupied by a tenant.

Tennessee. The State was so called from the Indian name of its principal river. The word signifies a curved spoon.

Tenpenny Nails. There is a well-known story of the great Greek scholar Dr. Parr giving his man-servant half-a-crown to pay for three tenpenny nails, under the impression that they were tenpence each. The word 'penny' in this and similar compounds, sixpenny, eightpenny, &c., is corrupted from 'pound.' Nails are *nominally* sold by the thousand, but they are not counted—each size has a given designation by weight which is supposed to be equivalent to a thousand if counted. Thus there are 8 oz., 12 oz., 16 oz., 2 lb., 4 lb., 10 lb., and so on, each representing a different size. The phrase 'ten pound nails' was first corrupted into 'ten-p'un' nails,' from which the transition to 'tenpenny' was easy.

Ten-pins. It has been stated that the game nine-pins having been interdicted in the United States, the Americans, with great ingenuity, evaded the law by introducing *ten*-pins. This seems very plausible, but it happens that ten-pins is an old English game

In a book published in 1600, 'Letting of Humours Blood in the Heade-vaine,' is this couplet :—

> To play at loggets, nine holes, or *ten pinnes*,
> To trie it out at foote-balle by the shinnes.

And in Moor's 'Suffolk Words,' p. 249, is the following : 'Nine, a favourite and mysterious number everywhere, prevails in games. We have, like others, nine-pins, which we rather unaccountably call "ten-pins," although I never saw more than nine used in the game.'

Tenter-hooks. Tenter is from the Latin *tentus*, stretched. Cloth, after being woven, is tentered or stretched by means of hooks passed through the edges or selvages. The hooks so used are tenter-hooks. A tent is a lodging-place made of canvas 'tentered' or stretched.

Termagant. This word is from the Anglo-Saxon *tyr*, very, and *magan*, mighty. It originally meant a turbulent, violent man. In the old romances it was applied to the god of the Saracens, and was generally coupled with the name of Mahomet. Bishop Hall speaks

> Of mighty Mahound, and great Termagaunt.

The word is now confined in meaning to a woman of ill temper, fierce disposition, and brawling tongue.

Terrier, from the Latin *terra*, earth. A terrier is a dog used in the chase for following *into the earth* animals which burrow. A 'terrier' of glebe lands is a catalogue of those lands.

Test. A *test* was originally, according to Blount, 1679, 'an instrument in which refiners do fine, refine, and part gold and silver from other metals, or (as we use to say) put them in the test or trial.' The Italians use the word *testo* for a goldsmith's melting-pot. The modern use of the word, it will be seen, is purely metaphorical.

Test and Corporation Acts. *Mansion House.*—In Conder's 'Historical Review of Religious Liberty during the last two Centuries,' it is stated that the City of London Mansion House was paid for out of fines levied upon Dissenters elected to fill the office of sheriff, but refusing to serve owing to the provisions of the Test and Corporation Acts. In one year—1806—these fines amounted to 10,306*l.* 13*s.* 4*d.*, and in 1815 to 9,466*l.* 13*s.* 4*d.*

Tetrarch. A tetrarch among the Romans was a governor of four provinces.

Thames. It is a common belief that this name is a compound of Thame and Isis, but it appears that the river now called the Isis has been known by the name of Thames for many centuries. The Anglo-Saxon Chronicle records that in 905 Ethelwald excited the East Anglians to rebellion, so that they overran all the land of Mercia until they came to Cricklade, where they forded the *Thames*. Canute also forded the *Thames* at the same spot in 1016. In Camden's 'Brittania,' an ancient charter granted to Abbot Adhelm is quoted, in which mention is made of certain lands on the east bank of the river *cujus vocabulum Temis juxta vadum qui appellatur Summerford*, this ford being in Wiltshire. In addition to these records is the fact that the country people on its banks know nothing of the name Isis, but up to its source in the Cotswold Hills, which they call 'Thames Head,' invariably call it 'Thames.'

Thames Tunnel. The Thames Tunnel was opened as a public thoroughfare March 23, 1843, and was closed preparatory to its being utilised for a railway, July 20, 1869.

Than is sometimes a conjunction, and sometimes a preposition. In the phrase 'He is wiser *than* I' it is a conjunction; in 'He is wiser *than* me' it is a preposition. Both are good English, but *than* is not often used as a preposition except before the word whom.

Thank, Think. 'Thank' and 'think' are more nearly allied to each other than is generally supposed. To be thankful is to be *thinkful* or mindful of a benefit received, and unthankfulness argues unthoughtfulness, forgetfulness, being unmindful of an obligation. The Anglo-Saxon verb for thank is *thancgian*, from *thencan*, to think.—*Dean Hoare*.

That. Mr Gould ('Good English,' New York, 1871) gives the following singular instances of the absurd practice of omitting the word *that* from carelessness or from a propensity to over-neatness of style:—'It was a long time before I ascertained [that] I had lost the book'; 'We all know [that] history repeats itself'; 'Those who are competent to judge say [that] he will never succeed,' and so forth. The word *that* in such cases gives precision, and precision, it will be admitted, is one of the great charms of composition. Some ingenious persons have constructed sentences in which the word 'that' is used seven times consecutively with correctness. The following example is from an old school book:—

> Five *thats* may closely follow one another,
> For be it known that we may safely write
> Or say that that *that* that that man writ was right;
> Nay, e'en that that *that* that that that has followed,
> Through *six* repeats, the grammar's rule has hallowed,
> And that that that (that *that* that that began),
> Repeated *seven* times, is right. Deny't who can.

Sir Richard Steele, in the 'Spectator,' No. 86, gives the following passage in ridicule of the too frequent use of the word *that*. The various sizes of type are intended to mark rising emphasis:—
'My lords, with humble submission that that I say is this, that that that that that gentleman has advanced is not that that he should have proved to your lordships.'

That's the cheese. In the Bengalee language, as spoken at Calcutta, the word *chiz* means thing; for example, 'That's the *chiz* for me.' The word has evidently been brought by some Anglo-Indian to England, and once here, the transition to *cheese* was inevitable. *Chiz* is pronounced cheese.

That's the ticket. This slang expression is a corruption of *that's the etiquette*—that's the proper mode of procedure. Etiquette is the French word for a ticket, and its present meaning in English arose from an old custom of distributing tickets, or etiquettes, upon which the ceremonies to be observed at any formal proceeding were duly set forth. The modern word 'programme' exactly corresponds to the old 'etiquette.'

Theatricals. The first notice of theatrical performances in England is by Matthew Paris, who relates that in the year 1110 one Geoffrey, a learned Norman, master of the school of the Abbey of Dunstable, composed the play of 'St. Catherine,' which was acted by his scholars. Geoffrey borrowed copes from the sacrist of the neighbouring Abbey of St. Albans to dress his characters. Fitzstephen, writing in 1174, says that 'London for its theatrical exhibitions has *religious plays*, either the representations of miracles wrought by holy confessors or the sufferings of martyrs.'

Theodore and **Dorothy** both mean 'the gift of God,' but the syllables are reversed. *Theodoric*, an old Gothic name usually borne by kings, although so like the other, is of totally different origin. It means 'chief of the people,' *theo*, people, *ric*, chief.

The other day is literally the day before yesterday. The word 'other,' as is shown in the article NUMERALS, was the Saxon nominal answering to the modern word 'second.' Now, as yesterday, reckoning backwards, is the first day from to-day, the day before yesterday is the second day; or, using the Anglo-Saxon nominal, it is the *other* day.

Thermometer. It is not known who invented the thermometer. It has been ascribed to Galileo, to Drebbel, to Paulo Sarpi, and to Sanctorio. Fahrenheit's thermometer was invented about 1710. In England the temperature is commonly denoted by the *Fahrenheit* scale, in France by what is termed the *Centigrade*. In the latter the space between the freezing and the boiling points is divided into 100 degrees, but in the Fahrenheit into 180. A degree of the Centigrade is therefore higher than a degree Fahrenheit in the proportion of 9 to 5. But, as the *zero* of the Centigrade is at the freezing point, and in the Fahrenheit is 32 degrees below it, this has to be taken into account when comparing the two. Suppose it is desired to express by Fahrenheit's scale the temperature of 10 degrees Centigrade, the 10 must first be multiplied by 9 and the product divided by 5, which will give 18; to this must then be added the 32 degrees of Fahrenheit which are not reckoned in the Centigrade, and the result will be 50 degrees Fahrenheit, which is the exact equivalent of 10 degrees Centigrade. Réaumur's thermometer is little used, except in Germany.

The sun never sets on the empire. This saying was not at first used in reference to England. In Howell's 'Familiar Letters,' 1623, we find it applied to Spain, the king of which is described as 'a mighty monarch; he hath dominion in all parts of the world; the sun shines all the four-and-twenty hours of the natural day on some part or other of his country, for part of the antipodes are subject to him.' Quaint old Thomas Fuller, too, speaking of Drake ('Holy State,' edit. 1840, p. 107), says, 'Though a poor private man, he hereafter undertook to avenge himself upon so mighty a monarch, who, as not contented that the sun riseth and setteth in his dominions, may seem to desire to make all his own where he shineth.'

Thicket is from thick. It means a small wood or coppice where the trees and shrubs are thickly planted.

Thief ' was anciently written *thieof*, and so appeareth to have been of two syllables. *Thie* was wont to be taken for thrift, so that *thie-of* is he that taketh of or from a man his *thie*—that is, his thrift or that by which he thriveth, his goods or commodities.'— *Verstegan, Restitution, &c.*, p. 263.

Thimble was originally thumb-bell, being worn on the thumb, as sailors wear theirs now. Thimbles were known to the Romans;

some were found at Herculaneum. They were first made in England by a Dutchman named Lofting, at Islington, near London, in 1695.

Things. 'By "things" I mean subjects as well as objects of thought, whatever one can "think" about.'—*Trench.* Tooke says, a 'thing' is 'whatever may be thought of.'

Thirteen at Dinner. The common superstition which makes it unlucky to have thirteen at dinner is no doubt a reference to the Last Supper of our Lord and his disciples, where thirteen were present and Judas was among them. He left first, and therefore the first of a party of thirteen to leave the table is the unlucky one.

This and That. Mr. Earle, in his 'Philology,' p. 413, calls attention to the rhetorical use of these two words, and points out that the word *this* may be used to imply contempt, instancing the case of Horne Tooke, who speaks of '*This* Mr. Harris, who takes fustian for philosophy'; whereas *that* is a symbol of admiration. To support this view he quotes a speech of Mr. Gladstone's, in which, speaking of justice, that great orator described it as '*That* rare, *that* noble, *that* imperial virtue.'

Thistle. 'The thistle is the emblem of Scotland; and the national motto is very appropriate, being—"*Nemo me impune lacessit*"—Nobody shall provoke me with impunity.'—*Brand.*

Those sort of things. This incorrect phrase is in frequent use even by people who should know better. 'Things of that kind' would be better English and quite as expressive.

Though lost to sight, to memory dear. The authorship or origin of this familiar line has long been a literary puzzle. A writer in 'Harper's Bazaar,' published in New York, says, 'It originated with Ruthven Jenkyns, and was first published in the 'Greenwich Magazine for Marines' in 1701 or 1702. The entire poem was as follows :—

>Sweetheart, good-bye! that fluttering sail
>   Is spread to waft me far from thee;
>And soon before the favouring gale
>   My ship shall bound upon the sea.
>Perchance all des'late and forlorn
>   These eyes shall miss thee many a year;
>But unforgotten every charm—
>   Though lost to sight, to mem'ry dear.
>
>Sweetheart, good-bye! one last embrace!
>   O cruel fate, two souls to sever!
>Yet in this heart's most sacred place
>   Thou, thou alone shalt dwell for ever.

> And still shall recollection trace
> In Fancy's mirror, ever near,
> Each smile, each tear; that form, that face—
> Though lost to sight, to mem'ry dear.'

Thought. The action of the mind which we call thought is expressed in most of the primitive languages by words signifying *internal speech*.

Thraldom is from the Anglo-Saxon *thrall*, a slave. Shakespeare says:—

> Look gracious on thy prostrate *thrall*.

Thrashing. When a father threatens to give his son *a good thrashing*, he is unconsciously alluding to the *threshing* of corn by the old-fashioned flail, in which repeated blows by a heavy rod are necessary in order to get out the whole of the grain.

'Three Goats' at Lincoln. There is an inn at Lincoln now called the 'Black Goats,' which was formerly known as the '*Three Goats*.' The house was originally named the '*Three Gowts*,' from the three drains, or gowts, which conducted the waters of a large lake which formerly existed to the west of the city into the river Witham near the spot where the inn stands. *Gowt* is still used as a name for the sluices which allow land-water to flow into the sea at low tide, but which are closed as the tide rises. Worcester derives it from 'go-out.' It is probably allied to the word gutter. A stream carrying water to a mill at Bristol is called the Gowte.

Three R's. The late Alderman Sir William Curtis, who was a very illiterate man, but was fully alive to the necessity of instruction, was once called upon at a public dinner to propose a toast, when he gave 'The three R's—reading, writing, and arithmetic'!

Threshold. This is a corruption of *threshwold*, the threshing *wood* or floor. The *threshwold* of a barn was not only the threshing floor, it was also the central bay into which the horses entered drawing the wains laden with corn. From this the name was first transferred to the entrance, bay, passage, or hall of a dwelling-house, and finally to the first step trodden upon in entering.

Thrill is allied to *drill*, and means to pierce, to perforate; hence 'a sensation as if produced by the action of boring or piercing' is a *thrilling* sensation.

Throwing Slippers at Weddings. Throwing an old shoe after a person was an ancient manner of expressing a wish for good luck. It is alluded to by most of the old poets and dramatists. Haywood has:—

> Now for goode lucke caste an old shoe after me.

Beaumont and Fletcher have:—
> Captain, your shoes are old, pray put 'em off,
> And let one fling 'em after us.

And in an old play called 'The Parson's Wedding,' printed by Dodsley, vol. ix., p. 499, we have :—
> Ay, with all my heart, there's an old shoe after you.

Thud. This expressive word is said to have been first used in English in the description given in the 'Times' newspaper of the pugilistic fight between Heenan and Sayers.

Thunderer, the. This term, so often now used to designate the 'Times' newspaper itself, was originally an epithet applied to Captain Edward Sterling, one of the most powerful writers ever employed on that paper. Sterling's connection with the 'Times' commenced in 1812. He died at Knightsbridge, September 3, 1847.

Thursday. 'Of the weekly day which was dedicated to his [Thor's] peculiar service we yet retain the name of Thursday, the which the Danes and the Swedians do yet call *Thorsday*; in the Netherlands it is called *Donders-dagh*, which being written according to our English orthography is *Thunder's-day*, whereby it may appear that they anciently therein intended the day of the god of thunder; and in some of our old Saxon books I finde it to have been written *Thunres-deag*. So, as it seemeth that the name of *Thor* or Thur was abreviated (*sic*) of *Thunre*, which we now write Thunder.'—*Verstegan, Restitution, &c.*, 1655, p. 62.

Thwart, from *athwart*, across. To thwart a person is to place an obstacle 'across' his path. 'Crossed in love' is thwarted in love. Addison has, 'By fortune crost.'

Thyme (the herb). So named from a Greek word signifying *sacrifice*, because from its sweet smell it was burnt upon the altars to diffuse pleasant odours.

Tiara. The *tiara* is the mitre of the popes. At first it was a round tall cap, differing from the double mitre of a bishop in being single. The first gold circlet was adopted about the year 860 by Nicholas I. as the symbol of civil power. The second was added by Boniface about 1300, and the third by Urban V. about 1365.

Tick. This is usually considered to be a slang word, but it has a good claim to be accounted classical. In Kerr's 'Blackstone,' chap. xv., p. 468, Chief Justice Holt is reported as saying : 'If a man send his servant with ready money to buy goods, and the servant buy upon credit, the master is not chargeable; but if the servant usually buy for the master *upon tick*, and the servant buy some things without the master's order, yet if the master were trusted by the trader he is liable.'

Tidy, from the Swedish *tidig*, which is from *tide*, timely, denoting done in good time, seasonably. Everything being done in good time will be well done and well arranged, tidy.

Tierce, from the French *tierce*, a third. A tierce is the third part of a pipe of oil or other liquid.

Tiffin. This is the Anglo-Indian name for luncheon. In the North of England a *tiff* is a draught of liquor, and *tiffing* means drinking or eating out of due season, or between meal times. This is, no doubt, the origin of tiffin, luncheon.

Tight is tied, ti'd, tight.—*Tooke, Diversions of Purley.*

Till. Horne Tooke thinks this is a word compounded of *to* and *while*. There is some probability in his theory; the people of the Northern counties invariably use *while* instead of *till* in such sentences as ' I'll stay *while* night,' ' I can't come *while* Monday,' &c.; and Shakespeare himself says:—

> We will keep ourself
> Till supper time alone; *while* then God bless you.

Timbered. Anciently this word was used in speaking of a man in the sense of constituted or adapted. Thus Beaumont and Fletcher speak of ' a goodly timbered fellow'; and Sir Henry Wotton, in his ' Short History of William I.' ('Collectanea Curiosa,' Oxford, 1781, vol. i. p. 221), says that the Conqueror ' left the succession upon his second son, not because he bare his name, though that perhaps might be some motive, but because he thought him the best *timbered* to support it.'

Timbrel. The timbrel mentioned in Exodus xv. 20, Job xxi. 12, Psalm cl. 4, and at other places in the Scriptures, was a musical instrument something like the modern tambourine. It consisted of a brass hoop over which was stretched a membranous disc of some material similar to parchment. It was used as a drum in the ancient Hebrew music.

Time and **Eternity.** Most people regard time as something entirely distinct from eternity. In reality it is not so. Eternity is 'never beginning, never ending,' and is going on now. Time, therefore, like a small segment of a great circle, is in fact a portion of eternity. Time is, for each individual, that portion of eternity which he is permitted to spend upon earth.

Time immemorial. By English law the reign of Richard I. is fixed as that of 'time immemorial.'

'Times' Newspaper. This great newspaper was started in the year 1785 as the 'Daily Universal Register,' of which 940 numbers were issued. On January 1, 1788, the additional words 'and Times' were added, but the numbering was continued, the first issue bearing the imprint 941. It was printed logographically— that is, all the more frequently occurring words were cast instead of being separately made up of single letters by the compositor. At that time there were many 'Red-letter Days,' which title included all the saints' days recognised by the Protestant Church, royal birthdays, and various other anniversaries. The dates on which these occurred were printed in the almanacs in *red ink*, and the days were kept as holidays at the Transfer Office at the Bank of England and at other public offices. On these days the title was printed in red ink, and the reason of the day being a red-letter day was specified. The following is taken from the 'Universal Register' for Friday, Aug. 11, 1786 : 'Princess of Brunswick born ; Holiday at the Bank, Excise Offices, and the Exchequer.' In 1803 the circulation was 1,000 per diem. The first double number was issued January 19, 1829, and the 'Table of Contents' first appeared January 29, 1869. The original 'City Editor' was a manufacturer and bleacher near the King's Bench Prison in the Borough. He gave up business in order to devote his time to the 'City articles,' and eventually became a partner in the 'Times' paper.

Tin. What are called by most people 'tin' kettles and 'tin' saucepans are made of sheet iron with a thin veneering or plating of tin. The adjective should properly be 'tinned.'

Tinder-box. The earliest known mention in literature of *tinder* for obtaining fire is in Shakespeare :—

> Strike on the tinder, ho !
> Give me a taper.

Tinker is a corruption of a compound Gaelic word *teine-ceard*, from *teine*, fire, and *ceard*, smith ; the word therefore means a firesmith, and is in no way connected with the English word *tin*. In Scotland a tinker is called a *caird*.

Tint is a double abbreviation of tincture, an old word for colour or stain. It was first contracted into *tinct*, in which shape it is found in Shakespeare, Bacon, and other old writers, and finally into *tint*, its present shape.

Tippler. This word originally meant a tavern-keeper or tapster. At Boston, Lincolnshire, in the year 1577, five persons were appointed '*tipplers* of Lincoln beer.' 'No other tippler or seller of ale and beer shall sell or draw any beer brewed out of the borough' under penalties. At Seaford, Sussex, a tippler in the reign of Elizabeth was bound 'not to use nor permit any unlawfull games during the said tyme of his *tiplinge*.'

Tipstaff. A tipstaff is an officer who attends judges at court or in chambers, and is so called from the staff of office he carries being usually *tipped* with a figure of the regal crown in gold or silver.—*Bouvier.*

Titter. Johnson gives 'from the sound' as the origin of this word. It, however, originally meant 'courtship,' and as, in the presence of their seniors, lovers sitting apart are apt to indulge in simpering and suppressed laughter, the name 'tittering' came in time to be applied to quiet or smothered laughter such as lovers indulge in.—*Dean Hoare, English Roots*, Dublin, 1856, p. 29.

Toad-eater. 'This slang phrase for a fawning, obsequious sycophant was first applied to a gluttonous parasite famous for his indiscriminate praise of all viands set before him. To test his powers of stomach and complaisance one of his patrons had a toad cooked for him, which he both ate and praised in his usual way.'—*Ogilvie.* Another authority says it is 'a metaphor taken from a mountebank's boy eating toads in order to show his master's skill in expelling poison.'—*Adventures of David Simple,* 1744.

Toast. It was formerly the custom to put toasted bread into liquor or wine. Pope alludes to the usage in the lines:—

> Some squire perhaps you take delight to rack,
> Whose game is whisk, whose treat a *toast in sack.*

The manner in which the word came to signify the 'health,' or other matter proposed at dinner-parties to be honoured by being mentioned in connection with a glass of wine, is thus told in No. 24 of the 'Tatler': 'It happened that on a public day a celebrated beauty of those times [of King Charles I.] was in the Cross Bath [at Bath], and one of the crowd of her admirers took a glass of the water in which the fair one stood and drank her health to the company. There was in the place a gay fellow, half fuddled, who offered to jump in, and swore, though he liked not the liquor, he would have the *toast* [making an allusion to the usage of the times of drinking with a toast at the bottom of the glass]. He was opposed in his resolution; yet this whim gave foundation to the present honour which is done to the lady we mention in our liquor, who has ever since been called a *toast.*'

Tobacco was first brought to England by Sir John Hawkins, but Sir Walter Raleigh and Sir Francis Drake are also mentioned as having first introduced it.—*Haydn.* Humboldt says that tobacco is the ancient Indian name of the pipe through which the herb was smoked. Columbus gave the name Tobago to the island where, to his astonishment, he saw the natives smoking. The 'Proceedings of the House of Commons' states that on " Wednesday, April 16, 1621, Sir William Stroud moved that he " would have tobacco banished wholly out of the kingdom, and that it may not be brought in from any part nor used amongst us"; and Sir Grey Palmer said "that if tobacco be not banished it will overthrow one hundred thousand men in England, for now it is so common that he hath seen ploughmen take it as they are at plough." '

Tocsin. This is a French term for an alarm-bell. It is compounded of the Old French *toquer,* to strike, and *sing* (Latin *signum,* a signal). 'The use of the terrible *tocsin* during the troubles of the Revolution to assemble the multitude has rendered the word almost proverbial.'—*Brand.*

Toddy. This word is the Indian name for the sweet juice of the unexpanded flowers of the cocoa-nut tree, from which the ardent spirit named arrack is distilled.

Tofore is an Old English word signifying before. It is used by several of the old poets. Shakespeare has two examples at least of its use, e.g. :—

    Farewell, Lavinia, my noble sister,
    O that thou wert, as thou *tofore* has been.
         Titus Andron., act iii. sc. 1.
    Some obscure precedence that hath *tofore* been sain.
         Love's Labour's Lost, act iii. sc. 1.

Fairfax also uses it :—

    With jolly plumes their crests adorned they have,
    And all *tofore* their chieftain mustered been.—*Tasso,* i.

Nares says : 'Some editors have printed it '*tofore,* as if it was an abbreviation of heretofore, but this is not proper.'

Toil comes from the Anglo-Saxon *tilian,* to till. Tilling the ground must, with the primitive implements in use in the Anglo-Saxon times, have been toil indeed.

Tolling Bells for the Dead. In an old English Homily for Trinity Sunday, cited by Strutt ('Manners and Customs,' vol. iii. p. 176), is the following :—'The fourme of the Trinitie was founded in Manne, that was Adam our forefadir, of earth oon personne, and Eve of Adam the secunde personne, and of them both was the third persone. At the death of a manne three Bellis schulde be ronge, as his knyll, in worscheppe of the Trinetee, and for a womanne, who was the secunde personne of the Trinetee, two Bellis schulde be rungen.' See NINE TAILORS MAKE A MAN.

Tomahawk was a word in use by most of the aboriginal tribes of North America to designate a *war hatchet*. The blade was of stone. It was customary to go through the ceremony of burying the tomahawk when peace was made; hence 'burying the hatchet' meant peace making. The word had different forms in the various tribes, as *tomehagen, tumnahegan, tamoihecan*, &c.

Tomb. This word comes from a Greek phrase denoting a place where a dead body has been burnt and a mound of earth raised to cover the ashes. The Latin word *tumulus* has almost the same signification. The Jewish tombs were generally hollows hewn out of the face of a rock.

Tomboy. Johnson derives this word from Tom, diminutive of Thomas, and boy, but Verstegan says it is from *tumbere*, a tumbler, from the Anglo-Saxon *tumbe*, to dance. A *tumbere*, he says, is 'a wench that skippeth like a boy.'

Tom Tiddler's Ground. This is a contraction of Tom the Idler's ground, thus—*Tom t'idler's ground*. It is a common expression in Hertfordshire for the garden of a sluggard or person too idle to pull up the weeds.

Tonsure. This is the name given to the crown or space on the top of the head kept shaven by persons in holy orders, or belonging to religious bodies in the Romish and other Churches. It is supposed to represent the crown of thorns worn by Christ. Tonsure was first rendered obligatory by the Fourth Council of Toledo, A.D. 633. As a priest advances in rank the tonsure is larger.

Tooley Street. The name of this street is a corruption of 'St. Olave Street,' from the church dedicated to St. Olave which stands at its western end. The name has undergone several transitions. In an advertisement, quoted in 'Ellis's Letters' (2nd Series, vol. iv.), the founder of Garraway's Coffee-house announces that 'Nicholas Brook, at the sign of the "Frying Pan" in *St. Tulie's Street*, is the only known man for making of mills for grinding of coffee powder.' This was in Cromwell's time.

Tooth and nail. This old phrase, meaning, of course, biting and scratching, is found in Shacklock's 'Hatchet of Heresies,' Antwerp, 1565. It is spelt '*tothe and nayle.*'

'**Too wise to err, too good to be unkind.**' The Rev. John East, of St. Michael's Church, Bath, is credited with the authorship of this line. He may have used the words as part of a hymn, but they were taken from a sermon by Dr. Adam Clarke on the text Gal. iv. 4-7, which the Doctor treated under these three heads :—

    1st. God is too wise to err.
    2nd. He is too holy to do wrong.
    3rd. He is too good to be unkind.

Top. 'To sleep like a top' is the English rendering of a French phrase meaning to sleep like a *taupe*, the word 'taupe' meaning a dormouse. The Italians have a proverb of exactly the same form and meaning, '*Egli dorme come un topo*'; *topo* being the Italian word for dormouse.

To pay the shot, i.e. to pay a proper share of a joint expense. The word shot in this phrase is a corruption of the word *scot*, Anglo-Saxon *scean*, a part or portion. The word *scot* as a legal term is still found in the phrase 'pay *scot* and lot.' It was first corrupted into *schotte*, in which shape it is used by Ben Jonson exactly in the modern sense in the line 'Let each pay his schotte.'

Tophet. An unclean place or pit near Jerusalem into which the Jews cast the bodies of beasts, or of men to whom burial was refused. A fire was kept burning to consume them. Hence metaphorically *hell*.

Topple means to fall *top* foremost or downwards—' Castles topple on their warder's heads.'—*Shakespeare.*

Top Sawyer. In a sawing pit the one who is underneath the log is not necessarily a skilled workman, but the top sawyer—the one who guides the saw and superintends the work—must be one of experience and knowledge; hence one who directs or takes the lead in any enterprise or work is metaphorically a 'top sawyer.'

Topsy-turvy. Many guesses have been made as to the origin and proper form of this proverbial expression. The following is at least a very old form. It is from Spenser's 'Faerie Queene' (b. v c. viii. s. xlii) :—

    At last they have overthrown to ground,
    Quite topside turvy.

Tervee is an old Anglo-Saxon verb still in use in some parts of Devonshire. To *tervee* is to struggle and tumble to get free. Perhaps topsy-turvy may originally have meant top side in a *tervee* or struggle. It is, however, generally thought to be derived from 'top-side, t'other way.'

Tor, applied to pointed rocks or hills in Cornwall and other parts of England, is from the same Anglo-Saxon root as the word *tower*.

To rights, Right away, Right off. In America all these expressions mean *directly*, e.g. 'I said I had never heard it, so she began *to rights* and told me the whole thing.'—*Story of the Sleigh Ride*. 'Uncle John,' said Nina, 'I want you to get the carriage out for me *right away*.'—Mrs. Stowe, *Dred*. 'I feel wonderfully consarned about that pain in your chest,' said the widow to Mr. Crane. 'It ought to be attended to *right off*, Mr. Crane, *right off*.'—*Widow Bedott Papers*.

Torpedo. In the 'Bath Chronicle,' September 10, 1807, was the following note :—' A Mr. Fulton has proposed to the American Government a plan to destroy the British navy. It is to be effected by an apparatus called a torpedo, filled with combustibles, placed under the bottom of the ships, and when exploded to blow them into the air.'

Tortoise (pronounced *tortus*). The origin of this word cannot be traced to any definite root. In Eden's translation of Oviedo's 'Natural History of the Indies,' 1555, the earliest known use of the word occurs as 'tortoyses (which are certain shell fishes).' What is called 'tortoiseshell' is the shell of the edible sea turtle.

Tory. Mr. George Olaus Borrow, in a very interesting paper contributed to the 'Norfolk Chronicle' in the year 1832, says that the word Tory 'may be traced to the Irish adherents of Charles II. during the Cromwellian era. The Gaelic words *Tar a Ri*, pronounced Tory, and meaning "Come, O King," having been so constantly in the mouths of the Royalists as to have become a by-word to designate them.'

Tot of Spirits. No derivation of this phrase is given by the dictionary-makers. A writer in 'Notes and Queries' is responsible for the following :—When Haydn, the composer, was in England, he was flattered and overwhelmed with the number of his visitors, and longed for the quiet of his German evenings, undisturbed except by the occasional lifting of his glass to his lips. At his most brilliant soirées he was in the habit of stealthily retiring now and then to his own room to moisten his lips. If he met any one on his way who wished to detain him, he would say, 'Excuse me, I have a *tot*' [a thought], tapping his forehead in a suggestive way. After a while his secret was discovered, and the *tot* became proverbial.

Toucher. 'As near as a toucher' is a cant phrase signifying a narrow escape. It is derived from an expression in use amongst London cab-drivers. A 'toucher' is when the wheels of a cab come in slight contact with another vehicle without actual damage. 'Touch and go' is from the same source.

Touching for the King's Evil. The once popular superstition that the touch of a king or reigning queen would cure the disease known as the evil may be to a certain extent explained by the circumstance that from the time of Henry VIII. it was usual to present to every person 'touched' a piece of gold from the Royal Privy Purse. Barrington ('Observations on the Statutes,' p. 107) mentions the cure of an old man, whom he was examining as a witness, who stated that when Queen Anne was at Oxford she 'touched' him for the evil. Barrington asked him if he was really cured, upon which the old man smilingly said that he did not believe he ever had the evil, but his parents were poor, and 'had no objection to the bit of gold.'

Tout-ensemble, a French phrase meaning the whole taken together. The English phrase 'the general effect' expresses nearly the same meaning.

Towel is the French *touaille*, which Landais says is a corruption of *toille*, linen, cloth.

Tower of London. The Tower was established by William I., and was completed by William Rufus, who surrounded it with the moat. The following is a very old account of its foundation: 'The Tower of London was builded by Belinus, of whose name the haven thereby [Billingsgate] continueth the memorye to this daye; but Lydgate the monk ascribethe it to Julius Cæsar. Howsoever that be, true it is that William the Redd walled it round about what tyme he layed the foundation of Westminster Halle.'—*Lambard*. The Duke of Wellington, when Constable of the Tower, had the moat dried and laid out as gardens, but the garrison still possess the power of filling it with water if occasion should require.

To wit. This ancient phrase, which has not even now disappeared from law-books and practice, is from the Anglo-Saxon *witan*, to know.

Town, from the Anglo-Saxon word *tune*, a hedge or fence. Verstegan says, 'Our ancestors in time of war, to defend themselves from being spoyled, would cast a ditch and make a strong hedge about their houses, and the houses so environed about with *tunes* or hedges got the name of *tunes* annexed unto them. As *Cote-tun*, now Cotton, for that his *cote* or house was fenced or *tuned* about; *North-tun*, now Norton, in regard to the opposite situation from *South-tun*, now Sutton. Moreover, when necessity, by reason of wars and troubles, caused whole *thorpes* to be with such *tunes* environed about, those enclosed places did thereby take the name of *tunes*, afterwards pronounced *townes*, and so gave cause that all *stedes*, now "cities," all *thorps*, now "villages," all *burghs*, now "burrows," and all places else that contained but some number of tenements in a neerness together, got the name of *Townes*, as vulgarly we yet, unto this day, call them.'—*Restitution*, edit. 1655, p. 232.

Toy. This word is used in Birmingham in a singular sense. It is applied to articles of utility made of steel. Purse mounts, small rings for keys, sword-hilts, purses, &c., and other small ornamental steel goods are called 'light steel toys.' Champagne-nippers, sugar-cutters, nut-crackers, and similar articles are called 'heavy steel toys.' Burke, as will be remembered, called Birmingham 'the toyshop of Europe.' The word 'toy' formerly meant a droll story or an odd fancy. Latimer, in 1550, in a sermon preached before the king, in introducing the legend of Tenterden steeple and the Goodwin Sands, says: 'And here, by the way, I will tell you a merry *toy*.'

Tozer. The 'Chronicles of Carlingford,' that charming *exposé* of the inner life of the dissent of half a century ago, has no more life-like portrait than that of Mr. Tozer the deacon. The name was not altogether a fictitious one. When Joanna Southcott in the early part of this century quarrelled with her chief disciple, Carpenter, she removed from Newington to Duke Street, Lambeth, where another enthusiast, a Mr. Tozer, built a chapel in which he preached the delusive stupidities which his patroness promulgated.

Tradesman, Trader. Johnson says a merchant is a *trader*, but not a *tradesman*.

Tradesmen's Signs. The origin of incongruous signs such as 'Bell and Candlestick,' 'Angel and Cucumber,' &c., may be accounted for by the following passage from the 'Spectator,' No. 28: 'It is usual for a young tradesman, at his first setting up, to add to his own sign that of the master whom he has served, as the husband after marriage gives place to his mistress's arms in his own coat.'

Tragedy. The literal meaning of this word is 'the song of the goat.' Some suppose that the name was given because the Greek actors were dressed in goat-skins to resemble satyrs; others that a goat was the prize for which the actors competed. The fact remains; the origin is lost.

Trammel. Trammels were ancient contrivances for teaching horses to 'amble,' that is, to move the legs on one side together, instead of alternating their motion with the legs on the other side. In G. Markham's 'Way to Wealth,' p. 48, is a description of the method of using trammels, which says that, after having provided strong pieces of web and proper straps and buckles, you are to fasten them 'one to his neer fore-leg and his neer hinder-leg, the other to his farre fore-leg and his farre hinder-leg, which is call'd among horse-men *trameling*.' The horse is then to be put to pasture for a time, and driven about occasionally, till 'you can see him amble swiftly and truly; then you shall take him back, and ride him with the same trammels at least three or foure times a daye, till you find that he is so perfect that no way can be so rough or uneven as to compel him to alter his stroke or to go unnimbly.'

Tramway. This is usually thought to be derived from the name of Mr. Benjamin Ou*tram*, who, it is stated, first made them in 1800. This is a mistake; the word was in use long before his time. A '*tram*' was a coal waggon or cart for carrying coal by the common roads from the pits to the ship. When wooden rails were used for coal waggons or trams to run upon they took their names from the vehicles. In 1794 an Act of Parliament was passed for making 'an iron dram-road, *tram-road*, or railway between Cardiff and Merthyr Tidvill.' This was six years before Mr. Outram was heard of.

Transpire means literally to breathe through the pores of the skin. The modern use of the word in the sense of to happen, to occur, to become known, &c., is greatly censured by accurate scholars, e.g.: 'Our newspaper writers talk of a business or an event "transpiring" when all they mean is that the business was transacted or the event happened.'—*Professor Malden.*

Trash. This word originally meant fine brushwood, such as the clippings of trees and hedges too fine to be used as firewood.

It was common to fill the middles of faggots with this fine stuff to swell the bulk. Evelyn, in his 'Discourse of Forest Trees,' speaks of 'the abuse too much practised of filling the middle part [of faggots] with *trash* and short sticks.' The word now means anything inferior or worthless.

Travail, labour, sorrow. This is purely Celtic in its origin. The Welsh *trafael* (*tra*, exceeding, and *fael*, work or labour) is conclusive on this point.

Treachery. This word is derived from an old Norman-English noun, *treacher*, a traitor. It was sometimes spelt *treachour*, and occasionally *treachetour*. Shakespeare uses it in 'Lear':—

Fools by heavenly compulsion ; knaves, thieves, and *treachers.*—Act. i. sc. 2.

Spenser spells it *treachour* in the following line from the 'Faerie Queene':—

No knight but *treachour*, full of false despight.—L. iv. 41.

But he uses another form in VI. viii. 7 :—

Abide, ye caytive *treachetours* untrew.

Treacle. This word literally means an antidote against poison or venom. 'Venice treacle was a common name for a supposed antidote to all poisons.'—*Trench*. 'A most strong *treacle* against these venomous heresies.'—*Sir T. More*. A curious example of Old English occurs in a black-letter Bible of Queen Elizabeth's time, where the verse Jeremiah viii. 22 stands thus : 'Is there no *triacle* at Gilead ? Is there no Phisition there ?' In making loaf sugar, the material when boiled is placed in moulds of the shape of a sugar-loaf, with the points downwards, near which are a number of small holes, through which the uncrystallisable portion *trickles*. This was probably the origin of the word *treacle* as applied to the syrup of sugar.

Treadmills were anciently used by the Chinese to raise water from their rivers for the irrigation of their rice-fields. They were adapted to prison use by the late Sir William Cubitt. The first was erected at Brixton Gaol in 1817.

Tree. 'The tree differs from the shrub in having its lowest branches at a greater height from the ground. The branches of a shrub proceed directly from the ground without a supporting stem.'—*Lindley*.

Trenchers. Trenchers were originally slices of bread (*tranchiors*) upon which the flesh-meat was served. They were succeeded by wooden 'platters' similar to the modern 'bread

platters'; and these were constantly used before the introduction
of metallic or earthenware plates. It appears to have been unusual
to change these trenchers, but to eat of various dishes from one.
Bishop Hall says that noblemen's chaplains had to stipulate 'never
to change their trencher twice.' Decker tells us that in those
days 'The Venetian carved not his meat with a silver pitch-fork,
neither did the sweet-toothed Englishman shift a dozen of trenchers at one meal.'—*Gul's Hand Book*, ch. i. Trenchers are now
used by cooks for chopping suet upon. 'A good trencherman' is
still a synonym for a heavy feeder.

Tresses. A woman's 'tresses' are composed of *three* locks or
portions of her hair braided together. When they are so braided
they form a 'tress.' The word is derived from a Greek word
implying threefold.

Tria juncta in unia. A Latin phrase meaning three joined in
one. It is the motto of the Order of the Bath, and was probably
at the first institution of the Order adopted in allusion to faith,
hope, and charity. It is now thought to signify the three classes
of those admitted into the Order, or perhaps to the three crowns
which are the armorial ensign of the Order.

Tricolour. The National Assembly of France, on July 13,
1789, decided that 'the cockade should be of the colours of the
city [of Paris], blue and red,' but, as these were already the colours
of the house of Orleans, white, the old colour of France, was
added on the proposal of M. de Lafayette.

Trifle. This is doubtless another form of the word *trivial*.

Trinidad was so named by Columbus from the fact that when
first seen from shipboard three mountain peaks upon the island
were thought to be as many separate islands, but when he found
only one he gave it the name of the Trinity, which it still bears.

Trinity. 'Theophilus, Bishop of Antioch, who flourished in
the second century, was the first who used the word *trinity*.'—
Haydn.

Trinity House. This celebrated Guild or Corporation, which
is so great a safeguard to navigation, was founded by Sir Thomas
Spert, who was Comptroller of the Navy to Henry VIII., and
commander of the great war-ship the *Harry Grâce de Dieu*. The
charter, which is dated March 20, 1529, designates the Guild as
'The Master, Wardens, and Assistants of the Guild, or Fraternity,
or Brotherhood, of the Most Glorious and Undividable Trinity,

and of St. Clement in the Parish of Deptford Strond, in the county of Kent.'

Trite. The literal meaning of this word is threadbare.

Trivet. This word is a corruption of trifeet—*tri*, three, and *feet*. The name expresses exactly the form of the instrument so well known in connection with Sunday dinners of baked legs of mutton, Yorkshire puddings, and potatoes.

Trivial, from the Latin *trivialis*, *trivium*, a place where three roads meet. 'Trivial is a word borrowed from the life. Mark three or four persons standing idly at the point where one street bisects at right angles another, and discussing there the worthless gossip, the idle nothings of the day; there you have the living explanation of the words *trivial*, *trivialities*, such as no explanation which did not thus root itself in the etymology would ever give you, or enable you to give to others. For there you have the *tres* [three], the *viæ* [ways], the *trivium*; and *trivialities* properly means such talk as is holden by those idle loiterers that gather at these meetings of three roads.'—*Trench*.

Trombone, from the Italian *trombona*, a large trumpet. See SACKBUT.

Trough. In Surrey and other Southern counties this word is pronounced as though spelt *trow*; a little further north we get the correct pronunciation, *troff*; whilst in the Midlands it is always called *truff*. How is a foreigner to learn the proper pronunciation of the English language?

Trousers. This word seems to be derived from the French word *trousse*, which signifies to tie or lace up tightly. It was first used in England in the form *truss*. We still *truss* a fowl for cooking, and we tie hay and pack drapery in *trusses*. One of the earliest examples of its use in connection with *trousers* is found in Wiseman's 'Surgery,' quoted by Johnson:—'The unsightliness and pain in the leg may be helped by wearing a laced stocking; a *laced trouse* will do as much for the thigh.' Spenser, in his work on Ireland, says, 'The leather-quilted jack serves . . . to cover his *trouse* on horse-back.' In Bulwer's 'Pedigree of the English Gallant,' it is said of the Irish, 'Their *trowses*, commonly spelt *trossers*, were long pantaloons exactly fitted to the shape.' The ancient *trowses* were probably long gaiters reaching to the thigh, worn separately on each leg, and kept in position by being fastened by a strap to the girdle. They were used when riding on horseback. Shakespeare ('Henry V.' act iii. sc. 7) has, 'You rode like a kerne of Ireland, your French hose off, and in your *strait* [that is, tight, narrow] trossers.' Trousers first began to be worn about the beginning of the present century. They were much ridiculed at first, and it was hardly considered respectable to be seen in them. The Rev. H. T. Ellacome, in a very interesting article on this subject in 'Notes and Queries,' November 22, 1879, says, 'I remember a clerical friend from a distance happened to call on me just when a funeral was announced; being busily engaged with a clothing club, I requested him to take it, but he declined *because he had trousers on*.' When Mrs. Siddons performed Imogen in the year 1802, her male dress was 'exactly the straight or frock coat and *trousers* of our modern beaux.' 'In October 1812, orders were made by Trinity and St. John's College that students appearing in hall or chapel in pantaloons or trowsers should be considered as absent.'—*Cooper's Annals of Cambridge.* There is considerable discrepancy as to the date when trousers were first adopted as a part of the dress of British infantry. Colonel Cadell, in his 'Narrative of the Campaigns of the 28th Regiment,' says that the men of that regiment, when despatched on the Walcheren expedition, were 'clothed in grey trowsers made loose, and half-boots.' When the regiments returned, 'the trowsers were nearly as good as when we started,' and 'trowsers as first worn by the 28th Regiment were adopted throughout the army to the great comfort of the soldier.' Two other statements follow. The first appears to refer only to a particular *shape* of the trousers used by the men under the Duke of Wellington. The date 1823 in the second is probably a mistake for 1813, but the compiler has been unable to ascertain which is correct. The Duke of York was Commander-in-Chief in both years.

'Senior,' in 'Notes and Queries,' December 27, 1870, says that 'trowsers were at first called Wellington trowsers, because the Duke introduced them during the Peninsular War, making the *pantaloon* loose from the leg downwards, with an opening at the sides as high as the calf of the leg, which was cleverly closed over the short boot (the Wellington boot) by a series of silk cord loops, so that the boot might be the more easily taken off in the case of a wound.' 'Up to 1823 the British soldiers as a rule wore breeches, leggings, or gaiters, and low shoes. On June 18, 1823, the Duke of York, who was Commander-in-Chief, announced by a General Order that "His Majesty has been pleased to approve of the discontinuance of breeches, leggings, and shoes as part of the clothing of the infantry soldiers; and of blue-grey cloth trousers and half-boots being substituted."'

The word 'trousers' is never used in America. The garments so called in England are known as '*pants*' in the United States, the word being a contraction of *pantaloons*, the old English name for a tight-fitting garment reaching to the ankle, worn by gentlemen about 1810 to 1820, with Hessian boots. See SANS CULOTTES.

Trousseau. A French word literally signifying a bundle. It is used in England to signify the outfit of a lady on her marriage, including her wardrobe, her jewellery, her ornaments, her toilet requisites, &c.

Troy Weight was so named from its having been first adopted at Troyes in France.

True Blue. This phrase originated in 1802 as the name of a dye discovered by a Mr. Scott, who made a fortune by it, and was afterwards known as 'True Blue Scott.' He built the original Adelphi Theatre.

Truro. The Bishop of this newly-created diocese signs ' E. W. Truro*n*.'

Truss. A truss of straw is 36 lbs.; a truss of old hay is 56 lbs., of new 60 lbs.

Truth, from the Anglo-Saxon *troth*. Tooke says that truth is 'the third person singular of the indicative *trow*, and was formerly written *troweth, trowth, trouth, troth*, meaning that which one *troweth* or believeth.' Other authorities dispute this etymon, and attribute it to the Sanscrit *dhru*, to be established, from which it is contended the German got *treu*, faithful, true. Truth, it is argued, is not what is *believed*, but what is fixed or immutable.

Tuition means defence, protection, or guardianship. Bishop Hall says: 'Proofs of an omnipotent *tuition*, whether against foreign powers or secret conspiracies.' Dr. Trench, speaking of this meaning of the word, says, 'One defends another most effectually who imparts to him those principles and that knowledge whereby he shall be able to defend himself; and therefore our modern use of tuition is a deeper one than the earlier, which made it to mean external rather than this internal protection.'

Tulip. The tulip is a native of the Levant, where it grows wild. It is not clear who brought it first to Western Europe, but

Gesner ('Gesneri Epistola Medicinales') tells us that he saw the first in the beginning of 1559 in the garden of John Henry Herwark at Augsburg. Soon after this they became pretty common in the gardens of florists. About eighty years afterwards, 1634 to 1637, arose in Holland the frantic piece of folly known as the *Tulipomania*, during which single roots of tulips were bought at fabulous prices. Beckmann ('History of Inventions') tells us that they were sold by weight, one root of a variety called *Admiral Leifkin*, weighing 400 *perit* (a weight rather less than a grain), having fetched 4,400 florins. Another buyer gave twelve acres of land for a single root of *Semper Augustus*. Munting gives from the trading books of the period a case where for a root of *Viceroy* some one agreed to deliver two lasts of wheat, four of rye, four fat oxen, three fat swine, twelve fat sheep, two hogsheads of wine, four tuns of beer, two ditto butter, 1,000 lbs. of cheese, a complete bed, a suit of clothes, and a silver beaker, the total value being estimated at 2,500 florins. The highest price Beckmann mentions is 7,000 florins, for which sum Henry Munting in 1636 sold a tulip root to a merchant of Alkmaar.

Tumble-down Dick is a sobriquet originally applied to Richard Cromwell after his fall.

Tune. 'The tune the old cow died of' was starvation. The following verse throws a little light upon the origin of the saying:

> There was an old man and he had an old cow,
>   And he had no fodder to give her,
> So he took up his fiddle and played her this tune:—
>   'Consider, good cow, consider;
>   This isn't the time for grass to grow
>   Consider, good cow, consider.'

Tureen is a corruption of the French word *terrine*, an *earthen* vessel in which soup is served. A silver or plated 'tureen' is consequently a misnomer.

Turkey. The ordinary name for this bird conveys the idea that it came originally from the East, which is an error. The turkey is a native of North America, from whence it was brought to Germany in 1536, and being domesticated there soon spread itself over Europe. Dugdale mentions that young turkeys were served at a great banquet in 1555. In a 'Bill of Charges' for a dinner given at Oxford by Lord Leycester, Chancellor of the University, is an item as follows: 'For vij. Turkes to Mrs. Cogene, iij. of them cokes and iiij. of them henes, at iiijs. a pesse and iiijd. over, in the whole xxviijs. iiijd.'—*Collectanea Curiosa*, vol. ii. p. 4. Tusser also mentions them in 1585 as though they were then well known. In his 'Five Hundred Points of Husbandry' are the following lines:

> Beefe, mutton, and porke, shred pies of the best,
> Pig, veale, goose, and capon, and *turkie* well drest,
> Cheese, apples, and nuts, jolie carols to heare,
> As then, in the countrie, is counted good cheare.

Turncoat. 'The name of turncoat took its rise from one of the first Dukes of Savoy, whose dominions lying open to attacks from both France and Spain, was obliged to temporise and fall in with that Power that was most likely to distress him, according to the success of their arms against one another. So being frequently obliged to change sides, he humorously got a coat made that was blue on one side and white on the other, and might be indifferently worn either side out. While in the Spanish interest he wore the blue side out, and the white side was the badge for the French. From hence he was called "Emmanuel the *Turncoat*," to distinguish him from other princes of the same name of that house.'—*Scot's Magazine*, October 1747, p. 477.

Turner the Painter. A correspondent, 'A. M.,' of 'Notes and Queries,' June 12, 1858, says that Mr. Tomkinson, the eminent pianoforte maker, told him the following story :—'My father was the first to discover the boy's talents. My father was a jeweller, and lived in Southampton Street, Covent Garden. Turner's father was a hairdresser, and lived in Maiden Lane, at a corner house in a little court; he operated on my father. On one occasion Turner brought his child with him, and while the father was dressing my father the little boy was occupied in copying something he saw on the table. They left, and after a few minutes they returned. Turner apologised for troubling my father, and begged to know what his son had been copying. On being shown the copy, my father said, "Your son never could have done it!" He had copied a coat of arms from a handsome set of castors which happened at that time to be on the table. Some time after, a gentleman died who had been long under Turner's razor, and left him a legacy of 100*l.* The moment my father heard this he begged Turner to allow him to dispose of the 100*l.* for the benefit of the boy by articling him to Malton, the distinguished architectural draughtsman of that day. This was done accordingly.'

Turning the tables upon us. This is a translation of an old Roman proverb. In the reign of Augustus, among other reckless extravagances, it was the rage in Rome to have tables made of mauritana wood inlaid with ivory. These tables were sold at extravagant prices. When the men rebuked their wives for the enormous sums spent upon dress, the ladies retorted by reminding their husbands of the large amounts they lavished upon their tables. They 'turned the tables' upon them.

Turnip, Purnsnip. *Nip* in these names is properly *nep*, from the Anglo-Saxon *næpe*, a tap-root.

Turnpikes were so called from poles or bars (*pikes*) swung on a pivot so that they could be *turned* round when the road was required to be opened for the passage of horsemen or vehicles. Ben Jonson says ('Staple of News,' act iii. sc. 1):

I move upon my axle like a *turnpike*.

Five hundred years ago, it is said, there was a monk whose self-appointed work it was to guard the shrine of St. Anthony on Highgate Hill. He was a man of some means, and had little to do. Being of an active turn of mind, he conceived the idea of taking gravel from the top of the hill to fill up the hollow way between Islington and Highgate so as to make a decent road for the pilgrims who came to St. Anthony's. In doing this he expended all his fortune, but the King came to the rescue, and published a decree addressed to 'our well-beloved William Phelippe,' in which, after approving the motives which had induced him to benefit 'our people passing through the highway between Heghgate and Smethfield, in many places notoriously miry and deep,' he authorises him to set up a bar and take toll, so that he might keep the road in order and himself in comfort and dignity. This was the first toll-bar in England.—*Timbs.*

Turret is *towerette*, a small tower. The word tower is from the Anglo-Saxon *torr*, the peak of a rock.

Turtle. This word, applied to the sea tortoise, first occurs in the works of Archer, an American, who wrote 'An Account of a Voyage to Massachusetts,' in which he says, 'I commanded some of my companions to seek out for crabbes, lobsters, *turtles*, &c., for sustaning us till the ship's return.' In 1610 mention is made of the animal in two accounts of Bermuda. The name does not seem then to have been fixed, for one says, 'The *tortoises* came in; one *turtle* (for so we called them) feasted six messes.' The other account has, 'Tortoises, which some call *turtles*.' In 1612 the name is spelt *turkle*, and in 1622 *turckle*.

''Twas in Trafalgar's Bay.' This song was written by **Mr.**

Samuel James Arnold, who was greatly annoyed at the alteration made by the publisher in the first two lines. Arnold wrote

> 'Twas in Trafalgar bay
> The saucy Frenchmen lay.

This the publisher altered to

> 'Twas in Trafalgar's bay
> We saw the Frenchmen lay,

which, of course, is ungrammatical. The author was a good deal 'chaffed' on the subject, and he altered them to

> 'Twas in Trafalgar's bay
> The boasting Frenchmen lay,

which Braham adopted, and ever afterwards used.

Tweed. This well-known name for a peculiar woollen cloth originated in an accident. A cloth in which the threads of the warp and the weft cross each other singly has a plain surface, but if they cross in ones and twos alternately a diagonal effect is produced. This diagonal cloth is called '*twill*' in England, and in Scotland '*tweel*.' In an invoice of 'tweels' sent to a dealer in London the letters had been blotted, and the dealer read the name '*tweed*,' and, as the goods came from the banks of the River Tweed, the name seemed so appropriate that he adopted it. It is now universally used as the name of the cloth.

Tweedledum and Tweedledee. The lines in which these words occur were written by Byrom—the inventor of the modern system of stenography—in 1725, when a musical charlatan named Bononcini was fashionable and Handel was neglected. They were published in 'Byrom's Remains' by the Chetham Society, and are as follows:

> Some say compared to Bononcini
> That Mynheer Handel's but a ninny
> Others aver that, to him, Handel
> Is scarcely fit to hold a candle.
> Strange all this difference should be
> 'Twixt *Tweedledum and Tweedledee.*

Twelvemonth in Law. 'This term, if it be in the singular, means an entire year; but if it be in the plural—twelvemonths—the months are computed at twenty-eight days to the month.'—*Wharton*. This is not the case as to *Acts of Parliament*, in which 'month' always means a calendar month. See MONTH.

Twenty, Thirty, Forty, &c. The *ty* in these words is the *tig* or ten of the Anglo-Saxons. *Twenty* is twain-tig, or two tens; *thirty*, three tens; *forty*, four tens, and so on.

Twig. To twig, to understand, as 'Do you twig?' 'Do you perceive?' This is not slang, as is commonly supposed; the Gaelic *tuig* signifies to discern, to understand.

Twilight is from the Anglo-Saxon *tweon*, signifying between, and *leoht*, light. The original meaning was *tween-light*.

Twin. Britton says that *ing* is a generic name for persons or people, often found with this signification in the names of places, as in *Leamington*, the town of the *ing* or people of the Leam [river]. The ancient name for twins was *twe-ings*, that is, two *ings* or persons. The surname *Twining* is derived from this source.

Twine, Thread. *Twine* means *two* cords *twiced* or twisted. Thread is *three* cords *three'd* or *thriced*.

Twinkling of a bedstaff. A bedstaff was a heavy rod with which chambermaids formerly beat up feather beds when 'making' the bed. The rapid following of blow after blow might suggest *twinkling* as a synonym for momentary. Hence the proverb, 'in a twinkling.' 'To run like winkin' was formerly commonly in use in the same sense.

Tyburn was the place of execution for London from 1196, when William Fitzosbert, or Longbeard, was hanged there, until 1783. The first execution in front of Newgate was on December 9, 1783.

Typhoon is from the Chinese words *tai*, great, and *foong*, wind. The Chinese pronounce the word *taifoong*, and it is spelt in that way by Europeans resident in China.

U

U as an initial letter. Formerly it was the practice to use the article *an* before every word beginning with *u*, whether long or short. It is now, however, held that, as the long sound of the *u* partakes of the sound *y* as in the word youth, all words beginning with the long *u* should have the article *a*. Thus we say '*a* united family,' '*a* useful servant'; but '*an* uncle,' '*an* urgent necessity,' '*an* ugly reptile.'

U and **V** were formerly considered to be the same letter, and were used indiscriminately the one for the other. At the beginning of the sixteenth century they were separated, *u* being marked as a vowel and *v* as a consonant.

Uhlan. This name came into general use at the time of the Franco-German War, and was then thought to be a new term for hussar. There is, however, a full account of them, under the spelling *Ulans*, in James's 'Universal Military Dictionary in English and French,' 4th edit. 1816.

Ultima Thule (Latin), the extreme end. The name given by the Romans to the most northerly part of Europe with which they were acquainted.

Ultramarine. Cotgrave (edit. 1611) has '*Terre d'ombre*, beyond sea azur, an earth used by painters.' *Asur* he defines as 'azure, skie colour.' '*Asur d'outre mer*, beyond sea azure; the best kind of azure, made of Lapis Lazuli.' The ' beyond sea ' of Cotgrave has been Latinised into ' ultramarine,' and now means the colour itself.

Ultra vires is a Latin term used in law to signify ' beyond the powers.' For instance, if a company be established for making iron, and the directors undertake the making of brass, and thereby lose money, the shareholders may charge the directors with the loss, because the making of brass was *ultra vires*, or beyond the powers delegated to them, which were limited to the making of iron. So, also, it would be *ultra vires* if the directors of the Bank of England were to become dealers in diamonds, or to set up a mint upon their premises.

Umbrella. There is a very general belief that umbrellas were invented and first used by Jonas Hanway, the celebrated philanthropist of the last century. This is an error. Hanway was perhaps the first *man* who walked London streets with an umbrella over his head to keep off the rain, and we are told that ' after continuing to use one for thirty years he saw them come into general use.' He died in 1786, so that the date when he introduced them must have been between 1750 and 1760. The earliest use of umbrellas, however, dates back two or three thousand years before this. On one of the ancient bas-reliefs brought from Nineveh by Layard, and now in the British Museum, there is a representation of a slave holding an umbrella over the head of the king as he rises in his chariot. And in Bohn's edition of ' Aristophanes,' vol. i. p. 413, the following stage direction occurs, ' Enter Prometheus, muffled up and covered with an umbrella.'

Coming to our own country, we find that there is a curious representation of a Saxon king with an attendant holding an umbrella over his head in a MS. of the tenth century, now in the British Museum ('Harleian MSS.,' No. 603). And in Quarle's 'Emblems,' published 1635, are the following lines:—

> Look up, my soul, advance the lowly stature
> Of thy sad thoughts, advance thy humble eye:
> See, here's a shadow found: the human nature
> Is made th' umbrella to the Deity
> To catch the sunbeams of thy just Creator:
> Beneath this covert thou may'st safely lie.
> Book iv. Emblem xiv.

In Kersey's 'Dictionarum Anglo-Britannicum,' published in 1708, we find: 'Umbrella or umbrello, a kind of broad fan or screen commonly used by women to shelter them from rain.' Swift, in 'A City Shower,' published in 1710, has the following couplet:—

> The tucked-up sempstress walks with hasty strides,
> While streams run down the oiled umbrella's sides.

And Gay, in 'Trivia, or the Art of Walking the Streets,' published in 1712, has:—

> Let Persian maids the umbrella's ribs display
> To guard their beauties from the sunny ray,
> Or sweating slaves support the shady load
> When eastern monarchs show their state abroad:
> Britain in winter only knows its aid
> To guard from chilly show'rs the walking maid.

Bailey, in his Dictionary, which was first published about 1720, says: 'PARASOL, a sort of little canopy or *umbrella* which women carry to keep off the rain.' 'UMBRELLA, *a little shadow*, an umbrella which women bear in their hands to shade them.' In 'Memoirs of the Reign of George II.,' by Horace Walpole, it is stated that in December 1758 one Dr. Shebbaire 'stood in the pillory, having a footman holding an umbrella to keep off the rain.'

When first introduced umbrellas were kept at coffee-houses to be lent to customers in case of a heavy shower. An advertisement in the 'Tatler' states that 'the young gentleman belonging to the Custom House who in fear of rain borrowed *the* umbrella from Wilk's Coffee-house shall the next time be welcome to the maid's pattens.' One Macdonald, who wrote his own life, says that in 1778 he had a fine silk umbrella that he brought from Spain, which he could not carry with comfort, as the people called out 'Frenchman, why don't you get a coach?' He also tells us that at that time there were no umbrellas '*worn*' in London except in noblemen's and gentlemen's houses, where there was a large one hung in the hall to hold over a lady if it rained between the door and her carriage.

Uncle Sam. This term is used in reference to America exactly in the same way as 'John Bull' is applied to England. It arose at the time of the last war between England and America. At a place named Troy, on the Hudson, a commissariat contractor named Elbert Anderson, of New York, had a store yard. A Government inspector named Samuel Wilson, who was always called 'Uncle Sam,' superintended the examination of the provisions, and when they were passed, each cask or package was marked 'EA—US,' the initials of the contractor and of the United States. The man whose duty it was to mark the casks, who was a facetious fellow, being asked what the letters meant, replied that they stood for Elbert Anderson and *Uncle Sam*. The joke soon became known, and was heartily entered into by Uncle Sam himself. It soon got into print, and long before the war was over was known throughout the United States. Mr. Wilson, the original 'Uncle Sam,' died at Troy in August 1854, aged eighty-four years, and the particulars just given were published in the 'Albany Argus' at the time of his death.

Uncouth. This word formerly meant unknown. Verstegan gives the explanation in his 'Anglo-Saxon Glossary' as follows: '*Kuth, known*, acquainted, familiar, as contrariwise *uncuth* is unknown,' &c.

Uncovering. Uncovering the head and ungloving the hand were knightly acts. The head uncovered—that is, the helmet removed—was significant of confidence, as he that did so was at the mercy of the other. The hand ungloved and bare was the sign that there was no lurking treachery.

Uncut Books. The term *uncut* as used by booksellers means uncut *by a bookbinder*, so as to cut away a portion of the margin. 'A book may have been cut open for reading, but it is still *uncut* in the proper trade sense.'—*Athenæum*, October 20, 1866.

Under the Rose. This phrase is said to have originated in Birmingham. A Jacobite Club, established in the early part of the eighteenth century, met in a room the ceiling of which was ornamented by the figure of an open rose. It was one of the rules of the Club that everything which took place there 'under the rose' was to be kept a profound secret. Perhaps, however, the founders of the Club placed the rose on the ceiling in allusion to the Latin phrase *sub rosa*.

Underwriter. Up to the year 1824 insurance companies were, with two exceptions, prohibited from negotiating marine insurance. The exceptions were two chartered companies, the *Royal Exchange* and the *London*, who established such rigorous rules and levied such high rates that their business fell off, and the whole system of marine insurance fell into the hands of private persons. The persons who engaged in this business met at a coffee-house kept by one Lloyd, and their room was eventually known as 'Lloyd's.' Unable to carry on any joint action because of the chartered monopolies just mentioned, the members of Lloyd's (acting practically in common) subscribed or *wrote under* the policy of insurance of a ship the sums for which they privately bound themselves in case the ship were lost or damaged. The prohibition of joint-stock marine insurance has long been abolished, but the traditional system of underwriting is still the practice which prevails more extensively than any other.

Unhouselled. Shakespeare makes the Ghost in 'Hamlet' complain that he was sent to his account 'unhousl'd and unaneled.' *Housel* was the Anglo-Saxon name for the Holy Sacrament, and to have partaken of it was to be *houselled*. To *anele* was to anoint, as in extreme unction. The Ghost therefore bemoans the fact that by being suddenly murdered he had no opportunity of partaking of the Sacrament before his death or of receiving the rite of extreme unction.

Unicorn. The chiru (*Pantholops Hodgsonii*), inhabiting the high plains of Thibet, is considered by many to have been the original unicorn. It has naturally two horns, but from its fighting propensities often loses one, and is more frequently seen with one horn than with two.

Uniforms. The colours of European soldiers are usually those worn as livery by the royal servants in each country, which are taken from the predominant colours in the armorial bearings. The English royal arms are *gules* or red, charged with golden lions, and the national uniform is red with yellow facings. The French adopted blue coats with yellow facings from the *azure* field and golden lilies of the Bourbons. The bearing of the Hapsburgs is '*argent*, a *fess gules*'— the Austrian uniform is white with red facings; and so of the other European nations.

Union Jack. The national flag of England was originally the banner of St. George—white with a red cross. It was called simply the 'Jack.' When James I. came to the throne of both kingdoms, the banner of St. Andrew, blue with a white diagonal cross, was added, the united crosses being thence called the 'Union' Jack. In 1801 the banner of St. Patrick—white with a diagonal red cross—was added. The word 'Jack' is supposed to be corrupted from the French *Jaque*, a jacket, and was applied to the early flags because the cross of St. George was embroidered on the jackets of the English infantry.

Unique. This French word is often erroneously used in England to express rarity, curiousness, or excellence. Not long ago an advertisement announced that a West End milliner had received from Paris a large number of hats and bonnets, all of which were perfectly unique! The word means *alone, without a parallel*, the only one of its kind. 'Perfectly unique' is nonsense; what is 'unique' requires no qualification.

United States. The United States declared their independence of England July 4, 1776. It was acknowledged by England September 3, 1783.

United States and Canada. 'The boundary line between these two countries is a tract thirty feet wide cleared of all trees or other growth. At the end of every mile is a cast-iron pillar, painted white, square, four feet out of the ground, and bearing in raised letters on its sides the names of the commissioners who ran the line, and the date.'—*Montreal Morning Courier.*

Unmarried. Burrill says that this word in a will denotes either never having been married, or not having a husband or wife living at the time.

Unnatural is something *contrary to* nature. 'Preternatural' is something beyond or beside nature. 'Supernatural' is something *above* natural. 'The miracles wrought by Christ were supernatural.'

Until. They have a curious use of this word in some parts of Ireland. Not long ago an application was made to the Court of Chancery for directions how to act in the case of a will drawn up by a Catholic priest, in which the testator left a certain sum to his nephew 'until he shall attain the age of 21 years.' It was ruled that the bequest was 'not to be paid' *until*, &c.

Upbraid, from the Anglo-Saxon *upgebiredan*, one of the meanings of which was regurgitation from the stomach. Grose, in his 'Glossary,' has '*Upbraid*, to rise in the stomach (North), e.g. My stomach *upbraids*.'

Upholder and **Upholsterer.** An upholder is an undertaker of funerals. An upholsterer is one who furnishes and fits up houses for residence.—*Smart.*

Upper Crust. This term is sometimes used as a slang term for the upper ranks of society. It seems that long ago the upper crust of a loaf of bread was the orthodox part to place before distinguished visitors. In Wynkyn de Worde's 'Boke of Keruinge' [carving] are these directions: 'Than take a lofe in your lyfte hande and pare ye lofe rounde aboute; then cut the ouer ernste to youre souerayne, and cut the nether cruste, and voyde the parynge, and touche the lofe no more after it is so serued.' In Mr. Furnivall's 'Manners and Meales in Olden Time,' some ancient directions are quoted, e.g. :—

> Furst pare the quarters of the loffe round alle about,
> Than kutt the vpper cruste for your souerayne and to him alowt.

Up to the hub. This is a proverbial expression in America signifying to the utmost, or to the extreme point. The allusion is to a vehicle sunk in the mud to the 'hub' of the wheels, which is as far as it can go. '"For my part," said Abijah, grimly, "if things was managed my way I shouldn't commune with nobody that didn't believe in election *up to the hub.*"'—Mrs. Stowe, *Dred,* vol. i. p. 311.

Up the Spout. This proverbial expression is an allusion to the custom of pawnbrokers of sending pledges up a spout or lift from the shop to a warehouse at the top of the premises.

Urbane is from *urbis,* a city. The allusion is to the polish or elegant manners of the inhabitants of cities, as compared with those of remote or country districts.

Urine of Birds. Birds have no urinary organs of discharge, so that the urine passes at once into the bowel, whence it is ejected with the fæces, generally in a solid form. It may be distinguished from the true fæces by being of a whitish colour.

Use of Animal Food. According to the Biblical account of the Fall and the subsequent Deluge, it would appear that men before the Flood did not eat the flesh of animals. The permission to do so was first given to Noah (Genesis ix. 3). Dr. Adam Clarke argues from this that after the Flood vegetal productions were less nutritious, and that the human constitution was consequently impaired, so that the normal duration of human life diminished from upwards of 900 years to the average of threescore years and ten.

Used up. This familiar expression for tired or exhausted took its rise in America. The first known use of the phrase in print occurs in Sam Slick's ' Human Nature,' p. 192, ' Well, being out, night arter night, she got kinder *used up.*'

Usher. An usher is an officer of a court whose duty it is to keep the door, to repeat in a loud voice from the door the names of witnesses who have been called by the court, and to preserve order and silence so that the proceedings of the court may go on undisturbed. The word is generally supposed to be derived from the French *huis*, a door; a French beadle, or door-keeper, is called a *huissier*. *Huis* is the Dutch word for house.

Utilitarian. John Stuart Mill, in his 'Autobiography,' says: ' The name I gave to the society I had planned was *the Utilitarian Society*. It was the first time that any one had taken the title of Utilitarian, and the name made its way into the language from this humble source. I did not *invent* the word, but found it in one of Galt's novels, " The Annals of the Parish." '

V

Vaccination. In the old churchyard of Worth, in Dorsetshire, is a tomb with the following inscription :—' Benjamin Jesty, of Donnshay; died April 16, 1816. He was born at Yetminster in this county, and was an upright honest man, particularly noted for having been the first person known that introduced the cowpox by inoculation, and who, for his great strength of mind, made the experiment from the cow on his wife and two sons in the year 1774.' This was two years before Dr. Jenner's 'attention was called to the subject,' and twenty years before he succeeded in introducing it generally.

Vade mecum (Latin), literally, ' Go with me.' A *vade mecum* is something portable that one should always have at hand ready for use.

Vagabond. In an old English statute vagabonds are defined as ' such as wake on the night and sleep on the day, and haunt customable taverns and ale-houses, and routs about, and no man wot whence they came nor whither they go.'

Vampire. This was a name formerly given by superstitious persons to a dead person who was believed to return in body and soul to wander upon the earth, doing every kind of mischief to the living; sucking the blood of persons asleep, and so causing their death. The only manner of getting rid of vampires was, according to Calmet, to disinter their bodies, to pierce them with a stake cut from a green tree, and to burn their hearts.—*Penny Cyclopædia.* There is a species of bat called 'vampire,' but the stories as to their fanning human victims with their wings while they suck their blood are altogether fabulous. Vampires sometimes attack men when sleeping in the open air, but such occasions are rare, and their bite generally awakens the sleeper.

Vapour and Gas. Gas and vapour are frequently spoken of as though they were identical. This is not so. Gas is a substance which ordinarily exists in a state of vapour. A true vapour is produced by the application of heat to a substance ordinarily either solid or liquid.

Varlet. Originally a follower of a knight, or any man servant or attendant.

> Call here my varlet, I'll unarm again.—*Shakespeare.*

Vaudeville. This word, which now means a play in which songs are introduced, is a corruption of Vaux de Vire, the name of two valleys in Normandy. A fuller in Vire, in the fifteenth century, composed some humorous and satirical drinking songs, which were very popular throughout France, under the name of their native place, 'Vaux de Vire.' The term seems to have been corrupted into *voix de ville*. A collection of songs was published at Lyons in 1561 entitled 'Chansons Voix de Ville,' and another at Paris in 1576 called 'Recueil des plus belles Chansons en forme des Voix de Ville.' Both these publications were probably reprints of the original songs. At any rate, the name Vaudeville has in some way grown out of them.

Vellum is the skin of the calf dressed so as to make a superior kind of parchment. The word is from *veel* or *veau*, the Old French and Norman names for calf. We retain the word in *veal*, the flesh of the calf.

Velvet is mentioned, under the name 'vellet,' by Joinville, A.D. 1272, and in the will of Richard II. in 1399. It was then made altogether in Italy. The manufacture was introduced into England on the revocation of the Edict of Nantes in 1685.

Veni, vidi, vici. These are three Latin words signifying 'I came, I saw, I conquered.' Plutarch, in his 'Life of Julius Cæsar,' says: 'In the account Cæsar gave to the Roman Senate of the rapidity and despatch with which he gained his victory over Pharnaces at Zela in Asia Minor, he only made use of these three words.' Suetonius says: 'It was an inscription upon a banner carried before Cæsar as suggestive of the celerity of the victory.' It might, however, have been both.

Venison is the flesh of any animal that has been hunted. The flesh of a hunted hare is more properly *venison* than that of a tame deer shot down in a gentleman's park by a gamekeeper. The limitation of the word to the flesh of deer is modern, and is quite erroneous.

Ventilate, in the sense of examine, sift, or discuss, is an old use of the word recently revived. Johnson mentions it as in use in his time; but Dr. Worcester, in his valuable Dictionary, published 1860, marks it as being obsolete.

Verandah. This word probably came to us from India, for in the Sanskrit *varanda* is a portico. The Portuguese, who use the word in the sense of balcony or terrace, spell it *varanda*.

Verb. A little girl the other day told the writer that 'a verb is a word which tells us what a noun has to do.' Trench says: 'The verb is the animating power, the vital principle, of every sentence, and is that without which, either understood or uttered, no sentence can exist.'

Verbatim et literatim, a mediæval Latin phrase, signifying copied accurately, not only as to words, but also as to letters. A copy *verbatim et literatim* is one where the *wording* and the *spelling* are accurately transcribed. The 'Quarterly Review' correctly stigmatises the word *literatim* as 'Low Latin.'

Verger. A *verge* is a staff carried as a mark of authority. The verger of a cathedral is an officer who carries the mace or verge of the dean, or as a substitute a white wand.

> The silver *verge* with decent pride
> Stuck underneath his cushion's side.—*Swift*.

Vermicelli. This Italian name is pronounced ver-me-chel-e. The delicate food so called is so named from its worm-like appearance (Latin *vermiculus*, a little worm).

Vermilion. Kermes was the Arabic name for the insect *coculus ilicis*, which gives the red dye. Kermes in Arabic means 'little worm.' This was Latinised into *vermiculus*, from which the French coined the name *vermilion*. We have adopted the

French word for a red pigment to which the name is wholly inapplicable, it being the red sulphuret of mercury.

Vermont, the State in America, was first so called by the inhabitants in their Declaration of Independence, January 16, 1777. The word is from the French *verd*, green, and *mont*, mountain.

Vest, Waistcoat. The garment called a waistcoat in England is styled a vest in America, whilst the under-garment which Englishmen call a flannel vest is in America always known as a flannel waistcoat.

Vestry, from the Latin *vestiarium*, a room attached to a church where the priestly *vest*ments are kept. In England the name is given to the room where the clergy attire themselves in canonicals or clerical vestments.

Vicar of Bray. The celebrated Vicar of Bray, who changed his religion four times in order that he might retain his living, was Symon Symonds, who was Vicar during the reigns of Henry VIII., Edward VI., Mary, and Elizabeth, from A.D. 1533 to 1558. He was twice a Papist and twice a Protestant.

Vice versâ (Latin), the condition or terms being exactly reversed; as, 'This is black outside, and the inside is white; the other is *vice versâ*, the inside being black and the outside white.' It is pronounced vi-ce ver-sa.

Victuals. This word, although of Latin origin, comes to us from the Spanish *vituallas*. The letter *c* in the word, although strictly in accordance with the Latin original, has an extremely disagreeable effect in English. It would be better to follow the Spanish example and omit the *c*. 'Vituals' would be a better word in all respects.

Vignette is from *vinea*, a vine. The capital letters in ancient illuminated manuscripts were so called from their being ornamented with flourishes in the form of vine branches or tendrils.

Viking (Anglo-Saxon *wicing*), a pirate. This word has nothing in common with sea-king. The sea-king was one of royal race who took charge of a galley or ship; vikings were pirates, deriving their name from the *vicks* or inlets on the coasts in which they harboured. 'Every sea-king was a viking, but every viking was not a sea-king.'—*Laing*.

Villain, originally a villager, a serf or peasant. Dr. Trench says, 'A villain was at first the serf or peasant because attached to the *villa*, or farm; secondly the peasant, who, it is taken for granted, will be churlish, selfish, dishonest, and of evil moral conditions. At the third step nothing of the meaning which the etymology suggests, nothing of *villa*, survives any longer; the peasant is quite dismissed, and the evil moral condition of him who is called by this name alone remains.'

Vinegar is the English form of the French *vin-aigre*, sour wine.

Vinegar Bible. The Oxford edition of the Bible published in 1717 contains a printer's error. The head-line over Luke xxii. has the misprint 'vinegar' for vineyard; hence the name applied to the edition.

Virginia, the American State, was so called in compliment to Queen Elizabeth.

Virgins of Cologne. At Cologne visitors are shown a large collection of bones, which are said to be those of eleven thousand virgins who were martyred. The legend seems to have arisen from a clerical error in some early martyrology. The name of one virgin who was martyred stood originally as 'St. Undecemilla'; the insertion of two letters changed this into *Undecem millia Virg. Mart.* Professor Owen says that the collection of bones comprises those of almost all the quadrupeds indigenous to the district.

Virtue, from the Latin *vir*, an heroic man. The word virtue originally signified bravery, courage, daring, or valour. Sir W. Raleigh says, 'The conquest of Palestine with singular *virtue* they performed.'

Viscount. *Comes* or *Count* was a title given to a nobleman to whom was entrusted the administration of the affairs of a *county*. His position in his county was analogous to that of the modern Lord Lieutenant. His deputy, or *Vice Comes*, was called in Norman-French *Vis Counte*, and his duties corresponded to those of a modern sheriff. In this sense it was used long before it became a title of peerage. As a title of nobility it was first conferred in 1440 by Henry VI. upon John, Lord Beaumont, and his heirs.

Visiting Cards. It was customary in the early part of the last century to utilise disused playing cards as visiting cards, by writing the owner's name thereon. Messages were also written and left in the same manner. In Plate IV. of Hogarth's 'Marriage à-la-mode' several of these cards are represented lying on the floor. On one of them the painter has satirised the ignorance of the upper classes of the time by inscribing on it 'Count Basset begs to no how Lade Squander sleapt last nite.'

Vivâ voce (Latin), 'by the living voice.' *Vivâ voce* evidence is spoken testimony as distinguished from written, or that which is given on affidavit. The phrase is divided into four syllables thus—vi-vâ vo-ce.

Vixen, a female fox. Verstegan says it was anciently written *foxen*. Todd says, 'A *vixen* is a fox's cub without regard to sex.' The first definition is the one generally accepted.

Viz. This little word is a contraction of *videlicet*, spelt incorrectly with a *z*. The proper symbol of contraction is identical with ʒ, the apothecaries' mark for drachm. This was an arbitrary sign used by the ancient scribes as a terminal mark of abbreviation, as in habʒ for hab*et*, and viʒ for *videlicet*. The form of this symbol being so nearly like that of the old form of the letter *z*, was probably the reason why the early printers, who had no type for the symbol ʒ, adopted the letter, and so perpetuated an absurdity.

Vogue is from the French *voguer*, to row, to sail, to be wafted. Hence to be in vogue is to go with the tide.

Voluble is from the Latin *volubilis*, the past participle of the verb *volvo, volutus*, to roll. Hence a voluble speaker is one whose words roll from his mouth apparently without effort.

Volume. The word volume (a book) is derived from the Latin noun *volumen*, which was derived from the verb *volvo*, to roll. An ancient 'volumen' 'was a long narrow roll of parchment or papyrus, generally divided transversely into pages or columns, the words written closely together without any separation by spaces; without distinctive forms of letters, capitals being employed for all purposes alike; without divisions of chapters, paragraphs, or periods; and frequently made still more illegible by complicated and obscure abbreviations of whole syllables, or even words, into a single character.'—*Marsh*. A sentence from Fuller's 'Worthies' is printed as an imperfect attempt to show the ancient method of writing, but as no contractions are used the example is far less difficult to decipher than an ancient manuscript must have been :—

'ITWILLPOSETHEBESTCLERKTOREADYEATOSPELL THATDEEDWHEREINSENTENCESCLAUSESWORDS ANDLETTERSAREWITHOUTPOINTSORSTOPSALL CONTINUEDTOGETHER.'

The sentence, printed in ordinary fashion, is as follows :—'It will pose the best clerk to read, yea to spell, that deed wherein sentences, clauses, words, and letters are without points or stops, all continued together.'

Vox populi, Vox Dei. This phrase was first used by Simon Mepham, Archbishop of Canterbury, as a text from which he preached a sermon after Edward II. had been dethroned by the people, and his son Edward III. made king.—*Hist. Angl.*, ed. Camden, p. 126.

Voyage, from the Latin *via*, a way, and *ago*, to pursue. A voyage formerly meant a journey, either by land or sea; it is now so used in France. On taking leave of persons going a few miles by railway, their friends do not wish them a pleasant journey, they say '*bon voyage.*'

Vulgar, from the Latin *vulgaris*, common. This word in its primitive sense implied nothing objectionable. It meant general, ordinary, or vernacular. 'The vulgar tongue,' for instance, simply meant the language commonly spoken.

W

W. This letter, at the time when V and U were identical, was generally printed VV. As the letter V was at that time called U, the name 'Double U' was then strictly accurate.

W, G, and Y as initial letters were anciently almost interchangeable. Thus we have yard, garden, and ward, as of a hospital or prison, from *geard*, an enclosure; ward and warden from the Anglo-Saxon *warian*, to beware, also guard and guardian from the same root, and having nearly the same significance. See WARDEN.

W and V. The substitution of V for W, and *vice versâ*, so common amongst the lower classes in the East of London, seems to be a remnant of the French language, formerly so much spoken in that locality by the thousands of French refugees who settled there after the revocation of the Edict of Nantes.

Wafers. Mr. Speiss says that the oldest seal with a red wafer that he has yet found is on a letter written by D. Krapf, at Spires, in the year 1624, to the Government at Beyreuth.—*Beckmann.*

Waifs and Strays. A 'waif' is an article which, having been stolen, is abandoned by the thief. A 'stray' is a domestic animal which has strayed from its owner's premises, so that the ownership is not ascertainable. Both waifs and strays are the property of the Crown, but may be claimed if the ownership can be satisfactorily proved.

Waitress. De Quincey, in his 'Autobiographic Sketches,' published in 1854, says: 'Social changes in London, by introducing females very extensively into the office (once monopolised by men) of attending the visitors at the tables of eating-houses, have introduced a corresponding new word, viz. *waitress*.'

Waits are mentioned as night musicians in the 'Liber Niger' of Edward IV., 1478. Waits are also mentioned in the 'Privy Purse Expences' of Henry VIII., edited by Sir Harris Nicolas. Sir Harris quotes the following two items, dated in 1532:—'Itm̄ the xi. daye (of October) paied to the Waytes of Caunterbury in rewarde ... vijs. vj*d*.' 'Itm̄ the xix. daye (of November) paid to the waytes at Caunterbury in rewarde ... xvijs. viij*d*.' In a copy of Johnson's Dictionary that formerly belonged to Burke, and is now in the British Museum, that great orator has written in MS. on the fly-leaf of vol. ii. as follows: 'Wait. n. s., from ye French guet (literally a sentinel on out-post duty). 2. Waits in ye pl., an old word signifying ye night Guard in ye City of London.'

Wake. Wakes were festivals formerly held in parishes, on the anniversary of the dedication of the parochial church.

Walk Chalks. To walk chalks is an ordeal used on board ship as a test for drunkenness. Two parallel lines are chalked for some distance upon the deck, and if the supposed delinquent can walk from one end to the other without overstepping either he is pronounced to be sober.

Wall. 'To go to the wall' or 'To be driven to the wall.'— These expressions mean that when a man in a fight is in extremity he places his back to the wall, so that it is only necessary to defend himself in front; his enemies cannot come behind him. Figuratively, it signifies the last chance.

Wall Papers. The first allusion to wall papers known to exist is in the account of the examination of Herman Schinkel, a printer of Delft, who was accused in 1568 of printing books inimical to the Catholic faith. Being interrogated as to certain ballads, he said they had been printed by his servant in his absence, and that 'when he came home and found they were not delivered, he refused to deliver them, and threw them into a corner, intending to print roses and stripes on the back to paper attics with.'

Wallsend Coals are so named from the fact that the collieries which produce them are situated near the east *end* of the *wall* built by the Romans to keep back the Picts and the Scots. The wall commenced at Bowness, near Carlisle, and extended to a point on the Tyne about three or four miles below Newcastle.

Walnut is a corruption of Gaul-nut, the nut of Gaul or France. As *Gallia* and *Wallia* both anciently signified Gaul, the transition from Gaul-nut to walnut is easily accounted for. See W, G, AND Y.

Walrus, the *whale-horse* (German *ross*, a horse). The animal is often called the sea-horse.

Waltzing. The German dance called the waltz was introduced at Almack's in 1813.

Want. Tooke, in his 'Diversions of Purley,' says that want is the past participle of *wane*, thus—wane, waned, want. The etymon seems far-fetched, but no other appears so feasible. The word want is used in different senses in various localities. In Norfolk it is confined in application to that which is actually needed. A man there may 'want' a dinner, and 'wish for' a new hat. In Scotland want means 'can't do without,' as in the sentence 'He is a man we can't want,' meaning 'He is a man whose aid, assistance, or advice is necessary to us.'

Warden, Guardian. Among the Anglo-Saxons there were many words and names beginning with *w*. When the Normans came, their language possessing no *w*, they used the letter *u* instead. To make the pronunciation easier to them, they placed a *g* before the *u*, and thus it comes that many Old English words formerly beginning with *w*, now commence with *gu*. In the cases of warden and guardian, both forms have been preserved, so that at the Tower we have *warders*, and at the Court, *guards*. Such Anglo-Saxon words beginning with *w* as the French have borrowed have undergone this process of alteration. Thus *war* has become *guerre*.

Warden Pie. This pie, which is often mentioned in old books, was made of large baking pears. These pears are still called 'wardens' in some counties. The 'warden pears' so celebrated for making the pies of the Middle Ages were so named from the

Abbey of Warden in Bedfordshire, the monks of which foundation cultivated them at an early period. The improved sort now grown is 'Uredale's Warden,' or 'Uredale's St. Germain.' Historical novelists sometimes erroneously describe these famous pies as being made of venison.

Ware in Hertfordshire is supposed to be the place where Alfred the Great constructed his *weir* across the Lea to cut off the retreat of the Danish fleet.

Warfare. The second syllable of this word means a journey or an expedition. It is analogous to the terms wayfaring, seafaring.

Warp and Weft. The warp consists of the longitudinal threads in a piece of cloth; the weft is composed of those running from selvage to selvage.

Wassail, Wassail-bowl. From two Anglo-Saxon words, *wesan*, to be, *hæl*, health. The Anglo-Saxons used the term '*wæs hæl*' as we use the words 'good health,' before drinking. The wassail-bowls corresponded to the punch-bowls of a couple of generations ago.

Watches are said to have been invented at Nuremberg in 1477. It is probable that the so-called watches of early times were small pendulum night clocks for ascertaining the number of the 'watch of the night.' Up to the time of Henry VIII. the time-keepers carried about the person were called pocket-clocks. The word 'watch' first appears in a 'Royal Household Book,' now in the Record Office, of the date 1542. Amongst other time-keepers mentioned is the following: 'Item, oone Larum or *Watch* of iron, the case being also iron gilt.' From this it would appear that the word 'watch' was first applied to something upon the same principle as our modern alarum. Watches of minute size seem to have been made at a very early period. In the will of Archbishop Parker, which is dated April 5, 1575, he makes the following bequest: 'I give to my reverend brother Richard, Bishop of Ely, my stick of Indian cane, which hath a watch in the top of it.' The Duke of Urbino is said to have possessed, in the year 1542, a watch which struck the hours, which had been made by an Italian. The Emperor Charles V. of Germany is also known to have had a watch inserted in a ring. In Nichols's 'Progresses of Queen Elizabeth' is an account of a number of watches presented to her by various noblemen, with full descriptions. One of these runs as follows: In the twenty-first year the Earl of Russell gave the Queen 'a ringe of golde called a paramadas, sett with vj. small diamonds, and garnished rounde aboute with small rubies, and two sparcks of ophals, and in the same backsyde a dyall.' The invention of the true *watch* to work by a spring and to be carried in the pocket has been ascribed with great probability to Dr. Hooke in the seventeenth century. He certainly invented the balance-spring, without which watches would be untrustworthy. A single ounce of steel, which is not worth a penny, will suffice to make 4,000 watch-springs, which if of the finest quality will be worth 4,000*l*.

Water has one property in which it differs from all other substances—it expands under the influence of both heat and cold. At about 40 degrees of heat it is at its greatest density; from this it expands by heat until it becomes steam, and by cold until it becomes ice, which it does at a temperature of 32 degrees.

Water-closets were invented by Sir John Harington, of Kelston, near Bath, about the year 1596.—Park, *Nugæ Antiquæ*.

Watered Silk. Silks which are intended for watering must be of good quality. In the process they are wetted, and then folded with particular care to insure the threads of the fabric all lying in one direction. The folded pieces are then placed in a machine and subjected to enormous hydraulic pressure. By this pressure the air is slowly expelled, and in escaping draws the moisture into curious waved lines which leave the permanent marking known as 'watering.'—*Chambers's Encyclopædia*.

Watershed. Some years ago there was a discussion in the 'Athenæum' as to the meaning of this word, the balance of authority favouring its derivation from the German *scheide*, to divide, in the same sense as parting the hair. Dodsworth, in his 'Yorkshire Collections,' quoted by Southey in 'The Doctor,' says, 'The River Don or Dun riseth in the upper part of Pennystone parish, near Lady's Cross, which may be called our Apennines, because the rain-water that falleth *sheddeth* from sea to sea.' This shows the meaning of *watershed* to be the ridge which causes streams to flow from it in opposite directions, thus parting them.

Waver. To waver is to be undecided, vacillating, unsettled, to be inclined to opposite directions, unstable. Its origin in the word 'wave' is obvious.

Waves mountains high. This is a mere figure of speech. It has been ascertained that waves do not rise more than twelve feet above the level of calm water. As, however, there is a corresponding 'trough' between every two waves, the highest crest of a wave is about twenty-four feet above the lowest depression. The water a few feet below the bottom of a 'trough' in a storm is perfectly tranquil, the storm causing only a superficial agitation.

Wax. 'Bees, even though fed upon pure sugar only, have the power of converting it into wax, which is therefore to be regarded as an animal secretion.'—*Miller.*

Wayzgoose. This name is applied to the annual holiday of the employés in printing offices. The name is synonymous with stubble-goose, and a stubble-goose is the principal dish on these occasions. The name and the custom are of considerable antiquity. Moxon, in his 'Mechanick Exercises,' 1683, says: 'It is customary for the journeymen every year to make new paper windows, whether the old will serve or no, because the day they make them the master printer gives them a *wayzgoose*. These wayzgooses are always kept at Bartholemewtide, and until the master has given the wayzgoose the journeymen do not work by candle-light.' A different etymology is suggested by Mr. Hazlitt. He says, in a note to Brand's 'Popular Antiquities,' 'I am of opinion that the ancient practice of holding a grand goose feast at Waes in Brabant at Martinmass is more likely to have given rise to our English phrase.'

We. Lord Coke says that the plural form was first used for a single person by King John, who introduced *nos* and *noster* into grants, confirmations, &c. His predecessors had been content with *ego* and *meus.*

Wearing the Hat. The Jews wear their hats in the Synagogues. The Friends also sit covered except during the offering up of audible prayer. It appears to have been formerly the case in the Church of England for men to be covered in sermon-time. In Peck's 'Disertata Curiosa,' it is stated that Richard Cox, Bishop of Ely, who died in 1581, was buried in Ely Cathedral, the congregation, 'a very great one, sitting in the choir to hear the funeral sermon, all covered.' In 1664 Evelyn mentioned in his diary that he had caught a severe cold 'by flinging off my hat at dinner.' A few pages further on he tells us that upon calling on the Lord Chancellor Bridgman, they walked up and down in the garden, 'and he would have me walk with my hat on.'

Weathercocks. 'Vanes,' says Du Cange, 'were anciently made in the form of a cock (hence called weathercocks), and put up in Papal times to remind the clergy of watchfulness.' A writer in the 'St. James's Chronicle,' June 10, 1777, says, 'The intention of the original *cock-vane* was derived from the cock crowing when St. Peter had denied his Lord.' Gramaye ('Historia Brabantiæ,' p. 14) says that 'the custom of adorning the tops of steeples with a cross and a cock is derived from the Goths, who bore that as their warlike ensign.'

Wed. This word was not originally confined to the sense of marrying. To 'wed' was to enter into a solemn pledge of any kind. Nobles and warriors were called 'weddyd brethryn' when bound by oaths of friendship and amity.—*Reliq. Antiq.* p. 85.

Wedding Customs in Old Times. Beaumont and Fletcher, in 'The Scornful Lady,' act i. sc. 1, have a few lines which give curious details of the wedding customs in use in their time. The Scornful Lady, in declaring her determination not to marry a boaster, says :—

>Believe me, if my wedding smock were on,
>Were the gloves bought and given, the license come,
>Were the rosemary branches dipped, and all
>The Hippocras and cakes eat and drunk off,
>Were these two arms encompassed with the hands
>Of bachelors, to lead me to the church,
>Were my feet at the door, were 'I John' said
>[That is, 'I John take thee Mary,' in the wedding service],
>If John should boast a favour done by me,
>I would not wed that year.

Wedding Rings. Rings are now put upon the woman's fourth finger at the time of marriage. The Jews, who originated the use of wedding rings, placed the ring upon the woman's finger at the time of espousal or contract *before* marriage. Wedding rings were originally signet rings. In ancient times, when few could write, seals were used in all important transactions as evidence of the binding nature of the bargain. Giving the wife a seal or signet at marriage was therefore a visible sign that the husband endowed her with equal rights with himself, and made her an equal partaker of all his 'worldly goods.' The custom of using plain gold wedding rings has come down to us from the time of the Anglo-Saxons, but there is no *law* upon the subject. The ecclesiastical rubric mentions 'a ring,' but says nothing as to its shape or material. Marriages have been solemnised where the ring of the church key has been used; and in one instance, where the proper ring had been lost or mislaid, a leathern ring cut from the finger of a glove, was used, and was held by the officiating clergyman to be sufficient.

Wednesday and **Thursday.** In the broad Northumbrian dialect these week-day names are still pronounced Wōdensday and Thŏrsday.

Weed. This word as applied to dress is now confined to widows' caps, which are still called *weeds*. Formerly it might mean any article of dress, but it was usually applied to an upper or outer garment. Spenser speaks of

A goodly lady clad in hunters' *weed*,

and Chapman mentions 'putting on both shirt and weed.' See LIVERY.

Weeping Willow. This tree came originally from Spain. Lady Suffolk, who was a favourite of George II. and his queen, received a present from Spain, the package containing which was enwrapped in twigs of willow. Pope the poet, who was present when the package arrived, perceiving that the twigs showed signs of life, said, 'Perhaps they may produce something that we have not in England.' He accordingly took some of them and planted them at Twickenham. One of them grew and became the parent of many others. The original tree was cut down by Lord Mendip soon after he purchased Pope's villa. Twickenham is still celebrated for the beauty of the willows which grow on the margin of the Thames at that place.

Weight of British Coins in Circulation. Professor Jevons calculates the weight of gold circulating as coins in Great Britain to be, approximately, 786 tons; of silver, 1,670 tons; and of bronze 2,652 tons. He tells us also that the average daily transactions in the London Daily Clearing House amount to about twenty millions of pounds sterling, which if paid in gold coin would weigh about 157 tons, and would require nearly eighty horses for conveyance.

We-ism, a jocose plural of the word egotism, applied by the 'Anti-Jacobin Review' to certain editors whose 'we' was used as though infallible.

Welcome. From the Anglo-Saxon *wel*, well, and *cuma*, a comer. The word *wilcuma* was strictly confined to its signification of a visitor who is gladly received. It was never applied to things, as in the sense of a welcome gift.

Weld (as applied to metal). Two or more pieces of iron are welded by being struck, when in a condition of intense heat, by a hammer which is '*wielded*' by a strong man, or by mechanical power.

We left our country for our country's good. These lines occur in a prologue written by the notorious pickpocket George Barrington for the opening of the first playhouse at Sydney, Australia, January 16, 1796. The performances on this occasion were entirely conducted by convicts, and the price of admission was a shilling, payable either in money, corn, meat, or spirits, at the market rate. The prologue opens as follows :—

> From distant climes o'er widespread seas we come,
> Though not with much éclat or beat of drum;
> True patriots all, for be it understood,
> We left our country for our country's good.

Welkin. This poetical word is the plural of an obsolete term *welc*, a cloud. The proper orthography is *welcen*, the *c* being hard.

Wellingtonia. This beautiful tree, which within the last quarter of century has been naturalised in England, was discovered by a hunting party at a place since called Mammoth Grove, Calaveras, Upper California. The tallest tree in the group they met with was 327 feet high, and 90 feet in circumference at its base. These dimensions, however, seem to have been exceeded by a tree that was found broken off at the height of 300 feet, where it was 18 feet in diameter. As it was 112 feet in circumference at the base, and tapered gradually to the broken point, it was computed that its entire height must have been 450 feet, or 85 feet higher than the cross of St. Paul's in London.

Welly. This word is in common use in the Midland Counties in the sense of almost. It is a contraction of the two words 'well nigh.' In the West of England it is used as an interjection implying pity. In this case it is a contraction of *well-a-day!* a phrase formerly in general use as an expletive.

Welsh. 'The Britains were a people of the Gaules, which the Saxons, according to their manner of speech, instead of calling Gallish called *Wallish*, and by abreviation Walsh or Welsh. In the ancient *Teutonick* it is very often found that divers names which the French are wont to begin with *g*, the Germans begin with *w*, as *ward* for Gard, *warduin* (whereof we yet keep the name of warden) for gardian, warre for guerre, and very many the like.' —*Versteyan, Restitution, &c.,* p. 120, edit. 1655. See WARDEN.

Welsh Origin of English Words. From the Welsh *llab*, a

stroke or blow, we get flap, slap, and clap; from *llag*, remiss, we have lay, lazy, laggard, flag, slug, and sluggard; and from *llai*, mud, we get clay, slab, and slabby.

Welsh Rabbit. This name for toasted bread and cheese is properly 'Welsh rare-bit.'

Welsher is a name applied on race-courses to one who, having lost a bet, absconds without paying. The term is understood in sporting circles to have originated in the old nursery ditty, 'Taffy was a Welchman, Taffy was a thief.'

Wench. This word had not originally, nor indeed has it now in the Midland Counties, any meaning of a derogatory character. It is supposed to be derived from the Anglo-Saxon *cwen*, a wife or woman, with the addition of something equivalent to the Dutch *je*, expressing familiarity or affection, as in *wijf-je*, little wife, or *kind-je*, little child. *Cwen-je* would easily, in pronunciation, fall into the sound of wench, and would signify 'little woman' in an affectionate sense. The words 'mah wench' from the lips of a Midland operative are probably the most tender form of expression he knows how to use in speaking to his wife or daughter.

Went is the past participle of the word '*wend*.'
    Uncompanied, great voyages to *wend*.—*Surrey*.

Westminster. It has been stated over and over again that Westminster was so named to distinguish it from the Abbey of Grace on Tower Hill, which was called Eastminster. Maitland, however, proves that a 'Charter of Sanctuary' was granted to 'Westminster' by Edward the Confessor, who died in 1066, whilst the 'Abbey of Grace' was not founded until the fourteenth century. Westminster was so named from its being west of the Cathedral of St. Paul's. In speaking of St. Peter's Church at Westminster the use of the word abbey is superfluous, as 'minster' means an abbey church, and is used to the present day in that sense in the cases of York Minster, Beverley Minster, and others.

Westminster Bridge. The old bridge was begun 1738; opened November 15, 1750; cost, 426,650*l*. The new bridge was commenced 1854, and opened May 24, 1862.

Westminster Hall was formerly liable to be flooded whenever high tides occurred. On November 19, 1242, boats floated from the river to the interior of the Hall. The coronation of George II. was announced for October 4, 1727, but as the day approached some one suggested that on that day there would be a spring tide, and that the ceremonial had better be postponed. It was accordingly postponed until the 11th. On the 4th, as predicted, the Hall was flooded. The floor of the Hall was afterwards raised several feet. Now that danger of inundation no longer exists, it would be well to restore the ancient proportions by lowering the floor to its original level.

Whalebone. In the time of Shakespeare it was commonly believed that ivory was the bone of the whale. There are many proofs that this error was common at the time, even among educated people. Shakespeare evidently thought so, for in 'Love's Labour's Lost,' act v. sc. 2, he has the line :—
> To show his teeth, as white as whale his bone.

And Spenser, 'Faerie Queene,' III. i. 15 :—
> Whose face did seem as clear as crystal stone,
> And eke, through fear, as white as whalës bone.

Lord Surrey, too, has :—
> A little mouth, with decent chin,
> A coral lip of hue,
> With teeth as white as whale his bone,
> Ech one in order due.—*Poems*, 1567.

Mr. Wright, however ('England in the Middle Ages'), speaking of chessmen, says, 'They were chiefly made of the tusk of the walrus, the native ivory of Western Europe, which was known popularly as whale's bone.'

Whales' Ribs. What are called 'whales' ribs,' which are sometimes seen as archways over carriage entrances in country places, are really the jawbones, which are usually about one-third the length of the entire body.

What is a Pound? Sir Robert Peel, in the great currency debates of his time, set everybody wondering by propounding the question, 'What *is* a pound?' The ablest financiers of his day were unable to give a strictly definite reply to the question. We are able, however, to say what a pound *was* when it was first instituted as a unit of value. It was simply a pound weight of pure silver.

What will Mrs. Grundy say? This question occurs in Morton's comedy, 'Speed the Plough,' where Farmer Ashfield, annoyed at his wife's continually bringing up the name of a neighbour's wife and her doings in contrast with theirs, exclaims petulantly : 'Be quiet, woolye? always ding, dinging Dame Grundy into my ears—" What will Mrs. Grundy say? what will Mrs. Grundy think?" Caunst thee be quiet ; let ur aloane and behave t yself pratty?'—Act i. sc. i.

Wheal. A large number of the Cornish mines have the word 'Wheal' as a prefix to the name, as 'Wheal Hope,' 'Wheal Unity,' &c. Formerly this prefix was written *Huel*, as 'Huel Friendship,' and so on. *Huel* in Gaelic signifies a tin mine.

Wheat came originally from the central land of Thibet, where its representative yet exists as grass with small mealy seeds.

Wheel Carriages. The earliest known mention of vehicles on wheels is in Genesis xlv. 27, where the Hebrew word *agaloth*, which is literally wheel carriages, is translated waggons.

Wherefore. Grose, in his 'Glossary,' gives whyfore or whyvore as a word in use in the West of England in the sense of wherefore. *Whyfor* is certainly a better word than wherefore when it is used interrogatively. '*Why*for have you done this?' is nearer the sense than '*Where*fore have you done it?'

Whetstone. 'It is a custom in the North, when a man tells the greatest lye in the company, to reward him with a whetstone. Matches are sometimes made called "lying for the whetstone."'— *Budworth*, ch. vi. This explains Lord Bacon's sarcastic remark to Sir K. Digby, when he boasted of having seen the Philosopher's Stone in his travels, but was puzzled to describe it. Bacon retorted, 'Perhaps it was a *whetstone*.'

Whig. In Scotland whig means a weak fermented liquor made from butter-milk. Nares, in mentioning this word, says: 'The nickname of Whig as applied to a party is commonly derived from this word, but Bishop Burnet derives it rather from "Whiggamoor," a cattle driver in the south-west of Scotland, by contraction "whig." His opinion as a Scotchman must have the more weight, because the name had been applied to the Scotch fanatics before it was taken up as a term of ridicule against the country party in England, which was about 1680.' Another and a very plausible theory as to the origin of this name for a political party, ascribes it to the initials of the motto of the Liberal party in Cromwell's time, 'We hope in God.'

While, Wile. These two words, utterly unlike in meaning, are frequently confounded. People who ought to know better write in newspapers and magazines '*while* away the time.' It ought to be '*wile* away the time.' While means time, as 'a long while,' but wile has the meaning of guile or beguile, and in the sentence quoted means to beguile away the time, or to make it pass without fatigue, or what the French call *ennui*.

Whimsey. When the steam engine was first used in Staffordshire to supersede horses in raising coals from a pit, the novelty caused a great sensation for miles round, and the miners congregated in great numbers to witness the strange sight. It was looked upon as a wild-goose scheme, and all sorts of evil prognostications were current. The whim or 'whimsey' of the crack-brained master miner was the laughing-stock of the district, and the term *whimsey* soon became the name by which the strange machine was known. At the present day the word 'whimsey' is applied universally to the apparatus, and is daily used by thousands who have no notion that the term originated in what was thought to be a foolish whim on the part of a far-seeing miner.

Whimwham. This is defined by the dictionaries as 'a duplication of whim.' It appears to have been used as the name of a flourish after a signature, &c. In a scarce book, 'Collectanea Curiosa,' Oxford, 1781, pp. 384-5, is a copy of a memorandum drawn up by the Protestant bishops, 1688, in which appears, 'How to demean ourselves in case of a Popish visitation. The way of writing to the Archbishop is for every man to write to a private friend, and for him to deliver the letter to my Lord Archbishop.' Several other secret means of communication are mentioned; letters for the Bishop of Elie are 'to be addressed to Madam Womock at Elie, in a woman's hand with a *whimwham*.' The woodcut is copied from the book mentioned.

Whisk, or **Wisk,** a light dusting brush made of feathers or very light twigs. The word is the Anglo-Saxon *wisch*, a word which was used in a similar sense; *fleder wisch*, or feather broom, was a dried goose-wing. The word 'whiskers,' the hair on the sides of a man's face, is from the same root.

Whisky. The Irish name of whisky is *uisge-beatha*, literally 'water of life,' being exactly equivalent to the Latin *aqua vitæ*, and the French *eau de vie*. It is curious that 'whisky,' which is the *uisge* of the full name, literally means water. On June 8, 1723, the first Agricultural Society in Great Britain was established at Edinburgh. At this meeting the Duke of Hamilton proposed and carried a resolution against drinking foreign liquors, so 'that thereby the distilling of our grain might be encouraged, and the great sums annually sent to France for brandy, generally smuggled, might be kept at home.' From this time it became a point of honour to drink only home-made whisky, which gradually became so popular that it has ever since been looked upon as the national drink.'—*Gentleman's Magazine*, August 1870.

Whist. Little is known of the origin of this game. Tayler, the Water Poet, writing in 1650, speaks of—

Ruffe, slam, trump, noddy, *whisk*, hole, sant, and new-cut.

Farquhar, in the 'Beaux' Stratagem,' 1706, makes Mrs. Sullen enquire, 'Dost think, child; . . . that my parents . . . had early instructed me in the rural accomplishments of drinking fat ale, playing at *whisk*, and smoking tobacco with my husband?' Pope, using the word *whist*, addresses Martha Blount thus :—

Some squire perhaps you take delight to rack,
Whose game is *whist*, whose drink a toast in sack,
Whose laughs are hearty, though his jests are coarse,
Who loves you best of all things—but his horse.

And Swift in 1728, thirteen years later, uses *whisk*—

The clergymen used to play at *whisk* and swabbers.

The game seems to have been gradually evolved from an older one called Triumph. Cotgrave's Dictionary, 1611, has '*Triomphe*, the card game called Ruffe or Trump.' The 'Compleat Gamester' (p. 86, edit. 1709), says, 'Whist is a game not much differing from this [ruff and honours].' Barrington, writing in 1787, says, 'Whisk seems never to have been played on principles till about fifty years ago, when it was much studied by a set of gentlemen who frequented the Crown Coffee-house in Bedford Row ; before that time it was confined chiefly to the servants' hall with all fours and put.' Alexander Thomson, who published 'A Poem in Eight Cantos' on Whist, says (p. 21, 2nd edit. 1792) :—

Let nice *Piquette* the boast of France remain,
And studious *Ombre* be the pride of Spain ;
Invention's praise shall England yield to none
While she can call delightful *Whist* her own.
But to what name we this distinction owe
It is not easy for us now to know :
The British annals are all silent here,
Nor deign one friendly hint our doubts to clear.

Whistle. The proverbial expression 'wet the whistle' is probably a corruption of 'whet the whittle.' 'Whittle' is a general term for cutting instruments, and was formerly a common name for a scythe. In harvest time, when a man stops work for the purpose of sharpening his tools, he generally takes the opportunity to quench his thirst by a draught of beer or cider. Hence 'whetting the whittle,' being usually accompanied by a draught of liquor, the phrase 'wet the whistle,' in the sense of moistening the throat, would very easily arise. See WHITTLE.

Whistle for it. The following paragraph went the round of the papers in 1856 :—'Mrs. Mary Dixon, widow of a canon residentiary of York, has presented two ancient silver tankards to the corporation of Hull. One of them is a whistle tankard which belonged to Anthony Lambert, Mayor of Hull in 1669. The whistle comes into play when the tankard is empty; so that when it reaches the hands of a toper, and there is nothing for him to drink, he must, if he wants liquor, *whistle for it.*' This may possibly be the origin of the singular phrase, or it may have arisen in the fact that whistling tankards of earthenware, holding about five or six pints, and bearing a date early in the eighteenth century, were formerly common in Dorsetshire. These tankards have four handles, in one of which is a whistle, the use of which is to 'whistle for more drink when the cup was empty.'—*Notes and Queries.*

Whitebait. The small fish caught in the Thames, and known to all London as 'whitebait,' are of a great variety of species. In February, when the season commences, the bait consists almost altogether of 'yawlings,' which are yearling herrings. A little later on the 'bait' is much smaller, and consists of 'heads and eyes,' a small transparent creature of which the name is very descriptive. At various periods, among the other minute creatures are 'polwigs' and 'Rooshans,' 'sticklebats,' 'buntings,' &c. Towards August young sprats appear in unnumbered myriads, and these, from their silvery whiteness, have given whitebait its distinctive name. It is called 'bait' from the fact that it was formerly exclusively used for baiting lobster and crab pots. It is stated that 'it was in 1780 that one Richard Cannon, a Blackwall fisherman, introduced it as a savoury dish.' The quantity caught is almost incredible, and the amount paid yearly to the fishermen who catch it is estimated by thousands of pounds. Cannon's 'introduction' was possibly a revival, for 'at a feast held in Stationers' Hall, May 28, 1612, there were six dishes of whitebait.' This is the earliest known mention of this delicacy.

White Feather. 'To show the white feather' is synonymous with 'to show cowardice.' The proverbial expression arose from the circumstance that a white feather in the tail of a game-cock is a certain sign that he is not thoroughbred.

Whiten. To whiten and to bleach or blanch have distinct meanings. To whiten is to 'cover with a coating of white,' so as to hide dirt or discoloration. To bleach or to blanch is to 'remove' the colouring matter, leaving only whiteness.

Whitlow. This is the name applied to a peculiar ulcer of a pale colour upon the fingers. The term is derived from the Anglo-Saxon *whit*, white, and *low*, a flame, from the colour of the ulcer and the burning sensation it causes.—*Dunglison.*

Whitsunday. Hearn, in the glossary to his edition of 'Robert of Gloucester,' under the head of 'Wyttesonetyd,' says: 'There are many opinions about the original of the name, all which I forbear mentioning, unless it be one not taken notice of by common etymologists, but occurs in folio liiij. of a very rare book printed by Wynken de Worde. . . . The words to our purpose are these:

'" ¶ In die Pentecostes.

'" Good men and wymmen, this day is called Wytsonday because the Holy Ghost brought wytte and wysdom into Cristis disciples, and so by her preching after in to all cristendom, and fylled hem full of ghostly wytte."'

Verstegan seems nearer the truth; he derives it from the Anglo-Saxon *wied*, sacred. He says, 'We yet say hallowed for halih*wied*; also we hereof retain the name of *Whitsonday*, which more rightly should be written *Weid Sonday*, that is, Sacred Sonday, so called by reason of the descending down of the Holy Ghost,' &c.—*Restitution of Decayed Intelligence*, edit. 1655, p. 188.

Whittington and his Cat. Mr. H. T. Riley, in the preface to his 'Munimenta Gildhallæ Londonensis,' p. xviii., tells us that in the fourteenth and beginning of the fifteenth century the French word *achat* was used by the educated classes in England to denote trading, or buying and selling at a profit, the word being written 'acat,' and probably so pronounced in England. To 'acat' of this kind Whittington was probably indebted for his wealth; and to ignorance of the French term on the part of some imaginative writer we doubtless owe the story with which we have all been familiar from our childhood. Chaucer has the word *acater* in the sense of a provider of provisions, or *caterer*.

Whittle was the Anglo-Saxon term for a knife. Hence the American 'whittling'—that is, from sheer restlessness cutting pieces of wood into small useless fragments. Shakespeare ('Timon of Athens,' act v. sc. 3) has:

There's not a *whittle* in th' unruly camp.

Chaucer has the word, but spells it differently:

A Scheffeld *thwitel* bar he in his hose.
Canterbury Tales, v. 3932.

See **Whistle.**

Wich (in the names of salt-making places). This affix is derived from the Norse word *wic*, a bay, and not from the Anglo-Saxon *wick*, a village. Salt was formerly produced by the evaporation of sea water in shallow *wychs* or bays. A salt-making house was thence called a 'wych-house,' and the inland places where rock salt was found took their names from the wych-houses built for its preparation and purification.

Wide-awake Hats. This phrase originated in the witty saying of some one who called the felted hats by this name because they never had a nap.

Widow. Among the Romans a woman was forbidden to re-marry for a year after the death of her husband, lest, bearing a child within that period, there might be dispute as to whether the paternity lay with the deceased or with the living husband.

Wig is an abbreviation of the word periwig, which was a corruption of the French *perruque*. Wigs were worn by bishops in the House of Lords until 1830, when Blomfield, Bishop of London, obtained the permission of King William IV. for the episcopal bench to discontinue the practice. The oldest wig in the world is of ancient Eygptian manufacture. It was found in a tomb at Thebes, and is now in the British Museum.

Wilderness is 'Wild-deer-ness,' and so it was anciently written. Its original meaning was a place of wild deer or wild beasts; for the word 'deer' formerly included all untamed beasts, and was not, as now, restricted to one species. Shakespeare ('King Lear,' act iii. sc. 4) has:—

> But mice and rats and such small *deer*
> Have been Tom's food for seven long year.

Will and **Testament.** These two words are usually thought to be synonymous, but in reality the word 'will' relates only to real, that is, freehold or landed property; while the word 'testament' relates merely to personalty. In 'Notes and Queries,' November 11, 1854, is a full copy of a will of the date 1635, in which the distinction is plainly shown. The 'testament' disposes of all personalty, and the bequests are described as 'being witnessed by four persons who are named, and 'with other moo.' Then follows: 'This is the last *will* of me, Robert Skynner, as concerning my landes and t'ents,' in which, reserving a third for his wife during her life, he devises all his landed possessions to his eldest son.

Wills. The wills formerly kept in Doctors' Commons are

now removed to Somerset House. The originals commence with the first year of King Edward V. (1483). A century later copies of all wills were made on parchment and bound in volumes. At first a small volume would contain the wills of ten or more years, but now the wills proved in London alone average about 10,000 a year, and those registered in the District Courts are probably from 15,000 to 20,000 additional.

William. This was originally a surname. In the ancient wars between the Goths and the Romans any northern soldier who killed a Roman leader was entitled to the gilded helmet of the victor as a reward. After the battle was over the helmet was placed upon his head with great formality, and he received the additional name of *Gildhelme*. This in French became Guilheme; was Latinised into Gulielmus; and, the initial letter being changed, it became William in English.

William the Conqueror. It is questionable whether this epithet should be applied to William. It certainly is not applicable in the ordinary sense. Edward the Confessor, it is well known, in accordance with the custom of the times, had bequeathed his crown to William, but the *Witen-agemôte*, or assembly of nobles, chose Harold to be king. William invaded England, therefore, not to *conquer* it, but to assert his right, in which he succeeded. At first his reign was mild and gentle, but the Saxon nobles stirred up so much rebellion against his rule that at length he adopted the usual course of conquerors and subdued all opposition by violence. Haydn says that English judges formerly rebuked barristers who spoke of 'William the Conqueror,' his proper designation being 'William the First.'

Willy-nilly is the ordinary pronunciation of *will-he nill-he*, meaning 'whether he will or not.' The Saxons had a negative form for every verb commencing with *w*, *h*, or a vowel. This consisted in prefixing the letter *n*, the initial of the negative particle, as a prefix. The word *nill*, in the phrase quoted, means therefore, 'will not.' Chaucer often used this form, saying, 'I nam' for 'I am not,' 'he nad' for 'he had not,' and 'I nas' for 'I was not.' Sylvester, at the end of the sixteenth century, uses this form in his 26th Sonnet:—

Who *nill* be subjects shall be slaves, in fine.

We continue to use it in the words 'none,' 'neither,' and 'never,' which are simply one, either, and ever with the negative prefix *n*.

Windmills were first introduced into England by the Crusaders, who had seen them in use among the Saracens

Window. A curious example of the use of this word to express the meaning of a blank space in a manuscript occurs in a letter of Archbishop Cranmer's ('Works,' Parker Society edit., vol. ii. p. 249) : 'And whereas there is a collation of a benefice now in my hands . . . . I will that you send me a collation thereof, and that your said collation have a *window* expedient to set what name I will therein.'

Window (anciently wind-dore, or wind-door). This word is common to all the Northern languages. In Danish it is *vindue*, literally wind-eye, an opening to admit the wind.

Window Glass. The manufacture of window glass was commenced in London in 1557, but for a long time it was a luxury only within reach of the opulent. In proof of this it may be mentioned that in 1580 the glass casements of Alnwick Castle, the residence of the Dukes of Northumberland, were removed during the absence of the family to prevent accidents to the glass.

Winter and Summer Temperature. The average difference between summer and winter temperature varies with the distance from the equator. Thus at Singapore it is but 2 degrees; at Bombay it is 6 degrees; at Calcutta 14; at London 23; at St. Petersburg 43; and at Quebec 54. The average summer heat at St. Petersburg is only 1 degree less than that of London. At New York, which is 11 degrees more south than London, the winter temperature is more than 9 degrees colder, whilst the summer is 9 degrees hotter.

Wire-drawing was invented by Rodolph of Nuremberg in the early part of the fifteenth century. Wire was first made in England at Mortlake in 1663.

Wisdom is active; prudence, passive. Wisdom leads one to what is proper; prudence prevents one from doing what is improper.

Wiseacre. The origin of this phrase is stated to be a retort given to Ben Jonson at the 'Devil Tavern,' a noted hostelry that stood next to Child's Bank in Fleet Street, and was a great resort of wits and players. One night a country gentleman was among the wits, and boasted interminably of his landed property, till Ben, chafed and angry, said, 'What signify to us your dirt and your clods? where you have an acre of land, I have ten acres of wit.' The countryman retorted by calling Ben 'Good Mr. Wiseacre,' to the great amusement of the bystanders. This is a very good story, but the term 'wiseacre' is a corruption of the German *weissager*, a wise-sayer or sayer of wise maxims or precepts; a prophet.

Wise Men of Gotham. Gotham is a village in the south-west of Nottinghamshire, containing about a thousand inhabitants. Wharton says that 'the mad pranks of the men of Gotham bore a reference to some customary land tenures of the neighbourhood now grown obsolete.' Hearne, too, confirms the view that the lands were formerly held there by some foolish 'sports and customs.' It has been said that, having found a cuckoo in a bush, the men of Gotham tried to fence it in, and that, seeing the reflection of the moon in a pond, they fetched a rake to get it out. There is still a bush in the village called the 'cuckoo-bush,' but how the stories and the proverb originated will perhaps never be known. The 'wise men of Gotham' have been notorious from the time of Henry VIII.

Wit, according to Dryden, consists in the resemblance of ideas, but every resemblance of ideas is not wit. The resemblance must be such as gives both delight and surprise. Where there is no surprise there is no wit. Thus, when a poet tells us that the bosom of his mistress is as white as snow, there is no wit; but when he adds, with a sigh, it is as cold, too, it then grows into wit. The old writers frequently used the word 'wit' as synonymous with wisdom. Pope says:—

> True wit is nature to advantage drest,
> What oft was thought, but ne'er so well exprest.

Within the Pale. This is a phrase familiar to students of Irish history, and is also often met with in theological works in such sentences as 'within the pale of the Church,' &c. The expression arose after the invasion of Ireland by Henry II., and the 'pale' was the boundary of that part of Ireland subject to English dominion. The limits 'within the pale' seldom exceeded the modern province of Leinster. The word pale is allied to the English paling, a wooden fence.

Without. There is a growing tendency in modern conversation to use this word where 'unless' is meant. 'I should not like to go *without* you give your consent'; '*Without* you go, I shall stay away,' and so on. Sidney certainly uses it in the following sentence: 'You will never live to my age *without* you keep yourself in breath with exercise.' In this, as in the other cases, the substitution of *unless* would greatly improve the sentence.

Witticism. Johnson says of 'witticism,' 'This word Dryden innovated'—
> A mighty *witticism*—pardon a new word.—*Dryden.*

Wizard. This word originally meant a wise man. Spenser has—
> And strong advizement of six *wisards* old.
> *Faerie Queene,* L. iv. 12.

And Milton calls the wise men from the East *wisards*—
> The star-led *wisards* haste with odours sweet.
> *Ode on the Nativity,* v. 23.

Woe-begone. The affix 'begone' in this term perpetuates an Old English word for decayed or badly worn. In the East of England the country people still use it, and it is no uncommon thing to hear a man say of the roof of a cottage, 'This thatch is badly *begone.*' The compound 'woe-begone,' with this meaning of begone kept in view, is singularly expressive and poetical.

Wolf. The last wolf in Scotland is said to have been killed in 1680—Sir T. Dick Lauder thinks by a man named Pollochock, or Pal à Chockain; but in the 'Catalogue of Mr. Donovan's Sale at the London Museum,' April 1818, is the following item : 'Lot 832. Wolf. A noble animal in a large glass case. The last wolf killed in Scotland, by Sir C. Cameron.'

Woman taken in adultery. According to Dean Alford the account of the woman taken in adultery (John viii. 3–11) is not to be found in the earliest copies of John's Gospel. It is printed within brackets in the revised edition of the New Testament for the same reason.

Woodbine and **Woodbind.** These are two distinct plants. The wood*bine* is the honeysuckle; the wood*bind* is the wild convolvulus, or bindweed. Nares suggested that in Titania's speech in the 'Midsummer Night's Dream' (act. iv. sc. 1) the word 'woodbine' should be altered to 'bindweed,' so as to get rid of an evident mistake on Shakespeare's part. Ben Jonson in the 'Vision of Delight' has an exquisite passage, in which he introduces the term bindweed correctly :—
> Behold
> How the blue *bindweed* doth itself infold
> With honey-suckle.

Wood Engraving was invented by an Italian named Cunio about the year 1285.

Wooden Walls of Old England. The expression 'wooden wals' appears in Spenser's 'Faerie Queene,' I. ii. 42. Grote, in his

'History of Greece,' says that the phrase was first used by the Delphic Oracle in reference to the Athenian fleet.

Woodman. Everybody is familiar with the engravings from Westall's picture of 'The Woodman,' which have been sold by hundreds of thousands. The following extract from the 'Gentleman's Magazine' for 1813 records the death of the man who sat as the model: 'Aged 107, Michael Baily, a native of Sherbourn, co. York, and the person who sat for the painting called "The Woodman." He was a very regular man, and from the age of fifty, when he first came to London, till he attained his hundredth year, he was a day labourer.'

Woolsack. An Act of Parliament was passed in the reign of Elizabeth to prevent the exportation of wool. In order to keep constantly in mind this source of our national wealth woolsacks were placed in the House of Lords as seats for the judges. The seat of the Lord Chancellor is to this day called the 'woolsack.'

Woolwich is Hill Reach, so called from its lying under Shooter's Hill.

Words. The English language is supposed to consist of about 60,000 distinct words. Mr. Max Müller is of opinion that the average farm labourer never uses more than 300; that an ordinarily educated man's vocabulary reaches to 3,000 to 4,000; and that a great orator may reach 10,000. The Old Testament contains 5,642 different words. Milton uses about 8,000, and Shakespeare nearly 15,000.

Words ending in 'our.' 'Of three hundred words formerly ending thus, not more than forty retain the *u* (as favour, honour), and these not always. It is probable, therefore, that the spelling of these forty will ultimately conform to the rest of the class.'— *Dr. Angus.*

World. To 'go to the world' formerly meant 'to be married.' In 'Much Ado about Nothing,' Beatrice complains that every one 'goes to the world but I, and I may sit in a corner and cry heigho! for a husband' (act ii. sc. 1). And in 'All's Well that Ends Well,' the Clown, in asking permission to marry the Chambermaid, says, 'If I may have your ladyship's good-will to go to the world, Isabel and I will do as we may' (act i. sc. 3). A 'woman of the world' then meant a married woman. Thus, in 'As You Like It,' when Touchstone says, 'To-morrow we will be married,' Audrey replies, 'I do desire it with all my heart, and I hope it is no dishonest desire to desire to be a woman of the world.'

Worsted was first spun at Worsted, in Norfolk, in the year 1340. Stockings made of this material were at first only used by the common people. Shakespeare uses the phrase 'worsted-stocking knave' as a term of contempt.

Wort, the terminal syllable in the names of plants, as colewort, spleenwort, liverwort, is the Anglo-Saxon word *wyrt*, a root. A *wart* is a fleshy excrescence deeply *rooted*.

Worth, as the terminating syllable in the names of places, signifies that the place stands on a tongue of land between two rivers, or formed by the loop-like bending of one. Tamworth is a good example, standing, as it does, at the junction of the Tame and the Trent. Kenilworth, Lutterworth, and Bedworth are also cases in point.

Worth. The use of this word as a verb has altogether gone out of use. It was formerly common in the sense of *betide*. Sir Walter Scott has :—

> Wo *worth* the chase—wo *worth* the day
> That costs thy life, my gallant gray.

And in the verse Ezekiel xxx. 2 we find, 'Thus saith the Lord God : Howl ye, wo *worth* the day.'

Worth a Jew's eye. This is a common proverbial synonym for a large sum. Its meaning is not very obvious, but it probably arose in the days of King John, who extorted large sums of money from the Jews under threats of mutilation. It is on record that John had the whole of the teeth of one Jew at Bristol drawn before he would satisfy the monarch's rapacity. The 'ransom' for an eye would probably be greater than for teeth, and so it became proverbial. There is another probable origin. In the 'Merchant of Venice' (act ii. sc. 5) Shylock has just been telling his daughter Jessica that a masque or procession is to pass the house, and, as he is going out, she is on no account to look out of the window, upon which Launcelot, very slily, advises Jessica, notwithstanding the parental prohibition, to look out, for—

> There will come a Christian by
> Will be worth a Jewess' eye.

That is, there will be some one coming by, whom, Jewess though you be, you will find *worth* looking at. As no reference to the proverb earlier than the time of Shakespeare is known, this speech, entirely misunderstood, may have been the origin of the saying.

Wreck. Probably derived from 'wrack,' the name given to sea-weeds cast upon the shore. The word 'wreckage' shows the analogy between the two words very clearly.

Wretch was formerly occasionally used by way of ironical pity, as 'illustrious wretch.' It was sometimes also used as an expression of tenderness, as—

> The happy *wretch* she put into her breast.—*Sir P. Sidney.*

Wretchlessness. This word occurs in the seventeenth Article of the Church of England. It is quoted by Earle in his 'Philology of the English Tongue' as a curious instance of the change of form in words. He says, 'To understand this word we have only to look at it when divested of its initial *w*, and then to remember that an ancient Saxon *c* at the end of a syllable commonly developed into *tch*, and in this way we get back to the verb *to reck*, to care for, so that *wretchlessness* really means recklessness, or caring for nothing, although the words look so unlike.'

Wright. In the North of England and throughout Scotland a carpenter is known by no other name than 'wright,' which in Scotland is pronounced *wrecght*. Amongst the Anglo-Saxons a carpenter was a wood-smith.

Write like an angel. The word angel in the common phrase 'write like an angel' is a corruption of Angelo. Isaac D'Israeli, in his 'Curiosities of Literature,' says, 'This fanciful phrase has a very human origin. Among those learned Greeks who emigrated to Italy, and some afterwards into France in the reign of Francis I., was one Angelo Verjecto, whose beautiful calligraphy excited the admiration of the learned. The French monarch had a Greek fount cast, modelled by his writing. His name became synonymous for beautiful writing, and gave birth to that familiar phrase, to "write like an angel."'

Writing. The earliest known mention of writing is in Exodus xvi. 14, where Moses is commanded to 'write this for a memorial in a book.'

X

X. This letter in English has two sounds, one where it is sounded as *ks*, the other *gs*. The rule seems to be that when the syllable after an *x* is accented, the *x* takes the *g* sound. Thus *ex'otic* is pronounced *egs'otic*, excavate as *eks*cavate. In the word export both sounds are used. The verb *to export* has the *y* sound, *egs*port, but in the nouns *export-duty* or *exports* the *k* sound is adopted.—*Earle*, p. 116.

Y

Yankee. This name originated in the first attempts made by the North-American Indians to pronounce the word English. Yenghies, Yanghies, Yankies are early forms of the word. It was first applied, offensively, to the New Englanders by the British soldiers about the year 1775. This is the generally received belief; but Jamieson, in his 'Scottish Dictionary,' has the word 'Yankie,' which he defines thus: 'A sharp, clever woman, at the same time including an idea of forwardness.'

Yankee Doodle. The real origin of the musical air called by this name has not been traced. It was known in England as 'Nankee Doodle' in the time of Charles I., and it is said to have been in common use by the agricultural labourers in the Netherlands for several generations. Kossuth, when in America, recognised it as a native Hungarian air; and Mr. Buckingham Smith, formerly Secretary of Legation at Madrid, says that it is the ancient music of the sword dance of the Biscayans. It was appropriated by the Americans, because it was the music to which the British soldiers marched out of Boston after the battle of Lexington.

Yard (the measure). William of Malmesbury, in 'Vita Hen. I.,' tells us that a new standard of length was established by Henry I., who ordered that the ulna, or ancient ell, which corresponds to the modern yard, should be the exact length of his own arm.

Y^e, Y^t, for 'the' and 'that,' are blunders arising from mistaking the Anglo-Saxon letter þ, which is equivalent to our *th*, for the letter *y*. The early printers, probably not having a type for printing the þ, used the *y* as the nearest, and so the error was perpetuated.

Yea and Nay, yes and no. There was formerly a clear distinction in the use of these two forms. Yea and nay were answers to questions framed in the affirmative, as 'Will he go?' *Yea* or *nay*. But if the question was formed in the negative, as

'Will he not go?' the answer was *yes* or *no*. Yea and nay are in the present day practically obsolete.

Year 'originally signified a revolution, and was not limited to that of the sun. Accordingly it is found by the oldest accounts that people have at different times expressed other revolutions by it, particularly that of the moon; and consequently that the "years" of some accounts are to be reckoned only months, and sometimes periods of two, or three, or four months.'—*Hutton*.

Year and a Day. This is a time fixed by ancient law within which certain things must be done. A stray horse or other animal must be claimed within a year and a day, or it becomes the property of the lord of the manor. A person wounded must die within a year and a day to make the person inflicting the wound guilty of murder.

Yeast, from the German *Geist*, spirit, essence. In Icelandic *geist* means fervent, fiery. This and the word gist (*g* soft) are evidently allied.

Yellow-hammer. The *h* in the name of this bird is an improper interpolation. The bird is a variety of the species *bunting*, the ancient English name for which was 'ammer.' In Germany the variety we call 'yellow-hammer' is known as the 'gold-ammer.'

Yeoman. 'The title *yeoman* is of military origin, as well as that of esquire, and other titles of honour. Esquires were so called because in combat they carried for defence an *ecu* or shield; and yeomen were so styled because, besides the weapons fit for close engagement, they fought with arrows and the bow, which was made of *yew*, a tree that hath more repelling force and elasticity than any other.... After the Conquest the name of yeomen, as to their original office in war, was changed to that of archers.'— *Gentleman's Magazine*, vol. xxxix. p. 408. The word yeoman may, however, be a corruption of *gentleman*. *G* and *y* were anciently, as is shown in the article YOLK, used interchangeably. The word gentleman, contracted as in modern times to *ge'mman*, might have been written *yemman*, from which the transition to the modern form would be easy. Verstegan gives the Anglo-Saxon word as 'gemæne,' which favours the hypothesis.

Yesterday. The use of this word in connection with the preposition 'on' seems to be confined to America. The following examples, one from a high-class newspaper, the others from speeches in Congress, sound strangely to English ears :—' It was the intention to send in the Treasury Report, which has been so long delayed, *on yesterday.*'—*New York Tribune,* January 9, 1852. ' I supposed that the House listened to the remarks of the gentleman from Texas *on yesterday.*'—*Speech of Mr. Brooks,* July 7, 1852. ' Mr. Speaker, when I arose *on yesterday* it was my intention,' &c.— *Mr. Quitman,* December 18, 1856.

Yew Trees in Churchyards. The common belief that the yew tree was planted in churchyards in order that a due supply of bow staves should be forthcoming seems to be erroneous. The bow staves were of foreign woods. Henry VIII. compelled shipowners to import bow staves in every ship in proportion to other cargo, and they were admitted duty free, which seems to prove that the native supply was inadequate. The true reason for planting yews in churchyards seems to be given in the following extract from ' Liber Festivalis,' printed by Caxton in 1483 : ' But for reason that we have non olyve that berith greene leef algate, therefore we take *ewe* instead of palme and olyve, and beren aboute in processyon, and soe is this daye called Palme Sondaye.' It is now known that anciently in England yew branches represented the palm branches on Palm Sunday, and the churches were decorated with yew on that festival. This is supposed to be the origin of dressing churches with yew and other evergreens at Easter. In Ireland at the present day Palm Sunday sees every Catholic peasant with a sprig of yew in his coat or hat, and in Kent yew trees are called palm trees. In the accounts of the churchwardens of Woodbury is the following entry:—' Memorandum, 1775—That a yew or *palm* tree was planted in the churchyard, yᵉ south side of the church, in the same place where one was blown down by the wind a few days ago, this 25th of November.'

Yokel. A name applied to an awkward rustic, originally applied to one who *yoked* oxen or other animals.

Yolk (of an egg). *G* and *y* were anciently used indifferently, the one for the other, as in yard, which was sometimes spelt *yard* and sometimes *gard* (garden). *Gealow* was Anglo-Saxon for yellow, and was also the name of the yolk of an egg. *Gealow* in time became *yellow, yelk* was contracted from yellow, and yelk has been corrupted into *yolk.*

York Street, a short street, leading from the north side of St. James's Square to Jermyn Street, was the first street in London to be paved for foot-passengers.—*New and Old London,* vol. iv. p. 203.

You. The Midland and Northern pronunciation of this word, 'yow,' is nearer to the original sound than the Southern 'yew.' Verstegan gives the Anglo-Saxon orthography *eow*, you, and *eower*, your.

You'll never set the Thames on fire. The word 'Thames' in this saying should be 'temse,' which is an ancient name for a sieve used by millers for separating flour from the bran, &c. Formerly the sieve was kept in motion by a man sliding it backwards and forwards on a wooden frame. A very active workman at the 'temse' would sometimes set fire to its rim by friction. An idle fellow would be too slothful to 'set the temse on fire,' hence the proverb. The word 'temse' is still used by brewers in Lincolnshire as the name of the sieve through which they strain their wort.

Your Petitioners shall ever pray, &c. The '&c.' of this phrase was formerly written at full length. In the case of a petition to a sovereign it ran: 'For your Majesty's most prosperous reign.' Where the petition was to Parliament the form was 'for the prosperous successe of this highe and honourable Court of Parliament.' Acts of Parliament are still in the form of petitions, but the prayer is now omitted, though *ante* Henry VI. the '&c.' meant 'for God's sake and as an act of charity,' the exact words used being 'Vos povers communes prient et suppliant, par Dieu et en œuvre de charité.'—*Rot. Parl.* 2 Hen. V. No. 22.

You've shot your granny. This is the American equivalent for the English saying, 'You've found a mare's nest.'

Yule. Brand ('Popular Antiquities'), speaking of *yule*, says of it, 'of which there seems nothing certain but that it means Christmas.' Mr. Fox Talbot has, however, discovered that both midsummer and midwinter were called yule, or jule, and he gives good reasons for the name being so applied. At each of these periods there is a *solstice*, or 'turning-point,' in the course of the sun. The Northern nations used the word 'wheel' to express this turning, and as the word wheel was variously spelt 'hiul,' 'hjul,' and so forth, it agrees well enough with *iul, iol*, and *yule*, to render it probable that this may be the origin of the term. This theory of Mr. Talbot's derives great support from the fact that so lately as 1823 'the inhabitants of the village of Konz, on the Moselle, were in the habit on St. John's Eve of taking a great wheel wrapped in straw to the top of a neighbouring eminence, and making it roll down the hill, flaming all the way. If it reached the Moselle before being extinct, a good vintage was anticipated.'—*Chambers's Encyclopædia*, art. 'Yule.' See JULY.

Z

Z. In America this letter, which we know by the name 'zed,' is always spoken of as 'zee.'

Zenith and Nadir. These are two Arabic words now naturalised in England—'zenith' to signify the point of the heavens immediately above a spectator; 'nadir' to denote the opposite invisible point immediately beneath him.—*Penny Cyclopædia*.

Zero is an Italian name for the arithmetical figure formed like the letter O, which we call *ought* or nought.

Zoölogical. By a large number of persons this word is mispronounced as though the first three letters formed one syllable, *zoo*. This is erroneous; they form two in this and all similar words. The music-hall song 'Walking in the *Zoo*' has done much to spread the vicious pronunciation. We should say *zo-o-log-i-cal, zo-ol-o-gy, zo-o-phyte*, &c.

Zounds. This profane expression is a corruption of the words 'God's wounds.' 'The first man of quality,' says Swift, 'I find upon record to have sworn by God's wounds' was Sir John Perrott, a natural son of Henry VIII., who was condemned to death for treason by Elizabeth. He 'died suddenly' in the Tower, September 1592.

THE END.

PRINTED BY
SPOTTISWOODE AND CO., NEW-STREET SQUARE
LONDON

[*Feb.* 1897.

LIST OF BOOKS PUBLISHED BY
CHATTO & WINDUS
111 ST. MARTIN'S LANE, CHARING CROSS, LONDON, W.C.

About (Edmond).—The Fellah: An Egyptian Novel. Translated by Sir RANDAL ROBERTS. Post 8vo, illustrated boards, 2s.

Adams (W. Davenport), Works by.
A Dictionary of the Drama: being a comprehensive Guide to the Plays, Playwrights, Players and Playhouses of the United Kingdom and America, from the Earliest Times to the Present Day. Crown 8vo, half-bound, 12s. 6d. [*Preparing.*
Quips and Quiddities. Selected by W. DAVENPORT ADAMS. Post 8vo, cloth limp, 2s. 6d.

Agony Column (The) of 'The Times,' from 1800 to 1870. Edited, with an Introduction, by ALICE CLAY. Post 8vo, cloth limp, 2s. 6d.

Aidé (Hamilton), Novels by. Post 8vo, illustrated boards, 2s. each.
Carr of Carrlyon. | Confidences.

Albert (Mary).—Brooke Finchley's Daughter. Post 8vo, picture boards, 2s.; cloth limp, 2s. 6d.

Alden (W. L.).—A Lost Soul: Being the Confession and Defence of Charles Lindsay. Fcap. 8vo, cloth boards, 1s. 6d.

Alexander (Mrs.), Novels by. Post 8vo, illustrated boards, 2s. each.
Maid, Wife, or Widow? | Valerie's Fate. | Blind Fate.

Crown 8vo, cloth, 3s. 6d. each.
A Life Interest. | Mona's Choice. | By Woman's Wit.

Allen (F. M.).—Green as Grass. With a Frontispiece. Crown 8vo, cloth, 3s. 6d.

Allen (Grant), Works by.
The Evolutionist at Large. Crown 8vo, cloth extra, 6s.
Post-Prandial Philosophy. Crown 8vo, art linen, 3s. 6d.
Moorland Idylls. Crown 8vo, cloth decorated, 6s.

Crown 8vo, cloth extra, 3s. 6d. each; post 8vo, illustrated boards, 2s. each.
Babylon. 12 Illustrations. | The Devil's Die. | The Duchess of Powysland.
Strange Stories. Frontis. | This Mortal Coil. | Blood Royal.
The Beckoning Hand. | The Tents of Shem. Frontis. | Ivan Greet's Masterpiece.
For Maimie's Sake. | The Great Taboo. | The Scallywag. 24 Illusts.
Philistia. | In all Shades | Dumaresq's Daughter. | At Market Value.

Under Sealed Orders. Crown 8vo, cloth extra, 3s. 6d.
Dr. Palliser's Patient. Fcap. 8vo, cloth boards, 1s. 6d.

Anderson (Mary).—Othello's Occupation: A Novel. Crown 8vo, cloth, 3s. 6d.

Arnold (Edwin Lester), Stories by.
The Wonderful Adventures of Phra the Phœnician. Crown 8vo, cloth extra, with 12 Illustrations by H. M. PAGET, 3s. 6d.; post 8vo, illustrated boards, 2s.
The Constable of St. Nicholas. With Frontispiece by S. L. WOOD. Crown 8vo, cloth, 3s. 6d.

Artemus Ward's Works. With Portrait and Facsimile. Crown 8vo, cloth extra, 7s. 6d.—Also a POPULAR EDITION, post 8vo, picture boards, 2s.

CHATTO & WINDUS, 111 St. Martin's Lane, London, W.C.

Ashton (John), Works by. Crown 8vo, cloth extra, 7s. 6d. each.
History of the Chap-Books of the 18th Century. With 334 Illustrations
Social Life in the Reign of Queen Anne. With 85 Illustrations.
Humour, Wit, and Satire of the Seventeenth Century. With 82 Illustrations.
English Caricature and Satire on Napoleon the First. With 115 Illustrations.
Modern Street Ballads. With 57 Illustrations.

Bacteria, Yeast Fungi, and Allied Species, A Synopsis of. By W. B. GROVE, B A. With 87 Illustrations. Crown 8vo, cloth extra, 3s. 6d.

Bardsley (Rev. C. Wareing, M.A.), Works by.
English Surnames: Their Sources and Significations. Crown 8vo, cloth, 7s. 6d.
Curiosities of Puritan Nomenclature. Crown 8vo, cloth extra, 6s.

Baring Gould (Sabine, Author of 'John Herring,' &c.), **Novels by.**
Crown 8vo, cloth extra, 3s. 6d. each ; post 8vo, illustrated boards, 2s. each.
Red Spider. | Eve.

Barr (Robert: Luke Sharp), Stories by. Cr. 8vo, cl., 3s. 6d. each.
In a Steamer Chair. With Frontispiece and Vignette by DEMAIN HAMMOND.
From Whose Bourne, &c, With 47 Illustrations by HAL HURST and others.
A Woman Intervenes. With 8 Illustrations by HAL HURST. Crown 8vo, cloth extra, 6s.
Revenge! With 12 Illustrations by LANCELOT SPEED, &c. Crown 8vo, cloth, 6s.

Barrett (Frank), Novels by.
Post 8vo, illustrated boards, 2s. each ; cloth, 2s. 6d. each.
Fettered for Life. | A Prodigal's Progress.
The Sin of Olga Zassoulich. | John Ford; and His Helpmate.
Between Life and Death. | A Recoiling Vengeance.
Folly Morrison. | Honest Davie. | Lieut. Barnabas. | Found Guilty.
Little Lady Linton. | For Love and Honour.
The Woman of the Iron Bracelets. Cr. 8vo. cloth, 3s. 6d.; post 8vo, boards, 2s.; cl. limp, 2s. 6d.
Crown 8vo, cloth extra, 3s. 6d. each.
The Harding Scandal.
A Missing Witness. With Eight Illustrations by W. H. MARGETSON. [April.

Barrett (Joan).—Monte Carlo Stories. Fcap. 8vo, cloth, 1s. 6d.

Beaconsfield, Lord. By T. P. O'CONNOR, M.P. Cr. 8vo, cloth, 5s.

Beauchamp (Shelsley).—Grantley Grange. Post 8vo, boards, 2s.

Beautiful Pictures by British Artists: A Gathering of Favourites from the Picture Galleries, engraved on Steel. Imperial 4to, cloth extra, gilt edges, 21s.

Besant (Sir Walter) and James Rice, Novels by.
Crown 8vo, cloth extra, 3s. 6d. each ; post 8vo, illustrated boards, 2s. each; cloth limp, 2s. 6d. each.
Ready-Money Mortiboy. | By Celia's Arbour.
My Little Girl. | The Chaplain of the Fleet.
With Harp and Crown. | The Seamy Side.
This Son of Vulcan. | The Case of Mr. Lucraft, &c.
The Golden Butterfly. | 'Twas in Trafalgar's Bay, &c.
The Monks of Thelema. | The Ten Years' Tenant, &c.
, There is also a LIBRARY EDITION of the above Twelve Volumes, handsomely set in new type on a large crown 8vo page, and bound in cloth extra, 6s. each; and a POPULAR EDITION of **The Golden Butterfly,** medium 8vo, 6d.; cloth, 1s.—NEW EDITIONS, printed in large type on crown 8vo laid paper, bound in figured cloth, 3s. 6d. each, are also in course of publication.

Besant (Sir Walter), Novels by.
Crown 8vo, cloth extra, 3s. 6d. each ; post 8vo, illustrated boards, 2s. each ; cloth limp, 2s. 6d. each.
All Sorts and Conditions of Men. With 12 Illustrations by FRED. BARNARD
The Captains' Room, &c. With Frontispiece by E. J. WHEELER.
All in a Garden Fair. With 6 Illustrations by HARRY FURNISS.
Dorothy Forster. With Frontispiece by CHARLES GREEN.
Uncle Jack, and other Stories. | Children of Gibeon.
The World Went Very Well Then. With 12 Illustrations by A. FORESTIER.
Herr Paulus: His Rise, his Greatness, and his Fall | The Bell of St. Paul's.
For Faith and Freedom. With Illustrations by A. FORESTIER and F. WADDY.
To Call Her Mine, &c. With 9 Illustrations by A. FORESTIER.
The Holy Rose, &c. With Frontispiece by F. BARNARD.
Armorel of Lyonesse: A Romance of To-day With 12 Illustrations by F. BARNARD.
St. Katherine's by the Tower. With 12 Illustrations by C. GREEN.
Verbena Camellia Stephanotis. &c. With a Frontispiece by GORDON BROWNE.
The Ivory Gate. | The Rebel Queen.
Beyond the Dreams of Avarice. With 12 Illustrations by W. H. HYDE.
Crown 8vo, cloth extra, 3s. 6d. each.
In Deacon's Orders, &c. With Frontispiece by A. FORESTIER.
The Revolt of Man. | The Master Craftsman. [May.
The City of Refuge. 3 vols., crown 8vo, 15s. net.
The Charm, and other Drawing-room Plays. By Sir WALTER BESANT and WALTER H. POLLOCK With 50 Illustrations by CHRIS HAMMOND and JULE GOODMAN. Crown 8vo, cloth, gilt edges, 6s.
Fifty Years Ago. With 144 Plates and Woodcuts. Crown 8vo, cloth extra, 5s.
The Eulogy of Richard Jefferies. With Portrait. Crown 8vo, cloth extra, 6s.
London. With 125 Illustrations. Demy 8vo, cloth extra, 7s. 6d.
Westminster. With Etched Frontispiece by F. S. WALKER, R.P.E., and 130 Illustrations by WILLIAM PATTEN and others. Demy 8vo, cloth, 18s.
Sir Richard Whittington. With Frontispiece. Crown 8vo, art linen, 3s. 6d.
Gaspard de Coligny. With a Portrait. Crown 8vo, art linen, 3s. 6d.

CHATTO & WINDUS, 111 St. Martin's Lane, London, W.C. 3

Bechstein (Ludwig).—As Pretty as Seven, and other German Stories. With Additional Tales by the Brothers GRIMM, and 98 Illustrations by RICHTER. Square 8vo, cloth extra, 6s. 6d.; gilt edges, 7s. 6d.

Bellew (Frank).—The Art of Amusing: A Collection of Graceful Arts, Games, Tricks, Puzzles, and Charades. With 300 Illustrations. Crown 8vo, cloth extra, 4s. 6d.

Bennett (W. C., LL.D.).—Songs for Sailors. Post 8vo, cl. limp, 2s.

Bewick (Thomas) and his Pupils. By AUSTIN DOBSON. With 95 Illustrations. Square 8vo, cloth extra, 6s.

Bierce (Ambrose).—In the Midst of Life: Tales of Soldiers and Civilians. Crown 8vo, cloth extra, 6s.; post 8vo, illustrated boards, 2s.

Bill Nye's History of the United States. With 146 Illustrations by F. OPPER. Crown 8vo, cloth extra, 3s. 6d.

Biré (Edmond). — Diary of a Citizen of Paris during 'The Terror.' Translated and Edited by JOHN DE VILLIERS. With 2 Photogravure Portraits. Two Vols., demy 8vo, cloth, 21s.

Blackburn's (Henry) Art Handbooks.
Academy Notes, 1875, 1877-86, 1889, 1890, 1892-1896. Illustrated, each 1s.
Academy Notes, 1897. 1s. [May.
Academy Notes, 1875-79. Complete in One Vol., with 600 Illustrations. Cloth, 6s.
Academy Notes, 1880-84. Complete in One Vol., with 700 Illustrations. Cloth, 6s.
Academy Notes, 1890-94. Complete in One Vol., with 800 Illustrations. Cloth, 7s. 6d.
Grosvenor Notes, 1877. 6d.
Grosvenor Notes, separate years from 1878-1890, each 1s.
Grosvenor Notes, Vol. I., 1877-82. With 300 Illustrations. Demy 8vo, cloth, 6s.
Grosvenor Notes, Vol. II., 1883-87. With 300 Illustrations. Demy 8vo, cloth, 6s.
Grosvenor Notes, Vol. III., 1888-90. With 230 Illustrations. Demy 8vo cloth, 3s. 6d.
The New Gallery, 1888-1895. With numerous Illustrations, each 1s.
The New Gallery, 1888-1892. With 250 Illustrations. Demy 8vo, cloth, 6s.
English Pictures at the National Gallery. With 114 Illustrations. 1s.
Old Masters at the National Gallery. With 128 Illustrations. 1s. 6d.
Illustrated Catalogue to the National Gallery. With 242 Illusts. Demy 8vo, cloth, 3s.

The Illustrated Catalogue of the Paris Salon, 1897. With 300 Sketches. 3s. [May.

Blind (Mathilde), Poems by.
The Ascent of Man. Crown 8vo, cloth, 5s.
Dramas in Miniature. With a Frontispiece by F. MADOX BROWN. Crown 8vo, cloth, 5s.
Songs and Sonnets. Fcap. 8vo, vellum and gold, 5s.
Birds of Passage: Songs of the Orient and Occident. Second Edition. Crown 8vo, linen, 6s. net.

Bourget (Paul).—A Living Lie. Translated by JOHN DE VILLIERS. With special Preface for the English Edition. Crown 8vo, cloth, 3s. 6d.

Bourne (H. R. Fox), Books by.
English Merchants: Memoirs in Illustration of the Progress of British Commerce. With numerous Illustrations. Crown 8vo, cloth extra, 7s. 6d.
English Newspapers: Chapters in the History of Journalism. Two Vols., demy 8vo, cloth, 25s.
The Other Side of the Emin Pasha Relief Expedition. Crown 8vo, cloth, 6s.

Bowers (George).—Leaves from a Hunting Journal. Coloured Plates. Oblong folio, half-bound, 21s.

Boyle (Frederick), Works by. Post 8vo, illustrated bds., 2s. each.
Chronicles of No-Man's Land. | Camp Notes. | Savage Life.

Brand (John).—Observations on Popular Antiquities; chiefly illustrating the Origin of our Vulgar Customs, Ceremonies, and Superstitions. With the Additions of Sir HENRY ELLIS, and numerous Illustrations. Crown 8vo, cloth extra, 7s. 6d.

Brewer (Rev. Dr.), Works by.
The Reader's Handbook of Allusions, References, Plots, and Stories. Eighteenth Thousand. Crown 8vo, cloth extra, 7s. 6d.
Authors and their Works, with the Dates: Being the Appendices to 'The Reader's Hand.
book,' separately printed. Crown 8vo, cloth limp, 2s.
A Dictionary of Miracles. Crown 8vo, cloth extra, 7s. 6d.

Brewster (Sir David), Works by. Post 8vo, cloth, 4s. 6d. each.
More Worlds than One: Creed of the Philosopher and Hope of the Christian. With Plates.
The Martyrs of Science: GALILEO, TYCHO BRAHE, and KEPLER. With Portraits.
Letters on Natural Magic. With numerous Illustrations.

Brillat-Savarin.—Gastronomy as a Fine Art. Translated by R. E. ANDERSON, M.A. Post 8vo, half-bound, 2s.

Brydges (Harold).—Uncle Sam at Home. With 91 Illustrations. Post 8vo, illustrated boards, 2s.; cloth limp, 2s. 6d.

Buchanan (Robert), Novels, &c., by.

Crown 8vo, cloth extra, 3s. 6d. each ; pos 8vo, illustrated boards, 2s. each.

The Shadow of the Sword.	**Love Me for Ever.** With Frontispiece.
A Child of Nature. With Frontispiece.	**Annan Water.** | **Foxglove Manor.**
God and the Man. With 11 Illustrations by FRED. BARNARD.	**The New Abelard.** | **Rachel Dene.**
	Matt: A Story of a Caravan. With Frontispiece.
The Martyrdom of Madeline. With Frontispiece by A. W. COOPER.	**The Master of the Mine.** With Frontispiece.
	The Heir of Linne. | **Woman and the Man.**

Crown 8vo, cloth extra, 3s. 6d. each.

Red and White Heather. | **Lady Kilpatrick.**

The Wandering Jew: a Christmas Carol. Crown 8vo, cloth, 6s.

The Charlatan. By ROBERT BUCHANAN and HENRY MURRAY. Crown 8vo, cloth, with a Frontispiece by T. H. ROBINSON, 3s. 6d. ; post 8vo, picture boards, 2s.

Burton (Richard F.).—The Book of the Sword. With over 400 Illustrations. Demy 4to, cloth extra, 32s.

Burton (Robert).—The Anatomy of Melancholy. With Translations of the Quotations. Demy 8vo, cloth extra, 7s. 6d.
Melancholy Anatomised: An Abridgment of BURTON'S ANATOMY. Post 8vo, half-bd., 2s. 6d.

Caine (T. Hall), Novels by. Crown 8vo, cloth extra, 3s. 6d. each. ; post 8vo, illustrated boards, 2s. each ; cloth limp, 2s. 6d. each.
The Shadow of a Crime. | **A Son of Hagar.** | **The Deemster.**
Also a LIBRARY EDITION of **The Deemster,** set in new type, crown 8vo, cloth decorated, 6s.

Cameron (Commander V. Lovett).—The Cruise of the 'Black Prince' Privateer. Post 8vo, picture boards, 2s.

Cameron (Mrs. H. Lovett), Novels by. Post 8vo, illust. bds. 2s. ea.
Juliet's Guardian. | **Deceivers Ever.**

Captain Coignet, Soldier of the Empire: An Autobiography. Edited by LOREDAN LARCHEY. Translated by Mrs. CAREY. With 100 Illustrations. Crown 8vo, cloth, 3s. 6d.

Carlyle (Jane Welsh), Life of. By Mrs. ALEXANDER IRELAND. With Portrait and Facsimile Letter. Small demy 8vo, cloth extra, 7s. 6d.

Carlyle (Thomas).—On the Choice of Books. Post 8vo, cl., 1s. 6d.
Correspondence of Thomas Carlyle and R. W. Emerson, 1834-1872. Edited by C. E. NORTON. With Portraits. Two Vols., crown 8vo, cloth, 24s.

Carruth (Hayden).—The Adventures of Jones. With 17 Illustrations. Fcap. 8vo, cloth, 2s.

Chambers (Robert W.), Stories of Paris Life by. Long fcap. 8vo, cloth, 2s. 6d. each.
The King in Yellow. | **In the Quarter.**

Chapman's (George), Works. Vol. I., Plays Complete, including the Doubtful Ones.—Vol. II., Poems and Minor Translations, with Essay by A. C. SWINBURNE.—Vol. III., Translations of the Iliad and Odyssey. Three Vols., crown 8vo, cloth, 3s. 6d. each.

Chapple (J. Mitchell).—The Minor Chord: The Story of a Prima Donna. Crown 8vo, cloth, 3s. 6d.

Chatto (W. A.) and J. Jackson.—A Treatise on Wood Engraving, Historical and Practical. With Chapter by H. G. BOHN, and 450 fine Illusts. Large 4to, half-leather, 28s.

Chaucer for Children: A Golden Key. By Mrs. H. R. HAWEIS. With 8 Coloured Plates and 30 Woodcuts. Crown 4to, cloth extra, 3s. 6d.
Chaucer for Schools. By Mrs. H. R. HAWEIS. Demy 8vo, cloth limp, 2s. 6d.

Chess, The Laws and Practice of. With an Analysis of the Openings. By HOWARD STAUNTON. Edited by R. B. WORMALD. Crown 8vo, cloth, 5s.
The Minor Tactics of Chess: A Treatise on the Deployment of the Forces in obedience to Strategic Principle. By F. K. YOUNG and E. C. HOWELL. Long fcap. 8vo, cloth, 2s. 6d.
The Hastings Chess Tournament. Containing the Authorised Account of the 230 Games played Aug.-Sept., 1895. With Annotations by PILLSBURY, LASKER, TARRASCH, STEINITZ, SCHIFFERS, TEICHMANN, BARDELEBEN, BLACKBURNE, GUNSBERG, TINSLEY, MASON, and ALBIN ; Biographical Sketches of the Chess Masters, and 22 Portraits. Edited by H. F. CHESHIRE. Crown 8vo, cloth, 7s. 6d.

Clare (Austin).—For the Love of a Lass. Post 8vo, 2s. ; cl., 2s. 6d.

CHATTO & WINDUS, 111 St. Martin's Lane, London, W.C.

Clive (Mrs. Archer), Novels by. Post 8vo, illust. boards, 2s. each.
Paul Ferroll. | Why Paul Ferroll Killed his Wife.

Clodd (Edward, F.R.A.S.).—Myths and Dreams. Cr. 8vo, 3s. 6d.

Cobban (J. Maclaren), Novels by.
The Cure of Souls. Post 8vo, Illustrated boards, 2s.
The Red Sultan. Crown 8vo, cloth extra, 3s. 6d. ; post 8vo, illustrated boards, 2s.
The Burden of Isabel. Crown 8vo, cloth extra, 3s. 6d.

Coleman (John).—Curly: An Actor's Story. With 21 Illustrations by J. C. DOLLMAN. Crown 8vo, picture cover, 1s.

Coleridge (M. E.).—The Seven Sleepers of Ephesus. Cloth, 1s. 6d.

Collins (C. Allston).—The Bar Sinister. Post 8vo, boards, 2s.

Collins (John Churton, M.A.), Books by.
Illustrations of Tennyson. Crown 8vo, cloth extra, 6s.
Jonathan Swift: A Biographical and Critical Study. Crown 8vo, cloth extra, 8s.

Collins (Mortimer and Frances), Novels by.
Crown 8vo, cloth extra, 3s. 6d. each; post 8vo, illustrated boards, 2s. each.
From Midnight to Midnight. | Blacksmith and Scholar.
Transmigration. | You Play me False. | The Village Comedy.

Post 8vo, illustrated boards, 2s. each.
Sweet Anne Page. | A Fight with Fortune. | Sweet and Twenty. | Frances.

Collins (Wilkie), Novels by.
Crown 8vo, cloth extra, many Illustrated, 3s. 6d. each : post 8vo, picture boards, 2s. each;
cloth limp, 2s. 6d. each.

*Antonina.
*Basil.
*Hide and Seek.
*The Woman in White.
*The Moonstone.
After Dark.
The Dead Secret.
The Queen of Hearts,
No Name.
My Miscellanies.

Armadale.
Man and Wife.
Poor Miss Finch.
Miss or Mrs.?
The New Magdalen.
The Frozen Deep.
The Law and the Lady.
The Two Destinies.
The Haunted Hotel.
The Fallen Leaves.

Jezebel's Daughter.
The Black Robe.
Heart and Science.
'I Say No.'
A Rogue's Life.
The Evil Genius.
Little Novels.
The Legacy of Cain.
Blind Love.

. *Marked* are the NEW LIBRARY EDITION at 3s. 6d., entirely reset and bound in new style.

POPULAR EDITIONS. Medium 8vo, 6d. each; cloth, 1s. each.
The Woman in White. | The Moonstone. | Antonina.

The Woman in White and The Moonstone in One Volume, medium 8vo, cloth, 2s.

Colman's (George) Humorous Works: 'Broad Grins,' 'My Nightgown and Slippers,' &c. With Life and Frontispiece. Crown 8vo, cloth extra, 7s. 6d.

Colquhoun (M. J.).—Every Inch a Soldier. Post 8vo, boards, 2s.

Colt-breaking, Hints on. By W. M. HUTCHISON. Cr. 8vo, cl., 3s. 6d.

Convalescent Cookery. By CATHERINE RYAN. Cr. 8vo, 1s.; cl., 1s. 6d.

Conway (Moncure D.), Works by.
Demonology and Devil-Lore. With 65 Illustrations. Two Vols., demy 8vo, cloth, 28s.
George Washington's Rules of Civility. Fcap. 8vo, Japanese vellum, 2s. 6d.

Cook (Dutton), Novels by.
Post 8vo, illustrated boards, 2s. each.
Leo. | Paul Foster's Daughter.

Cooper (Edward H.).—Geoffory Hamilton. Cr. 8vo, cloth, 3s. 6d.

Cornwall.—Popular Romances of the West of England; or, The Drolls, Traditions, and Superstitions of Old Cornwall. Collected by ROBERT HUNT, F.R.S. With two Steel Plates by GEORGE CRUIKSHANK. Crown 8vo, cloth, 7s. 6d.

Cotes (V. Cecil).—Two Girls on a Barge. With 44 Illustrations by F. H. TOWNSEND. Post 8vo, cloth, 2s. 6d.

Craddock (C. Egbert), Stories by.
The Prophet of the Great Smoky Mountains. Post 8vo, illustrated boards, 2s.
His Vanished Star. Crown 8vo, cloth extra, 3s. 6d.

Cram (Ralph Adams).—Black Spirits and White. Fcap. 8vo, cloth, 1s. 6d.

Crellin (H. N.) Books by.
Romances of the Old Seraglio. With 28 Illustrations by S. L. WOOD. Crown 8vo, cloth, 3s. 6d.
Tales of the Caliph. Crown 8vo, cloth, 2s.
The Nazarenes: A Drama. Crown 8vo, 1s.

Crim (Matt.).—Adventures of a Fair Rebel. Crown 8vo, cloth extra, with a Frontispiece by DAN. BEARD, 3s. 6d.; post 8vo, illustrated boards, 2s.

Crockett (S. R.) and others.—Tales of Our Coast. By S. R. CROCKETT, GILBERT PARKER, HAROLD FREDERIC, 'Q.,' and W. CLARK RUSSELL. With 12 Illustrations by FRANK BRANGWYN. Crown 8vo, cloth, 3s. 6d.

Croker (Mrs. B. M.), Novels by. Crown 8vo, cloth extra, 3s. 6d. each; post 8vo, illustrated boards, 2s. each: cloth limp, 2s. 6d. each.

Pretty Miss Neville.	Diana Barrington.	A Family Likeness.
A Bird of Passage.	Proper Pride.	'To Let.'
Village Tales and Jungle Tragedies.	Two Masters.	Mr. Jervis.

Crown 8vo, cloth extra, 3s. 6d. each.
Married or Single? | **In the Kingdom of Kerry.**
The Real Lady Hilda.

Beyond the Pale. Crown 8vo, buckram, 6s.

Cruikshank's Comic Almanack. Complete in Two SERIES: The FIRST, from 1835 to 1843; the SECOND, from 1844 to 1853. A Gathering of the Best Humour of THACKERAY, HOOD, MAYHEW; ALBERT SMITH, A'BECKETT, ROBERT BROUGH, &c. With numerous Steel Engravings and Woodcuts by GEORGE CRUIKSHANK, HINE, LANDELLS, &c. Two Vols., crown 8vo, cloth gilt, 7s. 6d. each.
The Life of George Cruikshank. By BLANCHARD JERROLD. With 84 Illustrations and a Bibliography. Crown 8vo, cloth extra, 6s.

Cumming (C. F. Gordon), Works by. Demy 8vo, cl. ex., 8s. 6d. ea.
In the Hebrides. With an Autotype Frontispiece and 23 Illustrations.
In the Himalayas and on the Indian Plains. With 42 Illustrations.
Two Happy Years in Ceylon. With 28 Illustrations.
Via Cornwall to Egypt. With a Photogravure Frontispiece. Demy 8vo, cloth, 7s. 6d.

Cussans (John E.).—A Handbook of Heraldry; with Instructions for Tracing Pedigrees and Deciphering Ancient MSS., &c. Fourth Edition, revised, with 408 Woodcuts and 2 Coloured Plates. Crown 8vo, cloth extra, 6s.

Cyples (W.).—Hearts of Gold. Cr. 8vo, cl., 3s. 6d.; post 8vo, bds., 2s.

Daudet (Alphonse).—The Evangelist; or, Port Salvation. Crown 8vo, cloth extra, 3s. 6d.; post 8vo, illustrated boards, 2s.

Davenant (Francis, M.A.).—Hints for Parents on the Choice of a Profession for their Sons when Starting in Life. Crown 8vo, cloth, 1s. 6d.

Davidson (Hugh Coleman).—Mr. Sadler's Daughters. With a Frontispiece by STANLEY WOOD. Crown 8vo, cloth extra, 3s. 6d.

Davies (Dr. N. E. Yorke-), Works by. Cr. 8vo, 1s. ea.; cl., 1s. 6d. ea.
One Thousand Medical Maxims and Surgical Hints.
Nursery Hints: A Mother's Guide in Health and Disease.
Foods for the Fat: A Treatise on Corpulency, and a Dietary for its Cure.
Aids to Long Life. Crown 8vo, 2s.; cloth limp, 2s. 6d.

Davies' (Sir John) Complete Poetical Works. Collected and Edited, with Introduction and Notes, by Rev. A. B. GROSART, D.D. | Two Vols., crown 8vo, cloth, 3s. 6d. each.

Dawson (Erasmus, M.B.).—The Fountain of Youth. Crown 8vo, cloth extra, with Two Illustrations by HUME NISBET, 3s. 6d.; post 8vo, illustrated boards, 2s.

De Guerin (Maurice), The Journal of. Edited by G. S. TREBUTIEN. With a Memoir by SAINTE-BEUVE. Translated from the 20th French Edition by JESSIE P. FROTHINGHAM. Fcap. 8vo, half-bound, 2s. 6d.

De Maistre (Xavier).—A Journey Round my Room. Translated by Sir HENRY ATTWELL. Post 8vo, cloth limp, 2s. 6d.

De Mille (James).—A Castle in Spain. Crown 8vo, cloth extra, with a Frontispiece, 3s. 6d.; post 8vo, illustrated boards, 2s.

Derby (The): The Blue Ribbon of the Turf. With Brief Accounts of THE OAKS. By LOUIS HENRY CURZON. Crown 8vo, cloth limp, 2s. 6d.

CHATTO & WINDUS, 111 St. Martin's Lane, London, W.C.

Derwent (Leith), Novels by. Cr. 8vo, cl., 3s. 6d. ea.; post 8vo, 2s. ea.
Our Lady of Tears. | Circe's Lovers.

Dewar (T. R.).—A Ramble Round the Globe. With 220 Illustrations. Crown 8vo, cloth extra, 7s. 6d.

Dickens (Charles).—Sketches by Boz. Post 8vo, illust. boards, 2s.
About England with Dickens. By ALFRED RIMMER. With 57 Illustrations by C. A. VANDERHOOF, ALFRED RIMMER, and others. Square 8vo, cloth extra, 7s. 6d.

Dictionaries.
A Dictionary of Miracles: Imitative, Realistic, and Dogmatic. By the Rev. E. C. BREWER, LL.D. Crown 8vo, cloth extra, 7s. 6d.
The Reader's Handbook of Allusions, References, Plots, and Stories. By the Rev. E. C. BREWER, LL.D. With an ENGLISH BIBLIOGRAPHY. Crown 8vo, cloth extra, 7s. 6d.
Authors and their Works, with the Dates. Crown 8vo, cloth limp, 2s.
Familiar Short Sayings of Great Men. With Historical and Explanatory Notes by SAMUEL A. BENT, A.M. Crown 8vo, cloth extra, 7s. 6d.
The Slang Dictionary: Etymological, Historical, and Anecdotal. Crown 8vo, cloth, 6s. 6d.
Words, Facts, and Phrases: A Dictionary of Curious, Quaint, and Out-of-the-Way Matters. By ELIEZER EDWARDS. Crown 8vo, cloth extra, 7s. 6d.

Diderot.—The Paradox of Acting. Translated, with Notes, by WALTER HERRIES POLLOCK. With Preface by Sir HENRY IRVING. Crown 8vo, parchment, 4s. 6d.

Dobson (Austin), Works by.
Thomas Bewick and his Pupils. With 95 Illustrations. Square 8vo, cloth, 6s.
Four Frenchwomen. With Four Portraits. Crown 8vo, buckram, gilt top 6s.
Eighteenth Century Vignettes. IN THREE SERIES. Crown 8vo, buckram, 6s. each.

Dobson (W. T.).—Poetical Ingenuities and Eccentricities. Post 8vo, cloth limp, 2s. 6d.

Donovan (Dick), Detective Stories by.
Post 8vo, illustrated boards, 2s. each; cloth limp, 2s. 6d. each.

The Man-Hunter. | Wanted! | A Detective's Triumphs.
Caught at Last. | In the Grip of the Law.
Tracked and Taken. | From Information Received.
Who Poisoned Hetty Duncan? | Link by Link. | Dark Deeds.
Suspicion Aroused. | Riddles Read.

Crown 8vo, cloth extra, 3s. 6d. each; post 8vo, illustrated boards, 2s. each; cloth, 2s. 6d. each.
The Man from Manchester. With 23 Illustrations.
Tracked to Doom. With Six full-page Illustrations by GORDON BROWNE.
The Mystery of Jamaica Terrace.

The Chronicles of Michael Danevitch, of the Russian Secret Service. Crown 8vo, cloth, 3s. 6d. [Shortly.

Doyle (A. Conan).—The Firm of Girdlestone. Cr. 8vo, cl., 3s. 6d.

Dramatists, The Old. Cr. 8vo, cl. ex., with Portraits, 3s. 6d. per Vol.
Ben Jonson's Works. With Notes, Critical and Explanatory, and a Biographical Memoir by WILLIAM GIFFORD. Edited by Colonel CUNNINGHAM. Three Vols.
Chapman's Works. Three Vols. Vol. I. contains the Plays complete; Vol. II., Poems and Minor Translations, with an Essay by A. C. SWINBURNE; Vol. III., Translations of the Iliad and Odyssey.
Marlowe's Works. Edited, with Notes, by Colonel CUNNINGHAM. One Vol.
Massinger's Plays. From GIFFORD'S Text. Edited by Colonel CUNNINGHAM. One Vol.

Duncan (Sara Jeannette: Mrs. EVERARD COTES), Works by.
Crown 8vo, cloth extra, 7s. 6d. each.
A Social Departure. With 111 Illustrations by F. H. TOWNSEND.
An American Girl in London. With 80 Illustrations by F. H. TOWNSEND.
The Simple Adventures of a Memsahib. With 37 Illustrations by F. H. TOWNSEND.

Crown 8vo, cloth extra, 3s. 6d. each.
A Daughter of To-Day. | Vernon's Aunt. With 47 Illustrations by HAL HURST.

Dyer (T. F. Thiselton).—The Folk-Lore of Plants. Cr. 8vo, cl., 6s.

Early English Poets. Edited, with Introductions and Annotations, by Rev. A. B. GROSART, D.D. Crown 8vo, cloth boards, 3s. 6d. per Volume.
Fletcher's (Giles) Complete Poems. One Vol.
Davies' (Sir John) Complete Poetical Works. Two Vols.
Herrick's (Robert) Complete Collected Poems. Three Vols.
Sidney's (Sir Philip) Complete Poetical Works. Three Vols.

Edgcumbe (Sir E. R. Pearce).—Zephyrus: A Holiday in Brazil and on the River Plate. With 41 Illustrations. Crown 8vo, cloth extra, 5s.

Edison, The Life and Inventions of Thomas A. By W. K. L. and ANTONIA DICKSON. With 200 Illustrations by R. F. OUTCALT, &c. Demy 4to, cloth gilt, 18s.

Edwardes (Mrs. Annie), Novels by. Post 8vo, illustrated boards, 2s. each.
Archie Lovell. | A Point of Honour.

Edwards (Eliezer).—Words, Facts, and Phrases: A Dictionary of Curious Quaint, and Out-of-the-Way Matters. Crown 8vo, cloth, 7s. 6d.

Edwards (M. Betham=), Novels by.
Kitty. Post 8vo, boards, 2s.; cloth, 2s. 6d. | Felicia. Post 8vo, illustrated boards, 2s.

Egerton (Rev. J. C., M.A.). — Sussex Folk and Sussex Ways. With Introduction by Rev. Dr. H. WACE, and Four Illustrations. Crown 8vo, cloth extra, 5s.

Eggleston (Edward).—Roxy: A Novel. Post 8vo, illust. boards, 2s.

Englishman's House, The: A Practical Guide for Selecting or Building a House. By C. J. RICHARDSON. Coloured Frontispiece and 534 Illusts. Cr. 8vo, cloth, 7s. 6d.

Ewald (Alex. Charles, F.S.A.), Works by.
The Life and Times of Prince Charles Stuart, Count of Albany (THE YOUNG PRETENDER). With a Portrait. Crown 8vo, cloth extra, 7s. 6d.
Stories from the State Papers. With Autotype Frontispiece. Crown 8vo, cloth, 6s.

Eyes, Our: How to Preserve Them. By JOHN BROWNING. Cr. 8vo, 1s.

Familiar Short Sayings of Great Men. By SAMUEL ARTHUR BENT, A.M. Fifth Edition, Revised and Enlarged. Crown 8vo, cloth extra, 7s. 6d.

Faraday (Michael), Works by. Post 8vo, cloth extra, 4s. 6d. each.
The Chemical History of a Candle: Lectures delivered before a Juvenile Audience. Edited by WILLIAM CROOKES, F.C.S. With numerous Illustrations.
On the Various Forces of Nature, and their Relations to each other. Edited by WILLIAM CROOKES, F.C.S. With Illustrations.

Farrer (J. Anson), Works by.
Military Manners and Customs. Crown 8vo, cloth extra, 6s.
War: Three Essays, reprinted from 'Military Manners and Customs.' Crown 8vo, 1s.; cloth, 1s. 6d.

Fenn (G. Manville), Novels by.
Crown 8vo, cloth extra, 3s. 6d. each; post 8vo, illustrated boards, 2s. each.
The New Mistress. | Witness to the Deed. | The Tiger Lily. | The White Virgin.

Fin=Bec.—The Cupboard Papers: Observations on the Art of Living and Dining. Post 8vo, cloth limp, 2s. 6d.

Fireworks, The Complete Art of Making; or, The Pyrotechnist's Treasury. By THOMAS KENTISH. With 267 Illustrations. Crown 8vo, cloth, 5s.

First Book, My. By WALTER BESANT, JAMES PAYN, W. CLARK RUSSELL, GRANT ALLEN. HALL CAINE, GEORGE R. SIMS, RUDYARD KIPLING, A. CONAN DOYLE, M. E. BRADDON, F. W. ROBINSON, H. RIDER HAGGARD, R. M. BALLANTYNE, I. ZANGWILL, MORLEY ROBERTS, D. CHRISTIE MURRAY, MARY CORELLI, J. K. JEROME, JOHN STRANGE WINTER, BRET HARTE, 'Q.,' ROBERT BUCHANAN, and R. L. STEVENSON. With a Prefatory Story by JEROME K. JEROME, and 185 Illustrations. A New Edition. Small demy 8vo, art linen, 3s. 6d.

Fitzgerald (Percy), Works by.
Little Essays: Passages from the Letters of CHARLES LAMB. Post 8vo, cloth, 2s. 6d.
Fatal Zero. Crown 8vo, cloth extra, 3s. 6d.; post 8vo, illustrated boards, 2s.

Pos 8vo, illustrated boards, 2s. each.
Bella Donna. | The Lady of Brantome. | The Second Mrs. Tillotson.
Polly. | Never Forgotten. | Seventy-five Brooke Street.

The Life of James Boswell (of Auchinleck). With Illusts. Two Vols., demy 8vo, cloth, 24s.
The Savoy Opera. With 60 Illustrations and Portraits. Crown 8vo, cloth, 3s. 6d.
Sir Henry Irving: Twenty Years at the Lyceum. With Portrait. Crown 8vo, 1s.; cloth, 1s. 6d.

Flammarion (Camille), Works by.
Popular Astronomy: A General Description of the Heavens. Translated by J. ELLARD GORE, F.R.A.S. With Three Plates and 288 Illustrations. Medium 8vo, cloth, 16s.
Urania: A Romance. With 87 Illustrations. Crown 8vo, cloth extra, 5s.

Fletcher's (Giles, B.D.) Complete Poems: Christ's Victorie in Heaven, Christ's Victorie on Earth, Christ's Triumph over Death, and Minor Poems. With Notes by Rev. A. B. GROSART, D.D. Crown 8vo, cloth boards, 3s. 6d.

Fonblanque (Albany).--Filthy Lucre. Post 8vo, illust. boards, 2s.

CHATTO & WINDUS, 111 St. Martin's Lane, London, W.C.

Francillon (R. E.), Novels by.
Crown 8vo, cloth extra, 3s. 6d. each; post 8vo, Illustrated boards, 2s. each.
One by One. | A Real Queen. | A Dog and his Shadow.
Ropes of Sand. Illustrated.

Post 8vo, illustrated boards, 2s. each.
Queen Cophetua. | Olympia. | Romances of the Law. | King or Knave?

Jack Doyle's Daughter. Crown 8vo, cloth, 3s. 6d.
Esther's Glove. Fcap. 8vo, picture cover, 1s.

Frederic (Harold), Novels by. Post 8vo, illust. boards, 2s. each.
Seth's Brother's Wife. | The Lawton Girl.

French Literature, A History of. By HENRY VAN LAUN. Three Vols., demy 8vo, cloth boards, 7s. 6d. each.

Friswell (Hain).—One of Two: A Novel. Post 8vo, illust. bds., 2s.

Fry's (Herbert) Royal Guide to the London Charities. Edited by JOHN LANE. Published Annually. Crown 8vo, cloth, 1s. 6d.

Gardening Books. Post 8vo, 1s. each; cloth limp. 1s. 6d. each.
A Year's Work in Garden and Greenhouse. By GEORGE GLENNY.
Household Horticulture. By TOM and JANE JERROLD. Illustrated.
The Garden that Paid the Rent. By TOM JERROLD.

My Garden Wild. By FRANCIS G. HEATH. Crown 8vo, cloth extra, 6s.

Gardner (Mrs. Alan).—Rifle and Spear with the Rajpoots: Being the Narrative of a Winter's Travel and Sport in Northern India. With numerous Illustrations by the Author and F. H. TOWNSEND. Demy 4to, half-bound, 21s.

Garrett (Edward).—The Capel Girls: A Novel. Crown 8vo, cloth extra, with two Illustrations, 3s. 6d.; post 8vo, illustrated boards, 2s.

Gaulot (Paul).—The Red Shirts: A Story of the Revolution. Translated by JOHN DE VILLIERS. With a Frontispiece by STANLEY WOOD. Crown 8vo, cloth, 3s. 6d.

Gentleman's Magazine, The. 1s. Monthly. Contains Stories, Articles upon Literature, Science, Biography, and Art, and 'Table Talk' by SYLVANUS URBAN.
₊ *Bound Volumes for recent years kept in stock, 8s. 6d. each. Cases for binding, 2s. each.*

Gentleman's Annual, The. Published Annually in November. 1s.

German Popular Stories. Collected by the Brothers GRIMM and Translated by EDGAR TAYLOR. With Introduction by JOHN RUSKIN, and 22 Steel Plates after GEORGE CRUIKSHANK. Square 8vo, cloth, 6s. 6d.; gilt edges, 7s. 6d.

Gibbon (Chas.), Novels by. Cr. 8vo, cl., 3s. 6d. ea.; post 8vo, bds., 2s. ea.
Robin Gray. Frontispiece. | The Golden Shaft. Frontispiece. | Loving a Dream.

Post 8vo, illustrated boards, 2s. each.
The Flower of the Forest. | In Love and War.
The Dead Heart. | A Heart's Problem.
For Lack of Gold. | By Mead and Stream.
What Will the World Say? | The Braes of Yarrow.
For the King. | A Hard Knot. | Fancy Free. | Of High Degree.
Queen of the Meadow. | In Honour Bound.
In Pastures Green. | Heart's Delight. | Blood-Money.

Gilbert (W. S.), Original Plays by. In Three Series, 2s. 6d. each.
The FIRST SERIES contains: The Wicked World—Pygmalion and Galatea—Charity—The Princess— The Palace of Truth—Trial by Jury.
The SECOND SERIES: Broken Hearts—Engaged—Sweethearts—Gretchen—Dan'l Druce—Tom Cobb —H.M.S. 'Pinafore'—The Sorcerer—The Pirates of Penzance.
The THIRD SERIES: Comedy and Tragedy—Foggerty's Fairy—Rosencrantz and Guildenstern— Patience—Princess Ida—The Mikado—Ruddigore—The Yeomen of the Guard—The Gondoliers— The Mountebanks—Utopia.

Eight Original Comic Operas written by W. S. GILBERT. In Two Series. Demy 8vo, cloth, 2s. 6d. each. The FIRST containing: The Sorcerer—H.M.S. 'Pinafore'—The Pirates of Penzance— Iolanthe—Patience—Princess Ida—The Mikado—Trial by Jury.
The SECOND SERIES containing: The Gondoliers—The Grand Duke—The Yeomen of the Guard— His Excellency—Utopia, Limited—Ruddigore—The Mountebanks—Haste to the Wedding.

The Gilbert and Sullivan Birthday Book: Quotations for Every Day n the Year, selected from Plays by W. S. GILBERT set to Music by Sir A. SULLIVAN. Compiled by ALEX. WATSON. Royal 16mo, Japanese leather, 2s. 6d.

CHATTO & WINDUS, 111 St. Martin's Lane, London, W.C.

Gilbert (William), Novels by. Post 8vo, illustrated bds., 2s. each.
Dr. Austin's Guests. | James Duke, Costermonger.
The Wizard of the Mountain.

Glanville (Ernest), Novels by.
Crown 8vo, cloth extra, 3s. 6d. each; post 8vo, illustrated boards, 2s. each.
The Lost Heiress: A Tale of Love, Battle, and Adventure. With Two Illustrations by H. NISBET
The Fossicker: A Romance of Mashonaland. With Two Illustrations by HUME NISBET.
A Fair Colonist. With a Frontispiece by STANLEY WOOD.

The Golden Rock. With a Frontispiece by STANLEY WOOD. Crown 8vo, cloth extra, 3s. 6d.
Kloof Yarns. Crown 8vo, picture cover, 1s.; cloth, 1s. 6d.

Glenny (George).—A Year's Work in Garden and Greenhouse:
Practical Advice as to the Management of the Flower, Fruit, and Frame Garden. Post 8vo, 1s.; cloth, 1s. 6d.

Godwin (William).—Lives of the Necromancers. Post 8vo, cl., 2s.

Golden Treasury of Thought, The: An Encyclopædia of QUOTA-
TIONS. Edited by THEODORE TAYLOR. Crown 8vo, cloth gilt, 7s. 6d.

Gontaut, Memoirs of the Duchesse de (Gouvernante to the Children of France), 1773-1836. With Two Photogravures. Two Vols., demy 8vo, cloth extra, 21s.

Goodman (E. J.).—The Fate of Herbert Wayne. Cr. 8vo, 3s. 6d.

Graham (Leonard).—The Professor's Wife: A Story. Fcp. 8vo, 1s.

Greeks and Romans, The Life of the, described from Antique Monuments. By ERNST GUHL and W. KONER. Edited by Dr. F. HUEFFER. With 545 Illustrations. Large crown 8vo, cloth extra, 7s. 6d.

Greville (Henry), Novels by.
Post 8vo, illustrated boards, 2s. each.
Nikanor. Translated by ELIZA E. CHASE.
A Noble Woman. Translated by ALBERT D. VANDAM.

Griffith (Cecil).—Corinthia Marazion: A Novel. Crown 8vo, cloth extra, 3s. 6d.; post 8vo, illustrated boards, 2s.

Grundy (Sydney).—The Days of his Vanity: A Passage in the Life of a Young Man. Crown 8vo, cloth extra, 3s. 6d.; post 8vo, illustrated boards, 2s.

Habberton (John, Author of 'Helen's Babies'), **Novels by.**
Post 8vo, illustrated boards, 2s. each; cloth limp, 2s. 6d. each.
Brueton's Bayou. | Country Luck.

Hair, The: Its Treatment in Health, Weakness, and Disease. Translated from the German of Dr. J. PINCUS. Crown 8vo, 1s.; cloth, 1s. 6d.

Hake (Dr. Thomas Gordon), Poems by. Cr. 8vo, cl. ex., 6s. each.
New Symbols. | Legends of the Morrow. | The Serpent Play.
Maiden Ecstasy. Small 4to, cloth extra, 8s.

Halifax (C.).—Dr. Rumsey's Patient. By Mrs. L. T. MEADE and CLIFFORD HALIFAX, M.D. Crown 8vo, cloth, 6s.

Hall (Mrs. S. C.).—Sketches of Irish Character. With numerous Illustrations on Steel and Wood by MACLISE, GILBERT, HARVEY, and GEORGE CRUIKSHANK. Small demy 8vo, cloth extra, 7s. 6d.

Hall (Owen).—The Track of a Storm. Crown 8vo, cloth, 6s.

Halliday (Andrew).—Every=day Papers. Post 8vo, boards, 2s.

Handwriting, The Philosophy of. With over 100 Facsimiles and Explanatory Text. By DON FELIX DE SALAMANCA. Post 8vo, cloth limp, 2s. 6d.

Hanky=Panky: Easy and Difficult Tricks, White Magic, Sleight of Hand, &c. Edited by W. H. CREMER. With 200 Illustrations. Crown 8vo, cloth extra, 4s. 6d.

Hardy (Lady Duffus).—Paul Wynter's Sacrifice. Post 8vo, bds., 2s.

Hardy (Thomas).—Under the Greenwood Tree. Crown 8vo, cloth extra, with Portrait and 15 Illustrations, 3s. 6d.; post 8vo, illustrated boards, 2s. cloth limp, 2s. 6d.

Harwood (J. Berwick)—The Tenth Earl. Post 8vo, boards, 2s

CHATTO & WINDUS, 111 St. Martin's Lane, London, W.C.

Harte's (Bret) Collected Works. Revised by the Author. LIBRARY EDITION, in Nine Volumes, crown 8vo, cloth extra, 6s. each.
Vol. I. COMPLETE POETICAL AND DRAMATIC WORKS. With Steel-plate Portrait.
„ II. THE LUCK OF ROARING CAMP—BOHEMIAN PAPERS—AMERICAN LEGENDS,
„ III. TALES OF THE ARGONAUTS—EASTERN SKETCHES.
„ IV. GABRIEL CONROY. | Vol. V. STORIES—CONDENSED NOVELS, &c.
„ VI. TALES OF THE PACIFIC SLOPE.
„ VII. TALES OF THE PACIFIC SLOPE—II. With Portrait by JOHN PETTIE, R.A.
„ VIII. TALES OF THE PINE AND THE CYPRESS.
„ IX. BUCKEYE AND CHAPPAREL.
The Select Works of Bret Harte, in Prose and Poetry. With Introductory Essay by J. M BELLEW, Portrait of the Author, and 50 Illustrations. Crown 8vo, cloth extra, 7s. 6d.
Bret Harte's Poetical Works. Printed on hand-made paper. Crown 8vo, buckram, 4s. 6d.
A New Volume of Poems. Crown 8vo, buckram, 5s. [Preparing.
The Queen of the Pirate Isle. With 28 Original Drawings by KATE GREENAWAY, reproduced in Colours by EDMUND EVANS. Small 4to, cloth, 5s.

Crown 8vo, cloth extra, 3s. 6d. each ; post 8vo, picture boards, 2s. each.
A Waif of the Plains. With 60 Illustrations by STANLEY L. WOOD.
A Ward of the Golden Gate. With 59 Illustrations by STANLEY L. WOOD.

Crown 8vo, cloth extra, 3s. 6d. each.
A Sappho of Green Springs, &c. With Two Illustrations by HUME NISBET.
Colonel Starbottle's Client, and Some Other People. With a Frontispiece.
Susy: A Novel. With Frontispiece and Vignette by J. A. CHRISTIE.
Sally Dows, &c. With 47 Illustrations by W D. ALMOND and others.
A Protegee of Jack Hamlin's, &c. With 26 Illustrations by W. SMALL and others.
The Bell-Ringer of Angel's, &c. With 39 Illustrations by DUDLEY HARDY and others.
Clarence : A Story of the American War. With Eight Illustrations by A. JULE GOODMAN.
Barker's Luck, &c. With 39 Illustrations by A. FORESTIER, PAUL HARDY, &c.
Devil's Ford, &c. With a Frontispiece by W. H. OVEREND.
The Crusade of the " Excelsior." With a Frontispiece by J. BERNARD PARTRIDGE.
Three Partners ; or, The Strike on Heavy Tree Hill. With 8 Illustrations by J. GULICH. [*Apr.* 8,

Post 8vo, illustrated boards, 2s. each.
Gabriel Conroy. | **The Luck of Roaring Camp,** &c.
An Heiress of Red Dog, &c. | **Californian Stories.**

Post 8vo, illustrated boards, 2s. each ; cloth, 2s. 6d. each.
Flip. | **Maruja.** | **A Phyllis of the Sierras.**

Haweis (Mrs. H. R.), Books by.
The Art of Beauty. With Coloured Frontispiece and 91 Illustrations. Square 8vo, cloth bds., 6s.
The Art of Decoration. With Coloured Frontispiece and 74 Illustrations. Sq. 8vo, cloth bds., 6s.
The Art of Dress. With 32 Illustrations. Post 8vo, 1s. ; cloth, 1s. 6d.
Chaucer for Schools. Demy 8vo, cloth limp, 2s. 6d.
Chaucer for Children. With 38 Illustrations (8 Coloured). Crown 4to, cloth extra, 3s. 6d.

Haweis (Rev. H. R., M.A.), Books by.
American Humorists : WASHINGTON IRVING, OLIVER WENDELL HOLMES, JAMES RUSSELL LOWELL, ARTEMUS WARD, MARK TWAIN, and BRET HARTE. Third Edition. Crown 8vo, cloth extra, 6s.
Travel and Talk, 1885-93-95: My Hundred Thousand Miles of Travel through America—Canada —New Zealand—Tasmania—Australia—Ceylon—The Paradises of the Pacific. With Photogravure Frontispieces. A New Edition. Two Vols., crown 8vo, cloth, 12s.

Hawthorne (Julian), Novels by.
Crown 8vo, cloth extra, 3s. 6d. each ; post 8vo, illustrated boards, 2s. each.
Garth. | **Ellice Quentin.** | **Beatrix Randolph.** With Four Illusts.
Sebastian Strome. | **David Poindexter's Disappearance.**
Fortune's Fool. | **Dust.** Four Illusts. | **The Spectre of the Camera.**

Post 8vo, illustrated boards, 2s. each.
Miss Cadogna. | **Love—or a Name.**
Mrs. Gainsborough's Diamonds. Fcap. 8vo, illustrated cover, 1s.

Hawthorne (Nathaniel).—Our Old Home. Annotated with Passages from the Author's Note-books, and Illustrated with 31 Photogravures. Two Vols., cr. 8vo, 15s.

Heath (Francis George).—My Garden Wild, and What I Grew There. Crown 8vo, cloth extra, gilt edges, 6s.

Helps (Sir Arthur), Works by. Post 8vo, cloth limp, 2s. 6d. each.
Animals and their Masters. | **Social Pressure.**
Ivan de Biron: A Novel. Crown 8vo, cloth extra, 3s. 6d. ; post 8vo, illustrated boards, 2s.

Henderson (Isaac).—Agatha Page: A Novel. Cr. 8vo, cl., 3s. 6d.

Henty (G. A.), Novels by.
Rujub the Juggler. With Eight Illustrations by STANLEY L. WOOD. Crown 8vo, cloth, 3s. 6d.; post 8vo, illustrated boards, 2s.
Dorothy's Double. Crown 8vo, cloth, 3s. 6d.
The Queen's Cup. 3 vols., crown 8vo, 15s. net.

Herman (Henry).—A Leading Lady. Post 8vo, bds., 2s. ; cl., 2s. 6d.

Herrick's (Robert) Hesperides, Noble Numbers, and Complete Collected Poems. With Memorial-Introduction and Notes by the Rev. A. B. GROSART, D.D., Steel Portrait, &c. Three Vols., crown 8vo, cloth boards, 3s. 6d. each.

12   CHATTO & WINDUS, 111 St. Martin's Lane, London, W.C.

Hertzka (Dr. Theodor).—Freeland: A Social Anticipation. Transated by ARTHUR RANSOM. Crown 8vo, cloth extra, 6s.

Hesse=Wartegg (Chevalier Ernst von).— Tunis: The Land and the People. With 22 Illustrations. Crown 8vo, cloth extra, 3s. 6d.

Hill (Headon).—Zambra the Detective. Post 8vo, bds., 2s.; cl., 2s. 6d.

Hill (John), Works by.
Treason-Felony. Post 8vo, boards, 2s. | The Common Ancestor. Cr. 8vo, cloth, 3s. 6d.

Hoey (Mrs. Cashel).—The Lover's Creed. Post 8vo, boards, 2s.

Holiday, Where to go for a. By E. P. SHOLL, Sir H. MAXWELL, Bart., M.P., JOHN WATSON, JANE BARLOW, MARY LOVETT CAMERON, JUSTIN H. MCCARTHY, PAUL LANGE, J. W. GRAHAM, J. H. SALTER, PHŒBE ALLEN, S. J. BECKETT, L. RIVERS VINE, and C. F. GORDON CUMMING. Crown 8vo, 1s.; cloth, 1s. 6d.

Hollingshead (John).—Niagara Spray. Crown 8vo, 1s.

Holmes (Gordon, M.D.)—The Science of Voice Production and Voice Preservation. Crown 8vo, 1s.; cloth, 1s. 6d.

Holmes (Oliver Wendell), Works by.
The Autocrat of the Breakfast-Table. Illustrated by J. GORDON THOMSON. Post 8vo, cloth limp, 2s. 6d.– Another Edition, post 8vo, cloth, 2s.
The Autocrat of the Breakfast-Table and The Professor at the Breakfast-Table. In One Vol. Post 8vo, half-bound, 2s.

Hood's (Thomas) Choice Works in Prose and Verse. With Life of the Author, Portrait, and 200 Illustrations. Crown 8vo, cloth extra, 7s. 6d.
Hood's Whims and Oddities. With 85 Illustrations. Post 8vo, half-bound, 2s.

Hood (Tom).—From Nowhere to the North Pole: A Noah's Arkæological Narrative. With 25 Illustrations by W. BRUNTON and E. C. BARNES. Cr. 8vo, cloth, 6s.

Hook's (Theodore) Choice Humorous Works; including his Ludicrous Adventures, Bons Mots, Puns, and Hoaxes. With Life of the Author, Portraits, Facsimiles, and Illustrations. Crown 8vo, cloth extra, 7s. 6d.

Hooper (Mrs. Geo.).—The House of Raby. Post 8vo, boards, 2s.

Hopkins (Tighe).—''Twixt Love and Duty.' Post 8vo, boards, 2s.

Horne (R. Hengist). — Orion: An Epic Poem. With Photograph Portrait by SUMMERS. Tenth Edition. Crown 8vo, cloth extra, 7s.

Hungerford (Mrs., Author of 'Molly Bawn'), Novels by.
Post 8vo, illustrated boards, 2s. each; cloth limp, 2s. 6d. each.
A Maiden All Forlorn. | A Modern Circe. | An Unsatisfactory Lover.
Marvel. | A Mental Struggle. | Lady Patty.
In Durance Vile. | The Three Graces.
Crown 8vo, cloth extra, 3s. 6d. each; post 8vo, illustrated boards, 2s. each; cloth limp, 2s. 6d. each.
Lady Verner's Flight. | The Red-House Mystery.
Crown 8vo, cloth extra, 3s. 6d. each.
The Professor's Experiment. With Frontispiece by E. J. WHEELER.
Nora Creina. | April's Lady.
An Anxious Moment, &c.
A Point of Conscience. [Shortly.

Lovice. Crown 8vo, cloth, 6s. [Shortly.

Hunt's (Leigh) Essays: A Tale for a Chimney Corner, &c. Edited by EDMUND OLLIER. Post 8vo, half-bound, 2s.

Hunt (Mrs. Alfred), Novels by.
Crown 8vo, cloth extra, 3s. 6d. each; post 8vo, illustrated boards, 2s. each.
The Leaden Casket. | Self-Condemned. | That Other Person.
Thornicroft's Model. Post 8vo, boards, 2s. | Mrs. Juliet. Crown 8vo, cloth extra, 3s. 6d.

Hutchison (W. M.).—Hints on Colt=breaking. With 25 Illustrations. Crown 8vo, cloth extra, 3s. 6d.

Hydrophobia: An Account of M. PASTEUR'S System; The Technique of his Method, and Statistics. By RENAUD SUZOR, M.B. Crown 8vo, cloth extra, 6s.

Hyne (C. J. Cutcliffe).— Honour of Thieves. Cr. 8vo, cloth, 3s. 6d.

Idler (The): An Illustrated Monthly Magazine. Edited by J. K. JEROME. Nos. 1 to 48, 6d. each; No. 49 and following Numbers, 1s. each. The first EIGHT VOLS., cloth, 5s. each. Vol. IX. and after, 7s. 6d. each.—Cases for Binding, 1s. 6d. each.

Impressions (The) of Aureole. Cheaper Edition, with a New Preface. Post 8vo, blush-rose paper and cloth, 2s. 6d.

Indoor Paupers. By ONE OF THEM. Crown 8vo, 1s. ; cloth, 1s. 6d.

Ingelow (Jean).—Fated to be Free. Post 8vo, illustrated bds., 2s.

Innkeeper's Handbook (The) and Licensed Victualler's Manual. By J. TREVOR-DAVIES. Crown 8vo, 1s. ; cloth, 1s. 6d.

Irish Wit and Humour, Songs of. Collected and Edited by A. PERCEVAL GRAVES. Post 8vo, cloth limp, 2s. 6d.

Irving (Sir Henry): A Record of over Twenty Years at the Lyceum. By PERCY FITZGERALD. With Portrait. Crown 8vo, 1s.; cloth, 1s. 6d.

James (C. T. C.).—A Romance of the Queen's Hounds. Post 8vo, picture cover, 1s. ; cloth limp, 1s. 6d.

Jameson (William).—My Dead Self. Post 8vo, bds., 2s. ; cl., 2s. 6d.

Japp (Alex. H., LL.D.).—Dramatic Pictures, &c. Cr. 8vo, cloth, 5s.

Jay (Harriett), Novels by. Post 8vo, illustrated boards, 2s. each.
The Dark Colleen. | The Queen of Connaught.

Jefferies (Richard), Works by. Post 8vo, cloth limp, 2s. 6d. each.
Nature near London. | The Life of the Fields. | The Open Air.
*** Also the HAND-MADE PAPER EDITION, crown 8vo, buckram, gilt top, 6s. each.

The Eulogy of Richard Jefferies. By Sir WALTER BESANT. With a Photograph Portrait. Crown 8vo, cloth extra, 6s.

Jennings (Henry J.), Works by.
Curiosities of Criticism. Post 8vo, cloth limp, 2s. 6d.
Lord Tennyson: A Biographical Sketch. With Portrait. Post 8vo, 1s.; cloth, 1s. 6d.

Jerome (Jerome K.), Books by.
Stageland. With 64 Illustrations by J. BERNARD PARTRIDGE. Fcap. 4to, picture cover, 1s.
John Ingerfield, &c. With 9 Illusts. by A. S. BOYD and JOHN GULICH. Fcap. 8vo, pic. cov. 1s. 6d.
The Prude's Progress: A Comedy by J. K. JEROME and EDEN PHILLPOTTS. Cr. 8vo, 1s. 6d.

Jerrold (Douglas).—The Barber's Chair; and **The Hedgehog Letters.** Post 8vo, printed on laid paper and half-bound, 2s. 6d.

Jerrold (Tom), Works by. Post 8vo, 1s. ea. ; cloth limp, 1s. 6d. each.
The Garden that Paid the Rent.
Household Horticulture : A Gossip about Flowers. Illustrated.

Jesse (Edward).—Scenes and Occupations of a Country Life. Post 8vo, cloth limp, 2s.

Jones (William, F.S.A.), Works by. Cr. 8vo, cl. extra, 7s. 6d. each.
Finger-Ring Lore: Historical, Legendary, and Anecdotal. With nearly 300 Illustrations. Second Edition, Revised and Enlarged.
Credulities, Past and Present. Including the Sea and Seamen, Miners, Talismans, Word and Letter Divination, Exorcising and Blessing of Animals, Birds, Eggs, Luck, &c. With Frontispiece.
Crowns and Coronations: A History of Regalia. With 100 Illustrations.

Jonson's (Ben) Works. With Notes Critical and Explanatory, and a Biographical Memoir by WILLIAM GIFFORD. Edited by Colonel CUNNINGHAM. Three Vols. crown 8vo, cloth extra, 3s. 6d. each.

Josephus, The Complete Works of. Translated by WHISTON. Containing 'The Antiquities of the Jews and 'The Wars of the Jews.' With 52 Illustrations and Maps. Two Vols., demy 8vo, half-bound, 12s. 6d.

Kempt (Robert).—Pencil and Palette: Chapters on Art and Artists. Post 8vo, cloth limp, 2s. 6d.

Kershaw (Mark). — Colonial Facts and Fictions: Humorous Sketches. Post 8vo, illustrated boards, 2s. ; cloth, 2s. 6d.

King (R. Ashe), Novels by. Cr. 8vo, cl., 3s. 6d. ea.; post 8vo, bds., 2s. ea.
A Drawn Game. | 'The Wearing of the Green.'

Post 8vo, illustrated boards, 2s. each.
Passion's Slave. | Bell Barry.

Knight (William, M.R.C.S., and Edward, L.R.C.P.). — The Patient's Vade Mecum: How to Get Most Benefit from Medical Advice. Cr. 8vo, 1s.; cl., 1s. 6d.

Knights (The) of the Lion: A Romance of the Thirteenth Century. Edited, with an Introduction, by the MARQUESS OF LORNE, K.T. Crown 8vo, cloth extra, 6s.

Lamb's (Charles) Complete Works in Prose and Verse, including 'Poetry for Children' and 'Prince Dorus.' Edited, with Notes and Introduction, by R. H. SHEPHERD. With Two Portraits and Facsimile of the 'Essay on Roast Pig.' Crown 8vo, half-bd., 7s. 6d.
 The Essays of Elia. Post 8vo, printed on laid paper and half-bound, 2s.
 Little Essays: Sketches and Characters by CHARLES LAMB, selected from his Letters by PERCY FITZGERALD. Post 8vo, cloth limp, 2s. 6d.
 The Dramatic Essays of Charles Lamb. With Introduction and Notes by BRANDER MATTHEWS, and Steel-plate Portrait. Fcap. 8vo, half-bound, 2s. 6d.

Landor (Walter Savage).—Citation and Examination of William Shakspeare, &c., before Sir Thomas Lucy, touching Deer-stealing, 19th September, 1582. To which is added, A Conference of Master Edmund Spenser with the Earl of Essex, touching the State of Ireland, 1595. Fcap. 8vo, half-Roxburghe, 2s. 6d.

Lane (Edward William).—The Thousand and One Nights, commonly called in England The Arabian Nights' Entertainments. Translated from the Arabic, with Notes. Illustrated with many hundred Engravings from Designs by HARVEY. Edited by EDWARD STANLEY POOLE. With Preface by STANLEY LANE-POOLE. Three Vols., demy 8vo, cloth, 7s. 6d. ea.

Larwood (Jacob), Works by.
 Anecdotes of the Clergy. Post 8vo, laid paper, half-bound, 2s.
 Post 8vo, cloth limp, 2s. 6d. each.
 Forensic Anecdotes. | Theatrical Anecdotes.

Lehmann (R. C.), Works by. Post 8vo, 1s. each; cloth, 1s. 6d. each.
 Harry Fludyer at Cambridge.
 Conversational Hints for Young Shooters: A Guide to Polite Talk.

Leigh (Henry S.).—Carols of Cockayne. Printed on hand-made paper, bound in buckram, 5s.

Leland (C. Godfrey). — A Manual of Mending and Repairing. With Diagrams. Crown 8vo, cloth, 5s.

Lepelletier (Edmond). — Madame Sans-Gène. Translated from the French by JOHN DE VILLIERS. Crown 8vo, cloth, 3s. 6d.; post 8vo, picture boards, 2s.

Leys (John).—The Lindsays: A Romance. Post 8vo, illust. bds., 2s.

Lindsay (Harry).—Rhoda Roberts: A Welsh Mining Story. Crown 8vo, cloth, 3s. 6d.

Linton (E. Lynn), Works by.
 Crown 8vo, cloth extra, 3s. 6d. each; post 8vo, illustrated boards, 2s. each.
 Patricia Kemball. | Ione. | Under which Lord? With 12 Illustrations.
 The Atonement of Leam Dundas. | 'My Love!' | Sowing the Wind.
 The World Well Lost. With 12 Illusts. | Paston Carew, Millionaire and Miser.
 The One Too Many.
 Post 8vo, illustrated boards, 2s. each.
 The Rebel of the Family. | With a Silken Thread.
 Post 8vo, cloth limp, 2s. 6d. each.
 Witch Stories. | Ourselves: Essays on Women.
 Freeshooting: Extracts from the Works of Mrs. LYNN LINTON.
 Dulcie Everton. Crown 8vo, cloth extra, 3s. 6d. [*Shortly.*

Lucy (Henry W.).—Gideon Fleyce: A Novel. Crown 8vo, cloth extra, 3s. 6d.; post 8vo, illustrated boards, 2s.

Macalpine (Avery), Novels by.
 Teresa Itasca. Crown 8vo, cloth extra, 1s.
 Broken Wings. With Six Illustrations by W. J. HENNESSY. Crown 8vo, cloth extra, 6s.

MacColl (Hugh), Novels by.
 Mr. Stranger's Sealed Packet. Post 8vo, Illustrated boards, 2s.
 Ednor Whitlock. Crown 8vo, cloth extra, 6s.

Macdonell (Agnes).—Quaker Cousins. Post 8vo, boards, 2s.

MacGregor (Robert).—Pastimes and Players: Notes on Popular Games. Post 8vo, cloth limp, 2s. 6d.

Mackay (Charles, LL.D.). — Interludes and Undertones; or, Music at Twilight. Crown 8vo, cloth extra, 6s.

CHATTO & WINDUS, 111 St. Martin's Lane, London, W.C. 15

McCarthy (Justin, M.P.), Works by.
A History of Our Own Times, from the Accession of Queen Victoria to the General Election of 1880. Four Vols., demy 8vo, cloth extra, 12s. each.—Also a POPULAR EDITION, in Four Vols., crown 8vo, cloth extra, 6s. each.—And the JUBILEE EDITION, with an Appendix of Events to the end of 1886, in Two Vols., large crown 8vo, cloth extra, 7s. 6d. each.
* Vol. V., bringing the narrative down to the end of the Sixtieth Year of the Queen's Reign, is in preparation. Demy 8vo, cloth, 12s.
A Short History of Our Own Times. One Vol., crown 8vo, cloth extra, 6s.—Also a CHEAP POPULAR EDITION, post 8vo, cloth limp, 2s. 6d.
A History of the Four Georges. Four Vols., demy 8vo, cl. ex., 12s. each. [Vols. I. & II. ready.

Crown 8vo, cloth extra, 3s. 6d. each; post 8vo, illustrated boards, 2s. each; cloth limp, 2s. 6d. each.

The Waterdale Neighbours.	Donna Quixote. With 12 Illustrations.
My Enemy's Daughter.	The Comet of a Season.
A Fair Saxon.	Maid of Athens. With 12 Illustrations.
Linley Rochford.	Camiola: A Girl with a Fortune.
Dear Lady Disdain.	The Dictator.
Miss Misanthrope. With 12 Illustrations.	Red Diamonds.

The Riddle Ring. Crown 8vo, cloth, 3s. 6d. [May, 1897.
'The Right Honourable.' By JUSTIN MCCARTHY, M.P., and Mrs. CAMPBELL PRAED. Crown 8vo, cloth extra, 6s.

McCarthy (Justin Huntly), Works by.
The French Revolution. (Constituent Assembly, 1789-91). Four Vols., demy 8vo, cloth extra, 12s. each. Vols. I. & II. ready; Vols. III. & IV. in the press.
An Outline of the History of Ireland. Crown 8vo, 1s.; cloth, 1s. 6d.
Ireland Since the Union: Sketches of Irish History, 1798-1886. Crown 8vo, cloth, 6s.
Hafiz in London: Poems. Small 8vo, gold cloth, 3s. 6d.
Our Sensation Novel. Crown 8vo, picture cover, 1s.; cloth limp, 1s. 6d.
Doom: An Atlantic Episode. Crown 8vo, picture cover, 1s.
Dolly: A Sketch. Crown 8vo, picture cover, 1s.; cloth limp, 1s. 6d.
Lily Lass: A Romance. Crown 8vo, picture cover, 1s.; cloth limp, 1s. 6d.
The Thousand and One Days. With Two Photogravures. Two Vols., crown 8vo, half-bd., 12s.
A London Legend. Crown 8vo, cloth, 3s. 6d.
The Royal Christopher. Crown 8vo, cloth, 3s. 6d.

MacDonald (George, LL.D.), Books by.
Works of Fancy and Imagination. Ten Vols., 16mo, cloth, gilt edges, in cloth case, 21s.; or the Volumes may be had separately, in Grolier cloth, at 2s. 6d. each.
Vol. I. WITHIN AND WITHOUT.—THE HIDDEN LIFE.
,, II. THE DISCIPLE.—THE GOSPEL WOMEN.—BOOK OF SONNETS.—ORGAN SONGS.
,, III. VIOLIN SONGS.—SONGS OF THE DAYS AND NIGHTS.—A BOOK OF DREAMS.—ROADSIDE POEMS.—POEMS FOR CHILDREN.
,, IV. PARABLES.—BALLADS.—SCOTCH SONGS.
,, V. & VI. PHANTASTES: A Faerie Romance. | Vol. VII. THE PORTENT.
,, VIII. THE LIGHT PRINCESS.—THE GIANT'S HEART.—SHADOWS.
,, IX. CROSS PURPOSES.—THE GOLDEN KEY.—THE CARASOYN.—LITTLE DAYLIGHT.
,, X. THE CRUEL PAINTER.—THE WOW O' RIVVEN.—THE CASTLE.—THE BROKEN SWORDS. —THE GRAY WOLF.—UNCLE CORNELIUS.

Poetical Works of George MacDonald. Collected and Arranged by the Author. Two Vols., crown 8vo, buckram, 12s.
A Threefold Cord. Edited by GEORGE MACDONALD. Post 8vo, cloth, 5s.
Phantastes: A Faerie Romance. With 25 Illustrations by J. BELL. Crown 8vo, cloth extra, 3s. 6d.
Heather and Snow: A Novel. Crown 8vo, cloth extra, 3s. 6d.; post 8vo, illustrated boards, 2s.
Lilith: A Romance. SECOND EDITION. Crown 8vo, cloth extra, 6s.

Maclise Portrait Gallery (The) of Illustrious Literary Characters: 85 Portraits by DANIEL MACLISE; with Memoirs—Biographical, Critical, Bibliographical and Anecdotal—Illustrative of the Literature of the former half of the Present Century, by WILLIAM BATES, B.A. Crown 8vo, cloth extra, 7s. 6d.

Macquoid (Mrs.), Works by. Square 8vo, cloth extra, 6s. each.
In the Ardennes. With 50 Illustrations by THOMAS R. MACQUOID.
Pictures and Legends from Normandy and Brittany. 34 Illusts. by T. R. MACQUOID.
Through Normandy. With 92 Illustrations by T. R. MACQUOID, and a Map.
Through Brittany. With 35 Illustrations by T. R. MACQUOID, and a Map.
About Yorkshire. With 67 Illustrations by T. R. MACQUOID.

Post 8vo, illustrated boards, 2s. each.
The Evil Eye, and other Stories. | **Lost Rose,** and other Stories.

Magician's Own Book, The: Performances with Eggs, Hats, &c.
Edited by W. H. CREMER. With 200 Illustrations. Crown 8vo, cloth extra, 4s. 6d.

Magic Lantern, The, and its Management: Including full Practical Directions. By T. C. HEPWORTH. With 10 Illustrations. Crown 8vo, 1s.; cloth, 1s. 6d.

Magna Charta: An Exact Facsimile of the Original in the British Museum, 3 feet by 2 feet, with Arms and Seals emblazoned in Gold and Colours, 5s.

Mallory (Sir Thomas). — Mort d'Arthur: The Stories of King Arthur and of the Knights of the Round Table. (A Selection.) Edited by B. MONTGOMERIE RANKING. Post 8vo, cloth limp, 2s.

CHATTO & WINDUS, 111 St. Martin's Lane, London, W.C.

Mallock (W. H.), Works by.
The New Republic. Post 8vo, picture cover, 2s.; cloth limp, 2s. 6d.
The New Paul & Virginia: Positivism on an Island. Post 8vo, cloth, 2s. 6d.
A Romance of the Nineteenth Century. Crown 8vo, cloth 6s.; post 8vo, illust. boards, 2s.
Poems. Small 4to, parchment, 8s.
Is Life Worth Living? Crown 8vo, cloth extra, 6s.

Marks (H. S., R.A.), Pen and Pencil Sketches by. With Four
Photogravures and 126 Illustrations. Two Vols. demy 8vo, cloth, 32s.

Marlowe's Works. Including his Translations. Edited, with Notes
and Introductions, by Colonel CUNNINGHAM. Crown 8vo, cloth extra, 3s. 6d.

Marryat (Florence), Novels by. Post 8vo, illust. boards, 2s. each.
A Harvest of Wild Oats. | **Fighting the Air.**
Open! Sesame! | **Written in Fire.**

Massinger's Plays. From the Text of WILLIAM GIFFORD. Edited
by Col. CUNNINGHAM. Crown 8vo, cloth extra, 3s. 6d.

Masterman (J.).—Half-a-Dozen Daughters. Post 8vo, boards, 2s.

Matthews (Brander).—A Secret of the Sea, &c. Post 8vo, illustrated boards, 2s.; cloth limp, 2s. 6d.

Meade (L. T.), Novels by.
A Soldier of Fortune. Crown 8vo, cloth, 3s. 6d.; post 8vo, illustrated boards, 2s.
Crown 8vo, cloth, 3s. 6d each.
In an Iron Grip. | **The Voice of the Charmer.** With 8 Illustrations.
Dr. Rumsey's Patient. By L. T. MEADE and CLIFFORD HALIFAX, M.D. Crown 8vo, cl. 6s.

Merrick (Leonard), Stories by.
The Man who was Good. Post 8vo, picture boards, 2s.
This Stage of Fools. Crown 8vo, cloth, 3s. 6d.
Cynthia: A Daughter of the Philistines. 2 vols., crown 8vo, 10s. net.

Mexican Mustang (On a), through Texas to the Rio Grande. By
A. E. SWEET and J. ARMOY KNOX With 265 Illustrations. Crown 8vo, cloth extra, 7s. 6d.

Middlemass (Jean), Novels by. Post 8vo, illust. boards, 2s. each.
Touch and Go. | **Mr. Dorillion.**

Miller (Mrs. F. Fenwick).—Physiology for the Young; or, The
House of Life. With numerous Illustrations. Post 8vo, cloth limp, 2s. 6d.

Milton (J. L.), Works by. Post 8vo, 1s. each; cloth, 1s. 6d. each.
The Hygiene of the Skin. With Directions for Diet, Soaps, Baths, Wines, &c.
The Bath in Diseases of the Skin.
The Laws of Life, and their Relation to Diseases of the Skin.

Minto (Wm.).—Was She Good or Bad? Cr. 8vo, 1s.; cloth, 1s. 6d.

Mitford (Bertram), Novels by. Crown 8vo, cloth extra, 3s. 6d. each.
The Gun-Runner: A Romance of Zululand. With a Frontispiece by STANLEY L. WOOD.
The Luck of Gerard Ridgeley. With a Frontispiece by STANLEY L. WOOD.
The King's Assegai. With Six full-page Illustrations by STANLEY L. WOOD.
Renshaw Fanning's Quest. With a Frontispiece by STANLEY L. WOOD.

Molesworth (Mrs.), Novels by.
Hathercourt Rectory. Post 8vo, illustrated boards, 2s.
That Girl in Black. Crown 8vo, cloth, 1s. 6d.

Moncrieff (W. D. Scott-).—The Abdication: An Historical Drama.
With Seven Etchings by JOHN PETTIE, W. Q. ORCHARDSON, J. MACWHIRTER, COLIN HUNTER, R. MACBETH and TOM GRAHAM. Imperial 4to, buckram, 21s.

Moore (Thomas), Works by.
The Epicurean; and Alciphron. Post 8vo, half-bound, 2s.
Prose and Verse; including Suppressed Passages from the MEMOIRS OF LORD BYRON. Edited by R. H. SHEPHERD. With Portrait. Crown 8vo, cloth extra, 7s. 6d.

Muddock (J. E.) Stories by.
Crown 8vo, cloth extra, 3s. 6d. each.
Maid Marian and Robin Hood. With 12 Illustrations by STANLEY WOOD.
Basile the Jester. With Frontispiece by STANLEY WOOD.
Young Lochinvar.
Post 8vo, illustrated boards, 2s. each.
The Dead Man's Secret. | **From the Bosom of the Deep.**
Stories Weird and Wonderful. Post 8vo illustrated boards, 2s.; cloth, 2s. 6d.

CHATTO & WINDUS, 111 St. Martin's Lane, London, W.C. 17

Murray (D. Christie), Novels by.
Crown 8vo, cloth extra, 3s. 6d. each; post 8vo, illustrated boards, 2s. each.

A Life's Atonement.	A Model Father.	Bob Martin's Little Girl.
Joseph's Coat. 12 Illusts.	Old Blazer's Hero.	Time's Revenges.
Coals of Fire. 3 Illusts.	Cynic Fortune. Frontisp.	A Wasted Crime.
Val Strange.	By the Gate of the Sea.	In Direst Peril.
Hearts.	A Bit of Human Nature.	Mount Despair.
The Way of the World.	First Person Singular.	

A Capful o' Nails. Crown 8vo, cloth, 3s. 6d.
The Making of a Novelist: An Experiment in Autobiography. With a Collotype Portrait and Vignette. Crown 8vo, art linen, 6s.

Murray (D. Christie) and Henry Herman, Novels by.
Crown 8vo, cloth extra, 3s. 6d. each; post 8vo, illustrated boards, 2s. each.

One Traveller Returns. | **The Bishops' Bible.**
Paul Jones's Alias, &c. With Illustrations by A. FORESTIER and G. NICOLET.

Murray (Henry), Novels by.
Post 8vo, illustrated boards, 2s. each; cloth, 2s. 6d. each.

A Game of Bluff. | **A Song of Sixpence.**

Newbolt (Henry).—Taken from the Enemy. Fcp. 8vo, cloth, 1s. 6d.

Nisbet (Hume), Books by.
'Bail Up.' Crown 8vo, cloth extra, 3s. 6d.; post 8vo, illustrated boards, 2s.
Dr. Bernard St. Vincent. Post 8vo, illustrated boards, 2s.

Lessons in Art. With 21 Illustrations. Crown 8vo, cloth extra, 2s. 6d.
Where Art Begins. With 27 Illustrations. Square 8vo, cloth extra, 7s. 6d.

Norris (W. E.), Novels by.
Saint Ann's. Crown 8vo, cloth, 3s. 6d.; post 8vo, picture boards, 2s.
Billy Bellew. With a Frontispiece by F. H. TOWNSEND. Crown 8vo, cloth, 3s. 6d.

O'Hanlon (Alice), Novels by. Post 8vo, illustrated boards, 2s. each.
The Unforeseen. | **Chance? or Fate?**

Ohnet (Georges), Novels by. Post 8vo, illustrated boards, 2s. each.
Doctor Rameau. | **A Last Love.**

A Weird Gift. Crown 8vo, cloth, 3s. 6d.; post 8vo, picture boards, 2s.

Oliphant (Mrs.), Novels by. Post 8vo, illustrated boards, 2s. each.
The Primrose Path. | **Whiteladies.**
The Greatest Heiress in England.

The Sorceress. Crown 8vo, cloth, 3s. 6d.

O'Reilly (Mrs.).—Phœbe's Fortunes. Post 8vo, illust. boards, 2s.

Ouida, Novels by. Cr. 8vo, cl., 3s. 6d. ea.; post 8vo, illust. bds., 2s. ea.

Held in Bondage.	Folle-Farine.	Moths.	Pipistrello.
Tricotrin.	A Dog of Flanders.	In Maremma.	Wanda.
Strathmore.	Pascarel.	Signa.	Bimbi.	Syrlin.
Chandos.	Two Wooden Shoes.	Frescoes.	Othmar.
Cecil Castlemaine's Gage	In a Winter City.	Princess Napraxine.
Under Two Flags.	Ariadne.	Friendship.	Guilderoy.	Ruffino.
Puck.	Idalia.	A Village Commune.	Two Offenders.

Square 8vo, cloth extra, 5s. each.
Bimbi. With Nine Illustrations by EDMUND H. GARRETT.
A Dog of Flanders, &c. With Six Illustrations by EDMUND H. GARRETT.

Santa Barbara, &c. Square 8vo, cloth, 6s.; crown 8vo, cloth, 3s. 6d.; post 8vo, illustrated boards, 2s.

POPULAR EDITIONS. Medium 8vo, 6d. each; cloth, 1s. each.
Under Two Flags. | **Moths.**

Wisdom, Wit, and Pathos, selected from the Works of OUIDA by F. SYDNEY MORRIS. Post 8vo, cloth extra, 5s.—CHEAP EDITION, illustrated boards, 2s.

Page (H. A.).—Thoreau: His Life and Aims. With Portrait. Post 8vo, cloth, 2s. 6d.

Pandurang Hari; or, Memoirs of a Hindoo. With Preface by Sir
BARTLE FRERE. Crown 8vo, cloth, 3s. 6d.; post 8vo, illustrated boards, 2s.

Parker (Rev. Joseph, D.D.).—Might Have Been: some Life
Notes. Crown 8vo, cloth, 6s.

Pascal's Provincial Letters. A New Translation, with Historical
Introduction and Notes by T. M'CRIE, D.D. Post 8vo, cloth limp, 2s.

Paul (Margaret A.).—Gentle and Simple. Crown 8vo, cloth, with
Frontispiece by HELEN PATERSON, 3s. 6d.; post 8vo, illustrated boards, 2s.

CHATTO & WINDUS, 111 St. Martin's Lane, London, W.C.

Payn (James), Novels by.
Crown 8vo, cloth extra, 3s. 6d. each   post 8vo, Illustrated boards, 2s. each.

Lost Sir Massingberd.
Walter's Word.
Less Black than We're Painted.
By Proxy. | For Cash Only.
High Spirits.
Under One Roof.
A Confidential Agent. With 12 Illusts.
A Grape from a Thorn. With 12 Illusts.
Holiday Tasks.
The Canon's Ward. With Portrait.
The Talk of the Town. With 12 Illusts.
Glow-Worm Tales.
The Mystery of Mirbridge.
The Word and the Will.
The Burnt Million.
Sunny Stories. | A Trying Patient

Post 8vo, illustrated boards, 2s. each.

Humorous Stories. | From Exile.
The Foster Brothers.
The Family Scapegrace.
Married Beneath Him.
Bentinck's Tutor. | A County Family.
A Perfect Treasure.
Like Father, Like Son.
A Woman's Vengeance.
Carlyon's Year. | Cecil's Tryst.
Murphy's Master. | At Her Mercy.
The Clyffards of Clyffe.
Found Dead. | Gwendoline's Harvest.
Mirk Abbey. | A Marine Residence.
Some Private Views.
Not Wooed, But Won.
Two Hundred Pounds Reward.
The Best of Husbands.
Halves. | What He Cost Her.
Fallen Fortunes. | Kit: A Memory.
A Prince of the Blood.

In Peril and Privation. With 17 Illustrations. Crown 8vo, cloth, 3s. 6d.
Notes from the 'News.' Crown 8vo, portrait cover, 1s.; cloth, 1s. 6d.

Payne (Will).—Jerry the Dreamer. Crown 8vo, cloth, 3s. 6d.

Pennell (H. Cholmondeley), Works by. Post 8vo, cloth, 2s. 6d. ea.
Puck on Pegasus. With Illustrations.
Pegasus Re-Saddled. With Ten full-page Illustrations by G. DU MAURIER.
The Muses of Mayfair: Vers de Société. Selected by H. C. PENNELL.

Phelps (E. Stuart), Works by. Post 8vo, 1s. ea.; cloth, 1s. 6d. ea.
Beyond the Gates. | An Old Maid's Paradise. | Burglars in Paradise.
Jack the Fisherman. Illustrated by C. W. REED. Crown 8vo, 1s.; cloth, 1s. 6d.

Phil May's Sketch-Book. Containing 54 Humorous Cartoons. A
New Edition. Crown folio, cloth, 2s. 6d.

Phipson (Dr. T. L.).—Famous Violinists and Fine Violins:
Historical Notes, Anecdotes, and Reminiscences. Crown 8vo, cloth, 5s.

Pirkis (C. L.), Novels by.
Trooping with Crows. Fcap. 8vo, picture cover, 1s.
Lady Lovelace. Post 8vo, illustrated boards, 2s.

Planche (J. R.), Works by.
The Pursuivant of Arms. With Six Plates and 209 Illustrations. Crown 8vo, cloth, 7s. 6d.
Songs and Poems, 1819-1879. With Introduction by Mrs. MACKARNESS. Crown 8vo, cloth, 6s.

Plutarch's Lives of Illustrious Men. With Notes and a Life of
Plutarch by JOHN and WM. LANGHORNE, and Portraits. Two Vols., demy 8vo, half-bound 10s. 6d.

Poe's (Edgar Allan) Choice Works in Prose and Poetry. With Intro-
duction by CHARLES BAUDELAIRE, Portrait and Facsimiles. Crown 8vo, cloth, 7s. 6d.
The Mystery of Marie Roget, &c. Post 8vo, illustrated boards, 2s.

Pollock (W. H.).—The Charm, and other Drawing-room Plays. By
Sir WALTER BESANT and WALTER H. POLLOCK. With 50 Illustrations. Crown 8vo, cloth gilt, 6s.

Pope's Poetical Works. Post 8vo, cloth limp, 2s.

Porter (John).—Kingsclere. Edited by BYRON WEBBER. With 19
full-page and many smaller Illustrations. Second Edition. Demy 8vo, cloth decorated, 18s.

Praed (Mrs. Campbell), Novels by. Post 8vo, illust. bds., 2s. each.
The Romance of a Station. | The Soul of Countess Adrian.

Crown 8vo, cloth, 3s. 6d. each; post 8vo, boards, 2s. each.
Outlaw and Lawmaker. | Christina Chard. With Frontispiece by W. PAGET.
Mrs. Tregaskiss. With 8 Illustrations by ROBERT SAUBER. Crown 8vo, cloth extra, 3s. 6d.

Price (E. C.), Novels by.
Crown 8vo, cloth extra, 3s. 6d. each; post 8vo, illustrated boards, 2s. each.
Valentina. | The Foreigners. | Mrs. Lancaster's Rival.
Gerald. Post 8vo, illustrated boards, 2s.

Princess Olga.—Radna: A Novel. Crown 8vo, cloth extra, 6s.

Proctor (Richard A., B.A.), Works by.
Flowers of the Sky. With 55 Illustrations. Small crown 8vo, cloth extra, 3s. 6d.
Easy Star Lessons. With Star Maps for every Night in the Year. Crown 8vo, cloth, 6s.
Familiar Science Studies. Crown 8vo, cloth extra, 6s.
Saturn and its System. With 13 Steel Plates. Demy 8vo, cloth extra, 10s. 6d.
Mysteries of Time and Space. With numerous Illustrations. Crown 8vo, cloth extra, 6s.
The Universe of Suns, &c. With numerous Illustrations. Crown 8vo, cloth extra, 6s.
Wages and Wants of Science Workers. Crown 8vo, 1s. 6d.

CHATTO & WINDUS, 111 St. Martin's Lane, London, W.C.

Pryce (Richard).—Miss Maxwell's Affections. Crown 8vo, cloth.
with Frontispiece by HAL LUDLOW, 3s. 6d.; post 8vo, illustrated boards, 2s.

Rambosson (J.).—Popular Astronomy. Translated by C. B. PITMAN. With Coloured Frontispiece and numerous Illustrations. Crown 8vo, cloth extra, 7s. 6d.

Randolph (Lieut.-Col. George, U.S.A.).—Aunt Abigail Dykes: A Novel. Crown 8vo, cloth extra, 7s. 6d.

Read (General Meredith).—Historic Studies in Vaud, Berne, and Savoy. With 30 full-page Illustrations. Two Vols., demy 8vo, cloth, 28s. [Shortly.

Reade's (Charles) Novels.
The New Collected LIBRARY EDITION, complete in Seventeen Volumes, set in new long primer type, printed on laid paper, and elegantly bound in cloth, price 3s. 6d. each.

1. Peg Woffington; and Christie Johnstone.
2. Hard Cash.
3. The Cloister and the Hearth. With a Preface by Sir WALTER BESANT.
4. 'It is Never too Late to Mend.'
5. The Course of True Love Never Did Run Smooth; and Singleheart and Doubleface.
6. The Autobiography of a Thief; Jack of all Trades; A Hero and a Martyr; and The Wandering Heir.
7. Love Me Little, Love me Long.
8. The Double Marriage.
9. Griffith Gaunt.
10. Foul Play.
11. Put Yourself in His Place.
12. A Terrible Temptation.
13. A Simpleton.
14. A Woman-Hater.
15. The Jilt, and other Stories; and Good Stories of Man and other Animals.
16. A Perilous Secret.
17. Readiana; and Bible Characters.

In Twenty-one Volumes, post 8vo, illustrated boards, 2s. each.

Peg Woffington. | Christie Johnstone.
'It is Never Too Late to Mend.'
The Course of True Love Never Did Run Smooth.
The Autobiography of a Thief; Jack of all Trades; and James Lambert.
Love Me Little, Love Me Long.
The Double Marriage.
The Cloister and the Hearth.
Hard Cash | Griffith Gaunt.
Foul Play. | Put Yourself in His Place.
A Terrible Temptation.
A Simpleton. | The Wandering Heir
A Woman-Hater.
Singleheart and Doubleface.
Good Stories of Men and other Animals.
The Jilt, and other Stories.
A Perilous Secret. | Readiana.

POPULAR EDITIONS, medium 8vo, 6d. each : cloth, 1s. each.
'It is Never Too Late to Mend.' | The Cloister and the Hearth.
Peg Woffington; and Christie Johnstone.

'It is Never Too Late to Mend' and The Cloister and the Hearth in One Volume, medium 8vo, cloth, 2s.
Christie Johnstone. With Frontispiece. Choicely printed in Elzevir style. Fcap. 8vo, half-Roxb. 2s. 6d.
Peg Woffington. Choicely printed in Elzevir style. Fcap. 8vo, half-Roxburghe, 2s. 6d.
The Cloister and the Hearth. In Four Vols., post 8vo, with an Introduction by Sir WALTER BRSANT, and a Frontispiece to each Vol., 14s. the set; and the ILLUSTRATED LIBRARY EDITION, with Illustrations on every page, Two Vols., crown 8vo, cloth gilt, 42s. net.
Bible Characters. Fcap. 8vo, leatherette, 1s.
Selections from the Works of Charles Reade. With an Introduction by Mrs. ALEX. IRELAND. Crown 8vo, buckram, with Portrait, 6s.; CHEAP EDITION, post 8vo, cloth limp, 2s. 6d.

Riddell (Mrs. J. H.), Novels by.
Weird Stories. Crown 8vo, cloth extra, 3s. 6d.; post 8vo, illustrated boards, 2s.

Post 8vo, illustrated boards, 2s. each.
The Uninhabited House.
The Prince of Wales's Garden Party.
The Mystery in Palace Gardens.
Fairy Water.
Her Mother's Darling.
The Nun's Curse. | Idle Tales.

Rimmer (Alfred), Works by. Square 8vo, cloth gilt, 7s. 6d. each.
Our Old Country Towns. With 55 Illustrations by the Author.
Rambles Round Eton and Harrow. With 50 Illustrations by the Author.
About England with Dickens. With 58 Illustrations by C. A. VANDERHOOF and A. RIMMER.

Rives (Amelie).—Barbara Dering. Crown 8vo, cloth extra, 3s. 6d.; post 8vo, illustrated boards, 2s.

Robinson Crusoe. By DANIEL DEFOE. With 37 Illustrations by GEORGE CRUIKSHANK. Post 8vo, half-cloth, 2s.; cloth extra, gilt edges, 2s. 6d.

Robinson (F. W.), Novels by.
Women are Strange. Post 8vo, illustrated boards, 2s.
The Hands of Justice. Crown 8vo, cloth extra, 3s. 6d.; post 8vo, illustrated boards, 2s.
The Woman in the Dark. Crown 8vo, cloth, 3s. 6d.

Robinson (Phil), Works by. Crown 8vo, cloth extra, 6s. each.
The Poets' Birds. | The Poets' Beasts.
The Poets and Nature: Reptiles, Fishes, and Insects.

Rochefoucauld's Maxims and Moral Reflections. With Notes and an Introductory Essay by SAINTE-BEUVE. Post 8vo, cloth limp, 2s.

Roll of Battle Abbey, The: A List of the Principal Warriors who came from Normandy with William the Conqueror, 1066. Printed in Gold and Colours, 5s.

Rosengarten (A.).—A Handbook of Architectural Styles. Translated by W. COLLETT-SANDARS. With 630 Illustrations. Crown 8vo, cloth extra, 7s. 6d.

Rowley (Hon. Hugh), Works by. Post 8vo, cloth, 2s. 6d. each.
Puniana: Riddles and Jokes. With numerous Illustrations.
More Puniana. Profusely Illustrated.

Runciman (James), Stories by. Post 8vo, bds., 2s. ea.; cl., 2s. 6d. ea.
Skippers and Shellbacks. | Grace Balmaign's Sweetheart.
Schools and Scholars.

Russell (Dora), Novels by.
A Country Sweetheart. Crown 8vo, cloth, 3s. 6d.; post 8vo, picture boards, 2s.
The Drift of Fate. Crown 8vo, cloth, 3s. 6d.

Russell (W. Clark), Novels, &c., by.
Crown 8vo, cloth extra, 3s. 6d. each; post 8vo, illustrated boards, 2s. each; cloth limp, 2s. 6d. each.
Round the Galley-Fire. | An Ocean Tragedy.
In the Middle Watch. | My Shipmate Louisa.
A Voyage to the Cape. | Alone on a Wide Wide Sea.
A Book for the Hammock. | The Good Ship 'Mohock.'
The Mystery of the 'Ocean Star.' | The Phantom Death
The Romance of Jenny Harlowe.

Crown 8vo, cloth, 3s. 6d. each.
Is He the Man? | The Tale of the Ten. With 12 Illustrations by G. MONTBARD. [Feb.
The Convict Ship. | The Last Entry. Frontis. [Shortly.
Heart of Oak.

On the Fo'k'sle Head. Post 8vo, illustrated boards, 2s.; cloth limp, 2s. 6d.

Saint Aubyn (Alan), Novels by.
Crown 8vo, cloth extra, 3s. 6d. each; post 8vo, illustrated boards, 2s. each.
A Fellow of Trinity. With a Note by OLIVER WENDELL HOLMES and a Frontispiece.
The Junior Dean. | The Master of St. Benedict's. | To His Own Master.
Orchard Damerel. | In the Face of the World.

Fcap. 8vo, cloth boards, 1s. 6d. each.
The Old Maid's Sweetheart. | Modest Little Sara.

The Tremlett Diamonds. Crown 8vo, cloth extra, 3s. 6d.

Sala (George A.).—Gaslight and Daylight. Post 8vo, boards, 2s.

Saunders (John), Novels by.
Crown 8vo, cloth extra, 3s. 6d. each; post 8vo, illustrated boards, 2s. each.
Guy Waterman. | The Lion in the Path. | The Two Dreamers.
Bound to the Wheel. Crown 8vo, cloth extra, 3s. 6d.

Saunders (Katharine), Novels by.
Crown 8vo, cloth extra, 3s. 6d. each; post 8vo, illustrated boards, 2s. each.
Margaret and Elizabeth. | Heart Salvage.
The High Mills. | Sebastian.

Joan Merryweather. Post 8vo, illustrated boards, 2s.
Gideon's Rock. Crown 8vo, cloth extra, 3s. 6d.

Scotland Yard, Past and Present: Experiences of Thirty-seven Years. By Ex-Chief-Inspector CAVANAGH. Post 8vo, illustrated boards, 2s.; cloth, 2s. 6d.

Secret Out, The: One Thousand Tricks with Cards; with Entertaining Experiments in Drawing-room or 'White' Magic. By W. H. CREMER. With 300 Illustrations. Crown 8vo, cloth extra, 4s. 6d.

Seguin (L. G.), Works by.
The Country of the Passion Play (Oberammergau) and the Highlands of Bavaria. With Map and 37 Illustrations. Crown 8vo, cloth extra, 3s. 6d.
Walks in Algiers. With Two Maps and 16 Illustrations. Crown 8vo, cloth extra, 6s.

Senior (Wm.).—By Stream and Sea. Post 8vo, cloth, 2s. 6d.

Sergeant (Adeline).—Dr. Endicott's Experiment. Cr. 8vo, 3s. 6d.

Shakespeare for Children: Lamb's Tales from Shakespeare. With Illustrations, coloured and plain, by J. MOYR SMITH. Crown 4to, cloth gilt, 3s. 6d.

CHATTO & WINDUS, 111 St. Martin's Lane, London, W.C. 21

Sharp (William).—Children of To-morrow. Crown 8vo, cloth, 6s.

Shelley's (Percy Bysshe) Complete Works in Verse and Prose.
Edited, Prefaced, and Annotated by R. HERNE SHEPHERD. Five Vols., crown 8vo, cloth, 3s. 6d. each.
Poetical Works, in Three Vols.:
Vol. I. Introduction by the Editor; Posthumous Fragments of Margaret Nicholson; Shelley's Correspondence with Stockdale; The Wandering Jew; Queen Mab, with the Notes; Alastor, and other Poems; Rosalind and Helen; Prometheus Unbound; Adonais, &c.
„ II. Laon and Cythna; The Cenci; Julian and Maddalo; Swellfoot the Tyrant; The Witch of Atlas; Epipsychidion; Hellas.
„ III. Posthumous Poems; The Masque of Anarchy; and other Pieces.
Prose Works, in Two Vols.:
Vol. I. The Two Romances of Zastrozzi and St. Irvyne; the Dublin and Marlow Pamphlets; A Refutation of Deism; Letters to Leigh Hunt, and some Minor Writings and Fragments.
„ II. The Essays; Letters from Abroad; Translations and Fragments, edited by Mrs. SHELLEY. With a Biography of Shelley, and an Index of the Prose Works.
₊ Also a few copies of a LARGE-PAPER EDITION, 5 vols., cloth, £2 12s. 6d.

Sheridan (General P. H.), Personal Memoirs of. With Portraits, Maps, and Facsimiles. Two Vols., demy 8vo, cloth, 24s.

Sheridan's (Richard Brinsley) Complete Works, with Life and Anecdotes. Including his Dramatic Writings, his Works in Prose and Poetry, Translations, Speeches, and Jokes. With 10 Illustrations. Crown 8vo, half-bound, 7s. 6d.
The Rivals, The School for Scandal, and other Plays. Post 8vo, half-bound, 2s.
Sheridan's Comedies: The Rivals and The School for Scandal. Edited, with an Introduction and Notes to each Play, and a Biographical Sketch, by BRANDER MATTHEWS. With Illustrations. Demy 8vo, half-parchment, 12s. 6d.

Sidney's (Sir Philip) Complete Poetical Works, including all those in 'Arcadia.' With Portrait, Memorial-Introduction, Notes, &c., by the Rev. A. B. GROSART, D.D. Three Vols., crown 8vo, cloth boards, 3s. 6d. each.

Signboards: Their History, including Anecdotes of Famous Taverns and Remarkable Characters. By JACOB LARWOOD and JOHN CAMDEN HOTTEN. With Coloured Frontispiece and 94 Illustrations. Crown 8vo, cloth extra, 7s. 6d.

Sims (George R.), Works by.
Post 8vo, illustrated boards, 2s. each; cloth limp, 2s. 6d. each.

The Ring o' Bells.
Mary Jane's Memoirs.
Mary Jane Married.
Tinkletop's Crime.
Zeph: A Circus Story, &c.
Tales of To-day.

Dramas of Life. With 60 Illustrations.
Memoirs of a Landlady.
My Two Wives.
Scenes from the Show.
The Ten Commandments: Stories.

Crown 8vo, picture cover, 1s. each; cloth, 1s. 6d. each.
The Dagonet Reciter and Reader: Being Readings and Recitations in Prose and Verse, selected from his own Works by GEORGE R. SIMS.
The Case of George Candlemas. | **Dagonet Ditties.** (From *The Referee.*)

Rogues and Vagabonds. A New Edition. Crown 8vo, cloth, 3s. 6d.
How the Poor Live; and **Horrible London.** Crown 8vo, picture cover, 1s.
Dagonet Abroad. Crown 8vo, cloth, 3s. 6d.; post 8vo, picture boards, 2s.

Sister Dora: A Biography. By MARGARET LONSDALE. With Four Illustrations. Demy 8vo, picture cover, 4d.; cloth, 6d.

Sketchley (Arthur).—A Match in the Dark. Post 8vo, boards, 2s.

Slang Dictionary (The): Etymological, Historical, and Anecdotal. Crown 8vo, cloth extra, 6s. 6d.

Smart (Hawley), Novels by.
Without Love or Licence. Crown 8vo, cloth, 3s. 6d.; post 8vo, picture boards, 2s.

Crown 8vo, cloth, 3s. 6d. each.
Long Odds. | **The Master of Rathkelly.** | **The Outsider.**

Post 8vo, picture boards, 2s. each.
The Plunger. | **Beatrice and Benedick.**

Smith (J. Moyr), Works by.
The Prince of Argolis. With 130 Illustrations. Post 8vo, cloth extra, 3s. 6d.
The Wooing of the Water Witch. With numerous Illustrations. Post 8vo, cloth, 6s.

Society in London. Crown 8vo, 1s.; cloth, 1s. 6d.

Society in Paris: The Upper Ten Thousand. A Series of Letters from Count PAUL VASILI to a Young French Diplomat. Crown 8vo, cloth, 6s.

Somerset (Lord Henry).—Songs of Adieu. Small 4to, Jap. vel., 6s.

Spalding (T. A., LL.B.).—Elizabethan Demonology: An Essay on the Belief in the Existence of Devils. Crown 8vo, cloth extra, 5s.

Speight (T. W.), Novels by.
Post 8vo, illustrated boards, 2s. each.

The Mysteries of Heron Dyke.
By Devious Ways, &c.
Hoodwinked; & Sandycroft Mystery.
The Golden Hoop.
Back to Life.

The Loudwater Tragedy.
Burgo's Romance.
Quittance in Full.
A Husband from the Sea.

Post 8vo, cloth limp, 1s. 6d. each.

A Barren Title. | Wife or No Wife?

Crown 8vo, cloth extra, 3s. 6d. each.

A Secret of the Sea. | The Grey Monk. | The Master of Trenance. [*March.*
A Minion of the Moon: A Romance of the King's Highway. [*Shortly.*

Spenser for Children. By M. H. TOWRY. With Coloured Illustrations by WALTER J. MORGAN. Crown 4to, cloth extra, 3s. 6d.

Stafford (John).—Doris and I, &c. Crown 8vo, cloth, 3s. 6d.

Starry Heavens (The): A POETICAL BIRTHDAY BOOK. Royal 16mo, cloth extra, 2s. 6d.

Stedman (E. C.), Works by. Crown 8vo, cloth extra, 9s. each.
Victorian Poets. | The Poets of America.

Stephens (Riccardo, M.B.).—The Cruciform Mark: The Strange Story of RICHARD TREGENNA, Bachelor of Medicine (Univ. Edinb.) Crown 8vo, cloth, 6s.

Sterndale (R. Armitage).—The Afghan Knife: A Novel. Crown 8vo, cloth extra, 3s. 6d.; post 8vo, illustrated boards, 2s.

Stevenson (R. Louis), Works by. Post 8vo, cloth limp, 2s. 6d. ea.
Travels with a Donkey. With a Frontispiece by WALTER CRANE.
An Inland Voyage. With a Frontispiece by WALTER CRANE.

Crown 8vo, buckram, gilt top, 6s. each.

Familiar Studies of Men and Books.
The Silverado Squatters. With Frontispiece by J. D. STRONG.
The Merry Men. | Underwoods: Poems.
Memories and Portraits.
Virginibus Puerisque, and other Papers. | Ballads. | Prince Otto.
Across the Plains, with other Memories and Essays.
Weir of Hermiston. (R. L. STEVENSON'S LAST WORK.)

Songs of Travel. Crown 8vo, buckram, 5s.
New Arabian Nights. Crown 8vo, buckram, gilt top, 6s.; post 8vo, illustrated boards, 2s.
The Suicide Club; and The Rajah's Diamond. (From NEW ARABIAN NIGHTS.) With Eight Illustrations by W. J. HENNESSY. Crown 8vo, cloth, 5s.
The Edinburgh Edition of the Works of Robert Louis Stevenson. Twenty-seven Vols., demy 8vo. This Edition (which is limited to 1,000 copies) is sold in Sets only, the price of which may be learned from the Booksellers. The First Volume was published Nov., 1894.

Stories from Foreign Novelists. With Notices by HELEN and ALICE ZIMMERN. Crown 8vo, cloth extra, 3s. 6d.; post 8vo, illustrated boards, 2s.

Strange Manuscript (A) Found in a Copper Cylinder. Crown 8vo, cloth extra, with 19 Illustrations by GILBERT GAUL, 5s.; post 8vo, illustrated boards, 2s.

Strange Secrets. Told by PERCY FITZGERALD, CONAN DOYLE, FLORENCE MARRYAT, &c. Post 8vo, illustrated boards, 2s.

Strutt (Joseph). — The Sports and Pastimes of the People of England; including the Rural and Domestic Recreations, May Games, Mummeries, Shows, &c., from the Earliest Period to the Present Time. Edited by WILLIAM HONE. With 140 Illustrations. Crown 8vo, cloth extra, 7s. 6d.

Swift's (Dean) Choice Works, in Prose and Verse. With Memoir,
Portrait, and Facsimiles of the Maps in 'Gulliver's Travels.' Crown 8vo, cloth, 7s. 6d.

Gulliver's Travels, and A Tale of a Tub. Post 8vo, half-bound, 2s.
Jonathan Swift: A Study. By J. CHURTON COLLINS. Crown 8vo, cloth extra, 8s.

CHATTO & WINDUS, 111 St. Martin's Lane, London, W.C. 23

Swinburne (Algernon C.), Works by.

Selections from the Poetical Works of A. C. Swinburne. Fcap. 8vo, 6s.
Atalanta in Calydon. Crown 8vo, 6s.
Chastelard: A Tragedy. Crown 8vo, 7s.
Poems and Ballads. FIRST SERIES. Crown 8vo, or fcap. 8vo, 9s.
Poems and Ballads. SECOND SERIES. Crown 8vo, 9s.
Poems & Ballads. THIRD SERIES. Cr. 8vo, 7s.
Songs before Sunrise. Crown 8vo, 10s. 6d.
Bothwell: A Tragedy. Crown 8vo, 12s. 6d.
Songs of Two Nations. Crown 8vo, 6s.
George Chapman. (See Vol. II. of G. CHAPMAN'S Works.) Crown 8vo, 3s. 6d.
Essays and Studies. Crown 8vo, 12s.
Erechtheus: A Tragedy. Crown 8vo, 6s.
A Note on Charlotte Bronte. Cr. 8vo, 6s.

A Study of Shakespeare. Crown 8vo, 8s.
Songs of the Springtides. Crown 8vo, 6s.
Studies in Song. Crown 8vo, 7s.
Mary Stuart: A Tragedy. Crown 8vo, 8s.
Tristram of Lyonesse. Crown 8vo, 9s.
A Century of Roundels. Small 4to, 8s.
A Midsummer Holiday. Crown 8vo, 7s.
Marino Faliero: A Tragedy. Crown 8vo, 6s.
A Study of Victor Hugo. Crown 8vo, 6s.
Miscellanies. Crown 8vo, 12s.
Locrine: A Tragedy. Crown 8vo, 6s.
A Study of Ben Jonson. Crown 8vo, 7s.
The Sisters: A Tragedy. Crown 8vo, 6s.
Astrophel, &c. Crown 8vo, 7s.
Studies in Prose and Poetry. Cr. 8vo, 9s.
The Tale of Balen. Crown 8vo, 7s.

Syntax's (Dr.) Three Tours: In Search of the Picturesque, in Search of Consolation, and in Search of a Wife. With ROWLANDSON'S Coloured Illustrations, and Life of the Author by J. C. HOTTEN. Crown 8vo, cloth extra, 7s. 6d.

Taine's History of English Literature. Translated by HENRY VAN LAUN. Four Vols., small demy 8vo, cloth boards, 30s.—POPULAR EDITION, Two Vols., large crown 8vo, cloth extra, 15s.

Taylor (Bayard). — Diversions of the Echo Club: Burlesques of Modern Writers. Post 8vo, cloth limp, 2s.

Taylor (Tom). — Historical Dramas. Containing 'Clancarty,' 'Jeanne Darc,' 'Twixt Axe and Crown,' 'The Fool's Revenge,' 'Arkwright's Wife,' 'Anne Boleyn,' 'Plot and Passion.' Crown 8vo, cloth extra, 7s. 6d.
*** The Plays may also be had separately, at 1s. each.

Tennyson (Lord): A Biographical Sketch. By H. J. JENNINGS. Post 8vo, portrait cover, 1s.; cloth, 1s. 6d.

Thackerayana: Notes and Anecdotes. With Coloured Frontispiece and Hundreds of Sketches by.WILLIAM MAKEPEACE THACKERAY. Crown 8vo, cloth extra, 7s. 6d.

Thames, A New Pictorial History of the. By A. S. KRAUSSE. With 340 Illustrations. Post 8vo, picture cover, 1s.

Thiers (Adolphe). — History of the Consulate and Empire of France under Napoleon. Translated by D. FORBES CAMPBELL and JOHN STEBBING. With 36 Stee Plates. 12 Vols., demy 8vo, cloth extra, 12s. each.

Thomas (Bertha), Novels by. Cr. 8vo, cl., 3s. 6d. ea.; post 8vo, 2s. ea.
The Violin-Player. | Proud Maisie.
Cressida. Post 8vo, illustrated boards, 2s.

Thomson's Seasons, and The Castle of Indolence. With Introduction by ALLAN CUNNINGHAM, and 48 Illustrations. Post 8vo, half-bound, 2s.

Thornbury (Walter), Books by.

The Life and Correspondence of J. M. W. Turner. With Illustrations in Colours. Crown 8vo, cloth extra, 7s. 6d.

Post 8vo, illustrated boards, 2s. each.
Old Stories Re-told. | Tales for the Marines.

Timbs (John), Works by. Crown 8vo, cloth extra, 7s. 6d. each.
The History of Clubs and Club Life in London: Anecdotes of its Famous Coffee-houses, Hostelries, and Taverns. With 42 Illustrations.
English Eccentrics and Eccentricities: Stories of Delusions, Impostures, Sporting Scenes, Eccentric Artists, Theatrical Folk, &c. With 48 Illustrations.

Transvaal (The). By JOHN DE VILLIERS. With Map. Crown 8vo, 1s.

Trollope (Anthony), Novels by.

Crown 8vo, cloth extra, 3s. 6d. each; post 8vo, illustrated boards, 2s. each.
The Way We Live Now. | Mr. Scarborough's Family.
Frau Frohmann. | The Land-Leaguers.

Post 8vo, illustrated boards, 2s. each.
Kept in the Dark. | The American Senator.
The Golden Lion of Granpere. | John Caldigate. | Marion Fay.

Trollope (Frances E.), Novels by.

Crown 8vo, cloth extra, 3s. 6d. each; post 8vo, illustrated boards, 2s. each.
Like Ships Upon the Sea. | Mabel's Progress. | Anne Furness.

24   CHATTO & WINDUS, 111 St. Martin's Lane, London, W.C.

Trollope (T. A.).—Diamond Cut Diamond. Post 8vo, illust. bds., 2s.

Trowbridge (J. T.).—Farnell's Folly. Post 8vo, illust. boards, 2s.

Twain (Mark), Books by.
The Choice Works of Mark Twain. Revised and Corrected throughout by the Author. With Life, Portrait, and numerous Illustrations. Crown 8vo, cloth extra, 7s. 6d.

Crown 8vo, cloth extra (illustrated), 7s. 6d. each; post 8vo, illustrated boards, 2s. each
The Innocents Abroad; or, The New Pilgrim's Progress. With 234 Illustrations. (The Two Shilling Edition is entitled **Mark Twain's Pleasure Trip.**)
The Gilded Age. By MARK TWAIN and C. D. WARNER. With 212 Illustrations.
The Adventures of Tom Sawyer. With 111 Illustrations.
The Prince and the Pauper. With 190 Illustrations.
Life on the Mississippi. With 300 Illustrations.
The Adventures of Huckleberry Finn. With 174 Illustrations by E. W. KEMBLE.
A Yankee at the Court of King Arthur. With 220 Illustrations by DAN BEARD.

Crown 8vo, cloth extra, 3s. 6d. each.
Roughing It; and **The Innocents at Home.** With 200 Illustrations by F. A. FRASER.
The American Claimant. With 81 Illustrations by HAL HURST and others.
Tom Sawyer Abroad. With 26 Illustrations by DAN. BEARD.
Tom Sawyer, Detective, &c. With Photogravure Portrait.
Pudd'nhead Wilson. With Portrait and Six Illustrations by LOUIS LOEB.
Mark Twain's Library of Humour. With 197 Illustrations by E. W. KEMBLE.

Crown 8vo, cloth extra, 3s. 6d. each; post 8vo, picture boards, 2s. each.
The £1,000,000 Bank-Note. | **The Stolen White Elephant.**
A Tramp Abroad.

Mark Twain's Sketches. Post 8vo, illustrated boards, 2s.
Personal Recollections of Joan of Arc. With Twelve Illustrations by F. V. DU MOND. Crown 8vo, cloth, 6s.

Tytler (C. C. Fraser-).—Mistress Judith: A Novel. Crown 8vo, cloth extra, 3s. 6d.; post 8vo, illustrated boards, 2s.

Tytler (Sarah), Novels by.
Crown 8vo, cloth extra, 3s. 6d. each; post 8vo, illustrated boards, 2s. each.
Lady Bell. | **Buried Diamonds.** | **The Blackhall Ghosts.**

Post 8vo, illustrated boards, 2s. each.
What She Came Through.   **The Huguenot Family.**
Citoyenne Jacqueline.   **Noblesse Oblige.**
The Bride's Pass.   **Beauty and the Beast.**
Saint Mungo's City.   **Disappeared.**

The Macdonald Lass. With Frontispiece. Crown 8vo, cloth, 3s. 6d.

Upward (Allen), Novels by.
A Crown of Straw. Crown 8vo, cloth, 6s.
Crown 8vo, cloth, 3s. 6d. each; post 8vo, picture boards, 2s. each.
The Queen Against Owen. | **The Prince of Balkistan.**

Vashti and Esther. By 'Belle' of *The World.* Cr. 8vo, cloth, 3s. 6d.

Villari (Linda).—A Double Bond: A Story. Fcap. 8vo, 1s.

Vizetelly (Ernest A.).—The Scorpion: A Romance of Spain. With a Frontispiece. Crown 8vo, cloth extra, 3s. 6d.

Walford (Edward, M.A.), Works by.
Walford's County Families of the United Kingdom (1897). Containing the Descent, Birth, Marriage, Education, &c., of 12,000 Heads of Families, their Heirs, Offices, Addresses, Clubs &c. Royal 8vo, cloth gilt, 50s.
Walford's Shilling Peerage (1897). Containing a List of the House of Lords, Scotch and Irish Peers, &c. 32mo, cloth, 1s.
Walford's Shilling Baronetage (1897). Containing a List of the Baronets of the United Kingdom, Biographical Notices, Addresses, &c. 32mo, cloth, 1s.
Walford's Shilling Knightage (1897). Containing a List of the Knights of the United Kingdom, Biographical Notices, Addresses, &c. 32mo, cloth, 1s.
Walford's Shilling House of Commons (1897). Containing a List of all the Members of the New Parliament, their Addresses, Clubs, &c. 32mo, cloth, 1s.
Walford's Complete Peerage, Baronetage, Knightage, and House of Commons (1897). Royal 32mo, cloth, gilt edges, 5s.

Tales of our Great Families. Crown 8vo, cloth extra, 3s. 6d.

Waller (S. E.).—Sebastiani's Secret. With Nine full-page Illustrations by the Author. Crown 8vo, cloth, 6s.

Walton and Cotton's Complete Angler; or, The Contemplative Man's Recreation, by IZAAK WALTON; and Instructions How to Angle, for a Trout or Grayling in a clear Stream. by CHARLES COTTON. With Memoirs and Notes by Sir HARRIS NICOLAS, and 61 Illustrations. Crown 8vo, cloth antique, 7s. 6d.

Walt Whitman, Poems by. Edited, with Introduction, by WILLIAM M. ROSSETTI. With Portrait. Crown 8vo, hand-made paper and buckram, 6s.

Ward (Herbert), Books by.
Five Years with the Congo Cannibals. With 92 Illustrations. Royal 8vo, cloth, 14s.
My Life with Stanley's Rear Guard. With Map. Post 8vo, 1s.; cloth, 1s. 6d.

Warner (Charles Dudley).—A Roundabout Journey. Crown 8vo, cloth extra, 6s.

Warrant to Execute Charles I. A Facsimile, with the 59 Signatures and Seals. Printed on paper 22 in. by 14 in. 2s.
Warrant to Execute Mary Queen of Scots. A Facsimile, including Queen Elizabeth's Signature and the Great Seal. 2s.

Washington's (George) Rules of Civility Traced to their Sources and Restored by MONCURE D. CONWAY. Fcap. 8vo, Japanese vellum, 2s. 6d.

Wassermann (Lillias), Novels by.
The Daffodils. Crown 8vo, 1s.; cloth, 1s. 6d.

The Marquis of Carabas. By AARON WATSON and LILLIAS WASSERMANN. Post 8vo, illustrated boards, 2s.

Weather, How to Foretell the, with the Pocket Spectroscope. By F. W. CORY. With Ten Illustrations. Crown 8vo, 1s.; cloth, 1s. 6d.

Westall (William), Novels by.
Trust-Money. Post 8vo, illustrated boards, 2s.; cloth, 2s. 6d.
Sons of Belial. Crown 8vo, cloth extra, 3s. 6d.
With the Red Eagle: A Romance of the Tyrol. Crown 8vo, cloth, 6s.

Westbury (Atha).—The Shadow of Hilton Fernbrook: A Romance of Maoriland. Crown 8vo, cloth, 3s. 6d.

Whist, How to Play Solo. By ABRAHAM S. WILKS and CHARLES F. PARDON. Post 8vo, cloth limp, 2s.

White (Gilbert).—The Natural History of Selborne. Post 8vo, printed on laid paper and half-bound, 2s.

Williams (W. Mattieu, F.R.A.S.), Works by.
Science in Short Chapters. Crown 8vo, cloth extra, 7s. 6d.
A Simple Treatise on Heat. With Illustrations. Crown 8vo, cloth, 2s. 6d.
The Chemistry of Cookery. Crown 8vo, cloth extra, 6s.
The Chemistry of Iron and Steel Making. Crown 8vo, cloth extra, 9s.
A Vindication of Phrenology. With Portrait and 43 Illusts. Demy 8vo, cloth extra, 12s. 6d.

Williamson (Mrs. F. H.).—A Child Widow. Post 8vo, bds., 2s.

Wills (C. J.).—An Easy-going Fellow. Crown 8vo, cloth, 6s.

Wilson (Dr. Andrew, F.R.S.E.), Works by.
Chapters on Evolution. With 259 Illustrations. Crown 8vo, cloth extra, 7s. 6d.
Leaves from a Naturalist's Note-Book. Post 8vo, cloth limp, 2s. 6d.
Leisure-Time Studies. With Illustrations. Crown 8vo, cloth extra, 6s.
Studies in Life and Sense. With numerous Illustrations. Crown 8vo, cloth extra, 6s.
Common Accidents: How to Treat Them. With Illustrations. Crown 8vo, 1s.; cloth, 1s. 6d.
Glimpses of Nature. With 35 Illustrations. Crown 8vo, cloth extra, 3s. 6d.

Winter (John Strange), Stories by. Post 8vo, illustrated boards, 2s. each; cloth limp, 2s. 6d. each.
Cavalry Life. | Regimental Legends.

Cavalry Life and Regimental Legends. LIBRARY EDITION, set in new type and handsomely bound. Crown 8vo, cloth, 3s. 6d. [*Shortly.*
A Soldier's Children. With 34 Illustrations by E. G. THOMSON and E. STUART HARDY. Crown 8vo, cloth extra, 3s. 6d.

Wissmann (Hermann von). — My Second Journey through Equatorial Africa. With 92 Illustrations. Demy 8vo, cloth, 16s.

Wood (H. F.), Detective Stories by. Post 8vo, boards, 2s. each.
The Passenger from Scotland Yard. | The Englishman of the Rue Cain.

Wood (Lady).—Sabina: A Novel. Post 8vo, illustrated boards, 2s.

Woolley (Celia Parker).—Rachel Armstrong; or, Love and Theology. Post 8vo, illustrated boards, 2s.; cloth, 2s. 6d.

Wright (Thomas), Works by. Crown 8vo, cloth extra, 7s. 6d. each.
The Caricature History of the Georges. With 400 Caricatures, Squibs, &c.
History of Caricature and of the Grotesque in Art, Literature, Sculpture, and Painting. Illustrated by F. W. FAIRHOLT, F.S.A.

Wynman (Margaret).—My Flirtations. With 13 Illustrations by J. BERNARD PARTRIDGE. Crown 8vo, cloth, 3s. 6d.; post 8vo, cloth limp, 2s.

Yates (Edmund), Novels by. Post 8vo, illustrated boards, 2s. each.
Land at Last. | The Forlorn Hope. | Castaway.

Zangwill (I.).—Ghetto Tragedies. With Three Illustrations by A. S. BOYD. Fcap. 8vo, cloth, 2s. net.

Zola (Emile), Novels by. Crown 8vo, cloth extra, 3s. 6d. each.
The Fat and the Thin. Translated by ERNEST A. VIZETELLY.
Money. Translated by ERNEST A. VIZETELLY.
The Downfall. Translated by E. A. VIZETELLY.
The Dream. Translated by ELIZA CHASE. With Eight Illustrations by JEANNIOT.
Doctor Pascal. Translated by E. A. VIZETELLY. With Portrait of the Author.
Lourdes. Translated by ERNEST A. VIZETELLY.
Rome. Translated by ERNEST A. VIZETELLY.

SOME BOOKS CLASSIFIED IN SERIES.

* *For fuller cataloguing, see alphabetical arrangement, pp. 1–26.*

The Mayfair Library. Post 8vo, cloth limp, 2s. 6d. per Volume.

A Journey Round My Room. By X. DE MAISTRE. Translated by Sir HENRY ATTWELL.
Quips and Quiddities. By W. D. ADAMS.
The Agony Column of 'The Times.'
Melancholy Anatomised: Abridgment of BURTON.
Poetical Ingenuities. By W. T. DOBSON.
The Cupboard Papers. By FIN-BEC.
W. S. Gilbert's Plays. Three Series.
Songs of Irish Wit and Humour.
Animals and their Masters. By Sir A. HELPS.
Social Pressure. By Sir A. HELPS.
Curiosities of Criticism. By H. J. JENNINGS.
The Autocrat of the Breakfast-Table. By OLIVER WENDELL HOLMES.
Pencil and Palette. By R. KEMPT.
Little Essays: from LAMB'S LETTERS.
Forensic Anecdotes. By JACOB LARWOOD.
Theatrical Anecdotes. By JACOB LARWOOD.
Witch Stories. By E. LYNN LINTON.
Ourselves. By E. LYNN LINTON.
Pastimes and Players. By R. MACGREGOR.
New Paul and Virginia. By W. H. MALLOCK.
The New Republic. By W. H. MALLOCK.
Puck on Pegasus. By H. C. PENNELL.
Pegasus Re-saddled. By H. C. PENNELL.
Muses of Mayfair. Edited by H. C. PENNELL.
Thoreau: His Life and Aims. By H. A. PAGE.
Puniana. By Hon. HUGH ROWLEY.
More Puniana. By Hon. HUGH ROWLEY.
The Philosophy of Handwriting.
By Stream and Sea. By WILLIAM SENIOR.
Leaves from a Naturalist's Note-Book. By Dr. ANDREW WILSON.

The Golden Library. Post 8vo, cloth limp, 2s. per Volume.

Diversions of the Echo Club. BAYARD TAYLOR.
Songs for Sailors. By W. C. BENNETT.
Lives of the Necromancers. By W. GODWIN.
The Poetical Works of Alexander Pope.
Scenes of Country Life. By EDWARD JESSE.
Tale for a Chimney Corner. By LEIGH HUNT.
The Autocrat of the Breakfast Table. By OLIVER WENDELL HOLMES.
La Mort d'Arthur: Selections from MALLORY.
Provincial Letters of Blaise Pascal.
Maxims and Reflections of Rochefoucauld.

Handy Novels. Fcap. 8vo, cloth boards, 1s. 6d. each.

The Old Maid's Sweetheart. By A. ST. AUBYN.
Modest Little Sara. By A. ST. AUBYN.
Seven Sleepers of Ephesus. M. E. COLERIDGE.
Taken from the Enemy. By H. NEWBOLT.
A Lost Soul. By W. L. ALDEN.
Dr. Palliser's Patient. By GRANT ALLEN.
Monte Carlo Stories. By JOAN BARRETT.
Black Spirits and White. By R. A. CRAM.

My Library. Printed on laid paper, post 8vo, half-Roxburghe, 2s. 6d. each.

Citation and Examination of William Shakspeare. By W. S. LANDOR.
The Journal of Maurice de Guerin.
Christie Johnstone. By CHARLES READE.
Peg Woffington. By CHARLES READE.
The Dramatic Essays of Charles Lamb.

The Pocket Library. Post 8vo, printed on laid paper and hf.-bd., 2s. each.

The Essays of Elia. By CHARLES LAMB.
Robinson Crusoe. Illustrated by G. CRUIKSHANK.
Whims and Oddities. By THOMAS HOOD.
The Barber's Chair. By DOUGLAS JERROLD.
Gastronomy. By BRILLAT-SAVARIN.
The Epicurean, &c. By THOMAS MOORE.
Leigh Hunt's Essays. Edited by E. OLLIER.
White's Natural History of Selborne.
Gulliver's Travels, &c. By Dean SWIFT.
Plays by RICHARD BRINSLEY SHERIDAN.
Anecdotes of the Clergy. By JACOB LARWOOD.
Thomson's Seasons. Illustrated.
Autocrat of the Breakfast-Table and The Professor at the Breakfast-Table. By O. W. HOLMES.

CHATTO & WINDUS, 111 St. Martin's Lane, London, W.C. 27

THE PICCADILLY NOVELS.

LIBRARY EDITIONS OF NOVELS, many Illustrated, crown 8vo, cloth extra, 3s. 6d. each.

By Mrs. ALEXANDER.
A Life Interest. | Mona's Choice.
By Woman's Wit.

By F. M. ALLEN.
Green as Grass.

By GRANT ALLEN.
Philistia.
Strange Stories.
Babylon.
For Maimie's Sake,
In all Shades.
The Beckoning Hand.
The Devil's Die.
This Mortal Coil.
The Tents of Shem.
The Great Taboo.
Dumaresq's Daughter.
Duchess of Powysland.
Blood Royal.
Ivan Greet's Masterpiece.
The Scallywag.
At Market Value.
Under Sealed Orders.

By MARY ANDERSON.
Othello's Occupation.

By EDWIN L. ARNOLD.
Phra the Phœnician. | Constable of St. Nicholas.

By ROBERT BARR.
In a Steamer Chair. | From Whose Bourne.

By FRANK BARRETT.
The Woman of the Iron Bracelets.
The Harding Scandal.
A Missing Witness.

By 'BELLE.'
Vashti and Esther.

By Sir W. BESANT and J. RICE.
Ready-Money Mortiboy.
My Little Girl.
With Harp and Crown.
This Son of Vulcan.
The Golden Butterfly.
The Monks of Thelema.
By Celia's Arbour.
Chaplain of the Fleet.
The Seamy Side.
The Case of Mr. Lucraft.
In Trafalgar's Bay.
The Ten Years' Tenant.

By Sir WALTER BESANT.
All Sorts and Conditions of Men.
The Captains' Room.
All in a Garden Fair.
Dorothy Forster.
Uncle Jack.
The World Went Very Well Then.
Children of Gibeon.
Herr Paulus.
For Faith and Freedom.
To Call Her Mine.
The Revolt of Man.
The Bell of St. Paul's.
The Holy Rose.
Armorel of Lyonesse.
S. Katherine's by Tower
Verbena Camellia Stephanotis.
The Ivory Gate.
The Rebel Queen.
Beyond the Dreams of Avarice.
The Master Craftsman.

By PAUL BOURGET.
A Living Lie.

By ROBERT BUCHANAN.
Shadow of the Sword.
A Child of Nature.
God and the Man.
Martyrdom of Madeline
Love Me for Ever.
Annan Water.
Foxglove Manor.
The New Abelard.
Matt. | Rachel Dene.
Master of the Mine.
The Heir of Linne.
Woman and the Man.
Red and White Heather.
Lady Kilpatrick.

ROB. BUCHANAN & HY. MURRAY.
The Charlatan.

By J. MITCHELL CHAPPLE.
The Minor Chord.

By HALL CAINE.
The Shadow of a Crime. | The Deemster.
A Son of Hagar.

By MACLAREN COBBAN.
The Red Sultan. | The Burden of Isabel.

By MORT. & FRANCES COLLINS.
Transmigration.
Blacksmith & Scholar.
The Village Comedy.
From Midnight to Midnight.
You Play me False.

By WILKIE COLLINS.
Armadale. | AfterDark.
No Name.
Antonina.
Basil.
Hide and Seek.
The Dead Secret.
Queen of Hearts.
My Miscellanies.
The Woman in White.
The Moonstone.
Man and Wife.
Poor Miss Finch.
Miss or Mrs.?
The New Magdalen.
The Frozen Deep.
The Two Destinies.
The Law and the Lady.
The Haunted Hotel.
The Fallen Leaves.
Jezebel's Daughter.
The Black Robe.
Heart and Science.
'I Say No.'
Little Novels.
The Evil Genius.
The Legacy of Cain.
A Rogue's Life.
Blind Love.

By E. H. COOPER.
Geoffory Hamilton.

By V. CECIL COTES.
Two Girls on a Barge.

By C. EGBERT CRADDOCK.
His Vanished Star.

By H. N. CRELLIN.
Romances of the Old Seraglio.

By MATT CRIM.
The Adventures of a Fair Rebel.

By S. R. CROCKETT and others.
Tales of Our Coast.

By B. M. CROKER.
Diana Barrington.
Proper Pride.
A Family Likeness.
Pretty Miss Neville.
A Bird of Passage.
'To Let.' | Mr. Jervis.
Village Tales & Jungle Tragedies.
The Real Lady Hilda.
Married or Single?
Two Masters.
In the Kingdom of Kerry

By WILLIAM CYPLES.
Hearts of Gold.

By ALPHONSE DAUDET.
The Evangelist; or, Port Salvation.

By H. COLEMAN DAVIDSON.
Mr. Sadler's Daughters.

By ERASMUS DAWSON.
The Fountain of Youth.

By JAMES DE MILLE.
A Castle in Spain.

By J. LEITH DERWENT.
Our Lady of Tears. | Circe's Lovers.

By DICK DONOVAN.
Tracked to Doom. | The Mystery of Jamaica
Man from Manchester. | Terrace.
The Chronicles of Michael Danevitch.

By A. CONAN DOYLE.
The Firm of Girdlestone.

By S. JEANNETTE DUNCAN.
A Daughter of To-day. | Vernon's Aunt.

By G. MANVILLE FENN.
The New Mistress.
Witness to the Deed.
The Tiger Lily.
The White Virgin.

By PERCY FITZGERALD.
Fatal Zero.

By R. E. FRANCILLON.
One by One.
A Dog and his Shadow.
A Real Queen.
Ropes of Sand.
Jack Doyle's Daughter.

Prefaced by Sir BARTLE FRERE.
Pandurang Hari.

BY EDWARD GARRETT.
The Capel Girls.

28   CHATTO & WINDUS, 111 St. Martin's Lane, London, W.C.

THE PICCADILLY (3/6) NOVELS—*continued*.

By PAUL GAULOT.
The Red Shirts.

By CHARLES GIBBON.
Robin Gray. | The Golden Shaft.
Loving a Dream.

By E. GLANVILLE.
The Lost Heiress. | The Fossicker.
A Fair Colonist. | The Golden Rock.

By E. J. GOODMAN.
The Fate of Herbert Wayne.

By Rev. S. BARING GOULD.
Red Spider. | Eve.

By CECIL GRIFFITH.
Corinthia Marazion.

By SYDNEY GRUNDY.
The Days of his Vanity.

By THOMAS HARDY.
Under the Greenwood Tree.

By BRET HARTE.
A Waif of the Plains. | A Protégée of Jack
A Ward of the Golden   Hamlin's.
  Gate. [Springs. | Clarence.
A Sappho of Green | Barker's Luck.
Col. Starbottle's Client. | Devil's Ford. [celsior.'
Susy. | Sally Dows. | The Crusade of the 'Ex-
Bell-Ringer of Angel's. | Three Partners.

By JULIAN HAWTHORNE.
Garth. | Beatrix Randolph.
Ellice Quentin. | David Poindexter's Dis-
Sebastian Strome. | appearance.
Dust. | The Spectre of the
Fortune's Pool. | Camera.

By Sir A. HELPS.
Ivan de Biron.

By I. HENDERSON.
Agatha Page.

By G. A. HENTY.
Rujub the Juggler. | Dorothy's Double.

By JOHN HILL.
The Common Ancestor.

By Mrs. HUNGERFORD.
Lady Verner's Plight. | A Point of Conscience.
The Red-House Mystery | Nora Creina.
The Three Graces. | An Anxious Moment.
Professor's Experiment. | April's Lady.

By Mrs. ALFRED HUNT.
The Leaden Casket. | Self-Condemned.
That Other Person. | Mrs. Juliet.

By C. J. CUTCLIFFE HYNE.
Honour of Thieves.

By R. ASHE KING.
A Drawn Game. | 'The Wearing of the Green.

By EDMOND LEPELLETIER.
Madame Sans-Gêne.

By HARRY LINDSAY.
Rhoda Roberts.

By HENRY W. LUCY.
Gideon Fleyce.

By E. LYNN LINTON.
Patricia Kemball. | The Atonement of Leam
Under which Lord? | Dundas.
'My Love!' | Ione. | The World Well Lost.
Paston Carew. | The One Too Many.
Sowing the Wind. | Dulcie Everton.

By JUSTIN McCARTHY.
A Pair Saxon. | Donna Quixote.
Linley Rochford. | Maid of Athens.
Dear Lady Disdain. | The Comet of a Season.
Camiola. | The Dictator.
Waterdale Neighbours. | Red Diamonds.
My Enemy's Daughter. | The Riddle Ring.
Miss Misanthrope.

By JUSTIN H. McCARTHY.
A London Legend. | The Royal Christopher.

By GEORGE MACDONALD.
Heather and Snow. | Phantastes.

By L. T. MEADE.
A Soldier of Fortune. | The Voice of the
In an Iron Grip. | Charmer.

By LEONARD MERRICK.
This Stage of Fools.

By BERTRAM MITFORD.
The Gun-Runner. | The King's Assegai.
The Luck of Gerard | Renshaw Fanning's
 Ridgeley. | Quest.

By J. E. MUDDOCK.
Maid Marian and Robin Hood.
Basile the Jester. | Young Lochinvar.

By D. CHRISTIE MURRAY.
A Life's Atonement. | Cynic Fortune.
Joseph's Coat. | The Way of the World.
Coals of Fire. | Bob Martin's Little Girl.
Old Blazer's Hero. | Time's Revenges.
Val Strange. | Hearts. | A Wasted Crime.
A Model Father. | In Direst Peril.
By the Gate of the Sea. | Mount Despair.
A Bit of Human Nature. | A Capful o' Nails.
First Person Singular.

By MURRAY and HERMAN.
The Bishops' Bible. | Paul Jones's Alias.
One Traveller Returns.

By HUME NISBET.
'Bail Up!'

By W. E. NORRIS.
Saint Ann's. | Billy Bellew.

By G. OHNET.
A Weird Gift.

By Mrs. OLIPHANT.
The Sorceress.

By OUIDA.
Held in Bondage. | Two Little Wooden
Strathmore. | In a Winter City. | Shoes
Chandos. | Friendship.
Under Two Flags. | Moths. | Ruffino.
Idalia. [Gage. | Pipistrello.
Cecil Castlemaine's | A Village Commune.
Tricotrin. | Puck. | Bimbi. | Wanda.
Polle Farine. | Frescoes. | Othmar.
A Dog of Flanders. | In Maremma.
Pascarel. | Signa. | Syrlin. | Guilderoy.
Princess Napraxine. | Santa Barbara.
Ariadne. | Two Offenders.

By MARGARET A. PAUL.
Gentle and Simple.

By JAMES PAYN.
Lost Sir Massingberd. | High Spirits.
Less Black than We're | Under One Roof.
 Painted. | Glow-worm Tales.
A Confidential Agent. | The Talk of the Town
A Grape from a Thorn. | Holiday Tasks.
In Peril and Privation. | For Cash Only.
The Mystery of Mir- | The Burnt Million.
 By Proxy. [bridge. | The Word and the Will.
The Canon's Ward. | Sunny Stories.
Walter's Word. | A Trying Patient.

By WILL PAYNE.
Jerry the Dreamer.

By Mrs. CAMPBELL PRAED.
Outlaw and Lawmaker. | Mrs. Tregaskiss.
Christina Chard.

By E. C. PRICE.
Valentina. | Foreigners. | Mrs. Lancaster's Rival.

By RICHARD PRYCE.
Miss Maxwell's Affections.

By CHARLES READE.
Peg Woffington; and | Love Me Little, Love
 Christie Johnstone. | Me Long.
Hard Cash. | The Double Marriage.
Cloister & the Hearth. | Foul Play.
Never Too Late to Mend | Put Yourself in His
The Course of True | A Terrible Temptation.
 Love Never Did Run | A Simpleton.
 Smooth; and Single- | A Woman-Hater.
 heart and Doubleface. | The Jilt, & otherStories;
Autobiography of a | & Good Stories of Men
 Thief; Jack of all | and other Animals.
 Trades; A Hero and | A Perilous Secret.
 a Martyr; and The | Readiana; and Bible
 Wandering Heir. | Characters.
Griffith Gaunt.

CHATTO & WINDUS, 111 St. Martin's Lane, London, W.C.

THE PICCADILLY (3/6) NOVELS—*continued.*

By Mrs. J. H. RIDDELL.
Weird Stories.

By AMELIE RIVES.
Barbara Dering.

By F. W. ROBINSON.
The Hands of Justice. | Woman in the Dark.

By DORA RUSSELL.
A Country Sweetheart. | The Drift of Fate.

By W. CLARK RUSSELL.
Round the Galley-Fire. | My Shipmate Louise.
In the Middle Watch. | Alone on Wide Wide Sea
A Voyage to the Cape. | The Phantom Death.
Book for the Hammock. | Is He the Man?
The Mystery of the | The Good Ship 'Mo-
 'Ocean Star.' | hock.'
The Romance of Jenny | The Convict Ship.
 Harlowe. | Heart of Oak.
An Ocean Tragedy. | The Tale of the Ten.

By JOHN SAUNDERS.
Guy Waterman. | The Two Dreamers.
Bound to the Wheel. | The Lion in the Path.

By KATHARINE SAUNDERS.
Margaret and Elizabeth | Heart Salvage.
Gideon's Rock. | Sebastian.
The High Mills.

By ADELINE SERGEANT.
Dr. Endicott's Experiment.

By HAWLEY SMART.
Without Love or Licence. | Long Odds.
The Master of Rathkelly. | The Outsider.

By T. W. SPEIGHT.
A Secret of the Sea. | The Master of Trenance.
The Grey Monk. | A Minion of the Moon.

By ALAN ST. AUBYN.
A Fellow of Trinity. | In Face of the World.
The Junior Dean. | Orchard Damerel.
Master of St. Benedict's. | The Tremlett Diamonds.
To his Own Master.

By JOHN STAFFORD.
Doris and I.

By R. A. STERNDALE.
The Afghan Knife.

By BERTHA THOMAS.
Proud Maisie. | The Violin-Player.

By ANTHONY TROLLOPE.
The Way we Live Now. | Scarborough's Family
Frau Frohmann. | The Land-Leaguers.

By FRANCES E. TROLLOPE.
Like Ships upon the | Anne Furness.
 Sea. | Mabel's Progress.

By IVAN TURGENIEFF, &c.
Stories from Foreign Novelists.

By MARK TWAIN.
A Tramp Abroad. | Tom Sawyer Abroad.
The American Claimant. | Pudd'nhead Wilson.
The £1,000,000 Bank-note | Tom Sawyer, Detective.

By C. C. FRASER-TYTLER.
Mistress Judith.

By SARAH TYTLER.
Lady Bell. | The Blackhall Ghosts.
Buried Diamonds. | The Macdonald Lass.

By ALLEN UPWARD.
The Queen against Owen | The Prince of Balkistan

By E. A. VIZETELLY.
The Scorpion: A Romance of Spain.

By WILLIAM WESTALL.
Sons of Belial.

By ATHA WESTBURY.
The Shadow of Hilton Fernbrook.

By JOHN STRANGE WINTER.
Cavalry Life and Regimental Legends.
A Soldier's Children.

By MARGARET WYNMAN
My Flirtations.

By E. ZOLA.
The Downfall. | Money. | Lourdes.
The Dream. | The Fat and the Thin.
Dr. Pascal. | Rome.

CHEAP EDITIONS OF POPULAR NOVELS.
Post 8vo, illustrated boards, 2s. each.

By ARTEMUS WARD.
Artemus Ward Complete.

By EDMOND ABOUT.
The Fellah.

By HAMILTON AÏDÉ.
Carr of Carrlyon. | Confidences.

By MARY ALBERT.
Brooke Finchley's Daughter.

By Mrs. ALEXANDER.
Maid, Wife or Widow? | Valerie's Fate.
Blind Fate.

By GRANT ALLEN.
Philistia. | The Great Taboo.
Strange Stories. | Dumaresq's Daughter.
Babylon | Duchess of Powysland.
For Malmie's Sake. | Blood Royal. [piece-
In all Shades. | Ivan Greet's Master.
The Beckoning Hand. | The Scallywag.
The Devil's Die. | This Mortal Coil.
The Tents of Shem. | At Market Value.

By E. LESTER ARNOLD.
Phra the Phœnician.

By SHELSLEY BEAUCHAMP.
Grantley Grange.

BY FRANK BARRETT.
Fettered for Life. | A Prodigal's Progress.
Little Lady Linton. | Found Guilty.
Between Life & Death. | A Recoiling Vengeance.
The Sin of Olga Zassou- | For Love and Honour.
 lich. | John Ford; and His
Folly Morrison. | Helpmate.
Lieut. Barnabas. | The Woman of the Iron
Honest Davie. | Bracelets.

By Sir W. BESANT and J. RICE.
Ready-Money Mortiboy | By Celia's Arbour.
My Little Girl. | Chaplain of the Fleet.
With Harp and Crown. | The Seamy Side.
This Son of Vulcan. | The Case of Mr. Lucraft.
The Golden Butterfly. | In Trafalgar's Bay.
The Monks of Thelema. | The Ten Years' Tenant.

By Sir WALTER BESANT.
All Sorts and Condi- | To Call Her Mine.
 tions of Men. | The Bell of St. Paul's.
The Captains' Room. | The Holy Rose.
All in a Garden Fair. | Armorel of Lyonesse.
Dorothy Forster. | S. Katherine's by Tower.
Uncle Jack. | Verbena Camellia Ste-
The World Went Very | phanotis.
 Well Then. | The Ivory Gate.
Children of Gibeon. | The Rebel Queen.
Herr Paulus. | Beyond the Dreams of
For Faith and Freedom. | Avarice.

By AMBROSE BIERCE.
In the Midst of Life.

By FREDERICK BOYLE.
Camp Notes. | Chronicles of No-man's
Savage Life. | Land.

BY BRET HARTE.
Californian Stories. | Flip.] Maruja.
Gabriel Conroy. | A Phyllis of the Sierras.
The Luck of Roaring | A Waif of the Plains.
 Camp. | A Ward of the Golden
An Heiress of Red Dog. | Gate.

By HAROLD BRYDGES.
Uncle Sam at Home.

TWO-SHILLING NOVELS—*continued.*

By ROBERT BUCHANAN.
Shadow of the Sword. | The Martyrdom of Madeline.
A Child of Nature. |
God and the Man. | The New Abelard.
Love Me for Ever. | Matt.
Foxglove Manor. | The Heir of Linne.
The Master of the Mine. | Woman and the Man.
Annan Water. | Rachel Dene.

By BUCHANAN and MURRAY.
The Charlatan.

By HALL CAINE.
The Shadow of a Crime. | The Deemster.
A Son of Hagar.

By Commander CAMERON.
The Cruise of the 'Black Prince.'

By Mrs. LOVETT CAMERON.
Deceivers Ever. | Juliet's Guardian.

By HAYDEN CARRUTH.
The Adventures of Jones.

By AUSTIN CLARE.
For the Love of a Lass.

By Mrs. ARCHER CLIVE.
Paul Ferroll.
Why Paul Ferrell Killed his Wife.

By MACLAREN COBBAN.
The Cure of Souls. | The Red Sultan.

By C. ALLSTON COLLINS.
The Bar Sinister.

By MORT. & FRANCES COLLINS.
Sweet Anne Page. | Sweet and Twenty.
Transmigration. | The Village Comedy.
From Midnight to Midnight. | You Playgme False.
| Blacksmith and Scholar
A Fight with Fortune. | Frances.

By WILKIE COLLINS.
Armadale.] AfterDark. | My Miscellanies.
No Name. | The Woman in White.
Antonina. | The Moonstone.
Basil. | Man and Wife.
Hide and Seek. | Poor Miss Finch.
The Dead Secret. | The Fallen Leaves.
Queen of Hearts. | Jezebel's Daughter.
Miss or Mrs.? | The Black Robe.
The New Magdalen. | Heart and Science
The Frozen Deep. | 'I Say No!'
The Law and the Lady | The Evil Genius.
The Two Destinies. | Little Novels.
The Haunted Hotel. | Legacy of Cain.
A Rogue's Life. | Blind Love.

By M. J. COLQUHOUN.
Every Inch a Soldier.

By DUTTON COOK.
Leo. | Paul Foster's Daughter.

By C. EGBERT CRADDOCK.
The Prophet of the Great Smoky Mountains.

By MATT CRIM.
The Adventures of a Fair Rebel.

By B. M. CROKER.
Pretty Miss Neville. | A Family Likeness.
Diana Barrington. | Village Tales and Jungle Tragedies.
'To Let.' |
A Bird of Passage. | Two Masters.
Proper Pride. | Mr. Jervis.

By W. CYPLES.
Hearts of Gold.

By ALPHONSE DAUDET.
The Evangelist; or, Port Salvation.

By ERASMUS DAWSON.
The Fountain of Youth.

By JAMES DE MILLE.
A Castle in Spain.

By J. LEITH DERWENT.
Our Lady of Tears. | Circe's Lovers.

By CHARLES DICKENS.
Sketches by Boz.

By DICK DONOVAN.
The Man-Hunter. | In the Grip of the Law.
Tracked and Taken. | From Information Received.
Caught at Last! |
Wanted! | Tracked to Doom.
Who Poisoned Hetty Duncan? | Link by Link
| Suspicion Aroused.
Man from Manchester. | Dark Deeds.
A Detective's Triumphs | Riddles Read.
The Mystery of Jamaica Terrace.

By Mrs. ANNIE EDWARDES.
A Point of Honour. | Archie Lovell.

By M. BETHAM-EDWARDS.
Felicia. | Kitty.

By EDWARD EGGLESTON.
Roxy.

By G. MANVILLE FENN.
The New Mistress. | The Tiger Lily.
Witness to the Deed. | The White Virgin.

By PERCY FITZGERALD.
Bella Donna. | Second Mrs. Tillotson.
Never Forgotten. | Seventy-five Brooke Street.
Polly. |
Fatal Zero. | The Lady of Brantome

By P. FITZGERALD and others.
Strange Secrets.

By ALBANY DE FONBLANQUE.
Filthy Lucre.

By R. E. FRANCILLON.
Olympia. | King or Knave?
One by One. | Romances of the Law.
A Real Queen. | Ropes of Sand.
Queen Cophetua. | A Dog and his Shadow.

By HAROLD FREDERIC.
Seth's Brother's Wife. | The Lawton Girl.

Prefaced by Sir **BARTLE FRERE.**
Pandurang Hari.

By HAIN FRISWELL.
One of Two.

By EDWARD GARRETT.
The Capel Girls.

By GILBERT GAUL.
A Strange Manuscript.

By CHARLES GIBBON.
Robin Gray. | In Honour Bound.
Fancy Free. | Flower of the Forest
For Lack of Gold. | The Braes of Yarrow.
What will World Say? | The Golden Shaft.
In Love and War. | Of High Degree.
For the King. | By Mead and Stream.
In Pastures Green. | Loving a Dream.
Queen of the Meadow. | A Hard Knot.
A Heart's Problem. | Heart's Delight.
The Dead Heart. | Blood-Money.

By WILLIAM GILBERT.
Dr. Austin's Guests. | The Wizard of the Mountain.
James Duke. |

By ERNEST GLANVILLE.
The Lost Heiress. | The Fossicker.
A Fair Colonist.

By Rev. S. BARING GOULD.
Red Spider. | Eve.

By HENRY GREVILLE.
A Noble Woman. | Nikanor.

By CECIL GRIFFITH.
Corinthia Marazion.

By SYDNEY GRUNDY.
The Days of his Vanity.

By JOHN HABBERTON.
Brueton's Bayou. | Country Luck.

By ANDREW HALLIDAY.
Every-day Papers.

By Lady DUFFUS HARDY.
Paul Wynter's Sacrifice.

By THOMAS HARDY.
Under the Greenwood Tree.

By J. BERWICK HARWOOD
The Tenth Earl.

TWO-SHILLING NOVELS—continued.

By JULIAN HAWTHORNE.
Garth.
Ellice Quentin.
Fortune's Fool.
Miss Cadogna.
Sebastian Strome.
Dust.
Beatrix Randolph.
Love—or a Name.
David Poindexter's Disappearance.
The Spectre of the Camera.

By Sir ARTHUR HELPS.
Ivan de Biron.

By G. A. HENTY.
Rujub the Juggler.

By HENRY HERMAN.
A Leading Lady.

By HEADON HILL.
Zambra the Detective.

By JOHN HILL.
Treason Felony.

By Mrs. CASHEL HOEY.
The Lover's Creed.

By Mrs. GEORGE HOOPER.
The House of Raby.

By TIGHE HOPKINS.
'Twixt Love and Duty.

By Mrs. HUNGERFORD.
A Maidenall Forlorn.
In Durance Vile.
Marvel.
A Mental Struggle.
A Modern Circe.
Lady Verner's Flight.
The Red House Mystery
The Three Graces.
Unsatisfactory Lover.
Lady Patty.

By Mrs. ALFRED HUNT.
Thornicroft's Model.
That Other Person.
Self-Condemned.
The Leaden Casket.

By JEAN INGELOW.
Fated to be Free.

By WM. JAMESON.
My Dead Self.

By HARRIETT JAY.
The Dark Colleen. | Queen of Connaught.

By MARK KERSHAW.
Colonial Facts and Fictions.

By R. ASHE KING.
A Drawn Game.
'The Wearing of the Green.'
Passion's Slave.
Bell Barry.

By EDMOND LEPELLETIER.
Madame Sans-Gene.

By JOHN LEYS.
The Lindsays.

By E. LYNN LINTON.
Patricia Kemball.
The World Well Lost.
Under which Lord?
Paston Carew.
'My Love!'
Ione.
The Atonement of Leam Dundas.
With a Silken Thread.
Rebel of the Family.
Sowing the Wind.
The One Too Many.

By HENRY W. LUCY.
Gideon Fleyce.

By JUSTIN McCARTHY.
Dear Lady Disdain.
Waterdale Neighbours.
My Enemy's Daughter.
A Fair Saxon.
Linley Rochford.
Miss Misanthrope.
Camiola.
Donna Quixote.
Maid of Athens.
The Comet of a Season.
The Dictator.
Red Diamonds.

By HUGH MACCOLL.
Mr. Stranger's Sealed Packet.

By GEORGE MACDONALD.
Heather and Snow.

By AGNES MACDONELL.
Quaker Cousins.

By KATHARINE S. MACQUOID.
The Evil Eye. | Lost Rose.

By W. H. MALLOCK.
A Romance of the Nineteenth Century. | The New Republic.

By FLORENCE MARRYAT.
Open ! Sesame !
Fighting the Air.
A Harvest of Wild Oats.
Written in Fire.

By J. MASTERMAN.
Half-a-dozen Daughters.

By BRANDER MATTHEWS.
A Secret of the Sea.

By L. T. MEADE.
A Soldier of Fortune.

By LEONARD MERRICK.
The Man who was Good.

By JEAN MIDDLEMASS.
Touch and Go. | Mr. Dorillion.

By Mrs. MOLESWORTH.
Hathercourt Rectory.

By J. E. MUDDOCK.
Stories Weird and Wonderful.
The Dead Man's Secret.
From the Bosom of the Deep.

By D. CHRISTIE MURRAY.
A Model Father.
Joseph's Coat.
Coals of Fire.
Val Strange. | Hearts.
Old Blazer's Hero.
The Way of the World.
Cynic Fortune.
A Life's Atonement.
By the Gate of the Sea.
A Bit of Human Nature.
First Person Singular.
Bob Martin's Little Girl
Time's Revenges.
A Wasted Crime.
In Direst Peril.
Mount Despair.

By MURRAY and HERMAN.
One Traveller Returns. | The Bishops' Bible.
Paul Jones's Alias.

By HENRY MURRAY.
A Game of Bluff. | A Song of Sixpence.

By HUME NISBET.
'Bail Up!' | Dr. Bernard St. Vincent

By W. E. NORRIS.
Saint Ann's.

By ALICE O'HANLON.
The Unforeseen. | Chance? or Fate?

By GEORGES OHNET.
Dr. Rameau. | A Weird Gift.
A Last Love.

By Mrs. OLIPHANT.
Whiteladies.
The Primrose Path.
The Greatest Heiress in England.

By Mrs. ROBERT O'REILLY.
Phœbe's Fortunes.

By OUIDA.
Held in Bondage.
Strathmore.
Chandos.
Idalia.
Under Two Flags.
Cecil Castlemaine's Gage
Tricotrin.
Puck.
Folle Farine.
A Dog of Flanders.
Pascarel.
Signa.
Princess Napraxine.
In a Winter City.
Ariadne.
Friendship.
Two Lit. Wooden Shoes.
Moths.
Bimbi.
Pipistrello.
A Village Commune
Wanda.
Othmar.
Frescoes.
In Maremma.
Guilderoy.
Ruffino.
Syrlin.
Santa Barbara.
Two Offenders.
Ouida's Wisdom, Wit and Pathos.

By MARGARET AGNES PAUL
Gentle and Simple.

By C. L. PIRKIS.
Lady Lovelace.

By EDGAR A. POE.
The Mystery of Marie Roget.

By Mrs. CAMPBELL PRAED
The Romance of a Station.
The Soul of Countess Adrian.
Outlaw and Lawmaker.
Christina Chard

By E. C. PRICE.
Valentina. | Mrs. Lancaster's Rival.
The Foreigners. | Gerald.

By RICHARD PRYCE
Miss Maxwell's Affections.

CHATTO & WINDUS, 111 St. Martin's Lane, London, W.C.

TWO-SHILLING NOVELS—*continued.*

By JAMES PAYN.
Bentinck's Tutor.
Murphy's Master.
A County Family.
At Her Mercy.
Cecil's Tryst.
The Clyffards of Clyffe.
The Foster Brothers.
Found Dead.
The Best of Husbands.
Walter's Word.
Halves.
Fallen Fortunes.
Humorous Stories.
£200 Reward.
A Marine Residence.
Mirk Abbey.
By Proxy.
Under One Roof.
High Spirits.
Carlyon's Year.
From Exile.
For Cash Only.
Kit.
The Canon's Ward.
The Talk of the Town.
Holiday Tasks.
A Perfect Treasure.
What He Cost Her.
A Confidential Agent.
Glow-worm Tales.
The Burnt Million.
Sunny Stories.
Lost Sir Massingberd.
A Woman's Vengeance.
The Family Scapegrace.
Gwendoline's Harvest.
Like Father, Like Son.
Married Beneath Him.
Not Wooed, but Won.
Less Black than We're Painted.
Some Private Views.
A Grape from a Thorn.
The Mystery of Mirbridge.
The Word and the Will.
A Prince of the Blood.
A Trying Patient.

By CHARLES READE.
It is Never Too Late to Mend.
Christie Johnstone.
The Double Marriage.
Put Yourself in His Place
Love Me Little, Love Me Long.
The Cloister and the Hearth.
The Course of True Love.
The Jilt.
The Autobiography of a Thief.
A Terrible Temptation.
Foul Play.
The Wandering Heir.
Hard Cash.
Singleheart and Doubleface.
Good Stories of Men and other Animals.
Peg Woffington.
Griffith Gaunt.
A Perilous Secret.
A Simpleton.
Readiana.
A Woman-Hater.

By Mrs. J. H. RIDDELL.
Weird Stories.
Fairy Water.
Her Mother's Darling.
The Prince of Wales's Garden Party.
The Uninhabited House.
The Mystery in Palace Gardens.
The Nun's Curse.
Idle Tales.

By AMELIE RIVES.
Barbara Dering.

By F. W. ROBINSON.
Women are Strange. | The Hands of Justice.

By JAMES RUNCIMAN.
Skippers and Shellbacks. | Schools and Scholars.
Grace Balmaign's Sweetheart.

By W. CLARK RUSSELL.
Round the Galley Fire.
On the Fo'k'sle Head.
In the Middle Watch.
A Voyage to the Cape.
A Book for the Hammock.
The Mystery of the 'Ocean Star.'
The Romance of Jenny Harlowe.
An Ocean Tragedy.
My Shipmate Louise.
Alone on Wide Wide Sea.
The Good Ship 'Mohock.'
The Phantom Death.

By DORA RUSSELL.
A Country Sweetheart.

By GEORGE AUGUSTUS SALA.
Gaslight and Daylight.

By JOHN SAUNDERS.
Guy Waterman. | The Lion in the Path.
The Two Dreamers.

By KATHARINE SAUNDERS.
Joan Merryweather.
The High Mills.
Heart Salvage.
Sebastian.
Margaret and Elizabeth.

By GEORGE R. SIMS.
The Ring o' Bells.
Mary Jane's Memoirs.
Mary Jane Married.
Tales of To-day.
Dramas of Life.
Tinkletop's Crime.
My Two Wives.
Zeph.
Memoirs of a Landlady.
Scenes from the Show.
The 10 Commandments.
Dagonet Abroad.

By ARTHUR SKETCHLEY.
A Match in the Dark.

By HAWLEY SMART.
Without Love or Licence.
The Plunger.
Beatrice and Benedick.

By T. W. SPEIGHT.
The Mysteries of Heron Dyke.
The Golden Hoop.
Hoodwinked.
By Devious Ways.
Back to Life.
The Loudwater Tragedy.
Burgo's Romance.
Quittance in Full.
A Husband from the Sea

By ALAN ST. AUBYN.
A Fellow of Trinity.
The Junior Dean.
Master of St. Benedict's
To His Own Master.
Orchard Damerel.
In the Face of the World.

By R. A. STERNDALE.
The Afghan Knife.

By R. LOUIS STEVENSON.
New Arabian Nights.

By BERTHA THOMAS.
Cressida. | The Violin-Player.
Proud Maisie.

By WALTER THORNBURY.
Tales for the Marines. | Old Stories Retold.

By T. ADOLPHUS TROLLOPE.
Diamond Cut Diamond.

By F. ELEANOR TROLLOPE.
Like Ships upon the Sea. | Anne Furness.
Mabel's Progress.

By ANTHONY TROLLOPE.
Frau Frohmann.
Marion Fay.
Kept in the Dark.
John Caldigate.
The Way We Live Now.
The Land-Leaguers.
The American Senator
Mr. Scarborough's Family.
Golden Lion of Granpere

By J. T. TROWBRIDGE.
Parnell's Folly.

By IVAN TURGENIEFF, &c.
Stories from Foreign Novelists.

By MARK TWAIN.
A Pleasure Trip on the Continent.
The Gilded Age.
Huckleberry Finn.
Mark Twain's Sketches.
Tom Sawyer.
A Tramp Abroad.
Stolen White Elephant.
Life on the Mississippi.
The Prince and the Pauper.
A Yankee at the Court of King Arthur.
The £1,000,000 Banknote.

By C. C. FRASER-TYTLER.
Mistress Judith.

By SARAH TYTLER.
The Bride's Pass.
Buried Diamonds.
St. Mungo's City.
Lady Bell.
Noblesse Oblige.
Disappeared.
The Huguenot Family.
The Blackhall Ghosts.
What She Came Through
Beauty and the Beast.
Citoyenne Jaqueline.

By ALLEN UPWARD.
The Queen against Owen. | Prince of Balkistan.

By AARON WATSON and LILLIAS WASSERMANN.
The Marquis of Carabas.

By WILLIAM WESTALL.
Trust-Money.

By Mrs. F. H. WILLIAMSON.
A Child Widow.

By J. S. WINTER.
Cavalry Life. | Regimental Legends.

By H. F. WOOD.
The Passenger from Scotland Yard.
The Englishman of the Rue Cain.

By Lady WOOD.
Sabina.

By CELIA PARKER WOOLLEY
Rachel Armstrong; or, Love and Theology.

By EDMUND YATES.
The Forlorn Hope. | Castaway.
Land at Last.

By I. ZANGWILL.
Ghetto Tragedies.